The SA

The SAS in Ireland

Raymond Murray

MERCIER PRESS

MERCIER PRESS
Douglas Village, Cork
www.mercierpress.ie

Trade enquiries to COLUMBA MERCIER DISTRIBUTION,
55a Spruce Avenue, Stillorgan Industrial Park, Blackrock, Dublin

© Raymond Murray, 1990
Revised edition 2004

ISBN 1 85635 437 7

IN MEMORIAM
BRIAN J. BRADY

Printed in Ireland by ColourBooks Ltd

Contents

The Untellable Story   9

Unravelling the SAS   13
    The Irish Connection   21
    The Sacred and the Profane   23

Six Phases of the SAS in Northern Ireland   29

Phase I: Intelligence Gathering and Torture   32

Phase II: The Sectarian Murders   41

    The Shooting of the Conway Brothers   45
    The Killing of Patrick McVeigh   47
    The Shooting at the Glen Road Bus Terminal 48
    The Case of Seamus Wright   50
    The Four Square Laundry and the Dolly Bird Spies 52
    The Killing of Daniel Rooney   56
    Loyalist Violence   60
    A Calendar of Incidents – 1972   61
        A Kidnapping   61
        The Murder of David Seaman 62
        Arrested by Plain Clothes Soldiers 64
        The Shankill Road Shooting 64
        The Attempts to Kill William Black 65
        The Bawnmore Incident 68
        The Leeson Street Shooting 69
        British Army Shoot-Out 70
        Plain Clothes Soldiers in Riverdale, Belfast 70
    Some 'SAS' Casualties 1972-76   70
    The Littlejohns   75
    Albert Walker Baker's Pseudo-Gang   91
        UDA Arms   93
        UDA Attacks on British Soldiers 94
        UDA/RUC Collusion 95
        Bombings in the Republic 1972 96
        End of Baker's Deal 100

MI5 and MI6   102
    SAS as Arm of MI5   103
    The Dublin Bombings 1974   107
    Holroyd/Wallace Revelations   110
    Captain Fred Holroyd   115
    Sectarian Murders in the 'Triangle of Death'   121
    The Murder of John Francis Green   125
    1975: Murders in South Armagh and 'The Triangle'   136
    UDR Incidents in Fermanagh/Tyrone 1974   144
    UDR Crime in the 'Triangle' Area   145
    Captain Robert Nairac   147
    The Case of Seamus O'Brien   154
    The Murder of Niall O'Neill   158

Phase III: The SAS in South Armagh   163
    The Murder of the Reavey Brothers   166
    'How the SAS moved in on the Terrorists'   167
    The Kidnapping of Seán McKenna   168
    The Shooting of Peter Cleary   169
    The Murder of Seamus Ludlow   175
    The SAS Incursion into the Republic   176
    SAS Jump the Border to make Arrests   180
    SAS versus Paratroopers   182
    The Shooting of Seamus Harvey, Crossmaglen   183

Phase IV: SAS Terrorism, 1977-78   185
    The Murder of Michael McHugh   186
    British Army Intelligence 1977-78   188
    SAS/Plain Clothes Soldiers Casualties   195
    The Shooting of Colm McNutt   199
    The Shooting of Paul Duffy   201
    The Shooting and Wounding of Desmond Mackin
        and Robert Gamble   208
    The Shooting of Denis Heaney   214
    The Ballysillan Massacre   221
    The Shooting of John Boyle   225
    The Shooting of James Taylor   236
    The Shooting of William Smyth   240
    The Shooting of Patrick Duffy   241

Phase V: Atkin's Secret Army   247
    The SAS on the Antrim Road   247
    'Our Secret Army'   249
    Undercover Soldiers Shot Dead   249
    The UDR and the SAS   252

Sir Maurice Oldfield   253
Operation 'RANC'   259
The Twinbrook Raid   265

Phase VI: Shoot-to-Kill   270
  IRA and SAS Casualties 1981-87   274
  The Shooting of Charles Maguire and
       George McBrearty   279
  The Shooting of Neil McMonagle   284
  The Shooting of Brian Campbell and Colm McGirr   289
  The Dunloy Killings   297
  The Shooting of William Price   304
  After the 'Brighton Bombing'   314
  The Shooting of Frederick Jackson   315
  The Shooting of Antoin Mac Giolla Bríde
       and the Death of Kieran Fleming   320
  The Shooting of Daniel Doherty and William Fleming   328
  Shoot-to-Kill in Strabane   333
  The Shooting of Francis Bradley   348
  The Killing of Seamus McElwain   365
  The Killing of Frank Hegarty   374
  The Loughgall Massacre   376
  Death in the Afternoon: Gibraltar   396
       Misinformation   422
       The Funerals   427
       The Inquest Verdict   434
  The Shooting of Ken Stronge: A Mistake   437
  Ambush at Drumnakilly   439
  Surveillance and Collusion   448
       The Shooting of Desmond Grew and Martin McCaughey   450
       The Shooting of Tony Doris, Lawrence McNally and Pete Ryan   452
       The Shooting of Kevin Barry O'Donnell, Seán O'Farrell,
       Peter Clancy and Daniel Patrick Vincent   456

Envoi 1990   462
Epilogue   466
Appendix I: *Rulings of the European Court of Human Rights*   476
Appendix II: *Interim Report on the Report of the Independent Commission
                of Inquiry into the Dublin and Monaghan Bombings*   480
Chronology   491
References and Notes   501
Bibliography   510
Index   517

The Untellable Story

On 30 April 1980 six Arab nationalists whose political aim was autonomy for the Arabistan or Khuzestan region of Iran invaded the Iranian embassy in London and for six days held twenty-six men and women hostage. Two of the hostages were killed during the siege. On 5 May millions of TV news-watchers saw black-clad soldiers swing on to the balcony of the embassy, place explosive charges and dive through billowing smoke. It made thrilling television. Five of the Arabs were killed. One was lucky to be taken prisoner. To read the *Sunday Times* Insight book *Siege*, the more personal account *Hostage* by Chris Cramer and Sim Harris and accounts of the subsequent inquests is to be faced with a sober question. Did the SAS soldiers who rescued the hostages murder the Arab gunmen? The Insight team posed such a question:[1]

> ... Abbas Fallahi, the Embassy doorman, did see what happened and takes up the story. 'The SAS began to shout: "The terrorists, who are the terrorists?" No one responded. We just couldn't do anything. Eventually Dr Ezzatti, the Cultural Attaché, who was almost mistaken for one of the gunmen, pointed one or two of them out. The SAS shot them where they sat with their backs to the centre of the room and their hands on the wall. Their bodies remained there, slumped against the wall and facing it. I thought they were merely unconscious but then I knew that the SAS had used real bullets'... The crucial question is: had the gunmen dropped all of their weapons and genuinely surrendered before they were shot? And if so, can their killings possibly be justified on any legal and moral basis?

The surviving gunman Ali was convinced that members of the SAS had tried to drag him back into the embassy and shoot him once they had discovered he was not a hostage. Some of the women hostages also believed this and tried to protect him as he lay on the grass outside the building.

Such serious questioning of the action of the SAS at the siege at Princes Gate, London, was lost in the euphoria and delight of the popular British daily newspapers, a delight enhanced by the SAS reconnaissance and three major offensive raids in the Falklands war. Jingoism enlivened the legend of supermen despite Mr Tam Dalyell, MP and others questioning the morality of the massacre of Argentinian soldiers at Goose Green and the legality and morality of the sinking of the Argentinian cruiser, the *Belgrano*.

The siege was not without its Irish connection. Corporal Tommy Palmer, who was seen on the television news running out of the embassy when the siege was over, his neck and shoulders scorched from his black hood which had caught fire, was to die three years later, 8 February 1983, in a car crash on the M1 motorway near Lurgan.[2] Another SAS soldier in the siege narrowly escaped death on 2 May 1980 when his CO, Captain H.R. Westmacott, was cut down by M60 machine-gun fire in Belfast. It is said that the SAS man who got himself entangled in his rope when swinging down from the embassy roof was one of the soldiers who served in Northern Ireland in 1973.[3]

SAS casualties are rarely released but in an unprecedented move the British Defence Ministry on 23 April 1982 released the names of eighteen members of an SAS unit and three others who were killed in Sea King helicopter ZA 294 which crashed into the sea during the Falklands war.[4] The Ministry did not disclose the dead as simply belonging to the SAS but recorded their parent regiments. Listed as dead were: Warrant Officer Lawrence Gallagher, Royal Engineers; Warrant Officer Malcolm Atkinson, Coldstream Guards; Staff Sgt Patrick O'Connor, Irish Guards; Sgt Philip Currass, RAMC; Sgt Sid Davidson, Parachute Regiment; Sgt John Arthy, Welsh Guards; Sgt William Hughes, Welsh Guards; Cpl Paul Bunker, RAOC; Cpl William Begley (RCT); Cpl William Hatton, Parachute Regiment; Cpl Philip Jones, Welsh Guards; Cpl John Newton (REME); Cpl Michael McHugh, Royal Signals; Cpl Stephen Sykes, Royal Signals; Cpl Edward Walpole, Royal Green Jackets; Cpl Robert Burns, Royal Signals; Cpl Douglas Mac Cormack, Royal Signals; L/Cl Paul Lightfoot, Royal Signals; Rifleman Raymond Armstrong, Royal Green Jackets; F/Lt Garth Hawkins, RAF; Cpl Michael Love, Royal Marines. Although the men were listed under their parent regiments it was an open secret that they were members of the SAS. An interdenominational service was held at Hereford Cathedral to mourn their deaths, the heaviest single loss by the regiment since establishing its headquarters at Hereford thirty years ago. The dead were 'professional but unassuming men, close to the hearts of Hereford-shire', said the Right Rev. John Eastaugh, Bishop of Hereford. 'They knew the risks, but that does not lessen our grief. We are immensely proud of the SAS here, and I hope to visit the families of all who died'.

It is an indication of the commitment of the British Government to the use of the SAS in Northern Ireland that eleven of the Falklands casualties who took part in Operation 'Corporate' served in Northern Ireland. Their obituaries are in the SAS magazine *Mars & Minerva* (Vol. 7, No. 2, 1982). A few phrases from them will illustrate the point. Sergeant Philip Preston Currass, QGM (Royal Army Medical Corps) joined 22 SAS in 1972. 'He saw active service in Dhofar, completing a number of operational tours, later serving in Northern Ireland. His efforts and enthusiasm earned him the award of the Queen's Gallantry Medal.' 24057552 Sergeant Sidney Albert Ivor Davidson joined 22 SAS in 1973. 'He served first in 'B' Squadron, joining 'D' in 1975, becoming a member of Amphibious Troop. He served both in Dhofar and Northern Ireland'. Sergeant John Leslie Arthy (Welsh Guards) – '"Lofty" came to the regiment in 1975 and joined 18 Troop (Mobility). In 1977 he transferred to Mountain Troop (18). He served with the Regiment in both Ireland and Oman'. Corporal Paul Bunker (Royal Army Ordnance Corps) joined 22 SAS in August 1976 and was posted to 16 Troop, the Free-Fall Troop. 'With 19 Troop he served in Northern Ireland, West Virginia, Florida, Bavaria and the Falklands'. 23969493 SSM Malcolm Atkinson joined 'G' Squadron 22 SAS in 1966. 'His career spanned 12 fully operational tours in Malaya, Borneo, Aden, Oman and Northern Ireland'. Staff-Sergeant P. O'Connor (Irish Guards) came to 22 SAS in 1966. 'He served with us in South Arabia, Belize, Northern Ireland, Dhofar, Norway and the United States. He was a specialist Signaller, skilful Freefall Parachutist and a qualified Norwegian Speaker'. 24154752 Corporal William Clark Hatton, QGM joined 'G' Squadron 22 SAS as a member of the Amphibious Troop in July 1978. 'He was present with his Squadron on four operational tours in Northern Ireland when his vast depth of experience in that theatre was of quite inestimable value'. 24442111 L. Corporal Paul Lightfoot enlisted in August 1977. 'During his time with 'G' Squadron he gained the GSM for service in Northern Ireland'. 24398223 Corporal Michael McHugh 'volunteered for service with 264 SAS Signal Squadron and completed the Signals Selection Course in June 1978. During his time with 'G' Squadron he was awarded the GSM with Clasp for Northern Ireland'.

There is no evidence to suggest that any of these SAS soldiers had any knowledge or involvement in the actions carried out by the SAS which are detailed in this book. Similarly, save where officers are named in relation to specific operations, there is nothing to suggest that any officer or man named in the book played any part in these activities. This is not to suggest that the SAS soldiers who were involved in the operations acted in a vacuum. They enjoyed a high degree of operational freedom. Their actions had official sanction. The SAS has been co-ordinated by the intelligence agencies, chiefly MI5 and MI6. On some occasions, such as the operation to trap an IRA bomb-team in Gibraltar, the intelligence agencies have worked hand in hand with the Ministry of Defence and the Cabinet in deciding how, when and where the SAS should be deployed.

Pride in the SAS, following the siege at the Iranian embassy and the Falklands war, renewed interest in the history of the regiment and ensured a flurry of new books. The older star-studded adventure stories, such as *The Phantom Major*, The Story of David Stirling and the SAS Regiment by Virginia Cowles, *Winged Dagger*, Adventures on the Special Service by Roy

Farran, *These Men are Dangerous* by Derrick Harrison, *Colonel Paddy* by Patrick Marrinan were back in fashion once more. A new edition of the 'official' history, or rather the one favoured by the SAS themselves, *The Special Air Service* by Philip Warner appeared in 1982 and then more solid but also partial and laudatory works, *Who Dares Wins*, The Story of the Special Air Service 1950-1980 by Tony Geraghty, A *History of the S.A.S. Regiment* by John Strawson (1984), *SAS Operations* by James D. Ladd (1986), and a personal account *SAS: Operation Oman* by Tony Jeapes (1980), an SAS man who was later to serve in Northern Ireland. A new biography of Lt Col. 'Paddy' Blair Mayne, *Rogue Warrior of the SAS* by Roy Bradford and Martin Dillon appeared in 1987. There were lighter books too for popular consumption: *This is the SAS*, A pictorial history of the Special Air Service Regiment (1982) by Tony Geraghty, *Elite Forces, The SAS* (1986), *True Stories of the SAS* by Robin Hunter (1985), *Secret Armies* (1988) by James Adams, and *Ambush*, The war between the SAS and the IRA (1988) by James Adams, Robin Morgan & Anthony Bambridge.

Geraghty has a chapter 'The Irish Dimension 1969' in *Who Dares Wins* but it is inadequate and he seems to have too much official approval from the regiment to be objective.[5] James D. Ladd includes Northern Ireland in his sketchy chapter 'Internal Security'. Major General John Strawson does not tell the story of the SAS in Northern Ireland but he remarks that the SAS could neither win victory nor draw there 'since there is no such thing as winning total control of Ulster's population, and therefore no such thing as defeating the IRA'. *Ambush* has a strong bias in favour of the SAS.

It is hoped to begin to tell the 'untellable story', to use Strawson's phrase, in this book.

Unravelling the SAS

The first SAS unit was founded in Egypt in July 1941 by Captain David Stirling of the Scots Guards. An ally and friend, David Lloyd-Owen of the Long Range Desert group, said of him, 'There was never a more convincing talker than Stirling once he had an idea in his head. On top of this he had a burning passion to fight the enemy and unbounded confidence that, given surprise, he would always be able to destroy them, despite the odds with which he might be faced. Failure meant nothing more to him than to generate fierce determination to be successful next time'.[6] 'He was the mildest mannered man that ever scuttled a ship or cut a throat' was Sir Winston Churchill's phrase to describe him, quoting Byron's *Don Juan*.[7]

The aim of the élite force, to be recruited from other regiments, was to carry out sabotage and intelligence operations behind enemy lines. Stirling's unbounded confidence and fierce determination were needed. The first actions were disastrous. In February 1941 thirty-six men of the 11th SAS were dropped in Northern Italy. All were captured. This is ignored in official histories but the regiment's official birthday, 16 November 1941, is hardly better. On that day sixty men were dropped behind enemy lines in North Africa with the task of destroying an airfield in Libya. Only twenty made it back to base, mission unaccomplished. Stirling himself was captured in 1943 and spent the rest of the war in a POW camp.

After a few years of action the SAS units were recognised as a regiment. A second regiment was formed in 1943 under the command of David Stirling's brother, William. These two regiments combined from 1944 with French and Belgian special forces. The war-time regiments saw action in the Western Desert 1941-43, in Italy and the Greek Islands 1943-45 and were parachuted into France before D-Day. The campaign in Greece ended in dishonour when British officers, acting on the instructions of Churchhill, Stalin and Roosevelt, were party to the massacre in Athens of their erstwhile comrades in arms, the left-wing ELAS.

The SAS regiments were disbanded in October 1945. A territorial unit, the 21st SAS (Artists), was formed in 1947. The Artists were an echo of the territorial regiment, the Artists' Rifles, dating back to 1859, whose members were drawn from professions and artists linked to the ruling class. Originally the idea was to call the new Territorial Army regiment the 12th regiment symbolically linking together the 1st and 2nd SAS regiments, but in case this would lead to confusion with the 12th Airborne TA the figures were reversed and the 21st SAS was born.

In 1950 Major J.M. Calvert, popularly known as 'Mad' Mike Calvert, a man with extreme right-wing views, raised the Malayan Scouts to oppose anti-colonialist guerrillas who had been fighting there since 1948. The guerrillas were tagged 'Chinese communists' in the British Press. The Malayan Scouts were drawn from ex-wartime SAS, SOE, Force 136, Ferret Force; together with M Squadron 21 SAS they combined to form 22 SAS now the only regular SAS regiment in the British Army. By 1952 the SAS had four squadrons in Malaya – 'A', 'B', 'C' and 'D'. An editorial in the SAS regimental magazine *Mars & Minerva*, November 1978, described them thus: "'A' was the 'SOP' outfit, straight-laced, formal, ultimately professional and probably the proud producer of more senior ranks in 22 SAS than any other – P de B, PFW, Lawrence, Tanky and Frank all spring readily to mind. 'B' were the tearaways, the humorists, the "livers of life" to the full, the unorthodox – even to the point of being disbanded ... 'D' was the old man's squadron, nasty, evil, tribalistic – even the Troops did not talk with each other, a mixture of 'A's' professionalism coupled with 'B's' humour, but with an evil touch...' The new regiment had a headquarters staff. In 1952 its soldiers were dropped behind the lines in Malaya with the objective of cutting off supplies to the Min Yuen. In June 1952 General Sir Gerald Templer, the Malayan High Commissioner, had said that the problem rested in the hearts and minds of the Malayan people. Such a phrase was taken up by SAS strategists and has ever remained a catch phrase of SAS philosophy. Paradoxically it is entwined with the SAS down-to-earth practicality of 'body count'.

In 1958 the 22 SAS withdrew from Malaya as the guerrilla war neared its end. The War Office had decided to reduce it from 3 Sabre (Combat) Squadrons to one small headquarter and base element but then the anticolonial uprising in Oman breathed new life into the regiment. Politically the British Government in 1958 did not wish to send troops in great numbers to reconquer the mountainous Jebel Akhdar, especially after the humiliation of Suez. The Foreign Secretary, Selwyn Lloyd, argued that the disadvantage of a large-scale operation was that 'after our troops had been withdrawn, the situation would progressively deteriorate, leaving us with no permanent military advantage to outweigh the political objections to military action of this type'. It was agreed by the defence committee to send in two squadrons of the SAS ('A' and 'D' of 22 SAS) 'provided that all possible steps were taken to avoid publicity for our action'. There was a reasonable chance, the committee said, that the moves would go unnoticed. To explain the SAS presence 'we should maintain...it was intended to assist in the training of the Sultan's own forces'. The Foreign Office was able to persuade the Prime Minister, Harold Macmillan, to intervene in covering up the role of the SAS in Muscat and Oman. FO minutes, now available, show that officials advised Ministers to offset a Labour Opposition debate in the Commons – 'It would be dangerous to say that operations by our forces continued throughout 1957-8: this would conflict with our contemporary statements that we were "assisting in training"'. As it happened the campaign added to the myth of SAS heroics. More importantly, some of the future top staff of the SAS regiments were blooded in the Oman campaign.

The SAS has become an 'élite' unit. While other regiments have been disbanded or have contracted, the SAS has grown in status and has been given special priority in provision of equipment. Anti-colonial guerrilla warfare since 1950 and the 'internal security' within states have added to its peculiar governmental patronage. Its development has been helped by its transitory nature. Officers are recruited for a 'tour of duty' and return to their own units. Junior Officers who commanded 22 SAS in Malaya and Oman are now senior officers and no doubt have influenced the protection of the SAS so that it has become powerful and established. Some institutionalism has gradually crept in. More SAS officers remain in the regiment and more return for repeated turns of duty. Its prestige has also been helped by the interweaving of other élite regiments. In Malaya the Paras provided the SAS with their third squadron and joint operations with the 'Guards Independent Para Company' enabled the SAS to form its own Guards Squadron 'G' in 1966. The 'Guards Independent Para Company' was disbanded in 1975. 'G' Squadron of 22 SAS picked up some twenty recruits from them. 'G' Squadron is distinguished from the rest of the SAS by the soldiers wearing their 'wings' on a dark red background and by having lance-sergeants. These guards have had two captains killed in Northern Ireland while on 'surveillance' duties, Captain A. Pollen (Coldstream) in Derry, Easter Sunday, 1974, and Captain Robert Nairac (Grenadier) in 1977.

22 SAS was at first housed at Malvern, Worcestershire. It moved to Hereford in 1960. The present SAS Group is commanded by a Director. The Group Headquarters/Regiment Headquarters is in the Centre Block of the Duke of York Barracks at the top of King's Road, London. Officially the Duke of York's Barracks is listed as the RHQ of the Royal Signals Corps (a unit with close relationships with the SAS), the 44 Parachute Brigade TAVR (= Territorial Army Volunteers Reserve) HQ (their section of the barracks was bombed by the IRA in September 1973), and the 'London Irish', a TAVR section of the Royal Irish Rangers. The SAS Regimental Museum is housed there and personnel from the RAF 'Special Services Air Crew' and 'Special Forces Parachute Detachment', who are attached to the SAS Group, are also accommodated within the Centre Block. The highest security is reserved for the SAS Group Intelligence which is also located in the barracks.

22 SAS Headquarters is at Bradbury Lines Barracks in the small market

town of Hereford. 'R' Squadron (TAVR) also have their base there. This is a reservist standby group of ex-22 Regiment members. SAS communications are provided by 322 Royal Signal Squadron and 264 (V) Signal Squadron.

22 SAS consists of four 'Sabre Squadrons', 'A', 'B', 'D' and 'G', a training wing and an Operational Research Section. Each squadron consists of seventy-two men and six officers. Each squadron is divided into five troops, an amphibious troop, an air troop, a surveillance troop, a mountain troop, each of these troops consisting of an officer and fifteen men, and finally a specialised signals troop of twenty-four men most of whom are seconded by the Royal Corps of Signals. It is interesting that the training wing has a special Northern Ireland cell. The SAS usually operates in teams of four, all with special skills, but at the same time all are trained in various skills. Much has been written about the SAS selection process and training. Needless to say the initiative tests are severe and the soldiers are well trained. They are intelligent and disciplined men, on occasion briefed direct from the Cabinet. On surveillance they try to adhere strictly to surveillance only but on special missions they 'take no prisoners'. They are backed in that event by the Government and well-orchestrated propaganda. In the event of mistakes and embarrassing situations the skill of lawyers is harnessed to protect them. The SAS is finding it increasingly difficult to recruit sufficient new personnel of the desired calibre, particularly officers. Whereas one in ten other rank volunteers pass their SAS selection course, the equivalent figure for officers has dropped to six per cent in recent years and, as the SAS has no lieutenants, it has a particularly high officer complement compared to most army units.

Recruits are drawn from other regiments. Peter Watson in his book *War on the Mind*, a study of the military abuses of psychology, says of the psychologists who test SAS recruits – 'The psychologists look for those who, on the tests, are: above average in intelligence; assertive; happy-go lucky; self-sufficient; not extremely intro - or extroverted. They do *not* want people who are emotionally stable; instead they want forthright individuals who are hard to fool and not dependent on others. The psychologists do acknowledge that occasionally with the SAS there are problems of too many chiefs and not enough indians'. Those who pass the selection course are formally given the beige coloured beret and its winged-dagger badge with the motto 'Who Dares Wins'. Officially the SAS maintains that the original cap badge was to be a flaming sword of Damocles but the tailor produced a design more like a winged dagger and this was retained. A more sinister interpretation is that there is in the SAS a warrior élite ethos derived from the Jacobite Freemasons of Scotland and the Winged Dagger is a vengeful symbol, a survival of a particular grade in their Lodge.[8] The motto is distastefully incorporated into a Regimental Collect:[9]

O Lord, who didst call on Thy disciples to venture all to win all men to Thee, grant that we, the chosen members of the Special Air Service Regiment, may by our works and our ways, dare all to win all, and in doing so render special service to Thee and our fellow-men in all the world. Through the same Jesus Christ, Our Lord, Amen.

There are two SAS TAVR regiments, 21 SAS (Artists V) and 23 SAS (V). In 1859 Edward Sterling, a student of Cary's School of Art, held a meeting in his studio with the intention of founding the Artists Rifles regiment. A second meeting took place in 1860 and first enrolments of the Artists Rifle Volunteers were organised. They became an official part of the British Army in 1863 and served in the Boer War. They were officially dubbed the 38th Middlesex (Artists) Rifle Volunteers. They were converted into the Territorial force in 1908 by Lord Haldane and supplied officers to other units in the First World War. In 1928 they were affiliated to the Rifle Brigade. On its formation in 1947, 21 SAS incorporated their title – 21st SAS (Artists).[10] They provide the Royal Academy Summer Exhibition Guard of Honour since the RA was originally the Artists HQ. They provide a guard for the Lord Mayor of London's Manor House Banquet. This connection with the city of London is also shown through the 'Glovers Company'. Their rank badge is against a black background instead of silver or white; their uniform has pompadour blue trimmings. The regimental toast is, 'Gentlemen of the Artists and men of the other Corps'. 21st SAS (Artists V) has its headquarters for 'A' and 'B' squadron at the Duke of York's HQ in London. 'C' squadron is based at Bedford Road, Hitchin, 'S' squadron at Tudor Crescent, Cosham, Portsmouth, where the 63rd Signal squadron (SASV) is located in Peronne Road.

The 23rd SAS (V), more proletarian in its style and origin, covers the industrial midlands and is important for monitoring social unrest. Its HQ and squadron 'A' are based at Kingstanding Road, Birmingham, 'B' squadron at Old Carlton Barracks, Leeds, 'C' squadron at Sanford Road Barracks, Doncaster, covering Tyneside, 'D' squadron covers industrial Scotland.

23rd SAS (V) was formed in London in 1959 but later transferred to Birmingham. It was formed from an existing unit, 'The Joint Reserve Reconnaissance Unit (TA)' which was originally known as 'The Joint Reserve Prisoner of War Intelligence Organisation (TA)', and before that again was called 'Intelligence School 9 (TA)', the post-war continuation of IS9 (d), the World War Two operational section of MI9, the British escape network commanded by Airey Neave and Lt Colonel James Langley.

Although the SAS regiments are officially under the command of HQ UK Land Forces, Wiltshire, in practice, like the Intelligence Corps, they work directly with the Ministry of Defence. The SAS Director has a direct line to the Prime Minister. The office of Director was created in 1970. He is not necessarily chosen from within the SAS but the SAS obviously influences the selection.

The 'SAS Group Intelligence' is the most secret section of the SAS. It is located in the Duke of York Barracks as is also the Special Branch 'telephone monitoring post' (tapping) and this is no coincidence. In Britain SAS members work on 'special detail' with the Special Branch in all major cities. The contacts with the British police go back many years. In 1970 the Home Office sent London Commissioner Robert Mark with the former 22 SAS OC Major General Deane Drummond on a world survey of police and anti-riot techniques. The setting up of the National Security Committee following the 1972 industrial unrest ensured further police contacts. The Labour Government renamed the committee the Civil Contingencies Committee (CCC) in 1975; responsibility for 'International terrorism' or anything the police could not deal with was delegated to the SAS. The CCC set out the three situations in which the Ministry of Defence, with the agreement of Ministers on the CCC, can order the military on to the streets: (1) *Military Aid to the Civil Power*, e.g. during the Provisional IRA bombing when units of the SAS and the Royal Military Police were on patrol in plain clothes, (2) *Military Aid to the Civil Community*, e.g. flooding (3) *Military Aid to the Civil Ministries*, the deployment of troops to maintain essential services during an industrial dispute.[11] SAS Group Intelligence reviewed security and prepared contingency plans for hijacks at British airports. Two SAS antiterrorist teams of twelve men with Range Rover transport are on a 24-hour, 3-minute alert, system, based at Hereford and London. They were employed at the January 1973 hijacking of a British Airways plane *en route* from Manchester to London and at the Balcombe Street siege of December 1975 where four IRA men were trapped by the Metropolitan Police. The SAS can now rank along with the four 'security agencies' in Britain: the Secret Intelligence Service (SIS or MI6 or DI6) under the control of the Foreign Secretary; the intelligence section within the Home Office, the Security Service (MI5 or DI5), the Defence Intelligence Staff at the Ministry of Defence, and finally the Special Branch. The Director of the SAS attends all Defence Intelligence committee meetings which co-ordinate British security.

The SAS saw nine years of jungle service in Malaya, 1950-59, a campaign in Borneo 1962-66, two campaigns in Oman 1958-59, 1970-76, and operations in Aden and Oman 1963-67. They served unofficially in Vietnam when they were attached to the Australian and New Zealand SAS but it is unlikely that they were used in Kenya and Cyprus. Their name has mistakenly been linked with the Queen Elizabeth II incident in May 1972. This was basically a Special Boat Section (SBS) operation, a unit now under the command of the Royal Marines but actually a part of the SAS during a period in World War Two. SAS latest assignments are Belize, Northern

Ireland and Cambodia where one officer and six soldiers of the Training Wing have helped to train CIA-backed guerillas.

Investigatory journalists who have turned their attention to the British-led mercenary operation in North Yemen, where the SAS fought on the Royalist side in the civil war, have revealed that the SAS returned secretly there in 1982. The mission took the form of giving Yemen troops a course in counter-insurgency. In his article 'Smiley's People – The SAS Men return' Morris Riley wrote (*Anarchy Magazine*, Issue 37, Winter 1984/4):

> History in North Yemen during the last two decades ... shows how the British public were not allowed to be cognizant about what was happening in North Yemen on their behalf. Publicly Prime Minister Sir Alec Douglas-Home professed a policy on 'non-involvement in the civil war in the Yemen'. Yet at the same time he had fully supported the operation, and was following ex-Prime Minister Harold Macmillan's attempt, executed by Julian Amery and a clutch of his old Albanian cronies, to fight the good fight in Yemen. This attempt included the involvement of British Intelligence operations.

Besides the clandestine war in North Yemen, mercenary operations[12] involving past and present associates of the SAS necessitate their inclusion in a history of the regiment. Tony Geraghty recognised that and included a chapter on mercenaries in his book. Duncan Campbell wrote an extensive article on the subject in *Time Out* magazine, 21-27 August 1978. In the article he researched KMS Ltd, nicknamed 24 SAS, a network for the employment of former SAS members. KMS, standing for Keeni-Meeni Services, (Keeni-Meeni is South Arabian slang meaning 'under the counter') was a mercenary recruiting organisation. Campbell mentioned the commanders in KMS, all former SAS commanding officers.

Colonel David Stirling who founded the SAS is also linked with the founding of the Capricorn Africa Society, an attempt (which failed) to win over in 1950-52 the African nationalist leaders for the pro-British middle class, and the setting-up in 1967 of the Guernsey based organisation Watchguard (International) Ltd (now defunct) to provide bodyguards and security training for leaders the British government approved. Watchguard was involved in 'Hilton Operation' which contemplated ousting Colonel Ghadaffi in Libya in 1970 after he had staged his coup against the pro-British regime in 1969. Industrial unrest in Britain in late 1973 and early 1974 led to the formation of 'patriot groups,' among them General Sir Walter Walker's Civil Assistance and David Stirling's strike-breaking force GB75. It is an interesting question whether the 'patriot groups' had semi-official backing. Stirling's documents say that the plans had been formulated after talking to 'varying ranks in the armed forces, local authorities, directors ... and some senior members of the late Conservative Government'. Walker had made contact with Field Marshal Sir Gerald Templer and Stirling with Field Marshal Lord Carver. Colin Wallace, formerly the British Army psy-ops expert in Northern Ireland, has written of 'covert assistance' from the British Intelligence agencies for the 'patriot groups', Unison, GB75 and Civil Assistance.

The combined SAS and Artist Rifles Association, with a membership of 1,200, many of whose officers now occupy high positions in the political and business world, is a great potential for intelligence collection and special security services.

On 14 August 1975 John Banks founded the firm of Security Advisory Services. He recruited mercenaries for the Angolan War, among them some ex-SAS members. The fact that Banks was able to recruit freely and send his men to Angola is an indication of the partial nod of the British Government. Banks had close links with the Special Branch and MI5. He outlined his relations with MI5 and the security services at the Old Bailey Trial of Sinn Féin member John Higgins in March 1977. In 1976 Banks had fooled John Higgins by offering him radio equipment and arms for the IRA. Higgins was not interested and was wary of Banks. He made the mistake of seeing Banks a second time. Banks had a tape recorder in his brief-case. When Higgins was charged Banks appeared as chief prosecution witness. At the trial Banks claimed he worked in 'close harmony' with Major Andrew Nightingale of SAS Group Intelligence and Detective Inspector Ray Tucker. Banks revealed under oath that when he heard of the alleged Irish arms plot he contacted SAS Group Intelligence ('The Kremlin') which he described as a 'regular SAS unit; it employs, controls and runs intelligence gathering and activities into alien paramilitary organisations in the UK'.

There are reports that the SAS serve unofficially in South Africa and that they served in Rhodesia against the nationalist guerrillas during the war of independence. It has been suggested that up to fifty former British SAS men were in the Rhodesian SAS and a slightly smaller number in the Selous Scouts. Other former SAS men served in Rhodesian intelligence while retaining British passports and were at the same time listed on the British Army's Reserve. The Rhodesian SAS is still officially designated as 'C' Squadron of the British SAS and its affiliation is printed in *Mars & Minerva*. Until UDI it ran joint training operations with the British. The article 'Zimbabwe and Britain' in *The Leveller*, November 1979, listed various SAS connections with Rhodesia: 'Last year the *New Statesman* reported that Major A. Nightingale accompanied Lord Carver as his bodyguard when he visited Rhodesia in November 1977. During the trial of John Higgins (see *Leveller* 6 & 25) John Banks named Nightingale as his SAS contact'.

The Irish Connection

A surprisingly high proportion of SAS men are Irish (and a high proportion are said to be Catholics). David Barzilay in his book *The British Army in Ulster* (Vol. 4, 1981) says, 'Much intelligence has been gathered by the SAS which is believed to have recruited a number of Irishmen to its ranks, both from the North and South of the Irish border'. An Irishman who gained a reputation as an SAS soldier was the Rt Hon. Sir Ambrose McGonigal, MC. When he died a memoir appeared in the SAS magazine *Mars & Minerva* (Vol. 4, No. 2., Dec. 1979). It is signed 'W.L.M.-B. D.G.C.S.' I include an extract here as it gathers a past and present Irish dimension together:

> When Ambrose McGonigal joined the SBS in Italy in August 1944 his reputation as a fighting soldier preceded him. For he had, as a young officer in the Royal Ulster Rifles attached to 12 Commando, taken part in numerous pre-invasion operations on the French coast, had been wounded and awarded the MC and Bar.
>
> From the earliest days the name McGonigal was familiar within the SAS. Ambrose's brother, Ian, joined David Stirling from the Scottish Commando and was killed on the first operation in the Western Desert in November 1941. Ambrose was determined to avenge him. Ambrose was a tall, dark, good-looking young man and a natural ally of Andy Lassen, with a talent for good-natured escapades, both on operations and in camp. I can only remember his being ruffled once, when he surprised us all by vehemently defending de Valera's action in mourning the death of Hitler in a speech he gave in Dublin. We had all been denouncing this as Free State treachery, but Ambrose regarded our comments as an insult to the Irish people as a whole.
>
> Ambrose's arrival in the SBS coincided with the unit's move from the Middle East to Italy where it came under command of Land Forces Adriatic based in Bari. The SBS were quickly involved in a series of operations in Greece, Albania and Yugoslavia against German garrisons in the coastal strip. Proceedings opened with Ambrose and his patrol landing on the Southern Yugoslav coast on 28th August, 1944. Over a period of several weeks the patrol carried out a number of successful ambushes against trains and trucks evacuating Germans from Greece. The success of these operations illustrated Ambrose's military and diplomatic aptitude as the area was full of Yugoslav Partisans and Ustashi. The former resented the British appearing when it seemed to them the war was nearly over and the latter were active German supporters.
>
> Early in 1945 the SBS established a forward base at Zadar on the Dalmatian coast. It was from here in March that Ambrose led two difficult attacks against strongly defended German positions. The first

was on the Villa Punta on the island of Losinj and the second on the bridge linking the islands of Losinj and Cres. The attacks involved heavy fighting at night. The Villa Punta was completely destroyed and the bridge garrison suffered heavy losses. There were SBS casualties but these would have been far more serious but for Ambrose's skill, determination and personal bravery. He was mentioned in despatches in 1945.

It was clear to us that whatever Ambrose did after the war he would excel for he was very able. As is well known, he followed his father's footsteps in a distinguished legal career in Northern Ireland. Ambrose rose to be a High Court Judge in 1968 and in 1975 became Lord Justice of Appeal at the Supreme Court of Northern Ireland being knighted and made a Privy Councillor in that year.

Two years ago I had an excuse for visiting Belfast.... It was clear in Belfast that he was under great strain. Bishops Court House, where they lived, was on the fringe of an airfield, protected by a detachment of the RAF Regiment and opposite a revolving searchlight which afforded some protection. Regular patrols came round at night, but there was a peep-hole above the entrance door so that no stranger could be let in. Even so Ambrose always carried a revolver and at night slept with one under his pillow.

A surprise, considering its Irish intake, is the strong anti-Irish racist tone of *Mars & Minerva*, the SAS Regimental Association Journal, and letters and addresses of its officers. For example:

'Have you heard about the Irish SAS man who fought his way into the zoo, shot all the ostriches and rescued the gorillas' (*Mars & Minerva*, No. 1, 1981).

'I rather like the story by the two *Daily Telegraph* reporters who wrote of interviewing an Irishman, who claimed he was God, in his two-storeyed bungalow. Perhaps he really was?' This went beside honouring Irishman Colonel Paddy Mayne – 'A wreath was laid on Colonel Paddy's grave at 0800 hrs on Sunday, 11th November, 1979, by Major Hector Gullan on behalf of all of us' (*Mars & Minerva*, Vol. 4, No.3, June 1980).

Another sample of anti-Irish humour appears in the same issue:- 'From 23 SAS ... WO 2 Chambers 'C' Squadron of this Regt wishes to attend the summer Olympic Games 1980. He coaches his Irish grandmother who participated in two track events in 1976 ... She took part in the 8,000 metres for men in 1976 and would certainly have got amongst the medal winners had her wellie not burst whilst cornering at speed...' This telex/teleprinter message appears to be a 'reply' to an official instruction that no military personnel were to attend the Moscow Olympics.

Major Tom Burt (aged 91, I am told) had an Irish joke letter in *Mars &*

Minerva, (Vol. 5, No.2, Spring 1982): 'Dear Son, Just a few lines to let you know I am still alive. I am writing this slowly because I know that you can't read fast. You won't know the house when you come home, we've moved. About your father he has got a lovely new job. He has got 500 under him, he cuts grass at the cemetery. Your sister Mary had a baby this morning. I haven't found out whether its a boy or girl so I don't know if you are an aunt or an uncle...'

Brigadier J.P. Foley, OBE, could not resist anti-Irish feeling in his speech at the regimental party of Major C.L. Newell, OBE, Regimental Adjutant SAS Group (popularly known as Dare):

> Dare has, of course, as has the SAS Association, achieved fame else-where, and some of you may not realise the permanent place that Dare and the Association played, in the 1970s, in the affections of Irish Republican terrorists. The association was known to them as The Kremlin, while Dare, mysteriously, was Clarence! Why, you may ask? Well, it was a case of the Irish dimension at work, for they somehow constructed Clarence from CLDN!! It reminds me of the story about the Irishman who couldn't understand why his sister had three brothers and he only had two...

Mars & Minerva is not an official British Army or Ministry of Defence publication. It can seemingly publish what it wishes about the Irish.

The Sacred and the Profane

> When you burst into a hut full of enemy soldiers you must remember the drill evolved for such occasions. Shoot the first person who makes a move, hostile or otherwise. His brain has recovered from the shock of seeing you there with a gun. He has started to think and is therefore dangerous. You must then shoot the person nearest to you, because he is in the best position to cause you embarrassment. Then deal with the rest as you think fit.
>
> – Lt Col. 'Paddy' Blair Mayne, DSO (3Bars)
> Légion d'Honneur.[13]

The SAS are trained to kill. The Loughgall and Gibraltar massacres, the stake-outs of arms' caches where the first person to arrive on the scene is murdered, the shooting of prisoners like Peter Cleary and William Price, all bear that out.

The British Army's own handbook, *Land Operations Manual* sanctions assassinations by the SAS. The third volume *Counter Revolutionary Operations* – prefaced with Mao Tse-Tung's comment 'Political power comes out of the barrel of a gun' – says in paragraph 225:

> SAS: SAS Squadrons are particularly suited, trained and equipped for counter-revolutionary operations. Small parties may be infiltrated or dropped by parachute, including free fall, to avoid a long approach through enemy-dominated areas, in order to carry out any of the following tasks:-
> a. The collection of information on the location and movement of insurgent forces.
> b. The ambush and harassment of insurgents.
> c. Infiltration of sabotage, assassination and demolition parties into insurgent-held areas.
> d. Border surveillance.
> e. Limited community relations.
> f. Liaison with and organisation, training and control of friendly guerrilla forces operating against the common enemy.

The SAS in service in Northern Ireland use the SLR, the Sterling sub-machine-gun, the Sterling MK5L34A1 which is collapsible, silent and flashless, the USA miniature Ingram MAC11 sub-machine-gun, which fires 1200 rounds a minute, HK (Heckler & Koch) 53 rifles, and Remington shotguns. The Sterling replaced the old Sten gun; it is accurate at about 150 yards with careful aim and fires fairly well on automatic; the magazine holds 34 rounds of 9 mm Parabellum cartridge rounds. The SAS also use foreign weapons that are used by the IRA, the Kalashnikov AK47, M1 carbines and in particular AR15s (Armalite rifles). All use the Browning pistol; it is gas operated, self-loading and used for close quarter killing. It is effective at 25 metres and uses 9 mm calibre rounds. All these weapons have been used in assassinations in Northern Ireland.

The SAS appears to enjoy immunity from prosecution for assassination. A number of murders became public knowledge and caused embarrass-ment. They were covered up by the publication of false information to the media, careful statements at inquests (phrased to bring them within the 'Yellow Card' engagement directives issued to members of the British Army in Northern Ireland), and the protective voice of government. The SAS Regiments are glorified by the establishment. How could members then be successfully prosecuted for murder?

For example, the *Daily Telegraph* reported on 4 April 1981, 'Britain's most celebrated regiment was given the freedom of the ancient city of Hereford yesterday by the back door of its ornate Victorian town hall ... A tight security cordon surrounded 22 Special Air Service Regiment as it was given the right to enter the city and march through its medieval streets with bayonets fixed, drums beating and flags flying ... But because of its top security role the regiment will never exercise the right because of the need to retain the anonymity of its operational soldiers ... None of the usual pomp surrounding freedom ceremonies was evident. Twenty senior officers of the SAS and their wives were taken into the town hall through the rear entrance for the freedom ceremony which was behind closed doors in the council chamber.'

On 5 June 1984 Queen Elizabeth II and the Duke of Edinburgh paid a private visit to 22 SAS headquarters at Hereford to meet soldiers who took part in the Falklands war and survivors of the SAS expedition to Mount Everest in which one SAS man died and three were injured.

If the assassinations and murders of the SAS are in truth a profanity, a counter 'sacredness' is cultivated. It is interesting to see this cult enshrined in an established religion service. The Rev. E.W. Evans, MBE, BA, former Regimental Chaplain, gave the following address at St Martin's Church, Hereford, on the occasion of the dedication of the Memorial Window, 19 May 1983:

'2 Samuel 2, Verse 23:
And it came to pass that as many as came to the place where they (he) fell down and died ... STOOD STILL.

'I stand before you today as the clerical representative of a great Regiment ... which Regiment the Mayor and Citizens of Hereford, together with many other friends from far and wide, have endowed by these gifts of a Regimental Window, a Book of Remembrance and a Memorial Chapel. They are to the honour and memory of the men of the Regiment over the years since its formation and stationed here in Hereford since 1960.

'The Regiment, as Regiments go in the British Army, is very young but it is already rich in inheritance, courage and valour, as its inscribed battle honours on the window bear tribute. There is no Regiment in the Army's Order of Battle today which is owed so much from so many to so few.

'For nigh on 15 years now I have had a close association with it and I, therefore, speak as I know with a sense of close affinity and affection.

'What I have to say today falls very naturally into three parts, each based on one initial of the Regiment's short tile – S.A.S. 'S' stands for *Sacrifice*, and there is plenty of Biblical background for this word. Even so, *Sacrifice* is not a popular word thought in men's minds today. The Oxford Dictionary defines it thus ... "The giving up of a valued thing for the sake of another that is more worthy, or more important, or more urgent – loss thus entailed to avoid greater loss, or to obtain compensating advantage".

'Some of the deeds of this Regiment will never be fully made clear, but one thing is certain ... worthy, important, urgent ... they certainly have been.

'*Sacrifice* makes these potent demands and from it all we learn this ... that a world cleansed from war and all that leads to it cannot be obtained except by faith in righteousness and a self-sacrificing loyalty to the will of God who is the Father of all men.

'*Sacrifice* calls for a readiness which this Regiment has never lacked – as it is enshrined in the words of the Regimental collect which I myself had the honour to put together many years ago now ... "That we may by our works and our ways dare all to win all". To dare all is to be ready to make any *Sacrifice*, should the need arise.

'*Sacrifice* – the supreme one at that – has been made, time and time again, as the tributes here today show. We who are left must never be afraid to use the word – honest men and true will never fail to see its meaning – as it has been so, in all history. The value of *Sacrifice* does not depend upon whether or not it achieves its object – the act of *Sacrifice* has permanent spiritual value and significance.

'A' – the second letter, stands for a host of words, all connected with the theme of the day. *Admiration, Appreciation, Affinity, Affection* and many more.

'Goodness knows the SAS are *admired* not only for the headline news items they sometimes make (and which they don't really like at all – it's against their creed and training) – but also for their local, more personal, impact right here in this City. When the floods came, when marathons need to be run, when the City is in any need the "know-how" and expertise of these very special people can make all the difference, as well we know.

Appreciation – it's a word that describes and says what this occasion is all about. The great generosity of a great many people who have made this possible is a mark of that *appreciation*. So much work and effort has been put into the occasion – the regiment's honour and standing have been greatly enhanced by the sheer *appreciation* of all concerned. It is an occasion for humble thanksgiving that God's House in the parish has been thus enriched, that the Committee's initiative has been so greatly rewarded. The definition of *appreciation* is "adequate recognition" and here we see it in its full array.

'S' – the second 'S' – stands for *sanctification* – which is really the core of the whole matter. It represents why all this is taking place in the Parish Church of St Martin, in the parish where the Regiment lives. Other cultures, other countries, would no doubt mark the *sacrifice*, show the *appreciation* elsewhere than in God's House. I like to think that in this country, with its age-long Christian heritage there can still be only one place for a Memorial of this kind – in this shrine surrounded as it is by the last resting-place of some and the Memorial plaques of others we remember now and especially those who passed from human ken exactly a year ago this very day.

'For the same reason that the Monarch is crowned in Westminster Abbey, not in the Houses of Parliament, or on Horse Guards Parade – it means that we wish to *sanctify* our efforts, to hallow the occasion and the memories, so that we may venerate the future of those we commend to Almighty God.

'Without this point being made – and demonstrated in the way it has been achieved – it would lack all spiritual meaning and strength. Here we now have a theme, a Chapel in which to pray for those remembered – "For this is the will of God, even your *sanctification*". All life must really be a process of *sanctification* – a making of Holiness in men's lives – a real preparation to fulfil the will of God for mankind.

'Over the months that this whole scheme has been in preparation, the theme of *sanctification*, the making Holy of men's lives, deaths and passing from us, ahead of us – it has been constantly in my mind. I have spent a lot of thought, trying to fit it all together and one day last November quite quite, suddenly, I got the answer. I went with my wife for a day to York – a city I had but briefly visited in 1947 and which I had never properly seen.There, in the Cathedral, are many memorials to Regiments of the Army from Yorkshire, to the Royal Air Force and also American Service-men of World War II. And in the middle of all these fine memorials, surrounding a Memorial Chapel, there is a plain wooden tablet, with a simple inscription upon it. The words are attributed to Monica, mother of St Augustine of Hippo, who lived at the turn of the fourth century. He was one of the great theologians of the day, of the early Church. He was a wayward man in his youth – "a bit of a lad" as you might say – but his mother worked and prayed urgently for his conversion to Christianity and thereafter his *sanctification* and much was the benefit later of his writings and stature as a Christian, spiritual leader. The words of his mother, inscribed there to remind all who looked on the memorials, express exactly what I mean about *sanctification* — making holy the memory of brave men who have passed out of our vision.

"Lay my body where you will
And be not anxious about it
This only I beseech you
Remember me at the Altar of God
Wherever you are" – Remember me at the
Altar of God, wherever you are …

'If you will believe and accept the Christian hope (and remember, there is no valid alternative before us) – that God does not write us off at death – that He takes us to himself – then it is in God's Holy Presence, at the Altar of God, wherever we are, that we can remember, sanctify the lives, draw resources for our future here on earth, for the time we have allotted to us in turn, till we ourselves pass into His presence.

Today we have gathered here to stand still –
To dwell on the sacrifices made

To show admiration and appreciation
To play our part in their sanctification at the Altar of God.
"And it came to pass, that as many as came to the place where they fell
down and died – stood still".

'And now the P.S. – the *post script* to this piece – something for you to do
about all this. It would be a great idea – would it not – that every Thursday
at 12 noon someone from the Regiment – perhaps members of the Wives'
Club or representatives of the Squadrons and Departments – just one at a
time would – could step into this Church and say a Prayer for those
remembered – something simple – the Prayer of the regiment and one or
two more, ready on a card – to keep going the *sanctification*, to build it up,
to deepen, to hallow the meaning of the place, and all it stands for.

'That's my thinking – see if you can do something about it – that it might
come to pass, that as many as come to this place where they fell down and
died, may *stand still*.' (*Mars & Minerva*, Vol. 6, No.1, Summer 1983.)

Six Phases of the SAS in Northern Ireland

The movement for social justice in Northern Ireland now stands out in headline dates of civil rights' marches; the first from Coalisland to Dungannon on 24 August 1968; Derry, 5 October 1968; 9, 16 October student marches from Queen's University in Belfast to the city centre; Armagh, 30 November 1968; January 1969 the Burntollet march. The resentment which calls for reform and justice caused among loyalists came to a head on 14 August 1969. A Shankhill mob invaded West Belfast with the collusion of the RUC whose machine-gun fire on the Divis flats killed nine-year-old Patrick Rooney; on the same night John Gallagher (29) was murdered by 'B' Specials in Armagh; there was shooting in Dungannon and the Battle of the Bogside raged.

Reforms had made little progress under the Labour Government; there were fine promises but the end results were always watered down and spurious. The Westminster election of 18 June 1970 brought a Conservative Government back into power. Within a month ties were renewed between the unionists of the North and the conservatives; it was accepted that violence from nationalists was the major problem. Lt General Sir Ian Freeland received orders to crush the nationalists of West Belfast; this led to the Falls Road curfew 3-5 July 1970. Relations between the British Army and the Catholic community broke down and have never recovered since. 3-5 July 1970, like 14 August 1969 and 9 August 1971 (internment day), is a date burnt into the minds of nationalists. It is in the context of that crushing of the nationalist population by force, following the Conservative return to power, that the SAS were sent into Northern Ireland in July 1970.

The story of the SAS in Northern Ireland and, indeed, in the Republic of Ireland has been kept secret as far as possible. Official SAS hagiographers generally make two points, that the first SAS came to Northern Ireland in 1969 to prevent the gun-running of loyalist paramilitaries (while there it is said they laid a wreath on the grave of Colonel Paddy Mayne) and that their main role was in South Armagh in 1976.

After the Falls Road curfew a decision was taken to send a group of SAS to Lisburn HQ to be attached to the 39th Brigade.[14] They received their orders from the Ministry of Defence and after six weeks special training for the Irish situation at an Army base in Honiton, North Devon, 45 SAS soldiers and some members of the Joint Service Intelligence Wing came to Northern Ireland. They were to form a core of intelligence officers who would prepare the interrogation techniques for internment, help run the

MRF (Military Reconnaissance or Reaction Force), and deal with pseudo-gangs.

The history of the SAS in Ireland since 1969 is not merely one of intelligence gathering. It is a history of torture, kidnapping, unjustifiable killing and murder. One can distinguish six phases in the operations of the SAS in Ireland since 1969.

1. *Intelligence Gathering*. The word to spell out here is Torture. The SAS, experts in 'deep interrogation' training and linked to the British Army Intelligence Centre in Ashford, Kent, were responsible for the 'Hooded Men' or the in-depth interrogation by sensory deprivation of fourteen men in Ballykelly Barracks in 1971. This was condemned by the European Commission on Human Rights at Strasbourg and the Strasbourg Court. Hundreds of detainees were also ill-treated by British soldiers and Special Branch RUC at Palace Barracks, Holywood, and Girdwood Barracks, Belfast.

2. *The Sectarian Murders*. Sectarian assassinations of Catholics were carried out by Protestant paramilitaries and pseudo-gangs, tolerated and often directed by the British secret service. The purpose of the murders was to break the nerve and sap the morale of the Catholic population, thus weakening its powers of resistance and drawing off its support for the IRA. This phase included British Intelligence support for the Ulster Workers' Strike in May 1974 (which brought down the power-sharing executive government in Northern Ireland), the two Dublin bombings, 1 December 1972 and 17 May 1974, and other bombings in the Irish Republic, and cross-border assassinations and kidnappings.

3. *The SAS in South Armagh, 1976*. On 7 January 1976 the British Prime Minister Harold Wilson announced that units of 22 SAS Regiment were to be sent into South Armagh following a period of violence when both Protestants and Catholics had been murdered in that area. The idea was to terrorise the nationalist people by propaganda and by nightly calls to scattered families threatening them with assassination. The SAS shot dead Peter Cleary and Seamus Ludlow. Seán McKenna was kidnapped and abducted across the border into the North. Patrick Mooney and Kevin Byrne were kidnapped by the SAS south of the border and brought to Bess-brook Army Centre where they were ill-treated. Seamus Harvey, an IRA man, was gunned down near Crossmaglen. The activity of the SAS in South Armagh led to the murder of the British Ambassador Christopher Ewart-Biggs, an MI6 agent, on 21 July 1976. Continued harassment in South Armagh led to the murder of Earl Mountbatten on 27 August 1979 and the attack on the Parachute Regiment in Warrenpoint on the same day when eighteen soldiers were killed.

4. *SAS Terrorism*. From 1977 to 1978 the SAS killed 11 people in stakeouts. The British Army Minister, Robert Brown, announced this intensification

on 9 December 1976 following a decision by the Prime Minister, James Callaghan. This policy was solidly backed by the Secretary of State for Northern Ireland, Roy Mason. As Minister for the Army between 1974 and 1976 Roy Mason took an interest in the SAS squadrons in Oman and the Arabian Gulf. He visited them frequently in the field. On 7 March 1978 he announced that the use of the SAS would be broadened and that every major army unit in Northern Ireland would have its SAS-style undercover operations. This was also the period of the stepping up of 'Ulsterisation'. It was a logical step, having weakened the Catholic population by the loyalist assassination campaign, harassment, ill-treatment and imprisonment, to arm the 'pro-British' and let the 'native' population itself defend the 'colony'.

5. *Atkins' Secret Army.* It was left to Secretary of State Humphrey Atkins to initiate the programme of plain clothes surveillance aimed at replacing British troops who would be withdrawn from the streets. This surveillance went hand in hand with 'Ulsterisation', the handing-over of security to the RUC and UDR. Atkins spoke publicly on the 'Secret Army' at a meeting of Newry and Mourne District Council on 3 September 1979 and to the Belfast Chamber of Trade on 30 October 1979. The job of co-ordinating the work of the SAS in the different units of the British Army and with the RUC was given to Sir Maurice Oldfield, former Director-General of Secret Intelligence Service in London. This is also the period of 'Operation RANC', the organised revenge killings for the shooting of Airey Neave.

6. *Shoot-to-Kill.* Assassination as administrative policy is not new in Northern Ireland. The 1980s, however, brought it to the level of a campaign. Any IRA member or suspected IRA member found in a compromising situation was to be executed. So that 'Ulsterisation' would be complete, a special RUC unit was trained by the SAS in their skills in order to eventually replace the SAS units in Northern Ireland. The SAS was brought into full action again after the RUC Special Support Unit and MI5 blundered in shooting dead six unarmed men and seriously wounding a seventh in three separate incidents in County Armagh in 1982. In the period 1981-89 the SAS, aided by RUC intelligence and sometimes accompanied by RUC personnel, has shot dead 31 people in Northern Ireland. On 6 March 1988 the SAS shot dead three IRA members in Gibraltar. The 'Shoot-to-Kill' policy became more ruthless after the Brighton Grand Hotel bombing of October 1984 when the IRA attempted to kill the Prime Minister, Mrs Margaret Thatcher, during the Conservative Party annual conference.

In the 1990s, there was almost a frenzied effort on the part of the British Army to wipe out the IRA in Co. Tyrone. In this campaign, nine IRA volunteers were shot dead by the SAS. This action conjoined with a widespread campaign of collusion with loyalist paramilitaries in the murder of Catholics. The story of the SAS from the IRA ceasefires to the present moves to the inquests, the domestic courts and the European Court of Human Rights at Strasbourg where relatives and lawyers of the victims of SAS and RUC killings, backed by human rights organisations, battle for the disclosure of the truth.

PHASE I

Intelligence Gathering and Torture

The time – 4.30 am, 9 August 1971. Conscious of a soldier standing in the bedroom. He hit me with the butt of a rifle to awaken me. I tried to get up and get dressed but I wasn't in fact given time. Just put on underpants and trousers – no vest or anything and had to go barefooted. I saw my father up. As soon as I had my trousers on I was forced at gunpoint down the stairs and on to the street. I was then forced to run 400 yards barefoot at gunpoint...

Then the hood was put over me ... The hood was double material, a square-shaped bag, about sixteen to eighteen inches square. It was darkish charcoal grey in colour. The double material was sufficient to black out all light. It came down to the shoulders and on to the chest. There was a peculiar smell of it. The stale smell of clothes piled for a period of time...

I was given a bottle-green boiler suit overall, about ten times too big for me... They forced me to stand against the wall in the search position, fingertips. I refused to do this. Each time I rolled into a ball. They kept kicking and beating me. I took a breather against the wall – then I discovered they weren't kicking me anymore and I decided to stand against the wall and get a break. I then spent God knows how long a time – nobody else had spoken – trying to figure out what was going on – continual noise going through the whole room and through my whole head. I was fully conscious of someone standing behind me all the time watching what I would do. There were occasions when I would move my hands down to get a better position, then my two arms would be lifted up against the wall to a very stretched position. Occasionally then I was punched, kicked and beaten. I could hear voices screaming all round. Screaming out same time as noise was going on...

On one occasion I heard screaming which I believed was Kevin Hannaway. This was when I pulled off the hood to see what was going on ... there were very bright lights shining. I was instantly grabbed and thrown to the floor – I had the hood off in my hand. Three boys were trying to put the hood back on my head and I was struggling with them. I could see the feet of four – two had red track suits and two had green track suits. I could only see their legs. They were wearing gym shoes...Working backways I think I was three days against the wall without food or drink. I remember collapsing three or four times, completely exhausted, kicked and beaten, then back up against the wall...

Around this time I suffered hallucinations. I thought I was in the company of friends and couldn't understand why they wouldn't take off the handcuffs. I thought another time I was in a big field. I kept walking but there was no end to it. There was always a wall about twelve foot high in front of me which stopped me from getting to the end of the field. There was a time when I believed I was dying and I felt very happy. Actually I prayed for death...

The above is an extract from a statement I took from Francis McGuigan of Belfast, one of 14 men hooded and tortured at the introduction of internment in Northern Ireland in 1971.[15] Two of the victims have since died, Seán McKenna and Patrick Shivers. The physical and mental torture suffered by the 'Hooded Men' has been recorded by Fr Denis Faul and myself in our book *The Hooded Men* and by John McGuffin in *The Guinea Pigs*. Brutality inflicted on those interned on 9 August 1971 has been documented by the Association for Legal Justice and in particular by one of its founders, Fr Brian J. Brady, who prepared much of the material for the Irish Government's case against the Government of the United Kingdom before the European Commission for Human Rights in Strasbourg. Brutality against prisoners was a planned policy vigorously executed by the British Army and officers of the RUC Special Branch.

Since it is the SAS who concern us here, one must point out their association with the brutality and torture in Ballykinler, Ballykelly, the Palace Barracks, Holywood, and Girdwood Barracks, Belfast. Until recently sensory deprivation was practised on candidates for the SAS selection course. *The Leveller* of June 1977 published an article by an ex-SAS soldier, 'How the British Army trained me in torture techniques'. He confessed that he not only suffered torture in training but that he in turn administered it. The training aimed at making one immune to suffering. In September 1977 the Ministry of Defence admitted – 'Practical training in resistance to interrogation is given to servicemen whose military employment in war render them particularly prone to be captured'.

The training programme of SAS men had aspects similar to the torture in Ballykelly. The ex-SAS soldier related in *The Leveller*:

As soon as a man was captured, he was brought in and his boots and everything was taken off him, even in winter. He was stripped right down to virtually nothing and put into a Nissen hut with a bare floor and this loud music playing day and night. Throughout their interrogation they would be deprived of food; when they weren't being interrogated they were left nearly naked in the Nissen hut with the lights on, the noise playing constantly and without liquid except cold water.

Some were made to lean against the wall for hours by their finger tips, with SAS regulars kicking them everytime they moved. The men were instructed to shout at the new recruits, threaten them with an 'accident', tell them the regiment would cover up with their families and the MOD if they died. This treatment would sometimes continue for days with a number of added refinements.

An SAS officer interviewed by Conor O'Clery in *The Irish Times* (June 1977) told him – 'My interrogator turned very nasty, and I was told I could be disposed of if I didn't help him. The exercise ceased being a game. The interrogator would say that a soldier could be written off as a "victim of an accident". Screams could be heard coming from the next room while this was happening. Many officers who failed were broken down for a long, long time'.

SAS soldiers are trained to resist 'deep interrogation' techniques. The British Army has used them in every major campaign from Kenya to Northern Ireland, including Oman, Aden and Cyprus. A BBC 2 documentary 'The Unleashing of Evil', 29 June 1988, examined the use of torture by special forces over the past thirty years and included the 'brutal, inhuman and degrading' treatment used against fourteen Catholics in Northern Ireland in 1971 in that survey. The producer, Mr Richard Taylor, interviewed victims and interrogators in the survey. A former British soldier described how special forces are trained in resisting deep interrogation at a secret base Bad Kohlgrub in Bavaria. A former interrogator told him that the American special forces based at Fort Bragg, Virginia, have a reciprocal training programme with the SAS.

The 'Hooded Men', the fourteen Irish Catholics, were spread-eagled against a wall for days, subjected to a high-pitched noise, deprived of food, drink and sleep, and were badly beaten.

The Leveller article pointed out that the SAS had been engaged in torture training since the early 1960s and the results were monitored at the Army Intelligence Centre in Ashford, Kent – 'It was from here that the team of intelligence officers went to Belfast to train their opposite numbers in the RUC at a special seminar held just before internment (See also *The Leveller*, Issue 2)'. The article sarcastically remarked that SAS men had served with the Shah of Iran's special forces for at least three years against the Kurds and no doubt the refinements of torture there were not lost on them.

When the European Commission for Human Rights found the Government of the United Kingdom guilty of inhuman and degrading treatment of prisoners in violation of Article 3 of the Human Rights Convention, *Hibernia* in its issue of 8 October 1976 carried two articles by Jack Holland, 'Strasbourg: The Men behind the Torture', and 'Strasbourg Report Decoded'. Not all the details discovered by *Hibernia* through extensive re-search were published but *The Leveller* of December 1976 gave a fuller story – 'Britain's Big Cover-Up is Blown – The Torturers' Who's Who'. 'Opera-tions Demetrius', as the Northern Ireland arrests and torture were called, was well planned. The tuition of RUC officers by British Army experts seasoned in colonial wars took place at a secret seminar in April 1971, four months before internment. Senior RUC officers were briefed and instructed in the use of the techniques by British intelligence officers. One of the police officers, it asserts, told the Commission on Human Rights that members of the Military Reaction Force (MRF) were present at Palace Barracks at the time of the detentions. The MRF, as we shall see, were pseudo-gangs operated by the British Army, backboned by soldiers, some of them SAS.

The history of torture and ill-treatment has been well covered in news-paper articles, pamphlets and books. It had reached such a pitch that on 1 November 1972 a statement calling for a judicial inquiry into torture signed by 387 priests in the North was sent to the media and human rights organisations. The priests said, 'We are convinced that brutality, physical and mental torture and psychological pressures have been inflicted on men arrested under the Special Powers Act. We believe these barbarities are still being inflicted on innocent people convicted of no crime – at the Palace Barracks, Holywood, under the protection of law by the Special Branch of the RUC'. I record here some information from my experience as prison chaplain in Armagh Jail. A personal account will illustrate the horror and throw some light on the SAS, RUC and the Northern Ireland executive.

From December 1971 until August 1972 some 130 men were held in Armagh Prison. They had been arrested under Special Powers, ill-treated at Palace Barracks, Holywood and Girdwood Park Barracks, Belfast, and then charged on the basis of statements made under duress. I saw the wounds, bruises, burns on their bodies, and heard allegations of the use of amphetamine drugs and electric cattle prods. These I reported to Cardinal William Conway who from this source and others documented in detail six cases complete with medical evidence. An independent doctor also visited Armagh Prison and recorded the bruising on the bodies of eleven men. One of these men was Joseph Rafferty, Belfast. Cardinal Conway told me he phoned General Tuzo and spoke to him about the brutalities meted out to prisoners in detention. When General Tuzo expressed incredulity, the Cardinal merely mentioned the name of Joseph Rafferty. Immediately the General promised an investigation.

One of the men I met in Armagh in early 1972 was Francis Maguire (31). He was arrested early in 1972 and was ill-treated in Girdwood Park Barracks. This is part of his testimony:[16]

I was handed over to the Special Branch in a cubicle room. There were four Special men ... One said he was a member of the SAS ... They made me stand against the wall. They took my jumper off and hooded me with it; made me put my hands down the back of my trousers, the back of my head and heels were against the wall. They started asking me questions. I said I didn't know what they were talking about, about the questions they asked. They started punching me in the stomach and kicking me on the privates and the stomach. They started kneeing me in the privates. This went on for an hour, an hour and a half. At one stage the SAS man pressed my eyeballs in with his thumbs saying: 'I have no Compton or anything to answer to; I could kill you and there wouldn't be a word; I have the right to do this'. He spat and said – 'that's what I think of you; it would not worry me in the least to kill you as I am a sadist and I enjoy hurting people'. He kept calling me my nickname 'Luger'. He said, 'You'll be tired listening to my voice before the night is through'. They kept asking me questions. I told them 'I don't know anything'. They kept kicking me. They told me to take my trousers down. They threatened to burn me with a cigarette. Then one said, 'Just take them up again'. They stood me in front of an electric fire. Then they said, 'Come on away before you get burned there'. They said, 'We told you this was only a wee bit; now the fun is going to start'. They started kicking, punching and kneeing me again. Put me against the wall, same position as before, head and heels. Started kicking me lightly on the privates and then they would land a hard kick in the privates. Then they threw me from one to another all over the room, punching me when in the air. I fell to the ground. Then all of them. The one who said he was an SAS man started choking me with his hands. He kept crying, 'I'll kill you, Luger, I'll kill you'. Five times he did this. One time I think I passed out for a short time. One other time my false teeth caught in my throat and I nearly choked; and one other time, as he was choking me, one was kicking me in the privates and the other was digging his head into my stomach. While this was going on they were always asking me questions and accusing me ...

The doctor's report on Francis Maguire showed the following:

Multiple bruising on the trunk of his body, legs and arms. Dark purple bruising about 8 inches wide and 4 inches high on the upper part of his abdomen, and numerous purplish, yellow, and brownish bruises on both arms.

A great purple bruising from above his wrist to his elbow on his right arm and numerous purple, yellow and brownish bruises on both arms. His left ankle was one uniform purplish black bruise and there was a smaller paler bruise about 3 inches by 4 inches further up the calf of his leg. There were other bruises on his lower legs and on his knees.

There was a great dark purplish bruise about 6 inches deep and 8 inches wide on his left upper leg stretching down the inner part of the leg from below his private parts which were reddened and tender.

In the debate on the Compton Report, an enquiry into the interrogation methods used in Northern Ireland, in the House of Commons 17 November 1971, Lord Balniel, in reply to a question from Mr Roy Hattersley (Labour, Birmingham, Sparbrook) as to whether Ministers at Westminster knew what was happening and whether they gave their approval said that the methods were the same as were used specifically at the time of Aden, Malaysia and Borneo. (These were places where the SAS had figured in intelligence work). To Mr James Callaghan (Labour, Cardiff, South-East) Lord Balniel said that the formal authorisation to remove certain detainees to the interrogation centre was necessarily given by the Northern Ireland Minister for Home Affairs, with the knowledge and concurrence of Her Majesty's Government; Ministers knew that the interrogation would be conducted within the guidelines laid down in 1965 and 1967 and the methods would be the same as had been used on numerous occasions in the past; their detailed application was necessarily a matter for the judgement of those immediately responsible.

The approval to ill-treat detainees affected all the structures of government up to Cabinet and Prime Minister level. The RUC and British Army carried out the ill-treatment. The administration seems to have co-operated in the cover-up. Victims and their families found that effective domestic remedies were lacking. There was no independent element in the investigation of complaints and it was unsatisfactory to have procedures whereby the RUC investigated the criminal actions of their colleagues and the British Army.

I soon realised that in my position as a prison chaplain. At the end of December 1971 I included a note in my annual prison report – 'Many of the prisoners arrive in prison with serious bruises on their bodies as a result of police interrogation. One man, Joseph Rafferty, had to be removed to the Musgrave Hospital for seven days from Armagh Prison. In my opinion severe mental damage has been done to many of the men due to interrogation with brutality'.

On 25 January 1972 the Ministry of Home Affairs wrote to me: 'Publicity was last week given in the press to a number of statements prepared by remand prisoners at Armagh Prison alleging brutal treatment by policemen and soldiers. The newspapers report that the statements were collected by Fr Denis Faul and yourself. As you know Rule 184 of Prison Rules prohibits officers of a prison from taking anything out of the prison for a prisoner save on the instructions of the Governor. Rule 188 prohibits an officer, unless authorised by the Ministry, from communicating with the

press on matters concerning prisoners and on any matters which have
become known to him in the course of his official duties. These provisions
are not intended to prevent investigation of abuses. If prisoners make
serious complaints of the kind described in the press to a prison chaplain or
any other officer of the prison it is obviously his duty to bring them without
delay to the attention of the Governor and of the Ministry so that steps can
be taken to have them investigated'.

In ensuing correspondence I made the following points:

Letter, 28 January 1972: 'On Friday 24 December 1971 Fr Faul visited
Armagh Jail at the request of relatives of three men, Joseph Rafferty,
Dominic Mallon, Eddie McCaffrey. He listened to their stories alleging
serious brutality by police officers and military personnel which took
place in Holywood and Girdwood Barracks, and saw in the case of
Rafferty appalling physical evidence on his body. Since Fr Faul has no
confidence in the Ministry of Home Affairs and believes that they
wouldn't investigate the brutality of police and soldiers against Catholics, he followed the usual practice of publishing his findings in the
press and communicating them to Members of Parliament at Westminster with a view to having brutality stopped...'

Letter, 9 February 1972: 'I would have thought that before this you would
have acknowledged my report and indicated what steps you were
going to take to deal with this urgent matter and others. Every blow
struck and every injury inflicted on a detainee is a violation of the law
constituting actual or grievous bodily harm – need I remind you of that?
I am satisfied, however, that important persons will see that these
complaints are pursued with energy and integrity to a just conclusion... In August 1971 His Eminence Cardinal Conway ... commented
on the ill-treatment of detainees – "For an official spokesman to say, as
he has done, that complaints should be forwarded to the police for
examination, must inevitably seem to those concerned, in the climate of
Northern Ireland at the present, as bordering on cynicism". Would the
relatives of the injured detainees accept an investigation by the Minister of Home Affairs? Would they not consider that an offer of investigation from such a source borders on the cynical?'

Letter, 7 March 1972: 'Since I last wrote to you, 9 February 1972, His
Eminence Cardinal Conway, Archbishop of Armagh, sent a telegram to
the bishops of Australia, and this appeared in the press, 11 February
1972. The telegram read – "Regarding the treatment of prisoners to
which you refer, I regret to say that an impressive body of medical and
other evidence indicates that physical assault of arrested and uncharged persons, especially during questioning, is continuing. Strenuous private efforts on my part to have this stopped appear to have

failed. As one who has frequently and publicly condemned in the strongest terms the shooting of policemen and others, I deeply deplore this. When those charged with upholding the law appear to violate it with impunity in this way, the foundations of respect for law and order disappear".

A number of things are clear from this telegram – the Cardinal, as an individual member of Northern Ireland society, had accumulated impressive evidence that brutality had been inflicted against prisoners detained without trial; he had made strenuous efforts to have this stopped and had failed. If an eminent individual person could accumulate such formidable evidence so that he could publicly stand over it, then the question arises – were the Ministry of Home Affairs in Northern Ireland also in possession of such formidable evidence? If they were, why did ill-treatment of prisoners detained without trial continue? Were officials in charge of men under custody, high-placed politicians, senior officers of the British Army, senior officers of the RUC, also in possession of such formidable evidence? If so, why did they allow ill-treatment of prisoners detained without trial to proceed? Are they a guilty party and were they guaranteed an immunity? If Cardinal Conway was in possession of impressive evidence and the Ministry of Home Affairs, Northern Ireland, was not aware that brutality was continuing, does the Ministry of Home Affairs, Northern Ireland, not then appear to be negligent in a serious manner?

In my Annual Report I said – "Many of them arrive in prison with serious bruises on their bodies as a result of police interrogation. One man, Joseph Rafferty, had to be removed to the Musgrave Hospital for seven days from Armagh Prison". You say this is unworthy of investigation because it is conveyed in general terms, and yet when Fr Faul makes detailed allegations about ill-treatment which is common knowledge to doctors, solicitors, and priests in the community, you are annoyed.

The real point here is the seriousness of the allegations of brutality inflicted on men arrested under Special Powers and imprisoned before trial. These allegations appear to involve a great number of people of high rank and low rank in the employment of the Ministry of Home Affairs.

In your letter of 25 January 1972 you say, and I quote:- "If prisoners make serious complaints of the kind described in the press to a prison chaplain or any officer of the prison it is obviously his duty to bring them without delay to the attention of the Governor and of the Ministry so that steps can be taken to have them investigated". May I quote to you from The Irish Times, Monday, February 28, 1972, where Dr Claire Palley, Professor of Public Law, the Queen's University, Belfast, says:

"Northern Ireland has no proper machinery for detainees and internees to complain against ill-treatment. The United Kingdom Government, being internationally responsible for its preventative detention
laws, should assert its authority, or act through the Westminster
Parliament, to ensure the passage of laws consistent with its international obligations and its democratic traditions". That is why complaints were directed to the Home Secretary. I am pleased to learn that
he is in touch with you. I feel that representations from such a source
will meet with your full co-operation'.

In February 1972 Amnesty International reported torture against detainees in Northern Ireland. A notable television programme, *A Question of
Torture* researched by the *World in Action* team, issued 25 September 1972,
broke the wall of silence in Britain. The European Commission of Human
Rights reported in 1976 and found the British government guilty of torture
in Northern Ireland in the 1971-1972 period. The European Court of Human
Rights at Strasbourg, 18 January 1978, found the British Government guilty
of violating Article 3 of the European Convention of Human Rights on two
counts.

When Paddy Joe McClean was being tortured at Ballykelly he saw some
of his torturers face-to-face when the hood was removed, bare-chested,
tanned, super-fit SAS men in drill trousers. He must have felt some sense
of redress to hear the European Court condemnation. The RUC Special
Branch and the SAS earned themselves a place in the legal textbooks. They
made history in Ballykelly, Holywood and Girdwood.

PHASE II

The Sectarian Murders

The policy of counter-insurgency aims simply at weakening in every way the political and economic structures of insurgency. Keeping the nationalists economically weak was policy in Northern Ireland since 1921. In the present conflict it is a matter of maintaining the system. From the beginning it was assumed by the unionist government of Northern Ireland, in typical precautionary fashion, that the Civil Rights movement of the 1960s was controlled by sinister militant elements. This was a mistake. Substantial reforms were ignored. The authorities curbed demonstrations in discriminatory fashion and used violence against protest marchers. Loyalist mobs attacked Catholic areas and the RUC tolerated the attacks and even joined them. The RUC were responsible for the first deaths, Samuel Devenney in Derry and John Gallagher in Armagh. By reacting in a violent way the government brought about a revolution, the very thing it feared. The Civil Rights movement in turn became violent and in a short time the local defence associations, the new IRA, moved from defence to offense. Since that time the Northern Ireland governing authorities have assumed that military members form the bone of nationalist political protest. Civil and military measures were therefore co-ordinated against nationalists. In practice this was spelled out in efforts to break the morale of the Catholic population on whom insurgents rely. Harassment, arrests, brutality and torture, internment, long prison sentences, housewrecking, selected murders, were administrative policy. The reaction of Catholics to this persecution, namely, rioting, bombing and shooting, was calculated and risked by the Government. The manipulation of the law was risked too. That has turned out to be the Government's most serious self-inflicted wound.

Much has been made of the writings of Brigadier Frank Kitson and his books, in particular *Gangs and Counter-gangs* (London, 1960, his Kenya experience), *Low Intensity Operations* (1971, written at Oxford in 1970) and *Bunch of Five* (1977). He is not to be credited as an innovator. British colonial policy and principles of counter-insurgency go back a long time before him. He is important in that he took part in the operation of such a policy. He researched its workings, updated it and commented intelligently on it. His theories did not work out in Northern Ireland. The British Government lacks the will to conquer. Kitson served as Army Commander in Belfast from the Spring of 1970 to April 1972. He had previously served in Kenya, Muscat and Oman, and Cyprus. He brought with him experience in counter-insurgency and he put it into practice in Northern Ireland.

When the British Army arrived in strength in Northern Ireland in 1969 the RUC was demoralised. For the next six years the British Army felt it could not rely on the RUC and so, more or less independently, set about its own information gathering, filling in the background of nationalists and protest movements, bringing information to the point of arrests and sometimes to the point of killing.

If we glance at Kitson's work in Kenya (where he played a minor role, described in *Gangs and Counter-gangs*), we see a parallel with the policy of the British Army in Northern Ireland in the 1970s. In Kenya his aim was to provide the information needed to destroy the Mau Mau in the area under his control. Apart from direct attacks, the methods were detention (which meant dossiers on the suspects), informers and infiltrators. Captured Mau Mau who would work against their former associates were obvious material for counter-gangs. In the nature of things high ranking Mau Mau were sometimes recruited. Hooded 'converts' pointed out members among lines of suspects. Units were formed who acted as regular Mau Mau but were really information gatherers.

When one turns to the situation in Northern Ireland in the post-1970 period, one can see the same pattern emerging, intelligence gathering, detention and internment, informers, infiltrators, pseudo-gangs. To this end plain clothes patrols were organised in every regiment in Belfast. They were staffed with regular soldiers, intelligence personnel of the regiment and sometimes strengthened by SAS men. The Military Reaction Force (MRF) was formed, made up again of soldiers assigned to intelligence work, some SAS men, and members or fringe members of the IRA – deserters who had in a sense been kidnapped. These deserters were enticed by bribery, by threat of imprisonment or worse, to work for the British Army.

The MRF was housed in two centres, Holywood Palace Barracks and Thiepval Barracks, Lisburn. It was made up of units with three or four British soldiers in charge of each unit. These were SAS men or Warrant Officers. The SAS was present from the beginning, commissioned to carry out initial experiments which included drawing up prototype plans for assassinations and 'dirty tricks' operations. It was not until March 1974 that an Army spokesman admitted the involvement of the SAS in the MRF (*The Times*, 19 March).

On the broader front the British Army welcomed the formation of the Protestant paramilitaries. These were manipulated as a third force, their assassinations of Catholics tolerated in order to strike terror into Catholic areas; the roads were left open to them, internment for them was practically nil; there was little raiding of their houses, and general immunity was understood. Only in the late 1970s, when the political situation was feasible, did the authorities move against them, when there was an 'acceptable level of violence' and Ulsterisation was well advanced in the recruitment and training of big numbers of RUC and UDR. Despite the fact that the UDA murdered hundreds of innocent Catholics they were rewarded by non-pro-scription. The British Army has brought its own patronised recruits right up to positions of power in the UDA under its pay; it is confident it can manipulate the UDA politically and militarily.

Some loyalist gangs were controlled by ex-soldiers who took orders from British Army intelligence. The SAS had close links with all this activity. Infiltration of the IRA also took place, how far it is difficult to say, but it would seem that British intelligence could criss-cross in the organisation of killings by giving information to both sides or by closer involvement. Political observers have long looked upon the complications as a jungle but are gradually finding paths towards the truth. As early as 12 December 1971 the *Sunday Press* alleged that 'the Special Air Service were Britain's under-cover commandos trained in murder, torture, black propaganda and other vile methods of warfare'. There was always a feeling that the SAS was in Northern Ireland but how could one reveal the operations of a secret army? The *Sunday Independent* of the same date ventured to say that the SAS was being moved to border duty under the name of another regiment. A few years later, 24 February 1974, the same paper was speculating as to whether it operated from Palace Barracks, Holywood, with the RUC Special Branch, or from a headquarters above the Northern Irish Tourist Office as reported in *Fortnight* magazine!

The SAS must be seen against the background of counter-insurgency operations. They were skilled men easily available for the Northern Ireland job, calculating surveillance men and ruthless assassins when that was necessary. To get a glimpse of them and the other undercover soldiers with whom they worked one must seek out incidents, sightings, wounding and killings perpetrated by undercover soldiers.

In its issue of Winter 1977, Bulletin No. 2 *The Workers Research Unit*, Belfast, published an article 'Statistics of assassination '72-'77' which showed that sectarian murders reached their highest level in 1972. This was proba-bly the most important year in the present struggle. Internment had taken place on 9 August 1971 and was a continuing operation. The British authorities then moved against the Catholic areas in force taking over the no-go areas in Belfast and reoccupying Derry in 'Operation Motorman', 31 July 1972. It was perfectly timed. On 21 July the Provisional IRA set off 22 bombs in Belfast killing nine people and injuring about 130. There was a strong revulsion from the Catholic community at the wanton loss of life. The British Army saw the psychological moment as favourable and moved into the 'no-go' areas. The activities of the SAS/MRF and the British agents within the Protestant paramilitaries prompted the sectarian murders of Catholics and created an atmosphere for massive security measures. 1972 was the climax of a steady campaign by the British Army, changing from a protective role in 1969-70, to one of confrontation and finally conquest. It began with the Falls Road Curfew 3-5 July 1970. The Catholic community was incensed by the killing of four people during the Curfew, the arrest of over 300 men and boys of all ages, and the destruction of homes. There followed two years of incessant brutal arrests. Arrested persons were thrown into army vehicles and made lie flat on the floor. Soldiers kicked them, beat them with rifle butts, shouted obscenities and degraded them. There were punitive measures against the population. The campaign of sectarian murders of Catholics continued unabated, posing, as the British knew, a serious problem for the IRA who did not wish their campaign to become bogged down in sectarianism. During this period the RUC issued hundreds of statements to the media calling the murders of Catholics 'motiveless murders'.

The July 1978 edition of *Troops Out*, a magazine of the Troops Out Movement, carried a statement from a former member of MRF. It throws light on the incidents to follow in a calendar of 1972. It is entitled 'The Army in Britain's Last Colony'.

> I was an infantry NCO. I served in the British army for 12 years. I have considerable experience of internal security in aid of the civil power, having carried out police action in six different territories, as well as having served three tours of duty in Ireland. The role of the British Army in the six counties, as propounded by the capitalist press, is one of keeping the peace. My experience of that role in practice, however, is one of repression through fear, terror and violence...
>
> Let me give you some examples. During early 1972 I was posted away from my battalion to a unit in Ireland as a military reconnaissance force, or MRF. I was based at the Army HQ, 39th Infantry Brigade Group, Lisburn. We operated in plain clothes, in civilian vehicles. We operated in teams of from two to four members, each one of which was a senior NCO or subaltern. Although it is not normal practice for members of the WRAC to even do weapon training, some women worked with us. We were instructed in the use of the Russian AK47 assault rifle, the Armalite, and a Thompson sub-machine-gun. All these weapons are favoured by the Provos... these weapons are not standard issue for the British Army. We used the Browning pistol and the Sterling sub-machine-gun only.
>
> One day in April 1972 I was on plain clothes surveillance duties with two other soldiers. We drove along Whiterock Road, Upper Falls. We had a death list with names and photos, with the orders, 'Shoot on sight'. One of the soldiers saw James - a man on the list, and another whose name I forget. We swerved our car in front of them, by some school gates, and leapt out, drawing our pistols, and opened fire. They

tried to run down an alley. We ran down it after them and the patrol commander gave the order 'bullets'. I scored several hits myself; both men were severely wounded. We radioed for a uniformed patrol. When it turned up the commander said to ours, 'you stupid bastards, you've shot the wrong fuckers'. The Army issued a press statement alleging that the men had shot at us and that the Army had a pistol to prove it. This was a lie. Both men were brothers, on their way to work – innocent men going about their lawful business.

In May 1972 another MRF patrol assassinated a man called McVeigh, with the intention of blaming the Protestants and taking the heat off the Army. A month later the MRF shot three taxi drivers in Andersonstown. A Thompson was used.

When soldiers are on rifle ranges in Germany or in England, it is normal practice to keep a couple of clips of ammunition for the paddies. This is illegal, but the NCOs turn a blind eye. These spare rounds can be used to replace any used rounds in Ireland when on patrol.

Let us examine the three incidents related here.

The Shooting of the Conway Brothers[17]

The Conway brothers, John and Gerard, of Ballymurphy Road, Belfast, fruit merchants who kept a stand in McQuillan Street, were shot in mistake for two well-known IRA men, two of the seven men who had escaped by swimming from the prison internment ship *Maidstone*.

The men left their home shortly after 7.30 am, 15 April 1972, and walked together to get a bus on the nearby Whiterock Road. They just missed the bus and decided to continue on to the Falls Road to catch another one. Approaching the gate of St Thomas' School, a bluish green car, like a 1100, pulled in a couple of feet in front of them. Three doors of the car, two front and one at the back, burst open suddenly and three men jumped out all armed with pistols. The Conways remembered their dress; one was of swarthy complexion dressed in blue pullover, blue jeans and hush-puppy boots; another had fair curly hair and wore a brownish pullover or jacket and flannel trousers; the third man had a dark blue jacket with a red stripe down the sleeve.

The brothers took fright. 'Run,' said John. The blue-jacketed one, immediately on jumping out of the car, had run over to Gerard Conway and pointed a gun in his face crying 'Hold it'. Gerard thought it was a hold-up, 'I've only £2 and a watch!' When John ran, followed by two of the men, one of them started shooting, grazing him with a bullet. At this the gunman holding Gerard was distracted and Gerard ran off. A couple of shots rang out and he was hit in the leg. Another bullet whizzed past his head. The story is taken up by a witness of the shooting, Noel O'Reilly:

Gerry Conway began to run again. I told my wife to keep watching and I ran downstairs and out my front gate. Gerry was then running past my old van parked at the door. I saw the gunman fire another shot. Gerry kept running. The gunman stopped opposite my gate in the centre of the road. He pointed the gun at me and said, 'Get in. I'm a soldier'. I shouted, 'No chance. You'll not murder anyone up here. There are too many witnesses'.

By this time Gerry Conway had stopped at the junction of Whiterock Road/Whiterock Gardens. The gunman fired another shot at him which I think hit Gerry because he started shouting – 'He's a soldier. He's trying to murder me'. Gerry was hysterical.

A car came up Whiterock Road from the Falls direction. It stopped. Gerry ran over to this car, threw his hands in the air and shouted – 'Take me away. He's a soldier. He's trying to murder me'.

The gunman ran up towards the car and Gerry threw himself on the bonnet and begged the driver to take him away. The gunman pointed his gun at the driver.

Within about thirty seconds a car came from the Ballymurphy direction and parked beyond Whiterock Gardens. Two men armed with pistols jumped out. They knelt on one knee at the corner of Whiterock Gardens. The fair-haired one ran back to the car, took a walkie-talkie and began to speak. A couple of minutes later two Saracens arrived. Soldiers of the King's Own Scottish Borderers got out. I heard the first gunman say, 'Bryson got away'. I also heard the name Toland mentioned. I also heard a ginger-haired soldier who got out of a saracen saying, 'You've got the wrong bloody man'. By this time two or three women had appeared in the street.

Meanwhile, Gerry Conway was over at the front of Francis Grant's car and had taken his coat off. He was shouting at the top of his voice, 'I'm not Toland. I'm not Toland. I've a wife and four kids'. I then saw them bundling Gerry into a saracen. I went back into the house and upstairs to my bedroom window. The ginger-haired soldier was talking to a couple of gunmen. The three gunmen got into the car they arrived in, reversed into Whiterock Road and went off towards Ballymurphy.

When a press report appeared quoting eye-witnesses' accounts of the shooting, the British Army Press Office issued a statement saying that a mobile patrol encountered two men, one of whom was a suspect, and the patrol returned fire after one of the men opened fire at them; the soldiers wounded one of them and he dropped his pistol.

The Conways were admitted to the Royal Victoria Hospital. They were interrogated by the RUC about the shooting. They were never charged despite the Army statement of their having a pistol and firing.

The Killing of Patrick McVeigh

The Catholic Ex-Servicemen's Association was set up in September 1971. The aim was to muster a passive resistance to the repression of Catholics in Northern Ireland and counteract gun-clubs freely conceded to loyalists who were considered to be well-armed, guns being a cult of their siege mentality. They vaguely threatened that although the association had no arms, they could get them. They looked forward to a membership of 10,000, hardly an exaggerated figure since Northern Ireland Catholics were always dominant in the British forces due to lack of work. There was an irony, also, in that it was thought that this Catholic 'loyalty' would impress the British and would emphasise the justice of the Catholic cause. CESA members acted as vigilantes against loyalist aggression. For such a simple policy CESA members paid with their lives. Bernard Rice, aged sixty years, was shot from a car at a fire station at the junction of Crumlin and Woodvale Roads on 8 February 1972. Police said that he had a Rangers football ticket in his pocket. On 27 May 1972 Gerald Duddy, Inishmore Crescent, Andersonstown, aged 20 years, said to have been at a CESA meeting in Andersonstown, went to visit a friend at Whiterock. He took a taxi. He was found shot dead at the same place as Patrick McVeigh. He was a boiler-maker in Harland and Wolf's shipyard. On 30 June 1972 another CESA member, Daniel Hayes, aged 43 years, left the bar in Skipper Street where he worked. His body was found at 1.26 am in Penrith Street off the Shankill Road. He had been beaten about the head and shot at least once in the head and twice in the chest.

On 12 May 1972 Patrick McVeigh, a vigilante member of CESA, aged 44 years, was shot dead from a passing car at a Catholic barricade at Riverdale Park/Finaghy Road North, in Andersonstown. He was a welder by trade, married and had six children.

It was just after midnight. Patrick McVeigh was talking to his friends. A car drove in from Finaghy Road North. One of the occupants opened fire on the five men. McVeigh was killed and his four friends seriously injured. Frank Doherty, writing in *Hibernia*, 30 March 1973, says:- 'The car continued along Riverdale Park for one hundred yards, made a three point turn on the narrow roadway, and drove at high speed past the scene of the shooting and down Finaghy Road North to a military road-check a few hundred yards away at a railway bridge. Here the driver showed a document to the troops and was allowed to proceed... It was several days before reports of the road-check clearance became current gossip in the area, and six weeks before the RUC informed the injured survivors that they had been shot by plain-clothes soldiers'.

Mary Holland reported the shooting in the *Observer*, 9 July 1972, revealing that a police detective said that it was the Army who had shot them. It was alleged that one of the wounded was told – 'We have four sworn statements from the occupants of the car that they were returning fire'.

At the inquest into the death of Patrick McVeigh, held on 21 December 1972, it was stated that forensic evidence showed that neither McVeigh nor his companions had fired weapons. Statements from the plain clothes soldiers claimed that they saw the men with rifles and revolvers and that one of these men fired at the car. The soldiers did not appear at the inquest so it was not possible to carry out a cross-examination. In their evidence the men who had been wounded maintained that they were innocent by-standers, that McVeigh had not been scheduled for vigilante duty that night but had stopped to chat with them. McVeigh lived only a hundred yards from where he was shot. Under cross-examination from Mr Charles Hill representing the next of kin, the British Army officer on duty in that area that night said that he had regarded the killing as a sectarian shooting until he heard statements from the soldiers read in court a few minutes earlier. A police officer told the coroner that no proceedings had been brought against the soldiers involved in the shooting.

In his article on the SAS in *Magill*, September 1978, Ed Moloney has revealed that the real target of the SAS hit squad was a leading republican. The bullets narrowly missed him but killed Patrick McVeigh and wounded his four friends.

The Shooting at Glen Road Bus Terminal[18]

Four men were shot and wounded at noon, Thursday, 22 June 1972, at the Glen Road Bus Terminal, Belfast. They were brought to the Royal Victoria Hospital. The men were Hugh Kenny of Rosapenna Square, a by-stander, Joseph Smith of Tullagh Park, a taxi-man, Jim Murray of Glenveagh Drive, a passenger and Thomas Shaw, hit in his bedroom in nearby Bunbeg Park.

The British Army issued a version of the incident:- 'Shortly after mid-day a mobile patrol wearing plain clothes and on surveillance duty was travelling eastwards on the Glen Road. A group of men standing at a bus turnabout opened fire on a patrol and shot through the rear window of the vehicle, narrowly missing a soldier. The patrol immediately fired back and the men were seen to fall'.

Eye-witnesses of the shooting, interviewed independently, said that the men had no guns and were not shooting at anybody.

The evening edition of the *Belfast Telegraph* carried another British Army statement, the first, issued shortly after the shooting. It said that about 18 shots had been fired in an incident in which the security forces were not involved; when a patrol of the 2nd Field Regiment Royal Artillery arrived at the scene, they found nothing.

Mrs Eileen Shaw of Bunbeg Park, wife of Thomas Shaw who was wounded, gave the following account to the Association for Legal Justice:

'About mid-day I was cleaning my window which looks to the Glen Road bus terminus. I saw a blue car with two men, the driver and one in the back, either moving very slowly or possibly halted opposite Mrs Hassett's house. Then it moved slowly down the Glen Road. Next I saw the rear window going down and a gun coming out of the window. I heard a volley of shots. I saw the three men fall and one of them bleeding. I stood petrified and screamed – "Tommy! Get up! There's three men lying on the roundabout". No answer came. I yelled again. Still no answer. I ran upstairs; on the way I saw bullet holes in the walls at the landing. I saw through the open door of the bedroom where Tommy was that the mirror of the dressing table was shattered. I realised that Tommy must have been shot and I was afraid to go in. I ran downstairs and on the street screaming – "Somebody come quick. I think Tommy is shot". Mrs McGuinness and my son Brian ran up to Tommy. They found him shot in the leg'.

Mrs Sheila McAree was sitting in the back seat of a taxi at the bus terminus. She also witnessed the shooting. A bullet hit the taxi she was in. In a statement she said – 'I tried to get out but couldn't. The taxi-man then opened the door for me and I ran screaming after the blue car but it disappeared out of sight. I ran back and helped to get Joseph Smith and Jim Murray, who were wounded, into the taxi I had been in. I travelled in the back seat with the two wounded men to the Royal Victoria Hospital. We kept saying Acts of Contrition on the way. Jim Murray kept saying – "I'm going. I can feel myself going" '.

Eight months after the shooting, on Tuesday, 27 February 1973, a captain, James Alistair McGregor, was charged with the unlawful possession of a Thompson sub-machine-gun and ammunition. When charged he allegedly told a detective – 'That ammunition had nothing to do with me. It belongs to the police at Castlereagh and was issued by the Special Branch'. It is interesting that a Thompson sub-machine-gun was used; in the early seventies it was still mythologically associated with the IRA.

A sergeant, Clive Graham Williams, whose unit was not revealed, was charged with the same offence and also with attempting to murder the three men at the bus terminal, causing them grievous bodily harm and with maliciously wounding Thomas Shaw.

On 2 May the charges against the soldiers relating to the firearm and ammunition were withdrawn. McGregor was then set free.

In court in June 1973, the sergeant said that in June 1972 he was a commander of a unit of the Military Reconnaissance Force attached to the 39th Infantry Brigade. He said that at the time of the shooting there were forty men in the force. He said there were fifteen men in his unit and that a squad was made up of between two and four men in a vehicle. His evidence was that on the morning of the shooting he instructed new recruits at Kinnegar in general weapons including Thompsons, although the Sterling was the usual weapon. A Sterling and automatic pistols, he said, were the usual armoury for a squad. He claimed that they came under fire at the bus terminal, returned fire and believed they hit three gunmen.

He was acquitted by the jury of all charges against him.

The Case of Seamus Wright[19]

Seamus Wright of Bombay Street, Belfast, aged 25 years, an asphalt layer by trade, was arrested from his home on Saturday 5 February 1972 at about 3 am. He was taken first to the military post in N. Howard Street and later to Palace Barracks, Holywood. After 48 hours his wife went to the Catholic Citizens' Defence Committee, a voluntary charitable organisation that tried to support people in trouble during the strife of the early 1970s. They made a phone-call for her and were told that he was on his way home. Later that day he hadn't turned up. She went to a priest in Clonard Monastery and he phoned the RUC. He was told that Seamus had been released at 5 pm on Sunday in the city centre. This made Mrs Wright suspicious as it did not tally with the previous information. The same priest phoned Springfield Road Barracks and they advised that he should be put on the 'list of missing persons'.

Next night, Tuesday 8 February, Seamus phoned John Devlin's shop at the junction of Kane Street, Kashmir Road. He used an expression his wife never heard him use before. He said that he had 'scarpered'. He left word that he would phone at 9 am the next day.

Next morning his wife got a letter postmarked 'Carrickfergus'. He didn't say much except that he had escaped from the Army, met another fellow and got his fare to England. She waited from 9 until 9.30 for the phone-call on Wednesday morning. Shortly after she left he phoned again and said that he would phone at 9 pm. He left the number of a call box in Birmingham. The Clonard priest phoned at the appointed time for her. He spoke to Seamus and also taped the call. Seamus gave an address in Birmingham. He asked for his wife to come over to England. She arranged to go over the next day with her father-in-law, William Wright, and Seamus said he would meet them at the airport.

The two arrived at the airport in Birmingham and Mrs Wright was called to the information desk. There was a message for her: 'Your husband has changed his digs. He will meet you in the airport tomorrow morning'. She began to cry.

A man dressed as a minister of religion came over to her and asked what was wrong. She told him the whole story and showed him the address. He said that he had just come from Belfast, which he often visited. He said that he had visited the family of the taxi- man shot on the Springfield Road that week. He said that his wife was there in a car and that he would take her to the address. When they got there there was nobody in. It was a block of flats. They sat there in the hallway and the minister stayed with them. He had already made a phone call before they left the airport.

Then Seamus Wright arrived with another man. The minister left at this point. Mrs Wright and Seamus' father were taken to a ground floor flat with almost no furniture – a settee, table and a couple of chairs. It didn't look lived in.

Mrs Wright asked Seamus if he could come with them to his aunt in London. He said that he couldn't. She asked him who the other man was. This man had gone into the kitchen of the flat. Wright said that his name was 'Colin', that he was a member of the SAS and that he had a gun. He said that during his interrogation in Holywood, he had been asked about different people. He also said that they should let it be known about the SAS man when they got back. 'Colin' was blond, fattish face and not too tall.

They were about ten minutes with him. The SAS man, 'Colin', called him into the kitchen. Seamus came back and said they had better go. He told them they were taking him back to Holywood in a couple of days. He arranged to meet them next morning in the railway station. The SAS man gave them the telephone number of a taxi company and they left before the SAS man and Wright.

Seamus Wright did not keep the appointment the next morning and they returned to Belfast.

Over the next few weeks Mrs Wright got letters from Seamus – one from Manchester and the other she thinks from London (going by the postmarks). He said that he was working at his trade. She phoned all the asphalt firms she could find but none of them knew anything about him. In one letter he said he would be home in a fortnight. In fact he didn't get back for about four weeks after that.

Seamus Wright arrived home on Good Friday, 31 March. He said that he had been taken from the flat to another part of England and flown back the next day to Belfast and then brought to Holywood Barracks. In Holywood, he said, he was billeted with others in two houses – two other young men together with a young girl, her mother and a couple of children. They were from other areas of Belfast. All the time they were guarded by a man with a gun. As far as he remembered, he said they were taken once a week to Bangor or Lisburn. He seemed to think they were with the SAS, although the MRF was also mentioned. He didn't say what he was asked to do during his time in Holywood. He reported what had happened to him to the local Provisional IRA and gave them information about the Four Square Laundry. He seemed to satisfy them as they didn't bother with him. After about a fortnight he went back to work until he disappeared again.

On two occasions during this period he had strange experiences.

One day he was walking up Leeson Street to get the bus to go to his mother's home. A car came slowly up the street behind him. He recognised one of the men in it from his time in Holywood. When he came downstairs in the bus to get off at Casement Park, he saw the man sitting downstairs in the bus. He got offside quickly as he believed he was being followed.

On another occasion he got off the bus at Casement Park. There were a number of men in the bus. He recognised one who got out and called 'Seamus'. He thought he was going to draw a gun. Again he got out of the way as quickly as he could.

On 2 October a Four Square Laundry van was ambushed in Twinbrook estate. One undercover soldier, according to an official report, was killed. When Seamus came home that evening from work he said that he would have to be careful because before his release he had signed a paper about the Official Secrets Act.

At 7pm that evening a car drove up to the door. Seamus answered the door. He had no jacket on and was in his slippers. His wife looked out and saw him talking to the driver. Then he opened the back door and sat in. Almost immediately the car drove off.

The fate of Seamus Wright so far is unknown. Both the British Army and the IRA have denied all knowledge of him. From that to 13 May 1973 when his wife gave a detailed statement to Fr Brian J. Brady of the Association for Legal Justice, on which the above account is based, great efforts were made to trace him by publicity in newspapers, by contacting General Tuzo, by correspondence with leading politicians, Edward Heath, Harold Wilson, Lord Grey, William Whitelaw, and Mr Jack Lynch. There were rumours and reports of various sightings. One wonders whether people were genuinely mistaken or false leads were deliberately given to hide the truth. In the end nobody was able to help his wife.

One presumes, since Seamus Wright is missing for 18 years, that he is dead, executed by the IRA or the SAS. Chapman Pincher in the *Daily Express*, 11 October 1972, reported the Army authorities insisted that they '"did not have Mr Wright..."; they believed he was taken up by the IRA after they shot up the Four Square Laundry van and killed the British intelligence man driving it. They fear Mr Wright may be executed as a British spy. And if that happens, and he is found dead, they suspect the IRA will blame the Army'.

The Four Square Laundry and the Dolly Bird Spies

As we have seen from the above account Seamus Wright blew the cover of the Four Square Laundry. The IRA probably had their suspicions. Obviously it is part of the intelligence work of insurgents to check suspicious vehicles. Such an operation led the IRA to three sources – the Four Square Laundry, operated from premises at 15 College Square East; the two operators of the laundry lived with two other agents at a flat at 247 Antrim Road; a premises at 397 Antrim Road housed the Gemini Health Studio, a massage parlour used by undercover agents to photograph and eavesdrop on people who might be thought to have valuable information. On 2 October 1972 the IRA struck, ambushing a van at Twinbrook and attacking both premises.

At 11.15 am three Provisional IRA men ambushed the green-lettered Four Square Laundry van in Juniper Park, Dunmurry. They arrived in a blue Cortina. They poured long bursts of automatic fire into the van. The British Army admitted that Sapper Ted Stuart of the Royal Irish Rangers, driver of the van, was killed in the attack. He was 20 years of age, a single man from Ardstraw, County Tyrone. He was shot five times from close range. In a second statement issued on 5 October the IRA claimed that two other 'British agents' had been killed in the van, allegedly in a concealed apartment under the roof from which they could spy or shoot. The bogus laundry was obviously a means of carrying out intelligence gathering, casually bringing agents in contact with people, providing an extra eye on areas, and selected clothing could also be forensically checked out for traces of use of arms and explosives. The bulk of the cleaning was given to another laundry who were under contract to the Army.

The British Army does not officially announce SAS casualties and indeed in the early 1970s the use of the SAS in Northern Ireland was hotly denied. The Royal Irish Rangers was obviously the sapper's parent regiment. SAS casualties abroad are sometimes conveniently brought home as 'car accidents in Germany'; 'swimming accidents' is another guise. A list of SAS killed in action (probably not all of them) is inscribed on the monumental tower clock at Bradbury Lines Barracks, Hereford, where Remembrance Day parades are held and wreaths laid. A few verses from James Elroy Flecker's play, *Hassan*, (Scene ii, Act V), form a prayer-motto on the monument:

> We are the Pilgrims, master; we shall go
> Always a little further: it may be
> Beyond that last blue mountain barred with snow
> Across that angry or that glimmering sea,
> White on a throne or guarded in a cave
> There lives a prophet who can understand
> Why men were born: but surely we are brave,
> Who take the Golden Road to Samarkand.

There is no free access to Bradbury Lines Barracks. Many SAS casualties will remain a mystery.

A member of the WRAC (Women's Royal Army Corps), who was with the laundry van, was in a house in Juniper Crescent collecting laundry when the attack took place. She was a member of the undercover team and used the code name 'Jane'. She was a native of Coleraine. A year later, on 18 September, she became the first WRAC to be awarded the Military Medal for an undercover operation in Northern Ireland. She was in a state of shock when the shooting took place. Locals sheltered her and gave her brandy and a nerve tablet until another plain clothes man came and took her away about half-an-hour later.

Intelligence is crucial in the Northern Ireland conflict. Incidents are only irritating faults in a smooth-running operation. Besides the pseudo-gangs and undercover agents, two regiments of Military Police comprising some seven hundred men were committed to Northern Ireland. The use of a member in the Four Square incident is proof that some WRAC have been recruited into the 'Intelligence Corps'. Four women of the Intelligence Corps were sent to the North in July 1975 following their training. The Intelligence Corps unit in the North, 'No. 12 Intelligence and Security Company' soon doubled its size from its formation at the end of 1971.

'The Dolly Bird Spies'– such was the huge title on the front page of the *Sunday Mail*, 8 October 1972. The writer told a story that a health studio with pretty girls giving massage treatment , and a taxi service, were part of the British spy-network. Chris Ryder also carried the story in the *Sunday Independent*, 8 October, 'Bond has nothing on the IRA Spycatchers'. It seems the health studio was located at Antrim Road. The *Sunday Mail* gave another address in Antrim Road as the luxury flat where girls lived, and added that nearby was another laundry which the Army used with agents posing as laundry men'. One must, however, treat stories in the popular press with caution.

David Lewis wrote up the 'Gemini' story in *Penthouse* magazine (Vol. 10, No. 12) in an article entitled 'On Her Majesty's Sexual Service', an expansion of a chapter in his book, *Sexspionage: The Exploitation of Sex by Soviet Intelligence*. Again his account has to be read with some caution. His story is that the first health clubs appeared in the Antrim and Stranmillis Roads in July 1970. Later there was a third on the Malone Road. They were organised by the Security Service in co-operation with Scotland Yard; a special intelligence service was set up in Churchhill House, Belfast, to operate the clubs. This unit hired the help of a Londoner (jailed for life in July 1975 for the murder of a racketeer) to run them. Lewis maintains that the operation scored a success in March 1971 which enabled the authorities to identify the alleged killers of the three Royal Highland Fusiliers shot dead in Belfast on 10 March 1971.

On Wednesday 4 October the Irish Republican Publicity Bureau claimed that the IRA shot dead two British agents at a flat on the Antrim Road. It said the victims were a former Army major, and a woman agent who was the daughter of a British officer. The RUC gave two versions of a shooting on the Antrim Road, firstly that a man was wounded in the left shoulder at the massage centre when a man entered the premises and fired two shots at another man in the waiting room but, later in the week, said that three shots had been fired at a man outside the premises and he had been slightly wounded in the chest. Girls next door to the massage centre told Chris Ryder that a wounded man came out of the massage centre and used the phone to call an ambulance; he had a towel wrapped round a wound on his arm.

Ryder also wrote in his article – 'About 12.40 pm on Monday two girls, one with a gun, pushed their way into an office block at College Square East, and they were followed by two men, one with a gun. One of the men tripped on the first step and his gun went off. They went up to the top floor and came down again quickly according to a worker in the building. Nobody was upstairs in the office at the time. The incident was not admitted by the British Army or the RUC until Thursday night. Then they did not specify the premises'.

The British Army made its defence in quite a long statement. It did include an admission that the flat on the Antrim Road was used by a plain clothes surveillance unit. On Thursday 5 October at mid-day Marine Commandos evacuated the Antrim Road flat. A wide area around the flat was cordoned off by troops and a search party broke into the first floor two-bedroomed flat. They entered the flat from a rear veranda. Troops carried army beds, furniture, bed clothes and boxes from the flat. The *Irish News* (6 October 1972) reported that after the Army search local shopkeepers talked about the 'brother and sister' who moved into the flat several months previous. One said – 'The girl was called Jane and she said her brother was called Bobbie. He had a beard and drove a motorbike. They said their father owned a laundry in Bangor. They spoke very well and they always had friends or other young people they said were cousins coming and going at the flat. Jane was slim and dark-haired. She was about 26 years of age and she spoke with a bit of a Scottish accent'. They had not been seen at the flat since Sunday 1 October.

The British Army statement of 5 October was as follows:

'Following an Army statement concerning the fatal shooting of Sapper Stuart in Twinbrook estate on 2 October, the Provisional IRA have made false claims. The true facts are these:-
1. At the time of the shooting there was only one man in the Four Square Laundry van – Sapper Stuart.
2. On 2 October, gunmen entered office premises in Belfast – evidently looking for the office of Four Square Laundry. One man fired his weapon accidentally. They were in the wrong office. No one was hurt.
3. On 2 October, a man was shot and injured in 397 Antrim Road. Neither the man, the premises, nor the shooting had any connection

with the Four Square Laundry or the security.

4. On 5 October, an office and a flat in Belfast were searched by troops. These premises had been used by a plain clothes detachment concerned with the Four Square Laundry. Precautions were taken against booby traps or ambush – but nothing appeared to have been touched. Claims that three soldiers and a girl concerned in Army surveillance duties have been murdered are completely without foundation.

In an earlier statement on 5 October the Army said: 'We wish to make it clear that the laundry and cleaning processing for the Four Square Laundry was operated on an agency basis as is customary in the laundry and dry cleaning business. The staff of the Four Square Laundry approached another firm to do the work for them. The firm concerned was in no way involved in any intelligence operations and neither they nor any members of their staff had any knowledge whatever of the true nature of the activities of the Four Square Laundry. Throughout the operation the firm was acting in good faith on what was to them a normal business transaction and the Army regret any inconvenience caused to the firm, or any employees, arising out of this operation'.

The Killing of Daniel Rooney[20]

In his book *Peace Keeping in a Democratic Society. The Lesson of Northern Ireland* (1978) Colonel Robin Evelegh makes a strong apologia for the use of plain clothes soldiers. As with Army 'census' or 'headchecking', as he calls it, he is annoyed at the 'inadequacy of the normal criminal prosecution or civil process for deciding on the legality of Security Forces' operating methods in the context of civil disorder'. It is interesting to pick some stray sentences from his thesis. He says that the security forces will be ineffective 'unless they have a proportion of some 20 per cent of their total strength in the terrorist-affected areas operating out of uniform'. Most of the vital arrests, identifications and locations of insurgents he attributes to the work of a small number of plain clothes soldiers who did the intelligence gathering. The Army did not use them more because of the political price, doubts about control and legal uncertainty. He says – 'There seemed to be an illogical extension of the principle that soldiers in a war against an external enemy should be in uniform into the situation of soldiers coping with internal terrorism. The matter came to a head after the "Four Square Laundry Murder" and I personally experienced an example of it. On 27 September 1972 I was interviewed for BBC radio the same day (*as Daniel Rooney was shot by soldiers*). During the interview (this part was not broadcast) the interviewer, Nicholas Woolley, asked me why the Army had been acting illegally by being in plain clothes. I said there was no law against soldiers being in civilian clothes in the United Kingdom. This appeared to be a new idea to him but, after further discussion, while agreeing that this might be the strict law, he said that it, nevertheless, seemed to him quite improper'.

The shooting of Daniel Rooney and the wounding of his friend Brendan Brennan on the night of 26-27 September 1972 is an example of the tragedies the Catholic population of West Belfast had to bear from 'undercover surveillance'.

Some weeks after the shooting of the Conway brothers in Ballymurphy, when the Association for Legal Justice issued a dossier on the incident, Mr Geoffrey Johnson-Smith, MP, a junior Minister of Defence, admitted in Parliament to the existence of plain clothes surveillance patrols. Many people, subsequently, were shot dead from passing cars. In a few cases, the Army admitted responsibility. In each case the claim was always made that the patrols were 'fired on first'. Few people believed them. The British Army admitted to the shooting of Daniel Rooney. Once again they said they were 'fired on first'. Colonel Evelegh said that Rooney got his 'just deserts'.

John Rooney and his wife Mary lived at Rodney Parade, Belfast, with seven of their eight children. One son was married and lived at St James' Road. From internment day, 9 August 1971, the family, with many others in the area, were systematically harassed by successive regiments of the British Army. Some were arrested, interrogated, and Seán was interned for a period. Daniel Rooney was a happy carefree type of person, always ready for banter and known as a wag, even friendly with the soldiers. 'When are you coming for me?' – he would often say to them without aggro.

One of the witnesses who gave a statement to the Association for Legal Justice, Mrs Canning, described the scenario of the shooting:

> My friend and myself were standing talking at St James' Road end of St James' Place at 12.05 am. Our attention was attracted by the glaring headlights of two cars which we could see speeding up the lower part of St James' Road. Knowing of the frequent car attacks in the area we immediately stood close into the hedge.
>
> We saw the first car turn into St James' Crescent. The other car proceeded past us and on up St James' Road. Seconds later the same car reappeared coming out of St James' Drive (the next street up from where we were standing). It then passed us again going down St James' Road where we saw it meeting up with another car which was coming out of St James' Crescent. The car leaving St James' Crescent turned out in front of the other car and, as they left the junction of St James' Crescent/St James' Road, shots were fired from the second car.

Just before the shooting two girls had come into the area and were chatting before parting for home. Two lads warned them that the same two cars that had been shooting in the area the week before were in again. A second warning was given to them as they moved to the corner of the street.

People had noticed the cars and were moving out of the way. The girls lay down in the hallway of a house. They got up and were just ready to move off again after the car had passed them when they saw a weapon coming out of the right hand side of the back window – 'About 10 automatic shots were fired, the flashes of the gunfire lighting the people's faces in the car. We saw four of these men, two in front and two in the back. We then heard moaning from the corner. We ran into the street; the car was making its way down St James' Road still firing. When we got to the corner, we saw two lads lying on the ground. We tried to comfort them telling them they would be all right'.

Daniel Rooney was standing with Brendan Brennan and another friend chatting at the corner of St James' Crescent and St James' Road. They saw a car coming out of St James' Crescent towards St James' Road. The friend shouted 'Run' and ran away. The other two stayed and laughed. The friend was hit on the left side of the head. He ran into a house. He ran back out and saw both boys lying on the ground. He bent over one of them and all he heard was – 'I am dying, I am dying'.

It is pure pathos that Daniel's sister Mary came on him as he lay dying:

> I was walking home down St James' Road about 11.55 pm. As I crossed the junction of St James' Road/St James' Place I saw a car coming slowly out of St James' Crescent and turn down St James' Road ahead of me. Suddenly I heard bursts of gunfire coming from both sides of the car and saw the flashes. I heard screaming and thought to myself, 'My God, someone has been hit'. I ran down to the Crescent. When I got to the Crescent I saw my brother Daniel lying flat on the footpath and bleeding. I also saw another boy bleeding whom I know now was Brendan Brennan. A crowd had gathered and moved me quickly away as I was extremely upset. I heard no other shooting in the district before, during or after the time I heard and saw the gunfire from the car. My brother was not a gunman and had been screened more times than I can remember by the security forces in the area. They knew him by name and I just cannot understand why they shot him down so callously. They have not been satisfied with gunning him down in cold blood. They have reached the depths of cruelty and said that he was a gunman and that he got his deserts. May God forgive them.

In its statement following the shooting the Army said that five shots had been fired by two gunmen at a security forces' surveillance patrol in the St James' Park area, that the fire was returned and that two hits were claimed; the security forces sustained no casualties. Colonel Evelegh, Commanding Officer of the 3rd Battalion, Royal Green Jackets, made the following points on TV, on Wednesday 27 September 1972: that this fellow was a gunman, that his activities could be traced back over a year, that a couple of weeks previously he was spotted with a gun by the security forces, that he was definitely engaged in a shooting incident at the time he was shot, that he got his just deserts.

Colonel Evelegh's statement was resented by the residents of the area and caused the Rooney family great pain. It prompted the priests of the parish to reply in a statement read at all Masses in the churches of St John and Corpus Christi the following Sunday:

> No one in the area has any doubt that Daniel Rooney was an innocent victim. He was talking peacefully with his companion when the fatal shots came from a passing car. The fact that the Army has since admitted that these shots were fired by military in plain clothes only increases the indignation felt by everyone about the brutal attack that led to his death.
>
> You have heard us frequently denounce and condemn in the strongest terms other murders committed in the parish. We would be quite inconsistent today if we did not make the point clearly that this kind of killing is totally indefensible, no matter who its perpetrators are. It is in direct contravention of the law of God. It is an assault on the most basic of all rights, the right to life itself. It calls in question the discipline and control of the forces supposedly devoted to the security of the community and it undermines any possibility of creating the understanding and trust that will ever be necessary if there is ever to be a solution to our problems.
>
> To the parents and family of Daniel Rooney we want to offer our deepest sympathy and the promise of our prayers for the happy repose of his soul. We will pray for the recovery of Brendan Brennan and for his parents and family also, and we give them our support in their ordeal.

The inquest was held on 6 December 1973. The six soldiers involved in the shooting did not appear. It was stated that at the time of the shooting they were stationed at Palace Barracks, Holywood (a centre for the SAS and MRF). Their statements were read by an RUC officer; they were referred to by letters. They said that Rooney and his companion had a rifle and a handgun. Soldier 'A' said that a third person, other than Rooney and Brennan, fired from a pistol. He said he fired three rounds from his Browning 9 mm pistol from the front passenger's seat and Soldier 'C' fired his Sterling submachine-gun from his position in the rear passenger seat. The court was told that lead tests were carried out on clothing worn by Rooney and his companion and on swabs taken from their hands and that these tests had proved negative. An open verdict was returned.

Accusations of plain clothes British Army murder squads increased after the shooting of Daniel Rooney. Mr Kevin McCorry of the Civil Rights Association speaking at Kildress, County Tyrone, said, 'Mr Whitelaw should come clean with the people and tell them honestly whether he has any control over the activities of these military personnel'. Another group, Cumann Saoránach na hÉireann, challenged Mr Whitelaw to deny that SAS units had been responsible for many of the shootings and bombings in Catholic districts. They accused the SAS of being responsible for the bombing of the Unity Flats social club on 27 September in which Daniel McErlean died.

Loyalist Violence

The Catholic population suffered grievously throughout 1972 at the hands of loyalist murder gangs. Loyalist violence was carried out by two main groups, the UVF and the UDA. The UDA was founded in the early 1970s, ostensibly as a defence group for Protestants in working-class areas. It quickly became involved in sectarian murders and armed robberies. The organisation has never been proscribed. In May 1973 at the height of the sectarian assassinations, a new group, the Ulster Freedom Fighters (UFF), emerged and claimed responsibility for many of the actions and sectarian murders carried out by the UDA. Since then the UFF has been used as a cover name by the UDA when claiming paramilitary activities.

It was not until 5 February 1973 that the first two Protestants were interned. After an attack on a workman's bus in Belfast a number of Protestants were arrested for questioning. Two of these men were later held under the Special Powers Act. Loyalist politicians called for a one day General Strike on 7 February in protest. The North was brought to a halt.

Why the British Government at this time should decide to intern loyalists became apparent on 25 March 1973 when the Secretary of State, Mr William Whitelaw, stated in Washington DC 'that if British troops are withdrawn from Northern Ireland there would be a bloodbath in which Protestants would attack Catholics'. By interning a few loyalists the British Government was simply continuing to propagate the myth of being the honest broker in the situation, projecting the image of holding the line and treating each side with equal repression to end the 'cycle of violence'.

During the period between internment on 9 August 1971 and 5 February 1973, when the first loyalist was interned, loyalist murder gangs were responsible for over one hundred deaths. Bomb attacks on Catholic property during this period were widespread. The scale of loyalist violence in the North was real and menacing. The British government's lack of urgency in dealing with it is clear in statements made by nationalist politicians. On 19 February 1973 Mr Ivan Cooper, MP said that Mr Whitelaw was still 'leaning' on the Catholic population. He stated that, in the 7-week period ending 31 January, 551 Catholics were arrested and 60 Protestants; 2,600 lbs of explosives were discovered in searches of Protestant areas compared with 1,200 lbs in Catholic areas; in spite of this only one ninth of all searches took place in Protestant areas where 13,700 out of a total of 19,000 rounds of ammunition had been found. Loyalist murder gangs assassinated 16 people during this same 7-week period. In one incident on 20 December 1972 five men were killed indiscriminately in a sub-machine-gun attack on a Catholic public house in Derry. They were Charles McCafferty, Bernard Kelly, Francis McCarron, Michael McGinley, all Catholics, and Charles Moore, a Protestant. On the same day David McAleese, a Catholic man going to work, was shot dead in Belfast and a Catholic youth Alphonsus McGeown suffered the same fate in Dungannon.

John Hume speaking in a debate in Stormont on 7 November 1973 referred to 'official figures for arms and explosives found in 1973'. He said that in June 1973 the figures were 3,708 minority area homes searched and 436 majority area homes searched; in June 563 guns had been found in minority areas and 438 in majority areas. He called for a radical review of the entire problem.

By November 1973 Frank Doherty, a Belfast journalist, was able to analyse the working out of Kitson's theory contained in *Low Intensity Operations* written just before he came to Belfast. The operations group of the MRF had committed sufficient blunders to bring them to the attention of the public press. In his article in *Hibernia*, 16 November 1973, Doherty claimed that the MRF had an intelligence section and a Special Methods' Group. The former consisted of junior officers with some back-up from 'other ranks'. The Special Methods' Group as explained by a sergeant in court was broken into cells of one junior officer, two sergeants and a private and what Kitson called 'indigenous' members. MRF had other sections. A Tactical Development section evolved operational techniques for use by regular units on the streets. The 'Hot Lips' tactic of hiding soldiers in ambush position in empty buildings (such an operation led to the shooting dead of Jim Bryson and Patrick Mulvenna in Ballymurphy on 31 August 1973) and the box formation of riot control were two examples. MRF had also an Equipment Research section at Thiepval Barracks, Lisburn. 'Its members', wrote Doherty, 'are officers and technicians drawn from the Royal Electrical and Mechanical Engineers, the Royal Corps of Signals and the Royal Engineers'. There were also assistant civilian scientists. Part of the technological development was the use of computers to store information and an elaborate VHF radio network established throughout the North.

A Calendar of Incidents – 1972

5 January. A Kidnapping[21]
In order to recruit members for the MRF, the SAS often had to kidnap their victims. There was a spate of these in the 1971-72 period. One such

kidnapping took place in the Clonard area on 5 January. Three men in civilian clothes drove at speed along the Falls Road at 1.45 pm and turned wildly into Clonard Street. There was a group of youths standing outside a bookmaker's shop on the corner of this street and the Falls Road. One of the men covered the group with a sub-machine-gun. Another jumped out and held a 9 mm Browning pistol to the head of a nineteen-year-old youth and forced him into the car. Not a word was spoken by the kidnappers. The youth was brought at speed to North Howard Street military post on the Shankill/Falls peaceline. He was told he was arrested under the Special Powers Act for being a member of the IRA. He was brought in a Saracen to Springfield Road RUC/Military Post where a uniformed RUC officer took his name, address, family details and then released him.

In the meantime a witness to the kidnapping had stopped a passing Army patrol and gave the number and description of the car. Instead of giving chase the soldiers arrested the witness and brought him in turn to Springfield Road station where he was held and questioned.

6 February. The Murder of David Seaman

On this day the hooded body of David Seaman, aged 31 years, of 32 William Street, Manchester, was found at Culloville, on the Dundalk-Castleblayney concession road, just ten yards into the North. The body was found by a showband returning from a dance. They first reported it to the Gardaí who then contacted the RUC when they discovered the body was inside the North. From the nose upwards the head was hooded by a mask of tape. Seaman had been shot five times in the head with a .38 revolver. The bullets had been fired into the back of the skull.

On 23 October 1971 David Seaman alias Hans Kruger alias Barry Barber had appeared at an Official IRA press conference. He said he had been sent to plant bombs which would injure civilians and thus discredit the IRA. He said that he and a fellow SAS man had planted the bomb on 29 September 1971 at the Four Step Inn on the Shankhill Road, Belfast, which killed two men, Alex Andrews and Ernest Bates. The explosion caused sectarian strife. It was disclaimed by both the Official and Provisional IRA. Seaman claimed he was trained by British intelligence. It was soon apparent that there was something crazy about him and the Official IRA stepped back, not wishing to appear foolish. Within a month he went back to his home at Anglesea Avenue, Manchester.

An in-depth article by John Burns in the *Belfast Telegraph*, 16 October 1973, shows clearly that this only son of John and Alice Barber was a psychiatric case. He lived in a dream world even as a boy. He joined the Paras in November 1957 but was dismissed after a month. He spent two terms in borstal. In October 1961 he was caught carrying a knife outside Castlemartin Camp, Pembrokeshire, where the 84 German Panzer Regiment was training. He appeared in Dublin in 1962 claiming to be a British agent and again in 1964 claiming to be an East German agent, Hans Kruger. In 1969 he was divorced from his wife and three children. He changed his name to Seaman. Again he made a few attempts to join the British Army. He met a girl in 1971 and with her two sons came to Ireland in October 1971 when he appeared at the press conference. He returned to Manchester and put an advertisement in the paper inviting volunteers for SEA (Secret English Army) to fight the IRA. It is said that he was visited in January 1972 by Irishmen not known in the area. On 25 January he appeared in Dublin again and the next day stayed with a friend in Howth, County Dublin. Burns relates that on 27 January he met a tall distinguished man at the Gresham Hotel, Dublin. Seaman appeared to be excited by their conversation. That evening a room was booked for him in a border hotel. He did not appear. The following evening he stayed with the Howth friend. He left on 29 January saying he had to contact an SAS man in Ulster. He came back the same night saying his mission was successful. On the last day of January he left Howth and disappeared for six days until his body was found in Culloville dumped on the grass verge on a cold misty morning.

Was Seaman, believed to be a crazy person, only a Walter Mitty type? Was he a criminal type that could be easily used by the SAS for a dirty job? Mr Joe Cahill of Sinn Féin has told me that Seaman once tried to kidnap him. At the time he appeared at the Official IRA conference, he also made a number of visits to Kevin Street Sinn Féin. The first time he came to the office he was looking for Joe Cahill; Cahill was not there. The second time he came he spoke to a senior official in the party, who was also one of the party treasurers. He said he and nine other criminal types had been recruited by the SAS but he was willing to become a double agent. To prove himself he asked the Sinn Féin official to phone British Army headquarters at Lisburn. Seaman then carried on a conversation. He asked them to send on two cheques for £50 each and put them in care of the seaman's mission, Dublin! He then told the Sinn Féin man he could lift them and cash them. He did so. Seaman called a number of times before he met Cahill. His proposition was that he would take Cahill to the border in the company of three other 'SAS'; this would enhance his standing with the British, that he had taken Cahill. Then near the border he would let Cahill escape; he then would be in a position to act as an agent for the IRA, having proved himself to both sides. Needless to say Cahill treated the scheme and the man as crazy.

It is known that Seaman did some probing around South Armagh. He was finally taken up by the Official IRA who executed him. He had embarrassed them too much.

A *Sunday Press* story, 12 August 1973, claimed that the Gardaí recovered a British War Department pistol following a bank robbery; interest was shown by the RUC who dispatched the markings on a bullet used to shoot

Seaman for comparison. The pistol which fired the bullet, it was claimed, was used in two other murders. The second killing was that of Private Robert Malcolm Benner (25), a member of the Third Queen's Regiment whose body was found also on the County Armagh border. He had been abducted after visiting his fiancée in the South; at that time Benner was stationed in the North. The other killing was that of Thomas McCann, of Sperrin Road, Drimnagh. He was a storeman with the British Army at Holywood Barracks. He went to Dublin to visit his widowed mother and disappeared after going to a local pub for a drink. His body was also found just over the border.

It is difficult to assess the authenticity of this *Sunday Press* article; it adds something to the mystery but could be mere speculation.

28 February. Arrested by plain clothes soldiers
A sixteen-year-old boy gave a statement to the Association for Legal Justice: 'On Monday, 28 February, first day at work, I was on my way home at lunch-hour. I stood for a moment at Cawnpore Street/Kashmir Road junction to speak to a friend. It was about 1 pm. A van came along Kashmir Road from Springfield Road and pulled up near the point where I was standing. Five men dressed in civilian clothes jumped out of the van holding guns (one of which was a rubber bullet gun) in their hands. They pointed the guns in our direction and shouted in English accents, "Stop where you are!" I was frightened and both I and my companion held up our hands and my companion shouted, "O God! No! No!" We thought they might be UVF.

'They waved us into the van and, as I was about to enter it, one of the men pushed me and I hit my head on the door. They took us both to North Howard Street military barracks. I was questioned for about 15-20 minutes by one of the men who arrested me. He asked me was I in the Fianna; he asked me to give him names of IRA men. He asked about the where-abouts of men and boys from the area and the location of arms dumps.

'After interrogation both of us were taken by Saracen to Springfield Road barracks where our photographs were taken. Shortly afterwards my mother arrived and I saw her speak to a policeman. A little later a policeman told me I was free to go home.'

26 May 1972. The Shankill Road Shooting[22]
Three Army Intelligence Officers were beaten up in Silvio Street, Belfast, in the early afternoon, by civilians. Four Protestant men travelling by car in Silvio Street, which lies between the Crumlin and Shankill Roads in Belfast, were intercepted by a gunman in civilian clothes who jumped from a blue Cortina. This car was driving towards them and had stopped at the junction of Silvio Street and Upper Charleville Street. The gunman

fired an automatic pistol at them and then returned to his car which made off at speed and according to locals then crashed. The Army said local people interfered with it. Residents seized the three men in the car, dis-armed them and beat them up. According to local community leaders one of the gunmen had a military identity card and inside the car an Army pocket-phone radio and three nylon masks were found. An Army spokesman said that a plain clothes patrol had chased a suspicious car and managed to stop it at Upper Charleville Street; when two men produced pistols a member of the patrol fired. The four men reported the incident at Tennent Street RUC barracks. An official RUC spokesman was quoted in the *Sunday News* as contradicting the Army version. He said the men and their car were checked and they were allowed to go. None of them was charged.

18 August 1972. The attempts to kill William Black[23]
On 26 January 1974 six armed men lay in wait at a cottage at Tully-West, County Down. One was armed with a sub-machine-gun fitted with a silencer. The gunmen had been lying in wait for three days. Two were SAS men. The other four were on secondment from the Royal Engineers. All six wore army uniform and army woollen caps. One of them, later recognised, was an Army Intelligence man who had been seen at the Giant's Ring following a mysterious murder a few months previous. Subsequently the British Army acknowledged the gunmen as members of the Special Investigations Branch, the Army's 'plain clothes' military police. These armed men were waiting to shoot William Black.

Black had rented a cottage outside Saintfield. On 26 January he arrived at the cottage with a colleague to whom he promised a water tank he had left there. He had brought his brother and another friend along. Black brought his sporting rifle with him intending to do some shooting. He got the keys of the barn where the water tank was and opened it. When he reached the top of the stairs he was shot with a Sterling machine-gun. He was left for dead. After a time, by rolling and sliding, he got down the stairs and struggled towards a nearby house. As he staggered up the hill he heard the sound of the Sterling machine-gun. The gunman was firing at him again. Blood was pouring out of him when he reached the house and called out for the police.

This was the third attempt on the life of William Black, a fitter at Harland and Wolf's shipyard. He was married with three sons, one of whom joined the RUC. He was a member of the Plymouth Brethern and led a strict religious life. He joined the UDR in November 1971.

The trouble in his life began on 18 August 1972. At 2 am he and his wife saw from their home three men tampering with a van belonging to a neighbour, Thomas Shannon. At this time the Blacks lived at Black's Road in south-west Belfast. They saw one of the men entering the van and the other two moving to a larger van owned by a neighbour. Black also noticed a large dark BMC 1800 saloon car nearby. He thought the hijackers were IRA men. He took his sporting rifle and ordered the men to halt. His action was to lead to the arrest of the hijackers. The engine of the car started up. The three ran towards it. Two climbed in and it drove off. The third fell as he tried to get in. Black held him under guard until the police arrived. Then the car came back again and the prisoner made a dash for it. At Black's warning a policeman sprang into the car and covered them. Later at the Army centre at Black's Road, some distance away, Black saw the BMC 1800 parked. The men who had been arrested were standing chatting. He saw that two had wigs in their hands and both wore their hair short. They abused him. He realised then that they were soldiers. The police had asked Black to come to the centre. The commanding officer told him that the men he had surprised were Special Investigation Branch men and turned nasty when he heard Black was in the UDR and reminded him about the Official Secrets Act. He explained – 'Certain vehicles are known and accepted in certain areas. When we want to get into them, we have to lay hands on those vehicles'. Meanwhile, back at home Mrs Black witnessed another hijacking. An Army land-rover with four men drove past and stopped. Two of the men were in uni-form and two in civilian dress, anoraks with coloured stripes on the sleeves. The men in civilian dress broke into a white Vauxhall car belonging to a young married couple called Darrem. One of them drove the car towards the Army centre. The next day an elaborate cover-up action took place to allay the fears of the neighbours. Darrem's car was found nearby. Explanations were given concerning the other vehicles. The Blacks were not consulted.

Black's action presumably had foiled a bombing mission on the part of the soldiers under the cover of well-known vehicles, especially his neighbour's; this man owned a light engineering works and his van would have been known in Andersonstown.

On 29 August Black's doorbell rang about 2.15 am. On answering the door he took the precaution of suddenly stepping to his right into the sitting room doorway. The action saved his life. A bullet came through the door at chest-high level and probably would have killed him. The Army arrived soon after and then the RUC but no statement was ever taken from the Blacks.

Shortly afterwards Black was dismissed from the UDR for 'failing to perform sufficient periods of duty'. There was no other explanation and he was told the decision was final. In all the incidents Black had probed too much and had looked for official investigations and answers. He was therefore regarded as dangerous. The Blacks moved to a new area, 174 Ainsworth Avenue in West Belfast. On 23 January 1973 the family was watching television when suddenly there were bursts of machine-gun fire outside the house. They threw themselves on the floor. Later Black went out and he and his son Tom collected spent cartridges. The house fired on was the house opposite, number 147. The Blacks suspected the gunmen had made a mistake in the numbers, their own being 174. To add to the suspicion both doors were painted yellow.

Black and his wife considered emigrating. The older children opposed the idea. They moved again, this time to Horn Walk. It was around this time that they became acquainted with Mr Kennedy Lindsay who took up their case and wrote a book on the subject *Ambush at Tully-West, The British Intelligence Services in Action* (1979).

Another incident occurred in August 1973. Shots were fired at Tom Black, then an RUC cadet, as he walked home in civilian dress after shopping. Because of previous incidents the Black family suspected that the British Army undercover forces were again at work, hoping to pressurise them to emigrate. Lindsay brought up Black's plight in the Northern Ireland Assembly. Pieces began to appear in the press. It has always been regarded as a sound principle to surround oneself with plenty of publicity in order to safeguard oneself against crimes of the state, but then came the attempted murder on 26 January 1974.

In chapter seven of his book, entitled 'The Instruction was:" Kill Black"', Kennedy Lindsay puts forward information from inside the officer corps of the SAS which alleges that one of them was sent to Northern Ireland to kill William Black:

> The assignment to assassinate an innocent married man with five children and strong evangelical Christian beliefs caused intense indig- nation among certain army officers who subsequently came to learn about it from army sources. One is known to have declared that he never believed the British Army could sink so low and to have consid- ered resigning his commission. Nor was the officers' mess at the regimental depot of the SAS at Hoarwithy Road, Hereford, immune from the indignation. It is a small, élite regiment with a strong sense of regimental honour and professional integrity. It is suggested, too, that the officer given the task had it emphasised to him that Black was an exceptionally dangerous subversive and that he had no opportunity during his brief, special visit to Ulster to check the truth of what he had been told.

In the emergency after he had been shot on 26 January 1974 a neighbour had brought Black to the Saintfield UDR post. While he was there he saw a regular soldier come up close and stand looking at him. He did not speak but looked at him in a hostile manner with a flint-like face – 'He was about six feet in height, well built and exceptionally fit with no surplus flesh. He had sharp features and wore combat green uniform (not camouflage green). He was a commissioned officer as he wore a pistol. His beret was blue or dark green and had a regimental badge which Black had never seen before during his years with the Territorial Army and UDR. It consisted of a Roman style sword supported by two upright hawk's wings'. Black described the badge to Robert Fisk of *The Times* and he identified it as the SAS badge. After the shooting of William Black, senior commanders of the British Army at Lisburn had the SAS unit arrested and placed in cells for one or two days. After the RUC investigation into the shooting the report was sent to the Northern Ireland Director of Public Prosecutions. As it had exceptional implications he forwarded it to the Attorney General for a decision. A reply from his Northern Ireland representative, with no mention of the involvement of the Attorney General, stated that on the evidence before the Director of Public Prosecutions initiation of criminal proceedings was not warranted. Lindsay says that the file is now at RUC Headquarters under a special classification with access only to the Chief Constable and a small number of his most senior officers.

Subsequently it was established that William Black was an innocent person and he was awarded £16,500 damages. Mr Archie Hamilton, the Armed Forces Minister, admitted in 1990 that Black was shot by a soldier in 1974 'while threatening the life of a soldier'.

There is an odd tailpiece to the story in that a Star pistol found in the settee of the cottage where Black was shot, serial number 1127606, had once belonged to a man in Belfast, a member of the UDR who had been shot dead by soldiers in a confrontation with residents in the Shankhill district on 17 October 1972. The weapon had disappeared then.

Star pistols have a habit of turning up in SAS-connected incidents. We will see that in the case of the murder of IRA captain, John Francis Green, the Star pistol used to shoot him was found at the scene of the Miami showband massacre in the possession of a UVF man who with Captain Robert Nairac of the SAS is alleged to have slain Green. A Star pistol also figures in the case of Denis Heaney of Derry shot by the SAS.

29 August 1972. The Bawnmore Incident[24]
An incident at the Bawnmore estate, Belfast, on this date when vigilantes came into contact with an undercover Army patrol led to the Civil Rights Association challenging the Secretary of State, William Whitelaw to 'come clean' and say whether the SAS was operating in Northern Ireland.

The Bawnmore and District Tenants' Association published documentation of the events which occurred on Tuesday at 1.15 am. Four vigilantes saw a powder-blue Hillman Hunter entering the area. They summoned the assistance of seven other vigilantes. The car cruised around but when it went to leave found its exit blocked by another car at Dandy Street. The vigilantes approached the car and questioned the occupants. The answers were not satisfactory. The one who spoke had a cultured English accent. The intruders would not identify themselves. The vigilantes tried to open the car doors which were locked save one of the rear doors. The back seat passenger was removed and a man was sent to alert the military. An attempt was made to remove the other occupant from the passenger front seat. He produced a gun and cocked it and only a quick action of a vigilante in striking the weapon down saved his life. The bullet lodged in the car. The vigilante pulled away from the car which then drove off at speed smashing into the car used to block it and escaping.

The man pulled from the car was frisked and a Browning pistol was found in a shoulder holster. He was removed to Bawnmore Park. A more thorough search revealed another full magazine for the pistol in his pocket. No identification was found. When harassed by the vigilantes he used the expression 'SAS' or 'ASSASS'.

Soldiers of the Marine Artillery arrived and the man was handed over to them. An explanation was given as to what happened. The captured man then gave his name as 'Peter Holmes' and Holywood as his address. Different investigations were set on foot by military and police after the incident. On the following night a local Army Commander had an interview with some of the vigilantes. He said he had been instructed to tell them that it had been a military operation that had gone wrong.

2 September 1972. The Leeson Street Shooting[25]
What has come to be known as 'The Leeson Street Shooting' involved IRA leader Brendan Hughes. He had been 'on the run' for some time and RUC and Army were looking for him. They had made a couple of attempts to capture him. On the morning of 2 September he was standing at the corner of Varna Street and Leeson Street awaiting a contact who was to bring him to a 'safe house'. While waiting for his contact another man joined him and while they chatted they noticed a large high covered van coming down Leeson Street. The driver glanced quickly at them and drove on down towards Grosvenor Road. Suspicious of the van, Hughes sent for weapons. Quite suddenly the van appeared again. It must have made a circle and was coming down the street once more. About twenty yards past Varna Street it suddenly stopped, the doors flew open and four men jumped out. Two dressed in bomber jackets, wearing jeans and carrying .45s, opened fire on Hughes who took to his heels into Sultan Street and dived through a window. The group pursuing constantly fired at him and a group of soldiers also opened up from a deserted house opposite Varna Street. Then two Saracens rumbled into the street and the firing ceased. One of the civilian gunmen ran to one of the Saracens and shouted to the occupants. Meanwhile the other Saracen had parked beside the deserted house. Residents saw uniformed soldiers come out of the house and get into the

Saracen. Minutes later the convoy left, the green van with its gunmen travelling between the two Saracens. The British Army statement issued after the incident made no mention of the four soldiers firing from the deserted house. Hughes escaped.

3 September 1972. British Army Shoot-Out[26]

Another shoot-out between uniformed and plain clothes soldiers took place at 4 am at the junction of Lepper Street and Stratheden Street in the New Lodge Road area of Belfast. In an hour-long battle more than 100 rounds were fired by both sides. Marine Robert Stephen Cutting (18) from Manchester was killed and another seriously injured. The Army admitted that both sides involved soldiers and stated that there would be an enquiry. According to eye witnesses one of the men in civilian clothes was shot by a soldier at point-blank range. He was reported pleading for his life. It was stated that he spoke with a Belfast accent. This casualty, however, was not officially listed.

Plain Clothes Soldiers in Riverdale, Belfast

25 November 1972. 'On Saturday 25 November about 12.30 pm I was taking out the hose to wash the car, when I noticed a group of young men run into my garage. I went to speak to them and asked what they were doing. One with black curly hair and carrying a pistol told me not to worry; it was just a routine check.

'They were not in uniform as worn by the British Army; they were wearing green trousers, some in blue anoraks, some in waterproof jackets, but none wore berets or badges or insignia of any kind. I think they were soldiers because they had Scottish accents'. (Statement to the Association for Legal Justice.)

1 December 1972. 'Late on Friday night about 12.30 am, 1 December, I was returning home with my husband; from my garden path I saw a man leaning on the gate of the house next door quite casually. I thought at first it was my neighbour's husband but when he turned I saw he carried a pistol; his sandy-coloured hair was uncovered; he wore an anorak. Just then I saw another man crouching behind the wall wearing a knitted cap and carrying a rifle. Because they were openly displaying arms I formed the opinion they were the British Army. The man leaning on the gate wore no beret or badge of any kind'. (Statement to the Association for Legal Justice.)

Some 'SAS' Casualties 1972-76

In the early 1970s the British Army was active in community relations work. It was a major thrust at the time, a very different front from internment, torture and the manipulation of sectarian killings. British Army personnel appeared at all kinds of meetings, anything from the setting up of a play school, the allocation of houses, to the planning of youth outings. The motive was ulterior, intelligence gathering plus gaining a grasp on the communities.

One of those active in the 'hearts and minds' campaign was an SAS soldier.[27] He and another SAS soldier were taken prisoner by a mixed group of Provisional and Official IRA in Leeson Street, 14 June 1972. Both became victims of a 'punishment shooting'. One was kneecapped; the other was so badly injured he was left for dead. The wounding of these two were the first SAS casualties.

Another soldier was found seriously wounded in an entry off the Ormeau Road, Belfast, at the end of April 1973.[28] He had been shot twice in the head. He was brought to the Royal Victoria Hospital and later transferred to the military wing of Musgrave Park Hospital for his safety. He had joined the British Army in 1969 but deserted a short time afterwards. He is then reputed to have joined the Provisional IRA. He was picked up by the Army while manning a barricade in Andersontown in 1972. The Army looked on him as fair game to pressurise into joining the Military Reconnaissance Force. The Army admitted in May 1973 that he was a member of this force and that rather than face a charge of desertion he agreed to work as an undercover agent, helping to identify IRA men whilst they conducted him around in unmarked vehicles. One thing is clear. He and others were expendable human beings whose lives were impaired or destroyed in a jungle-type world.

On 20 March 1974 in a case of mistaken identity Corporal Michael Francis Herbert (31) and Corporal Michael John Cotton, undercover soldiers, were shot dead by the RUC in Mowhan, South Armagh. 1974 was an important date in SAS activity; the SAS operating then were caught in the MI5/MI6 power struggle. I deal later in detail with their deaths in that context.[29]

Captain Anthony Stephen Hungerford Pollen (27) (parent regiment, the Coldstream Guards) was shot dead by the Provisional IRA on Easter Sunday, 14 April 1974 in the Bogside, Derry.[30] He and another SAS soldier were on surveillance duty but were foolhardy and made themselves obvious by photographing the Sinn Féin Easter commemoration. Some IRA members spotted them and realised that the plain clothes men were undercover soldiers. They were chased and Captain Pollen was shot dead. His companion escaped. The IRA said Pollen also opened fire and that they took possession of his pistol. They claimed he was a member of the SAS. The British Army statement denied this and denied that he exchanged fire.

Brian Shaw (21) an ex-Royal Irish Rangers soldier was shot dead in a derelict house at Arundel Street in West Belfast on 20 July 1974.[31] Two conflicting stories were issued concerning his death. The IRA said he admitted membership of the SAS under interrogation. The British statement said he had bought himself out of the Army three months before his death and denied he was in the SAS.

A British Army captain was killed on 4 April 1975 when his jeep struck a telegraph pole on a road near Trillick, County Tyrone.[32] His death was not reported by the RUC or the British Army until the afternoon of the next day. He remains unnamed. Army Headquarters in Lisburn would only confirm that he was killed; they said he was attached to a unit in the area and was driving a civilian car; he was 'non-operational' at the time. Local sources said he died at 4 am (two hours earlier than the Army report) and that he was in a jeep; that he was stationed at Middletown, County Armagh and that he had been visiting a retired British Army officer who lived at Kilskeery on the road from Trillick to Errington. Local SDLP politician, Mr Tom Daly, commented at the time, 'With the number of sinister events which have happened in the area the incident is bound to make people suspicious that units such as the SAS are at work, and such suspicions are disturbing'.

Suspicions in 1975 were increased by the revelations of some ex-soldiers. One was the case of a soldier from the South.[33] He belonged to a large family which gave many soldiers to both the Irish and British armies. He was arrested in south-east London in June 1975 and had to face a court-martial. He denied desertion but admitted being absent from his base at Ballykelly from 21 June 1972. His one-year job in Northern Ireland was not disclosed in court. His solicitor handed in a document to the president of the Board, saying – 'There are certain elements which preclude me from addressing you further in the present atmosphere of the court, as it is now constituted. The implications of his service in Northern Ireland exposed him to more danger than normal'. Later he said, 'We cannot allow his face to be seen or published in any way. For his own protection I do not want him to be photographed. I cannot say any more about the situation but it is delicate'. An Army spokesman refused to comment on the soldier's job – 'We have very good reason for not wanting to answer any questions about that'.

Another English-born soldier, who had been attached to the First Royal Tank regiment and was stationed at Omagh from August 1973 to October 1974 gave an interview to *Sunday World* journalist Cathal O'Shea for his paper's issue, 14 September 1975. He said he deserted from the Army because he was sickened by their attitude to the Irish. He spoke of the plain clothes intelligence men who worked in the Republic of Ireland gathering information on the Provisional IRA – 'Sometimes they would be absent from the camp for three or four days at a time. Their main points of infiltration were Dundalk, Monaghan, Castleblayney, Clones, Bundoran, and other areas where there were known republican sympathisers. No one would ever have guessed that the intelligence boys were Army men. Some of them dressed as business men, others wore their hair long and operated under the guise of being students. They used family-type saloon cars for travelling in but the registration numbers were false. Each month a differ-ent number was placed on their cars'.

An Phoblacht in its issue of 19 March 1976 claimed that three soldiers involved in a motor crash on the afternoon of Saturday 13 March 1976 near Newry were members of the SAS. Two were killed when the unmarked van in which they were travelling collided with a single-decker Ulster bus. *An Phoblacht* put forward a number of points to argue that they were SAS – their plain clothes; their unmarked van; their unit of three; their age. The Army, however, said that they belonged to a bomb disposal unit and were based in Lurgan; the republicans said they were based in an Army post in South Armagh and had been under observation by their intelligence officers.

Ten weeks into the 1975 ceasefire between the Provisional IRA and the British Army, the IRA shot and wounded a British soldier dressed in plain clothes on the Falls Road on Saturday 18 April 1975.[34] The IRA maintained that he was part of an undercover squad of four whose activities in the Falls Road district were observed before an order to shoot was given. The IRA captured an expensive miniature recorder with tape from the van and radio manuals. The material on the tape listed the names of approximately 30 members of the republican movement who had been shadowed and their movements noted. The IRA said they regarded such activity as a breach of the truce. To embarrass the British Government leading members of Sinn Féin invited journalists to hear the tape recording. The recording used code names. Some people were referred to by their names, like Seamus Loughran of Belfast Sinn Féin, but others were referred to by such codes as 'Delta Nine, X-Ray 21'. The Falls Road incident centre was referred to as 'Lincolnshire'. There were reports on people going in and out of the centre. There were remarks like: '1600 hours. Delta Six is in the bookies in Clonard Street, dressed very smart!'. Suspected male Provisionals were reported as 'cocks' and female suspects as 'turkeys', with such remarks as: 'A young turkey and a young cock in Waterford Street having a hamburger and things!'. The IRA alleged that the wounded soldier was one of a team from the SAS.

In June, 17 weeks into the ceasefire, Catholics in Belfast were highly disturbed when the *Sunday Times* of 8 June claimed that compromising British Army dossiers containing detailed information about IRA suspects had been handed to loyalist paramilitaries by British soldiers. The news increased fears of Catholics at a time when there was a wave of sectarian killings of Catholics in Belfast. A loyalist gave the paper four documents. One document was marked 'restricted', part of a large dossier of suspected IRA men compiled at British Army headquarters at Lisburn, and distrib-uted in blue plastic folders to Army units throughout Northern Ireland. It contained photographs taken of republicans during interrogation and screening, their addresses and Army code numbers. Underneath the pho-tographs were potted biographies, giving sometimes place of work and car registration. The second document contained photographs of Provisional IRA suspects in Ardoyne. The other two contained information on republican internees in Long Kesh Prison. One listed 60 internees released at a certain date; the other had the names of more than 400 internees with the names and addresses of their visitors at the prison.

The June revelations in the *Sunday Times* led Kevin Myers to recount in *Hibernia* (13 June 1975) British Intelligence/loyalist links. Early in 1973 he was shown some of the UVF files on the IRA. Among them were official documents, many listed as 'restricted'; one was a street map of Ligoniel in north Belfast drawn up by British Army patrols – every house where an IRA man occasionally billeted or lived was listed, with some photographs attached. Jim Hanna, a UVF leader, once told him that in an IRA/UVF gunbattle which lasted two days a British Army patrol allowed him and two others to enter Corry's timber yards overlooking Catholic Ballymurphy and were present when one of the three shot a young Catholic – they were not arrested. Myers alleges that by 1973 Hanna had become the senior military commander for the UVF in Northern Ireland. He had also become a close friend of members of the 39th Brigade Intelligence at Lisburn and another man who is not listed as a member of Intelligence Corps but was possibly an SAS man attached to Intelligence. They were frequent visitors to Hanna's home near Lisburn, and group photographs of Hanna and themselves were taken away by police after Hanna was murdered. Hanna (27) was found shot dead in a car in Mansfield Street, Shankill Road, Belfast on 1 April 1974. He was a victim of internal loyalist dissension; they possibly suspected him of being an informer. Myers, who knew Hanna well, was told by Hanna that he was on good terms with the soldiers; these men often spoke to him about his involvement in the UVF.

On the evening of 8 July 1975 a British soldier in plain clothes, presumed to be a member of the SAS, crashed his car at the public library near Leeson Street on the Falls Road, Belfast.[35] It was 9.40 pm. Realising that he was in danger he grabbed his radio and made a run for it. He was set upon by a group of men and given a beating but managed to escape. An angry crowd gathered and set fire to the crashed car. Provisional IRA and Official IRA members shared out the spoils that were in the car. In Dublin on Monday 14 July the Official IRA produced photographs of an American made Ingram M10 sub-machine-pistol which they said they had found under a coat in the soldier's car. In February the British Ministry of Defence stated that fewer than 100 of these weapons had been issued and only to the SAS and the Royal Marines Special Boats Service. At that time it was emphasised that it had been bought for the Army for specialist purposes and had not been used in Northern Ireland. Fitted with a silencer and a flash guard, the Ingram M10 is a 9 mm weapon well suited for undercover operations. The seizure of such a weapon was an indication that the soldier was an SAS member. A British Army spokesman at Lisburn Army Headquarters then said on 15 July:- 'The statement issued on February 5 was inaccurate because we discovered soon afterwards that the weapon had been issued to other units in the United Kingdom and Northern Ireland as well as to the SAS'. Ingram sub-machine-pistols have, of course, turned up listed in official inquest documents in Northern Ireland as a weapon used by SAS soldiers in various stake-outs. For example it was one of the weapons used to kill Patrick Duffy in Derry on 24 November 1978. The *Republican News* issue of 12 July 1975 displayed a copy of the soldier's identity card; he was also carrying a 'Joint Services Movement Card' bearing a serial number. The British Army admitted that the soldier's weapon was missing but commented – 'He was engaged on routine military duties. Obviously in a period when assassinations continue to be a matter of grave concern it is important that the Army should not lower its guard'. The Provisionals also claimed that other equipment captured included a book containing the names of 51 suspected Provisionals. It also produced tape recordings made at the time of the accident which were alleged to come from an Army radio network. On one a man with a Scottish accent was heard to say: 'This is a very sensitive situation due to the car which is involved'.

The Littlejohns

Kenneth Littlejohn, ex-paratrooper, allegedly dismissed ignominiously from his regiment, was a member of an Official IRA unit, and later a break-away group, in the 1971-72 period.[36] This IRA unit operated in the South Down/South Armagh and County Louth region. For a short while he was joined by his brother Keith. They were spies for MI6. Both men were highly intelligent and had criminal records. Kenneth's wife Christine described him thus – 'He was always surrounded by glamorous women. He liked the best wines and lived in the best hotels. His whole life was modelled on the James Bond image. He saw every Bond film. Late at night when I had gone to bed he used to come into the room and practise drawing a gun from a shoulder holster in front of a mirror. He had several guns. He was mad about them. He had a book on karate because Bond was an expert on self-defence. He kept fit by doing yoga'.

Perhaps the 'Walter Mitty' type better describes Kenneth Littlejohn. Both brothers acted as *agents provocateurs*. Their case lifts the cover on the British secret service in Ireland and we see the wider canvas of which the SAS was part.

The Littlejohn brothers became a total embarrassment to the British Government. It was soon sorry it ever meddled with them. Kenneth Littlejohn was out for his own gain. It is unclear how much he did for the British secret service but he used it for immunity purposes. When he was arrested in London for armed robbery in the Irish Republic he revealed his connection with MI6 in order to avoid extradition. The story actually begins with his younger brother Keith. In the first half of 1969 Keith Littlejohn was the young released borstal boy making good, with a steady job and even featuring in the *Observer* colour supplement. During his borstal days he became friendly with Lady Pamela Onslow, a voluntary social worker. That friendship was to have great political repercussions.

In 1970 Kenneth Littlejohn went to Ireland to avoid the British police who wanted him for questioning about a £38,000 wages robbery at Smethwick near Birmingham. He had already served five years imprisonment for larceny. He lived a very carefree life in Ireland, stayed in the best hotels, mixed with high society and sheltered behind high promises and a bogus clothing business. For what it is worth, his story, which he revealed in his trial in Dublin after his arrest in 1972, was that in Galway he was shown a Russian designed Kalashnikov rifle which had been landed with others by submarine. He returned to London, told his brother and he introduced him to Lady Onslow. It is probable that the brothers concocted this story from the start. It seems that the friendship between Keith Littlejohn and Lady Onslow had continued in post-borstal years. One of Keith's friends, school teacher Mrs Barbara Hughes, said that he had taken her to Callcott Street, Kensington and introduced her to Lady Onslow – 'He seemed very at home with her, and they chatted away like old friends. There was no mention of espionage or anything like that, of course; they just talked about old times when Lady Onslow, a prison visitor, had seen him in jail'. Lady Onslow was the daughter of the 19th Viscount Dillon. Her late ex-husband, the Earl of Onslow, was Tory Assistant Chief Whip in the House of Lords from 1951-60. Through her friendship with Lord Carrington, the Defence Minister, an arrangement was made by him whereby Kenneth Littlejohn had a two-to-three hour meeting with Geoffrey Johnson-Smith, Under-Secretary for the Army at the Ministry of Defence, on 22 November 1971 in Lady Onslow's house. The meeting resulted in Littlejohn's recruitment to the Intelligence services. In 1973 a third brother in Birmingham claimed that Kenneth and Keith had been armed by the British secret services and paid £5,000 a year to spy on the IRA. On 7 August 1973 Lord Carrington was to justify his action in recruiting Littlejohn. In a radio interview he said – 'I am the Minister responsible for the Services and for sending British troops to Ireland. British troops and innocent people are getting killed and murdered because of arms smuggled in by the IRA. This man said he had information about the sources of those arms and would only give that information to a Minister whose face he recognised. Would I have gone back and slept happily in my bed, knowing that there might be information which I was refusing to get which could save the lives of British soldiers in Ireland? I could never have held my head up again'.

On the next day after his meeting with the Under-Secretary, Littlejohn met his main contact and boss, 'Douglas Smythe' alias 'Michael Teviott', an ex-marine much better known in Ireland as 'John Wyman'. At the meeting they discussed the situation in Ireland and the sectarian assassinations. He was to send arms back to England for ballistic tests. He was told that if he was arrested in the Republic then he was on his own. In court in 1973 Kenneth Littlejohn said – 'In the event of my death it was guaranteed that my son would have a place in Sandhurst when he was old enough. Douglas Smythe indicated that I could put myself up as an operative for these people (the Official IRA). I was told that under no circumstances was I to endanger civilians but, if it came to a member of the IRA or even British troops, I could shoot and, as long as I was back in England, I would be safe'. Littlejohn said that Smythe was a member of the Ministry of Defence in England and that he lived in Kettering, Northamptonshire. 'He has appeared in court earlier', said Littlejohn 'and I think he gave his address in Swan Walk'. Swan Walk, Chelsea, was the false address given by John Wyman when he was arrested in Dublin just before Christmas 1972.

Kenneth Littlejohn was a wanted man at the time he met the government minister. Lord Carrington, however, said that when Littlejohn met the Under-Secretary he was no longer wanted by the police. Kenneth's brother-in-law Brian Perks (36), a wages clerk, was found bound and gagged near an empty safe at the time of the £38,000 robbery at Smethwick. Perks had been sentenced for the robbery but this was quashed on appeal in 1971. Perks said – 'It was common knowledge at my trial that he was wanted for questioning in the case'. The West Midland Constabulary confirmed, in response to Lord Carrington's denial, that Kenneth Littlejohn was a prime suspect and was still wanted for questioning at the time of his meeting with Mr Johnson-Smith. On 11 September 1970 the *Police Gazette* reported that Littlejohn, alias Kenneth Austen alias Charles Durverne, was wanted for the Smethwick robbery. After Perk's successful appeal the word 'Wanted' was altered to 'a desire to interview'. The notice was only cancelled in October 1972 when police interviewed Littlejohn in Pentonville Prison. It is significant that both brothers travelled freely back and forth to Ireland without being questioned about the Birmingham robbery. Obviously they had been granted immunity.

As part of the deal Littlejohn alleges he was given two telephone numbers, an ex-directory number of an MI6 office in Central London and the Scotland Yard extension number of an inspector. In case of arrest he was to ring this latter number and he would be sure of release. The British Home Secretary, Mr Robert Carr, in August 1973 in a reply to Lord Wigg who had queried the role of the inspector said he understood the inspector, Cameron Sinclair was not concerned with Littlejohn's affairs until August 1972 when he agreed – 'in my view quite properly – that his name might be given to

Littlejohn as a point of reference if it became necessary for his involvement in intelligence work to become known to the police. In the event Littlejohn was shortly afterwards arrested in connection with the Irish robbery and he asked ... to see that the officer from MI6, with whom he had been concerned, should be informed of his arrest. This was done'. On 4 August 1973 after Kenneth Littlejohn was sentenced to 20 years in a Dublin court, his wife at 6 pm picked up the phone and asked to speak to 'Douglas'. After a moment's hesitation the switchboard voice came back, 'Sorry you have the wrong number'.

It is not clear how often Littlejohn spoke to or met Johnson-Smith. Little-john's wife Christine alleged he had several meetings with him in Hyde Park. Kenneth Littlejohn says he only met him once but that he spoke to him on the telephone on a number of occasions and maintains that Johnson-Smith phoned him after the Aldershot bombing on 22 February. This atrocity was carried out by the Official IRA. Six people were murdered in revenge for the fourteen civilians murdered by paratroopers in Derry on 29 January 1972. Johnson-Smith thanked him for the good job he was doing in Ireland.

Soon after Kenneth's meeting with Johnson-Smith the Littlejohns trav-elled to Ireland. Their first action was the kidnapping and abduction of Seán Collins on 13 January 1972 from a bar in Dundalk. Collins was brought to Newry, charged with offences, including attempted murder, and was imprisoned in Armagh Jail. I met Seán Collins in Armagh Prison as chaplain there and published his story 'Kidnapped' in *British Army and Special Branch RUC Brutalities* in March 1972. At the time of Littlejohn's trial, Collins, then an internee (charges against him having been dropped) recognised Little-john from pictures as the man who kidnapped him. The text of his statement to his solicitor Mr Paschal O'Hare was released to the press.[37] The text of his statement reads:

> *Dundalk.* On January 13 1972 shortly before 9 pm, two men in a car called at my home. My wife told them that I was probably in Mulligan's bar in Crowe Street, Dundalk. Some time afterwards they arrived at the bar. One of them spoke to me, said that he had been sent down from Waterfoot and told to contact me for help. He asked me to go outside with him. When we got outside, he drew a gun on me and forced me into a car which I think was a dark red Fiat 850. I didn't get the number of it but I think that the registration letters were either NZH or MZH. There was a driver in the car. (When the photographs of the Littlejohn brothers were published in the press in July and August of this year – 1973 – I recognised Kenneth Littlejohn as the one who kidnapped me at gunpoint in January 1972).
>
> We drove to Newry via an unapproved road. They said that mem-bers of the Official IRA wanted to have a talk with me. On the way,

Kenneth Littlejohn kept the gun on me all the time. In Newry, the driver parked the car in a street diagonally opposite the RUC Station. They said: 'The boys are in here'. The driver got out, went over towards the house. Littlejohn was nervous and shaking. Within a few minutes the car was surrounded by soldiers.

Newry. We were taken out of the car and put against the wall and frisked. While Littlejohn was being frisked he still had the large pistol in his hand against the wall. Then there was some commotion followed by shots. I glanced around sufficiently to see the driver running towards the barracks and a soldier firing a shot up in the air.

I was then taken into Newry RUC Barracks but kept in military custody. I was stripped naked and my clothes were searched. Then I was allowed to dress again. I was kept spread-eagled against the wall and guarded by three soldiers who had been ordered by the officers to shoot if I moved. At one point, I was turned around and there was an Englishman in civilian clothes in front of me. He said 'Yes that's the man'.

Then they made four attempts to take me out of the barracks. Each time there was somebody in the street and they ordered the street cleared of everybody except men in uniform. Eventually I was taken out and driven to Palace Barracks, Holywood.

Palace Barracks, Holywood. I arrived about 1 am in Palace Barracks, Holywood, on Friday, 14 January 1972. I think that I was interrogated practically continuously for about 12 hours. My interrogators were two members of the RUC from Newry and the Englishman already mentioned...[38] They asked me what I was doing in Newry. I told them that I had been kidnapped. They laughed sarcastically at that. The fat Special Branch man said that my two companions had escaped but that they thought one of them had a 'hot arse' since they felt they had shot him. They suggested that the alleged escapees were Martin Meehan and 'Dutch' Doherty. During my interrogation I was kicked, punched, spread-eagled against the wall and threatened with electric shocks. They brought out a machine but did not give me shocks. At the end of it all my thighs were black and blue, my face cut and one of my arms was very badly twisted. My arms were in such a state I could not lift them on to the table for fingerprinting and had to be helped to do so. I was examined by a doctor before and after interrogation.

At one point I was taken out to Musgrave Park Hospital for X-rays. My arm was bandaged and put in a sling. I was taken back to Holywood where I sat facing the wall for the night.

Magherafelt RUC Station. About 11 am. I was taken to Magherafelt RUC Station. There I was questioned... I was not physically ill-treated although I was threatened often enough. They alleged that I was

supplying arms to the IRA in S. Derry. They wanted to know who was
getting them. Eventually, I was charged with the attempted murder of
Michael Magill of Gulladuff in July, 1969. Even after I was charged I was
still interrogated, offered bribes for information, etc.

I spent Saturday night in the cells and appeared before a JP at a
special court, Sunday, 16 January 1972.

Armagh Prison. I was remanded in custody to Armagh Prison. I
appeared regularly in the magistrates' court every couple of weeks.

Trial and Re-arrest. On April 26 1972 I was due to have depositions
taken at Magherafelt Court. There had been a postponement at the
request of the Crown two weeks before. My lawyers were Kevin
Agnew, solicitor, and Tom Cahill, barrister. The police inspector called
the names of his principal witnesses but no one came forward. He said
that he had no other evidence and the case was dropped.

I waited in the court for a few hours to avoid re-arrest. Eventually I
was re-arrested in the solicitor's room of the court in the presence of my
solicitor. I was taken to Ballykelly for interrogation.

Long Kesh. On April 28 1972 I was interned in Long Kesh and I am
here since.

I have instructed my solicitor, Mr Paschal O'Hare, to sue for damages
for false arrest and false imprisonment and to inform the Attorney
General in Dublin and the Director of Public Prosecutions in Belfast of
the criminal act of my kidnapping.

An alleged former member of the Provisional IRA, in the High Court in
Great Britain in December 1973, argued against his extradition to the
Republic of Ireland claiming that he feared for his life due to his part in the
abduction of Seán Collins; it apppeared that he was an informer. Ex-
Officials say that it was this Provisional who called Collins out of the bar.

In early 1972 Kenneth Littlejohn lived in a housing estate in Rostrevor,
County Down. He soon gained an introduction to IRA circles in Newry and
district through an Official IRA man from Newry who lived in Rostrevor.
The sister of this man's wife had married a British soldier in England and
he was a relative of the Littlejohns. The Newry Official became acquainted
with the Littlejohns through this relationship and, knowing their expertise
in bank robberies, introduced them to the South Down Official IRA.
Kenneth Littlejohn frequented the Newry, Warrenpoint, Rostrevor and
Dundalk public houses and mixed with members of the Official IRA.
Newry, Warrenpoint and Rostrevor had been a stronghold of the Official
IRA from the beginning of the campaign for civil rights. Most of the IRA
operations in that area were carried out by the Officials. In general there
were harmonious relations with the Provisionals. When the Officials declared a ceasefire on 29 May 1972 the Newry and district units to a large
extent did not accept it. The result was that from that time on most Officials

there were 'irregulars'. Without proper leadership due to internment and in the midst of dissension they broke into dissident groups who carried out armed robberies mainly for their own gain. Some members were 'on the run' and, since there was no organised help for families nor a proper supply of weapons, they took to sharing the spoils. The continuing assistance of Kenneth Littlejohn was accepted by the main dissident unit on the word of his 'relative' from Rostrevor. The mixed gang proved effective. Bank robberies followed in Rostrevor, Warrenpoint and a major robbery of Allied Irish Banks, Hill Street, Newry, on 12 June 1972.

The leader of the dissident unit was Paul Tinnelly from Rostrevor. Tinnelly as a youth had joined the IRA in the 1950s. In the late 1960s he became involved in the Civil Rights Movement and was promoted OC of the Official IRA in South Down/South Armagh. He gained a reputation among republicans as an idealist and a fearless militarist. He commanded about thirty men, most of whom had crossed the border to a base in Omeath. Some were from Belfast. Former members say he was a disciplinarian but they respected him. From early 1972 Tinnelly argued strongly against the growing Official IRA emphasis on politics. He saw it as detrimental to the military campaign. He was suspended for a term, though contacts remained, but after the May 1972 Official IRA ceasefire the rupture was complete. A group of nine men joined him in an independent unit which became popularly known as 'Tinnelly's Brigade' and 'the Pimpernels'. Such dissension heralded the IRSP split led by Seamus Costello, 8 December 1974.

Many Officials met Kenneth Littlejohn for the first time in Woolsey's pub, the Ulster Bar in Warrenpoint. They knew him as Kenneth Austen. They describe him as arrogant, one who professed superior tastes, a gourmet, reserved in manner. He drove an automatic E-type Jaguar car and had also a Triumph Spitfire. He boasted that he had a boutique in England, that he mixed with the 'best' people; he said he knew Lord Carrington personally. He was not social-minded and did not drink much; only once was he seen drunk. Although the 'dissidents' were wary of him, and Tinnelly especially, because he was English, there was little attention at that time to 'spying'. Once across the border IRA men thought they were safe.

In an interview to *Time Out* magazine, August 1973 (cf. Geoff Robertson, *Reluctant Judas*, 1976), Kenneth Littlejohn stated that he was involved in illegal acts and this meant the possibility of shooting to kill:

> The only way you can get involved with men who are on the run from the British Army is to be doing the things they're doing. And so I became involved with them. If I was told about any illegal act before it happened, I would always discuss it with London. I was always told to go ahead and to use my own discretion and try to make sure that no one

got hurt, which is what I did. But I was to take part in anything that they did ... I was carrying M1 rifles, issuing them to various people who were out on the road waiting for the Prods to come down. I was actually in Rostrevor village itself, my point was in the Square. If they had actually come into the building, I was to stop them. I said to Smythe 'If it comes to this what am I to do?' and he said, 'If there is any shooting, do what you've got to do'. I said, 'Well obviously I'm going to shoot to kill' and he just assumed that if I had to do it I would do it.

Former Officials are amused by such a statement from Kenneth Littlejohn and regard as nonsense a sentence like, 'I was carrying M1 rifles, issuing them to various people'!

Time Out, 10-16 August 1973, carried an article on 'The Littlejohn Affair'. Some of it was based on statements made to it by Kenneth Littlejohn in February 1973. He said his first operational meeting with 'Douglas'(John Wyman) followed the Aldershot bombing. British Intelligence carried out major bombings and assassinations of Catholics in the build-up to 'Operation Motorman', 31 July 1972. When Kenneth Littlejohn alleges that 'Douglas' before and after 'Operation Motorman' provided him with a death list of prominent IRA men, Provisional and Official, whom he was to assassinate, there is a ring of truth about it. Among the names were Seamus Costello and Seán Mac Stiofáin. One is suspicious, however, that Littlejohn could have made up this story. These were household names. Kenneth Littlejohn did not, of course, assassinate any of them. There is some suspicion, however, of his involvement in the shooting of Joe McCann. Joe McCann was a leading nationalist much thought of in Belfast. Littlejohn always claimed that at the first meeting with Johnson-Smith in Lady Onslow's house he gave information concerning assassination plans on the part of the Official IRA to shoot John Taylor, a Junior Minister in the Ministry of Home Affairs in Stormont. The attempt on John Taylor's life took place in Armagh. On Friday, 25 February 1972 he was hit by six bullets as he got into his car. Kenneth Littlejohn named Joe McCann in his statement to *Time Out* as leader of the attempt. A Special Operations Unit had been set up by the Official IRA to carry out important tasks. McCann and Tinnelly were prominent members of this group and the shooting of Taylor was probably one of the operations planned by it. However, neither of them would have been involved in the actual shooting. That would have been carried out by North Armagh Officials.

The suspicion of Littlejohn's involvement in the McCann case is also contained in *The Plough* (Vol. 1, No. 5, 1974), the publication of a dissenting group of Officials in the South Down/South Armagh area:[39]

Joe McCann was shot dead by British paratroopers in April 1972 as he walked unarmed through the Markets area of the city (Belfast). His death was not only the work of those who fired the shots, but of those who had followed his movements and watched his every step.

At the time of his death, Joe travelled regularly from Belfast to Dublin and back. Often his route took him through Rostrevor, where he stayed many times overnight. At this same period in Rostrevor two other gentlemen were in residence. They were English and the local people knew them as Keith and Kenneth Austen.

The brothers spent their time in the company of a group of local criminals who were in the Official IRA at that time. Because of the ability to spend large sums of money, the brothers were very popular in the village and Kenneth even managed to have two steady girl friends from Rostrevor... The local people did not question what the brothers were doing in the village. The local gang did not question them either as they simply regarded them as fellow criminals and the police records of both parties would bear this out.

A report on the activities of both groups was sent to IRA headquarters but no notice was taken of either the brothers or the local criminals who acted under the banner of the IRA.

It is not known if Joe McCann actually came face to face with the brothers, but it is highly unlikely that they could have missed each other, as all three drank in the same pub at about the same time. There was certainly some contact between McCann and the Littlejohns because, as he claims himself, Kenneth had advance notice of the attempted assassination of John Taylor which, as he says, was carried out by McCann.

If McCann was involved in the Taylor affair it is highly unlikely that he told Kenneth Littlejohn but it is quite probable that he did confide in some of the local 'Republicans' who often arranged military affairs for him. They, knowingly or unknowingly, passed this information on to the Littlejohns who in turn informed the British government.

If Kenneth Littlejohn passed on information on a plan to assassinate John Taylor at his meeting in November 1971, then it points to some contact in the Rostrevor area before he went to live there in early 1972.

In the summer of 1972 Kenneth Littlejohn rented a house, Smugglers Cottage, at Clogherhead, from Mrs Sheila Heany of Dunleer. [40] Mrs Heany has said that the brothers stayed in Clogherhead for not more than two to three weeks in all in the May to October period. The longest single visit, she remembers, lasted not more than four to five days. Christine Littlejohn claimed in the *News of the World* that in August 1972, before the bank raid in Dublin which led to his arrest, Kenneth persuaded her to spend a week with the IRA men and their wives in Clogherhead. 'I knew at the time,' she says, 'he was working for the Intelligence service. I was frightened because I saw the IRA men cleaning guns and all that sort of thing. At the end of the week I demanded to be put on a plane back to England.' Such a statement is denied by the ex-Officials. They say they never even bothered cleaning guns in those days and would never show guns openly for fear of a raid from the Gardaí. One of his hopes according to Mrs Littlejohn was that the warrant against him would be dropped if he provided information about the IRA. She says – 'He used me to gain the confidence of the IRA Provisionals. I knew at the time he was working for the British and I hated him for it'.

One of the Officials who stayed in a caravan at Clogherhead says that Kenneth Littlejohn had a long-barrelled Luger pistol but he thought little of his marksmanship. He went for a walk with him along the sea shore and Littlejohn had a few pot shots at bottles but missed every time. When Littlejohn first made acquaintance of the IRA 'irregulars' he had an old .45 revolver. One of the Belfast IRA men swopped him a better gun that had been used in operations in Belfast. He thought he was clever getting rid of it but Littlejohn may have been happy to hand it on to British Intelligence for ballistic tests. Littlejohn later sported a .22 semi-automatic pistol which he said was given to him by a solicitor in Dublin.

On 18 September 1972 Edmund Woolsey (31), owner of a public house in Warrenpoint, was killed when he went to collect his car at Glassdrum-mond near Crossmaglen. It had been stolen in Dundalk the week before. After a call to the local police Woolsey thought it had been cleared and was safe. When he opened the door he was killed and his two companions were injured. One of those injured was Jack Tinnelly, a cousin of Paul and a member of his unit. Official IRA men said that the three men were on the fringe of their organisation and suspected that they were deliberately lured to their death. Paul Tinnelly had been using this car. In hindsight, relatives say he suspected that the British Army or British agents had taken it to engineer his death. On 10 August 1973 the *Irish People* published a piece, 'Did Littlejohns help in Woolsey killing?' The paper claimed to be in possession of a document written by Kenneth Littlejohn as part of his defence in his extradition case which was held in secret in London early in 1973. Littlejohn, it alleges, inferred in the document that he had played a part in organising the death and says, 'this made the situation very difficult for me, but they (IRA) accepted that I had nothing to do with it'. The paper did not publish the document and therefore the allegation must be treated with extreme caution. Ex-Officials say the car had been stolen by the Provisional IRA from outside the Derryhale Hotel, Dundalk. They set a booby trap for the Army who then saw an opportunity of turning the tables.

On 22 September 1972 the Littlejohns, as they later claimed, carried out petrol bomb attacks on Garda stations at Louth and Castlebellingham. The purpose was to push the Government in Dublin under Mr Jack Lynch to move quicker in its preparation of anti-IRA legislation. After the petrol bombing and a riot in Dundalk, the Minister for Justice, Mr Desmond O'Malley, began to draft his amendment to the Offences Against the State Act. That was the last thing the IRA wanted. In this affair the Littlejohns could claim success.

On 12 October 1972 the brothers, together with four others, carried out the biggest bank raid in the history of the Irish Republic. Keith seems to have been brought over from England for the raid. Three armed men held the wife, sister-in-law and two children of Noel Curran, manager of Allied Irish Banks in Grafton Street, Dublin, and then forced him to help them and three other raiders rob the bank of £67,000. The raid was carried out in military style. It lasted a few hours and was a real professional job.

A week later, 19 October, Kenneth Littlejohn, his wife Christine and Robert Stockman, a friend, were arrested at Stockman's flat in London. (Stockman was later released.) It is not clear how the Gardaí got on to their trail. It is said they found money in Smugglers Cottage or in a Dublin flat. Another story says they picked up useful hints from a Dublin bank. When they appeared in Bow Street Magistrates Court on 24 December 1972 Kenneth Littlejohn seized the opportunity of revealing 'official involvement'. The day before the hearing the accused had asked through their lawyers that Mr Johnson-Smith, Lady Onslow and others should be called as witnesses. The 10-11 January 1973 hearing was held *in camera*. The extradition hearing was also held *in camera*. When the Irish Attorney-General, Mr Colm Condon, gave an assurance that the Littlejohns would not be tried for political offences, an extradition warrant was granted by the Lord Chief Justice, Lord Widgery. Christine was not sent back. On 9 November 1972 Brian Mathers had been charged in Dublin with taking part in the Grafton Street bank raid. He was sentenced to five years on 2 March 1973 and this was doubled in the Court of Criminal Appeal.

Mrs Littlejohn says she joined her husband in London after the October bank raid, spent a day visiting solicitors and other people. 'I waited three hours while he had a meeting with his Intelligence controller. He came back and said he'd had a row. He said he was doing his job but British Intelligence wasn't doing theirs. Next day we went to a friend's house and later the police marched in and took us to Scotland Yard. Ken had been told that if he got back to England after the robbery he would be safe. He kept telling me that if he was arrested it would just be a formality and he would be released very quickly. But it did not work out that way. I was charged with conspiracy and spent eight days in Holloway Jail ... Then I was allowed bail'.

Kenneth Littlejohn is more revealing on his meeting with his Intelligence controller the day he was arrested. In a 1973 statement he said:[41]

Douglas and Oliver were fully aware that the IRA members with whom

I had been staying had been committing a number of bank raids in the North and the South of Ireland. I was told to do nothing to stop this, partly because it might break my cover and also because they were happy for pressure to be brought to bear on the Lynch government to tighten up control on the IRA. I should mention that I met Douglas and Oliver at Mrs Foggs, a bar in Regent Street off Piccadilly Circus, when I came to London and on one occasion I also met Douglas at Buswells Hotel in Dublin...

My last meeting was with Oliver on 19 October; early on the same day I was arrested. I met him in Trafalgar Square that morning underneath the statue of the Admiral.

Was 'Oliver' Christopher Ewart-Biggs? The article 'The British Secret Service in Ireland', *Magill*, June 1979, points to the research of Chapman Pincher, defence correspondent of the *Daily Express*, who, it says, states that Ewart-Biggs was a senior man in MI6. *Magill* says very vaguely, 'other intelligence services have leaked the word that, in their encounters with the SIS (Special Intelligence Service), the Littlejohn brothers met Ewart-Biggs. At one such meeting, Lord Carrington is reported to have dropped in. Another meeting is alleged to have taken place at a favourite SIS watering hole, the Volunteer pub in London's Baker Street'.

On 18 December 1972 'Douglas' alias John Wyman was arrested at the West County Hotel, Chapelizod, about five miles from the centre of Dublin.[42] He admitted that he was an agent of a British Ministry. Wyman, according to evidence later laid against him in court, said he had paid a number of visits to Ireland to obtain information about the IRA and the sources of arms being sent to the North. On 19 December, Patrick Crinnion of the Garda Síochána, who worked in section C.3 of the Irish Special Branch Office as a detective garda doing clerical work, was arrested when he went to the Burlington Hotel in Dublin to meet Wyman, not knowing that Wyman was already in custody. Ten documents of a highly confidential nature were found under the carpet in Crinnion's car and other documents were found later in a search of his residence. Crinnion was an important contact for Wyman. It is often the case that a man in lower ranks with access to office documents is a more valuable mole than a top-ranking figurehead.

On 28 December 1972 the prosecution made application to have the Wyman/Crinnion case held *in camera* on the plea that the charges were brought under the Official Secrets' Act 1963. The trial opened at the Special Criminal Court in Dublin on 1 February 1973. The Chief Justice ordered the proceedings to be held *in camera*. On 13 February both Wyman and Crinnion were acquitted of six charges under the Official Secrets' Act. Without the production of documents upon which the charges were based, evidence was too limited and secondary. On 27 February they were found guilty of summary charges, Crinnion of having in his possession or under his control official documents at the Burlington Hotel, Dublin, on 19 December 1972, and Wyman of attempting to obtain information from Crinnion then holder of a public office. They were both sentenced to three months imprisonment, dating from their arrest. It was disclosed in court that Wyman was born in East Africa in 1937 and that he had no previous convictions. His address was given as Swan Walk, Chelsea, London.

In March 1973 the Littlejohns' appeal against extradition was refused. On 19 March they were flown to Dublin. This coincided with the ending of the sentences of Wyman and Crinnion and they were flown to Britain.

Rumour had it then that the British Government asked Dublin to hush up the affair by trying the Littlejohn brothers in a closed court. The Irish Government refused, fearing that it would lead to further damaging suspicion. On 3 August 1973 both brothers were found guilty of armed robbery in the Special Criminal Court. Kenneth was sentenced to 20 years penal servitude and Keith to 15 years. When sentenced Kenneth shouted, 'Thank You, England' and 'Ask Lord Carrington what he thinks of that lot'. There was no enquiry in Britain into the Littlejohn affair. Obviously the governments were privy to a lot of the underhand crimes committed but the full story was withheld from the public. The Irish Government was disappointed that the British Government did not give a public expression of regret. It was not merely a case of seeking information on the IRA; there was suspicion in government and in the media that British agents were fomenting violence in the Republic. Not only the petrol bombings and bank raid carried out by the Littlejohns indicated that but, to add to the hurt, two bombs exploded in Dublin on Friday, 1 December 1972 killing two people and injuring 83. This happened during the second stage of the Offences Against the State (Amendment) Bill in Dáil Éireann. The bombs had the desired effect. The Bill was passed by 70 votes to 23 at 4 am on Saturday. Who was responsible for the Dublin bombings? On 11 August in an interview with Geoffrey Archer on ITN, the former Taoiseach Mr Jack Lynch said that he was 'suspicious' that they had been caused by British agents especially as no organisation claimed responsibility. Mr Lynch was to suffer a grave embarrassment a few days later. He admitted on 13 August 1973 that he knew about the Littlejohn brothers being used as British agents in the South; he had previously denied any knowledge of their activities. A written report was received by courier on 3 January 1973 from the Irish ambassador in London containing information on the Littlejohns. Mr Lynch blamed his earlier statement on a lapse of memory.

It may be possible to fit together a theory from two accounts, both of which dovetail in naming one of the organisers of the bombings as 'Fleming'. On 21 August 1973 the *Evening Herald*, Dublin, reported that a dossier compiled by the Irish Special Branch had been handed to the Government which contained information that two of four men working under the code names of Fleming and Thompson, who stayed in the Belgravia Hotel in Belfast, were members of the SAS; that they drove down to Dublin and placed the bombs on 1 December 1972. On 4 January 1986 Frank Doherty contributed an exclusive article to the *Sunday World* giving some of the revelations of Albert Baker who had been jailed on 15 October 1973 for the murders of Catholics in Belfast. The Englishman, 'Fleming' figures in it too:

> On the Dublin bombings Baker has claimed that the cars were driven from Belfast by UDA men but that the explosives and cars were supplied by a leading member of the UDA in Derry who also provided weapons and explosives for operations in Monaghan and Donegal. Like Baker this man, whose name has been given to the *Sunday World*, had a close association with British Intelligence. On December 20, 1972, the same man organised a machine-gun attack on the 'Brow of the Hill' in the Waterside area of Derry which left five customers, one Protestant and four Catholics, dead.
>
> The planning of the Sackville Place bombing, on December 1 1972, was carried out in the Rangers Club, Chadolly Street, in the New-townards Road area of Belfast. One of the cars which exploded in Dublin had been rented from a Belfast car firm by a 'well-dressed Englishman'. The man used a driving license belonging to a Mr Joseph Fleming of Derby. The license had been stolen [*without the owner's knowledge*]. But the identity of that 'well-dressed Englishman' is known to *Sunday World*.

One repercussion of the Littlejohn Affair was the discrediting of Wyman's MI6 team. As Peter Gladstone Smith put it in the *Sunday Telegraph*, 'A network of British agents has been withdrawn'.[43]

Before turning to the story of a pseudo-gang led by Albert Baker, a man controlled by British Intelligence, who joined in the slaughter of Catholics in the fateful year of 1972, it is necessary to conclude the Littlejohn saga with a relation of the assassination of Paul Tinnelly by the Official IRA. The conflict between Tinnelly and the leadership of the Official IRA came to a head when he publicly opposed the policy of the Officials standing for the Assembly elections through the Republican Clubs. This led to a fracas and subsequent to this his condemnation to death was read out in a public house in Rostrevor in June 1973. From then on he was 'on the run' from British forces and the Official IRA. He made a short trip home to see his family at Christmas 1973. By summer 1974 he had ceased his activities. He was tired of his situation and this led him to bring his family south. He returned to Rostrevor again for his uncle's funeral on 2 June 1974. His uncle, Edward Cooper, was a foundation member of St Bronagh's GAA club, Rostrevor. Tinnelly himself had been a star footballer in County Down and in Dublin where he won two county championship medals playing for Clann na Gael. At 6 pm on 2 June he had just entered his home with his mother when he was attacked by armed men. He was struck by 3 or 4 bullets from an M1 carbine and died instantly. His mother Kathleen was injured in the face in the shooting. Some 4,000 people attended Tinnelly's funeral, a mark of his popularity. In the ensuing war of words there were more defections locally from the Officials.

Following revelations in the *Sunday Times*, 8 June 1975, of collusion of the British Army with loyalist paramilitaries, an article appeared in the *Irish Independent* of 12 June claiming that it was in possession of documents found on a rubbish dump in Bessbrook, South Armagh, where there was an Army camp.[44] This batch of documents was purported to contain photographs, addresses and other details of two men, Paul Tinnelly and another, unnamed in the paper but assumed to be the man who had introduced the Littlejohns to South Down. Tinnelly's photograph was published with the instruction underneath: 'Not to be arrested unless suspected of or just seen committing a crime'. Security authorities will not comment on the authenticity of these documents. Relatives of Tinnelly believe they are forgeries planted by the Official IRA to smear Tinnelly as an informer and counter the odium they suffered after Tinnelly's death. Another explanation put forward is – if they are genuine, the instruction may be peculiar to the post-ceasefire period before loyalties clarified. Relatives of Tinnelly also find it suspicious that, contrary to custom, the British forces did not look for Paul on the day of his uncle's funeral and seemed to ignore the presence of Official IRA personnel who were in Rostrevor from 10 am and the shooting team who made their escape in two green Cortina cars which were never traced.

The Littlejohns have expressly said that Tinnelly and his companions did not know that they were acting as agents for the British secret service. When Kenneth Littlejohn was in prison in Mountjoy, Dublin, there were constant rumours that he was writing a book on his case. The book has not appeared. However, in a letter from Winston Green Prison, Birmingham, to his brother Keith in Mountjoy, Kenneth seems to confirm that he had the intention of writing his story and comments on his former associates in Tinnelly's gang:

Jack (*Tinnelly*) needn't worry about Paul's children because I will make another 'Myth' arise from the dead so that they'll even build a statue to perpetuate his memory. You can take that as a firm promise because it is something that I have been concerned about for all of the boys. I hope that this will make Kay's (*Brian Mathers' wife*) life a little easier as well. By the time I'm finished her husband will be lionised throughout God's own country. This probably sounds flippant but you should know me well enough to know that I only joke when I'm serious. Those lads were the best friends I've ever had and no matter what they think of me, as far as I'm concerned I'd still go out on a limb for any of them. Or their families.

In a letter from Mountjoy Prison to Seán Tinnelly, brother of Paul, 4 April 1975, Keith Littlejohn shows that he was anxious to clear Paul's name as an informer and also absolves the introductory party as an 'unwitting vehicle'. He pays tribute to Tinnelly's own political principles:

I apologise for the long delay in forwarding this letter. Following Paul's murder last June, I received many letters from the Rostrevor area asking me to make comment. When the 'Official IRA' issued a statement calculated to bury your brother with ignominy, I didn't believe it was an authentic Republican press release and was surprised that it wasn't challenged. The reference to Paul being the responsible party for introducing 'the Littlejohns to the South Down/South Armagh area' is peculiar for two reasons. The Official IRA have indicated the identity of the unwitting vehicle and given the accurate basis for the association between that person, my brother and myself, and it must be remembered that I was not known in any Northern area. As the plural was used, it is indicative of an ill-informed source attempting to grind an axe for obscure political reasons.

The possibility that many people would interpret comment from myself as substantiation of the allegations against Paul also caused me to delay writing. It seems to be the vogue to disown one's friends when they are the subject of rumour, and even participate in bringing about their unjustified downfall. I have no intention of subscribing to this fashion and have no hesitation in describing Paul as a respected friend. The qualification that he held polar political views, was a ruthless opponent of my Country and at all times a potentially dangerous adversary, doesn't in any way detract from my respect. Paul was a traditional Republican and I never at any time knew him to compromise his beliefs, or speak or act in a manner to suggest that such compromise was a possibility. His awareness of a responsibility to the minority community, which he fulfilled in accordance with his martial honour, placed him high on the Security Forces wanted list. Paul's murderers acted in accordance with the wishes of the hawks in British service. The Border Unit with which he was involved, known widely as the 'Pimpernels', was a means for the Official IRA to condone military action by the simple method of knowing but pretending not to see.

In so far as the allegation of Paul being an informer on his comrades, I would echo your own question, to whom, what information was passed, and who did it concern? It is ironic but had I been asked to indicate the person least likely to be compromised in such a way, Paul would have been one of the few in this category. The alcoholic patriots who earn pieces of silver to feed their habit, even to the extent of sitting with their backs to television cameras, are evidently regarded by the Intelligence Units of the Official IRA as reliable sources. As the so-called Intelligence Officers are little more than 18-year-old boys with an eroded grasp of the value of human life, the freedom of speech and political expression, it is an unfortunate aspect of alternative politics that they are in a position to influence the taking of a mature life.

The letter is brief and void of much detail which would perhaps influence opinion away from the suspicion levelled at Paul. I have written sufficient to refute the allegations, but in the event of non-acceptance, will write extensively and publish the views of certain parties who have written to me about this matter. My own beliefs remain constant, as does my obligation to my Country. By writing to you, I wanted to indicate that no consideration, threat or promise, would deter me from acknowledging Paul's qualities. The attempt by all sides to conceal their own shortcomings by presenting the period when my brother and I knew Paul, and opposed his intent with ours, as a convention for informers, makes me believe we were involved in the only honourable confrontation of the campaign.

If it isn't presumptuous or a poor gesture, I send sincere, belated condolences to Paul's Widow and to his Family, for their loss. The situation is outside my experience and I write only in what I feel is the best interests of Paul's children. This is one of the reasons I didn't write a detailed account on principle, and the kids would be the ones to endure the gossip.

Albert Walker Baker's Pseudo-Gang

Albert Walker Baker joined the Royal Irish Rangers in Belfast in March 1970 at the age of 19 years.[45] He turned out a crack shot and won prizes in shooting competitions during his training in Ballymena. From there he proceeded to Warminster in England and served with the Second Battalion of this regiment. Then it was abroad, first to serve with an élite group doing special training in Fort Hood, Huston, Texas, USA, and thence to the Persian Gulf where he served in the company of 22 SAS.

When Albert Baker was sentenced to life imprisonment on 15 October 1973 for the murders of four Catholics, Judge Robert Lowry said, 'I believe that but for the troubles in Northern Ireland you may have continued to live a blameless and useful life'. It seems a fair statement; so often the machinery of a violent organisation carries human beings relentlessly along with it, not only in the case of the paramilitary organisations but also the underground British Army, the SAS, with all its dirty tricks, including murder.

According to counsel at his trial and other statements made by Baker he deserted from the British Army in July 1971 after a drinking spree. Along with six others he took the boat to Belfast. The UDA with its flourishing money operations attracted him. He soon learned that the aim of the UDA was to kill 'members of the IRA'; he offered his army skills to train members; in practice the UDA methods were savage, ranging from mutilation to murder.

There is another theory which questions the 'desertion' of Baker from the Army. Supplementary evidence comes from his family who would have heard details from Albert and pub gossip on the Newtownards Road, Belfast. Some members of the family tell stories about Albert being seen in Belfast at times when he was supposed to be in Germany and when they had received postcards from him in the Persian Gulf. On one occasion he was accosted by an old school friend, a woman, in Donegall Quay, who asked him if he had left the Army. This was long before his 'desertion'. He told her he was on special duties watching the cross-channel boat for deserters. She told the family, pointing out that his hair was too long for a soldier. On another occasion he was spotted on the Shankhill Road.

Whether he was a 'deserter' or on 'special duty', the truth is that Albert Baker was able to move freely around Belfast with his gang and commit the notorious 'Romper Room' murders where Catholics were beaten and tortured before being mutilated and shot. Baker claims that the answer is simple. It fitted into British Intelligence's plan to terrorise the Catholic community and push off IRA support. British Intelligence in the form of the SAS used the UDA to this purpose and one of their link-men was Albert Walker Baker.

He met his 'handler' regularly in the Candlelight Inn, Rosemary Street, Belfast. He knew him as 'Captain Bunty'.

Baker maintained through his counsel at his trial that he returned to England sickened with the murders he had committed and determined to make a new start. After his court martial he was later discharged from the Army. He then decided to give himself up and make a clean breast of his actions. He allegedly told the English police, 'I am really sorry. Thank God I have told someone'. He was charged in August 1973 with the murder of a Catholic. On 30 August 1973 he was charged with the murder of four Catholics, 11 robberies, some of them armed, involving £15,000 and 24 firearms charges.[46] On 15 October 1973 he was tried and pleaded guilty. He was sentenced to life imprisonment, to serve a minimum of 25 years for murder, and was also sentenced to a total of 20 years for his part in robberies.[47]

Baker admitted murdering Philip Anthony Faye, a 19-year-old waiter, in East Belfast on 18 August 1972, 52-year-old Paul McCartan on 26 September 1972, 21-year-old James Patrick McCartan on 4 October 1972. His last victim was Patrick Eugene Heenan aged 46 years whom he killed with a grenade.

Philip Anthony Faye had been a head waiter in the Girton Lodge Hotel and had just moved to the Stormont Hotel. He lived in East Belfast. Baker went to his door at night, knocked and when Faye opened the door asked him whether he was a Catholic. Faye replied 'yes' and Baker shot him five times in the head. Barman Paul McCartan was walking home on the Newtownards Road the night he was killed. He had some drink taken. He was stopped by a UDA patrol who took him to the local headquarters. When they found out he was a Catholic, Baker shot him twice in the face and through the back of his head. James Patrick McCartan went to a party in the Park Avenue Hotel. He was taken out by a number of people, beaten up, tied and hooded before being shot three times on wasteland at Mersey Street. Mr Babbington the prosecutor in the case said – 'We have details of how the young man made pitiful attempts to find refuge'. A .762 Browning pistol was used in all the shootings. The RUC recovered it. The last murder happened when a workers' bus carrying Catholics to a building site in Cherryvalley was ambushed. A limping youth halted the bus and then Baker threw a grenade into it. There were fourteen workers in the bus. Patrick Eugene Heenan was killed by the shrapnel.

Baker said that he was paid £10 for killing Heenan. The £15,000 he had stolen went to a UDA unit in East Belfast.

Fr Denis Faul visited Albert Baker in Albany Prison on 1 November 1985. On 4 November Baker wrote him three letters. These together with a 12-page memorandum, foolscap size, written by Baker in 1986, make serious allegations about collusion between the UDA and security forces and other undercover operations on the part of the RUC and the SAS.

UDA Arms

Baker alleges that on the night he returned to Belfast after surrendering himself to the police he was taken to Mountpottinger RUC station in East Belfast. He was questioned by CID officers of the 'Inner Circle Murder Squad', a group set up by the Secretary of State, Mr William Whitelaw, to combat sectarian murders. He says he gave the RUC details of houses and premises where arms could be found. One of these was a house in East Belfast where a comrade-deserter from the Royal Irish Rangers lived. A big cache of arms was discovered including pistols, revolvers, shotguns, an SLR rifle, magazines and five or six thousand rounds of ammunition. The SLR was a UDR rifle handed over to the UDA in the Shankhill and later passed on to East Belfast in a weapons' swop. This weapon, according to Baker, was used to shoot three British soldiers in two separate incidents at the top of Church Street East at the junction of the Newtownards Road. Baker insisted that the family in the house where the arms were found should not be charged and his request was accepted. The family was brought in for questioning but none were charged. Such, Baker points out, is the dictating power of the 'Supergrass'!

A raid on an East Belfast house is recounted in the *Belfast Telegraph* (16 October 1973). Edward McCreery (27) went on trial, 16 October 1973, accused of having an M1 rifle and 3 magazines with 45 rounds of .30 ammunition at his Derwent Street home on 5 June. They were found on the roof of his coal shed at the rear of his house. A balaclava helmet with traces of lead was found in his home. He was acquitted on the grounds that the prosecution had not proved that he knew they were on his property.[48] Baker specifically mentions a UDA man he informed on; a .45 revolver was found in his home and he was charged; arms were also found on his word at a UDA headquarters. Baker said that he had every reason to believe that M1 carbines found were taken from the headquarters of the Department of Forensic Science at Newtownbreda which had been raided by armed men on 31 March 1973.

On 3 April 1973 the body of David McQueen was found dumped along the roadside at Ballyhalbert near Portavogie.[49] He had been shot three times, twice in the neck and once in the chest. The 28-year-old man had left his parents' house where he lived at 8.50 pm. His movements can be traced to within 70 minutes of his death. His parents said he had had a phone call before leaving but didn't seem anxious about it; he continued to watch his favourite TV programme *Alias Smith and Jones* to the end. He dressed up before leaving. McQueen had gone to Canada in 1963 at the age of 18 years but came back three years later after he lost the girl he loved and became homesick after a visit from his mother. He was a popular singer and liked entertaining people. On the night he went missing he was seen both at the Vulcan bar at the corner of Dee Street and the Clock bar. His parents thought he was not involved in organisations. 'He didn't appear to have much faith in them,' said his father. After his death there was a message of sympathy in the *Belfast Telegraph* from the Loyalist Prisoners' Association. His death seemed a mystery. His father said, 'Anytime I ask questions I just get blank stares. No one heard anything or saw anything. No one wants to know'.

Was David McQueen assassinated because of his part in the raid on the Department of Forensic Science? Baker recalls that McQueen, a UVF man from the Ballybean estate, was supposed to drive his vanload of arms up the Shankill, but drove instead to East Belfast. He could have been the victim of East/West Belfast paramilitary rivalry or of UDA/UVF factionism.

UDA Attacks on British Soldiers[50]

In his statements Baker says that the UDA was quite aware that professional killers from different branches of the British Army were operating in the North to stir up sectarian strife and that their aim was to turn loyalist guns on Catholics. This of course suited the UDA but they did not like to be controlled.

He mentions an East Belfast incident similar to the Shankill Road incident of 20 May 1972. In this incident two SAS men were attacked by loyalists. Their car crashed into a phone-box outside Stewart's supermarket on the Newtownards Road near the corner of Dee Street. The UDA vigilante patrol seized a 9 mm Browning pistol from the car. However, an Army land-rover came to the rescue. The soldiers radioed for an ambulance and the SAS men were taken away.

Baker says that on two different occasions he himself was involved in the shooting of three British soldiers. The incidents occurred at the junction of Church Street East and the Newtownards Road, on one occasion when a land-rover was turning and on another occasion when a lorry was turning. There were numerous occasions played down by the media when, as he says, there were gun battles between loyalist paramilitaries and British soldiers in East Belfast, all co-ordinated by the UDA except one which was carried out by the UVF. It was a time when the UDA suffered splits in its organisation, exemplified by the sudden departure of one of its leaders to England with his wife and family. Ernie 'Duke' Elliot, a senior UDA member, was assassinated on 7 December 1972 and Tommy Herron in September 1973. The UDA at this time drove many Catholic families out of East Belfast. Little attempt was made to protect them. On 18 October 1972 when the UDA called off its 'war' with the British Army, following an agreement between them on control, Mr Paddy Devlin, then SDLP MP for Falls, called the action 'horse-trading'. This followed a clash between the UDA and the British Army on 17/18 October night. John T. Todd with dual membership of the UDR and UDA was found dead in the Shankill Road area; he had been shot by the Army. Baker points out two incidents in UDA/British Army shouldering for power. One was a 'debacle ambush' on British soldiers on the Newtownards Road, 16 June 1972. One man was found wounded beside an Armalite rifle, one of those stolen from the Department of Forensic Science. Secondly, Baker connects the late evening rioting and stoning of security forces in the neighbourhood of East Belfast on 16/17 February 1974 with raids for arms on UDA depots. In a battle a 19-year-old youth Kirk Watters was shot dead and two others seriously injured. The incident occurred in Belvoir Street off the Newtownards Road. The UDA and the Army gave conflicting versions of what happened.

UDA/RUC Collusion

These allegations are amongst the most serious that Baker makes. He names an RUC inspector who, he alleges, handed over a Sterling sub-machine-gun from the armoury in Mountpottinger RUC station to Tommy Herron, vice-

chairman of the UDA, at its headquarters on the Newtownards Road. He
first spoke about this to the Corruption Squad of the RUC in Crumlin Road
Jail and made a statement to an inspector in Wansworth Prison, London,
shortly after sentence.

Baker was very frightened on his return to Belfast; he thought he would
be assassinated by the UDA. In this regard he relates a bizarre incident.
After being questioned in Mountpottinger Road RUC station he was taken
to Newtownards RUC station. On the day he was to appear in court in
Belfast he alleges that a detective sergeant and two other CID officers were
to accompany him. He recognised one of the officers whom he names as a
'deep penetration UDA man' operating inside the very squad the Secretary
of State had set up to combat sectarian murders. He related his fears to the
detective sergeant that the man he recognised might drive him to UDA
headquarters. He was told not to worry. On the way the sergeant stopped
at Dundonald RUC station. Baker presumed the sergeant made a phone call
there for when he got back into the vehicle he smiled as if to say 'everything's all right'. When they got to Chichester Street a chief inspector came
to question him about the UDA/RUC man. Baker also feared for his
mother's safety. As it happened two men did call at his mother's home
probing Albert's whereabouts but she had been forewarned and disclosed
nothing. The suspicion remained that the two paramilitaries had been
tipped off.

Baker alleges that the same UDA/RUC man was involved in an abortive
assassination attempt outside Du Barrie's bar in Prince Street near the
Albert clock. His story is that UDA men on an assassination operation were
foiled when an RUC land-rover unwittingly occupied their pre-planned
parking place. The problem was solved when their RUC member took
charge of the guns and took them back to the safety of East Belfast.

Bombings in the Republic 1972

Mention has already been made of Baker's disclosures of UDA activity in
Donegal, Monaghan and the 1 December 1972 bombings in Dublin. Frank
Doherty in his *Sunday World* article of 4 January 1976, 'Probe uncovers
Dublin car bombers', uses information from Baker which states that one of
the Dublin bombers of 1 December was a member of the UDA Inner
Council. Doherty writes – 'At least two others have since gone to jail in
Belfast for other offences, while a third had been shot dead. Baker claims
that Tommy Herron knew of the Dublin bombings and gave his approval.
Baker's family claims that Albert told them that Herron would be killed to
keep him quiet, while others involved would never be charged because of
a deal they had to remain silent about British involvement. A few weeks
after Baker made his prediction, Herron was found dead near Lisburn'.

Baker in his memorandum says that he informed the RUC that Tommy Herron was responsible for all sectarian assassinations of Catholics in and around Belfast. Herron sanctioned them.

Baker suggested that if Herron was stopped at a road block he would be found carrying £500 'underground money' in the event of his having to go into hiding. He knew that because he had been bodyguard for the Inner Council. Such a road block was set up, he claims, and Herron was found to be carrying more than £500. He says he told the RUC of Herron's pending assassination but wasn't treated seriously until after it happened. When it did he was the first person questioned about it while still in Crumlin Road Prison.

Baker wrote to the East Belfast MP Mr Peter Robinson on 6 January 1984 giving much the same information on the Herron case. He had already received a letter in answer to his correspondence on 'supergrasses' from Andy Tyrie, chairman of the UDA. When Tyrie informed him that a member was willing to visit him Baker said he hoped to discuss Herron's murder with him.

On 14 September 1973 Tommy Herron was reported missing from the Newtownards Road area. On the evening of 16 September his body was found at Glen Road, Drumbo.[51] He had been shot dead and his body dumped. There was immediate speculation that the murder was an internal UDA affair. There had been some reshuffling in UDA titles and appointments and Herron had ostensibly been moved from vice-chairmanship. There was talk of more militant young people taking power. There was gossip of embezzlement of funds. Herron's brother-in-law and bodyguard, 18-year-old Michael Wilson had been assassinated in Herron's home on 15 June 1973 and to some it looked like an abortive attempt on Herron. But many people, like Ian Paisley who did all but mention the SAS by name, the UDA press officer Sammy Doyle, and both republican groups were convinced that the killing was the work of British counter-insurgency, and for many that meant the SAS. The UDA shot Wilson themselves because he was a police informer. It was thought Herron was party to his death. Part of the UDA cover-up was to shoot dead two Catholics in 'retaliation'; 17-year-old David Rouse, Riverdale Park South, Belfast, was abducted by four men at Trench Park and killed on 15 June and the body of James Joseph Kelly (former UDR man), native of Larne, was found at Corr's Corner near Glengormley on 17 June.

Some light was thrown on the murder of Herron when the UFF claimed responsibility for the murder of a 27-year-old Protestant, Gregory Brown, shot dead on the Woodstock Road on 13 May 1976. They alleged he was involved in the murder of Herron. The information had been passed on to the loyalists by the IRA in Crumlin Road Jail.

On 10 May 1974 the RUC raided a house in Myrtlefield Park in the residential Malone area of Belfast and captured the republican leader Brendan Hughes. They discovered tapes and a scrambling device attached to the house. The IRA had been recording telephone conversations from 39th Brigade, Lisburn headquarters. They also discovered the famous 'Doomsday' document, an emergency plan drawn up by the IRA in the eventuality of UDI or large-scale civil war. MI5 leaked the document to deceive Harold Wilson and the loyalists into thinking that it was a current IRA operational plan. In prison Hughes and other IRA leaders became suspicious of Myles Vincent McGrogan and Vincent Patrick Hetherington who had been remanded in custody accused of the murder of two RUC men, John Malcolm Ross and Brian Edward Bell on Friday, 10 May 1974 at Finaghy Road, Belfast. They were not members of the Provisional IRA and the killing of the policemen had been an IRA operation, an apparent revenge for the arrest of Hughes. The IRA regarded them as 'planted'. No information was obtained from McGrogan but some information was obtained from Hetherington. An IRA leader questioned Hetherington for some days. The task proved difficult for it seemed Hetherington had received training in anti-interrogation techniques and mixed misinformation with the truth. Furthermore it is alleged McGrogan had sent him a note – 'Talk and you're dead'. The story allegedly obtained by the IRA was as follows: Hetherington had been arrested when a member of the Fianna and had been taken by the British Army to a police station; there he broke and gave names and addresses; plain clothes people took him out in a car to Hannastown where they opened fire on a Gaelic football match with a machine-gun and then handed the gun to him; he was released and then arrested again and threatened he would be charged with possession of the gun and the shooting in Hannastown; Hetherington, then demoralised and under intense pressure, agreed to work for the British undercover service; he was brought to England where he was trained at a large country estate in the company of Myles McGrogan, Seamus O'Brien (subsequently executed by the IRA) and some others; this pseudo-gang had a house on the Antrim Road, a caravan in Finaghy Road North and a flat in Dublin near Connolly railway station where they met their contacts, a man and a woman; the gang was allegedly responsible for the bombing of the Long Bar in Leeson Street, with loyalists from Sandy Row, and Benny's bar; they received their explosives from their English contacts in Dublin and brought them north on the train; at the time of the Dublin bombings they received instructions not to come to Dublin. Republican analysis of Hetherington's revelations was that, in the turmoil of the IRA position of 1974 and 1975, an atmosphere of catastrophe was being deliberately cultivated by the British secret service using pseudo-gangs like that of O'Brien, McGrogan, Hetherington, Brown and their companions. This involved the sabotaging of nationalist areas, threats of civil war. The 1974 loyalist strike, so welcome to MI5, fitted into this scenario. The British secret service had deeply infiltrated the UDA and UVF. The pseudo-gangs saw their function as helping to cause as much confusion as possible within the nationalist areas, all leading to the discrediting of republicans and a security take-over. On the personal side the British cultivated the pseudo-gang by plenty of money, drink, women and adventure, all crimes being guaranteed immunity. One of the bizarre offshoots of the confusion campaign was the discovery in Crumlin Road Jail at this time of an alleged plot to poison republicans by putting a lethal dose into the kitchen boilers. The poison, it was alleged, was to be brought into the jail to the loyalists by a prison officer. Hughes brought the matter to the attention of the authorities who admitted poison had been discovered but that it was a matter of a loyalist internal feud. The republicans reported the matter to a lawyer and Fr Brian Brady as a pre-emptive measure to secure their safety by publicity.

To return to the murder of Gregory Brown. The republicans informed the loyalists that the 'planted' group in Crumlin Road Jail had revealed that Gregory Brown had told them that he had been one of four people involved in Herron's death. Brown had free access to visit his counterparts in Andersonstown. He had a grudge against Herron, having been beaten up on Herron's orders. He was a central man in the gang which killed Herron. David McKittrick set out the information that was gradually surfacing on Brown's pseudo-gang in his article 'East Belfast killing linked with Herron case' (Irish Times, 15 May 1976) – 'It consisted of a Protestant, a Catholic, a policeman and a woman. The Catholic once lived in east Belfast, in either Cregagh or Castlereagh, and was last heard of living in Craigavon, County Armagh. His life is now in danger. The policeman is an RUC detective constable who in 1973 was stationed in east Belfast. The woman may have been either a foreign journalist who is reputed to have been working for British military intelligence or a Belfast woman who has since married a soldier and emigrated. The Protestant was Gregory Brown.' McKittrick put forward a theory that Herron may have been murdered because the policeman feared inordinate demands from Herron in their mutual information-swopping.

Subsequent events allow an addition to this theory. The same detective sergeant worked with the SAS. After the murder of Herron he moved into the north County Antrim territory into a pseudo-gang run by the SAS from its base at Ebrington, Derry. There he worked closely with a British agent, a Provisional IRA man, an ex-internee trained by the SAS. The policeman was the link-man in a gang which operated in the north-west and as far south as Ballymena and the Glens of Antrim.

There is also a tailpiece to the Gregory Brown story. Following his murder and an article in the Sunday News, 16 May 1976, linking him with the Herron killing, a reader sent an alleged picture of Brown to Republican News.

It was published in its 22 May issue. The picture was taken from the British service paper *Visor*, 18 March 1976. *Republican News* reported – 'On page 6 of the paper there is a photograph of Brown sitting in a pony-trap which is being "searched". The soldiers in the picture are members of the Royal Horse Artillery from which the SAS get many of their personnel. A glance at the picture shows that it is a "staged exercise"'.

McGrogan and Hetherington were acquitted of the RUC murders in March 1975. Republicans believed that they were supplied with arms by Gordon Catherwood, Upper Hightown Road, Belfast. He was shot dead on 30 October 1974 by a sniper (*Irish News*) or as the *Belfast Telegraph* reported, 'shot dead through the kitchen window by a man on high ground with a revolver'. Catherwood had many friends in the UDR. Death notices of sympathy from the officers, NCOs and men of 'C' company 10th (city of Belfast) Battalion and officers, men and female members of 'G' company, appeared in the *News Letter* and *Belfast Telegraph*.

The IRA did not move against Hetherington and McGrogan for some time. Members in 1974 and 1975 who had knowledge of British undercover work had dropped out, were in prison or had other priorities following two 'bad years'. It was not until 1976 and later that they were able to put some of the story together. On 6 July 1976 Vincent Hetherington's body was found at Colin Glen, Andersonstown, near his home. He had been blind-folded, had his hands tied behind his back and was shot through the head. An IRA statement said he had been guilty of 'complicity with British forces'. Vincent Hetherington was 21 years of age. Myles McGrogan (22) was found shot dead on the Colin Glen Road between Andersonstown and Lisburn on 9 April 1977. He was probably killed by the IRA. Like others they had been pressurised into working for the British forces and found no way out. Their tragedy is the tragedy of many other young people caught up in the spiral of violence.

End of Baker's Deal

In his memorandum (1986) and letters from prison Baker alleges a deal was made if he gave evidence. While in prison in Crumlin Road Jail Baker was anxious for the safety of his family. He thought the RUC used his predica-ment to squeeze as much information as possible out of him and he complained of their delay in getting his family out of Belfast. He then took action, barricaded himself in his cell, crushed the light bulb into a cup and then made his demands on the threat of suicide. He asked for the Secretary of State to come to speak to him. Since Mr Whitelaw was in London, a junior minister visited him with a Stormont official. Promises were then made regarding the housing of his family. Before he was sentenced Baker was transferred 'suddenly and without reason or warning, during the hours of darkness in a British land-rover to Musgrave Park Hospital'. After sentence he was brought there again and in the presence of his family, he says, a prison officer produced two yellow forms to sign which stated that his life was threatened by the UDA. He maintains that he was assured of Special Category Status before he signed. He never received such conditions in England. He was escorted out of the hospital ward, placed in an armoured car, driven a short distance to a waiting helicopter, then flown to a military airport and from there by a Hercules transport plane to RAF Northolt. From there he was brought to Wandsworth Prison and isolated in the hospital ward. In Wandsworth Prison, he alleges, he was visited by an RUC officer who told him that if he gave Queen's evidence against the UDA he would be released after ten years. His family suffered by this transfer to England. In February 1974 he was taken to Northern Ireland to give evidence. He claims that he received visits in jail from the RUC and was tutored in the evidence he was to give. On 14 February 1974 seven UDA men from Belfast, accused of murdering James Patrick McCartan (21), causing him bodily harm and possessing a pistol with intent were found not guilty. [52] Baker had claimed that the seven accused had tortured McCartan in a club and were all present when one of them gave Baker the order to shoot him. At the court a British Intelligence Officer said that, after McCartan had been kidnapped, he appealed to the UDA to help in the search. After submissions by defence lawyers Sir Robert Lowry gave his decision that the evidence of Albert 'Ginger' Baker was 'manifestly unreliable'.

In his memorandum Baker concludes his story. After his trial he was taken back to Parkhurst Prison. From there he made an escape attempt. He grabbed a prison officer, held him hostage and demanded a helicopter to fly him to the South of Ireland. The attempt ended when he was jumped by four fellow-prisoners who, he says, made a deal with the governor. Albert Baker's brother maintains that the 'prisoners' who overpowered Baker were SAS men, one of them a Belfast man whom Albert recognised. He says Albert refused to go into the helicopter and that rather he ran away, thinking that the SAS would throw him out of it when airborne.

From prison Baker has written letters and memoranda to draw attention to his harsh conditions and to promises unfulfilled in his regard. He especially sought help in the 'Supergrass' period 1981-84 when he saw parallels with his own case. In July 1988 Mr Ken Livingstone, MP interviewed him in Frankland Prison, Durham, and included an edited transcript of his conversation with him in his book *Livingstone's Labour*, detailing allegations of RUC/UDA collusion. In December 1989 the Irish Embassy in London asked the British Home Office's permission for a consular visit to Baker. In a letter to the Minister for Foreign Affairs, Mr Gerry Collins, Baker offered information on the handing over of classified documents by RUC and UDR officers to the UDA.

MI5 and MI6

MI6 arrived in Northern Ireland in 1971 but only on a very limited scale and, apparently, Maurice Oldfield, effective head of MI6 at the time, was opposed to it.[53] The move came on the order of the Prime Minister, Mr Edward Heath. After the debacle of internment and the realisation by the British Army that the information of the RUC Special Branch was minimal, intelligence was reorganised and expanded and most information was kept only in the hands of the Army. Information was the main philosophical drive of Kitson and the other British commanders. In 1972, MI6 in Northern Ireland was greatly enlarged. The use of MI6 is a sign of the dichotomy of Northern Ireland, officially part of the United Kingdom but policy-wise linked with the whole of Ireland. This attitude is an inheritance of Britain's fear that Ireland is a security risk, the backyard of past intrigues and present subversion. In this expansion of MI6 perhaps as many as twenty members operated at a time.

The Littlejohn affair tarnished MI6's reputation. There was rivalry with Army intelligence. The Falls Road Curfew, internment, the controlled sectarian murders, the massive census taking and screening, the wrecking of houses, all made the nationalist people wary of 'underground government' on the part of the British. MI6's mistakes broke the cover. In late 1973 MI5 moved in to form another rival intelligence faction. This followed the IRA bombing campaign in Britain. At Stormont Castle the chief of intelligence, an MI6 man, was replaced by an MI5 man. Denis Payne was in the 'Political Secretariat', N. Ireland 1972-76. Paul Foot says in *Who Framed Colin Wallace?* (p. 28), 'During 1973, there was a decisive shift in the organisation of Intelligence in the North. At Stormont, the seat of Northern Ireland government which was controlled by Britain, a new post called 'Chief of Intelligence' was created and filled by a senior M15 officer, Denis Payne. Soon afterwards, the MI6 officer at Lisburn, Craig Smellie, left Northern Ireland. He was replaced by an MI5 officer, Ian Cameron. Effectively, MI6 dropped out of the picture and intelligence in Northern Ireland became almost the exclusive preserve of MI5'.Two former British Army officers, Colin Wallace and Fred Holroyd, victims of the factional rivalry, and victims in a sense of their own 'dirty tricks', have in recent years made startling revelations of the 'secret governing' by intelligence groups. All three, MI5, MI6 and British Army Intelligence moved heavily into the political field, kept the government much in the dark about security operations and carried out their own subversion, discrediting politicians and destabilising government. The revelations of Holroyd and Wallace form part of this story. One must look first, however, at the manipulation of the SAS by MI5.

SAS as Arm of MI5

In the phase-in to the MI5 takeover from MI6, information was leaked to the media revealing the hitherto 'secret' presence of the SAS. It was a double blow dealt by MI5. It felt it would discredit MI6 who had continually denied the presence of the SAS. On the other hand the SAS could be phased in as MI5's men in intelligence to replace Army SMIU (Special Military Intelligence Unit). Then there was what British writers consider an SAS asset – the very name of the presence of the SAS would make republican paramilitaries quake, would make them scale down their efforts out of pure fear!

It was easy to leak the story to the press and what better way to do it than by means of giving a reporter an exclusive. Robert Fisk of *The Times* reported from Belfast on 18 March 1974. He accepted that 'republican sympathisers' who had alleged the SAS presence hitherto were incorrect. He took the story from an Army spokesman, that all were volunteers from five squadrons of 22 SAS and 'between 40 and 50 SAS men are serving in Northern Ireland'. The *Irish Press* was not so gullible and published a hard-hitting editorial on 20 March 1974 – 'Three years ago the *Irish Press* reported their presence; the report was officially denied. Since then, more than once we have reported and commented on SAS activities especially in connection with interrogation procedures, the notorious Four Square Laundry case, and the pattern of sectarian assassinations and other inter-communal provocations. Each time the reports have been denied or ignored by the British military authorities'.

No sooner had MI5 leaked its story than a blunder occurred almost to match MI6 embarrassment over the SAS. On the morning of 20 March the RUC mistakenly shot dead two undercover soldiers in South Armagh.

Shortly before midnight on 19 March an orange-coloured Commer van, probably containing four soldiers, developed engine trouble and stopped outside a house in Glenanne. They made a phone call at a nearby grocer's house informing headquarters in Gosford Castle in nearby Markethill that the bearings on the engine of the van had gone. However, they obtained oil at the house and were able to continue. The grocer said that the four young men were in plain clothes and spoke in English accents. He saw no sign of any weapons. The engine failed again on a lonely road beside Shaw's lake. Then the first shooting took place. An RUC mobile patrol came on the scene. They were suspicious of the van. A policeman carrying a Sterling sub-machine-gun saw a similar one in the hands of the van-driver. He opened fire and shot him through the head. The other occupants in the van surrendered when the police surrounded the van.

A middle-aged garage owner, driving south along the road an hour later saw the van beside a low wall:- 'It was right next to the wall with sidelights on and pointed north. I slowed down and saw a Sten gun lying underneath the front bumper. Then I saw a man lying on the ground next to the offside front wheel. He was a civilian and his legs were pointing towards the centre of the road. The windscreen had been smashed out.

'I decided to telephone for help and squeezed my car past the van. I drove up the road but after a few yards I was stopped by two policemen in uniform. There was a red Cortina car next to them and they were covering the van with a Sten. They asked me my name and I refused to give it – you do not give your name willingly round here – but they said they had sent for help. I looked back at the van and the back door was open. There was no one else and no sign of life in the van' (*The Times*, 20 March 1974).

Meanwhile an Army relief vehicle had set out from Gosford Castle following the emergency call. It pulled into the forecourt of the post office at the little village of Mowhan. A soldier carrying a hand-gun got out to make a phone call in the post office coin box. He was gunned down from a police vehicle concealed on the far side of the road. The postmistress Mrs Sarah Davidson and her husband William ventured to look out when the shooting stopped. They saw the body of a man beside the telephone kiosk. A second man was standing with his hands up. There was a small group of armed police. The police had emerged from a red car. The other vehicle was a white-topped land-rover.

Later on the morning of 20 March a short statement from the British Army and then a joint Army-RUC statement gave little information, merely that the soldiers were on their way home from mid-term leave in Germany and were shot in two incidents, the second involving a relief vehicle which had come to pick them up after the civilianised vehicle had broken down.

Little credulity was attached by journalists to these official statements released by the RUC and British Army eight hours after the deaths. The Secretary of State, Mr Merlyn Rees, reported officially in Parliament on 21 March that the soldiers were returning from leave to Newcastle, County Down; they had a driver and an escort when the Commer van in which they were travelling broke down. The more acceptable theory to observers was that the plain clothes soldiers were SAS men. The IRA said they were part of a unit involved in bombing and assassination missions and had been seen previously in the area. The leader of the SDLP, Mr Gerry Fitt, said, 'If the SAS have to be here, they should wear their uniforms'. The casualties were officially listed as Corporal Michael Francis Herbert (31) from Prestwick, married with one child, and Corporal Michael John Cotton (36) from Nottingham, with a son of sixteen, who had been married a second time in January to a Women's Royal Army Corps private serving in Germany. Both soldiers were said to be members of the 14th/20th King's Hussars.

Robert Fisk's article in *The Times* (19 March 1974) emphasised the surveillance nature of the SAS in Northern Ireland, that they had been sent to serve as military intelligence agents in Belfast and Derry. Fisk said the 'newcomers' were given photographic training 'because troops in plain clothes in Ulster regularly use the Pentax camera with telephoto and fixed-focus lens during intelligence operations'. He said that the MRF progressed to soldiers within their own battalion districts carrying out intelligence work as 'civilians' and then to the SAS assisting these. He feared the political implications of using the SAS in Northern Ireland, hinting at 'Shoot-to-Kill' and quoting an army officer that they were trained 'to kill swiftly and silently behind enemy lines'.

Fisk returned to the intelligence theme in an article 'Army goes in to battle with a filing cabinet' in *The Times* (18 April 1974). He said – 'An estimated 40 per cent of the adult and juvenile population of Northern Ireland have their names and family details on an intricate system of card indexes built up by the Army'. Information came not only by census and surveillance but Fisk also mentioned paid informers and blackmail. He returned to the photography aspect of intelligence work – 'In some areas of Belfast soldiers carry with them a card containing miniature photographs of all the wanted men in their areas. These photographs cross refer to a card index at company headquarters. Every four months, soldiers in certain districts re-check the contents, calling at houses to make sure that the same people with the same children and the same elderly relatives still live there'. Fisk wondered, if the Army controlled the more mundane intelligence operations, then who gave directions to the Littlejohns? Would the techniques perfected in Northern Ireland provide a precedent for other parts of the United Kingdom? In Luton, for example, where Kenneth Lennon lived; Lennon alleged blackmail by the English Special Branch and was later found shot dead.

The card file data base was transferred in 1974 to a £500,000 computer in Lisburn Army HQ. The Army Intelligence Corps added the movement of cars and details of resistance to questions at check-points to the basic material. The main computer in operation in the North, an index of vehicles, is codenamed 'Operation Vengeful'.

On 14 August 1974 Fisk in *The Times* returned to the theme of the SAS again, this time to reveal that the SAS had been sent to Northern Ireland in January 1974. He quoted the British Army as saying that they had returned to 22 SAS Regiment headquarters at Hereford in April. Since Fisk prefaced his remarks by emphasising the secrecy surrounding the SAS and the unwillingness of the British Government to discuss the role of the SAS, one can only assume that the Army statement that they had left in April was misinformation. Fisk quoted the Army spokesman as saying: 'We had a manpower shortage at the start of the year and we filled this gap by the introduction of people who had just finished their SAS training. We got over the manpower shortage in the early spring and they returned to their former units or to such places as the Army may have chosen to send them'. Fisk mentioned that it was possible the SAS were present when soldiers shot a former member of the UDR (Black) and – 'when three young men tried to drag a Protestant extremist from a public house in Portadown, County Armagh, some months later, a patrol of plain clothes soldiers, including a member of the SAS, was believed to have been in the area. The SAS may well have been involved in helping to capture some of the four IRA brigade commanders in Belfast who have been arrested this year; the fourth … was captured last week'.

The UFF actually issued a statement on 21 March 1974 on the Portadown incident involving the SAS referred to by Fisk and alleged SAS responsibility for a more serious one.[54] The bar incident, the statement said, occurred on 19 March in West Street when five men with English accents carried out a carefully planned attack on a loyalist customer: two of the Englishmen had been in the bar for about an hour; they attacked the customer and dragged him from the bar with a gun in his back; two fought them off and reported it to the police but no action was taken. This is a very different story from that of *The Times* reporter but Fisk's account is nearer the mark. The second incident is more mysterious and was probably the result of internal loyalist feuding. The UFF accused the SAS of planting a bomb in the car of UDA officer James Redmond (41) near his Derryclose Gardens home; it exploded at 5.55 am just as he was setting out to his work in the Metal Box factory; he suffered serious injuries to both legs; the fact that he kept his driving-side door open while reversing, because of the early morning frost, minimised the force of the blast. The UFF statement alleged that 11 SAS men were operating in the Portadown area and warned the RUC and Army to leave the loyalists alone or 'bear the consequences of a fierce terrorist campaign'.

The authors of *The Technology of Political Control* (Pelican, 1977) in their analysis of Kitson's theory in his book *Low Intensity Operations* touch on his keynote of the 'process of tying civil and military measures together into a single effective policy'. One aspect of the preparatory work for this was the holding of joint civil-military seminars. It mentions one held in secret in 1974 at Lancaster University, 'to promote discussion between academic thinkers and serving officers on the practical problems in understanding revolutionary warfare'. They say:

> The list of people who attended it reads like a north-western Army and police *Who's Who*, plus military experts in academia and journalism and the right wing of the Tory Party. The Army delegation was led by GOC, North-Western District. The police contingent included three Chief Constables and four Assistant Chief Constables; there were seven

university professors, and the Tory Party was represented by William Deedes, a member of the Monday Club and editor of the *Daily Telegraph*. Also present was Robert Moss, correspondent on counter-insurgency for *The Economist*. The topics discussed included the Clay Cross councillors, urban guerillas, the SAS (Special Air Services) and the necessity for a 'third force'.

This academic exercise only underlines that Northern Ireland was good training ground for British counter-insurgency and as surely as the theory was tested in Northern Ireland the lessons learned would be useful in any forthcoming 'security' crisis in Great Britain.

Army intelligence also carried out surveillance on journalists. Robert Fisk revealed this in March 1975. He himself was among them. Liz Curtis in her book *Ireland: The Propaganda War* wrote:- 'The file on Fisk included a report submitted to the Army's Special Investigation Branch by a former member of the SAS, who had invited Fisk to dinner and questioned him about the sources for several of the stories he had written. Suspicious of the officer's motives, Fisk invented several names and fictitious contacts, all of which appeared in the army file'.

The Dublin Bombings 1974

On 17 May 1974, on the fourth day of the Ulster Workers Council strike aimed at overthrowing the power-sharing executive set up at Sunningdale, bombs went off in Dublin and Monaghan killing 33 people. 28 people died in the Dublin blast and 100 were injured. The car bombs went off in the city centre in Talbot Street, Parnell Street and South Leinster Street off Nassau Street. It was at the height of the evening rush. No warning was given. Hundreds of people were walking home due to a bus strike. Two of the cars used in the bombings were hijacked in Protestant areas of Belfast, one on the Shankill Road, one in the Oldpark district. The third was hijacked in West Street car park in Portadown. The Hillman Minx which carried the Monaghan bomb was stolen in Portadown. Five people were killed in the Monaghan explosion.

The bombings were carried out by Portadown loyalist paramilitaries. At that time UVF/UDA paramilitaries in the Portadown area were quite interchangeable. The UDA Press Officer said – 'I am very happy about the bombings in Dublin. There is a war with the Free State and now we are laughing at them'. On the BBC programme, *Scene Around Six*, the day before the bombings, Mr William Craig, MP, Ulster Vanguard Leader, said, 'The British Government will have to recognise that it cannot ratify the Sunningdale Agreement or implement it in any way. If they do there will be further actions taken against the Irish Republic and those who attempt to implement it'.[55] Robert Fisk in his book on the loyalist strike, *The Point of No*

Return, 'The Strike which broke the British in Ulster,'quotes 'a well-known, generally respected figure who is not quite of Craig's importance – who played an important part in the UWC strike', as saying, 'outside humanitarian feelings, slap it into you fellahs – you've deserved every bit of it'.

The UDA motive was obviously to warn the Irish Government not to interfere in the crisis. It was also meant as a death warning to Catholics in the North. The global planning of the bombs came from MI5. The power-sharing executive had been set up by Mr Heath following the Sunningdale Agreement of December 1973. In February 1974 Mr Harold Wilson became Prime Minister with a small majority. MI5 did not like him and started a smear campaign against him and his government. MI5 in Northern Ireland also worked against him. It disliked his soft line on Northern Ireland. In his article 'Setting Spy against Spy' in *The Irish Times* (24 April 1980) David McKittrick wrote:- 'Another officer said that the army, and MI5, watched the fall of the power-sharing Executive with some glee. "We could tell from the start that the UWC strike could develop into something serious. We didn't want to get caught in the middle between the Prods and the Provos, and our assessment was that, while we could run the power stations at ordinary times, we couldn't have coped with major faults, or with sabotage. For those reasons we advised Rees not to move against the strikers. But some of us also hoped that the strike would make progress and Wilson and Rees would be defeated. We thought that if the Protestants won, Wilson would be discredited. And we hoped that if power-sharing failed, the United Kingdom population would say Ulster had had its last chance politically and would advocate an all-out effort for military victory"'.

On 22 March 1987 Barrie Penrose published a story in the *Sunday Times* which helps to confirm that MI5 'plotted' the Ulster workers' strike. One man told Penrose that he was recruited by Army intelligence and MI5 in 1970. He was an Englishman married to an Irish Protestant and lived in County Antrim. He was an engineer who travelled all over Northern Ireland, a factor which enabled him to make contacts. He infiltrated the UDA on behalf of MI5 and became one of its military commanders for almost five years. His case officers instructed him to use his position to promote the strike. He told Penrose – '... I could never understand why my case officers ... wanted the UDA to start a strike in the first place. But they specifically said I should get UDA men at grass-roots level to "start pushing" for a strike. So I did'. Home Office officials working with MI5's legal adviser confirmed that this man had worked for the security forces in Northern Ireland... Admiral William Higgins, secretary to the D-Notice Committee at the Ministry of Defence, requested the *Sunday Times* not to identify this man's present whereabouts or his case officers.

Part of the British Army plan was an all-out effort against the Catholic people to break them from the IRA. It paralleled the 1972 period. I remember on 8 September 1974, when Fr Denis Faul, Fr Brian Brady and I met the Gardiner Committee we attacked the illegal activities of the British Army in the previous months, its census-taking, its photographing and arresting people for the sole purpose of intelligence gathering.[56] MI5 neatly set a tone for an anti-IRA drive, a good preparation for the strike and a climate for the bombing of Dublin and Monaghan by putting 'disinformation' in the hands of Mr Wilson. Wilson innocently disclosed in the House of Commons what he thought was an IRA plan intended to provoke a civil war. The IRA, it alleged, proposed to take over the centre of Belfast and place car bombs in Protestant streets. The plan documents had been seized in Belfast on 10 May. What the Intelligence did not explain to Wilson was that they were merely contingency plans in a hypothetical doomsday situation. Wilson took them for real. Probably the intention too was that the UDA and UVF would fall for them as well. The ground was prepared for the Dublin bombings. The loyalist paramilitaries had an agreement – 'They are going to bomb our streets, let's bomb them first'. Paul Foot in *Who Framed Colin Wallace?* (1989) reveals that Wallace, a Senior Information Officer at British Army HQ Lisburn, noticed the steep rise in assassinations of Catholics by loyalist paramilitaries in 1974; 'He learnt for the first time in September, for instance, that the explosives used to kill nineteen people in the indiscriminate bombing of a main Dublin street during the UWC strike might have been supplied by British Intelligence. He suspected too that some personal assassinations carried out by the UDA or the UVF had been inspired by British Intelligence. He was concerned in case the huge increase in assassinations in November had been planned to coincide with the secret ceasefire talks between the government and the paramilitaries of both sides'.

In a report in the *Sunday News*, 1 March 1987, taken up by *The Times* on 2 March, Fred Holroyd said the bombs were planted by a loyalist gang based in Portadown which had links with an MI6 officer through a Royal Ulster Constabulary detective sergeant. Obviously there was MI5/MI6 overlapping in agents and 'informants'. One stole from the other. The report in the *Sunday Times* (15 March 1987) that Thomas Clarke was the innocent victim of secret operations run by the RUC and MI5 specifically states that the same killers of Anthony Duffy of Portadown were also responsible for the Dublin car bombings. On 23 March 1987 the Belfast *News Letter* quoted a Sunday newspaper that two loyalist paramilitary chiefs in league with British agents were living in Scotland, with their wives and grown-up families. One of them was a battalion commander with the UDA and the other held similar rank in the UVF. One of them had links with the Dublin bombings and they both played leading roles in the murders in the 'murder triangle' around Portadown.

In May 1987 Captain Holroyd sent the names of six people, three RUC officers and three UVF men to the Gardaí, alleging that they were involved in the Dublin and Monaghan car bombing plot. He gave the names in a written statement to the *Sunday World* which published the statement without the names on 6 December 1987. It said:- 'To my certain knowledge Sgt X of the RUC Special Branch was controlling key members of the UDA/ UVF. These included the nominal UDA commander for County Armagh and the most active terrorists (3 names) and (*I*) can also state from first hand knowledge that Sgt X abused his authority by protecting these people from prosecution. During the years mentioned above Sgt X worked closely on operations with a special unit of SAS trained soldiers, the Second in Command of which was Robert Nairac who personally related to me his participation in the murder of John Francis Green. The weapons used in the Miami Showband murders of military origin were obtained from a cache of weapons whose location I revealed to Sgt X ... at least two members of the Portadown UDA have identified Nairac as being with them on plan- ning sessions for terrorist outrages ostensibly initiated by (*two names*). The SAS unit was controlled through SAS or ordinary staff officers attached to HQ3 Infantry Brigade based at Lurgan and SAS officers based at Lisburn. There were two similar units based in Belfast ... and Ballykelly. Nairac's unit posed as an SAS survey team and the Ballykelly unit as a signals squad.

'On one occasion while on duty with Sgt X during a surveillance operation, he confided in me that the Portadown UDA/UVF were respon- sible for the car bombs that detonated in Dublin and Monaghan ...'.

Captain Holroyd said that the three loyalist paramilitaries named by him 'were aware that their terrorist operations were being influenced by the security forces'.

Holroyd/Wallace Revelations[57]

Let us turn our attention now to the revelations of Captain (retired) Fred Holroyd and Mr Colin Wallace concerning the MI5/MI6 conflict in the 1974-76 period.

Colin Wallace at one time was head of production services at British Army Headquarters (NI). In his capacity as a senior civil servant he had a rank equivalent to that of major or colonel. Whilst a senior information officer he served as a part-time 2nd lieutenant in (County Antrim) UDR. He was an expert parachutist who had trained with the SAS in New Zealand. He married an English colleague, the confidential secretary to the Chief of the Secret Service (MI6) in Belfast. His career is summed up in *Lobster* (No. 11):

'*John Colin Wallace* 1968-76
Ministry of Defence (Army Department): Army number 474964. Commis-

sioned 1962 (TAVR Gen. List) Officer Cadet, Cadet Training Officer, St Patrick's Barracks, Ballymena and later with the Field Marshal Earl Alexander Cadet Company Irish Guard. Appointed Assistant Command Public Relations Officer, HQ Northern Ireland in 1968 and engaged in a wide variety of information work both as a serving officer (Captain) in the Ulster Defence Regiment and as a civilian information adviser. Overseas work during this period included assignments in West Germany, Malaysia, Australia, Hong Kong, New Zealand, Berlin and the U.S. Appointments held included:

1. Senior Information Officer (Psychological Operations) Army HQ, Northern Ireland.

2. Member of the Northern Ireland Information Co-ordinating Committee.

3. Member of the tribunal of inquiry set up under Lord Widgery – the 'Bloody Sunday' tribunal.

4. Commander of the Army's free fall parachute team 'The Phantoms', 1972-75. BPA number 3150: 'D' license No. 1416.

5. Staff Officer (Information Policy) Ulster Defence Regiment.

6. Head of Production Services (cover title for Senior Information Officer, PSYOPS) Army HQ, Northern Ireland.'

In the early 1970s information control was part of counter-insurgency operations. A secret department for psychological operations (Psy-ops) called Information Policy was set up in Northern Ireland. Its existence is still denied by the Ministry of Defence. It worked under cover as a separate unit from the Army's Public Relations office at Army Headquarters. Part of the set-up was a sophisticated printing press which forged driving licenses, identity cards, posters, press ID cards, bank statements. It was also used in smear campaigns, individuals being selected by MI5 and MI6. One of the things Wallace felt keenly about was the Intelligence link with the Kincora Boys Home, and this was one of his first public revelations. It has been suggested that MI5 knew that young boys in this home were being buggered and withheld the information so that they could blackmail Protestant politicians.

Wallace sums up the MI5/MI6 conflict in *Lobster* (No. 11): 'The 1973/74 period was particularly critical because it was, in my opinion, a watershed in the battle for supremacy between MI5 and the SIS (MI6). In the UK the problems associated with the increases in international terrorism, the miners' strike, the 3-day week, alleged increases in power and influence by Left Wing activists, etc, all had a profound effect on the roles of these two services... As you can imagine, Ireland was, at that time, the "in" place to be both in military and intelligence terms. If one examines most of the top posts held in these fields today, the incumbents have, almost without exception, had experience in Northern Ireland...

'There was a strong difference of opinion between MI5 and the SIS over who should have overall responsibility for the Irish problem – particularly in the case of operations in the Republic of Ireland. To make matters worse, the two services regarded Army Intelligence as amateurs and the RUC Special Branch as totally unreliable. You can imagine the problems such a situation created for joint operations, the channels of reporting, etc... When MI5 gained control of the overall intelligence operation they tried to replace those who were already in key posts with others with total loyalty to them. For example, in 1974, there was an attempt to use SAS personnel to replace the normal Army SMIU men (Special Military Intelligence Unit). This was a total disaster. Not only did MI5 have much less experience of running agents in a hostile environment than SIS, the SAS at that time had no experience of Northern Ireland-type operations – they had been prohibited from taking an active part (officially at least) for purely political reasons. After a number of quite amazing blunders the SAS were withdrawn from plain clothes duty in the Province. As the hostility between the various intelligence factions increased they began to "nobble" one another's operations. The Army had a number of key agents "taken out" by the terrorists and a FINCO (Field Intelligence Non-Commissioned Officer) in Belfast committed suicide.

'It became quite clear that MI5 were trying to get the SIS removed from the Province completely – this they almost achieved by late 1976'.

Lobster (No. 11) listed incidents which it said, if investigated, would throw light on the MI5/MI6 conflict:

'1. A bank robbery in Coleraine carried out by the SAS (The soldiers were ex-Para and ex-Royal Irish Rangers).

2. The shooting of William Black in 1974 (*a case of mistaken identity*). This is said to have been a bungled SAS operation to "take out" ... a UDA commander.

3. Explosions caused by the parachute Regiment in 3 Brigade area.

4. The bombing of the Alliance Party HQ in 1974 during the general election – suspected of being the work of the security forces.[58]

5. SAS activities in the Irish Republic, including the arrest of two patrols in plain clothes by the Irish police.

6. The plot to recruit an ex-professional football player to assassinate...

7. The leaking of material by MI5 on MI6 operations, including the production of a booklet on the Littlejohns, and information on Howard Marks.

8. An attempt to assassinate ... in Holland where he was involved in a drugs ring which supplied arms to the IRA. (cf. "The Secret War in Ireland" by Stephen Scott in *Hibernia*, 19 July 1979).

9. The bombings in Dublin in 1974 by Protestants linked to the security

forces, and in particular, an RUC Special Branch officer.

10. A bomb attempt on Enoch Powell, MP by the security forces.

11. The Miami Showband killings by Protestants linked to the security forces.

12. The smearing of ... trust which was the conduit for money from MI6 to the political organisations it supported in Northern Ireland.

13. "The Ulster Citizens' Army" – a "black" operation *not* set up by Wallace and Information Policy (cf. *Lobster,* No. 14 and *Who Framed Colin Wallace?*, p.102 ff).

14. The assassination of Catholics in 1975 by Protestant groups linked to the security forces. The increased killings were designed to break the Provisional IRA truce arranged with the help of MI6.'

Wallace became disgusted with some of the operations he had to perform. He says – '1974 was the watershed because the intelligence game ceased to be just directed against legitimate terrorist targets. It became much more political and the friction between the intelligence agencies became more pronounced. As the interfactional rivalry intensified so the activities became more bizarre. There was less control and political clearance. Most of my work during this period was being used by others for totally unconstitutional ends.' Wallace showed opposition, was posted out of Northern Ireland, disciplined and charged with 'leaking' to the press, a charge full of irony since that had been his job. He was convicted of manslaughter on 20 March 1981.[59] He claims he was framed. Naturally this has added to his grievances.

Besides intelligence gathering and the attempt to move the Catholic population away from IRA support by the terror of the sectarian murders of the early 1970s, MI6 worked in the greater political field. It encouraged the formation of the SDLP (Social Democratic and Labour Party), the Alliance Party, supported the Northern Ireland Labour Party, the New Ulster Movement, and the politicisation of the loyalist paramilitaries.

MI6 also sought the politicisation of the IRA, quite aware of the influence of the 'politicals' in the IRA Army Executive. This political manoeuvring and softer line which was developing, particularly under the Wilson Labour government, was watched with horror by MI5 and powerful elements within the British Army in Northern Ireland. The Army in particular resented Rees' moves to end internment and their Intelligence went so far as to give him false information; IRA suspect 'biographies' were concocted and the number of ex-internees returned to IRA activity was falsified. All ran parallel with the MI5 campaign in Britain against the Wilson government, Edward Heath and his supporters, and the liberals. Much of this is now described in Peter Wright's *Spycatcher.* There is a serious omission in his book, however, since he does not deal with the Northern Ireland dimension.

In 1976 Mr Litterick, MP asked the Secretary of State for Defence a written question on the functions of the Information Policy Branch in Northern Ireland, and what the figures were showing the current establishment, together with the corresponding figures for 1975 and 1974, showing in each case the numbers of military and civilian personnel employed. Mr Robert C. Brown replied:- 'There is no Information Planning section which is a part of the Army Information Service at Headquarters Northern Ireland. It has a very small staff whose function is to advise the GOC on the public relations aspects of Army operations and to prepare public information programmes. The Army Information Service maintains a close liaison with the NIO Information Department and is also responsible for running a 24-hour Press desk, providing a wide range of Press facilities and producing a newspaper for the forces in Northern Ireland'. Mr Ken Livingstone, MP returned to the question of an Information Policy Unit in the House of Commons on 24 March 1988. The Parliamentary Under-Secretary of State for Northern Ireland, Dr Brian Mawhinney, denied the existence of such a unit in his department. Mr Livingstone got no satisfaction when he pursued the question – 'I thank the Minister for his response. But will he explain why members of the security services have been involved in exercises entailing the use of Government facilities to forge documents; the passage of arms, including guns and bombs, to members of the civilian community, to be used against members of the security services and individuals in southern Ireland; and political disinformation programmes such as "Clockwork Orange" during the 1974 election? Who was authorising all that, if there was no such unit?' Mr Livingstone in a written question (answered on 26 April 1988) asked the Prime Minister Mrs Thatcher what action was taken relating to the case of Mr Colin Wallace following information forwarded by the Treasury and Civil Service Select Committee relating to false job descriptions, psychological warfare and propaganda. She replied: 'Following consideration of the papers by the Ministry of Defence and other Departments involved, I wrote to the Chairman of the Treasury and Civil Service Select Committee explaining that the various allegations made by Mr Wallace over many years had been fully investigated and no evidence had been found to substantiate any of them'.

Mr Livingstone in 1988 also pursued a series of written questions on Psychological Warfare. The Secretary of State for Defence, Mr Freeman, would not comment on his question as to how many members of the armed forces and civil servants from his Department were engaged in psychological warfare in Northern Ireland each year from 1972 to 1987. Mr Livingstone asked how many members of the armed forces and civil servants from his Department were trained in psychological warfare in each year from 1972 to 1987 in England, in the United States of America, or both. The Minister said that the Ministry of Defence no longer used the term 'psychological

warfare' but in common with the rest of NATO used the term 'psychological operations'; it ran courses intended to familiarise Ministry of Defence
personnel with the background to and the concept of psychological operations; records of Ministry of Defence personnel attending such courses
were only available from 1983; a small number of armed forces personnel
also attended psychological operations training courses run in the USA. To
Mr Livingstone's question where courses were held Mr Freeman replied on
6 May 1988 that they were held, until their closure, at the joint warfare establishment at Old Sarum, Salisbury (1972-78) and at the joint warfare wing
of the National Defence College at Latimer (1978-82); since 1978 responsibility for the courses was transferred to MOD central staff.

Mr Tom King on 21 March 1988, to a question by Mr Livingstone, MP,
said that he was not aware whether Mr Colin Wallace was ever personally
interviewed by an official inquiry or by other official persons in connection
with (a) psychological operations, (b) an alleged shoot-to-kill policy, (c)
alleged political disinformation and (d) any alleged use of forged documents.

Captain Fred Holroyd

Colin Wallace's view is shared be another ex-officer, Fred Holroyd. Captain
Holroyd came from a military family. He was educated at a Yorkshire
Grammar school. He enlisted as a private in the gunners and three years
later was commissioned into the Royal Corps of Transport. He volunteered
to be a Military Intelligence Officer (MIO) after attending and passing a
course at the Joint Service School of Intelligence at Ashford, Kent. He was
then posted to a unit called Special Military Intelligence Unit (SMIU,
Northern Ireland). This unit provided MIOs who were mostly volunteers
from all the regiments and corps in the Army. It also provided FINCOs,
who were all Intelligence Corps personnel, to the RUC. Normally one MIO
and one FINCO went to each RUC division. The HQ element was at HQ
RUC at Knock. The HQ personnel was headed by the CO, a Lt Colonel, Int.
Corps (E5). Subordinates in SMIU (NI) referred to him as RUC LO (RUC,
Liaison Officer). (RUC CO was a title used for Army personnel attached to
the RUC, such as Battalion NCOs). The SMIO or RUC LO was supported by
his deputy, the Assistant Senior Military Intelligence Officer (ASMIO), a
Major, usually from any corps or regiment in the army, and a small team of
clerks from the Intelligence Corps. They were located in an office next door
to that of Head of Special Branch at HQ RUC Knock. There were about 50
MIOs and FINCOs in SMIU (NI) who had access on the Army side to
technical support from 12 Intelligence and Security Company (Intelligence
corps) based at HQ (NI), Lisburn. They also had access to Intelligence Staff
at HQ (NI) Lisburn. Ostensibly the duties of the MIOs were to liaise at what-

ever level they were at (usually Brigade HQ) with the Special Branch in the RUC division, further the passage of intelligence both ways and build up the trust between the Army and the RUC. They recruited and ran 'sources' and passed intelligence to the CO at Knock; he and the Head Special Branch RUC then decided how to disseminate it back down through the Army system, to Brigade HQs.

Captain Holroyd first made his startling revelations on the underground operations of British security forces in Northern Ireland on the Channel 4 programme *Diverse Reports* on 2 May 1984, a programme researched and reported by Christopher Hird and Duncan Campbell. Campbell followed this up with three reports on Holroyd's revelations in the *New Statesman* (4, 11, 18 May 1984).

Holroyd maintains that his case was complicated. His sources were so good that he was asked to bring information on all matters to do with his cross-border activities to Craig Smellie (MI6) and HQ (NI) at Lisburn. This caused ill-feeling at his own Brigade Headquarters (3 Infantry Brigade, Lurgan). Brigadier Wallis-King was annoyed at his mode of operating in his area, feeling himself 'cut out' of information. It was Craig Smellie of MI6 who organised the small group for cross-border operations.

Holroyd also worked with an undercover SAS team and this gave him knowledge of their sensitive activities. This SAS unit was under the command of Captain Julian A. Ball who had joined the SAS from the Kings Own Scottish Borderers. Second in command was Captain Robert Nairac ex-Grenadier Guards. It went under the cover of Royal Engineers 'Survey Troop' but was not a signal Corps detachment. It was not based, as is sometimes thought, at the Army Mahon Road camp, Portadown, but at Castledillon House near Armagh, one of the gentry houses once belonging to the Molyneux family but in recent years used as a mental home and just before internment as an open prison. It is now an old people's home. It had been taken over as a barracks for a Royal Engineer Regiment. The 'Survey Troop' was housed in a special guarded compound at the rear of the main house, in portocabins. This SAS unit operated with a Special Branch Officer who partially handled local Portadown loyalist paramilitary organisations. This officer was the organiser of a gang which included renegade Catholics as well as Protestants. He was closely associated with Nairac and was the same officer who had a hand in the Dublin bombings of 1974 and in the murder of IRA Captain John Francis Green.

On 29 February 1988 the Secretary of State for Defence, Mr Freeman, in a written reply to Mr Ken Livingstone, MP confirmed that a Royal Engineer survey troop was stationed at Castledillon but denied there was a Northern Ireland training and advisory team stationed there. To a further question he said that there were two Northern Ireland training and advisory teams responsible for advising and assisting in the training of all units due to deploy to Northern Ireland in the internal security role; a team of 41 officers and men for units of the United Kingdom Land Forces and a team of 43 for units of the British Army of the Rhine. Mr Freeman replied to a further question on Castledillon on 28 March 1988:

Mr Livingstone: To ask the Secretary of State for Defence
(1) which members of the Royal Engineers survey troop stationed at Castledillon in 1974-75 belonged to Army units other than the Royal Engineers;
(2) how many officers and of what rank served in the Castledillon, Royal Engineers survey troop in 1974-75;
(3) what role the Royal Engineers survey troop was carrying out whilst stationed at Castledillon in 1974-75.
(4) how many service men and women served in the Royal Engineers survey troop stationed at Castledillon, from 1974-75.
Mr Freeman: Detailed information on this unit, which is not now deployed in the Province, is no longer available. The role of a Royal Engineer field survey is to provide or process aerial photographs, ground surveys and mapping for the army as required. The strength of such a unit at that time varied between about 30 and 40, depending upon its specific task, and usually included two officers.

Asked by Mr Livingstone by what unit the survey troop at Castledillon was guarded Mr Freeman replied that the RE squadron based at Castledillon would have been responsible for the overall security of the base. He further revealed that the numerical designation of the survey troop at Castledillon was 4 Field Survey Troop, Royal Engineers. On 6 May 1988 in answer to a further question from Mr Livingstone, MP he said that there were no other Royal Engineer survey troops stationed at Castledillon in 1974-5. To further questions he said that 4 Field Survey Troop Royal Engineers was formed in early 1973 at Castledillon and disbanded in late 1975 since there was no longer a requirement for the unit.

An obituary on Captain Julian A. Ball, commander of the SAS team in Castledillon, appeared in *Mars & Minera*, Vol. 5, No. 2, Spring 1982. It is an unusual obituary in style and format:

LT COL J. A. BALL MBE. MC. KOSB
Sultan of Oman's Special Forces

Julian Ball was commissioned into the Kings Own Scottish Borderers in 1970 having previously served with the Parachute Regiment and 22 Special Air Service Regiment in the ranks.

In a very short space of time he established an unequalled reputation for being an original thinker, outstanding leader and tactician.

Over the next few years he became one of the Service's foremost authorities on operations in Northern Ireland. The personal contribution which he made to the fight against terrorism and his cool gallantry resulted in him being awarded a number of unique decorations for the campaign. He was also recommended for several others.

However, Julian was as compassionate as he was ruthless, and he showed a great deal of sympathy for the common people's problems in Ireland. His loping figure will be missed in many different areas of Belfast, as well as in more familiar places.

He later returned to the SAS for two tours where he once again made a considerable and long-lasting impact, both on operations and in training.

Always restless he elected to leave the Army and had just started to establish himself as a tough and uncompromising Commanding Officer of the Sultan of Oman's Special Forces when he was tragically killed in a road traffic accident in May, 1981. He was only 38.

He leaves behind an indelible impression on all who have come into contact with him, be they friend or enemy. He was a natural soldier and leader who was happiest when the going was rough. As an individual his energy, personal bravery and keen sense of humour cannot be surpassed.

The Regiment and the Army mourn the loss of a very fine officer and companion. We extend our deepest sympathies to his wife, Jeanette, and to his son and daughter.

Holroyd himself took part in covert operations, disguised with heavy beard and long hair, his .45 pistol at the ready under his dirty clothes, a hidden transmitter strapped to his back, the microphone like a necklace strapped around the throat, below the collar. As MI5 took control and the 'dirty tricks' became more bloody involving the murder of innocent Catholics, Holyroyd's unco-operative attitude was noted. He fell victim to the MI5/MI6 rivalry. An attempt was made to remove him on the grounds of mental instability. Embittered by his treatment in the Army he resigned his commission. Since that he has tried to get proper investigation of his own case and the methods used by British intelligence in the North.

Details of 'dirty tricks' revealed by Captain Fred Holroyd are:[60]

1. An attempt to kidnap Eamon McGurgan, native of Portadown, from County Monaghan. It failed because the kidnappers were reportedly stopped at a road block. The Gardaí handled by British agents were not able to 'freeze' the area. (On the same night 11 March 1974, by coincidence, Senator Billy Fox was killed at a farmhouse near Clones).

2. An attempt on 29 March 1974 to kidnap Seamus Grew and Patrick Loughlin, natives of Armagh City living in Monaghan: For conspiring to assault Seamus Grew, three Protestant men from Lisburn were sentenced to five years imprisonment. They were James O'Hara (34) a machine operator of Hugenot Drive, William McCullough (36) a salesman of Grove

Hill Avenue, and John Flynn (22) a joiner of Ava Street. McCullough had been a member of the British Army for nine years and O'Hara had been a champion boxer in the Territorial Army.

3. The setting-up of Mrs Bernadette O'Hagan and her son Kevin by planting ammunition in the O'Hagan household in April 1974. (The British Army had found two IRA weapons in Lurgan; they proceeded to plant the two magazines at O'Hagans').

4. A plan to discover the escape route from Belfast for wounded and wanted men. For this a 17-year-old boy was set up and ammunition was planted in his home in September 1974. He was forced to act as an IRA infiltrator. Having been interrogated by the IRA in prison he gave false information out of fear, listing his Protestant milkman as a collaborator with the British. Another milkman who took this man's place for one day, Christopher Main, was gunned down on his milk round on 11 February 1975.

5. On 5 October 1974 Eugene McQuaid, a 35-year-old Newry man, was blown to pieces when his motorbike exploded just north of the Border on the main Belfast-Dublin Road. He was not a member of the IRA but was doing a 'job' for them, transporting bombards on his motorcycle. The bombards had been doctored by 3 Brigade's Intelligence officers in the Irish Republic. The repercussions of a British Army undercover group crossing the border to set up a murder should have been great. There were none. (On 6 December 1975 two IRA volunteers Seán Campbell and James Loughrey were killed at Killeen, South Armagh, when a landmine they were preparing exploded prematurely. It may have been doctored by an SAS team).

6. On 8 November 1974 a train was deliberately derailed at 'The Tunnel' in Portadown. It had already been hijacked by the IRA in South Armagh and set in motion with a warning that bombs were planted in it. The SAS plot, of which Ball and Nairac, plain clothes SAS men, were part, was designed to have disastrous consequences in the Portadown Catholic district and thus throw odium on the South Armagh IRA who frequently hijacked trains at Kilnasaggart. The train was derailed; there were no bombs and no one was injured.

Holroyd has revealed that he ran three senior Garda officers in border towns and gathered intelligence from them.

The most important contact was 'The Badger'. Brendan O'Brien interviewed him for the *Irish Independent*, 20 January 1987. The report gave the following details. In 1972 he said he was approached by a friend with connections in County Armagh who said a fellow in the North wanted to meet 'some kind of a policeman'. He drove his car to Lurgan hospital and met four guys in plain clothes. A trade agreement was made between them to exchange intelligence. One of the Army men present gave his name as 'Bunny' Dearsley. (Staff Sergeant Bernard 'Bunny' Dearsley died in 1977).

He met Dearsley often afterwards in his house and once in the Garda station. He gave detailed information on members of the Provisional IRA and later on members of the INLA including their names, addresses and how to get to their houses, even their photographs. In return he got information on loyalist paramilitaries. Between 1972 and 1983 he made contacts with six British Army men. When he was asked if he was aware that his information was being used for cross-border kidnappings and possibly assassinations he said, 'I wouldn't lose any sleep over retaliation or tit-for-tat in some cases but I would if innocent people got killed'. One of the people he gave information on was Seamus Grew. (This information, of course, was not used when Grew was shot dead by the RUC in 1982.) He recognised a photograph of Captain Holroyd when shown it; he remembered being introduced to him by 'Bunny' Dearsley. 'I remember well meeting that Fred fellow one night between Middletown and Tynan.' Those meetings were in a car in the dark and he assumed his conversations were recorded. He recalled the night when the Gardaí raided the house of a Monaghan Official IRA man – 'Bunny Dearsley and an RUC Special Branch man … turned up as well. They were just told to go away'.

Most of Holroyd's allegations centre in 1974 and 1975 when Mr Edmund Garvey was Garda Commissioner.

Holroyd regarded 'The Badger' as a first-class source. 'Bunny and I ran "The Badger" for about two-and-a-half years. On my own I ran him for about nine months'. He says he met him often and ran two other Garda informants through him. Holroyd delivered his information personally to Craig Smellie of MI6. Smellie decided how much went down through the Brigade to RUC Special Branch.

The competitive intelligence operations in the North in the 1974-75 period led to Holroyd's undoing. The Army resented his close association with and working directly for MI6 whose controller was based at Army headquarters but whose activities were kept secret from Army staff. Furthermore Holroyd worked with an undercover SAS team. Army resentment was brought to a head in April 1975 when at the invitation of Assistant Commissioner Garvey, as Holroyd alleges, he went to Garda Headquarters at the Phoenix Park, Dublin. His commander told him not to go but he went accompanied by an RUC CID officer. Holroyd's IMCO drove both of them to the border where the Gardaí met them and took them to the Phoenix Park. They examined the haul seized by the Gardaí from the IRA bomb factory at Donabate. The party crossed at Newry and drove straight to Dublin with an escort of Irish Army Panhard armoured cars and another escort with four Gardaí inside. The Panhards peeled off just on the outskirts of Dublin. No military escort was provided on the return trip nor any other Garda car. One Garda car took them to the border where they were met by the IMCO who took them to Portadown. Assistant Commissioner Garvey has denied all knowledge of the meeting or that he ever met the particular Chief Inspector. Holroyd was removed from his post without warning on 27 May 1975. His last meeting with his intelligence commander before leaving Ireland was not with his usual handler, Craig Smellie of MI6, but with the MI5 man whom he believes replaced him, Ian Cameron. He alleges, 'Before I left the meeting I was grabbed by Keith Farnes SAS, the G2 Intelligence of Army HQ, who pulled me into a doorway and told me that ten of our IRA deep sources had just been murdered by the IRA who had discovered them all within the week, that the information had been handed over to MI5. The handler, a staff sergeant in the Army whom I knew, had gone into an Army bunker and shot himself'. (cf. Robin Ramsay, *The Tribune*, 23 January 1987; Farnes was a former CO 21 SAS). However, I find no record of ten informants having been shot by the IRA at this time.

Duncan Campbell followed up his *New Statesman* articles of 4, 11 and 18 May 1988 and the Channel 4 *Diverse Reports*, 2 May 1984, with an article in the *New Statesman*, 'MI5 subverts "dirty tricks" investigation', 14 December 1984. The two-year RUC investigation into Holroyd's allegations resulted in insufficient evidence to 'warrant the initiation of criminal proceedings against any person'. Holroyd was informed of this by the Director of Public Prosecutions, Northern Ireland. Campbell alleged that in 1983 MI5 intervened to obstruct the police investigation.

He added:

> Since the cover-up began, the RUC have refused to return critical evidence to Captain Holroyd, including a photograph given to him by the late Captain Robert Nairac, GC, of a senior IRA figure whom Nairac claimed to have assassinated, in the Irish Republic. Other evidence includes photographs of a train derailed during an Army and SAS investigation, and tape recordings in which another intelligence officer, now dead, described his personal knowledge of the 'dirty tricks' campaign.

Sectarian Murders in the 'Triangle of Death'

The MI5/MI6 conflict came to a head over the IRA ceasefire, 22 December 1974 to 2 January 1975. The ceasefire was welcomed by MI6 who saw it as part of their scheming to politicise the IRA. MI5 resented the overtures being made to the IRA at this period. Rees was also winding down internment. Wallace and Holroyd both testify to the murder campaign by Protestant paramilitaries in the triangle area of Armagh, Portadown, Dungannon as an orchestrated one. The loyalist teams worked with the security forces across the border and assassinated IRA Captain John Francis Green. It was a deliberate act aimed at provoking a reaction and breaking the ceasefire. To understand the context it is necessary to look at sectarian murders of Catholics in the triangle area in 1974. At the end of that year came the ceasefire. Then came the murder of John Green. The murders of Catholics and retaliation from the IRA formed the pattern for 1975 in the South Armagh and 'triangle' areas.

In a letter to the Prime Minister, Mrs Margaret Thatcher, in December 1986 Colin Wallace provided details of some 30 assassinations of Catholics in the late 1974/1975 period in the 'triangle of death' area, territory enclosed by the towns of Portadown, Armagh and Dungannon and their immediate surrounding area, pointing out the links between some of the killers and the security forces. I have no access to that letter of Wallace but one can easily list the murders in those areas at that time. The murder gangs, I suspect, were a combination of SAS/UDR/loyalist paramilitaries. UDA and UVF are interchangeable for that area at that time. They worked closely together and even sometimes combined membership.

Fr Denis Faul and I wrote of the murders in a pamphlet entitled *The Triangle of Death*, coining a name which has since stuck. Daniel Hughes (73) was the first victim in 1974. He was killed by machine-gun fire on 17 January as he stood in the doorway of Boyle's pub at Cappagh, near Dungannon.

On the evening of 19 February 1974 I was filling in marriage papers in the Parochial House, Armagh, when I heard the dull thud of a bomb in the distance. Almost immediately the phone went. The call was from Traynor's pub on the Moy-Armagh road to say that a bomb had just gone off in the bar and two men had been killed. I arrived at the pub within minutes, made my way into the wrecked bar, then piled up with debris and whiteish dust. I anointed the two men. Soon afterwards I learned the dead men were Patrick Molloy, a Catholic neighbour of the area, and a Protestant friend, Jack Wiley. A little road beside the pub leads to Bond Plantation and Tullyroan. Fr Faul and I had long suspected that this was the hideout and planning area for the sectarian assassination of 19-year-old Alphonsus McGeown on 21 December 1972 in Dungannon and the shooting dead of Francis and Bernadette Mullan at their home in Moy on 5 August 1973.

On 3 December 1975 William Thomas Leonard (21), a UDR man, of Dungannon, was sentenced to life imprisonment for the murder of James Devlin (46) and his wife Gertrude near their home at Congo a few miles from Dungannon on 7 May 1974. He was a member of the UVF. The Crown said he had driven two gunmen in a car to the spot where the crime was committed. He admitted doing a dummy run the night before. Mrs Devlin and her daughter Patricia had driven to Coalisland to collect Mr Devlin after his day's work. Mrs Devlin was driving; her daughter was in the front seat and Mr Devlin was in the rear. As they turned into a lane close to their home they saw a man dressed in British Army uniform step from a hedge and hold up his arm. They thought it was an Army checkpoint. Then they saw a gun in his hand. Many shots were fired into the car and the three occupants were hit but not killed. Mr Devlin tried to leave the car to get help when there was a second burst of shots and both he and Mrs Devlin were killed and Patricia injured. Patricia ran to a neighbour's house for help. Later an examination of the scene revealed 29 9 mm calibre shells and other fragments of bullets. A Sterling sub-machine-gun and .45 revolver had been used.

William Thomas Leonard (UDR), Laurence Tate (29), also a UDR member, Main Road, Dungannon, Howard Henry McKay (25), Dunore Avenue, Dungannon, and John Nimmons (45) of Far Circular Road, Dungannon, were sentenced to jail – Nimmons for 10 years, the others for 12 years for sectarian explosions, including that of a public house, in December 1975. Counsel for Nimmons said he had acted out of a misguided sense of loyalty to the security forces. On 29 March William Thomas Leonard received a further sentence of 8 years for armed robbery and causing £12,000 damage to a CIE bus. The robbery was from a passenger on the bus. The bus was en route to Letterkenny and was stopped near Aughnacloy by a man 'waving a red light'.

Michael McCourt, a factory manager, was blown to pieces by a booby trap set in a transistor radio at his factory in Pomeroy, County Tyrone, on 16 September 1974. It was a skilfully made bomb. Local people suspected British Army expertise in its making. The British Army then stationed in Pomeroy put out a series of statements implying that McCourt's was a bomb factory. They arrested and ill-treated many Catholics in the area. Pomeroy people suspected loyalist UDR paramilitary people of the murder.

There was little attempt by the RUC in the Portadown area to prevent the sectarian murderers of Catholics at this time. Jack McCabe was assassinated in his own bar on 12 July 1972. Felix John Hughes (40) disappeared on 15 July 1972. His body was taken from a drain channel of the Bann river off Watson Street, tied to a mattress and weighted with stones, on 4 August 1972. On 15 May 1973 a 16-year-old boy was ordered to be detained for eight years in connection with the crime. Some 12 men were known to be involved in it. Eamonn McMahon disappeared on 26 August 1972 on his way home from visiting his girlfriend in Lurgan. Two were accused of his murder but when the RUC presented their case the judge said he had to reduce it to manslaughter. The two men got 5 and 3 years. Patrick Connolly (23) was killed on 4 October 1972 when a grenade was thrown through the window of his home at Deramore Drive. Joseph Weir (48) was shot dead on 18 January 1973 in the car park off West Street. One man was convicted and sentenced to life imprisonment. Denis Gorman was found dying in Obins Street on 25 August 1973 as a result of a blow. On 9 March 1973 Patrick James Turley of Burnside, Craigavon, was beaten up by a number of men as he left a bar in Portadown. He was then taken on a 'death ride' to a lonely spot where he was shot and left for dead. Although he survived he was confined to a wheelchair. One man was convicted of attempting to murder Turley and another man pleaded guilty to the assault and firearm charges in the crime.

There was a link-up among elements of the UDA/UVF, Special Branch and SAS in the Portadown area at that time. Allegations have been made that a particular RUC Special Branch man ran the mid-Ulster UDA commander ... and another notorious paramilitary member ... as 'sources of information' or agents of the Special Branch. This Special Branch man was linked via the SAS Covert Troop based at Castledillon to HQ 3 Brigade. He provided weapons not handed in to RUC Forensic to the SAS commanders ... and ..., who in turn used their SAS Troop facilities and the Special Branch man's introductions to arm and task the Portadown loyalist gangs, using information from the Garda nicknamed the 'Badger' and his Garda friends to clear areas across the border for SAS/UDA/UVF operations. The loyalist gangs in Portadown also recéived British Army uniforms and weapons 'stolen' from a TA base.

On 27 October 1974 Anthony Duffy (18) was found beaten and shot dead in Portadown. On 15 March 1987 the *Sunday Times* carried an article by Barrie Penrose stating that Captain Fred Holroyd had first-hand evidence that Thomas Clarke, found guilty of murdering Duffy in 1975, was innocent. He said that Clarke and Wilfred Cummings, also found guilty, 'took the rap' to protect the real killers, a UVF gang which had been carrying out 'deniable' cross-border operations for the RUC and MI5. He claimed that one of this UVF gang was a police informant and had to be protected. On the day Duffy died Holroyd was watching Cummings's house. Army intelligence had information of Cummings's association with UVF members including those whom Holroyd is convinced actually shot Duffy. At the time of Holroyd's disclosure Cummings independently sent out a letter from the Maze Prison clearing Clarke of any involvement in the murder and admitting that he himself was the driver in the killing.

Patrick Falls of Aughamullan, Coalisland, was assassinated by machine-gun fire while helping in his brother's bar at 9 pm on 20 November 1974. In 1981 James Joseph Somerville (37) of Moygashel Court, Dungannon, was sentenced to 35 years imprisonment for the murder of the Miami Showband musicians on 31 July 1975 . Two other members of the UDR, Thomas Raymond Crozier and James Roderick McDowell of Lurgan, got similar terms of imprisonment for the murders in October 1976.   Somerville's brother, Wesley Somerville, and Harris Boyle, also members of the gang, died in a premature explosion at the scene.   James Joseph Somerville had already pleaded guilty to the murder of Patrick Aidan Falls, the attempted wounding of a customer at that attack and also causing an explosion at a bar in Dungannon on 3 April 1973.

September, October 1974 also saw a flurry of sectarian killing and wounding in Belfast similar to the bloody conflict of 1972/73. There were retaliatory killings in the loyalist/republican strife but British intelligence also took revenge for the Guildford pub bombings which killed five people and the IRA murders of judge Rory Conaghan and resident magistrate Martin McBirney.

There was a proliferation of 'underground literature' in Belfast from the British secret services; while MI6 attempted to smear the assassins, MI5 promoted communal conflict. The Ulster Citizens' Army, probably a tiny 'political' grouping controlled by MI6, re-emerged in mid-1974 accusing named members of the UDA and UVF of being responsible for assassinations.[61] A broadsheet was circulated in October 1974 entitled 'Wanted for Murder'. The anonymous authors, claiming to be former members of the UDA and UVF, blamed those two organisations for the assassinations and named five members of the UDA who they said were chiefly responsible for the killings. (The combined British Army/RUC Task Force set up in 1972 to deal with assassinations had been disbanded in early 1974!). In December the Ulster Citizens' Army circulated leaflets containing the names of 13 men allegedly responsible for the sectarian assassination campaign of the past year. One of the names was that of a senior officer in the UDA, another that of a man lately released from internment. The British intelligence propaganda effort was not directed at the loyalists only. Nationalist papers like the *Andersonstown News* received a document from the 'Catholic Defence Volunteers' – 'We shall go on the offensive,' it said, 'against those known to have planned or executed attacks against the minority community and honest Protestants who have opposed them. These names shall be given to us by our intelligence sources which include a number of well-known politicians, civil servants, a few members of the RUC itself, honest Protestants and our own agents, all of whom are reliable'. Soldiers of the 1st Battalion, the Gloucestershire Regiment, pushed propaganda broadsheets through letterboxes on the Falls Road, Belfast in December 1974. The forged broadsheets purported to be copies of republican newssheets, *The Vindicator* and *The Nation* but were a not too clever mix of British and IRA propaganda.

The Murder of John Francis Green

On a sad, sullen January day
The faceless men in Britain's pay
Came to murder brave John Green...

On 10 January 1975 John Francis Green, OC, 2nd Battalion, North Armagh, IRA, was assassinated at Mullyash mountain, near Castleblayney, County Monaghan. He was 28 years of age. He left a wife, Ann, and three children, Ursula, Gerard and Francis. On 12 January nearly three thousand people attended the removal of his remains from the morgue at Monaghan County Hospital and walked in procession to St Mary's Church. Relays of mourners carried the coffin through the streets of Monaghan. A Provisional IRA guard of honour flanked the bearers. A drummer sounded the 'Dead March'. A bugler attended to sound the last post. As the coffin was placed in the hearse the President of Sinn Féin, Ruairí Ó Brádaigh, addressed the crowd. He told them not to have revenge in their hearts but to trust in the leadership of the republican movement. He said that John Francis Green was killed at a time of peace during the Provisionals' ceasefire; it showed there were still people in Ireland who did not want peace. There was a similar crowd and display of honour in Lurgan for his burial on 14 January. A guard of honour waited near the church; the tricolour covered the coffin; the RUC saluted the cortège as it passed. It sounds strange now but that was the climate of those days. It was truce time and Green was recognised as a man of honour and a soldier by all sides. Castleblayney looked on Green as an adopted son. When the funeral passed through, the whole town was shut down. The Gardaí saluted the coffin.

All this public honour was a reflection on Green. He was recognised as the clean-living idealist republican in the old style, a man who loved his country. He had been missed out at the time of internment. His house was raided but he wasn't there. He was popular in the estate in which he lived in Lurgan; many people were willing to offer transport to whisk him away in time of danger. He was picked up finally on the Armagh-Portadown road on 16 December 1971 and interned. On 9 September 1973 he escaped from Long Kesh prison on a day his brother, Fr Gerry Green, visited his compound. The priest was seized and tied up. His brother donned his clothes and walked out calmly through all the security stations.

Green then took up residence in Castleblayney. He was a man in a hurry. At that time the Provisional IRA in North Armagh was poorly organised. He set about reforms. He frowned on drinkers, investigated freelance robberies, moved the rowdies off. He divided command with Michael McVerry. McVerry looked after South Armagh and district but was shot on 15 November 1973 on a raid on Keady joint RUC/Army barracks. He died in hospital. Green took charge of North Armagh with authority from Castleblayney and Monaghan town across to Armagh City, Portadown and Lurgan.

On 10 December 1974 a group of Protestant churchmen met members of Sinn Féin and the IRA at an hotel in Feakle, County Clare. The talks were fruitful. There was a desire to open up dialogue and continue channels of communication. As a demonstration of peace the IRA on 20 December announced a ceasefire to begin from midnight 22 December to 2 January 1975. Although the Northern Ireland Office was careful not to make a reciprocal move publicly, it diplomatically declared that there would be a 'more relaxed atmosphere' regarding detention if the ceasefire were to be extended. Ruairí Ó Brádaigh replied that the ceasefire would continue while the British Army refrained from taking a military advantage. At midnight 20 December the IRA ceasefire came into effect. House searches and screenings by the British Army ceased. A gentleman's agreement was abroad.

MI5 did not like the truce. It thought the IRA was using it as a shield to regroup. Robert Nairac of the SAS was ordered to kill Green, then the high-ranking Provo of the Border area and a man of standing.

John Francis Green went back to Lurgan on Christmas Eve. He was no sooner home than the Army came to the door. The soldiers observed the niceties however and didn't enter. Green was suspicious. He stayed a few days and then secretly returned to Castleblayney. A lot of people thought he was still at home in Lurgan. There was an atmosphere of euphoria. Returned Provos were celebrating at home and went out to entertainment with their friends

At this period in Castleblayney John Francis Green was staying with Eamon McGurgan and his family. McGurgan was from Portadown and his wife Kathleen was from Lurgan. McGurgan had been a prospective candidate for kidnapping by Nairac and his gang in March 1974. The McGurgans had ten children but they lived in a huge barrack of a house and there was plenty of room. Another republican from the Portadown area but a native of Lisburn, Eric Dale, also lived there. In 1983 Eric Dale was found shot dead by the roadside at Clontygora near Killeen in South Armagh. The INLA said they had executed him because he gave information about the movements of Seamus Grew and Roddy Carroll who were gunned down by the SAS trained Special Support Unit of 'E' Department, RUC Headquarters, on 12 December 1982. This was not true.

It was festival time in Castleblayney but Green cut a lonesome figure. His republican friends were still celebrating across the border. He missed especially fellow Lurgan man Feilim O'Hagan. On 9 January an Armagh City man who had settled in Castleblayney met him outside the Spinning Mill in Castleblayney. Green was a jolly type and would welcome an occasion to go into a pub for a chat although he did not drink himself. His friend couldn't delay but said he hoped to be free later. Green talked about going to the annual dinner dance of Castleblayney Faughs' GAA club. He was interested in football. The Armagh man got the impression that Green was not in good form and that was unusual.

Green was busy at this time investigating local IRA internal affairs. He had been active since his return carrying out an inquiry about money, robberies and weapons. It had been particularly upsetting because it involved the conduct of a fellow Provo who was close to him. Green himself had conducted the inquiry, completed it and had it typed. After he was murdered a letter from Provisional IRA HQ about missing cash in Lurgan, a reply from the Provos being investigated explaining on what it had been spent and Green's report were found in his car.

He took his dinner in the McGurgan household on the evening of 10 January. He seemed anxious and was awaiting the return of Feilim O'Hagan. The McGurgans knew he was going to the Faughs' dinner later that evening. Mrs McGurgan was also going. He announced he was going out the road for half an hour. He left in his dark green Volkswagen. It was 6.20 pm.

The evening was cold, wet and windy. He left the town behind and headed for the home of Gerry Carville who lived alone in a two-storey farmhouse on Mullyash mountain. Carville, a man in middle age, was a humourous warmhearted character. Mullyash is a remote area, very bare, intersected with a maze of tiny roads pointing towards the border east to Tullyvallen and Newtownhamilton and more west to Darkley and Keady.

Green himself often stayed at Carville's. Local Protestants ceilied there too. Few Catholics lived in the area. The vein of 'Protestant territory' extended from the edge of Castleblayney across the border to New-townhamilton and Armaghbreague. Protestants and IRA often met there casually. Naturally the house attracted the attention of both Gardaí and British Army. Three weeks or a month before Green's death the Gardaí raided the house and searched it and the outhouses. In that period a British Army helicopter also crossed the border and circled the house several times. It had even followed two men to the house hovering over their car. A few years previously soldiers of the British Army had actually come across the border and searched the house. Carville had been alerted by neighbours and when he hurried home he found soldiers leaving the sheds. They did not speak but moved across his lane and headed over the fields and rocks. On that occasion the Gardaí intercepted them on the road and conducted them back to the border.

Two weeks before the murder of John Francis Green, Gerry Carville and a friend, Kevin Nugent, were sitting chatting in the living room of the house. Nugent was startled by a movement outside the house. 'There's some fellas out there,' he said. 'It's the sow,' said Carville jokingly. Carville went out and was just in time to see two men wearing masks running down by the little plantin' of trees on the entry lane to the house. He ran towards them and saw them jumping into a car and moving off at speed. If such warnings were not enough, those who frequented Carville's home were aware of a white car moving around in the district. It roused suspicion. In fact Garda investigations after Green's murder produced reports of a white Mercedes or Audi in the area thought to contain three men. Carville had often said to Green over a number of months, 'John Francis, it's getting dangerous'. Green passed it off lightly, 'You're getting afraid, are you?' Those who stayed took precautions. Many slept with a gun at the bedside and sometimes posted a guard at the door all night. Two nights before the shooting Green visited Carville in the company of two other men.

On the evening of 10 January Green drove out to the house purely by chance. The house was obviously under surveillance for some time.

Gerry Carville outlines the events from the time Green arrived at his house at 6.30 pm:

> I was doing the milking for Frank King, a neighbour. Always went about 7 pm. In the early evening I had been up at King's and came down home around 5 pm. I was making dinner and Tommy Laverty landed here. He came in for dinner. The dinner was around 6 pm. We were just finished when John Francis Green arrived. I said to John, 'There's no milk. Will you go down to Joe Hamilton's for a bottle of milk?' He took the bottle out of my hand and went down to Joey Hamilton's for the milk. When he came in I says, 'You'll have a bite of dinner'. ' No', he says, 'I'll take a mug of tea'. So I made tea for the three of us. When the tea was over it was just seven and that was my milking time. So Tommy Laverty says, 'You'll be up the road with me'. I says, 'Right'. So I put on my working coat and whatever I had to take with me and I says to John, 'You'll be here whenever I come back?' He says, 'I might. I was going to have a wash'. I says, 'You may put on the electric kettle for the fire isn't lit'. So I went out.
>
> Tommy turned the tractor on the street. There was a wee hedge, a wee wall at the front and I walked out and stepped on the back of the tractor. When I got off the tractor at King's I looked back and saw that the lights were all on. I thought to myself – 'What is he doing with the lights on?' I went to milk my cows.
>
> There was another wee man there they called Willie Smith of Madden. So we had gone over the road and foddered a few heads of cattle that was lying out over Jerry Carville's. We foddered and I came back over and filled a bottle of milk and headed down the road. It was blowing and teeming wet. Coming home I met Joe Hamilton and Hugh William Clarke on the road. I says, 'King's cow is going to calve, and you needn't be going far away'.
>
> I came over here and when I landed at the front door, the door was lying wide, busted open. I looked in sideways and John Francis was lying on the flat of his back on the floor. I ran back to the end of the lane. I threw the bottle of milk in the wind. I ran on down ahead to get ahead of Joe. He was on or about McKelvey's church, the Meeting House. I

says, 'Joe, John Green is dead'. Joe says, 'He's at his ould laughs again'. Clarke says, 'You better tell me anyway'. I says, 'Willie, John Green's shot at the house'. He says 'Don't be talking'.

We went back. Me and Willie stayed out. I says to Joe Hamilton, 'Joe, will you go over and look. Turn out the light for fear of somebody coming in'. Joe came back and said,'He's shot and well shot'.

Duncan Campbell wrote on the circumstances of John Francis Green's assassination in his article 'Victims of the "dirty war"' in the *New Statesman*, 4 May 1984. It is essential to add it to the above account. It has provoked controversy but the case it states has not been answered. The answer lies with the Gardaí and RUC. It would take a public inquiry in both parts of Ireland, especially in the Republic, to bring out the truth. Basic reports like the inquest transcripts, the forensic details and the pathologist's report would help solve the mystery. Why are they not readily available?

Campbell alleged:

According to the official ('Restricted') manual on 'Counter- Revolutionary Operations', the SAS's tasks included the 'infiltration of ... assassination parties...into insurgent held areas', and 'liaison with...forces operating against the common enemy'. Ball and Nairac visited intelligence officers in the Armagh areas, including Holroyd in Portadown, asking for suggestions of worthwhile intelligence targets. They told Holroyd that they were under the direct orders of SIS and army headquarters intelligence staff.

On 10 January 1975, in a remote mountain side farmhouse in County Monaghan, a mile south of the Irish border, a leading republican, John Francis Green, was murdered. Careful planning and good intelligence was evident in his killing, for he had only visited the farm at short notice. The killers waited until Green was alone and then burst in on him, emptying the contents of two pistols into him.

Soon afterwards, Captain Nairac called routinely on Holroyd at the Army's Mahon Road camp in Portadown. The subject of Green's death came up – Green, aged 27 (*recte 28*), a local republican hero after an escape from internment in Long Kesh in 1973, had by 1975 become the IRA commander in North Armagh. After an SAS sergeant major left the room, Nairac said that he had killed Green. When Holroyd expressed disbelief, Nairac produced a colour Polaroid of Green's bloodsoaked body, taken soon after his death. Green was pictured from the waist up, lying on his back. With some reluctance, Nairac allowed Holroyd to keep the picture. It remained in Holroyd's photo album until 1982, when it was handed over to ... of the RUC.

Who took the Polaroid picture is still a mystery. Nairac implied that he had done so. RUC detectives investigating the case suggested to Captain Holroyd in 1983 that the picture had been taken by the Irish Police. But a very senior Garda source says that no Garda officer in the area had either the equipment or any official reason to take such a picture. He said that the morning after the crime, a fully equipped Garda photographic team travelled up from Dublin and took pictures using standard (black and white) film.

Nairac told Holroyd that he and two other men had done the killing. He then described in detail how they had crossed the border during the evening and driven down a country road. Green was at first in the company of farmer Gerry Carville... But the old farmer, said Nairac, had left at a set time, known to the killers. One man stayed with the car, while the other two crept up a lane to the isolated farm and watched Green through an uncurtained window. They kicked down the door and shot him repeatedly, emptying one of the guns into his body as he lay dying.

Nairac's account of the killing, as provided to Holroyd, is chillingly exact. Irish police investigations produced reports of an unknown vehicle in the area at the time of the killing – a white Mercedes or Audi – which eye witnesses thought contained three men. Farmer Gerry Carville has told us that for more than one month he had left his farm at the same time each evening to tend a neighbour's cow. In the last month it has been revealed that, at the time, there were two well-placed informers working for British security inside IRA circles in the nearby town of Castleblayney.

Garda investigation of the killing confirmed many aspects of Nairac's account. The room in which John Francis Green was shot was indeed uncurtained at the time. The front door frame was kicked in, and still bears the cracks. Forensic experts, whose reports we have also seen, later established that two guns were used to shoot Green, one is thought to be a Luger, the other a Spanish-made Star automatic pistol.

The writer of the piece 'Undercover Murder' in *New Hibernia*, December 1985, confirms from his sources the allegations of Captain Holroyd in the John Francis Green murder but claims that his sources 'suggest that the actual killer involved with Nairac was a well-known UVF man from Lurgan who has been involved in many killings since the early seventies, but has never been convicted of murder. However, loyalists suggest that in fact Nairac, although involved in setting up the murder, did not go along with the UVF team which brought back the Polaroid photo as proof that the job had been carried out. The same sources say that the Lurgan man's connection with military intelligence in the mid-seventies was well known locally'.

This 'Lurgan man' was involved in an early morning UVF raid on the Territorial Army depot at Lurgan, 23 October 1972, when the guards were overpowered and 104 guns and an assortment of amunition were stolen. British Army soldiers later recovered most of the weaponry but 36 guns and some ammunition remained missing. The raiders were dressed in British Army uniforms and the operation was co-ordinated by UVF men in the Ulster Defence Regiment. One of the weapons found at the scene of the Miami killings was from this haul. The 'Lurgan man' was spotted among onlookers the morning after the Miami disaster watching as police and firemen cleared up. The *New Hibernia* article claims that he is believed to have played a part in the murder of a loyalist suspected by the UVF of giving information to the police.

One of the stolen weapons was also said to be used in the murder of Patrick Campbell (34), Banbridge, at 10.04 pm on the night of 24 October 1973. Patrick Campbell worked at Down Shoes Ltd, Banbridge. He was an outstanding cross-community and parish worker and a staunch trade unionist. He had Lurgan connections. There were constant callers at his home on matters of work and union problems. On 24 October his wife answered a knock at the door. There were two men there unmasked and wearing identical black shower proof coats, like police clothes, and black gloves. One asked, 'Is Pat in ?', using the usual familiar form of his name. A minute or so later Mrs Campbell heard her husband saying, 'No. I'm not going with you'. Mrs Campbell moved to the door and saw the three men jammed there, Pat in between. He was trying to move into the house and there was a struggle. The man on his left, whom we have been calling 'the Lurgan man' (he is also known as 'The Jackal') had a hand-gun and Mrs Campbell heard the single shot as he fired into Pat. The other man then opened up indiscriminately at close quarters with an automatic cutting Patrick Campbell down in a hail of bullets and narrowly missing Mrs Campbell. It is reckoned five men took part in the operation – the two killers, a man in a waiting car on the main road, a look-out in the estate at the scene of the murder, and a man in the transfer car which was placed at Tullyear road. Mrs Campbell identified a man at an identification parade. He was charged but later the charges were dropped. One of the intrigues of the case is that investigating police have been mystfied by Mrs Campbell's insistence that a hand-gun was used and gave the impression that they had no evidence of it; she says she saw the gun and heard the shot. 'The Jackal' had worked for a time at Down Shoes Ltd and therefore Patrick Campbell would have known him. The murdered man was 'fingered' by an ex-UDR man who subsequently was jailed for paramilitary activities and arms charges. 'The Jackal' was an informer for a Special Branch man. An article in the *Sunday World*, 27 May 1984, said that a loyalist gunman known as 'the Jackal' was back in the Portadown area; he was reputed to have killed upwards of 15 people, was associated with Captain Nairac and involved in the Miami Showband murders; 'He was personally identified in two sectarian murders'. There has been further speculation that 'the Jackal's' companion in the Campbell shooting was Wesley Somerville who died in the Miami Showband explosion. The *New Hibernia* article adds that 'the Jackal' was an associate of a former RUC constable, convicted in 1971 for sectarian murder in Portadown and that he played a part in the subsequent murder of a loyalist suspected by the UVF of giving information to the police – 'The Lurgan man is also a former associate of RUC Constable ..., who is now serving life for murder and kidnapping. In at least one confession statement made to RUC in Castlereagh Holding Centre, the Lurgan man is named as the actual killer of William Strathearn, an Ahoghill grocer shot dead in 1977. To date, however, the Lurgan man's only conviction has been short term for possession of a weapon. According to a loyalist source, when finally arrested he was on his way to carry out another sectarian assassination. He is currently at liberty again'.

The same article also touches on the shooting of Seamus Grew and Roddy Carroll in Armagh on 12 December 1982. The RUC on the information of a Castleblayney informer had expected INLA leader Dominic McGlinchey to be with them. McGlinchey was staying with the informer, and Carroll and Grew called at this man's house. McGlinchey, however, in an instinctive intuition changed his mind. During the subsequent trial of Constable Robinson for the murder of Carroll and Grew, the informer fled to the North and took refuge in a RUC station. No doubt he sensed danger when Constable Robinson gave evidence of an unnamed informer. Many republicans have asked since – what information did this informer disclose to British intelligence over the years, since he was privy to much IRA information and operations from 1971? *New Hibernia* also speculates that he was probably the local contact in the 1974 attempted kidnap of Grew. Republicans in Castleblayney say that John Francis Green never liked this person and studiously avoided him.

In its issue of 2 September 1987 *The Independent* carried a full page purporting to 'unravel the truth in Ulster's dirty war'. Most of the writing was by *The Independent*'s Irish correspondent David McKittrick, a skilled journalist and acknowledged authority on the loyalist paramilitaries. David McKittrick had often carried the allegations of Colin Wallace in *The Irish Times* and had relayed Duncan Campbell's articles (drawn from the revelations of Captain Holroyd) in *The Irish Times* where he was once the Northern Ireland correspondent. In *The Irish Times* of 21 March 1981 he had described Wallace's Army role:

It was clear that he had access to the highest levels of intelligence data.

He had an encyclopedic memory which he occasionally refreshed with calls made on his personal scrambler telephone to the headquarters intelligence section a few floors above his office. He was astonishingly frank. He would freely give the names, addresses, phone numbers and names of mistresses of paramilitary figures both Republican and Loyalist. He was also ready to admit mistakes made by the British Army and to acknowledge that the Provisionals or any other group were doing well.

Part of the knocking of Wallace's allegations in *The Independent* special page was written by John Ware. The attack on Wallace's credibility led to a 41 page refutation by Robin Ramsay and Stephen Dorril of *Lobster*. They took the arguments and innuendos of McKittrick and Ware apart. Their logical analysis and documentation received little attention from McKittrick or Ware or *The Independent*. Robin Ramsay followed with a further criticism in *Lobster*, 15, 'Smearing Wallace and Holroyd'. On 30 January 1990 Mr Archie Hamilton, Minister of State for the Armed Forces, announced in a written House of Commons answer that documents had been discovered supporting Colin Wallace's claims that he was wrongly dismissed for leaking a classified document to a journalist in Belfast on 4 February 1975. In March 1990 the Press Council upheld a complaint against *The Independent* by Colin Wallace arising out of articles in that newspaper on 2 September 1987.

Since it is Holroyd's allegations that mainly concern us here, it is necessary to examine the attack on them. McKittrick's main thrust is that the general assumption in Northern Ireland is that Green's murder was the work of extreme loyalists; there is no proof that Captain Nairac was involved. Holroyd had alleged that Captain Nairac had given him a photograph of Green's body taken after he had shot him. McKittrick then quotes Holroyd on a BBC interview – 'Nairac disclosed to me that he'd carried out an assassination operation with two other chaps across the border on John Francis Green. He gave me a photograph – which the RUC have confiscated and refused to return and in fact I'm taking legal action to get it back – which indicated to me that the person who took the photograph must have been the murderer, because the window outside was showing complete blackness. The police didn't arrive until daylight because they were afraid of mines'. *The Independent* professed to have examined the original photograph and obtained a copy. Holroyd is reported as having said that the RUC obtained it. McKittrick says that it does not match Holroyd's description – there is no window and since flash was used it is unclear whether it was taken in daylight or at night; it is clear from the congealed blood that it was taken many hours after Green's death, about 18 hours according to forensic science. In fact *The Independent* says it has 'established' it was taken by the Garda Technical Bureau the following day and later sent to the RUC in the North and circulated to Garda stations; an RUC detective recollected giving it to Holroyd, a collector of such memorabilia. *The Independent* also claimed to have seen Holroyd's scrapbook dealing with Green and obtained a copy of it. On the back of the photograph Holroyd had written 'Found assassinated by the Garda in a farm near Castleblayney. Evidence suggests the IRA were the murderers in an internal feud. 9 mm and .38 automatic used. – Later found to have been shot by UVF'. McKittrick also adds that it was 'established' that Green was not, as Holroyd alleged, shot with handguns of 9 mm and .38 calibre. McKittrick apart from using the word 'established' does not provide us with the pathologist's report on Green's wounds nor the forensic scientist's ballistic reports on the firearms used in the killing. One must ask – did McKittrick see the original photograph of Green's dead body? How did he procure a copy, since, as he emphasises, the photograph is RUC property? Obviously the photograph copy is a hand-out. The story could be an MI5/RUC counter attack against the Wallace/Holroyd revelations. One simply asks – was the photograph shown to McKittrick really the original which once belonged to Holroyd?

Duncan Campbell who first investigated and published Holroyd's allegations in the *New Statesman*, 4 May 1984, replied to McKittrick's arguments in the *New Statesman*, 25 September 1987. Campbell argues:

> In attacking Holroyd, *The Independent* evaluated only one of his allegations, against Nairac. Some of the remarks made about Holroyd reflect not only a distorted view held by the RUC, but also directly contradict McKittrick's own reportage of 1984. For example, a photograph of Green's dead body allegedly taken by Nairac and given later to Holroyd – a colour polaroid print – is a key piece of evidence. It is at least circumstantial evidence that Nairac took the picture himself, since according to senior Garda (Irish police) sources, such colour polaroid pictures were never officially taken by the Garda who attended the scene of the crime. Thus, in McKittrick's *Irish Times* 1984 version, it was reported 'RUC sources have suggested the photographs might have come from the Garda, but Garda sources deny this'. But in *The Independent* 1987 version it is reported that 'we have established that it was taken by the Garda Technical Bureau, which circulated it...' The Garda Technical Bureau did not use colour polaroid cameras – and in any case, a polaroid photograph normally has no negative and cannot be copied for circulation.
>
> Perhaps most tellingly, *The Independent* reproduces the page of Holroyd's notebook on which the Green body picture was stuck, with five other pictures. Only four of these other pictures are to be seen in *The Independent*, however. The fifth has been removed, leaving a blank space. What is missing is a picture of Green taken from an SAS hide

concealed near a farm he was seen visiting. The SAS team who took the picture was commanded by Nairac and another officer....

Last week, McKittrick refused to discuss the sources of the picture or information from RUC reports used in *The Independent*. ... The article states that the picture had not been returned to Holroyd because 'the RUC takes the view that the picture is police property'. Asked this week if an official leaks enquiry had been launched into how *The Independent* had obtained and published a photograph that was their property, chief RUC press spokesman Bill McGookin told the *New Statesman* that he had just been on holiday. Mr McGookin's former deputy, Chief Superintendent Bill Wilson, is rumoured to have been the RUC official who was authorised to hand the picture and RUC files on Holroyd to a *Sunday Times* reporter and then to *The Independent*. Wilson said this week that these rumours were untrue. But he agreed that the report in *The Independent* 'fitted in with the facts that we (the RUC) related – very much so'.

There is no reason to expect a 'leak' enquiry over the RUC Holroyd's files; their leakage was patently 'official'. In reproducing parts of the story as the RUC tells it, *The Independent* has done its readers a disservice. The paper certainly cannot assert, as its headline proclaims, to be an objective attempt at 'unravelling the truth in Ulster's dirty war'. Instead, the evidence suggests that it has become enravelled in an RUC propaganda ploy.

1975: Murders in South Armagh and 'The Triangle'

1975 is known as the year of the 'truce' engineered by the Secretary of State Mr Merlyn Rees and assented to by the Provisional IRA. The setting up of recognised 'incident centres' by Sinn Féin was meant to encourage political movement on the part of the republicans. 1975, however, was a year of feuding among republican groupings and saw a great increase in sectarian murders. MI5 did not agree with the political overtures of Rees towards the republicans and no doubt played its part in encouraging sectarian murders. Let us go back to the 'triangle area' and South Armagh to follow the repercussions of the murder of John Green.

In the 'triangle area' there was a spate of attacks against Catholics and this was followed by retaliatary IRA action:

On 10 February 1975 Arthur Mulholland (60) and Eugene Doyle (18) were shot dead in Hayden's Bar, Gortavale, Rock. A Sterling sub-machine-gun was used.

On 19 February 1975 James Breen of Lurgan was shot dead at his own door.

Mrs Dorothy Trainor (45), Portadown, was assassinated on the night of

31 March-1 April 1975 on her way home from the British Legion Club at 1.30 am. Her husband Malachy was seriously injured by several shots.

Martin McVeigh (22), Portadown, was gunned down on 3 April 1975 at 10.15 pm as he cycled home from his work at the Metal Box factory, Portadown.

On 11 April 1975 Owen Boyle (41), Glencull, Aughnacloy, was shot five times by assassins who fired through the back window of his bungalow. The marks of military style boots were found outside the window.

On 21 April 1975 Mrs Marion Bowen (21) and her seven-month pregnancy, her two brothers Seamus McKenna (25) and Michael McKenna (27) were blown up by a booby-trap explosion at Killylis, Dungannon. The bomb was set in Bowen's house which they had been repairing almost daily for two months.

Three men, Michael John Feeney (45), Joseph Toman (45), and Brendan O'Hara (40) were killed in a machine-gun attack on a dart club at Bleary near Portadown on 27 April 1975.

If the murder of John Francis Green stands out amongst all the other tragedies from a publicity point of view at the beginning of the IRA ceasefire, the related murder of members of the Miami Showband captured the headlines in mid-term. Captain Holroyd has revealed that the SAS was behind the massacre. The Castledillon SAS unit organised the gang which was made up of members of the UVF, some of whom were also members of the UDR, providing the weapons and explosives. The murder of innocent Catholics was part of an officially approved counter-insurgency plan.

On 31 July 1975 the five-man party of the Miami Showband were returning from playing at a dance in Banbridge when they were stopped by what seemed a UDR checkpoint at Buskhill on the Banbridge-Newry Road. A red light was flashed. At least three men were seen in UDR uniform and berets. The showband were asked their identity, put out of the vehicle and questioned, names, date of birth. Two of the hold-up gang went to the showband van with a parcel which contained a 10 to 15 lb bomb. It exploded prematurely, the van was cut in half and the two UVF men Harris Boyle of Portadown and Wesley Somerville from Dungannon were killed instantly. In the panic that ensued the bandmen made a run for it. The remaining members of the gang opened fire on them. Tony Geraghty was struck by eight bullets fired from behind. Fran O'Toole was struck by at least 18 bullets; he was lying on the ground when he was hit by some of them. Brian McCoy was struck by bullets fired at him from both sides. Stephen Travers was hit by a dumdum bullet in the hip; it exploded inside him before exiting under his left arm. He survived. Des McAlea also survived. He was knocked down by the explosion, heard the shooting, called to his companions, later came to and ran for help. He remembered the patrol being stopped by a military man with a torch. He said he thought it was a joint UDR-Army check because he heard an English accent and local accents. 'Some had berets on,' he said in evidence in court. 'They had standard military weapons like rifles and sub-machine-guns.' In fact three green berets, a Sterling sub-machine-gun, a magazine containing 32.9 mm bullets and a .38 pistol were found in the debris.

In October 1976, James Roderick McDowell (29), Princetown Drive, Lurgan, an optical worker, a sergeant in 11 UDR, and Thomas Raymond Crozier (25), Queen Street, Lurgan, a painter and lance corporal in the UDR, were sentenced to life imprisonment for the Miami band murders. As already stated another member of the gang James Joseph Somerville (37), brother of Wesley Somerville killed in the explosion, was also imprisoned for life, November 1981.

Crozier in evidence mentioned two other men in uniform besides himself. Probably all the gang were in UDR dress. It is possible that some of the gang who emerged from the hedge at the scene, and who could have come in a different car, were unknown to McDowell and Crozier. Who was the member of the gang with the English accent? An SAS man? Captain Robert Nairac was a companion of Harris Boyle. Both of them are suspected of the plot to assassinate John Francis Green. (RTE *Today Tonight* programme, 18 March 1987). Was Nairac present at the Miami Showband killings?

Harris Boyle was 24 years of age when he was killed.[62] There were massive shows of UVF strength when he and Wesley Somerville were buried. Both were given paramilitary funerals. Three volleys of shots were fired over Somerville's coffin outside his home at Moygashel Park, Dungannon. For Boyle, described in death notices as a UVF major, double-decker busloads of UVF from Belfast and other parts poured into Portadown. Many of them had earlier attended Somerville's funeral. A volley of shots was fired when the cortège left Boyle's home at 20 Festival Road, Killicomaine. Many of the UVF were in battle dress. An Ulster flag with black rim covered the coffin and eight girls wearing black glasses and carrying wreaths bearing initials 'HB' walked in front of the cortège. Two minutes silence was observed outside the Ulster Social Club in Bridge Street.

Boyle had a previous conviction.[63] In February 1973, then described as a telephone wireman, he and two others, Robert John Kerr (29) unemployed weaver of Florence Court and William Ashton Wright, a full-time member of the UDR attached to Seagoe Fort, faced charges of carrying a loaded firearm in public without lawful authority and under suspicious circumstances. All admitted membership of the UDA. Judge Rory Conaghan directed the jury to find all the accused 'not guilty' of possessing with intent two revolvers and 13 rounds of ammunition at Teghnavan, Lurgan, on 9

September 1972 and stealing a car. One was acquitted on the grounds that the loaded .38 revolver in his possession was service issue and he was permitted under statute to carry it. He said that he had been intimidated out of his home in Churchill Park, Portadown, after a Protestant, Paul Beattie, was shot dead by loyalists on 11 July 1962 near his home. Boyle in court admitted ownership of a black woollen mask found in the dashboard of the car. He had used it, it was claimed, the previous evening at a UDA parade in Dungannon. The other denied throwing a .45 revolver on to the road when they were stopped at an RUC checkpoint. Boyle was fined £75 for driving without insurance.

The Somerville brothers James Joseph, lorry-helper, and William Wesley, textile worker, had appeared in court in 1974 on charges in connection with a bomb which exploded in the Mourne Crescent housing estate, Coalisland, on 5 March 1974 injuring 12 people including a five-week-old baby. The RUC said that two breadservers had been set upon in their depot at Gortnaglush by four or five masked men who tied them up and put them into a breadvan from which they had removed the shelves. They drove off in the van and in one of the breadservers' cars. The two men were later transferred from the van into the boot of the car before being released near Moy. A bomb was placed in the van and taken to Coalisland where the van was abandoned in the housing estate. Two men were seen running from the scene and getting into a car; they drove off at speed. The Somervilles were remanded on bail. They were later acquitted of the charges. [64]

At the Miami trial John Wright gave evidence of parking his car outside his home in Portadown on the night of 30 July shortly after 10.30 pm. At 7 on the following morning police arrived at his house and he saw that his white Ford Escort with black bonnet was missing. It had been stolen during the night. Wright identified two pictures of a car shown to him as his vehicle. *The Craigavon Times (Portadown Times)*, August 1975, reported that the owner of a Ford Escort which was found at the scene of the explosion lodged a complaint against the RUC alleging ill-treatment and claiming that he was detained longer than the 72 hours without being charged. He said the police arrived at his house to ask for his help in tracing his car. 'He was escorted to Portadown police station and later to Newry where he said the tone of the investigations switched from his car to the murders. During several lengthy interrogations he claimed the police tried to make him sign statements which they had contrived, and offered him a £3,000 bribe with guarantees that he and his family would be taken safely out of Northern Ireland if he were to reveal the names of the people involved in the incident. He also alleged that he was shown plastic bags containing parts of the bodies of the victims in an attempt to make him sign the statements, and further alleged that he was deprived of sleep and had to lie on the hard floor of the cell to get some rest'.

At Newry Crown Court on Saturday 10 January 1976, two detectives won their appeal against conviction for assaulting Robin John Jackson (26) of Lurgan during an interview in Bessbrook RUC station on 7 August 1975. Judge James Brown allowed the appeals of CID Detective Constables Raymond Buchanan and Norman Carlisle of Newry RUC barracks who had been fined £10 at a special court. In evidence Jackson told the court he was being questioned about the Miami Showband murders and that Carlisle and Buchanan and three other detectives ill-treated him. [65]

Following the Miami Showband murder, the IRA shot dead a 22-year-old former UDR man George McCall on 2 August 1975. [66] They suspected him of taking part in sectarian murders in the Moy area. He died in a hail of bullets as he and his wife walked through the village of Moy after a Saturday night drink in a local pub. The attack took place just before midnight. The couple had almost reached their home in Jockey Lane when white-masked gunmen stepped out from behind a clump of bushes and started to shoot. Alarmed by Sandra McCall's screams three of the men ran off but a fourth continued to pump bullets into his victim while she desperately wrestled with him in an attempt to save her husband. George McCall had retired from the UDR in 1973. His funeral took place from his father's residence at Tullyroan.

On the morning of 14 August the IRA shot dead Norman 'Mooch' Kerr (28), a native of Portadown, in the Carrick Bar, Market Street, Armagh. The shooting happened shortly after closing time. Norman Kerr was a disc-jockey who played in this bar every Thursday night for a year previous. He was a friend of Harris Boyle who sometimes accompanied him to Armagh to give him a hand. In fact two weeks previous to the Miami massacre Boyle was in the bar with him. They rarely talked about their friends or mixed much with the clientele. It may be significant that Kerr played in Banbridge four nights a week; also the sleeve of a Miami record was on display in the Carrick.

On the night he was shot, Kerr had just finished loading his gear into his van which was stationed outside with its sidelights on. He returned to the bar and sat chatting to his girlfriend with his back to the door. Suddenly three IRA members appeared on the scene. Two stood guarding the door. The third ran straight to him and shot him in the back of the head.

The gunman retreated quickly to the door covering himself with the gun. As he went out the door one of the barmen threw a stool at him catching him on the back of the legs. In a moment all three had disappeared. In private the IRA let it be known that they had shot him because of his relationship with Captain Robert Nairac. The IRA was in possession of Harris Boyle's diary, a member having stolen it from his clothes while he was swimming at Portadown baths.

After Norman Kerr's death, Mrs Evelyn Boyle, mother of Harris, said, 'I think that Mooch was picked out because he was a friend of Harris. They often went out together. Harris used to help Mooch run the disco. He often warned him about playing in Armagh, but he never mentioned this bar in particular'. Laurence Erwin (27), the road manager who normally attended discos with Kerr, said, 'I believe Mooch was killed in retaliation for the Showband killings'. He said he went everywhere with Kerr but on that Thursday night decided not to go as he had 'an uneasy feeling about the place'.[67]

At the weekend Cardinal Conway condemning the series of murders and other violent deeds said, 'Even on earth the memory of what they have done will haunt them later in life. Each of the victims of these murders had years of life ahead of him, many of them long years of happy family life. What kind of monster can wipe that out in a single instant?'

Until Captain Holroyd pointed the finger at Captain Robert Nairac for the John Green killing, the common surmise and gossip was that the IRA found out the names of the killers of John Green when they took William Meaklin of Newtownhamilton prisoner. Meaklin, a former RUC reservist, went missing on 14 August 1975. He owned a 'travelling shop'. The van was found near Crossmaglen and his badly disfigured body was found on the Newtownhamilton-Castleblayney road. This murder was followed by the revenge killing of Seán Farmer (32) of Moy and Colm McCartney (22) in Tullyvallen between Castleblayney and Newtownhamilton.

A number of murders of Protestants which seemed to emanate from the murder of William Meaklin followed in a wide ring around Newtownhamilton. Some were members of the UDR. The rash assumption was that the IRA had tortured him and gained some information.

On 30 August 1975 Robert Frazer (50), a council worker and part-time UDR member, was shot in the head at point blank range as he got out of his car at his farm in Ballymoyer. The Army spotted the fleeing car heading in the direction of Newtownhamilton. A helicopter followed the car but lost it as it crossed the border. The next day another part-time member of the UDR, Joseph Reid (46) of Fennalog, Madden, near Keady, a Unionist member of Armagh District Council, was shot dead. His daughter answered a knock at the door. A man asked for her father. The daughter went upstairs for her father who was getting ready for bed. When he appeared at the door he was shot three times in the chest and stomach.

On 1 September five Protestants were shot dead at Tullyvallen Orange Hall on the Altnamackin Road. Just before 10 pm two masked men burst open the door and sprayed the hall with machine-gun fire. The men who died were, James McKee (70), Ronald McKee, John Johnston (70), Nevin McConnell (40) and William Heron.

On 6 November a UDR man, John Bell, of Whitecross, Newtownhamilton was shot dead and on 10 November Joseph Nesbitt of Darkley, also a

UDR member, was shot dead.

The killings moved on into 1976. Robert McConnell of the UDR was shot dead in Newtownhamilton on 5 April 1976.

Hugh William Clarke who had gone to Carville's house with Gerry Carville and Joe Hamilton the night Green was murdered was himself gunned down beside his digger at Mullaghbawn in South Armagh on 2 April 1977.

More murders of Catholics followed William Meaklin's murder:-

Two Gaelic football fans were shot dead on 24 August 1975. Suspicion for their murder falls on the Nairac (SAS)/UDR/UVF alliance.

22 August 1975 John McGleenan and Patrick Hughes were killed in a bomb attack on McGleenan's pub in Armagh City. Thomas Morris, who was injured in the explosion, died on 27 August.

1 September 1975 Denis Mullan was shot dead at his home in Moy.

22 September 1975 Mrs Margaret Hale died from injuries sustained in a bomb attack at McCann's public house near Loughgall.

23 October 1975 Peter McKearney and his wife Jennie were shot dead at their home in Moy.

29 October 1975 James Griffin was shot dead at his home hear Lurgan.

19 December 1975 Trevor Bracknell, Michael Donnelly and Patsy Donnelly were murdered in a gun and bomb attack on a pub in Silverbridge, South Armagh.

31 December 1975 Seamus Mallon died from injuries after an explosion at Vallely's pub, Loughgall, on 26 December.

The murder of Seán Farmer (32) of Moy, County Tyrone, and Colm McCartney (22) of Castledawson, County Derry, took place just a month after the Miami Showband massacre when a UVF/UDR gang struck again on 24 August. The two men were on their way home from the Dublin/Derry All-Ireland semi-final match in Dublin when they were stopped at a bogus Army checkpoint and murdered. Obviously they would have thought it was a normal Army checkpoint. At the inquest held in July 1976 members of an RUC patrol gave evidence that they also had been flagged down at this bogus UDR patrol checkpoint a short time before the Gaelic fans were shot.[68] A man waving a red torch, dressed in full military combat uniform with camouflage jacket, trousers and a green beret which had its cap badge blacked out, stopped them. The police saw another man in the ditch with an SLR. The RUC sergeant became suspicious. He knew there were no UDR or Army patrols out from Newtownhamilton. However, he thought it possible that a UDR patrol had wandered from the Keady direction by accident or design. The 'UDR man' who accosted them started back when he saw they were policemen. The police car then sped off. When the RUC men looked round they saw one of the men noting their car registration number. Some time later they heard shooting and when they went back they discovered the bodies of Farmer and McCartney some fifty yards apart lying face down near where their own car had been stopped. Tullyvallen, where they were murdered, is beside the County Monaghan border and only a few miles distant from Mullyash where John Francis Green was shot.

Fr Denis Faul complained about this illegal roadblock and gave other examples. 'The British authorities,' he said, 'have constantly refused to deal with complaints about illegal roadblocks and illegal happenings at roadblocks. For example on 20 August 1974 I was stopped at Lower Cloughfinn crossroads, near Ballygawley, at 10.30 pm by the UDR operating from a Morris Oxford car. When I pointed out that they were operating illegally I was threatened. I made a complaint to UDR HQ that night with no result. On 26 August 1974 I made a complaint that three young men were severely assaulted at Ballinderry Bridge, County Derry by UDR personnel who had operated a roadblock all evening. I was told from UDR Headquarters that no UDR patrol was in the district that night. Under pressure a senior British officer admitted to me – 'They are probably cooking the log book'. It must be pointed out that Councillor Patrick Kelly of Trillick, County Tyrone, was almost certainly abducted and killed by uniformed men operating a roadblock illegally near his home in June 1974. He assured his wife many times that he would only stop his car for a uniformed roadblock.'[69]

The *Sunday News* of 31 August 1975, just after the murder of the Gaelic fans, had an article entitled – 'UVF say "Our Boys are in the UDR"'. It pointed out that shortly after the deaths of Boyle and Somerville the UVF magazine *Combat* carried a full page of sympathy notices to the relatives. Two of the notices were published by members of the UDR in Portadown, Lurgan, Dungannon and Carrickfergus. Each of the notices was printed under the regimental crest of the UDR. A UVF spokesman was quoted in the article as saying – 'We do not stop our members from becoming involved in the security forces. Some of them are attached to the RUC, UDR and several full-time army regiments. They are not only active members of the UVF but they also feed us vital information on security and Republicans through the UCIA'. The *Irish Press,* 15 September 1975, had an article by Aidan Hennigan reporting from London on an interview given to the BBC on behalf of the UVF. The interviewee claimed that the UVF had the best intelligence network in Northern Ireland. He said – 'I can guarantee that 90 per cent of the people we have taken action against, we have an Army photograph to go along with their obituary. We must face it; there are security forces' personnel who agree with our standpoints. Let us say there is a thin line between UVF membership and security forces membership in certain cases'.

UDR Incidents in Fermanagh/Tyrone 1974

In County Tyrone and Fermanagh the UDR bore the burden for the loyalist paramilitaries. It was an area where loyalists were not organised. Protestant paramilitaries were organised in the north-east, Belfast/Lisburn, Portadown/Lurgan, and the Waterside, Derry, and its hinterland in County Derry. UDR subversives in Tyrone and Fermanagh linked up with the Waterside and Dungannon paramilitaries. Dungannon in turn fitted in with Portadown/Lurgan. A chronology of Fermanagh/Tyrone UDR incidents shows the UDR/IRA struggle:

17 January: Robert Jameson, UDR, Trillick, shot dead.

21 February: Four UDR men injured in a landmine attack on their land-rover near Augher, County Tyrone.

23 February: A gas cylinder was thrown through the window of a house in nationalist Carrickmore, County Tyrone, causing damage but no injuries.

3 March: Cpl Robert Moffett, UDR, of Blacktown, Newmills, Dungannon, killed in a landmine attack at Donaghmore, County Tyrone. Cpl Moffett, a former RUC 'B' Special was a member of the Bloomhill Purple Star Orange Lodge and Stewartstown Apprentice Boys of Derry Walker club.

3 March: Four UDR men were injured by an explosion at Eskaraghlough, County Tyrone.

5 March: A van bomb exploded in a housing estate in Coalisland, County Tyrone.

18 March: A 43-year-old Catholic schoolteacher was shot and wounded at his home in Cookstown, County Tyrone. The next day the UFF claimed responsibility. It said further steps would be taken against Catholics in County Tyrone in retaliation for recent land mine attacks against the UDR.

5 April: 'Red Hand Commandos' of Fermanagh/Tyrone warned that five Catholics would be killed for every Protestant.

11 April: Sgt David Sinnamond, UDR, was killed by a booby trap in Dungannon, County Tyrone.

21 April: James Murphy, a Catholic garage owner, was found shot dead at the Hilltop filling station at Kinawley, County Fermanagh.

2 May: Mrs Eva Martin, UDR, was killed in a gun attack on Clogher UDR post, County Tyrone.

7 May: Jim Devlin and his wife Gertrude were shot dead by gunmen near their home at Congo, Edendork, County Tyrone. Their daughter Patricia was wounded. (William Thomas Leonard, UDR, was sentenced to life imprisonment for the murders).

19 July: A car bomb exploded without warning outside a Catholic bar in Carrickmore. Two people were injured.

23 July: Tyrone Civil Rights Association criticised the UDR as sectarian. It said good relations depended on 'halting the bullies who are at present provoking and terrorising innocent people'. It singled out UDR platoons in the Trillick, Dromore and Fintona districts.

24 July: Mr Patrick Kelly, an Omagh councillor, was reported missing.[70] On the road near his home bloodstains and shirt buttons were found. He lived in Golan not far from Trillick. During the day he managed the Corner Bar in Trillick. He had taken over the management after the previous owner, Michael McCourt, had sold it because of threats. A UDR man was shot dead in Trillick on 21 January. On that same night a Catholic was shot dead at Boyle's bar at Cappagh, County Tyrone; three were injured. After the UDR man's murder McCourt's bar was attacked by gunmen using Sterling sub-machine-guns (British Army issue). Three men were injured. Threats were made to Michael McCourt. He sold the bar to Gilbert Tunney who asked Mr and Mrs Kelly to manage it. When Patrick Kelly's body was found the UFF claimed responsibility saying that his public house had been used by the IRA. (cf. ' "Clean up UDR", order', *Sunday World*, January 1984).

7 November: A bomb exploded outside the UDR centre in Dungannon.

20 November: Patrick Falls shot dead in a gun attack on a bar near Coalisland. (James Joseph Somerville was sentenced to life for this murder).

3 December: A bomb damaged the town hall in Omagh. The 'Protestant Action Group' claimed responsibility for that bomb and a bomb at the public toilets at Beragh, County Tyrone and in Cookstown on 5 December. The statement said the bombs were token protests at harassment by the RUC Special Branch, Omagh, and the British regiment stationed in Omagh, of UDR personnel in Mid-Ulster. The caller stressed that the group had 'no connection' with the UDR but supported it.

UDR Crime in the 'Triangle' Area

It is interesting to see the tip of the iceberg of UDR/loyalist paramilitary involvement in the 'triangle area' in the 1970s by looking at occasions when they came before the courts. The evidence illustrates the unsuitability of certain members and the laxity of vetting. Recommendations for UDR membership are usually given by Protestant clergymen but the final vetting is done by the RUC. Convictions included stealing guns, possession of ammunition, discharging guns and possession of guns in public while under the influence of alcohol, arson, drunken driving with previous convictions, photographing an RUC man, stealing goods, making a false report and wasting police time, sexual offences against children. Six other UDR members appeared in court during this period on various charges but they were acquitted.

In November 1973 ex-UDR member, Winston Buchanan, Horse Shoe Lane, Portadown, was charged with possession of explosives, detonator and a grenade. Bail £600. He was found guilty in January 1975 and sentenced to one year imprisonment. (*Irish News*, 2 November 1973; 30 January 1975.)

In November 1973 William Hanna (44), Houston Park, Lurgan, was charged with possession of one round of ammunition and two six-volt batteries wired together, found in his home. He was a former member of the RUC 'B' Specials, the Royal Irish Fusiliers, and an ex-sergeant instructor in the UDR. (*Irish News*, 16 November 1973.) According to the *Lurgan Mail*, 18 April 1974, he was fined £25 for having no firearm certificate and £15 for having one round of ammunition. Hanna was alleged to have been a high-ranking UVF member when he was shot dead by other loyalists during the UDA/UVF feud, 27 July 1975.

In November 1973, UDR member James Henry Hutchinson (31), a gun dealer of Drumnasoo, Portadown, was charged with possession of nine guns and 1,848 rounds of ammunition and explosive materials. (*Portadown News*, 23 November 1973.) He was found guilty. He received a two-year sentence for firearms and a two-year sentence to run concurrent for possession of 34 lbs of explosives on 13 July 1973. (*Portadown News*, 8 November 1974.)

In February 1974 ex-UDR member Private Roger Lockhart (27), Mullalish, Richhill, Armagh and non-member David Ritchie (27), Union Street, Portadown, were charged with bombing incidents in Armagh. Lockhart was jailed for ten years and Ritchie for seven years (*Portadown News*, 4 October 1974.) Lockhart faced nine further charges in 1975 including the planting of a bomb, armed robbery and the possession of 10 weapons. (*Belfast Telegraph*, 16 April 1975; *Portadown News*, 18 April 1975.)

June 1975, UDR part-time member Evan Alexander Irwin (23), Moygashel Park, Dungannon, who had been in the regiment for five years, was charged with and later convicted of possessing explosives and 11 bullets under suspicious circumstances at his home in May 1975. He also had a UVF rule book and three UVF presentation diaries (*Irish News*, 11 June 1975; *Dungannon Observer*, 14 June, 27 November 1975.)

January 1976, UDR member Joseph Denis McConville (24), Meadowview Drive, Annaghmore, Portadown, was charged with possession of 100 9 mm bullets, ammunition which he stole from Magilligan Army Camp and sold to a UVF member William Corrigan also of Meadowview Drive for £2.

McConville was arrested on 21 January. The court heard that McConville had been dismissed from the UDR. Lord Justice McGonigal said this was the sort of supply of ammunition which at that moment was responsible for deaths and seriously wounding people in that particular area. (*Belfast Telegraph*, 27 January 1976; *Irish News*, 28 January 1976.) McConville was given a two-year prison term on 14 September 1976 by Judge Richard Chamber. (*Belfast Telegraph*, 15 September 1976.) Corrigan also received a two-year suspended sentence when he admitted handling the stolen ammunition and having it in suspicious circumstances. William Corrigan (41) was shot dead outside his home at Annaghmore by the IRA on 14 October 1976. As he was driving his car into a driveway, the gunman opened up with a Kalashnikov rifle firing at least 25 shots. His son Leslie working at a car nearby was shot in the back several times and died on 25 October. Two miles away, a Catholic, Peter Woolsey, had been shot dead by a loyalist gang at Cornascriebe on 11 October. (*Belfast Telegraph*, 14 October 1976; *News Letter* 15 October 1976: 26 October 1976.) Thomas McGrath was convicted of the killing of the Corrigans in January 1979. Extraordinary forensic evidence was given at his trial that his teeth marks were left on a half-eaten apple thrown on the ground in the nearby orchard of Corrigan's home. Republican circles are adamant that McGrath was not there.

In July 1977 two part-time UDR men, Mervyn Joseph Faloon (28), The Mount, Tandragee, a Lance Corporal, and Kenneth Young (32) of Dawson Green, Portadown, were charged with the attempted murder of William James Keeley on 12 July 1977 and possessing a .22 Walther pistol with intent to endanger life. Both were remanded in custody. (*Belfast Telegraph*, 14 July 1977.) On 1 February 1978 they were both found guilty of shooting into houses in Obins Street, Portadown, a 'flashpoint' just before the Orangemen were due to march; they were sentenced to five years imprisonment. (*Irish News*, 2 February 1978.)

Captain Robert Nairac[71]

1900 hrs. August 1973.
Tomorrow the Grenadier Guards advance party arrive and I have to show the platoon commander assigned to me the Shankill in all its glory...I'm still at the Ops. Desk at ten o'clock in the morning, having had a brief respite for a wash and shave followed by breakfast, when the OC comes in with the grenadiers advance party, to introduce me.

'Tony, this is Bob Nairac who will be assigned to you for the handover period'.

I shake hands with a stocky guy with curly black hair, far removed from the normal type of Guards' officer you usually meet. I take in the broken nose and cheerful grin and think 'Thank God I haven't got one of those guys with a mouthful of marbles'. The pleasantries over, he goes off to dump his kit and I'm left alone again with my thoughts and the radio operator gabbling away in my ear...

Bob is the one with all the questions, insatiable for knowledge, expressing disappointment that his Coy is not in the Ardoyne and not convinced when we tell him that we, the Shankill Coy, have had more finds and by far the biggest contact of the tour. He is no sooner in the place then he wants to get on the first patrol. It just so happens that I'm due out with one of my sections in an hour's time so he goes away happy, to get his kit together. Clive and I look at each other in disbelief. There's no way we would be so keen to get out there and certainly not at this stage in the tour. In fact the OC had to hound us to get us out into the street. Well, each to his own. Right now I want to stay safe.

Out in the street and Bob is like a foxhound, digging into everything, questioning everything, wanting to cram five months knowledge into one short two-hour patrol. The lads are working well, putting on their best performance to impress the 'crap-hats' and the two hours goes past quickly without incident.

This vignette of Nairac is taken from A.F.N. Clarke's book *Contact* (1983). Clarke served as a paratrooper officer in Belfast and Crossmaglen.

Robert Nairac was a native of Standish Court, Stonehouse, Gloucestershire, son of a distinguished opthalmic surgeon, Dr Maurice Nairac. They were a religious family; his father a Catholic, his mother Barbara an Anglican. Nairac went to Ampleforth College which is attached to the Benedictine Abbey of St Laurence in North Yorkshire. The Preparatory School is at Gilling Castle; the Upper School, the College itself, is in North Yorkshire. There is a strong military tradition in the school. It has a Territorial Army Cadet Force with a staff of five officers. A high proportion of officers in the British Army is Catholic. SAS officers educated there include David Stirling, the founder of the SAS, Lord Lovat and members of his family, and Sir Hugh Fraser. Cardinal Basil Hume knew Robert Nairac when he was abbot there. When he went missing the Cardinal expressed his deep personal sorrow: 'This is a terrible blow. He is a very fine and very courageous young man. I am deeply saddened by the reported death of Robert. I remember him well from his school days. It makes me realise even more vividly what anguish and pain so many people have suffered in the long years of civil disturbance'.

After Ampleforth Robert Nairac went to Lincoln College, Oxford, where he studied history. He is best remembered for reviving the university boxing team; he boxed himself, hence perhaps the broken nose. He boxed for a season for the Gloucester City Club. He was also a rugby player. He had a flair for touches of eccentricity or showmanship; he kept a pet kestrel at Oxford and matched this later by keeping a huge dog at the Castledillon

SAS post. He received his military education at Sandhurst and joined the Grenadier Guards, passing from there in to 22 SAS. He did an Intelligence course at the Army's Intelligence Centre at Ashford in Kent and was picked for special training for MI6 in Northern Ireland. It is said that he worked as a labourer in Irish districts in London to try to pick up an Irish accent.

It is clear from A. F. N. Clarke's account that he served a term in Belfast. In March 1979, the official magazine *Soldier* stated that, by 1973, 'he spent a lot of time on the peace line between the Shankill and Ardoyne working with the "Local Fianna and Tartan gangs"'. He was SAS at this time working as an Intelligence officer in his parent regiment. The next move was to Castledillon where he was second in command at the SAS centre there, liaison man with Holyroyd, MI6 and the local RUC in the form of a Special Branch man who was in tow with loyalist paramilitaries; Nairac also worked closely with loyalist paramilitaries.

Holyroyd had the feeling that Nairac wanted to succeed him as the local intelligence officer when MI5 took control. This seems to have happened and has enabled the authorities and some authors to classify him as non-SAS when he was killed. When the SAS was sent in to South Armagh in big numbers in 1976, Nairac was its guide and mentor. He was still based in Castledillon but had a bedroom in Bessbrook Army centre and often stayed there. Nairac became a familiar figure in Crossmaglen and the South Armagh area. Sometimes he appeared in uniform with the resident regiment; other times he moved around in his donkey jacket and sported a moustache. He continually tried to make conversations with local people and attended republican commemorations in cemeteries. He went on uniformed patrols in Crossmaglen and went out of his way to chat people up. In fact photographs of Nairac circulated freely around Crossmaglen before he was assassinated. They were hastily burned when he was shot.

Captain Robert Nairac was 29 years of age when he was abducted from the Three Step Inn near the village of Dromintee in South Armagh on 14 May 1977. He is presumed dead. His body has never been found. He left Bessbrook Army Camp at 9.25 pm on 14 May 1977 in a red Triumph Dolomite car. He was last seen by Captain David Allan Collett of the Worcester and Forresters Regiment who was the operations officer responsible that evening for logging personnel in and out. Nairac was armed with a Browning pistol, serial number IT 7774. The gun had special modifications: the usual safety catch had been replaced by a larger one and the hand grip had been filed. He wore the loaded pistol under his arm in a special holster he himself had bought. Presumably with a full-type jacket, it would not be seen. (Captain Collett said in court that Captain Nairac had a small personal pistol in his room at Bessbrook). He had a spare magazine for the pistol. He also carried 80 rounds of 8.82 ammunition for his SLR rifle; the rifle however had not been taken from the armoury in Bessbrook. His car was equipped with a high-powered transmitter camouflaged as a car radio. The microphone was under the seat. There was a panic button on the dashboard. Captain Collett received a message from Nairac at 9.58 pm just before he went into the Three Step Inn. He was due to call again at 11.30 pm. The fact that he was logged out and that further check-calls were arranged prove that he was acting under orders. Whatever his mission, it was official.

It is said by some in South Armagh that Nairac was in and out of the Inn a number of times the week before he was abducted. That may be rumour. He was certainly there on Friday, 13 May from 9 pm. He left at 10.15 pm. He returned on Saturday night. It is thought that he had made a contact with a member of the Provisional IRA in the district. Whether this person played a game as a double agent or was an informer, one does not know. Nairac was wearing a black donkey jacket, a pullover, flared grey trousers and worn brown suede shoes. One witness described him that night as having a black droopy moustache, black shaggy hair and wearing a long black coat. There was no premeditated plan to abduct Nairac. He was recognised as an undercover soldier; his name had already been linked in gossip with the death of IRA member Peter Cleary. There was also a suspicion of 'dirty tricks' following the deaths of two IRA men, Jim Loughrey and Seán Campbell, in a bomb explosion at Killeen on 6 December 1975. The bomb had been moved a few times by the IRA: they finally decided to prime it and await a target since they did not want it lying about lest it prove a danger at the Jonesborough mart. The night they were killed Loughrey and Campbell approached the bomb; two other IRA men took up positions at two distant points; Loughrey and Campbell came back and remarked that there was fresh earth around the bomb. 'The rabbits must have been tearing at it,' one of them said. It was more a light-hearted remark than a serious worry. Unknown to them the bomb had been primed by British soldiers; Campbell and Loughrey returned to prime it; it exploded, killing them when one of them touched it.

There were a number of IRA men in the Inn on Saturday night, 14 May. They recognised Nairac and began to plot to abduct him. They checked on his conversation with various people. One of the stories was that he said he was home from Canada and wanted to visit some relatives in Dundalk; he enquired the shortest route by side-roads to Dundalk; when told to go the Tiefcrum Road by Forkhill he said he did not want to go by the barracks. He said his name was 'Danny'. The common opinion is that Nairac must have thought the people very 'green' not to recognise him. He put on an Irish accent; some people said it sounded genuinely local; others say it had a Belfast ring. There was a great crowd in the bar. An IRA man watched Nairac in the mirror behind the bar. Nairac twice bought a pint of Guinness and a packet of twenty cigarettes. He went to the toilet at least three times. At about 11.15 pm when he was coming out of the toilet, he asked one of the musicians could a Belfast man sing a song. He was asked to write the request down on a piece of paper. He said, 'No, just call it out'. He gave his name as Danny McErlean. He sang two republican songs, one of them 'The Broad Black Brimmer'. He told the band what key he wanted to sing in and was quite a good singer. When he had finished singing he went back to the bar and joined the same people there he had been talking to before he sang. The band finished playing at 11.35 pm and started to pack up. Nairac was still there at 11.35 pm because one of the musicians accidentally hit him on the head with his guitar when he was detaching it; he apologised to Nairac and he accepted it. At about 12, one of the musicians heard a scuffle at the top of the car park as he was getting into the van but took no notice of it thinking it was an ordinary fight.

After the band stopped, a youth was asked by an IRA man to scout the road, to go as far as the Border Inn and see if there was any Army about. He left with another man, scouted the road, saw no Army and came back. When Nairac left the pub he was followed out by an IRA man. The impression was that Nairac seemed to panic a little before he left the pub; perhaps it was just a sign that he was late in contacting Bessbrook. Nairac headed for his car. The IRA man called on him to halt. Just as he got to the car Nairac stopped and reached inside his coat for his pistol; the IRA man, well-known for his boxing ability, closed on him, hit him a punch on the jaw, at the same time throwing his arm wide and knocking the pistol out of Nairac's hand. Both men closed in a wrestling struggle. Three men who had followed closely on the IRA man leaving the pub ran up and joined in the struggle, kicking and punching Nairac. They overpowered him. A car was brought forward and Nairac was bundled into it. Perhaps as many as nine altogether gathered round Nairac to overpower him. The gun was picked up and brought with the party. Four men accompanied Nairac in the car. A second car followed. They drove to Ravensdale Park, taking a little road to the left on the Newry-Dundalk Road, crossed over a little humpbacked bridge that spans the Flurry stream. Nairac was taken into the field on the left beside the bridge as one turns into the park. He was beaten there and interrogated. The holster, magazine of bullets and a driving license with a Belfast address were taken from him. Matches and lighters were lit. Nairac stuck to the one story, that he was from Belfast, that he was a 'Stickie' (member of the Official IRA); he named an Official IRA man from the Dromintee area – the name was authentic. He never admitted that he was a soldier. Two men went on to Dundalk for a more senior IRA man. A .32 revolver was collected from a wall near the border. When they arrived Nairac was too weak. One IRA member discharged a shot and grazed one of his companions. Two of the IRA walked Nairac up the centre of the field supporting him; another walked behind. The more 'junior' of those present walked to the gate. Half-way up the field Nairac collapsed on to the ground.

He asked for a priest. One of the IRA men pretended he was a priest but Nairac did not say anything. He was taken further into the field. One of them hit him a few times over the head with a stick. Two men moved off leaving one IRA man with him. This man then fired a shot. The group scattered. They did not return to Nairac's car lest a back-up Army group would have it under surveillance. Someone, however, must have moved the body that night. It was seen as late as 10.30 am the next day in a sitting position, legs stretched out, propped against the wall of the bridge. The body must have been removed on Sunday, 15 May.

On 18 May a Garda car was stopped by two fishermen. They explained how they found two bullets, a small sum of money and a piece of metal with a spring attached at the Flurry river bank. The Gardaí went to the scene and saw blood stains on the grass and stones of the bridge. There were signs of a struggle. On the grass near the bridge the Gardaí found a small amount of money in copper and silver and a spring clip. A piece of lead from a 7.65 mm bullet was found in a ledge of the bridge. Ten days later the Gardaí went to a different part of the field where they found two areas of blood and blood-stained stones, also a round of 9 mm ammunition.

Nairac was given some leeway at Bessbrook when he did not report back at 11.30 pm. Sometimes he was late. When he did not check in by midnight Captain Collett became anxious. He consulted his commanding officer and a search party was sent out to look for him. It was not until 9 am on Sunday that his car was located by a helicopter standing alone in the car park of the Three Step Inn.

There is always a military back-up for a solitary SAS man or intelligence officer. Surely the Army knew where he was when he radioed base at 9.58 pm? Why was there no back-up for him on that fateful night? Why did it take the Army nine hours to find his car at the Three Step Inn? Surely even before he left his base he would have pin-pointed the object of his mission, a rendezvous with an 'informer' at or near the Three Step Inn? Standard procedure for surveillance is known. Troops are landed by helicopter. They make their way across country and seal off an area. Surveillance lasts two or three days. When an undercover soldier moves into danger there is external cover and soldiers ready to 'move in'. Brigadier David W. Woodford, under whom Captain Nairac served, when questioned by journalists after his disappearance, admitted that it was not normal for Nairac to work alone and the circumstances were being looked into.

An RUC constable found Nairac's car locked in the car park at the Three Step Inn on 15 May. It was intact save for the broken outside mirror. The car keys were found near the driver's door. There was a trail of blood from a spot seven feet from the car, along the edge of the car park in the Forkhill direction. Coins and cigarettes were also found near the car.

On 28 May Liam Townson, an unemployed joiner from Dromintee

living in Dundalk, was arrested by Gardaí. He was charged with the murder of Captain Robert Nairac and possession of firearms with intent to endanger life. Garda evidence at his trial maintained that he brought them on 30 May to Thistle Cross and showed them where blood-stained clothes and shoes were hidden in a plastic bag under a pile of stones and nearby, also in a plastic bag, two guns, a holster, a magazine and some ammunition. One of the guns was Nairac's Browning pistol. The magazine and holster were also his. A forensic examination showed that the bullets found at Ravensdale had been marked by the firing pin of the second gun, a revolver, which was defective and prone to misfire. This may have led to the accidental shooting at the scene of the murder. The second gun, a .32 revolver, was procured apparently because of an IRA ruling that a man is not to be executed with his own gun. At his trial a case was made by the defence that Townson had been threatened by the Gardaí that he would be handed over to the SAS; attention was drawn to his long hours of interrogation. He was found guilty of murder on 8 November 1977 and given the mandatory sentence of penal servitude for life. He was also convicted of possession of firearms with intent to endanger life and given a concurrent sentence of five years. On 4 November the Special Criminal Court had ruled as admissible two verbal statements of Townson confessing to the murder of Captain Robert Nairac but excluded five other alleged statements including one allegedly dictated to Gardaí in a patrol car parked near the Border.

On 15 December 1978 five men from South Armagh were jailed at a Diplock court in Northern Ireland by Lord Justice Gibson for their part in Captain Nairac's abduction and murder. The case involved the Criminal Jurisdiction Act of 1975 which allows certain serious prosecutions to be carried out on either side of the Border. It was the first murder case to be conducted in Northern Ireland when the victim's body was still not found. Their conviction also took place at a time when serious allegations were made regarding ill-treatment of detainees in the interrogation centres of Castlereagh and Gough barracks. Those convicted were Gerard Patrick Fearon (20), Thomas Patrick Morgan (18), Daniel Joseph O'Rourke (32), Owen Francis Rocks (33) and Michael Joseph McCoy (19). Fearon was jailed for life for murder with no recommendation for any specific term and to a total of 22 years for grievous bodily harm, kidnapping, possession of a pistol and membership of the IRA. Morgan was ordered to be detained during the pleasure of the Northern Ireland Secretary for murder and was given a total of 22 years for possession of the murder weapon, grievous bodily harm and kidnapping. O'Rourke was given 10 years for manslaughter and 7 years for kidnapping. McCoy was given 5 years for kidnapping and Rocks received two 3 year sentences for withholding and failing to given information. All sentences were to run concurrently. The impression of observers at the trial was that the British Army was embarrassed by the whole affair and did not push the case to extremes; all the men sentenced in the North were released in minimum periods. It was accepted that other men had escaped the law. Townson alone remains in prison in the Republic.

Cardinal Hume, Archbishop of Westminister and former Abbot of Ampleforth, made an appeal for the safe return of Captain Nairac when he disappeared. He knew Nairac when he was a student. Captain Nairac's sister Rosamund said, 'Since he has always loved Ireland and the Irish it is ironic that he may have died while trying as a volunteer to contribute to peace in Ireland. If he is dead he died trying to do what he felt and stated to be his duty'. The Army officially denied that he had anything to do with the SAS. Fr Anthony McCabe of St Joseph's Catholic Church, Stonehouse, said: 'Captain Nairac was a very charming man. He was a regular worshipper when he was with his family. I never asked him about his career in the Army but I gathered he was fulfilling a normal peace-keeping role'.

When Cardinal Hume made his appeal for the release of Captain Nairac, before it was realised that he must be dead, British Intelligence was in hot water. His disappearance hit the headlines. It had questions to answer. It directed attention from itself by making him a hero. He was given the George Cross in record time. Medals usually come slowly and proceed from citations down the line. This one came from the top. The move diverted the press from investigating. His tragedy was used in propaganda abroad. An article 'Keeping up ... with Youth', appeared in *Parade* magazine distributed with the *Sunday Free Press* in the USA: ... 'He was tall, handsome, intelligent and friendly. He felt deeply about the war in Northern Ireland and, rather than take part in parades in front of Buckingham Palace, he volunteered for intelligence duty. He loved Ireland and the Irish and thought somehow he might contribute to peace'.

The Case of Seamus O'Brien

Another West Belfast man who fell victim to the machinations of the SAS was Seamus O'Brien of Turf Lodge, Belfast. His story was written up by Roger Faligot in *Britain's Military Strategy in Ireland*, 'The Kitson experiment'. Faligot's version is that O'Brien (24) left his wife Sheila at Easter 1973 and went to live with a girlfriend, a young Protestant in Larne. They moved to Bangor and O'Brien socialised with his girlfriend in loyalist paramilitary clubs. There he was taken under the wing of a British agent, 'Bobby', who posed as a former British soldier interested in socialism and ran his own little organisation (it did not really exist) within the Red Hand Commandos; 'Bobby's' purported object was to collect information on those committing sectarian murders in order to stop them This British intelligence agent succeeded in persuading O'Brien to go back to Turf Lodge to establish links with the military wing of the IRSP; an exchange of republican/loyalist information was to follow, benefiting of course the British agent. Faligot maintains that O'Brien also went to live in the Short Strand Catholic ghetto where 'Bobby' introduced him to another agent 'Brian'. Faligot's theory is that the IRA grew suspicious of him when he supplied them with a detailed account of Rev. Ian Paisley's movements; this led to his assassination by the IRA.

There is another 'republican' version of the fate of Seamus O'Brien. This theory maintains that in the first week of August 1975 a wallet belonging to O'Brien was found and that he was living in Bangor at the time. The wallet contained the following items:-

(1) Photocopies of republicans

(2) Two phone numbers (a) a Craigavon number with six digits; Craigavon, however, had only five digits; the six numbers were dialled – the RUC answered (b) the second number was dialled; the person who answered gave another number; when this number was rung a woman who answered asked who the caller wanted; the caller at a loss said 'Michael'; the republican caller must have hit on a security number because he heard somebody at the other end say 'keep him talking, we'll get a tag on where the call is from'; the caller rang off and the phone was watched from a safe distance; a car pulled up and four men got out; two had weapons drawn.

Other items in the wallet included airplane tickets, an identity card for selling *Encyclopædia Britannica*, membership cards for clubs in Bangor. O'Brien was pulled in for questioning in depth by the IRA about the contents of the wallet. They found out that he was going with a girl from Bangor; he had left his wife who was from Andersonstown; he got a house almost immediately he went to live in Bangor in an estate run by the Red Hand Commandos; the girl he was living with had strong connections with paramilitaries; father and uncles; he admitted that he had met a Protestant who had 'felt' for the Catholics; this man got material out, e.g. photographs of wanted men (that is how O'Brien explained the photographs of republicans in his wallet); the man who gave O'Brien this information was later arrested and charged with possession and membership of the Red Hand. Even with this information it was decided to let O'Brien go, since there was no real proof that he was working with the Special Branch or loyalists at that time (August 1975).

On Saturday, 10 January 1976 it was noticed that O'Brien and a girl were visiting a few social clubs in Belfast. Later the same girl was caught trying to take a bomb into a Catholic bar. In her statement she implicated O'Brien. The flat used by them as a base was staked out and then raided by an IRA Active Service Unit. O'Brien was then interrogated about his involvement with loyalists and the Special Branch. He admitted this.

On the afternoon of Saturday, 17 January 1976 the body of Seamus O'Brien was found by British soldiers in a ditch at Hannastown on the outskirts of Belfast. The location was the corner of the Glen and Glenside Roads. He was in a kneeling position, his hands tied behind his back and he had a gunshot wound in the back of his head. In a statement the Belfast Brigade of the IRA said that Seamus O'Brien had been killed for spying for the British Army and a loyalist paramilitary group. They claimed that he had been discovered planting a bomb in a Catholic area of Belfast. A statement supporting O'Brien came from a loyalist organisation calling itself the 'Ulster Army', (from 'Bobby' and 'Brian' the undercover British soldiers?). It said that O'Brien had been working for it, that he was a 'true Ulsterman and good Catholic who wanted to break the stranglehold of the republicans over ordinary Catholics'.

Following his death Alan Murray wrote an article in the *Irish Press*, 20 January 1976, 'The Spy who Died after a Lover's Tiff'. It was based on 'loyalist sources'. According to the article O'Brien, known as Shay to the loyalists, had been spying on the Provisionals, the Officials and the IRSP for almost eighteen months. That would send the story back to mid-1974. It dates his first 'arrest' by the Provisionals as mid-1974 when he was held for 28 hours in Bingnion Drive, Andersonstown. The 'loyalist' version is that he deliberately left his wallet containing photographs of the top Provisional active service unit in a taxi. This was to draw the IRA. When they picked him up he claimed he had inroads into the RUC. They released him then as a 'friend'. The article states:-

'O'Brien supplied names, addresses and locations of arms dumps to loyalists in the 18 months and helped build up a comprehensive file on the republican movement. Shortly before his death he had compiled the names and addresses of the officers in the Provisional IRA and volunteers from the New Lodge Road. He supplied names and addresses, nicknames and haunts. O'Brien was regarded by loyalists as a shrewd and fearless man. He claimed that he had carried out on his own a number of operations against the Provisionals and the Officials and had made them appear as part of an internal dispute. O'Brien was the chief "intelligence man". His contact on the loyalist side was a man he referred to as "Michael". These two had regular meetings in the Green Briar pub and it was there O'Brien passed on his reports. This was on the Provisionals' doorstep and it was a pub O'Brien frequented quite often ... he was able to pass himself through every republican area, including Crossmaglen and Dundalk, where he compiled lists of active Provisional men and women from the areas. O'Brien lived one time around the Carrickfergus area and sold loyalist newspapers at one stage. He moved to Bangor, County Down and lived with a woman there. The woman is a Protestant ... His last meeting with the loyalists was at the end of December ... O'Brien was picked up... on Sunday, 11 January . He was taken to a house in Andersonstown and was there tortured by the Provisionals ... the loyalists denied that O'Brien had intended to blow up the social club in a Catholic area, as the Provisionals had suggested. They said the bomb was intended for use at a meeting where some members of the Belfast Brigade of the Provisionals would be present on Friday last. O'Brien had apparently requested that the bomb be left at a flat in The Mount area of east Belfast, where he and his girlfriend were living. The device was left on either Friday or Saturday of the week before last. It was left by a loyalist paramilitary man and when he arrived at the flat, O'Brien's girlfriend apparently said to him "Don't I know you?" The man bluffed his way out of the flat. But O'Brien, according to the loyalists, had a row with the girl over another girl and had struck her. She apparently decided she would go and "inform" on O'Brien because of the argument. The loyalists with whom O'Brien had contact say he informed them of the row and was anxious about what the girl might do. Before they could do anything, however, the girl fled the flat and O'Brien was picked up by the Provisionals shortly afterwards. The main thing the loyalists wished to make clear was that O'Brien had not worked for the British Army. They claim that he had worked entirely for the loyalists and that he was in their words a "true Catholic Ulsterman"'.

The theories on O'Brien certainly diverge. Was he a spy solely for a loyalist organisation or, unknown to the loyalists, was he an agent for British undercover soldiers who used the loyalists as his cover?

Republican News, 24 January 1976 and *An Phoblacht,* 30 January, published O'Brien's photograph and carried the same article – 'The Belfast Brigade, Óglaigh na hÉireann, are maintaining a discreet silence on the Seamus O'Brien case until all the evidence uncovered by IRA intelligence units is examined in detail. O'Brien, disturbed while priming a 25 lb satchel bomb outside the fire-doors of a local club in Andersontown, was apprehended later after a republican patrol had trailed him to his home. A .32 semi-automatic Japanese pistol was seized when an Active Service Unit arrested O'Brien. Although the Belfast Brigade are not issuing any comprehensive statement for the time being, one will be made later; it is thought the loyalist agent was planning to bomb pubs and clubs in and around Andersontown'. The account then goes on to quote extensively from Alan Murray's article in the *Irish Press.* The Belfast Brigade, however, never issued any detailed statement on O'Brien.

O'Brien worked as a roofer in the Short Strand area for a firm owned by a man from the Suffolk area, Belfast, and often gave workmates lifts home when he lived in Tullymore Gardens, Andersonstown. He is remembered as a womaniser. Since he worked in the Short Strand area and lived there in The Mount area, suspicion has fallen on him of being connected with attacks on pubs and clubs there. The clubs are very near Mount Street, all within 100 yards. On 6 April 1975 there was a bomb attack on the CESA club in Clyde Street. On 12 April the Strand Bar on the corner of Anderson Street and the Short Strand was attacked shortly before closing time. It was a bar frequented by pensioners. A number of men drew up in a white Hillman, fired six or seven shots into the pub, then threw in a cylinder bomb containing about 20 lbs of explosives. Five people were killed and 39 injured. The five victims were Mrs Elizabeth Carson (64), a widow of Anderson Street, Mrs Agnes McAnoy (63) of Thompson Street, married with three children, Mrs Mary McAleavey (57) of Mountpottinger Road, married with eleven children, Mrs Marie Bennett (42), of Clyde Street, married with seven children and Mr Arthur Penn (33) of Altear Street married with three children. A sixth victim, Michael Mulligan, died of injuries on 19 April 1975. On 31 December 1975 at 8.45 pm a bomb exploded at the Bridge End bar in the Short Strand. A group of teenagers had gathered for a drink before going to a disco. The bomb went off at 8.45 pm without warning. One teenager was severely injured. He lost his legs in subsequent operations. *Republican News*, 10 April 1976, carried a letter protesting about harassment of the same boy by British soldiers when he was being pushed in a wheelchair by a friend. Soldiers gathered round the wheelchair and sang 'Dance to your daddy'. After O'Brien's murder three people were injured in an attack on Kelly's bar on the Short Strand on 29 January 1976.

O'Brien was most active in 1975, a time of rivalry and shoot-outs between paramilitary organisations. It was the year of the uneasy 'truce'. From the British Army point of view the dissension, internecine murders and confusion were welcome. It was in the interest of their undercover soldiers to foment strife. It also drew the heat off British forces; for example, in September 1975 there was not a single British Army, RUC or UDR casualty.

The Murder of Niall O'Neill

The murder of Seamus O'Brien had a strange sequel. A magazine called *Shatter* (not in British Library lists) contained an article on the SAS under the title 'Spyfile'. The magazine is undated and may have been for private circulation. It is well printed and illustrated, reminiscent of the jingo-type magazine circulated among soldiers. On the SAS in Northern Ireland it carried (a) the story of the IRA leader who stopped bomb manufacturers from using contraceptive sheaths, (b) the use of brothels by British intelligence, (c) an account of an SAS man pitching an IRA sniper from a roof to the concrete below (I do not know of this incident), (d) SAS booby-trapped bomb planters' cars, (e) how The Four Square Laundry was used by SAS assassination squads, (f) how the number of Protestant/Catholic terrorists, IRA and enemy agents eliminated by SAS is less than two score, (g) a veiled reference to premature detonation by radio triggering, citing the killing of a bombmaking mastermind blown up along with three accomplices in Bann Street, Belfast (I know of no such incident in Bann Street; three

IRA men were killed in a premature explosion in Clonard Street on 9 March 1972; 8 people including 4 members of the IRA were killed in an explosion in Anderson Street, Short Strand, Belfast, 28 May 1972 – it may have been an accidental detonation), (h) a piece on Seaman – 'One man who served with SAS, 31 year-old Englishman David Seaman, started betraying SAS secret operations to the Dublin Press; his body was found in a County Armagh ditch in early 1972', (i) how when the Government sent in 150 SAS in January 1976 those pictured on television and in press were decoys; the SAS operated in secret, (j) how SAS units operated in all kinds of vehicles with souped-up engines, (k) Kenneth Littlejohn affair, (l) the capture by Irish security forces of an SAS agent sent into the south to assassinate IRA leaders.

Of special interest is the reference to the assassination of Niall O'Neill: 'In retaliation for the (Russian trained) IRA Special Intelligence Unit's assassination of Top British agent Seamus O'Brien, the SAS carried out a reprisal raid. "It was a cold Belfast night. Inside a semi in Thirlmere Gardens, in the suburb of Cavehill, IRA, SIU man Niall O'Niell (*sic*) is sleeping off a night's drinking. Outside three black-clad figures get out of a Ford Cortina parked nearby. Silently they vault over a gate and file along the alley at the side of O'Niell's house. In less than a minute, the first man had slipped the catch on a back window, letting his two companions into the house. Their gym shoes make no sound as they climb the stairs. One waits outside the bedroom door as the other two enter, each with a silenced 9 mm Browning hi-power automatic in their hands". On the morning of Thursday, January 22, 1976, the life of Niall O'Niell ended with two bullets in the back of his head'.

Niall O'Neill was shot by an MRF team, a mixture of loyalists and SAS. The shooting took place between 3.45 am and 4 am. The O'Neill family, especially Mr O'Neill senior, was security conscious because of murders of Catholics in North Belfast and therefore kept the inner doors downstairs locked at night. One of the gunmen, who must have been slim and agile, gained entrance to the house through a ventilation window which opened out and was about 15 feet from the ground. The window was at the back and gave access to the living room. The living room door was the one door downstairs left unlocked that night. The gunman unlocked the dining room door, then the kitchen door and finally the back door to admit his companions. Niall's sister was awakened from sleep by a creaking on the stairs. She thought it was the wind. The gunmen must have had torches because she saw a light. In her half-sleep she thought someone had left the landing light on. The father and mother were awakened by the shooting. They thought at first it was in the street. The father got up and fumbled for his slippers, intending to go downstairs and investigate. The action probably saved his life. By the time he found them the gunmen were gone. One of them had paused on his way out to lift a diary from the table in the hall. He had examined it and had thrown it on the floor. Mrs O'Neill ran into Niall's bedroom and found him slumped dead between two beds. She knelt and said an Act of Contrition. Róisín, his sister, joined in the prayers. When his brother, Fr Paddy O'Neill, arrived at 4.30 am the RUC and British Army were already there and also other members of the family. Fr McGarry had anointed Niall. Later Fr O'Neill brought the family to the Somerton Road oratory where he said Mass for the deceased.

Niall O'Neill had been shot six times. The RUC did not collect the cartridge shells from the bedroom floor and only made one gesture at forensic in fingerprinting the ventilation window. Niall O'Neill was not a member of the IRA. However, one of his lifelong friends was a member. He had been with this companion socially the night he was shot. He told him that he was aware that his movements were being watched for some time and expressed a fear that he might be shot. He actually gave the number of the car following him to his friend saying, 'If anything happens to me, you'll know'. He accepted that he had received a clear warning a few days before his death when in the company of this same friend he was stopped by a British Army patrol. One soldier, whom he described as, 'nice and not like the rest', said to him, 'You are out of your depth and out of your area'. Indications went back even further than that. He had been on the staff of British Midland Airways. One night an official of the firm came to his home and told him that his services were no longer required, that the Airways did not have enough work. Niall always thought that was not the full story. His next job, managing a number of licensed premises, brought him to areas as diverse as Carrickfergus, frequented by the UDA, and a pub in Andersonstown frequented by the IRA.

On 23 January 1976 the family of Niall O'Neill issued a statement denying reports which had linked their son to an explosion in Belfast. The family said 'they were deeply distressed by news media reports of circumstances surrounding his death'. They were particularly upset by a report attributed to a police spokesman which said that shortly after the explosion in North Street arcade which killed four people, Niall had left his work as an off-license manager and that since then detectives had not known his whereabouts. Their statement continued:- 'Niall's employer has confirmed to the O'Neill family that the dead man was not absent from work during the period stated. The family hope that even at this late hour this stain might be withdrawn from the good name of their son'. Protestant neighbours also gave statements asserting that he was not absent from his home at that time.

When the family's statement was carried in the newspapers and on television a senior policeman called at their home to complain that the RUC was upset by their action, that it could have been a reserve policeman who had issued the RUC statement. Fr O'Neill replied that his family was even more upset and that the issuing of a false statement by the RUC was their own responsibility.

On 13 January a bomb exploded prematurely on the first floor of a do-it-yourself shop in North Street Arcade, Belfast. Twenty-one people were injured. Four people died, Ian Gallagher (42) part owner of the shop, Mrs Mary Ellen Dornan (30) a part-time shop worker and two others who were later claimed by the Provisional IRA as members, Martin McDonagh (22) and Rosemary Bleakley (19) of Newington Avenue, North Belfast. Martin McDonagh's address was given as Thirlmere Gardens off the Antrim Road, the same avenue where Niall O'Neill lived. A caller to the home of Mrs McDonagh, mother of Martin, said that her son had been killed. Martin McDonagh had not been immediately identified. Nobody has been made amenable for the murder of Niall O'Neill.

Niall O'Neill is not claimed as an IRA volunteer or officer in the republican 'Roll of Honour'. Martin McDonagh is claimed as a volunteer in 3rd Battalion, Belfast. In a later chapter I deal with other SAS activity in the Antrim Road area in 1976. Inter-connected dates are:-

13 January, premature explosion in North Street arcade; IRA volunteers Martin McDonagh (Thirlmere Gardens) and Rosemary Bleakley killed.

17 January, assassination of Seamus O'Brien by the IRA. 22 January, assassination of Niall O'Neill of Thirlmere Gardens.

26 March, rape of Mrs Irwin, wife of police surgeon Dr Robert Irwin allegedly by an SAS soldier.

4 April, Mrs Margaret Gamble stabbed to death.

The murder of Niall O'Neill fits into a demographic pattern. In the 1970s Catholics from the New Lodge Road district off the Antrim Road were moving across the Antrim Road into the suburban areas of Cavehill Road, Cliftonville Road and on to the Antrim Road itself. Loyalists and British Intelligence adopted a policy of assassination to prevent this. Here is a catalogue of murders of Catholics in the area in 1975-76.

At 1 am on 27 February 1975 a gunman firing a machine-gun from a passing car killed Michael Convery and very seriously wounded another man at the junction of the Antrim Road and Limestone Road. Michael Coyle and Kevin Kane were killed in an explosion at a pub on the Antrim Road on 5 April 1975. Thomas Murphy was killed in an explosion at his shop on the Antrim Road on 2 October 1975. Four members of the ACE Taxi company were killed between 1969 and 1975. On 17 October 1975 Jack Greer (38) of ACE Taxis received a call to go to a house on the Upper Cavehill Road. The house had been taken over by gunmen. When he knocked on the door he was immediately shot dead, hit in the face and chest at point-blank range.

Niall O'Neill, as we have seen, was murdered on 22 January 1976. On 24 January Patrick J. Quaile was shot dead in Clifton Street. On 29 January Joseph McAlinden (42), a well-known publican who ran the Washington

Bar for his father, was shot dead by gunmen in his home. The killers entered the house by a ladder. They had pushed aside some protective hardboard on a broken bedroom window. When Mr McAlinden switched on the light to investigate he was gunned down. Ten days before killers shot Jack Greer three youths arrived at McAlinden's house, tied up his wife and tried to lure a taxi-driver to the house by telephone. On 27 May Gerard Masterson (33) was shot dead in front of his wife (a Protestant) in their bedroom. Mrs Elsie Masterson described how they heard footsteps coming up the stairs and her husband ran to try and close the bedroom door. The gunmen pulled it partly open and shot him five times in the back. They had broken down the front door. Early on 5 June two gunmen burst into a house in Camberwell Terrace and shot dead Colm Mulgrew (26). On the same morning a 55-year-old Catholic man was seriously wounded at his home in Upper Cavehill Road when gunmen called at his house and fired into his chest. On 1 August Cornelius Neeson was beaten to death on his way home from a bingo hall. He was found at the junction of Manor Street and Cliftonville Road. On 17 September Peter Gerald Johnston (28), an accountant, was found shot dead by his girlfriend in his upstairs bedroom at his home in Cooldarragh Park, Cavehill Road. He had been shot twice through the head, Mrs Catherine O'Connor (68) and her son-in-law Frank Nolan (34) were murdered in their house at Victoria Gardens, Cavehill Road, on 6 October at 2 am. Two men broke into the house through a kitchen window at the back. They went first to Mrs O'Connor's first floor bedroom and stabbed her at least 14 times. They then shot her son-in-law who had heard her screaming and had run out off his room. His wife crawled under the bed when they fired at her and pleaded with them not to shoot her. Mrs O'Connor was found dead still clutching her rosary beads. Twenty-one Catholics and eight Protestants died in explosions and shootings in the Antrim Road area in 1976; two RUC officers were shot dead.

PHASE III

The SAS in South Armagh

'The Government has decided to further reinforce the Army in Northern Ireland with elements of the SAS. These troops will be used in County Armagh for patrolling and surveillance tasks to which the SAS are particularly well suited'. This statement of 7 January 1976 from Downing Street was the first government announcement that the SAS was being sent to the North. It was stated that the soldiers would wear their uniforms and use standard Army weapons. On 13 January, however, Mr Roy Mason, the British Secretary of State for Defence, declared that they would not always operate in uniform. This was in reply to former SAS officer Mr Stephen Hastings, MP (Conservative, Mid-Bedfordshire) who had asked him if he was satisfied that enough SAS had been sent to Armagh. The SAS unit sent to South Armagh was estimated at 150 men. It supplemented an extra 600 ordinary troops. In South Armagh 49 British soldiers had been killed to date; there were no IRA casualties.

On 13 January Chapman Pincher maintained in the *Daily Express* that the number of SAS troops sent was less than 20. Later he wrote that the exact figure was 11. Mr Biggs-Davison, MP voiced concern in Parliament. Mr Roy Mason would give no figures but said the number of SAS in Northern Ireland would grow. Journalist Chris Walker estimated the figure between 50 and 70 in *The Times*, 24 March 1976.

Robert Fisk in *The Times*, 9 January 1976, reported that the identity of the man in charge of the SAS in the North was being kept secret but speculated that he was from the North, a colonel born in the West who had previously served in the Royal Irish Rangers at Enniskillen. He gave his official title as 'Director of the SAS and Special Forces'. There is, however, no such command or title. Generically speaking the British 'Special Forces' include, as well as the SAS and their associated Signals units, the reconnaissance units of the Parachute Regiment, a special task-designated RAF logistics squadron and the Special Boat Squadron of the Royal Marines (and arguably the RM Commanders themselves). The idea that in 1976 the Director of the SAS controlled Paras, never mind Royal Marines, is ridiculous. There is hostility between the units. A few years ago the Ministry of Defence set up the nucleus of a 'Special Forces Command' to co-ordinate these units but it is still very much in its infancy and has drawn opposition from vested interests.

The Director of the SAS in 1976 was not, as Fisk claims, a mere colonel. The Director of the SAS, in effect, commands the equivalent of a small brigade – 22 SAS, 21 SAS and 23 SAS Regiments plus R Sqn SAS and 63 Signals Sqn; a command whose importance has been recognised since the early 1970s as warranting a Brigadier's rank.

Mr Airey Neave, Conservative spokesman on Northern Ireland, welcomed the announcement of the sending in of the SAS to South Armagh but SDLP members were angry. Mr Gerry Fitt, the party leader, compared the SAS to the CIA and said that the people of Northern Ireland would regard it in the same light. Mr Paddy Devlin, SDLP, said, 'It is only a cosmetic exercise. The SAS have always been here'.

The announcement provoked comment from journalists who recalled the 1974 announcement of SAS presence in Northern Ireland by a British army spokesman and the various allegations and denials of SAS operations. The Northern Ireland Civil Rights Association had been prominent in making such accusations; accusations had followed reports of plain clothes soldiers operating from unmarked cars and from Belfast hospitals amongst other headquarters. *The Irish Times* recalled that as far back as October 1971 information that 22 SAS had sent several members to Northern Ireland on missions was given in a series of articles. The 1976 announcement prompted journalist Claud Cockburn in the same paper to ask, 'Is South Armagh so short of terrorist gangs of one kind or another that it needs a new one to be imported? In this connection some British spokesmen make feeble efforts to pretend that the SAS are not terrorists, saboteurs and spies like others. It is in that sense, apparently, that they are 'special'. Most people understand that the SAS have been operating in the North for a long time so why the particular public announcement?...The SAS became famous during World War II and their deeds were treated as heroic rather than reprehensible. All such actions are applauded in an acknowledged war by people who find them horrifying or illegitimate unless a genuine war is going on. Now the Government is in the awkward position of continually denying that it is waging war and yet defending the use of forces such as the SAS'.

A different point of view was expressed by Lt Colonel J.C. Wakerley (Retd) who was Assistant Director of Army Legal Services, Headquarters, Northern Ireland from 1972-74. He wrote to *The Times* (published 20 January 1976) pleading that the SAS operating in South Armagh be allowed to waive the rules for opening fire listed on the Army's yellow card – '...Otherwise we shall have to face the spectacle of another spate of prosecutions of soldiers in Northern Ireland in which, to the delight of our enemies and the amazement of almost everyone else, we parade the law-enforcers before the same courts and on the same charges as the terrorists themselves'. Lt Colonel Wakerley's worries were largely unfounded. None of those paraded before the courts of the coroners' inquiries suffered more than an embarrassment.

Chris Ryder and Tony Geraghty of the *Sunday Times* (11 January 1976) pictured the SAS men watching suspects and isolated houses and farms where residents might be liable to murder – 'Each is equipped with a so-called 'bingo book' containing lists of wanted men and vehicles and suspect addresses. They also carry infra-red night sights and image intensifiers for night vision are fitted to their weapons. In addition to radio, they carry two sophisticated technical aids – Iris, an infra-red intruder detection system, effective over three miles by remote control, and ground surveillance radar, a three-piece portable unit with a scanning range of 10,000 metres'.

Lord Chalfont, former defence correspondent of *The Times* and former Minister for Disarmament in Mr Harold Wilson's first government, contributed an article to the *Sunday Independent* (11 January 1976) arguing that the role of the SAS in South Armagh would be one of surveillance, improving the intelligence-gathering effort so necessary for counter-insurgency; better he thought than giving way to the machine-gun school who wanted the Army to function without 'one arm tied behind their backs'. The aim was to suppress the level of violence. On 8 January the BBC showed a 12-minute programme on the SAS practising and training at Hereford barracks. One section – a sequence showing an SAS man about to strangle a pretended 'enemy' with wire – was omitted. On the *News at Ten* programme (8 January) the Prime Minister, Mr Wilson, said that the images people had of the SAS were like science fiction. He defended his decision to send them because of the deteriorating situation in South Armagh where 'there was a danger of a "gun law regime" developing'.

The reason the Prime Minister sent the SAS into South Armagh was to appease outraged loyalist opinion. A series of gruesome murders organised by undercover gangs from the security forces had provoked terrible revenge actions from republican paramilitaries. This was the period December 1975-January 1976. Trevor Bracknell, Michael Donnelly and Patsy Donnelly were killed by a mixed loyalist-security force pseudo-gang in Silverbridge on 19 December 1975. Seamus Mallon died on 31 December from an explosion at a Catholic pub in Loughgall on 26 December. Three Protestants, Richard Beattie, William Scott and Mrs Sylvia McCullough were killed in an explosion at a pub in Gilford on 31 December.

Three members of the SDLP, 19-year-old Declan O'Dowd and his brother Barry (24) and their uncle Joseph O'Dowd (61) were killed on 4 January 1976 when men burst into their home near Gilford and shot them. There had been a family reunion in the house for the return home of the two brothers to Ballydougan near Gilford, County Down. However, it was the murder of the Reavey brothers in Whitecross which provoked the worst revenge killing, the massacre of ten Protestants from Bessbrook. All these killings led to the public announcement of the SAS presence in South Armagh and this sets the scene for the South Armagh phase.

The Murder of the Reavey Brothers

Brian Reavey (22), a joiner, and John Martin Reavey (25), a bricklayer, were shot dead in their home on the same day as the O'Dowd family. A third brother Anthony Reavey (17) was severely wounded and died 30 January 1976. Anthony, the survivor, told the story of the shooting to his father who told it to me.

The fourth of January 1976 was a Sunday.[72] There were 12 children in the Reavey family. Sunday was a meeting day for the greater family; all gathered into the Reavey parents' home. There were three married sons and they and their wives and seven children often invaded the home on a Sunday. Normally there were many family members and neighbours gathered for a Sunday social evening. On the evening of the murders, due to a number of coincidences, only three brothers were in the house.

The Reavey cottage is half-a-mile distant from the village of Whitecross. It is enclosed by a circle of roads. A small road over the fields leads across to the road to Deverna and thence to Newry. An intersecting road cuts the main road just beside the house. The killings happened after six o'clock soon after the Reavey parents had left the house. The three brothers were sitting in the living-room, John Martin and Anthony at each side of the fire, Brian in the middle of the room opposite the fire. No car sound was heard. The killers had obviously got out of their vehicle on the side road and came up the field into the cottage garden and then round to the front door. The key was in the door. One of them turned the key and two of them walked in. From his armchair Anthony looked up at the door of the living-room as it opened and saw a masked man in khaki filling the door. A smaller man also in khaki wearing a black mask stood behind him. As Anthony recollected, in those seconds the brothers showed no alarm and were not afraid. They thought the intruders were the Army. Raiding and searching houses was the common lot of Catholics. As he looked up Anthony thought at first their faces were blackened in the usual Army fashion to disguise their features. Then he saw they were wearing black masks. The taller man advanced into the room. He shot John Martin out of the chair riddling his chest with sub-machine-gun fire. Brian let out a shriek. Then both brothers charged for the bedroom door behind Anthony, Anthony dragging the armchair for protection. The gunmen spread their fire over the chair shooting at the door. A bullet caught Brian in the doorway going through his back and heart. He fell into the room, twisting as he fell and his face smashed against the fireplace hearth. There were two single beds lengthwise against the wall opposite the door. Anthony dived under one of the beds. He couldn't get his legs drawn under the bed. The gunman entered and saw where Anthony was from the light of the living room falling into the bedroom. He walked over to Anthony, stood on his feet and fired six bullets into his thighs. He thought Anthony was dead. Anthony stayed under the bed. He heard the gunmen opening and closing doors as they searched the house. When they had gone he crawled from under the bed, over Brian's dead body, out into the living-room and out the front door. He called at a car going by but the driver did not realise his plight. He crawled about 300 yards to a neighbour's house. It was then twenty-two minutes past six. The neighbours phoned for an ambulance and he was brought to Daisy Hill hospital, Newry. Although Anthony was released from hospital before the end of January, he died suddenly on 30 January at home.

At twenty-five minutes past six another brother, Oliver, arrived home and walked into the house to find his two brothers John Martin and Brian crumpled dead in pools of blood.

The next day at 5.30 pm 10 to 12 masked and armed men waved down a workers' minibus at Kingsmills with a red torch. The workers were returning from the linen factory of John Compton Ltd in Glenanne to Bessbrook where most of them lived. The driver, a Catholic, was told to walk on quickly. The gunmen then lined up the 11 Protestants and riddled them with gunfire killing ten. One man, Alan Black (30), miraculously survived. The dead men were James Lennon (50), Kenneth Wharton in his late twenties, Walter Chapman (33) and his brother Reggie (25), John McConville (19), Robert Chambers in his twenties, Robert Freeburn (50), Robert Walker (40), James McWhirter in his mid-fifties, John Bryans in his forties. It was the worst single shooting massacre of the present conflict.

'How the SAS moved in on the Terrorists'

The title is taken from Simon Winchester's article on the SAS in the 11 December 1976 issue of *The Guardian*. When Winchester wrote that article he probably did not realise that he created a myth. The substance of it has been trotted out in every official account of the SAS in South Armagh ever since. 'Well, we got four of them', said F, 'and the other six have been chased away down south. The area is pretty clear of them now – you can tell how much quieter it has become.' This was the main thrust of one of the most senior officers of the SAS, dressed like a gentleman, over coffee in a two-hour frank discussion on the SAS with the journalist in a night train from Scotland to the English midlands. The senior officer put it all in context: the SAS had been in the North in 1972 and in 1974 'on quick jobs'; 'members of enemy units had been to use the CIA's favourite phrase "terminated with extreme prejudice"'. The SAS in South Armagh at first patrolled with the resident Scottish regiment (the paras were to follow) but after two months, when morale was low, they hit on a better plan, the elimination of the ten top IRA men. The senior officer explained some of the circumstances of their operations – Seán McKenna was arrested 'after having supposedly been dragged over the border from his hidey-hole in the south; two were arrested by the Gardaí on SAS advice; and one Peter Cleary was shot dead at point blank range on April 16'. The officer explained that Cleary was shot trying to escape.

The Kidnapping of Seán McKenna

Seán McKenna of Newry, one of a family of six, was the son of Seán McKenna, one of the Hooded Men of the internment period who died at the early age of 42 on 5 June 1975 from the effects of sensory deprivation torture inflicted on him by his SAS torturers. Seán junior was arrested in August 1971 at the age of 17 years and was interned for 3 years. When he was released he went to live in the family summer cottage situated a few hundred yards south of the border in Edentubber.

Seán gave an account of his kidnapping following a family visit to Crumlin Road Jail:[73]

> I was arrested at 2.45 am on Friday morning, 12 March 1976. I was in bed in my home at Edentubber, Ravensdale, Dundalk, Republic of Ireland, when two men came in through the bedroom window. They came through the kitchen and tried to open my bedroom door – I had a chair against it – but they kicked the door open. One of them put a short against my head; it was a 9mm Browning; he told me not to move or he would blow my head off. He shone a small flashlight in my face and told me to get out of bed slowly. I got out and he walked me into the kitchen. I put the light on. He asked for my clothes and then saw them on the chair. He searched them thoroughly, then handed them to me. I dressed and then one of them said, 'I want to explain the case to you. Do you realise that I could have shot you? If you want to put up a struggle or if you don't want to come, say so. I will have no hesitation about shooting you now'. I said that I would go with them.
>
> At this they took chairs from the front door and I saw another one standing outside with a Sterling. He was wearing an ordinary jacket, but had Brit trousers on. They took me out and across the wall and down the fields, two or three, until we came to the Flurry River; he said that I wasn't to get wet. He stressed this. We walked until we came to a spot where we could jump the river. We walked through another couple of fields until we met three Brits in uniform behind a wall. One had a radio and the officer told him to call in and say 'We have our friend' and to get the pick-up arrangement for the same spot where they were dropped. It was to be at 3.15 am. The ones who arrested me then

took off their jackets and put the civilian jackets in a hold-all. The officer then told all the men that if I made a wrong move they were to shoot me. We crossed another field into the North and we were at Kelly's Road, Killeen. I was made to kneel on the ground with one Brit over me. He called the others to a spot about ten yards away and all I could hear him say was something about the methods of the SAS. Then he said, 'If the word gets out about this, the man responsible will be shot'. The officer then came over and put his hand on my shoulder and informed me that he was arresting me. A blue Volkswagen van pulled up. I was put inside it; three men were already inside it; and then I was taken to Bessbrook Station where I was questioned. I said that I had been taken illegally from the Republic and the CID man said that this was a load of nonsense. He then said, 'So you realise your position; you could have been shot tonight'. I replied, 'Then you acknowledge that I was lifted in the Free State'. He didn't answer but informed me that no one knew that I was there and that I could end up with a hole in my head, so I had better start talking. Realising the danger I was in, I felt compelled to agree to sign a statement.

On 14 May, the day Captain Nairac disappeared, Seán McKenna was sentenced to 25 years imprisonment for what Judge Babbington described as 'the whole catalogue of terrorist offences', including two murder bids, two bombings, kidnapping, hijacking, possession of firearms and explosives and belonging to the IRA. McKenna told the court that he had been taken by three soldiers wearing civilian clothes from his house 250 yards over the border. Eight members of the SAS gave evidence that they had been patrolling north of the border when they came across McKenna in a field. The bulk of the evidence against McKenna was in the confession he gave to the police. Counsel for the defence said he had been ill-treated in Newry police station.

Seán McKenna was one of seven men who went on hunger strike in the H-Block Prison, Long Kesh, 27 October 1980 until Christmas 1980.

The Shooting of Peter Cleary, 15 April 1976[74]

When paratroopers shot Martin Walsh in the head on 7 April 1973 intending to kill him, his neighbour Peter Cleary and some other men were taken from their homes near Belleeks village in South Armagh and brought to Bessbrook Military Barracks. On that occasion the soldiers kicked Peter Cleary on the legs when he could not follow their English accents. In 1975 he went 'on the run' across the border to Dundalk. He was later convicted at a Special Criminal Court, Dublin, for unlawful possession of arms and ammunition and given a suspended sentence of three years. After his death, republican notices referred to him as Staff Captain, 1st Battalion, South

Armagh.

After the Kingsmills massacre the SAS sought to show results. Their 'official' entry into Armagh had been accompanied by enormous publicity. On Wednesday 31 March a mixed group of Scottish soldiers and SAS raided the Cleary home at Magee Terrace, Belleeks at 9.30 am when they were preparing to go to Mass. They wore steel helmets and carried chisels and axes. People in nearby Forkhill village claimed that three weeks before Cleary's death a group of SAS men visited houses disguised as Provisionals and wearing masks. They inquired about Cleary and said they were IRA men. However, their British accents betrayed them.

On 31 March three members of the Royal Scots, David Ferguson, Roderick Bannon and John Pearson, were blown up by a land mine at Belleeks, Cleary's home village. It prompts one to ask if there was a motive of revenge in the killing of Cleary. Certainly the IRA 'coup' in face of the SAS and the 600 extra Spearhead Battalion made the British Army look foolish. Christopher Walker wrote in *The Times* (2 April 1976) – 'Almost all (*SAS*) are operating in plain clothes, often spending days at a time in specially concealed dugouts near cross-border routes. Those who operate in uniform are understood to wear the cap badges of the regiments to which they are attached, often The Royal Scots, whose men were killed on Wednesday night'.

In his statement at the inquest on Peter Cleary, 28 January 1977, the SAS officer designated 'A', serving with the SAS unit in Bessbrook Camp, said that on or about 8 April he had been ordered by his Unit Commander to arrest Peter Cleary about whom information had been received that he was regularly visiting his fiancée who was staying with her sister at Tievecrum. A description had been given of him including special characteristics, that he had a stammer and was in the habit of carrying £200 in cash on him and that he was usually armed. The IRA suspect that a local man who had a grudge against Cleary set him up. Their suspicions were hardened by the fact that he was taken into protective custody by the British Army within hours of Cleary's death.

On Monday, 12 April a patrol commanded by officer 'A' was dropped at 9.45 pm near the house of Raymond Fagan, Tievecrum. A communications' base was set up and a close observation point about 120 metres east of the house. A support was stationed a further 300 metres east and a few metres north of the border.

On Thursday at 9.40 am Cleary was noticed driving from the house across the border. Officer 'A' says they decided then to take no action. He was sighted again at 5 pm. At 7.45 pm three explosions and a prolonged burst of automatic fire were heard in the distance. A helicopter coming into land at Crossmaglen was attacked by rockets and machine-guns. At 9 pm Officer 'A' led his group forward to the close observation point. He says in

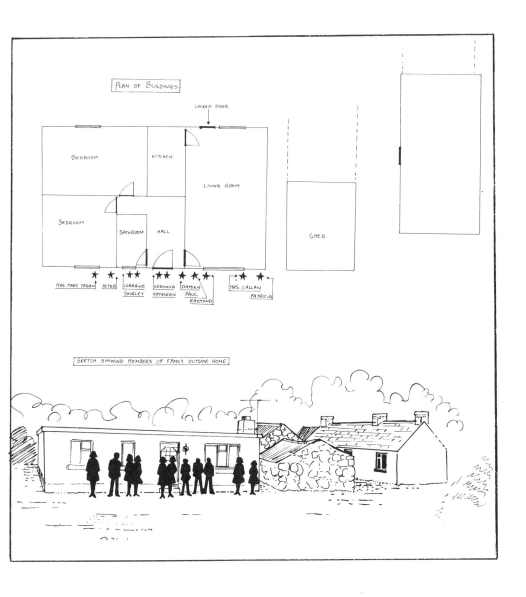

The Shooting of Peter Cleary

his statement, 'At approximately 21.45 hours, having decided that Soldier 'B' and I would cover the front of the house, Soldier 'C' led the remaining troopers towards the rear of the house. Soldier 'B' and I gave them a few minutes start and then we moved off. By 22.00 hours we were in position behind a bank about fifteen feet on the opposite side of the road to the drive-way entrance. At that time about six people were tinkering around a car in the drive, all illuminated by a bright light on the wall of the house. I spotted the man whom I believed to be Cleary. We were then discovered by a male civilian who was carrying a large torch. There was a certain amount of confusion and movement amongst the people in the drive. We both shouted that everyone was to stand still and, as there was still movement, Soldier 'B' fired a single shot in the air from his sub-machine-gun. I ordered everyone to go outside and started to place them against the wall...'

Peter Cleary had come to see his girlfriend Shirley Hulme on the night of 15 April. Their wedding was to take place on Tuesday 27 May. He left his car on the Republic side of the border, only fifty yards away. This was about ten minutes to nine. He went to see a friend and came back about 10 pm. Damian Hulme, brother to Shirley and Patricia, and his wife Kathleen arrived also at Fagans. They were to buy a car from Raymond. Mrs Mary Callan, a neighbour, had called. Also in the house was Lorraine the seven-year-old daughter of Raymond Fagan. The other children, Mark aged six and Rachel aged three, were in the grandparents' house just behind Fagans' new house. Around 10 pm the men had gathered round the car outside. A last minute job was being done on the car before it finally changed hands. Paul Mulkearns, a neighbour, had called over. He mentioned something about a helicopter incident being on the news. Raymond, Damian and Peter Cleary went into the house to watch the rest of the news on television.

Outside Patricia Fagan and Paul Mulkearns were talking. The dogs were barking. They walked across the road. Paul stood up on the ditch and shone his torch. Two soldiers were lying on the other side. They jumped up and one fired a shot over their heads.

Inside the house Peter said to Raymond, 'I'm dead. What will I do?' Everybody was ordered out of the house and made to stand against the wall. Officer 'A' had taken his position at the front door. As he was looking at those against the wall, a young man walked past him out of the house. He ran after him and threw him to the ground. He was joined by Soldier 'B'. When asked his name, Peter Cleary was supposed to have said 'Eamon McCann'. He was taken to one of the out-offices. They were joined by two more soldiers. Cleary was then stripped and his body and clothing searched. They had a photograph of him and easily identified him. 'A' says it was then 22.30 hours. He radioed and requested a helicopter.

The witnesses at the wall saw the soldiers kicking Peter as he was led off to the outhouse. They were then brought into the house where they were subjected to obscenities and insults by a solider 'with a fine accent'. He asked, 'Which of you is Shirley? You are, aren't you? It won't be long till the wedding now. I have news for you. You are not going to have one'. His words were prophetic. Peter Cleary was waked in his wedding suit.

Damian Hulme was brought outside and questioned about the car. The car was searched. He was questioned about Peter. A red-haired soldier pushed him down and crushed his head into the ground with his boot. He thinks Peter Cleary was about fifteen minutes in the outhouse with the other soldiers. Later when he and others went into that house they concluded that a good deal of beating had gone on; a lot of the furniture was disturbed and thrown around. Damian was still outside at the car when the SAS men re-assembled and Peter was dragged up past him by two of them, moving very slowly. His head was down and they were pulling him by the arms. Damian saw this clearly under the outside light. They took him across the road.

Damian was sent back into the house. When the 'educated' soldier and a small soldier called 'George' left, they broke the outside lights, after giving a warning to those inside not to move. Those inside recall a rattle of gunfire after the light was shot out.

Less than ten minutes after the soldiers left the house three shots were heard. Raymond Fagan heard a stone falling from the stone ditch at the top end of the little field opposite their house. Beyond this field is the park of Captain Johnston's estate. The trees have been removed from the park. About 400 yards further is the garden of the old house, square in shape, surrounded by broken-down walls. When the three shots were heard, two helicopters, one with a search light, were still in the air about 150 yards up the road from Fagans' house. The witnesses at the house say that the SAS raided the house at 10.20 pm judging by the 'news'. They stayed until near 11 pm. Less than ten minutes later they heard three shots. They concluded that Peter Cleary was shot by the SAS as soon as they crossed the fields opposite the house.

The SAS officer 'A' in his statement says they brought him to the walled garden. Guards were deployed around the walls and at the gateway. 'A' was alone with Cleary. The helicopters approached. At this point no lights were on. He was standing with the butt of the SLR in his armpit. The rifle was cocked. As the lights were switched on, he alleges that Cleary hurled himself at him. In the next sentence, however, he says it was dark; he was alone with an IRA man who had attempted to escape at the house before he was brought down; he believed him to be a killer; his instinct as an SAS soldier took over; he released the safety catch and started shooting and continued to fire until the danger to his life was past; he had no chance to warn him; the first bullets knocked Cleary down and backwards; as he was going down he fired the first of a further two shots but ceased fire when he realised the Cleary was no longer a threat.

The officers's statement allows 55 minutes from the time the SAS left the house until he shot Peter Cleary. He says they withdrew at 22.40 hours and it was 23.35 hours when the helicopters approached. The witnesses at the house claim that the SAS withdrew at 11 pm and Cleary was shot less that ten minutes later.

Peter Cleary's body was taken by helicopter to Bessbrook Army Camp. Brigadier Peter Morton, battalion commander of 3 Para in South Armagh received a radio report from the SAS patrol while he was returning by helicopter from Crossmaglen to Bessbrook – 'Have a bodybag waiting on the LS for us when we arrive'. At Bessbrook Captain A.H. McMillan of the Royal Army Medical Corps certified him dead. Brigadier Morton delayed releasing the news of his death or the body for a few hours so that the story would be too late for the newspapers and give time to release a statement. The body was then brought by RUC tender to the Mortuary at Daisy Hill Hospital. At 5.15 am Michael Philip Hughes, a neighbour of Peter Cleary, identified the body.

The SAS soldiers are described by witnesses as being dressed in dark green uniform that had little black checks all over it and gave the appearance of a black uniform. All wore black gloves. Only one had dark civilian trousers and a chequered jacket which was lying open. They wore no badges or caps. Their faces were blackened. Some carried sub-machine-guns and one a gun about two and a half foot long, short-barrelled and green sacking wrapped around half the barrel. The British Army statement of 16 April said Cleary was killed by the SAS while attempting to escape, that he was wanted by the police for questioning in connection with several serious crimes, that he had been convicted in a court in Dublin in 1975. This was elaborated by the British press. John Ware of *The Sun* under a large heading 'Storm after SAS shoot killer' wrote: 'Cleary, aged 25, was a member of the gang which had slaughtered 10 Protestants at Bessbrook; he also killed three soldiers with a landmine in March, and was wanted over the massacre of five Protestants at an Orange Hall in September'. Niall Kiely in *The Irish Times* quoted the proper distinction made by an RUC spokesman (17 April) that Cleary was wanted for questioning but that did not mean he was guilty of any crime. The RUC adopted the same attitude to the family. It is clear from the minutes of the Twenty Seventh Meeting of the Police Division 'H' Local Security Committee held at Newry on Tuesday, 11 May that Councillor J. Murphy was assured that in no statement by the RUC or the British Army had Cleary's name been associated with the Kingsmills' massacre; the Press release had said he was wanted in connection with unspecified serious crimes (Document marked 0411/11, Standard Distribution, Headquarters, 3 Infantry Brigade, British Forces Post Office 801). The British Army was willing to clear Cleary's name in private but they left it open to the British popular press to connect him with specific crimes.

The *Cork Examiner* commented on the killing of Peter Cleary in its editorial 'An Act of Utter Folly', 17 April: 'It is tragically true to describe Eastertide as a potentially explosive time in Northern Ireland ... In this context the shooting by the SAS of a prominent member of the Provisional IRA in South Armagh was an act of stupidity, particularly at this time. "Shot while trying to escape" is one of the oldest and least credible excuses put forward by armies throughout the world down the years. It has usually been greeted with cynicism and deservedly so'.

On 22 June, in an extraordinary move, the British Ambassador to Ireland, Christopher Ewart-Biggs visited Bessbrook Army Camp where the SAS were based. He is widely believed to have been an MI6 agent. On 21 July the South Armagh IRA killed him in a bomb explosion in revenge for the shooting of Peter Cleary.

The Murder of Seamus Ludlow[75]

On 1 May 1976 the SAS crossed the border in search of a well-known republican who lived in Ravensdale, County Louth. They made a grave error. They shot a man who greatly resembled him, Seamus Ludlow aged 48 years of Thistlewood, Mount Pleasant, Dundalk. His body was found on Sunday, 2 May in a laneway at Culfore near Dundalk, lying on top of a grassy bank with the head uppermost. The body was about 20 yards from the main road. There was a stab wound on the left side of his chest and what the pathologist has described as 'two curious abrasions' on the right side of the chest and on the back of the left hand. He died as a result of bullet wounds in his heart, right lung and liver. Two bullets were retrieved from his clothing and a third bullet was removed from his chest.

Seamus Ludlow was last seen alive on Saturday night, 1 May, outside Smith's garage just north of Dundalk thumbing a lift as he so often did. About £7 was found in his pocket, his shoes were clean, and there was no sign of struggle, facts which led the Gardaí investigating the crime to believe that he was murdered elsewhere and dumped.

Seamus Ludlow was a quiet person, unconnected with politics and known for his charitable activities. The Provisional IRA claimed the SAS were responsible for his death. John Keane in the *Sunday World*, 16 May 1976, advanced the common theory in the Ravensdale area that it was a case of mistaken identity; he was the double of a top Provisional IRA man who was on the wanted list of the SAS.

Further suspicion of British army involvement in his murder was aroused when British soldiers called on his sister Mrs Donegan, Dromintee, four or five days after the burial. They said they were acting on the instructions of the Gardaí and wanted to ask questions. Mr and Mrs Donegan refused to comply and said they would talk to the police but not to the Army. They wanted to take Mr Donegan over to Forkhill Barracks. He said he would go over on his bicycle. There was no policeman when he went there. He was taken by helicopter to Bessbrook Army Camp where the SAS was stationed. There he was questioned about his brother-in-law Seamus Ludlow. His interrogators implied that Seamus was involved in the IRA.

In the meantime Mrs Donegan telephoned local councillor James Murphy. She was greatly distressed. Mr Murphy spoke to an officer at Bessbrook by phone. The officer said it had nothing to do with Murphy. Mr Murphy said he was acting as a councillor and asked the officer why the soldiers were acting outside the state, having no instructions from the Gardaí. The Army then denied they had mentioned the Gardaí. Mr Murphy was then put on to the Intelligence Officer. Mr Murphy told him that many people in Armagh, Louth, and in fact in the whole of Ireland were convinced that the British Army was involved in Ludlow's murder, and that the Army's going to his relatives and questioning them added weight to this. It looked, he said, as if the Army was trying to justify itself by branding him as IRA. Mr Donegan was then released and Councillor Murphy took him home.

The SAS Incursion into the Republic

Four days after the murder of Seamus Ludlow the SAS were back in the Republic.[76] This time they were caught. On a bright moonlight night, 5 May 1976, at 10.40 pm two SAS men, Private Illisoni Vanioni Ligari (37) and Private John Michael Lawson (37), crossed the border into the Republic in a yellow Triumph 2000. They travelled on the little road known as the Flagstaff Road which runs from the Newry-Dundalk Road down to Omeath. What their mission was one cannot say. It has been suggested that it was in connection with the escape of nine INLA prisoners from Long Kesh the night before. Ligari, a native of Fiji, was dressed in a white overcoat and green shirt. Lawson was dressed in a brown jersey and white shirt. In the boot of their car was a Sterling sub-machine-gun, a Browning pistol and 82 rounds of ammunition. They had come from the SAS base in Bessbrook Military Camp. An Irish Army/Garda checkpoint was cleverly concealed 700 yards inside the Republic. Lawson carried a Browning automatic pistol loaded with a magazine and he also had a spare magazine. Ligari had a Sterling sub-machine-gun loaded with a magazine and a second magazine taped underneath.

Sergeant Patrick McLoughlin and Garda Murray stopped the car in the middle of the road. Sergeant McLoughlin spoke to them and arrested them under Section 30 of the Offences against the State Act 1939. Sergeant McLoughlin asked them how they had crossed the border. They said they were going to Bessbrook. Lawson said he was a member of the British Army and that he had crossed the border due to a map-reading error. He said he was not a member of the SAS, that he was off duty and testing the car which was an official one. There was a military log book in the car. Ligari had a large map with which he tried to conceal his machine-gun. Ligari said, 'I cannot tell you the mission we were on'. The Gardaí then brought the two men to Omeath Garda station.

When the SAS men failed to return to their base six more SAS men in civilian dress and armed were dispatched to find them. They crossed the border at exactly the same spot, obviously aware of the route of the first mission and making nonsense of the map-reading error. They ran into the same checkpoint. Garda Murray signalled to them to stop. The first car was a white Hillman Avenger. Two of the four men in it were in civilian clothes. The driver was Private Vincent Thompson (32). He wore a sweater. The front seat passenger Private Neill Garvock McClean (26) was dressed in a black leather jacket. Staff Sergeant Malcolm Rees (34) and Corporal Ronald Nicholson (32), a dark haired man with a moustache, were in the back seat. These two wore military uniforms and had black camouflaged faces. The four carried between them two Browning automatic pistols, one Sterling sub-machine-gun, one sawn-off pump-action shotgun and 196 rounds of ammunition. The second car, a Vauxhall Victor contained two SAS men dressed in civilian clothes, Private Nigel Anthony Burchell (28), moustached, wearing a grey sweater, and Private Carsten Rhodes (26), also wearing a sweater. Burchell and Rhodes had Sterling machine-guns and 116 rounds of ammunition. All the magazines of their guns were loaded.

The driver of the first car gave his name, Vincent Thompson, and explained that they were searching for two of their colleagues who had been reported missing earlier. When asked how they came into the South, they said they must have taken a wrong turning. The Gardaí informed them that their companions were in Garda custody and asked them to hand over their weapons.

They refused each time. The Irish Army members present then surrounded the cars and they surrendered their weapons. The shot-gun and pistols were cocked. In the first car the Gardaí recovered a holdall with a torch and a night sight. In a packbag was a ranger type radio. While they were being held at the road check one of the soldiers put through a message to Bessbrook that they were being stopped on the road at a Garda checkpoint.

Among the weapons was a dagger in a sheath. Later Thompson is alleged to have said they would have opened fire only they saw the Irish Army insignia badges. The SAS men said little under interrogation. McClean revealed that his wife's people came from Dundalk and that he was a Presbyterian of Scottish descent. Staff Sergeant Rees said he was a member of the 3rd Parachute Regiment. He admitted he was qualified in map reading. He also admitted that on three occasions he had refused to allow his men to hand over their weapons and is said to have asked, 'Let us go back. If the roles were reversed, we would let you back. We are doing the one bloody job'.

The SAS men appeared at a special sitting of the Special Criminal Court in Dublin on 6 May. They were represented in court by Mr Peter Sutherland, barrister-at-law. He applied for bail and Mr Laurence Farrell, Chief State Solicitor, said he would not object. Mr Justice Pringle, presiding, then fixed bail at £5,000 each. The hearing was attended by the Military Attaché to the British Embassy in Dublin, Brigadier Frank McMullen.

The arrest of the SAS men brought cries of rage from the British press. Pride in the regiment was hurt. Far from seeing it as a breach of sovereignty, the British press looked on it as a misjudgement on the part of the Gardaí. *The Times* editorial of 8 May said they should have sent the SAS men back with a wigging; diplomatic, not legal channels, should have been the means to pursue the matter. The *Sunday Times* editorial, 'No way to win a war' linked the Irish Government's persistence in this case with its pursuit of the British Government in the European Court at Strasbourg on the question of torture, a comment ironic to Irish readers since it was SAS men who trained the torturers at Ballykelly, Holywood and Girdwood and were present in an instructive role! For the *Daily Mail* the SAS's only wrong was to get caught, and added, 'It would be naive to imagine that the SAS, if they are to do their job effectively as undercover soldiers, do not cross it, too, both accidentally and deliberately'. *The Guardian*'s editorial, 'Border Panto-mime' thought it was a political decision of the Government in Dublin to charge them. The absurd comment, however, was left to William Hunter and John Ley reporting in the *Daily Express*, 7 May, 'A misleading blaze of light in the night sky led the eight soldiers into the arms of the Irish police in the early morning darkness. It is thought they mistook the glare of floodlights for a British army checkpoint on the Newry Road'.

In January 1977 Mr Roy Mason, Secretary of State, visited Dublin for the first time since his appointment and discussed the case of the SAS men.

They were still on £40,000 bail paid by the British Embassy at the initial hearing. By this time they had left Northern Ireland and some were living overseas. When they were brought together for the trial in March 1977, some came from the Middle East. The British Government was nervous about the trial. A high level meeting of officials from the Foreign Office, Ministry of Defence, and the Northern Ireland Office took place in London on 2 March 1977. They had already decided at a previous meeting that it would be bad policy to 'jump bail'.

The SAS men were flown into Baldonnel airport shortly before 8 am on 7 March. An Army/Garda convoy consisting of three Army personnel carriers and six land-rovers accompanied them to Green Street courthouse. Among the attendance at the court were the British Ambassador Mr Robert Hayden, the British Military Attaché Brigadier Frank McMullen and other members of the British Army staff.

The eight men were cleared of the charge of taking weapons into the Republic with intent to endanger life, a charge with a maximum penalty of 20 years jail. They were each fined £100 for taking weapons into the Republic without firearms' certificates. The weapons were to be handed back by the Gardaí to the British authorities.

Of great interest in the trial was the evidence of Major Brian Baty, commanding officer of the SAS at Bessbrook Camp. He said that all soldiers under his command were subject to normal restrictions including the yellow card, a summary of legal instructions regarding the opening of fire; he added that it was dangerous for soldiers in South Armagh to travel in military uniform whether alone or in convoy. The soldiers carried weapons and ammunition which were normal British army issue. The carrying of those weapons was authorised by him. (This would not explain the pump-action shotgun and the dagger.) The eight SAS men were on duty in Northern Ireland just over four weeks at the time of the offences; that night he had given instructions for a surveillance party to be mounted; they acted under the same rules as the rest of the British Army. 'But,' he said, 'we employ possibly slightly different tactics.'

Major Baty resurfaced in Irish affairs in 1986 when Patrick Brazil (34), of Belcamp Avenue, Dublin, William Grimes (43), of Cherryfield Road, Dublin and Dr Máire O'Shea (66), a retired consultant psychiatrist of Birmingham, were tried in Manchester Crown Court on charges of conspiracy.[77] (Both O'Shea and Brazil were acquitted.) It was alleged that he was the target of an alleged INLA plot. His statement was read at the trial by prosecuting counsel Mr Rhys Davies. The colonel (as he was then) stated that his anonymity was blown at the trial of the eight SAS men in Dublin. He said he had been in the British Army between February 1951 and October 1984 when he retired. As an SAS officer it was policy to preserve anonymity. The colonel said he had seen a piece of paper which police found in the house of a fourth defendant, Peter Jordan, containing his name, military decoration, service number, date of retirement and his honorary rank. It is possible to trace some of his career by using non-classified sources:- Serial number 22548546; Sgt Argyll and Sutherland Highlanders, 1965; awarded Military Medal, 1965, for campaign in Borneo; commissioned (Short Services Officer) Lt A & SH (serial no 480027), 21 September 1965 (the date 21 September 1963 is given in some subsequent editions of the Army List); promoted Captain A & SH, 21 September 1967; awarded Long Service Good Conduct Medal, 25 February 1969; promoted Acting Major, 8 September 1971, confirmed, 30 June 1973; transferred from A & SH to General List, 16 October 1975, promulgated, February 1976; mentioned in dispatches, 11 January 1977 (Northern Ireland Service, May-July 1976); appeared in defence in SAS trial, Special Criminal Court, Dublin, March 1977; promoted Local Lt Colonel, 1 December 1979; transferred from General List to Parachute Regiment, 1 April 1982, retired, retired officer's pay, 27 October 1984 with honorary rank of Lt Colonel; awarded MBE.

After the incursion by the SAS into the Republic the British Army Minister, Mr Bob Brown, appealed to the Irish Government in the House of Commons on 6 May 1976 to take a 'constructive view'. 'There can be no doubt,' he said, 'it resulted purely and simply from a map-reading error on the part of the men concerned. Given the increasing co-operation between us in enforcing anti-terrorist measures in the Border area, we had hoped it might have been possible to obtain the early release of these men. But now the process of law has been engaged and they have been charged and are appearing in court this evening. We hope a constructive view of this mistake will be taken.' Serious British papers treated the excuse with the same contempt as Irish politicians and people who lived in the border area. 'It had been pointed out,' wrote Derek Brown in *The Guardian* (7 May 1976), 'that the cross-border road to Omeath where the men were arrested is not exactly an unmarked country lane. The border itself is marked with bombed wreckage of an old British Army checkpoint and the road is deeply pitted by abortive British attempts to close the unauthorised crossing-point with barricades, and by subsequent, more successful operations by local people, to remove the obstructions. The crossing, is, in fact, one of the most noticeable along the entire border!' Similarly William Elisworth-Jones writing in the *Sunday Times*, 9 May 1976, said that it would be very difficult to take this border road by mistake.

In the four months of the SAS presence in South Armagh, it was repeatedly claimed by local people on both sides of the border that the SAS sent plain clothes patrols into the Republic. Dr Garret Fitzgerald revealed in the Dáil on 13 May that there had been 304 recorded cross-border incursions by British soldiers since 1973: 63 on foot; 18 in armoured vehicles; 55 in other transport (of these groups five cases related to civilian attire); 151 by helicopter and 17 in other aircraft. In the debate in the Dáil Mr Dowling raised the question of civilian attire and pump-action shotguns – 'These guns,' he said, 'were not issued by any army in the world, but were used mainly by thugs and criminals'.

When the embarrassment eased, the SAS returned to 'normal' functioning but again blundered.

SAS Jump the Border to make Arrests

Not far from the spot where they killed Peter Cleary, the SAS on 12 July 1976 made another incursion into the Republic.[78] The drama began at 10 pm at

Flurry bridge. A Newry man, a 32-year-old furniture dealer and haulier, Patrick Mooney, went with his wife and three children to visit a scrap dealer and warehouse keeper Arthur Mullen who lived some 30 yards on the southern side of the border near Jonesborough. An unemployed labourer, Kevin Byrne, was there at the same time to talk to Mullen about prospects of a job. Byrne described the incident, 'Arthur went over to the gate to talk to Mr Mooney. After a while I heard the screeching of brakes and when I looked around, I saw two cars, one of them a white saloon and the other a light-coloured Triumph, pulling up on the northern side of the border. Within seconds, all the doors flew open and four men from one of the cars ran through a gap in the wall and came into the yard which is in the Republic'. Some of them were carrying automatic pistols and others had machine-guns. Mullen took to his heels heading for Dromad Garda Station a short distance away. Two other SAS men had come into the yard and one took up a firing position and aimed at Mullen as he ran. There were women and children unloading turf from a lorry and as they were in his line of fire he changed his stance. Seconds later a plain clothes man ran up to Byrne and put a gun to his ear and screamed, 'Don't move, don't talk, just don't say anything'. Uniformed soldiers, who looked like paratroopers, then jumped the wall and ran into the yard. Mrs Mooney described the SAS as being dressed in sweaters and slacks. She thought they were paramilitaries because it was the Twelfth night. She saw an SAS man with a gun to her husband's head against the wall and Byrne held in a similar fashion. Both men were then shoved and pushed across the border. The children were crying. Mooney was ordered to stop speaking by a man with an English accent. A man in an Army uniform then pulled his face around and looked at him. Both captives were ordered to trot and were marched up the mountain. On the way they were given a stream of orders, to walk slow, fast, to stop. They were made to lie face down on the grass a few times. They reached a camp where three tents were pitched. They were put lying down on their faces. A uniformed soldier arrived and questioned them about their money. Their papers were taken and put into a plastic bag. Then they were moved up the mountain again. They were told to keep their heads down – 'If he lifts it again, give him a kick in the ear'. A helicopter arrived and Mooney was put in first. He was told to lie face down and Byrne was forced to lie on top of him. Mooney held on to what seemed to be a seat-belt during the journey. There were two soldiers in front and two behind. His legs from the knees stuck out of the helicopter into the air. At least four times the soldiers threatened to throw Byrne out of the helicopter, jerking him towards the door. He was made repeat, 'I'm a filthy Irish bastard and I hate all the fucking Fenians'. Fingers were stuck into his mouth and he was repeatedly thumped. At Bessbrook they were put through preliminaries of photographing and weighing. After several hours of abuse and insult they were released. It was another man the SAS were after and they talked openly of 'moofing it' and the 'mess-up'. The man's warehouse had been broken into four times from the beginning of the year. British Army soldiers had also found 70 lbs of explosives in it. His property straddled the border. The man said he knew nothing about the explosives and had no interest in politics.

On 17 February 1983 Kevin Byrne of Muirhevnamore, Dundalk, won a claim for compensation. He sued the Ministry of Defence for unlawfully arresting and detaining him and brought the case to the High Court in Belfast. It was settled out of court for an undisclosed figure.

SAS Versus Paratroopers

At the beginning of April 1976 the 3rd Battalion, the Parachute Regiment, moved into Bessbrook Army Camp and South Armagh to relieve the Royal Scots Regiment. A.F.N. Clarke, author of *Contact*, who had met Captain Nairac in Belfast in August 1973, was back on another stint in Northern Ireland and was stationed with the paratroopers in Crossmaglen. His comment on the role of the SAS in South Armagh is unfavourable:-

May 1976.
I grunt an acknowledgement. I wonder what's going through his mind? What went through mine when I was that age? Envy? Thinking to himself and wondering what it must be like to come under fire like that?

Don't think. I've been there and it is a scary thing. Something you can best do without, I want this to be a nice peaceful tour. What I am saying, we hadn't been here two minutes and a chopper was hit, then some idiot of an SAS officer shot some guy he said was trying to take his rifle off him and caused a storm because nobody believed a word of it. Then a whole car-load of SAS got picked up in the Republic in a civilian car in civilian clothes and armed to the teeth. The excuse was that they got lost. Well, if that's the élite then what the fuck must the rest of us be like? Cowboys, the lot of them; there are some guys I've recognised who have failed our selection tests, so how did they get into the SAS? I wouldn't give them the time of day. A few years ago after the Belfast tour, we took part in an exercise as enemy, with them. After a couple of days we were asked to take twenty-four hours off to give them a chance to regroup because we had completely compromised all their R.V. points. They are a joke.

Still, it's not worth getting hot under the collar, it just annoys me when guys like us, who spend all the time on the ground doing the donkey-work, get the worst equipment and the cannon-fodder tasks. Shit, this whole mess is getting to me.

The Shooting of Seamus Harvey, Crossmaglen[79]

On 22 November 1975 the IRA ambushed four soldiers at their hide on the hill of Drummuckavall near Crossmaglen. Three of the soldiers were killed, Peter McDonald, James Duncan and Michael Sampson.

The Harvey family lived near Drummuckavall. In October 1976 they and other families were terrorised by the Royal Marine Commandos. Fr Denis Faul and I called on them and later published a pamphlet 'Terror Tactics of the British Army, Royal Marine Commandos at Crossmaglen'. We listed the following brutalities:-

1. Beating citizens with rifle butts.
2. Kicking, thumping.
3. Long hours in the British Army search position.
4. Threatening death. Using army photographs to send death messages.
5. Attempted murder by interfering with mechanism of cars.
6. Degrading treatment in Army vehicles.
7. Simulated executions. Putting guns to heads of citizens and clicking them.
8. Shining torches into eyes.
9. Inflicting knife wounds.
10. Attempted suffocations.
11. Night assaults on isolated farmhouses.
12. Continuous visits to houses. Psychological torture of the older members.
13. Damaging, stealing and destroying private property.

The Harvey family told us that soldiers arrived at their home on 9 October at 10.30 pm. Patrick Harvey and his wife were there. They gaped in through the windows, hammered on the door, searched all the outhouses. They arrived the next morning at 6 am and got the sons up out of the house outside where they had temporary sleeping accommodation since the dwelling house was being renovated. On 13 October they came again and took Patrick Harvey's photograph. They threatened to shoot the dog. They shouted in through the window that they would get him and his son. They came again on 18 October 1976 at 11 pm. They kicked the door. They took oil out of one of the cars and spilled it over drawers and presses, the living quarters of the sons, on boxes of tools, on glue for setting tiles. They took one of the sons, put him against the wall, kicked his ankles, put a gun in his back and threatened to shoot him. Earlier they had stopped the same son in his car, suddenly stepping out in front of it. They threw everything in the car on the road, threatened to kick his head off and then threatened to shoot him.

On 16 January 1977 members of the Provisional IRA in South Armagh moved into the Cooldery area to examine a car abandoned on the road about three miles outside Crossmaglen on the border with County Louth. One of the men was Seamus Harvey, son of Patrick who had been threatened by the Marine Commandos the previous October. He was dressed in combat jacket and armed with a sawn-off pump-action shotgun, a type used by the SAS. He was masked and wore an ammunition belt with cartridges. Harvey, a building worker, was a staff officer in the Crossmaglen battalion IRA. Other IRA men covered while he went forward to examine the car.

The car was a decoy set up by the SAS who were lying in bracken and nettles nearby. The IRA claimed that they opened fire when the SAS shot Seamus Harvey dead without warning. A gun battle ensued. The fact that the IRA had taken cover saved them from being cut down. It was estimated that fifty shots were fired in the exchange. The British Army version was different. The SAS unit was approached by Harvey at 2.15 pm. The unit heard a van drive up to them while they were on surveillance duty. They crept down to intercept Harvey as he moved forward. They were then spotted by two other IRA men. They fired 28 rounds in reply when they were attacked. Later 20 cases from IRA automatic rifles were found.

A strange paradox ensued. The British Army statement announced that the SAS unit shot Seamus Harvey. The IRA claimed he was shot by soldiers from the Royal Highland Fusiliers. It was an indication of pride on both sides. In accordance with the wishes of the Harvey family there was no military style funeral for Seamus Harvey. Members of the Rangers GAA football team, of which he was an esteemed member, attended.

After the death, Mr Airey Neave MP, pleased with the success of the SAS in South Armagh, appealed in the House of Commons on 17 January for increased use of the SAS in Northern Ireland. The Government, he said, should make 1977 the year of victory over terrorism in Ulster. He offered to back Mr Roy Mason, Secretary of State, in taking severe measures. In future Ulster should be the first priority of the SAS regiment.

PHASE IV

SAS Terrorism 1977–1978

On 2 December 1976 the SAS was given a new brief to step up undercover operations in Derry and Belfast and other parts of Northern Ireland extending its role from the emergency zone of South Armagh. The killing of Peter Cleary in South Armagh in April 1976 was followed soon by the killing of Seamus Harvey in January 1977. The killing of Michael McHugh in County Tyrone on 21 January 1977 was generally accepted as a murder planned by British Army Intelligence. The new decision was taken by the Prime Minister, James Callaghan, despite the impending trial of the eight SAS men who had violated the sovereign territory of the Irish Republic. The new move was elaborated on in a written answer from the Army Minister, Robert Brown. He said the SAS had 'a significant effect in reducing terrorist activity in the rural and border areas in County Armagh. It has therefore been decided that their skills and the experience gained will be used, where appropriate, in other similarly troubled areas'. Mr Brown's answer followed a written question in the House of Commons by the Conservative MP Mr Alan Le Williams and was delivered on 9 December 1976. A Ministry of Defence spokesman added that the SAS normally operated in uniform but when the occasion demands they use plain clothes as did other units of the British Army in Northern Ireland. The general British opinion both from politicians and media was that the SAS had a deterrent effect. The very thought of ruthless highly-trained soldiers roaming the country in plain clothes should instil fear into the hearts of paramilitaries. The keen interest of the Secretary of State, Mr Roy Mason, in the SAS while in the Ministry of Defence increased the enthusiasm to deploy them in greater numbers in Northern Ireland. The move was welcomed by loyalists such as the Vanguard leader, William Craig, and Ernest Baird, one of the leaders of the loyalists' coalition. Mr Paddy Devlin of the SDLP believed that the move was a cover up for a more general withdrawal of British troops. Mr Seamus Mallon of the SDLP described them as experts in sabotage and *agent provocateur* type operations, the British Army's 'dirty tricks unit'. It was at this time, 11 December 1976, that Simon Winchester published his article in *The Guardian*, 'How the SAS moved in on terrorists'. He claimed it was based on a conversation with a senior SAS officer on a train travelling from Scotland to England. This article couldn't have appeared at a more auspicious time to back the Government's new policy. Winchester says his chance encounter couldn't have been more civilised. It couldn't have been more timely from a propaganda point of view. Significantly it has been trotted out by official SAS historians ever since.

On 6 December Christopher Walker in *The Times* quoted the reaction of a senior officer in Belfast to the extension of the use of the SAS. 'This is one story where we are happy for as much press speculation as possible. Nothing could suit us better.' Walker wrote, 'Although its operations have been shrouded in secrecy, it is known that the SAS regularly operates in units of four or six men who specialise in long-term surveillance of suspected terrorists. With their specialised training, SAS men often stay in camouflaged hideouts for several days, building up a comprehensive picture of Provisional IRA activity. One group is said to have spent 36 days "in the field" without returning to base. Often dressed in plain clothes and driving unmarked cars, the men have proved they can deter hardened terrorist units with little publicized involvement in violent incidents. The few incidents in which its presence has come to public notice have served only to reinforce its reputation as a shadowy force specialising in under-cover operations...'

The Murder of Michael McHugh[80]

On 21 January 1977 Michael McHugh (32), a forestry worker, was machine-gunned to death by two members of the UDA, one of them a British Army agent, at Aghyaran or Corgary near Castlederg, County Tyrone. Because of the agent it might be described as an undercover British Army murder. Michael McHugh was active in Sinn Féin. He was chairman of the local branch for a period but had resigned this position before he was assassinated. His family insist that he was never a member of the IRA.

His house was often raided by the British Army. They continually arrested him and stopped him, so much so that after his death his wife accused the British Army of 'putting a name on him'. When he was shot Fr Denis Faul disclosed that he had sent copies of a letter threatening McHugh to the RUC and British Army in Omagh for investigation. The letter had been sent to McHugh on 29 October 1976. Fr Faul maintained that the style of the letter was 'British', drawing attention to the use of words like 'kiddies', 'kids', 'dad' and 'cheerio'. It is thought now the letter was typed in a UDR base and posted in Belfast. The death letter read:-

Dear Michael,

Just a few lines to let you know your name has been added to our list. By our 'List' we mean our vermin extermination list.

It's really too bad that your kids will not have a Daddy, but on second thoughts, none would be better than the rat they have for one now.

We know you work part-time in the Forestry-Division and your old yellow lorry ... has been followed by some of us time and again.

We already have our plans made and are just about waiting for the correct time to carry out the execution. Won't the world be a better place without scum like you? Where you are going you won't be able to make any more false accusations or write to any newspapers.

Remember, when you are doing a bit of farming, keep looking behind. No, don't worry, we won't take you from behind. We like scum like you to see what's coming to them.

Wouldn't it be a sin if anything happened to your kiddies? All because of the action of their dad.

See you soon, Michael
Cheerio.

It is true that Michael McHugh was continually followed by a UDR man who threatened and harassed him. In fact he had a set-to with him in late August 1976 on Chapel Lane. He noticed him afterwards on a number of occasions following him on the road. A week before he died Michael mentioned him to his wife and said, 'If anything happens to me he will have something to do with it'.

The British Army also posed a sinister threat. On 3 October 1975 a splinter republican gang kidnapped a leading Dutch industrialist, Dr Tiede Herrema, director of a steel firm in Limerick. He was rescued in Monasterevan after a siege of sixteen days, 22 October-7 November. Since Castlederg is near the Donegal border, there was a suspicion that two of the kidnappers, Marion Coyle and Eddie Gallagher, might have sought refuge there with their quarry. Houses were raided including McHughs'. The sinister element is that two 'civilian representatives' from the British Army barracks began to call at Michael McHugh's house. They were English men and they acted in a friendly manner. They often drew the conversation into political problems. They were seen on occasions walking the fields in wellington boots. On one occasion they offered Michael McHugh a gun for his protection. The McHughs were frightened of their ways.

The murder was carried out 'to the letter' on 21 January 1977. Michael McHugh had just left his wife Mary, a schoolteacher, and two little girls, aged four and two, and travelled down the lane in his yellow lorry, on his way to work at Killeter forest. His wife heard three bursts of machine-gun fire. When she looked out she saw the lorry with its headlights still on. 'I ran out,' she related, 'and my husband's body was lying beside the lorry. I knelt down and said some prayers.' Later an anonymous telephone caller in Derry claiming to represent the UFF admitted responsibility for the killing and claimed that McHugh was the west Tyrone commander of the Provisional IRA. The caller said that the murder had been carried out by the west Tyrone unit of the UFF.

Ten years later, following the evidence of an informer, nine UDA men were sentenced on 20 November 1987 for crimes ranging from robbery and hijacking to murder. They were all from the Derry area. One of them William Bredin (38), originally from Moville, County Donegal, was sentenced to life for the murder of Michael McHugh. He pleaded guilty and so few details were revealed in court. Peter McClay (30) was convicted of murdering Kevin Mulhern in the Waterside, Derry, on 3 October 1976. Both men received concurrent sentences for other offences including possession of guns, hijackings and conspiring to murder Kevin Agnew, solicitor, Maghera, between October 1976 and December 1977.[81] Former UDR man, David Hamilton (59) of Church Brae, Derry, was acquitted of murdering Mulhern and Eglington bar-owner, John Toland, on 22 November 1976. Lord Justice Turlough O'Donnell accepted his claim of police ill-treatment. Hamilton was jailed for five years for possessing guns. The judge said his crime was the more serious because he used his position in the UDR as a cover to transport guns. Robert Rutherford was jailed for ten years for armed robbery; he pleaded guilty and was given concurrent sentences for possession of guns and burglaries. Five others who admitted charges ranging from hijacking to having a gun were freed when given recorded or suspended sentences. Trevor Brace (32) and Aubrey Mills (35) were given two-year suspended sentences. Derek Kennedy (30), Alexander Collins (42) and David Simpson (31) were given four-year recorded sentences.

William Bredin, ex-RUC reserve policeman, now in Long Kesh (Maze) Prison, has revealed to Fr Denis Faul that he did not know at the time of the shooting that a threatening letter had been sent to Michael McHugh; he had been told that McHugh had shot two UDR men. Only after the shooting did his colleague inform him of the letter. His companion had a British Army issue map on which were marked roads and McHugh's lane and house. His companion was never charged; he was outside the country when an informer gave the evidence against this group of Derry UDA men; this man, a native of Castlederg, worked in close liaison with the British Army; he is now in Saudi Arabia; according to local people he is thought to have returned for his father's funeral. The murder of Michael McHugh was a classic combination of British undercover soldiers, UDR and UDA.

Information from a loyalist source alleges that Bredin's companion supplied Albert 'Ginger' Baker with British Army-supply grenades. The same source also suggest that a .38 revolver used in the killing of three Catholics in Derry in 1976, namely, Kevin Mulhern, 3 October, John Toland, 22 November, and James Loughrey, 25 November, was passed by this British agent to the security forces who used it to commit murder in 'No Man's Land' in South Armagh.

British Army Intelligence 1977-78

By 1977 the British Army had completed a circle in intelligence operations in Northern Ireland. It had taken over the role from the Special Branch RUC in the 1971-72 period and by 1977, following 'Ulsterisation', shared it again with the RUC. Further co-ordination was to come in 1979 with the advent of Sir Maurice Oldfield. David A. Charles summed up the role of the British Army Intelligence in an article 'Intelligence and Psychological Warfare Operations in Northern Ireland' in the *Journal of the Royal United Services Institute for Defence Studies* (September 1977):

1. Army Intelligence Corps personnel seconded to the RUC Special Branch;
2. close Army/RUC co-operation, maintained by joint operations centres;
3. local censuses to build up a street-by-street register of the population, and a card index of known or suspected terrorists, their families, friends, habits – the index is cross-referenced to reports and intelligence summaries so that a complete dossier, including photographs, can be put together for any person;
4. constant mobile and foot patrols, which allow troops to familiarise themselves with their area and to pick up background information;
5. snap searches, particularly vehicle checkpoints established at short notice;
6. joint Army/RUC patrols, and a special Army/RUC murder investigation squad to deal with sectarian killings;
7. covert operations – specially trained plainclothes patrols; use of the Special Air Service Regiment (SAS) in South Armagh; and use of infiltration, captured documents, informers and defectors to gain information;
8. interrogation techniques.

These methods are designed to destroy the subversive organisation by increasing the flow of information to the security forces, by immobilising or eliminating members of the organisation, and by denying them arms, explosives, refuge, recruits and intelligence. This in turn will break the organisation's hold on the population and will prevent expansion of the 'rival state'.

On 1 March 1977 Conor O'Clery, London editor, *The Irish Times*, reported in his paper that a full squadron of SAS, believed to be 120 men, was engaged in undercover military activity in Northern Ireland. A NATO troop deployment map for early 1977, contained in an annex to a defence White Paper published in 31 April 1977 in London, showed that Northern Ireland had 'one SAS squadron'. It had been believed that the number of SAS in South Armagh had been 30. The same White Paper confirmed the British policy of 'Ulsterisation', a policy that was to occupy the Secretary of State in a vital way in Northern Ireland for the next year.

A 'Training Paper' dated April 1977 gives the structures of the Intelligence bodies in Northern Ireland:

AGENCIES AVAILABLE TO THE UNIT IN NORTHERN IRELAND FROM
WHICH INFORMATION/INTELLIGENCE CAN BE OBTAINED

Military
1. Brigade Headquarters G (Int) including the Brigade Intelligence Section.
2. Brigade Weapons Intelligence Section (WIS).
3. Other units.
4. Own sub-unit.
5. Operation VENGEFUL.
6. Reconnaissance Interpretation Centre RAF (RIC).
7. 120 Security Section.
8. Royal Military Police Pointer Teams (39 Bde units only).
9. Province Search Centre Intelligence Cell (PSCIC).
10. Royal Navy (where applicable).

Police – Royal Ulster Constabularly (RUC)
11. Special Branch (SB). (Normally through MIO or FINCO).
12. Criminal Investigation Department (CID).
13. Uniform Branch.
14. Criminal Records Office (CRO). (Normally through Bde HQ or MIO, FINCO.)
15. Data Reference Centre (DRC). (Through Bde HQ, MIO or FINCO.)

Civilian
16. There are many of these to choose from and from some of them information has to be requested through another agency such as Special Branch. Examples:-
    a. COLERAINE – Vehicle Taxation Office (Direct).
    b. Vehicle Licensing Office. Through MIO/FINCO to SB.
    c. Housing Executive. Through MIO/FINCO to SB.
    d. Registrar of Births and Deaths. (Through Bde HQ.)
    e. Newspaper Editors. (For photographs.) (Direct.)

Formation HQ Staffs. These are made up from officers of all arms supported by Int Corps intelligence sections at HQ Northern Ireland and Bde HQs...

Liaison Intelligence NCOs (LINCOs). These are senior NCOs of the Int Corps or any arm, having been trained at the School of Service Intelligence for this role. They are on the establishment of 12 Int & Sy Coy. They are attached to a unit or sub-unit and co-located with them. They are not accredited to Special Branch, and the appointment does not imply the right of direct access to the Branch. Any business with Special Branch must be done through the local MIO of FINCO. The function of a LINCO is to provide intelligence liaison and continuity services within a battalion in Northern

Ireland. He is under the command of the brigade in whose area he operates but in support of the unit to which he is attached. He is under the command of 12 Int & Sy Coy for administration, apart from daily administrative functions. He serves a tour of two years. Every roulement unit has a least one LINCO. A total of 30 LINCO posts are now established for Northern Ireland.

Military Intelligence Officers (MIOs) and Field Intelligence NCOs (FINCOs). The former are any arm, the latter are senior NCOs of the Int Corps. They have all been trained at the School of Service Intelligence for their role. They are held on the establishment of the Special Military Intelligence Unit (SMIU), and are administered by 12 Int & Sy Coy. They serve for two years and are accredited and integrated into Divisional Special Branch staffs.

As subordinate members of Special Branch, they are under the direct command of the local Head of Special Branch (HSB) and give their primary allegiance to him. Their prime function is to provide the direct link for the passage of information between SB and the Army, and vice versa, at police Divisional and Sub-Divisional level. It is important to stress that unit IOs should on no account by-pass the MIO or FINCO when they are authorised to deal direct with SB, otherwise one of the main functions of the MIO/FINCO, i.e. providing continuity, is lost. In most cases SB prefer to deal with units only through the MIO or FINCO...

Security and Intelligence (SI) Personnel. Intelligence Corps personnel forming an element of 12 Int & Sy Coy, who are responsible for military security throughout Northern Ireland.

Weapons Intelligence Sections (WIS). These are co-ordinated by the SO2 Weapons Int at HQ NI but work and are commanded by the OC Weapons Int Section at Bde HQ. They comprise small teams of Ammunitions Technical Officers (ATOs), RMP and Int Corps NCOs. Their job is to collect and collate information on weapons, ammunition, explosives, devices and subversive personnel associated with this form of activity, concentrating on the technical methods of operating and the production of intelligence from it.

Data Reference Centre, Int Support Teams, Special Collation Teams. The functions of these organisations are dealt with in detail in the precis 'The Royal Ulster Constabulary'...

Reconnaissance Intelligence Centre Northern Ireland (RIC(NI)). The RIC (NI) became operational in May 1973. It is located at RAF ALDERGROVE. The function of the Centre is to produce aerial photography as requested by units. It is commanded by an RAF officer with RAF and Army (Int Corps) personnel to assist. It is essential that all unit IOs make a visit to RIC (NI) to see the equipment available and the photographic support they can expect

COMPOSITION OF FORMATION INTELLIGENCE STAFFS
IN NORTHERN IRELAND (1978)
HQ NI
Staff HQ NI
Col GS
GSO1 (Col)
2 x GSO2 (Majors)
4 x GSO3 (Captains)
SO2 Wpn Int (Captain)
SO2 Production
SO1 IDM (WO)
2 x SO2 IDM (Sgts.)
Attached civilians (Civil Servants)
Int Sect (20 Clerical)

PORTADOWN	LISBURN	DERRY	
3 Bde	39 Bde	8 Bde	12 Int & Sy Coy
GSO2 Int	GSO2 Int	GSO2 Int (Major)	30
GSO3 Int	GSO3 Int A	2 x GSO3 Int (Capt)	
GSO3 Int/Liaison	GSO3 Int B	GSO3 Int/Liaison (Capt)	
Int Sect (A desk =	GSO3 Int/Liaison	Int Sect	
Catholics B desk =	Int Sect		
Protestants).			
124 Sect	121 Sect	123 Sect	

Wpns Intelligence Sections (W18)	Data Reference Centre (DRC)	Regional Crime Squads Int Sp Teams	Special Collation Teams	Special Military Intelligence Unit
(9 each brigade Felix + 2 Int Corps + 2 RMP)	(5 RUC Insp + civilians)	(50 WO + Capt other NCOs)	(20. 1 x NCO at each location)	(30. Headed by Capt. FSC)

NOTE:- GSO = General Staff Officer

WO = Warrant Officer

FSC = Field Sources Controllers. Deals with all handlers. Made up of personnel from Sgt to Major, one for each RUC division.

SO2 Production = Capt. Production of Tasks (i. e. Internal organisation of intelligence staff duties).

to receive. Requests for such support are channelled through Bde HQ. RIC is ideal for photographing pin-point targets and areas smaller than 1 1/2 grid squares approximately. The response time should be about two hours, weather permitting. The advantage of having a locally based aerial photographic unit means that brigade and battalion officers can speak to the OC, the photographic interpreter and, indeed, the pilots about their tasks and requirements.

A week after the SAS soldiers were fined on minor charges in the Dublin court, David Blundy, in one of the first articles on the subject (*Sunday Times*, 13 March 1977) drew together a series of incidents depicting the British Army's bizarre secret war in Ulster. This included soldiers setting off plastic bomb explosions in border areas to create confusion about IRA activity; planting ammunition on suspects; concocting letters from Ulster civilians supporting the troops. Specifically he mentioned an over-enthusiastic bomb explosion set off by soldiers which destroyed Gerry King's weighbridge at Killeen causing more than £2,000 damage (set off according to RUC records by 'person or persons unknown' in November 1974); in February 1976 soldiers of the Black Watch regiment were given sentences for planting ammunition on civilians in Andersonstown; the planting of ammunition in the car hub of a UDA man Jackie Hutchinson; the machinegunning of citizens at the Glen Road bus terminal in 1972; the shooting of William Black in January 1974; the falsification of statistics of released internees returning to violence to hoodwink Merlyn Rees because the Army was unhappy about his policy of releases and the dialogue with Sinn Féin. The secret war included the discrediting of politicians. Blundy wrote:- 'Towards the end of 1974 a committee consisting of representatives from the Northern Ireland Office, the Army and the Royal Ulster Constabulary met at Stormont Castle and discussed among other things, ways of discrediting politicians judged hostile to Government policy'. Blundy continues by naming some members of the committee, one of whom, a senior British Army official, stated that the meeting 'was like a newspaper's editorial conference... Some of the ideas thrown up might be daft and never eventually appear in the paper'. Nevertheless, our sources maintain that, following a series of meetings, which continued into early 1975, the Committee issued a report which went to Army, Stormont and police officials, but was quickly withdrawn after protests from the RUC about possible political consequences'.

In 1976 Robert Fisk reported in *The Times* that British soldiers were using faked cards which bore the name Inter-Press Features. The danger it posed to journalists was acknowledged then by Mr Roy Mason. However, the practice of undercover soldiers using press cards to infiltrate loyalist and republican areas to take photographs seems to have continued. David Blundy in the *Sunday Times*, 31 July 1977, published four cards, two fakes and two genuine. The fakes were based on genuine cards with new data superimposed. One bore the name of an Army captain, a photograph and a signature. In 1976 the British government gave an assurance that plain clothes soldiers in Northern Ireland would no longer use the fake press cards. This time Mr Fred Mulley, spokesman for the Secretary of State, Northern Ireland and the Ministry of Defence said that after investigation no evidence was found to connect them with the Army. It was acknowledged that individual undercover soldiers could have used them without permission. The officer who provided the *Sunday Times* with them and an unnamed NCO who had served in Northern Ireland told the *Sunday Times* that such fakes had been used in Northern Ireland in the previous two years.

The advent of Mr Roy Mason as Secretary of State brought an 'intensification', to use his own word, of existing security measures, the strengthening of 'Ulsterisation' of security forces and the 'criminalisation' of political prisoners; harsher penalties for political offences were legislated for. On the border deployment of the SAS to the whole of the six counties, an *Irish Times* editorial of 9 June 1977 issued a word of warning:- 'And there must be grave misgivings about an increase in "SAS-type activity", which will certainly not enhance the acceptability of the regular security forces in some of the most difficult areas, and which would seem to some extent to run contrary to the main lines of policy'.

Such warnings fell on deaf ears. In November 1977 Major-General Timothy Creasey was appointed the Army's new commanding officer in Northern Ireland.[82] He was understood to be a friend of Brigadier Kitson and like him had a long career in 'counter-insurgency'. He was commander of the Sultan's armed forces in Oman between 1972 and 1975; SAS soldiers were part of his command there. He held a senior post in the 39th Infantry Brigade in Northern Ireland in 1956 at the time of the IRA Border Campaign. He was a bustling 'up and at 'em type' who, whatever about 'Ulsterisation', would not play second fiddle to the RUC.

In the period of December 1977 to the end of 1978 the SAS and undercover soldiers shot dead 11 people; Colm McNutt in Derry, 12 December 1977; Paul Duffy near Ardboe, County Tyrone, 26 February 1978; Denis Heaney in Derry, 10 June 1978; Jim Mulvenna, Denis Brown, William Mailey and William James Hanna in Belfast, 20 June 1978; John Boyle in Dunloy, 11 July 1978; James Taylor near Coagh, County Tyrone, 30 September 1978; William Smyth in Belfast, 24 October 1978; Patrick Duffy in Derry, 24 November 1978.

In the same period SAS/plain clothes soldiers suffered a number of casualties.

SAS/Plain Clothes Soldiers Casualties

Sergeant Hubert Shingleston, King's Own Scottish Borderers, attached to 16/5 Lancers at Kitchen Hill died when his SLR went off accidentally in an observation post in a hedgerow at 1.30 am on 25 November 1977.[83] A Royal Marines Sergeant, who was with him at the time, said at the inquest that the shooting happened in a field at the rear of Kilwilkie Estate, Lurgan. He said he was handing Shingleston an SLR when it went off, shooting Shingleston in the head. The body was taken by military ambulance to Craigavon area hospital. A doctor said he examined the body of a man dressed in combat uniform in an Army ambulance outside Craigavon hospital. The body was then taken by helicopter to Musgrave Hospital, Belfast. A Warrant Officer in the Intelligence Corps gave evidence of identification. (Why not an officer from his own regiment?) An armourer attached to the 1st Gordons said he examined the SLR weapon which killed Shingleston; it was old, having been made in 1957 but still in working order but the gas regulator would have needed adjustment to ensure the weapon recocked properly. The two soldiers had also a sub-machine-gun in the observation post.

'On Wednesday the 14th December 1977 we caught and executed Intelligence Officer Paul Harman.[84] He was operating under the name Hugill, and was engaged in SAS activities in West Belfast.'

So ran the opening sentence in the *Republican News* account of the killing of Paul Harman on 7 January 1978. It was officially admitted by the British Army on the night of 14 December 1977 that Harman was a member of the Intelligence Corps attached to 39th Brigade stationed at Lisburn. Lance Corporal Paul Harman (alias Paul Edward Hamnan) was 27 years of age and was a native of Orpington in Kent. He was a member of 14 Company Intelligence Corps; son of a career diplomat he was born in Ankara, Turkey; he served in Cyprus during the Greek-Turk war and came to Northern Ireland in 1977 when he was selected for special duties. The corps to which he belonged assessed the general political and military situation in the North, interliaising with the subsidiary intelligence officers in the regiments and directly with the SAS units. As with Captain Nairac, moving from one to another was logical.

The plain clothes soldier was driving a red Marina car near the junction of Monagh Road and Monagh Drive in the Turf Lodge area of Belfast when he was shot in the back of the head. The car crashed into the railings. An emergency call for an ambulance brought the first people to the scene. He was found dead beside the car. After the ambulance left the scene and before the police arrived, the car was set on fire and destroyed.

The IRA account stated that his complete intelligence data, personal firearm and a slim 'transistor-like' set of flares were taken by them. The folder contained miniature photographs of 73 republicans, including Billy McKee, Sinn Féin Ard-Chomhairle member Gerry Adams, advice centre worker Mary Kennedy. The article continued – 'Five weeks ago a people's taxi was fired at from a passing car in West Belfast. The number of this civilian vehicle, as well as a long list of others, were among the spy's file. Much of the information and a few photographs were of non-republican civilians.' The codes were as follows:- buildings were named after fruits – 'grape' meant a 'church'; 'pear', 'taxi'; 'apple', 'pub'. Towns and republican areas throughout the six counties were named supposedly after English football teams – Derry was 'Oxford'; Dromore in County Down 'Celtic', Crossmaglen, 'Notts'. Some republican centres were called after planets. Inside a copy of *Amateur Photographer* were intelligence maps of Belfast and its environs. Spy routes were plotted out. The paper published enlarged copies of some of the photographs.

14 Co. or HQ company to which Harman belonged was the eyes and ears of the Secretary of State. It was based at Portadown, Palace Barracks Holywood, Ebrington and Lisburn. There were 15 officers at each location. These were trained at SAS headquarters in Hereford, in weapons, signals, driving and local dialect and accent recognition.

Former SAS member Lt Colonel Iain Gordon-Lloyd was killed when his helicopter was shot down by the IRA using an M60 machine-gun at Jonesborough in South Armagh on 17 February 1978.

Two undercover soldiers were shot and wounded near Maghera in South Derry on 16 March 1978.[85] One of them, who died the next day, was named as Lance Corporal David Jones (23) from Worcestershire. He was seconded to the SAS from the 3rd Parachute Battalion. His companion who was wounded was Lance Corporal Kevin Smyth. They were hit in a shoot-out with IRA man Francis Hughes and another IRA volunteer. Hughes was subsequently captured. He died on hunger strike in Long Kesh (Maze) Prison on 12 May 1981. There is a vivid description of the gun battle in David Beresford's book *Ten Men Dead* (1987).

Tony Geraghty in his history of the SAS, *Who Dares Wins*, gives in Appendix A to his book a list of SAS casualties, 1950-80, the names of those killed in training or in action. Only two are officially listed for Northern Ireland, S. Sgt D.J. Naden, 1978 and Capt. H.R. Westmacott, 1980. The extraordinary thing is that Staff Sergeant D.J. Naden of the SAS was killed in an accident on the Garvagh to Limavady Road at the Shanalongford Bridge, County Derry on 7 June 1978. The *Northern Constitution*, 5 August 1978, reported the inquest on David John Naden of 8th Brigade, Ebrington Barracks, Derry. There was a verdict of misadventure. It stated that he died from multiple injuries after his car skidded on screening and crashed into Shanalongford Bridge. The force of the impact split the car in two, the rear remaining on the road and the front section ending up on the opposite bank of the river. Mystery is added to his death since he is listed as an official SAS 'casualty'.

Lance Corporal Alan David Swift was killed in Derry on 11 August 1978.[86] The shooting occurred on the edge of the Bogside. The IRA accepted responsibility. His age was given as 25 years. He was single and it was said he served with the 2nd Battalion, Scots Guards. He was from Formby, Liverpool. A British Army statement said, 'L. Cpl Swift was in plain clothes and on duty when he was shot as he sat in his car on the Letterkenny Road.'

Two soldiers were killed in a road accident near Nutts Corner while on undercover work on 5 October 1978.[87] Sergeant John Roeser (30), a married man from Colchester and Corporal Michael Bloor (28), a single man from Stevenge in Hertfordshire, died instantly when their blue 120Y Datsun car was in collision with an Army lorry.

On the same day, 5 October 1978, the IRA shot and wounded Corporal Richard Alan Bonnett, an undercover soldier in Dungannon.[88] They claimed he was a member of the SAS. He was in plain clothes and travelling in an unmarked car when the attack was mounted.

On 19 March 1978 the *Daily Mirror* claimed that the SAS was being secretly withdrawn from Northern Ireland. The Northern Ireland Office promptly described the report as a 'load of rubbish'. Mr McCusker, MP raised the report in Parliament. He was concerned because he said he thought the SAS had been effective in Northern Ireland; more were needed, not less. 'The UDR should also be trained in SAS techniques,' he said.

On Thursday 28 September 1978 a tragedy occurred in West Belfast which indicated that SAS/undercover work was still in operation. Three Belfast youths, Anthony Fisher (21), Springfield Road, Samuel McHugh (20), Springhill Avenue and Peter Lavery (21) of Glenalina Road were knocked down on the Glen Road by an undercover soldier who killed Fisher and McHugh in a hit and run accident. A few weeks after it occurred *Hibernia* (19 October) reported that the three youths signalled an approaching car as they walked past the Bass Brewery, assuming it to be a taxi – 'According to eye witnesses the car swerved to hit all three youths killing McHugh and Fisher and seriously injuring Lavery'. The *Irish News* (23 March 1979) reported the inquest. The undercover soldier of the 1st Battalion Queen's Regiment, said he drove on because he feared he would have been killed if he had stopped. In his statement he said – 'I left barracks at about midnight in civilian clothes armed and on duty. I saw three men stagger across my path after a pair of headlights had interrupted my vision. I struck them. The windscreen smashed and the bonnet buckled up. I was sure to be identified by unfriendly members of the population if I had stopped. My life would be in danger. I decided to drive on and report to the authorities as soon as possible'. The DPP decided to take no action in the case. The jury at the inquest returned an open verdict.

One of the SAS who served in Northern Ireland in 1978 and, apparently, in the 1974-75 period was Major Mike Kealy, DSO (1945-79). He ranks among today's SAS heroes. His parent regiment was the Queen's. His obituary appeared in *Mars & Minerva*, Vol. 4, No. 1, June 1979. He was awarded the DSO for bravery in a battle against odds at the Fort of Marbat in the 'Jebel' in the Oman province of Dhofar, 19 July 1972. The obituary states:-

> Michael John Anthony Kealy was born at Farnborough on 29 May, 1945. He was the only son of Colonel and Mrs John Kealy, whose only other child died tragically young.
>
> Mike leaves behind a devoted wife, Maggi and three children; two of these, Amy and William, are twins born on Christmas day only 2 months ago.
>
> He was educated at Eastbourne College and then commissioned from RMA Sandhurst into the Queen's Surreys in 1965 and posted to BAOR. As a member of The Queen's Regiment he served in Bahrain and with the Junior Infantryman's Battalion at Shorncliffe.
>
> In 1971 he was selected into 22 Special Air Service Regiment with whom he served throughout the world. He returned to 1 Queen's for 18 months in 1974-75 and again in 1978 for service in Northern Ireland and BAOR. From 1976-77 he was GSO3 in HQ SAS and SAS Group. He took command of 'D' Squadron 22 SAS in December 1978...

Another SAS soldier mentioned in an obituary in *Mars & Minerva* (Vol. 7, No. 2, 1985) as serving in Dhofar and Northern Ireland is S. Sgt Ray Abbots. The dates, however, are not pinpointed.

> Ray served with the Royal Tank Regiment before passing selection and joining 'G' Squadron 22 SAS in 1973. He joined the Mobility Troop and soon established himself as a hard-working and conscientious soldier, attaining excellent results in all courses that he attended. During the Squadron's tour of Dhofar and Ulster he proved himself to be a man of deep integrity and one with a sense of purpose ... Tragically, Ray died in a training accident on 16th January, 1985.

At this time the Secretary of State, Mr Roy Mason, explained why he had extended SAS work – 'Covert intelligence and covert surveillance and the effect of the SAS in Armagh proved worthwhile and I decided therefore to take the decision that the SAS should operate province-wide'. It was stated, however, although this may have been a ploy to draw away criticism from the SAS if mistakes were made, that there were not enough men available to cover all six counties and so a decision was taken to train members of every major unit going to Northern Ireland in SAS type of work. Mr Mason said, 'Now within the battalions we have small numbers of trained people in that particular sphere of operations, in which the SAS are famed to do the job, in the province'.

In the following year there were numerous incidents of farmers stumbling on undercover soldiers in bushes and dug-outs; in Derry and Belfast they were discovered in vacant houses.[89] English newspapers continued to create an image of a terrifying élite unit, even 'more dangerous than they are'! This was state-sponsored psychological warfare.

The truth is, SAS blunders brought tragedy and grief to many Irish homes.

The Shooting of Colm McNutt[90]

Colm McNutt of Derry knew no other world than the disturbed state of conflict in Northern Ireland. He grew up in it. He was 18 years of age when he was shot dead on 12 December 1977 by an undercover British Army officer in plain clothes. NcNutt was a section leader in the INLA. He seems to have been carrying out a plan to hijack a car in the company of another youth, Patrick Heslin Phelan, when the incident occurred. The undercover soldier had been provided with a back-up. The shooting happened at a car park at the junction of Little James Street and William Street, Derry. A British Army spokesman denied that the soldiers involved in the incident were SAS.

His mother pointed out to me when I visited her that he was only nine when the 'troubles' broke out. She added that he wouldn't have been in anything had his father been alive. Colm was constantly harassed by the Army from an early age. He was terrified of them. They arrested him frequently. When he grew up he spent six months in the Irish Army. He worked for some time at Wellworth's. He was off sick before he was shot and he did not leave the house much. He was going with a girl and was often in her company in the house. It was his custom to stay in the house from four in the afternoon until bedtime. The doctor had certified him for sickness benefit. At that time he was waiting for a card to come from the Labour Exchange so that he could collect some money. The card failed to arrive on Saturday but he was happy when it arrived on the Monday. In buoyant spirits he talked to his mother about getting a motorbike; he had been saving up for one.

His mother remembers him getting up on the fatal day, 12 December 1977, taking his cup of tea and setting off. Since his money arrived by post the day after the tragedy, his mother concluded that he must have gone to the Labour Exchange. Mrs McNutt never saw him alive again after he left the house. She knew no more until 3.30 pm. She was standing in the living room doing her daughter Una's hair when a woman from Creggan Heights came into the house and told her she thought Colm had been shot.

Statements made to the RUC by Hessie Phelan and a statement of an Army Captain of 8th Brigade Headquarters, Derry, help to give us a picture

The Shooting Of Colm McNutt

of what happened.

According to Phelan's accounts to the police he left the garage where he worked as an apprentice mechanic at 12.45 pm and went to William Street where he met Colm McNutt. They went to Nelly's cafe and had a cup of tea. McNutt asked him to accompany him to Great James Street and they returned a little later, about 2.30 pm. Phelan said he had only been in the INLA/IRSP three or four weeks at this time. When they came back from Great James Street they went to the car park at the junction of Little James Street and William Street to hijack a car. He thought there was a plan to do something at Maybrook dairy, perhaps a robbery. Phelan noticed a red Hillman Hunter drive into the car park with one person in it. The car stopped and he is alleged to have said to McNutt, 'There's a car now. We'll get this one'. They went to the car and told the man to put down the window. He screwed down the window a bit. McNutt told him they wanted the car. The driver said he wasn't giving it. McNutt then took a Webley revolver from the waistband of his trousers. Apparently it wasn't loaded. The man got out of the car and they told him they were taking the car and he should go to the Lion Bar. Phelan got into the driver's seat. McNutt walked round the car to get into the front passenger's seat. The man then ran round and began to shoot. Phelan dived out of the car and took cover behind another car. McNutt started to run. The man shot at him with a pistol-type gun which he held in both hands. McNutt was hit three or four times in the right side. The soldier then got into his car and drove off up William Street. Local people recall that other cars moved off with him. Phelan states that he picked up McNutt's gun and ran over to the Lion Bar and shouted at the barman to ring for an ambulance. He hid the gun at the back of the public house. Later it was recovered by police. Phelan accompanied McNutt in the ambulance to the hospital. McNutt told him to speak to his girlfriend and tell her what happened. He had been hit in the stomach and once in the arm.

In his statement Captain ... said that he had briefed a soldier in the presence of three other members of staff for a particular task which included the use of five unmarked saloon cars. Each car was equipped with covert radio. Each member was in possession of 'various items of very sensitive military equipment' concealed from view in each car. The sensitive equipment of the soldier involved in the shooting was contained in a shopping bag in his car. He was to operate alone in the general area of Bogside and Brandywell and was not to be separated from his vehicle except on a military order. At 3pm the captain received a message regarding the shooting and in a few minutes met up with him.

A crowd of people demonstrated on 13 December at the place where the shooting took place and then marched to protest at RUC headquarters in the Strand Road. The march was led by women carrying black flags and placards. They then moved to demonstrate at Guildhall Square.

A large crowd attended McNutt's funeral. It was a paramilitary funeral. A party of men wearing black berets and dark glasses accompanied the hearse. One of them was Raymond Gilmour, later to gain notoriety as an informer. The graveside oration was given by Mrs Maolíosa Costello, widow of Seamus Costello, former IRSP leader who had been murdered in Dublin a few weeks previous.

The Shooting of Paul Duffy[91]

On Sunday 26 February 1978 Paul Duffy (23), a carpenter of Carnan near Stewartstown, County Tyrone, came home after 11 am Mass and had his dinner. He was intent on going to a football match in Ardboe. Before leaving he asked his mother to leave planning permission papers in Cookstown for him; he intended building a house down the road from where his parents lived. He had no car with him; he had lost his licence for having no car insurance. He went to the match, spent some time with his friends around Ardboe and sought the loan of his brother-in-law's car. His brother-in-law was Gerry Forbes married to his sister Anne. Martin McGuckin, a friend, drove the car.

While he was at the match Paul heard that explosives brought from Dungannon had been left at a derelict house; fearing that they might present a danger to two old men, brothers of the name Quinn, who lived near it, Paul took a decision, apparently on the spur of the moment, to remove them. One lad, however, at the match told him there was a lot of Army activity in the area and to watch himself.

Paul had been arrested under Emergency Powers and ill-treated in an RUC station in February 1977. The ill-treatment took the form of slapping about the head, kicks on the ankles, pushing and boxing around the interrogation room, warnings that he would be killed. The police knew that he had had an accident and had lost his kneecap. They forced him to bend and squat, with his knees bent and his arms held straight out. They knocked him on the knee and kicked and twisted his foot from under him. All this caused him excruciating pain. He was stripped naked and made do press-ups. At first they allowed him to keep his underpants on but then made him take them off and put them over his head. They tried to smother him with a coat and then with a plastic bag.

After the torture in the RUC station a relative brought him to Dublin, secured a job for him and tried hard to dissuade him from involvement in any organisation. Paul returned home. In the year before he was shot by the SAS everyone was convinced that his involvement had ceased. He had started to plan the erection of a new house for himself. Despite the beating in the police station which resulted in his having to be removed to Tyrone County Hospital for treatment, his people thought he was not involved. His mother used to always ask him whether he was in anything. He would just say 'No' and use his charm to tell her not to worry. Upon his release from hospital and until he was shot he and his family were continually harassed by RUC and Army.

After the football match in Ardboe, Martin McGuckin drove Paul to the deserted farmhouse at Killygonland near The Diamond. The farm was a walled-in complex of an old dwelling house and outhouses, hay sheds and a single storey house with a loft. An open street led into it. Duffy and McGuckin drank Lucozade at Forbes' around 5.30 pm. They must have gone to the old house shortly after that. The farmhouse is about 400 yards from Forbes'. McGuckin dropped him off at the roadside, unaware of the purpose of Duffy's visit. Duffy walked alone the forty yards or so into the cul-de-sac yard. It would seem that he did not know exactly in which building the stuff was hidden. He did not know of course that the yard and houses were staked out by the SAS. When he at last moved towards the house where the explosives were, he was shot dead through the forehead. McGuckin had driven a piece after leaving Duffy off, had turned the car and had just drawn level with the entrance when he heard the volley of shots. He drove off; shots were fired after him and he was hit in the back. He stopped the car at Gerry Forbes' byre, a building at some distance from the dwelling house and got help. Some friends drove him to the house of the parish priest and phoned for an ambulance. Neighbours had heard the shooting. They knew Paul Duffy had gone that way and feared something had happened to him.

The following is part of the text of a proposed statement prepared by Mr P.A. Duffy, solicitor and uncle of Paul Duffy:

> Paul's killing must rank as the most bizarre in which the British Army has been involved. I just cannot say if the mortars shown on television and in photographs were found at the scene or whether they were simply a propaganda or justification exercise but there is no doubt that Paul was unarmed and he was shot in an enclosed yard surrounded by members of the British Army. When I saw Paul's body after the shooting it was clear that he had been shot through the forehead from the front with his back against the wall. There is not the slightest shadow of doubt that he was not even given a chance to surrender or allow himself to be arrested. It will be recalled that after the shooting of Patrick McElhone and the judicial justification given in that case to the shooting of a person when he is attempting to escape that I personally pointed out to the Secretary of State, and to the public at large the great risk that rose from that decision. That decision simply gave to the British Army a free hand to shoot down any person on the allegation that that person was attempting to escape. This is now the third occasion in which the British Army have used that statement in order to justify a killing. There is an immediate necessity for the Secretary of State to clearly set out the circumstances in which the British Army are justified in shooting down unarmed persons or indeed armed persons who want to surrender.
>
> The conduct of the British Army after the shooting was despicable and degraded Christian values and human life to a degree lower than those associated with the La Mon tragedy. Having clearly shot a young person dead without ever giving him a chance to live, they proceeded to degrade the human body. When I personally, along with the parish priest, approached them on two occasions and asked if someone had been injured they assured both of us that there was no one injured, despite the fact that they knew that within twenty yards the body of my

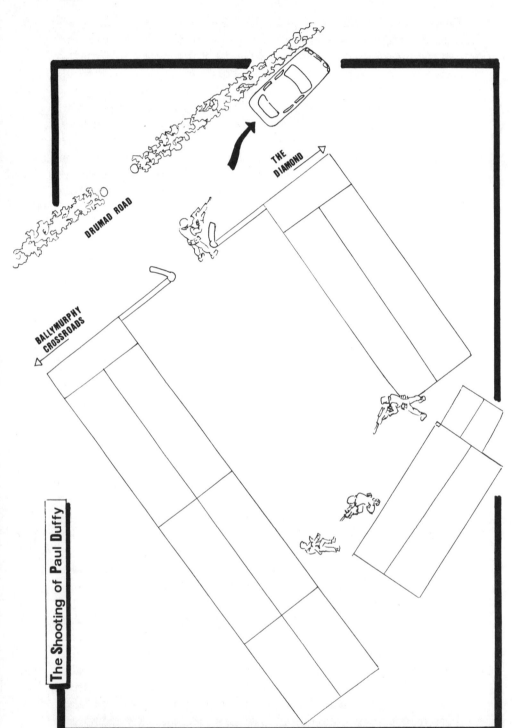

DRUMAD ROAD

THE DIAMOND

BALLYMURPHY CROSSROADS

The Shooting of Paul Duffy

nephew was lying. They refused to give him the right to be anointed by a priest which from the beginning of Christian time has been acknowledged as the one basic right that no authority, however despicable or desperate, has taken away.

I want on behalf of the parents and myself to thank sincerely the RUC and in particular Inspector Murphy of Cookstown who on taking charge of this incident immediately granted the local curate an opportunity to administer to the deceased. Indeed I want to place on record that the RUC gave to everyone concerned that consideration which the dead and those that are bereaved are normally entitled to. In this regard I want to condemn the shooting of a young police constable in Derry on Tuesday night last. The only factor that makes that killing less despicable than the killing of my nephew is that Paul Duffy was killed by a force that is supposed to be disciplined and subject to authority. Any effort to use the death of Paul as a justification for revenge is deplored by every member of Paul's family. In the past the Provisional IRA have not needed any justification for some of the most despicable crimes ever committed, and I see no reason now why they should seek such justification in carrying out another bloody crime in the name of the people of Ireland...

No charges were brought against the SAS for the shooting of Paul Duffy. He could have been arrested and need not have been shot. On 22 August 1978 the inquest on Paul Duffy commenced and although it was adjourned a basic frustration was immediately apparent. Mr Tom Cahill, QC had been instructed to act on behalf of Duffy's parents. The Ministry of Defence had quite a back-up team. The Northern Ireland Office had clearly not properly briefed their barrister. He had only got the file that morning and had only learned on his way to Cookstown that, in fact, the Army personnel were not going to give evidence. He had been advised that the DPP had directed that there would be no charges brought against the Army. The position in *Inquest under the Coroner's Act* is that if a person is likely or possibly to be charged with a criminal offence then that person is not a compellable witness, although he is a competent witness. This means that he cannot be compelled to give evidence. This section usually applies to cases where death results from a car accident and where the driver usually elects not to give evidence but simply puts his statement in evidence. In the Duffy case the DPP Office had decided that there was not to be any prosecution. This means one would have expected the Army to have given evidence. Not only were they not prepared to give evidence but they were not even at the inquest.

There were three relevant statements, namely the statement of the two soldiers and the statement of Inspector Murphy the police inspector in charge of investigations. The soldiers who were called Bravo A and Bravo

B each made statements which were quite inconsistent with each other. Bravo A said that he shot Paul Duffy as Duffy came out of a house. Bravo B said that he shot him as he ran across the yard. Their statements were quite inaccurate in saying that the car had gone up and down the road several times that morning. The car in question was in Dungannon and had not been on the road that morning at all apart from 8 am when Paul Duffy's sister had to go to Dungannon to nurse in the South Tyrone hospital. She did not return until the afternoon and the car was at Dungannon hospital all the time.

A further relevant point was that Chief Inspector Murphy, who was not at the inquest due to the fact that he was shot by the IRA early in the week of the inquest and was recuperating, stated that he had seen three mortars in the house when he inspected it. He then went on to detail the position and at the end of his statement said that he saw another mortar lying 6 feet away from Duffy's body. Mr P.A. Duffy personally inspected the body with Chief Inspector Murphy when he had given him permission to enter the yard contrary to the Army. He looked particularly to see if there was anything at or near the body. He is quite adamant he saw nothing at or near the body.

The inquest on 22 August 1978 was adjourned indefinitely. It resumed on 15 December 1978. Mr Tom Cahill, QC for the next of kin, described the non-appearance of the three soldiers who were directly involved in the shooting of Paul Duffy as 'a total negation of facts'. He said they should have turned up to clear up any doubt as to whether the young man had been shot improperly; all lived under a rule of law and this applied equally to Army as well as citizens; they could not shoot people in circumstances they could not justify.

Soldier 'B' said in his statement that he shot Paul Duffy. He said his commander woke him at 17.30 hours and he knew something was going on. 'I jumped down from the loft and I heard shots. I saw a man at my left; he had something in his hand. I shot him and he fell back'. He then ran to the roadway and fired shots at the rear of the escaping car; the car swerved but drove on. The statement was read out by a detective and in cross-examination Mr Cahill asked him whether the statement was taken under caution. The detective said it wasn't. Mr Cahill pointed out that it was an impossible situation; nobody knew whether the soldier who made a statement without caution was telling the truth, and the same soldier who shot a youth dead was not there for examination. Soldier 'A' (who was in charge) and Soldier 'C' both said that warnings were shouted at Duffy but he paid no heed. Mr Cahill said the statements were not worth the paper they were written on as the names of the soldiers making them were unknown. Chief Inspector Murphy gave evidence of going to the scene and taking charge of investigations. He said Duffy's body was lying on its back just outside the door of an outhouse; his feet were pointing towards the farmyard and his head was propped up against the hinge. He said he saw what appeared to be a rocket between two bales of hay about 6 feet away from the body in the beam of his torch. Mr Duffy, solicitor and uncle of Paul Duffy, said that he went to the body with Father McParland. Chief Inspector Murphy was helpful; he showed him the body by torchlight and he could see nothing close by; he contested a photograph presented at the inquest by a police photographer; he claimed that the photograph showed a rocket close by the body which was not there when he saw his dead nephew; he said he could not contest the Chief Inspector's evidence of a bomb some 6 ft from the body.

A member of staff of the forensic laboratory gave evidence of examining swabs taken from the dead man's hands with a view to ascertaining if he had been handling firearms; nothing was found.

In conclusion Mr Cahill said that, having heard the evidence, members of the jury could not be wiser as to how Paul Duffy died; the only witnesses of the shooting were the three soldiers and the Army had not thought fit to allow them to come along to the inquest and tell their stories; the parents of Paul Duffy would have liked to have known through the evidence presented at the inquest if the life of their son could have been saved; there was nothing to show in the evidence that the Army were apprehensive in the situation about their own safety and therefore could not have arrested Paul Duffy.

About 2,000 people attended Paul Duffy's funeral at Mullinahoe, Ardboe. Although the IRA claimed him as a member, there was no paramilitary presence. His companion who had been wounded, Martin McGuckin, had been brought to the Mid-Ulster hospital and was later transferred to Crumlin Road Prison, Belfast; all charges against him were eventually dropped.

There is a strange SAS sequel to the shooting of Paul Duffy. Within the year the SAS made a 'hide' in the yard of Paul's sister and brother-in-law, Gerry Vincent and Anne Forbes. They concealed themselves under a large old van which the Forbes used for growing mushrooms. The wheels had been removed and it made a handy shed. The SAS were discovered by accident. A scrapman called at the house and when Gerry went searching for old scraps of iron in the yard his eye fell on a man's finger with a ring on it when he looked under the van. He raised the alarm. A crowd gathered. The family rang the RUC and the local priest. The people gathered round the van, then called on those concealed to come out. It seemed hardly possible but three men with blackened faces emerged from under the van. They reversed on foot into a nearby field away from the people until they reached a helicopter which they must have called for by radio. The story is one of several examples of SAS hideouts discovered at this time, some of them in Carrickmore, County Tyrone.

*The Shooting and Wounding of Desmond Mackin
and Robert Gamble[92]*

Desmond Mackin (22) and Robert Gamble (26) were mates. On Wednesday night, 15 March 1978 they spent the evening drinking together in the Andersonstown Social Club, Belfast. About 11.30 pm Mackin discovered that his taxi was missing. They made an arrangement that Gamble would lift Mackin the next morning and they would search around the estates for the taxi. The next morning Gamble turned up between 11 am and 11.30 am. They went over the Ramoan Drive area which is at the head of the Glen Road thinking it might be there. Gamble drove around for a while looking out for the taxi. He then parked his car and they searched on foot. They looked into lock-up garages off the streets behind the flats. They began to notice some men acting suspiciously; they did not recognise them; one was sitting in a car. This went on for about half-an-hour. They decided to get out of the way. As they were walking across the Glen Road they noticed a man crossing the Glen Road also; he was glancing up the Glen Road towards them. He walked on towards the bus stop. He was about 23 to 24 years of age, short hair, wearing a blue snorkel jacket just like Robert Gamble's; they were fashionable at the time. Mackin said he thought he had seen him before. As they were both members of the republican movement, they were conscious from time to time of surveillance.

Gamble stated: 'As we approached where the man had been standing he started to open his coat and put his hand inside his coat. I thought that he was going to draw a gun; I threw my hands up and brought them down on top of his hands and as soon as I did this I heard the shots. I started running across the Glen Road and felt being shot in the right leg. I stumbled on; as I reached the Green I felt being shot in the back and I started to stumble and eventually fell; before I hit the ground I was shot in the left arm. As I lay on the ground I tried to lift my head to see who had been shooting and I saw figures running towards me where I was lying. They were coming from the corner of Ramoan and Clonelly. Somebody had shouted, "Don't move". I heard a shot at the same time and I felt it hit me. When they reached me one of them dragged me for a few feet and I think he asked me about a gun. I said, "I have not got a gun". The next thing I knew I seen soldiers in uniform and someone shouted "Get a doctor". Then the crowd just gathered round. I was given some medical attention as I lay on the ground. I was taken to the Royal Victoria hospital in an ambulance. I received seven gun shot wounds, two in my right arm, two in my right leg, two in my left shoulder or left back and one in my left arm. All these entered from the back'.

Mackin's version is as follows – 'As we walked past him he made some remark, and we looked towards him and I saw him pull a gun. In the panic afterwards a struggle took place between the three of us and I heard shots.

At this here I broke free and bolted across the Glen Road and on to a green.

At this time figures appeared all round the place and started shooting. I was shot in the nose but I kept running and as I reached the bottom of the Green I was shot in the left foot. I ran into the garages and I turned to my left and tried to get into a woman's back door. I heard English voices and I still heard the shooting. At that I turned round and I saw a person facing me with a gun in his hand; he was firing at me. I jumped to the ground and all I heard was, "Throw out your gun". I shouted back, "I have no gun, I have no gun". I shouted, "I'm wounded badly and bleeding badly". At that he said, "Get up and put your hands over your head". Just as I got up he fired two shots; they missed so I dived to the ground behind a coalbunker. I saw him walk towards me and fire a shot into me; it hit me on the left side. I am convinced he was going to kill me only women came out and started to scream and he stopped. They all got round me. The soldiers kept the people back till an ambulance came and took me away'.

Some local people gave statements to the Association for Legal Justice which give some picture of the activity of the SAS at the time of the incident. Shortly after 1 pm three of the SAS, all wearing Snorkel jackets buttoned up to their faces, burst into a flat where a young baby-sitter was minding two small children. They ordered the baby-sitter out. When the family arrived after the alarm was raised, they found a curtain in the living-room had been pulled up and a window opened which overlooked Rosnareen Avenue; obviously SAS men covering the area near the shooting. Another local witnessed the shooting, 'Whenever I heard the first shot, I looked out the window and seen one man standing in the middle of the Green; he was shooting at a man who was running. They were all in plain clothes. One was wearing a black anorak with no hood. He was the one who was doing most of the shooting. I saw one man falling and getting up. I think the other man shot him in the leg. He started shooting at another man, whom I now know to be Bobby Gamble. Then this one who was doing the shooting (he had a beard) at Bobby Gamble started shooting at him as he lay on the ground with his hands stretched behind his back. He fired twice at him and he was only a couple of feet from him. After he shot Bobby he brought the other fellow (soldier) whom I think was wounded because he was hopping and he sat on the wall beside the fence pointing the gun at Bobby while the one with the beard started to search Bobby. All this time there was a grey mini van, parked half on the lay-by and half on the footpath. A plain clothes man dressed in a sports jacket was kneeling down at the front end of the van, pointing his gun down Ramoan Gardens away from the shooting and giving cover to others. I seen all this from the window. After this I ran out the back; there was another plain clothes man out there. He was pointing his gun at a man whom I believe now to be Dessie Mackin, whose hands were held behind his head. When the plain clothes man saw me, he shouted,

"Get into the kitchen or I'll blow your fucking head off". Whenever I walked back into the kitchen I said to my father, "there's a man out there with a gun and he said get in or he'd blow my fucking head off". Then we heard shooting and we ran out the front as we heard them shouting and knew they were English. I then ran up the street to Bobby Gamble and helped to give First Aid. All this time the plain clothes men were still covering them. Then the Paras came on the scene. We were putting bandages on for Bobby's leg was lying wide open. One Para gave me three or four pressure bandages when he seen the wound on the leg. When the plain clothes men seen the Paras, they stood with their hands in the air waving their guns...'

The Paras were the resident regiment in the area who arrived on the scene shortly after the shooting.

Soldier 'A' was the soldier at the bus stop. In his statement he said he recognised Mackin and Gamble in the Glen Road because he was operating in that area and was familiar with photographs and descriptions of persons relevant to his duties. He said – 'As they approached ... I turned my back on them and Mackin came round behind me and caught hold of my left shoulder and pulled me round to face him. Gamble was about one pace behind Mackin. Mackin asked me who I was and what I was doing in the area. He then told me to take my hands out of my pocket which I did. At the same time I saw Mackin place his hand inside his coat jacket in the area of the waistband. I then took about five paces backwards and drew my pistol. At the same time I also saw Gamble place his hand inside his jacket. In both cases it appeared to me that they were about to make a cross draw. Gamble then came towards me and tackled me around the lower part of my body. I fired one aimed shot at the upper part of Gamble's body. Both of us the fell to the ground and were struggling. I was still holding my pistol in my left hand. I did not see any pistol in Gamble's hand but felt a thump in the thigh as if I had been kicked. Following this there was a general struggle, during which I fired more shots at Gamble. There was a lot of confusion, and the next thing I remember is being on my own and trying to stand. I managed to get to my feet, and crossed the Glen Road, and walked down Ramoan Gardens. At this stage I saw soldier 'B' who was standing on the grassed area on the corner. He had his weapon out, and was covering a man who was lying on the grass. I then saw Mackin running across Rossnareen Avenue into the estate, and I fired one aimed shot at him. I made my way to the bottom corner of 76 Rossnareen Avenue, where I sat down and covered the man lying on the ground whilst Soldier 'B' was trying to keep civilians out of the area ... I was subsequently taken by military ambulance to the MPH and during the journey I handed my pistol ... to the Medical Orderly in the vehicle. During the incident I fired 13 shots, and sustained a gunshot wound in my right thigh.'

Soldier 'A' states that he recognised Mackin and Gamble; they were IRA suspects. Would an armed man turn his back on men he believed to be armed terrorists? He says he saw Gamble and Mackin move as if to draw. No gun was ever found despite the fact the incident happened from start to finish in a small area along a direct line taken by the two wounded men; neither men were ever shown to have been armed on that day. The soldier drew his gun and fired at Gamble and continued to shoot at him. In the court case the soldier said that he had his gun directly down the front of the waist band of his trousers. If Gamble and Mackin were armed why would they not simply have shot him? It was odd behaviour for Gamble, as the soldier asserted, to tackle a soldier who had a gun in his hands if he knew that Mackin also had a gun. If Gamble had a gun why should he ignore that fact and come straight at another man who had a gun in his hands in a frontal tackle. The soldier discharged 11 shots in the struggle. He described feeling what he thought was the barrel of a pistol against his right thigh and then he felt a thump. He did not know who shot him. He did not ascribe it to Gamble or Mackin. There were other soldiers in the area and there is the possibility that one of them shot him. The soldier said in the Gamble case that he thought there were four vehicles for the 8 plain clothes soldiers in the patrol; they were saloon cars except for a very small van. Soldier 'B' said there were 8 vehicles in the patrol for the eight soldiers! Mackin thought there were many more than 8 plain clothes soldiers. Another thing. It is extraordinary that a professional soldier who had fired a weapon should hand his pistol to a Medical Orderly.

Soldier 'B' was parked in a vehicle at the junction of Ramoan Gardens and Clonelly Avenue. He saw soldier 'A' at the bus stop and recognised Mackin and Gamble who walked across the road in the direction of Soldier 'A'. He said that when they reached Soldier 'A' Mackin tapped Soldier 'A' on the shoulder from behind. He continued in his statement, 'By this time Soldier 'A' had turned to face the two men and a few words appeared to be exchanged. I saw Soldier 'A' attempt to walk away, but was restrained by both men who caught hold of his clothing. A struggle ensued with Gamble and Soldier 'A' on the ground. Mackin moved a few paces backwards and I saw him produce a pistol from the front of his clothing in the area of his waistband, whereupon he commenced to fire at Soldier 'A'. I heard at least two or possibly three shots from the minute I saw the encounter taking place. I left my vehicle and went towards Soldier 'A' in order to assist him. As I left the vehicle and on seeing Gamble draw a weapon, I also drew my 9 mm pistol. As I heard the shots being fired I started to engage Mackin and fired a number of aimed shots at him. I do not know if I hit him. By this time Mackin had seen me and started to run across the open area in front of 82-74 Rossnareen Avenue towards the area of 100 Ramoan Gardens. I still continued to fire at Mackin until I considered him to be out of range. I noticed by this time that he had difficulty in running and assumed that he had been wounded. By this time also I noticed that the struggle between Soldier 'A' and Gamble had finished and Gamble was running in the same direction as Mackin. I also started to fire at Gamble as I understood him to be armed. I fired a number of aimed shots at him hitting him at least once. He collapsed after what I considered to be my second hit whereupon I approached him. He was lying on his left side and he was conscious. He was bleeding profusely from the legs and stomach. I searched him but found no weapon. I then questioned him as to the whereabouts of his weapon and he replied "I dropped it on the grass". I also asked him where he had been hit and he replied, "The leg, arm and chest or stomach". By this time Soldier 'A' had moved to the end of the pathway beyond 74 Rossnareen Avenue and I shouted to him to cover Gamble whilst I carried out a cursory check of the grass for Gamble's gun. At this time a person who identified himself as a civilian doctor arrived on the scene and asked if he could attend Gamble. He was allowed to do this. I then continued with a cursory search of the area over which Gamble had travelled but no weapon was found ...'

Soldier 'B' says that when Gamble and the soldier fell to the ground Mackin then stepped back a couple of paces, produced a handgun and began firing 'two possibly three shots'. Since no gun fired by Mackin or Gamble was found, it would seem the shots 'B' heard were the shots Soldier 'A' had admitted firing at Gamble and Mackin. He states that when he left his car he began running towards and firing at Mackin. He states that Mackin started to run away and did not return fire. He admitted that when Mackin ran past him he did not see any gun in Mackin's hand.

When Mackin was out of range of 'B's' gun 'B' began firing at Gamble, on the excuse 'I believed him to be armed'. Yet he never saw Gamble with a gun even when he passed him at a distance of less than 15 yards. 'B' was pressed on this by Mr Desmond Boal, QC representing Gamble.

> Q 1865. So you had not seen him with a gun before; you had not seen him with a gun during the tussle; you did not hear any report of a gun that might have come from him and now you have got a perfect view of him at one point, no more than 15 yards away and there is no gun. Witness B, what were the grounds of your belief that he had a gun? A. Because of what had happened ...
>
> Q 1884. Do your instructions allow you to fire on somebody who might have a gun as distinct from somebody who has a gun? A. I believed him to be armed because he was a danger to Soldier 'A' and I thought he was a danger to myself.
>
> Q 1885. A danger perhaps in the sense that he was grappling with Soldier 'A' physically but that is a far cry from a danger in the sense that he would be prepared to shoot Soldier 'A'. You see away at the very beginning of my cross examination you told the court that your under-

standing of the yellow card instructions was that you used a gun only in the event of you believing that your own life was in danger or that somebody else's life was in danger. When this man was running across 15 yards from you, intent upon obviously getting away, without you having seen a gun, what led you to believe that your life was in danger? A. As I have said because of the prior incident that had occurred.

Q 1886. That led you to believe that your life was in danger? A. Yes.

Q 1887. He had not directed any shots at you; he had not directed any shots at your colleague? A. I did not know that.

'B' does not mention having heard any of the 11 shots that 'A' fired including the shot he fired before Gamble and 'A' fell to the ground. Why would an armed man wrestle on the ground with another armed man? Why did 'B' feel the need to hit Gamble seven times before stopping fire? 'B' says Gamble admitted to having a gun; why was 'B' unable to find it in a small area in the line that Gamble took from the bus stop to the green? If Mackin had a gun and 'B' says he was able to see it at a distance when Mackin was at the bus stop, why was he unable to see it when Mackin ran close to him? Both men were apprehended – how would it be possible, if they had arms, that these could not be found? 'B' refers to Gamble and Mackin as 'my two assailants', yet these two men never fired a shot at him.

Gamble and Mackin gave separate statements in separate locations while they lay in hospital wounded; there was no possibility of collusion; their statements are in agreement apart from a minor point on the night before the incident.

On Monday, 20 March 1978 Desmond Mackin's mother was in the hallway of Ward 16 of the Royal Victoria Hospital at 5 pm talking to her son. She did not get into the ward to see him. She was informed by a detective that Desmond had been arrested under Section 10 of the Emergency Provisions Act (1973) and that he was being transferred to the Musgrave Park Military Hospital where he would be in charge of the CID. Mrs Mackin through Fr Denis Faul made a complaint about the way Desmond was treated in his transfer:-

Desmond was taken out of the back of the RVH in a wheelchair with a soldier holding the drip. A student nurse was pushing the wheelchair and four Special Branch men and a few soldiers and a couple of RUC men were walking all round him. A freak snowstorm was on. Desmond had no blanket on him; he had the coat of his pyjamas around his shoulders. The soldier said, 'Get in'. Desmond was not under shelter; he could not get out of the chair. He was sitting with the snow coming down on him. His uncle took off his overcoat and put it over Dessie's head. By the time they got the stretcher his uncle had lifted him off the chair and on to the stretcher which was covered with snow. I asked,

'Have you a blanket to put round him'. They took one out and put it over him. I want to complain about this. They brought him out like an old dog.

On 5 October 1979 Robert Gamble was found guilty of wounding the SAS soldier and of possessing a pistol on 16 March 1978. He was found not guilty of attempted murder. He was sentenced to 8 years concurrent on each of the two charges. On 28 February 1980 he was freed following a three day re-trial at Belfast Crown Court before Lord Justice Gibson. Desmond Mackin had fled to the Republic of Ireland and later to the USA. He was arrested in New York by immigration officials in October 1980 and was held in custody. The British Government made a formal request to the State Department for his extradition, as he was being deported to the Republic at his own request. The US Court of Appeals in a judgement on 23 December 1981 upheld the ruling of Federal Magistrate Namoi Buchwald that he could not be extradited to Northern Ireland, as the British Government had requested, because his alleged offence was 'political' in character. Mackin agreed to deportation before an immigrant judge and returned to Ireland on 30 December 1981.

The Shooting of Denis Heaney[93]

Denis Heaney was born on 1 November 1956. He was 12 years of age, the youngest of four boys in a family of thirteen, when the violence first erupted in Derry in October 1968. He witnessed the harassment and ill-treatment of the Catholic population by the British Army. He was 14 years of age when the paratroopers murdered 14 people on the streets of Derry. Denis left school when he was sixteen and started work as an apprentice fitter. Six months later he was returning home from work when someone threw a bolt from the bus in which he was travelling, breaking the windscreen of a police vehicle. Everyone on the bus was arrested. All but Denis were released after two hours.

He was kept spread-eagled against the wall for several hours. A soldier kicked his feet from under him several times. Eventually he was interviewed by the RUC and released at 11.30 pm.

Denis Heaney completed his apprenticeship and was employed as a fitter in the DuPont factory on the outskirts of Derry. He belonged to the culture of his day, beloved by his family who called him 'Wee Denis', and naturally joined in the discussions in pub and home about what was happening in Northern Ireland. He had a steady girlfriend, played football twice weekly; his favourite pastime was music, the strange extremes of listening to heavy rock music and playing Irish traditional music on the fiddle given to him by his father.

In May 1978 the British Army and RUC raided the Heaney home and arrested him under the Prevention of Terrorism Act. He was kept in Strand Road RUC Barracks for three days. He made allegations of ill-treatment: He was made to stand to attention for hours on end. Interrogation sessions lasted an average of three hours with an hour's break and then more interrogations. During that time he was punched and slapped about the room by three different police officers. He said that when one got tired knocking him about another took over. At one point an RUC man put his knuckles behind Denis's mastoid bones, lifted him clean out of the chair and held him several inches off the ground. When the pain became unbearable Denis knocked the policeman's hands away, whereupon he was punched savagely in the stomach as he fell. RUC officers presented him with statements written by themselves and tried to force him to sign them. Before he was released they told him they would bide their time and shoot him.

Denis Heaney led a double life. He had many friends and a steady girlfriend but neither they nor his family knew he was a member of the IRA. His girlfriend and other friends were not involved. At the time he was arrested the youth, who was later to accompany him on the hijacking that led to his death, was also arrested. This companion was released shortly before Denis. Mrs Heaney spoke to him when he came out of the police barracks, asking him about Denis. Obviously, being a member of an organisation, he wasn't going to give anything away. 'I don't know your son, Mrs Heaney', he said. No one knew at that time that Denis was in the IRA.

Denis stayed with his brother Seamus at Clarendon Street, Derry, on Friday, 9 June 1978. It was customary for him to stay there on Friday and Saturday nights in order to meet his girlfriend. Seamus saw him last about 1 am on Saturday morning. Denis got up early and left before Seamus and his family were awake. He went to his parent's house at Greenhaw Road. He arrived home at about 10 am or 11 am. His mother remembers him sitting in the armchair at the fire reading a book, *Vanishing Derry*, which his brother Bernard had bought. 'It's not worth the money,' he commented. His mother looked at him bemusedly, noting his brown head of hair, his red moustache and the black hair on his stomach. 'If I wasn't your mother,' she teased, 'I would say you were dying your hair.' 'O, mother, you're terrible!' he said. His mother went upstairs bringing clothes up to the hotpress. Gabrielle, his sister, was in the bathroom. Denis came up, saw the bathroom door closed, went back downstairs, shouted, 'Cheerio, Pops', to his father and went off.

That was the last any of the family saw of him. He left home between 1.30 pm and 2 pm.

Denis teamed up with a fellow-IRA man, the same person who had been arrested with him, and they went to hijack a car. By coincidence the car they attempted to hijack was driven by an SAS soldier in plain clothes who was on surveillance patrol. He was backed up by a second SAS man in a car immediately behind him. In the incident that followed Denis was shot dead and his companion was fired on but escaped. Like other incidents of the kind it all happened within a few minutes.

Richard McCarron, a bookmaker's clerk, witnessed some of the events:

I am employed as a clerk in William Gallagher's betting shop, at 14a Chamberlain Street, Derry. On Saturday, 10 June 1978 there was a newspaper strike on in Northern Ireland. I usually put the papers for the racing up on the walls at 10 am. I knew in advance that there would be no papers and I made arrangements with my nephews who were coming home from England to have some English papers delivered to the shop. My nephews arrived with these at about 2.15 pm. We exchanged greetings and they left. It was about 2.30 pm.

I started to put the papers on the walls, just inside the door of the shop which was open. I heard a burst of gunfire, about four or five shots and a screech of brakes of a car. I saw two cars speeding over Chamberlain Street, towards William Street. The car in front was red in colour, the car behind chocolate brown. Both cars turned to the left at William Street. Then I saw the fellow lying in Harvey Street. He was in a crouched position, half on the footpath and the gutter; his knees were doubled up and he was facing the wall.

I ran over and turned him on his back. I thought he had been knee-capped. His hands were covering his face. He was wearing what I took to be grey industrial gloves. I am not sure if he had one or two.

Another man arrived beside me. I pulled the injured man's knees down and I saw blood on his clothes, at the stomach and chest. There was also blood on the knees of his trousers. I pulled down his hands to see if I recognised him. His eyes were open and staring. I did not know him so I put my hand into the inside pocket of his jacket. There were some papers in the pocket but they were covered in blood. By this time, a lot of people had gathered and someone shouted to get an ambulance. The Army arrived and I heard the Radio Officer report that he was at the scene of a shooting and he could not see any gun or shells.

I would estimate the time between the first shots and the Army's arrival to be about four minutes. The ambulance came and I went back to the betting shop.

Robert Barrett, a bus driver, who lived in Chamberlain Street also witnessed some of the details:

I was in my home on Saturday, 10 June 1978 watching racing on TV. It was somewhere between 2.30 pm and 2.45 pm as the race I was watching went off at 2.45 pm, and it had not commenced. I heard a burst of gunfire, about three or four shots. I ran to the door and as I reached it, I heard a second burst of gunfire. I think it was two shots. I saw a man running from the bookie's and I thought something had happened there. I made to go across the street and, as I did so, two cars came around the corner at Harvey Street. They were flying and I had to jump back on the footpath or I would have been run over.

The first car was a red Cortina. I got a clear look at the driver. He was in his middle thirties, wearing a grey sports coat. He was clean shaven with a full face. I didn't notice the colour of his hair. He was the only occupant of the car.

The second car was brown-coloured, but I didn't make out the company name. The driver who was the only occupant was wearing what appeared to be a denim jacket. He was in his early twenties, with a fair bushy moustache and longish straggly fair hair.

I ran across the street towards the 720 Bar. I turned the corner and as I did so I saw a man whom I now know to be Dickie McCarron turning over a fellow who was lying on the edge of the footpath, beside the grating. My first thought was that someone had been knee-capped but when I looked he was either dying or dead, because his face was grey-white. I knelt down and started to say the Act of Contrition. A lot of people gathered, and as I finished the prayer the Army arrived.

On the day Denis Heaney was shot a new Stewarts' supermarket was opened in Derry. Paula Heaney went to the opening. Mrs Heaney and Joan were sitting in the house. Mrs Heaney's cousin, Betty Henderson, called. She had seen the crowd gathered in William Street. She had gone over and recognised Denis. There was a lot of confusion. Denis was like Gerry O'Hara. News had even been brought to Gerry O'Hara's wife and people sympathised with her. She knew, however, that Gerry was all right. Betty Henderson found it hard to tell Mrs Heaney straight out. She told her that there was some shooting. At the back of her mind Mrs Heaney knew it was Denis and that he was dead. At 3.30 pm Gabrielle went to her brother Seamus and said some fella had been shot over in the Bog. Seamus was working at documents which he had to collect. He did not bother about the news since there was no indication that it was Denis. He was still working when a caller came to the door at 5 pm and said, 'Are you Seamus? I want to speak to you privately'. Seamus took him into the kitchen. The caller said, 'I have some very bad news for you. Your brother Denis has been shot'.

'Is he bad?' asked Seamus.

'He's dead'.

Seamus then said that he knew people in the Bog and they would check it. He went to the hospital and arrived about 5.30 pm. He met a priest and gave a description of Denis to him. He was then taken to the morgue and identified his brother.

Great crowds attended the funeral Mass for Denis Heaney on Tuesday,

13 June at Our Lady of Lourdes Church in Shantallow. Many people lined the route as a uniformed piper, playing laments, led a guard of honour from Na Fianna Éireann, Cumann na mBan and Cumann na gCáilíní. At the gates of the cemetery a volley of shots was fired from rifles in a last farewell.

The inquest was held in November 1979. An open verdict was returned. Exact details of the shooting were not given after an objection by Mr Michael Nicholson, QC, instructed by Mr R.B. Campbell who appeared for the next of kin. He objected to depositions from two detective inspectors and a detective sergeant which related to interviews between them and two soldiers, 'A' and 'B' who were involved in the shooting. Mr Nicholson objected to verbal evidence unless he was given an opportunity to cross-examine the soldiers in the witness box. He said that, unless the Ministry of Defence intended to call the soldiers or make them available, it was his submission that it was quite wrong to have any statement made or some explanation or excuse for the shooting put in. He said that if he was not given an opportunity to cross-examine the soldiers then it was only hearsay evidence.

The Coroner Mr B. W. McCloskey expressed his judicial discretion and would not allow the evidence to be admitted.

The Ministry of Defence Counsel said he reserved the right to question the Coroner's decision by judicial review. Mr McCloskey also refused to allow a statement of a third soldier described as Soldier 'C'.

Professor Thomas K. Marshall who performed a *post mortem* examination said that death was caused by bullet wounds to the trunk. The deceased had been struck by five bullets, three of which were fatal. These bullets had entered from the rear, a fact established from the examination of Heaney's jacket. A fourth bullet also hit him in the back of the chest but was not fatal. A fifth bullet hit him in the back of the calf of the right leg. No bullets were recovered.

Mr Marshall said he could not determine from what distance the bullets were fired but they were not near and by this he meant two feet. The three fatal bullets had travelled horizontally and the fourth which hit the deceased in the back could have struck him as he was bending backwards.

Mr Nicholson asked, if deceased had been standing at the time the fourth bullet had been fired, then could the person who fired the bullet be kneeling and firing from an angle of 30 degrees. Mr Marshall agreed. In answer to a further question he said that, assuming the deceased was standing at the time he was hit by the fourth bullet, then the person firing could have been holding the pistol 15 inches above the ground; if the deceased was perfectly erect, it would not be consistent with the bullets being fired from a car. The wound on the leg would have in-activated the leg for a short while. He said the deceased might have fallen over or been able to hop off.

Mrs Sheila NcNabb who came on the scene of the shooting attended him, but by then he had practically no pulse. She did not recall seeing any glove or firearm; he could have had a glove on his right hand as he lay on his right side.

Richard McCarron also gave evidence at the inquest.

A member of the police patrol group said the deceased was wearing a brown glove on his right hand. Forensic evidence revealed no firearm residue. Although residue and barium particles were detected from the swab from the right palm of the deceased, it was admitted that such particles could be got from working at a car.

Following the open verdict at the inquest, Denis Heaney's father, Denis Heaney senior, initiated an action claiming damages against the Ministry of Defence under the Fatal Accidents (NI) Order 1977 and the Law Reform (Miscellaneous Provisions) Act (NI) 1937 for loss and damages suffered by the dependants and estate of the deceased by reason of his death caused by the negligence and assault and battery of the soldiers. Denis Heaney senior died 25 April 1985. The action came to a trial in the name of his mother, Elizabeth Heaney, as *administratrix de bonis non* of his estate. Judge Kelly dismissed the action. It suffered from a serious weakness in that there were no other witnesses of the actual shooting except the soldiers who fired the shots. Heaney's companion was in prison in the Republic of Ireland. The High Court damages action assured the presence of the SAS soldiers. Captain 'C' said he had detailed soldiers 'A' and 'B' to carry out a plain clothes patrol in the area of Bogside, Brandywell and city centre. He briefed them about 2 pm. Each carried a Browning automatic pistol. The patrol began about 2.30 pm. Their duty was to observe, note and report anything significant and they had no instructions to engage any persons unless their lives were threatened.

Soldier 'A' testified that he was driving an unmarked red Renault 12TL saloon car. Soldier 'B' followed in a gold-coloured Vauxhall Magnum saloon car. Two-thirds of the way down Chamberlain Street and heading to William Street, he noticed a group of five or six young men standing near the Cladagh Bar (formerly the 720 Bar); two came from the crowd towards his car, pointed at it and seemed intent on stopping it; each pulled aside their jackets to show they had guns in the waistband of their trousers; he slowed and stopped; they came to different sides of the car, Heaney to the driver's side. Soldier 'A' alleged that Heaney tapped the driver's window with the pistol motioning that he open the door; he thought it was a Colt .45 automatic and the hammer was in the half-cock position. Soldier 'B', some ten yards behind, had seen what had happened although signalled to stop by Heaney's companion. 'B' got out of his car; Heaney's companion made to draw a gun whereupon he fired two shots at him. 'B' then observed that at his right Heaney was aiming a pistol at him and he fired two shots at Heaney who fell to the ground apparently struck by one of the bullets; he saw him raising his left hand holding a pistol.

Soldier 'A' had by this time got out of his car. Heaney had moved up to the rear of 'A's' car. 'A' was then behind him. Soldier 'A' then has to account for shooting Heaney in the back. How does he do it?

Soldier 'A' says he saw Heaney, still on the ground with his back to him, raise his left arm and bring it round holding a pistol in his direction as if to aim at him. He then from 10 to 12 feet away fired four shots at Heaney, coolly and deliberately with the intention of killing him. The four shots struck him. Heaney sprawled over on the pavement and his pistol fell from his hand. 'A' picked it up and threw it into the car and drove off quickly. He radioed Captain 'C' and he, Soldier 'B' and Captain 'C' then met in the Railway car park. Heaney's companion, it was alleged, was seen running into the 720 Bar.

The pistol recovered, allegedly belonging to Heaney, was a 9 mm calibre Spanish Star BS self-loading pistol. Mystery remains as to whether Heaney was wearing a glove or two glove or any gloves. Richard McCarron thought he was wearing grey industrial gloves. Nurse McNabb did not notice any glove. A member of the Royal Army Medical Corps who arrived at the scene of the shooting in the ambulance says Heaney was wearing a light brown suede glove on the right hand. The point is not significant. Whether he was wearing gloves or not, he did not fire. Heaney was armed with a defective gun. Often the mere showing of a gun is reckoned enough to hijack a car. To shoot a person while hijacking would be very counter-productive from an IRA viewpoint. His companion was unarmed.

The High Court action for damages brought the SAS men before the public. Captain 'C' is described by relatives of Denis Heaney as Arab-like in appearance, swarthy olive skin, handsome, with a great head of hair, brown moustache, piercing eyes, about 40 years of age, about 5'10", very broad shoulders; he was known in Derry for a few years previous. Soldier 'B' is described as non-descript in appearance, an 'ordinary bloke', small, fat and sandy-haired, about 34 years of age. Soldier 'A' was very tall, well over 6', receding hair, gingery beard, blotchy skin, well-built, tough-looking, longish face with deep-set eyes; he gave the impression of being callous by nature; he admitted frankly that he did not shoot Denis Heaney in panic but shot him deliberately with the intention of killing him.

All the bullets struck Denis Heaney in the back and on the back of the calf of his leg. Relatives still believe that he was shot running away and could have been arrested once he had fallen. They cannot prove it. Heaney's companion, who did not appear at the inquest or at the court, told me that the object of their mission was to hijack a car. They did not realise that the cars contained SAS men. For them it was an unfortunate coincidence.

The Ballysillan Massacre[94]

At 9 pm on 20 June 1978 Daniel Devlin was rudely interrupted while showing films in the Shamrock Club in Flax Street, Ardoyne, Belfast. The doorman told him he was wanted outside. He went to the main door and saw four men there. One of them asked him for the keys of the car, just for ten minutes. He was annoyed. 'You're not getting them,' he replied. One of them said, 'Well, we'll be back'. At that he handed over the keys. No firearm was produced. His Mazda estate car had been taken for use by the Provisional IRA.

In the incident that followed the seizure of this car four men from north Belfast were shot dead by a group of SAS and one RUC man. Three of those killed were IRA volunteers – James Gerard Mulvenna (28), of Ballycastle Street, Denis Emmanuel Brown (28), of Ballynure Street, William John Mailey (30), Chatham Street. William James Hanna (28) of Alliance Road, an innocent passer-by, was the fourth victim.

The IRA active service team were in possession of bombs when they were shot. They aimed to sabotage the GPO Depot on the Ballysillan Road, Belfast. The firebombs they carried were all of the same pattern, contained in blue webbing packs, surrounded with rubber, and made up of a timing and primer unit contained in a small box, together with a plastic container of petrol, detonators and a piece of rectangular section metal girder.

The Depot was staked out by a combined force of five SAS men armed with Armalite rifles and one RUC man armed with a Sterling sub-machine-gun. The presence of an RUC man is significant. It points to the initiation of the RUC into SAS tactics with a view to 'Ulsterising' such operations. This was later brought to fruition in the SSU (Special Support Unit) of 'E' Department, RUC Headquarters. The RUC officer fired 22 shots in the ambush. His name was not revealed at the inquest; he was referred to as witness 'F' in the manner of the anonymity of SAS soldiers; it is unusual for a police officer's name not to be revealed at an inquest.

A story in the *Belfast Telegraph* (22 June 1978) surmised that the decision to watch the Depot had been taken in RUC Headquarters after an article in *Republican News* on 10 June stating that the Provisionals intended concentrating on transport and communications targets. Six days after the article, the Post Office's Dial House in Belfast city centre was attacked and that was followed by incendiary attacks on depots in Derry and Martin's Buildings, Belfast. The alternative theory is that the RUC received information. On 19 January 1981 Maurice Gilvarry (24) of Butler Street, Ardoyne, Belfast, was found shot dead. The IRA claimed that he was a former member who had been giving information to the RUC. His name was linked to giving information on the Ballysillan operation.

A British Army statement issued on the day of the shooting, 21 June 1978, said, 'The men were challenged, and there was an exchange of gunfire. Four men were shot dead'. Part of the propaganda game on the part of the state is to get a message across to the public quickly; it is difficult then to contradict the first story; things are made easy for the British Army and RUC in Northern Ireland where the media are favourable to them. The media in this case immediately took up the theme of a gun battle and set at large the idea that the men died in a fair fight. The three IRA men were unarmed; no guns were recovered; there was no forensic evidence that they had guns; the fourth man was an innocent passer-by; the sole survivor, another Protestant and the companion of William Hanna, makes it clear in his statement that the shooting was sudden and there was no warning. The SAS in their statements emphasise that they were under fire and that they issued warnings. The four men were gunned down in cold blood. Mr Roy Mason, MP, the Secretary of State, muscled in on 22 June to announce that there would be no special inquiry into the role of the SAS in the shooting. One calls to mind the wry remark of Claud Cockburn in *The Irish Times* after the SAS were sent into South Armagh, that what makes the SAS 'special' is that British spokesmen pretend that the SAS are not terrorists.

The British tabloid newspapers went a stage further to show that the IRA men deserved to die. Because the firebombs were similar to those used in the La Mon hotel fire, when twelve people were burned to death the previous February, they took the liberty of linking these same men with that atrocity. The *Daily Mirror* headline of 23 June ran, 'Dead IRA "La Mon Suspects"– Depot Bombers Carried Napalm'.

From reading the statements of the SAS men at the inquest with caution one can try to piece together the events of that night. Four IRA men, Mulvenna, Brown and Mailey and a fourth unnamed man (as we shall see, he escaped) drove to Wheatfield Drive in the Mazda estate car taken from Daniel Devlin. Wheatfield Drive is a cul-de-sac with a vehicle turning point at the innermost end. The driver presumably did a 'U' turn to have the car facing outwards again. A lane runs from Wheatfield Drive to the Ballysillan Road and is bounded by the GPO Depot on one side and the Ballysillan Playing Fields on the other.

The SAS staked out the immediate area of the Depot. Soldier 'D', a Lance Corporal, and Soldier 'E', a trooper, were positioned in bushes close to the lane and just down from the GPO. Soldier 'D' in his statement said, 'At approximately 12.10 am I saw an estate car turn in the entrance of flats behind the GPO Depot. This car then stopped in the entrance to the flats. From my position I saw two men leave the car from the passenger side. One of these men got out of the front passenger seat and the other from the rear passenger seat. As soon as these men got out of the car I moved back slightly into better cover. The next thing I saw was three men walk past my position. These men were walking in single file approximately 2-3 yards apart. The front two were carrying small green rucksacks and the third one was carrying what seemed to be a bag over his shoulder. When they passed me I moved position and watched them walk up the laneway which runs alongside the GPO Depot out on to the Ballysillan Road. I lost sight of these men after they had walked approximately 35 metres from my position. I remained in my position and about a couple of minutes later I heard shouting from the top of the laneway, followed by gunfire.'

The commanding officer Soldier 'A' takes up the story; he mentions a fourth man; this can not be the fourth IRA man who remained in the car but he is introduced to explain away the shooting of William Hanna; the impression given is that Hanna is thought to be one of the IRA party.

Soldier 'A': 'We had been in concealed position for approximately one hour from approximately 23.10 hrs. Four men including myself and the RUC Officer were concealed in a garden facing the depot and convenient to a lane running down the side of it. At the bottom of this lane two more of my soldiers were concealed in a bush watching the rear of the depot. I was carrying an AR15 Colt Commander rifle and 60 rounds of ammunition for the same. At 00.00 hrs I received information from another observation post that a group of men were acting suspiciously in the lane at the side of the GPO Depot. We reacted to this message by the four of us leaving our concealed positions. The other two men concealed at the bottom of the lane remained concealed. I saw what appeared to be four men grouped at the corner of the lane and Ballysillan Road. I identified one man holding a large green bag, which from information previously supplied to me I identified to be a bomb. Soldier 'B' who was to the left of me shouted to the men, "Stop, stop, stop". Soldier 'C' had a strong torch attached to his weapon and this was shining on the men.' (*Soldier 'C' in his statement says*: 'I saw the Police Officer begin to break cover and on looking back towards the lane I saw a small number of men one of whom attempted to throw a container over the fence which fell back into the lane. At this point I moved out of cover and when I was in the centre of the road I switched on a powerful torch; just prior to this I heard one of the members of the patrol give a verbal warning, "Stop! Stop! Stop!". I shouted "Stop" and then engaged the man who didn't stop whom I believed was responsible for firing in my direction...') Soldier 'A': 'At this I heard shots. I don't know exactly who fired first but Soldier 'B', 'C' and I opened fire after coming under fire ourselves from their direction. We continued to fire down the lane at these men. I fired a total of twenty rounds in all. I believed all the men to be armed at the time in view of the fact they were carrying bombs and we had come under fire. I ordered my men to stop firing...'

Meanwhile Soldier 'D', who is with Soldier 'E', continues his story – 'I moved out onto the laneway followed by Soldier 'E'. I then saw a group of about 4 men running down the laneway towards us. One of these men stopped, and seemed to take up a kneeling firing position and the other three kept running on towards us. At this stage I thought we were under fire from behind and in front. I moved out into the centre of the laneway and shouted at these men which were still running towards us to "Stop, Security Forces". These men did not stop running and the person who had taken up the firing position remained where he was and I thought he was firing at soldiers above me. I immediately fired a burst of 4 to 5 rounds at this kneeling man. I am unable to say whether I hit this man or not. The men that were running ran towards the hedge and as gunfire was very close to me I told Soldier 'E' to move back into the sports field and I followed him. He ran about twenty metres into the field and I ran after him. He then stopped running and I stopped about 5 metres from him. On looking on my left I saw a man running towards us. This man was about 30 metres away from me and seemed to be carrying a handgun. I shouted at him, "Stop, Security Forces" and he made no effort whatsoever to stop. As I was under fire and as there was a lot of gunfire in the immediate vicinity I fired an aimed burst of shots at him. Soldier 'E' also fired at this man. This man fell to the ground...'

As one can see the statements are well spiced with imaginary firing from phantom gunmen, shouts of warning and escaping men in 'firing positions' and seemingly 'carrying a handgun'. The shooting of William Hanna is even more indefensible; a man on the ground surrounded by skilled soldiers is deliberately finished off because he is thought to be an IRA man.

David Alexander Graham of Wheatfield Drive was William Hanna's companion the night he was shot. In his statement he relates that on 20 June 1978 at about 9 pm he called for William Hanna at his home in Alliance Avenue. They went to drink at the Mountainview Club at Olive Street in the Shankill. They left the club about ten past eleven. They took a taxi up to the top of the Bilston Road and Crumlin Road and set out to walk the rest of the way home. They walked down Bilston Road to the Ballysillan Road and across into the lane which runs onto the Ardoyne Road. He continues – 'When we got about two thirds way down the lane Billy and I were walking side by side and engaged in conversation. I don't know whether he was on my right or my left. I didn't see anyone else about, either in uniform or in civilian clothes. All of a sudden and without any warning I heard shooting very close at hand. Although I had a few drinks in me, as I have already said, I hit the ground immediately. The shooting lasted for a few seconds; then I heard English accents speaking. In the time between me first hearing the shooting and hearing the accents I rolled into the bushes at the side of the lane. When I heard the voices I shouted, "I'm over here mister". A soldier in uniform came over to me and I saw that he had a rifle. I was put against the wall at the side of the lane and searched. I was later taken to North Queen Street Police Station ... I want to say that when the shooting started I was very scared and I'm still scared when I think about it...'

William Hanna must have been hit by the shooting that Graham heard close at hand. His killing is described in the SAS statements. 'A' the commanding officer says – 'Approximately 20 metres further on we came across a third man lying on the ground. Soldier 'C' ordered the man to stay still and put his hands on his head. He moved as if to go for a weapon and both soldiers opened fire on the man. I checked this man and found he was still alive. I quickly searched him for a gun but he had none...We continued on down the lane to where a fourth man was lying on the ground. Soldiers 'B' and 'C' ordered the man (*Graham*) to put his hands on his head and remain still. The man did this ...'Soldier 'B' says – 'As we were clearing the alleyway there was another body laid on the left of the alleyway. This person appeared to be still alive and Soldier 'C' told him not to move. He then told him to put his hands on his head and as he did so he made a twisting movement as to go for a weapon, and as I believed he was reaching for a weapon I and Soldier 'C' opened fire on this person. We then disregarded his body and made a further search finding another body who in my opinion was still alive. We told him (*Graham, who had shouted out to them*) to be still and to put his hands on his head...' Soldier 'C' says – 'At this point the man on the ground twisted and started to turn towards us and appeared to me to be making a movement with his right hand. At no time did the man try to identify himself and when he made the movement I interpreted it as going for a weapon. I and the man covering me simultaneously opened fire. The man appeared to be hit and I left him for another member of the patrol to cover...'

The escape of the fourth unnamed IRA man was seen by Witness 'H' who was in Wheatfield Drive on the night of the shooting. He saw the parked Mazda there and one man in the driver's seat. He walked up to the pedestrian walk at the side of the GPO yard; when he looked up the walk he saw three or four 'fellas' standing about half-way up the walk – 'They were just standing there close together. I walked away and I heard shooting. I then saw the blue Mazda car reverse up Wheatfield Drive and stop in Wheatfield Drive. Its front wheel went up the kerb. This man then jumped out of the car and left the front door open. He ran up Wheatfield Drive and scaled a wall beside the block of maisonettes'.

The Shooting of John Boyle[95]

The eleventh of July 1978 was a glorious summer day. Many people in customary Irish fashion would have said, 'It's great to be alive'. It was an unhappy day, however, for the Boyle family of Dunloy, County Antrim. Sixteen-year-old schoolboy John Boyle was shot dead on that day by two SAS soldiers, Sergeant Alan Michael Bohan (28) and Lance Corporal Joseph Temperley (26). The series of events that led to his death began the day previously. John visited the small graveyard about half-a-mile from the village. He went through the gate and up the path flanked with hedges. It is a graveyard no longer in use, surrounded with walls, hedges and some trees. To the right just at the end of the path there is a little ruined building, really only the remains of the walls. A large yew tree faces you at the opposite end of the graveyard when you reach the end of the path. The graveyard is of interest for its old stones and John had moved round the cemetery looking for ancestral names. It was then he came across an arms cache in a plastic bag which had been pushed under a fallen headstone, the leaning slab forming a roof of protection. John told his brother Hugh. He took him to the cemetery and showed him the cache. Hugh told their father and he also came and visited the spot. The cache included an Armalite rifle, a revolver, an incendiary bomb, a face mask, combat jacket and black beret. Cornelius Boyle, the father, then telephoned Ballymoney RUC Station and spoke to Detective Constable Millar. Police from Ballymoney came out and inspected the package.

The RUC and the SAS were to stake out the cemetery. The Dunloy area is a small nationalist island surrounded by loyalists. It was easy to assume IRA connections with the weapons. The RUC informed the British Army's brigade headquarters at Ebrington of the find. An army liaison officer with the RUC acted as co-ordinator in the plan. He was later to say in court that the detective who first heard of the arms' find in the cemetery from Mr Boyle told him that the family had been 'warned off' and that he, the detective, would telephone again to 're-emphasise the warning'. Constable Robert George Millar attended a meeting on the night of 10 July; at the midnight meeting were Army officers whom Millar believed, as he said in court, were SAS men; none of the soldiers was identified to him by name; Millar said that he had warned the Army officers on at least three occasions during the briefing that the information had come from a family with children between the ages of ten and twenty-four and advised them to be careful in case any returned to the scene out of curiosity. He went over the aerial map with the Army members and pointed out to them that ninety per cent of the people who lived there were Catholics. He also remarked to them that there was an Orange parade there the following morning but denied suggesting or discussing with the soldiers that the parade could be the intended target for those who were to pick up the guns.

A second briefing took place in the graveyard. The SAS took up their positions around 3 am and were then left alone. There were four SAS soldiers observing the cemetery. Two soldiers armed with an SLR rifle and an Armalite rifle were positioned in the little ruined house and the two others, Bohan and Temperley, armed with Armalites, hid about twelve yards from the arms' cache in a hedge near the stone wall of the cemetery. It was Bohan as sergeant (at the outset of the trial Mr Michael Nicholson, QC referred to Bohan as a sergeant and Temperley as a corporal) who was in charge of the three other men and who located the observation positions; the major briefing, however, was done at Ballymoney RUC station by Soldier 'F', an SAS captain, who Bohan later said in court had left the Army.

On the morning of 11 July Detective Constable Millar phoned the Boyle family at 9.40 am to warn them, as he said, in case of a booby trap as they might lose their legs. When he rang, John Boyle, his brother Hugh and Cornelius their father had just left the house. He told Mrs Boyle to make sure that none of the family went back to the graveyard. The call was minutes too late. They had left at 9.30 am. Asked in court why he had not mentioned in his statement that he had cautioned the SAS men about the safety of the family on three occasions, Constable Millar said that he had mentioned it in his original statement and that the statement before the court was one typed and sent to him for signing from the officer of the Director of Public Prosecutions in February 1979; he assumed that it had been deleted from the statement for a legal reason.

At 10 am on 11 July John Boyle entered the graveyard again. Curiosity had obviously got the better of him.

For what happened next we are dependent on Bohan and Temperely as witnesses. Both made statements but only Bohan testified in court. The circumstances of their statements are a matter of interest. In court Constable Millar said that he went to Ballykelly Barracks after the shooting. He saw Bohan and Temperley but they were introduced to him as Soldier 'A' and Soldier 'B'. He was not aware of their proper names. 'A's' face was still blackened with camouflage. Statements were given to him in the presence of Major T.B. Wright from the British Army's legal service. Major Wright handed the statements to another detective. A formal caution was read to the soldiers who signed them 'Soldier A' and 'Soldier B'. The police did not interview the accused. (An RUC order, numbered 136/76, issued in October 1976, directed that in shooting incidents, involving soldiers, the soldiers should be referred to by letters of the alphabet, in the initial stages of inquiry, so as not to disclose their identity). The other detective was probably Constable James Bell who was to testify at the trial that he went to interview the accused at Ballykelly Army Camp on the afternoon of the shooting. 'People were produced,' said Constable Bell. 'I had never seen them before. I tried to ask who they were and things were discussed in general terms. It was a situation I had never come up against before.'

In court Detective Constable Bell read statements by Bohan and Temperley made to him a month after the shooting. In his statement Bohan said that a detective constable had taken him to the graveyard with another soldier and had briefed him about the area. The detective had also assured him that the family who found the bundle under the gravestone would not be back to the site of the find...'I believed we would be up against armed terrorists.

Our mission was to capture the terrorists. To apprehend a terrorist would be of great value for long-term intelligence'. He said that when he saw the boy at the gravestone on the morning of 11 July, he thought it was a terrorist whose photograph he had seen and who was believed to be an expert in explosives. (Detective Constable Millar who was cross-examined on this point denied that he had suggested the name of a man wanted by the police as a possible 'collector' of the bomb and weapon in the graveyard. He also denied mentioning any particular person to the army officers, whose names he did not know either, who were at the briefing in the police station after midnight on the morning of the shooting). Bohan continues, 'I did not challenge because of the possibility of other terrorists supporting him. He started to remove the rifle from the bag, and turned, bringing it to bear on us. We fired, and he fell'. Temperley said he saw the young man standing with the weapon at his right side at hip level – 'Sergeant Bohan stood up, and I thought he was going to make a challenge. There was a noise like the rustling of clothing or branches. The man turned round and the rifle came up, pointing towards the observation post. Sergeant Bohan fired, then I fired three shots at "single fire"'. Temperley also alleged in his statement that at the briefing with the police they were told that the cache had been discovered by a 10-year-old child. The previous day the detective constable denied this in court.

The prosecution case argued that John Boyle was shot at one of three stages: either when he was looking into the hole; or having checked, stood up with his back to the two accused; or, having taken the rifle and turned away, was shot without warning and without challenge. Mr Michael Nicholson, QC said that the force used was not reasonable in the circumstances and therefore the Crown said that John Boyle was murdered. While Boyle had his back to them they opened fire; he was wounded once in the head and twice in the back, in the right shoulder, and was killed immediately.

The Deputy State Pathologist Dr John Press told the court of a *post-mortem* examination he carried out on Boyle. He stated that the three bullets which killed Boyle came from behind. There was an entrance wound at the back of the youth's head with an exit wound on the left eyelid and two other entrance wounds in the right back below the shoulder. Mr Michael Lavery, QC, defending, argued that defence medical experts would say that the boy had been shot in the head first from the front with the bullet entering the left eye – 'As he was falling forward towards the gunmen and collapsing over, the other two bullets struck his back...' In cross-examination Dr Press agreed with the defence that the wound in the back of the head did look more like an exit wound and the wound in the eye could have been either. He insisted that bullet fragment tracks inside the head and body showed definitely that the fragments had been travelling forward. In his summing up Lord Chief Justice Sir Robert Lowry said that a number of unsatisfactory features of Dr Press's evidence had been identified, such as wrong measurements, inaccurate location of landmarks, and failure to note a number of essential features. He concluded that John Boyle could not have been shot in the back in the ordinary sense. He said, 'I consider the most probable thing is that Soldier 'A' (Bohan) shot the deceased in the head when the deceased's head was facing him. The deceased fell forward, his left shoulder coming under his body and while in that position two bullets from Soldier 'B' (Temperley) entered his back, and made a downward track towards the left hip'. It must be noted that Judge Lowry did not abort the case when the independent medical evidence was argued during the trial. He said, 'The basic allegation is that the man was killed by the intentional discharge of a firearm with the intention or knowledge that he would be killed or severely injured. There is no doubt that the Crown set out to prove he was shot in the back. Suppose they fail to do that, the issue of the primary fact is still there'.

The kernel of the clearing of the soldiers was the judge's acceptance of the claims of the SAS men that they fired because they believed that their lives were in danger. The case was not proven beyond doubt. The judge remarked:

> The Army and Soldier 'A' (Bohan) and the patrol gravely mishandled the operation because they shot an innocent boy, who, whether he was holding a gun or not, had no capacity to harm them...The strength of the defence is its simplicity. If in a statement it is reasonably possible that Boyle did in any way turn the rifle towards the defendants, it is impossible to say the Crown have refuted the evidence.

The judge was critical of the military handling of the operation. He said that the soldiers had raised a case of justifiable homicide on the grounds of self-defence and, unless they knew that the rifle was not loaded, they may well have believed that their lives were in danger. 'The belief of the two soldiers here was mistaken, but even a mistaken belief is enough. The defendants knew, or ought to have known, that they were dealing with one person and all they had to do was to jump on him before he could get the rifle into his hands'.

One of the strange features of the trial was the switch in the identification of the ranks of the accused. At the outset they were referred to as Sergeant Bohan and Corporal Temperley. In the witness box Bohan described himself as corporal and Temperley as trooper. Various media then adopted various titles for the defendants. Sir Robert Lowry criticised Bohan strongly in his summing up. 'I found him wholly untrustworthy and eager to make meritorious points, and he alleged that a 10-year-old child had found the cache which I am sure was untrue. Soldier 'A' was quite definite that the plan was to capture whoever came to the cache but he was unsatisfactory when questioned as to the details of the plan'. 'If he thought he was a terrorist,' he concluded, 'one wonders why he allowed him to get a rifle into his hands. The deceased did not attack or consciously menace the soldiers.'

In this matter one must ask a crucial question. How could security forces who plan a stake-out possibly leave their own personnel in danger by leaving loaded weapons as bait and allow the person or persons coming to retrieve them to take such loaded weapons in their hands? To the public this is incredible.

In his evidence Bohan said that months after the killing he was told by one of the soldiers ('D' and 'E') who were posted as lookouts that they did not see who was coming into the graveyard because their vision was obscured by the wheel of John Boyle's tractor. This was why he did not get a radio message to tell him someone was approaching the cemetery. 'Were they unable to move their heads to look around the wheel?', he was asked. He could not say. He revealed that he joined the British Army twelve years previously and six years later became a member of the SAS. Since he gave his age as 28 this would mean that he joined the Army at the age of 16. He served in Northern Ireland prior to his previous stint, two four-month tours and an 18-month tour; he had been one month in the North prior to the Boyle shooting.

According to Tony Geraghty in his history of the SAS, Bohan and Temperley, who were friends, were relaxing in a depot a few miles away when they were summoned with three others to Ballymoney police station for the briefing.

Bohan lost his temper a few times during cross-examination. When asked whether he had been told to shoot the first person who approached the cache because he was likely to be a terrorist, he replied, 'I do not believe you can go around shooting people. No one can tell me to get out and shoot somebody'. During questions about records of his use of ammunition prior to the Dunloy incident, Sir Robert Lowry remarked that such records should have been made available to the RUC. Bohan could not remember whether he had fired at Boyle from a sitting position or a standing position, or whether he fired from the hip or the shoulder, and he could not even say what part of Boyle's body he fired at. On tactics he commented irritably, 'Tactics are like opinions. Everyone has one. We cannot dictate tactics to terrorists'. Mr Nicholson, QC pointed out that both men had exposed themselves and thus showed they knew Boyle was unaccompanied. Bohan ran to the body of the dead boy after shooting him despite the fear of other terrorists in the vicinity. He removed the plastic bag despite the possibility of a booby trap. Bohan agreed that he was a marksman but denied that he had fired at Boyle in a cool calm manner. 'I don't think anyone sitting 12 yards from a person with a weapon is in a calm state of mind'. He agreed that photographs of the dead youth lying in the graveyard gave the impression that Boyle had just emptied the cache when he was shot. The truth was that he lifted the plastic bag at the boy's feet and emptied the contents out.

Some detail emerged in the evidence in court as to what happened after John Boyle had been shot. His brother Hugh heard the shooting as he was working in a field just opposite the little cemetery. He headed over and was taken captive by the SAS with blackened faces. They made him raise his hands in the air and then forced him to spread-eagle on the ground. Likewise, Con Boyle, the boy's father, was passing the cemetery at the time of the shooting; he saw some movement and the next thing was also taken prisoner and also spread-eagled on the ground. As soon as the SAS shot the schoolboy they radioed the Quick Reaction Force, a back-up group, who arrived to take charge.

The shooting of John Boyle on 11 July 1978 brought criticism from all sections of the community. There was public revulsion at the plot to use the cache as a bait following information from a concerned member of the public who wished to save life. At that time it was twinned with revulsion at the murder of Constable William Turbitt by the IRA whose body was only recovered after being missing for three weeks in South Armagh. Both funerals took place on the same day, uniting the two villages of Dunloy and Richhill in grief. The entire population of Dunloy turned out for John Boyle's funeral. After the Requiem Mass Mr Con Boyle, the boy's father, said that if his son's death brought solace to a community that needed help he would not have died in vain. The Secretary of State, Mr Roy Mason, MP, who initiated the intensification of the use of the SAS, promised a full RUC investigation and public inquiry. Bishop Edward Daly of Derry said it gave further credence to a growing conviction among some observers that a 'new and extremely dangerous policy' was being implemented by the British Army. Belfast City Councillor Alastair McDonnell, SDLP, a native of North Antrim himself, sent a strong protest by telegram to the Prime Minister James Callaghan. Fr Denis Faul said, 'The Security Forces and the RUC appeared to have lost the proper sense of responsibility in regard to the lives of the public they are supposed to protect in a prudent and sensible way. What appears to be the logic of the Dunloy incident is that bombs will be left until their 'owners' come for them to get killed – anybody who manifests curiosity by their presence or their actions can be shot dead and a story made up to justify it'. The expressions of condemnation and outrage in the immediate aftermath of the shooting were made without the benefit of a judicial inquiry into the circumstances surrounding the stake-out. The disquiet was in no way appeased by the verdict when the two SAS soldiers were acquitted of any wrong-doing.

Fr Faul's words would seem to have gone unheeded. Time and time again the SAS and the RUC continued to stake out arms caches and both paramilitaries and non-combatants were shot down in cold blood. Incredible accounts were then put forward to justify the killings. The *Irish Press* in its editorial of 13 July summed up the public apprehension that the SAS had been issued with orders to shoot first and ask questions afterwards. There was resentment at Mr Mason withholding judgement until after an official inquiry and the inquest.

> Mr Mason is obviously playing for time, but the public has already made up its mind. When we find the SDLP, the Alliance Party and Rev. Ian Paisley joining in the universal condemnation of the killing, and the unequivocal statement by the RUC that John Boyle was an innocent victim, it is not to be wondered at that the Secretary of State should be showing signs of panic. The killing shows unmistakable indications of being the handiwork of the SAS. They can scarcely be described as soldiers in the ordinary sense, but as professional killers who are subject to no laws but their own decision on when to shoot. Wherever they have operated, from Aden to Northern Ireland, they have left a blood-stained trail. We can only pray that there will be no reprisals for John Boyle's death.

What aroused the wrath of the public most was the issuing of conflicting statements by the British Army. The first statement said a patrol spotted three men acting suspiciously and when challenged one pointed a rifle at them. One of the soldiers then fired five shots killing John Boyle. The second statement said only one man was present and he pointed a rifle at the soldiers when challenged; later two other men came to the scene and they were arrested and handed over the the police. The third statement said no challenge was made to the man, that this was impracticable as he was 10 yards from them, pointing a rifle in their direction. This prompted the *Belfast Telegraph* to ask in its editorial:-

> Why did the Army issue conflicting statements? Why are the statements of the Army and police at such variance? Why did the police take so long to warn the Boyle family to keep away from the area where the arsenal was found, so that the message came after the boy was shot? Why were the boy's father and brother treated like common criminals when they went to investigate what had happened? Why did the troops open fire? Would a warning to the boy or a challenge not have been enough? Why was there such an apparent breakdown in communications between the Army and the RUC? What are the Secretary of State, the GOC and the Chief Constable to do to prevent such tragedies in future?

The North Antrim MP, Rev. Ian Paisley, who visited the Boyle family said, 'I feel that the Army, even at this late stage, should be prepared to simply state that a terrible mistake was made'. Mr John Turnly of the Irish Independence Party, also a North Antrim man, later to be assassinated in an SAS/UDA plot, condemned the Army for shooting the boy when they were in a position to challenge. In the House of Commons Mr Gerry Fitt, MP led public opinion in a campaign to force action on the part of the British government and the RUC to bring charges for what was commonly described as the 'murder of the innocent'. When he raised the point of the use of minimum force and the instructions of the yellow card, he was shouted down by Conservative MPs. Mr Mason, MP said that some soldiers were killed by hesitating. The shadow Northern Ireland spokesman, Mr Airey Neave, MP, nodded vigorously at Mr Mason's remarks. David McKittrick entitled his column Northern Notebook, *The Irish Times* for 15 July, 'Tragic results of Mason's policy' and commented, 'Roy Mason himself has always been attracted by the glamour of the SAS, dating back to his days as Minister of Defence. He speaks glowingly of their capabilities and it came as little surprise a year ago when he announced that many more soldiers were to have special training in "SAS-type activities". We are now seeing the fruits of that policy: shoot-outs and killings, sometimes in dubious circumstances, with soldiers often acting with more enthusiasm than attention to detail. And of course there is the occasional plain clothes soldier that the Provos have got their hands on'.

On 21 July 1978 the British Defence Minister, Mr Fred Mulley, revealed that the SAS soldiers involved in the killing of John Boyle were still on duty on the streets. On 8 September 1978 the Chief Constable of the RUC informed a delegation from the SDLP that the RUC would pass a file on the killing to the Director of Public Prosecutions. By February 1979 some of the file's contents had been leaked to the Press Association, namely, that Dr Press had said that Boyle had been hit from behind and that John Boyle's fingerprints were not found on any of the guns in the arms cache. After five months Rev. Ian Paisley, MP tabled a question for the British Attorney General, Sam Silkin, on the lack of response to the submitted RUC file. He was infuriated that the Commander of Land Forces in Northern Ireland, Major General Richard Brooking Trent, had called him an 'enemy of the Army' because he criticised them over the Boyle case in front of others.

On 1 February 1979 the RUC announced that two soldiers would be charged with Boyle's murder. There was an extraordinary scene in Bally-mena Magistrate's Court on 6 February when the two SAS men, formally charged, appeared before resident Magistrate Arthur Jack and were granted bail at £2,000 per man and remanded into military custody. The two SAS men were crammed into the small dock with five others, all in plain clothes (three were recognised by local journalists as policemen). There were shouts of 'sham' and 'travesty of justice' from the Press. At no point was it made officially clear who were the defendants amongst the group. All

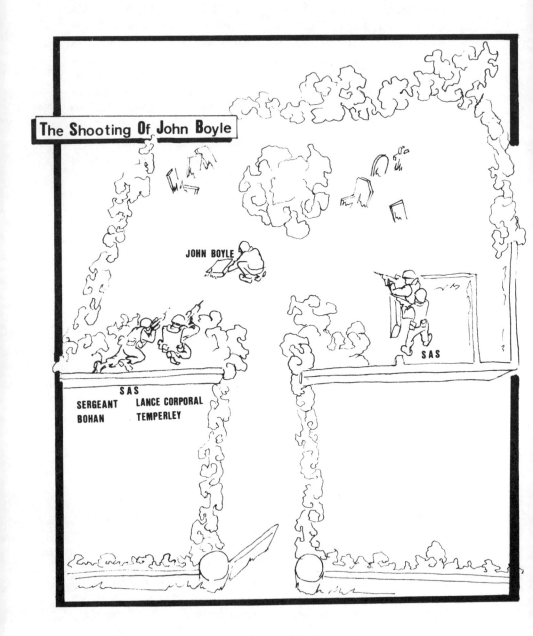

The Shooting Of John Boyle

JOHN BOYLE

SAS
SERGEANT   LANCE CORPORAL
BOHAN   TEMPERLEY

SAS

seven rose and sat in unison and all left the dock together. An officer gave an undertaking that both SAS men would remain in military custody.

A forensic report on the weapons found in the graveyard was made public. It said that the rifle was used in three murders including that of Clifford Evans at Toomebridge in January 1976 and William McCutcheon in April 1976; it had also been used in murder attempts on civilians and the security forces in Moneyglass, Portglenone, Draperstown, Castledawson and Ahoghill between 1976 and 1977. It said that the revolver was used in a shooting incident in Ballymena and in an armed raid and planting of a bomb in a shop in Armoy in North Antrim in April 1978.

At their second hearing the SAS men were identified. They appeared dressed in sports jackets among a guard of RUC and prison wardens.

When the SAS men were cleared of murder on 4 July 1979 there was public anger and dismay. It did not seem enough that the Lord Chief Justice described the plot as a 'badly-planned and bungled exercise'. The boy's father said the police had let him down. 'I know some of the RUC and I trusted them', he said. 'I did what I felt was right and they let me down. They did not give us a warning until the boy was dead. Had the police given me any kind of warning, I would have taken it and John would still be alive. I thought that they owed me this much. For anything the police have done for me I thank them, and for anything they could have done and did not do, it is they and not I who have to live with it. I have little to say about the Army. They have not deviated one inch from the path ever trod by their predecessors in Ireland. Having killed the boy they tried to discredit him, and defame him and in this they have failed miserably, as they were bound to do.'

There was anger both from unionists and nationalists at the good wishes to the SAS expressed by Mr Harold McCusker, MP in the House of Commons. He asked a Northern Ireland Junior Minister, Mr Michael Alison, 'Will you join with me in expressing good wishes to those two members of the SAS who were acquitted in the murder trial in Northern Ireland. And will you now encourage their colleagues to take the sort of action they took last year when, in fact, they managed to kill a few terrorists – quite apart from a number of people that were being killed by terrorists in my constituency'. He was immediately criticised by Mr Gerry Fitt, MP and the Rev. Ian Paisley, MP.

Almost immediately after the court's decision acquitting the two SAS men, the British Army Commander in the North, Sir Timothy Creasey issued a statement. He had no word of sympathy for the Boyle family. He said that he had never doubted that the two acquitted men had acted in good faith. He pledged that the Army would continue the task of defeating terrorism in support of the civil power, 'willingly, cheerfully and with good nature and tolerance. The dilemma that those two NCOs faced on making their split-second decision is one that can face any soldier in the Province at any time. A major part of their operations are out of sight until the focus of public attention is directed on their actions, but they have learned to live with the constraints made by the rules of *sub judice* which have to be accepted, often in the face of wild allegations'.

The Shooting of James Taylor[96]

James Taylor, a 23-year-old civil servant who worked as a water surveyor, was shot dead by the SAS on Saturday, 30 September 1978. He was shot in the back. His case bears a resemblance to that of John Boyle in that he was not a member of any paramilitary organisation. It was another incredible 'blunder' on the part of the SAS and, coming so soon after the killing of John Boyle, it said little for the concern of government in such matters. The only softening was that this time there was a word of regret from the British Army. Taylor was a Presbyterian and his death drew the same kind of anger from a united community as that of Boyle. At his funeral service in Coagh Presbyterian church the Rev. W.J. Crossley Mercer said, 'Let it be known that we are as concerned about the lives of our harmless Catholic fellow countrymen as we are about our Protestant neighbours in the pursuit of innocent happiness'.

James Taylor lived at Windsor Avenue in the village of Coagh, County Tyrone. He was married with two children. After tea on Saturday, 30 September, he and two friends, his cousin William George Hamilton McCollum (20), a cabinet maker of Moneymore, and William Robert Devenney (16) of Bridgend, Coagh, went duck shooting on the Ballinderry River, down at the end of the Ballygoney Road. They had three dogs with them. Taylor and McCollum had shotguns but Devenney had no gun. They fired a few shots at pigeons and returned to the car after dark. They put the three dogs in the boot, got into the car, started the engine but the car would not move off. George McCollum got out of the car and to his intense annoyance found all the tyres deflated. He was so angry that he fired three shots into the air from his shotgun. There was nothing to do except seek for help. He lived with his uncle, Given Shuter; he decided to head for home, get a pump and with good luck get the loan of his uncle's car. Taylor and Devenney took two of the dogs with them and accompanied him to Shuter's house. He got the pump and the car after explaining the situation to his uncle. The three men then returned down the Ballygoney Road.

On his way home McCollum had noticed the lights of a car travelling along the Ballygoney Road in the direction of the river. He then saw it turning into a laneway on the right hand side of the Ballygoney Road as one travelled towards the river. On their return to the abandoned car he drove into the same laneway. In front of a derelict house down the laneway he saw two cars parked. The men decided to return home as the cars looked suspicious, so they went back to consult with Given Shuter. James Taylor asked Shuter if he should contact the police about the two cars. They did not tell the police. At Shuter's suggestion the four took courage and decided to set out once again and travel back to the abandoned car with the intention of pumping up the tyres. Just as the four were getting into Shuter's car, the lights of the cars appeared coming towards them. McCollum drove his uncle's car into the side of the road to let the oncoming cars pass. But the cars stopped and reversed back up the road. He followed them up the road. The two cars in front turned and drove off in the direction of the river ahead of him. When McCollum and his companions got to the river where the abandoned car was, they found the two cars parked near it. McCollum pulled his uncle's car within four or five yards of the front of his own car and left the lights on so that they could see to pump the tyres. He got out and, overcome with frustration, shouted at the occupants of the two cars, 'Are you the boys that are so good at letting down tyres?', or something to that effect. There was a word of reply from the second car but he couldn't make out what was said and he shouted again. McCollum continues in his statement at the inquest in Magherafelt (5 September 1979):-

> Before I got finished speaking, I think three shots rang out. I cannot say whether the driver had his door open or whether he fired through the open window. Immediately the shots were fired, the occupants of both cars, except the driver of the first car, jumped from their cars and pointed guns towards us. They shouted 'Stand still and put your hands up'. I put my hands up and saw a number of men rushing towards us with guns pointing at us. I think they were nearly all handguns except for one. It was about one foot long and two inches broad. At least four persons got out of these two cars.

McCollum, Devenney and Shuter were made stand with their hands on top of the car. McCollum said to his uncle, 'They have shot Jim'. He was told to shut up by one of the soldiers. He heard the driver of the first car say to one of the other soldiers, 'He cocked the gun at me'. The headlights of Shuter's car were left on until about ten or fifteen minutes after the shooting. All this time McCollum could see Taylor lying on his back on the ground, motionless. One of the soldier's took Taylor's right arm as if to feel his pulse. McCollum said, 'At no time did I see my own shotgun or Jim Taylor's shotgun out of the car at the scene of the shooting'. He never had the shotgun in his hand at any time before the shooting and at no time did he hear the sound of a gun being clicked. He was familiar with the sound of a slide being slashed on an automatic shotgun and felt he would have heard it had it been done. He did not remember hearing or seeing James Taylor load or cock his shotgun either to or from his uncle's place *en route* to the abandoned car. He asked the car occupants who they were but they told him to shut up. Twice he asked if they were members of the security forces and on the second question one of them said 'Yes'. He heard them speak on the radio in the front car.

Devenney in his statement at the inquest corroborated much of what McCollum said except that he thought that Taylor had his shotgun with him getting out of the car. Shuter in his statement at the inquest said that the shooting took place as they were getting out of the car. The shooting took place about ten to twelve feet away from his car; there was no warning, no call to halt, and he thought two men did the shooting. As far as he could recollect he did not see any of his companions with a weapon. They were asked no questions when they were put against the car; indeed they were not permitted to speak. The two men who searched them were dressed in civilian clothes and both had what appeared to be English accents.

At the inquest the state pathologist, Dr T.K. Marshall, said that James Taylor was struck by three bullets. The first bullet struck him in the middle of the back, about one inch to the left of the spine; the other two bullets struck the right side of the chest, near the back fold of the armpit. In his view the second and third bullets struck Taylor as he was collapsing forward and twisting to his left. It was possible but most unlikely that after being struck by the first two bullets in the side Taylor then became erect and was struck by the third bullet in the back.

The three SAS soldiers designated 'A', 'B' and 'C' denied that they had interfered with the tyres of McCollum's car. Soldier 'A' did not appear at the inquest. His statement was read out by a senior police officer. He said he was on plain clothes duty in the Coagh area, driving a military civilianised car accompanied by the two corporals, 'B' and 'C', who were in another civilianised military car. He said that earlier they had been parked in a laneway and on the way back along the Ballygoney Road, they had come to a house where a car was blocking the road. 'B' and 'C' in the car in front of him told him by radio that they had seen a shotgun with the people involved in movement between the house and the car blocking the road. They therefore reversed down the road and turned their cars. They were followed closely by the car blocking the road. (McCollum said they had pulled into the side of the road to let the soldiers pass.) They all drove down to the immobilised car. On stopping he opened the driver's door and swung his legs to get out. He continued:

> I drew my 9mm Browning pistol and held it out of sight behind my right leg. I immediately saw a person walking behind the immobilised car between it and the hedge which went up both sides of the road. As the person came round the nearside boot of the car, he was walking 'crabwise' with his back and right-hand side facing me. I could see him clearly in the headlights of the vehicles. I saw the stock and barrel of a gun protruding from his left side pointing downwards and the butt protruding upwards through his right armpit. I realised it was an automatic shotgun. I saw his right arm making pushing movements as if to load the weapon and I could hear the magazine spring clicking as if it was loaded. Then I heard the noise of the working parts go forward. I am sure of what these sounds were as I own and use this type of gun. All the time the man was backing into me and trying to conceal his gun.

The working parts went forward as he reached the rear outside of the immobilised car. This meant he had moved backwards the width of the immobilised car and was now eight feet from us. As the working parts went forward, he swung the gun round in a clockwise direction. As he swung it round fast, I could see the barrel being raised. I immediately feared for my life and took my 9 mm pistol which was in my right hand beneath my right leg, and fired in quick succession three shots. At the time of firing, the man was approximately 90 degrees to me with his back side still facing me, but he was swinging round fast. At the time I fired all three shots the man was upright. He fell to the ground and the shots sent him and the shotgun closer to the hedge.

Corporal 'B' and Corporal 'C' were present at the inquest. 'B' said they were trying to get away from the men without confrontation. After they reversed he thought they were being pursued by the other party. He did not want to address the men lest his English accent would give away the fact that he was a soldier. At the immobilised car he saw Taylor with the shotgun and believed a direct confrontation with armed civilians was imminent. Under cross-examination he said it was pure coincidence that they arrived at the place where the immobilised car was. Corporal 'C' did not add further detail to 'B's testimony.

At the funeral of James Taylor, the Rev. W. J. Crossley Mercer said that on the facts as they knew them there had been ample time for the Army to check out the number of the car of Taylor and his friends and later the house they had been seen to enter. If this had been done and if a closer link had been established between the police and the security forces, there would have been no case of mistaken identity.

On 18 April 1979 the RUC announced the decision by the Director of Public Prosecutions that there would be no prosecutions in the case. Mr Paschal O'Hare, SDLP expressed amazement. He said the killing of James Taylor was a calculated covert operation sanctioned by the highest military authority and appeared to be one of a pattern of such killings tantamount to summary execution. He thought an alternative to murder, namely manslaughter, ought at the very least to have been preferred. Taylor's uncle, Given Shuter said, 'These soldiers seem to have a licence to go round shooting anybody they think is doing wrong, which Jim wasn't, and they know it. There seems to be one law for them and another for civilians. If we had shot one of these chaps without reason, would the DPP have reacted in the same way?' Again after the inquest in September 1979 relatives of James Taylor were still adamant that he was murdered and the Army was twisting the facts. George McCollum insisted again that neither Taylor's shotgun nor his own were out of the car and at no time prior to the shooting did he hear a gun being cocked. Given Shuter said, 'The Army has cooked up the whole story'.

The Shooting of William Smyth[97]

On Tuesday, 24 October 1978 William Smyth, the Catholic manager of an ex-servicemen's club set out home around midnight. He had only a few hundred yards to walk. As he passed the corner of Ballynure Street on the Oldpark Road he was shot dead through the back of the head. Witnesses saw the murderer leaving the scene walking down Mayfair Street but by the time they reached the corner of the Oldpark Road he had disappeared. He appeared to be man of about 5' 4" in height.

Radio bulletins on 25 October reported that the RUC had a detailed description of the murderer. He was described as wearing a large-patterned check coat. The possibility was put forward that it was a feud killing.

Events subsequent to the shooting however led to the interpretation by residents of the area that the murder was the work of undercover soldiers.

On Wednesday 25 October Hughie Hunter went to his shop on the Oldpark Road and found twelve soldiers inside. The lock had not been broken and so he asked them how they had got in. They said they found the door open. At 2.20 am on Sunday, 29 October Brendan Duffy who lived on the Old Park Road heard noises from Hunter's shop which was next door to his home. The top floor of the shop was used as a storeroom and he knew it would be unoccupied. The noises continued to 7 am, keeping Duffy and his wife awake. The next day he went at 2.30 pm to Hughie Hunter who lived in Ballycastle Street and told him about the noises in his shop.

The two men went to the shop and went upstairs to the store. Everything seemed normal and then they saw a soldier standing with a gun, up in a hole in the ceiling. Hunter shone a torch on him and was promptly told to put it out or he would get his head blown off. The soldier dropped from the ceiling and ordered them to lie flat on the ground. Hunter explained that he was just out of hospital but the soldier put his foot on his back and pushed him to the ground. Mrs Hunter then came into the shop and shouted up the stairs. She was about to go up when the soldier threatened to shoot her. Another soldier dropped from the roof space and both put their guns to the men's heads. They were made stand face to the wall while the soldiers gathered their gear from the roof space. Hunter was told to go down the stairs and not let anyone up. After 10 minutes the soldiers came down with Duffy. Two Saracens came into the street and one of them backed into the doorway of the shop. Neighbours had gathered and they now pulled at the bag one of the soldiers was carrying. It revealed sleeping bags and other gear. A soldier grabbed Duffy, put a gun to his head and shouted at everyone to keep away. The soldier was nervous and when Mrs Duffy attempted to approach he shouted that he would shoot. The soldiers got into the Saracen, taking Duffy with them. One of those who joined the neighbours around the Saracen thought that Duffy had been wrapped up in a blanket the soldiers were carrying. Some of the women jumped into the Saracen and refused to move. The blanket was pulled open and witnesses saw a red and tan check jacket or coat. One witness remarked to her husband that this was the description of the coat which the killer of William Smyth was wearing.

At Flax Street Army Post where he was taken, Duffy saw a group of soldiers wearing a kind of uniform, light green tunic top, like tracksuits. When they went to take the gear out of the Saracen, they were told not to until Duffy had been removed. After some minutes a man in plain clothes spoke to the soldier guarding Duffy. He had an English accent. He said the soldiers were there because they thought there was going to be another murder. Duffy noticed that the two sets of soldiers kept apart.

Hunter reported the incident at his shop at Oldpark RUC Station. A few days later three plain clothes detectives came to his home and asked him to go the station to make a statement.

No one to date has been made answerable for the murder of William Smyth.

The Shooting of Patrick Duffy[98]

'Members of the British Army here seem to be able to act outside the law with immunity from the law. The shooting dead of a person merely because he enters a house or place where illegally-held guns or explosives are stored is quite unjustifiable. This policy gives soldiers the power to act as judge, jury and executioner.' So spoke Bishop Edward Daly of Derry after members of the SAS shot dead Patrick Duffy in Derry city. Patrick Duffy was a married man with six children. He was fifty years of age, a fitter by trade but was off work. He was shot dead at approximately 9.30 pm on 24 November 1978 after entering an unoccupied house. Duffy was an auxiliary member of the IRA and had called to collect or inspect an arms cache stored in a wardrobe in the front room on the first floor of a house at 2 Maureen Avenue off the Abercorn Road, in Derry. The cache had been discovered and was staked out by the SAS.

At 8.30 pm on Friday, 24 November 1978 Patrick Duffy, accompanied by two other men, went into the Rocking Chair bar, Waterloo Street, Derry and one of them asked the bar manager for the loan of his car for five minutes. He gave them the car, a black BMW 2002, after he took time to do a message. Patrick Duffy drove off in it. He called at his own house at Clark's Terrace. His daughter Margarita was at home, baby-sitting for her sister. Martin the baby was crying as he was teething. Patrick said he would take both of them out for a run, saying that the motion of the car would soothe the baby. Margarita suggested that they would call on her aunt who lived on the Waterside and who recently had a stroke. She had never seen the baby.

They left shortly after 9 pm, drove down Anne Street, up Bishop Street

242 THE SAS IN IRELAND

and down Abercorn Road. Patrick then turned down Lower Bennet Street saying that it would be quicker to take the under-deck bridge. When he reached the bottom of the street he appeared to Margarita to remember something. 'I almost forgot,' he said, 'I have to see a man about a car; it will only take a few minutes.' He then drove over Foyle Road and up Ferguson's Lane and into Maureen Avenue. He stopped the car outside the last house and got out. He said, 'I'll only be a few minutes Margarita'.

Margarita sat in the car playing with the baby which by this time had stopped crying and was biting on the steering wheel to soothe its gums. She heard a door close and almost immediately the sound of shots being fired. The gunfire was also heard by Margaret Isobel Wade who lived at 4 Maureen Avenue. She was making a phone call when she heard a very loud continuous noise. She put down the phone and ran to the living room to see if everything was all right. She thought the noise was a machine-gun. She ran to the front door. She saw a small black car with a person sitting in it. She came in and phoned a neighbour who said she did not hear anything. She put down the phone.

The next observation is important. At this point she heard the same type of noise again but it did not last as long as before. This means there was a considerable interval, of about five minutes, between the bursts of gunfire. Patrick Duffy was hit at close range by the first gunfire. Why was it necessary to fire again?

Margaret Wade was back and forward to the door. She saw uniformed soldiers arriving in 'pigs'. There was a lot of police and Army activity. At one stage she saw two men coming out of 2 Maureen Avenue. They got into an Army vehicle. 'Both men,' she said, 'seemed to be like workmen and one was carrying a bag.'

During the inquest it was alleged that it was information given to the RUC that led to their request to the Army to apprehend the person or persons entering the house. The 'Special Surveillance Unit' or SAS then staked out the house. The familiar pattern was to follow: the killing was done; the élite soldiers declared they thought their lives were in danger; decisions had to be made in split seconds; examination of the arms haul showed that the weapons had been used in terror atrocities.

At the time of the shooting No. 2 Maureen Avenue was unoccupied; the owner had a plan to have it repaired. As far as he was aware, there were only two front-door keys both held by his mother-in-law. When work was to be done at the house a key was obtained from her. There was a wardrobe in the bedroom midway between door and window. An odd-job man was doing some work in the house; he also gained access by getting a key from the same lady. The workman was also aware of the wardrobe. In his statement at the inquest he said that on the first day he had been in the house he noticed that this wardrobe was locked but after the first day it was open. On the day

The Shooting of Patrick Duffy

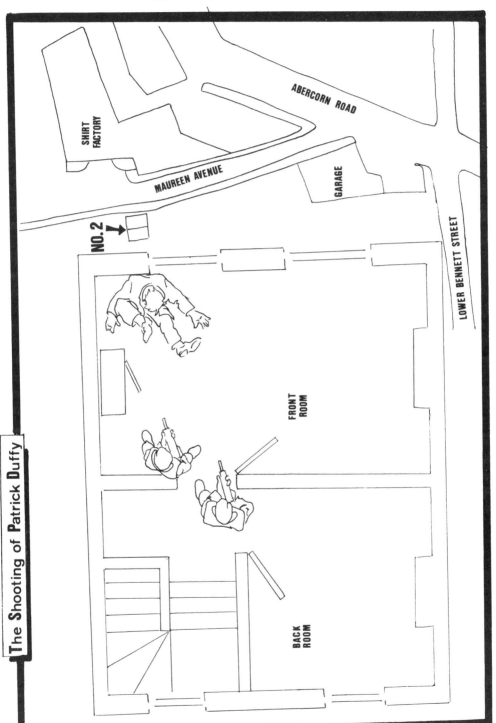

SHIRT FACTORY

ABERCORN ROAD

MAUREEN AVENUE

GARAGE

NO.2

LOWER BENNETT STREET

FRONT ROOM

BACK ROOM

before the shooting he went with another workman to check some foundations. This time he noticed that the wardrobe was once again locked. This
was the early afternoon of 23 November. He tried to open the wardrobe but
couldn't. He shook it from side to side but it was very light and seemed
empty. He returned again on 24 November at 11 am with a building-control
inspector of the Northern Ireland Housing Executive. They did not examine
any of the rooms or the wardrobe.

Soldier 'E', an SAS officer stationed at Ebrington Barracks, in his state-
ment gave the outlines of the observation of the house. At 01.00 hours on 23
November 1978 he deployed Soldiers 'A', 'B' and 'C' to search No. 2
Maureen Avenue. He said his briefing covered the following points:-

1. Soldier 'A' was to command the party.
2. If no illegal arms, ammunition or explosives were found during the
initial search, the party was to monitor all movement to and from the
building from the attic.
3. If illegal arms, ammunition or explosives were found the party was
to keep the aforementioned items under close observation in order to
apprehend anyone handling the stated items.
4. The party was instructed to enter the premises in civilian clothes,
carrying their uniforms consisting of camouflage combat jackets and
trousers and also their weapons in canvas holdalls. Once on the
premises they were instructed to change into uniform and complete
their task.
5. The party was instructed to carry the following weapons – one
Browning 9 mm pistol each; one Armalite rifle carried by soldier 'S'; one
Sterling SMG carried by soldier 'B'; one Ingram SMG carried by soldier
'C'. Ammunition was issued for each weapon.
6. Each man carried an individual radio-set for communication between themselves and a main radio-set to communicate to 'E' at base.
7. The orders given to the three SAS men on anyone seen to handle
illegal arms, ammunition or explosives on the premises was to challenge and apprehend, only opening fire under the conditions of the
Yellow Card, if it became necessary.

Officer 'E' presented in his statement a record of the radio messages sent
back to base, date, time, event, remarks. On 23 November, 21.41 hours, it is
recorded:- 'Two men enter the house. Move around stealthily. Go upstairs.
Enter front upstairs bedroom. Dragging noises heard; it is thought these
men left by the rear door of the house'. 24 Nov., 01.17 hours: 'The house is
searched again. Illegal weapons and ammunition are found in a wardrobe
in the front upstairs bedroom; the wardrobe door was prised open and then
re-closed by the same method'. 02.03:- 'One man heard moving around
downstairs, thought to be waiting for something; Soldier 'A' is in the attic

and soldiers 'B' and 'C' in the upstairs back bedroom at this stage...' 21.22:- 'A car stops outside the house. A man enters the house. Goes upstairs, opens the wardrobe, leans inside, re-locks wardrobe; the man is challenged, reacts as if about to use a weapon and is shot'.

The three SAS men all say they thought more than one man was coming up the stairs; 'A' and 'B' thought there were two. An attempt is made to build up the danger. 'B' makes the extraordinary statement, continuing in the plural – 'if they weren't armed already they had access to arms in the wardrobe'. As in the case of John Boyle this poses the question: why do élite soldiers make it difficult for themselves by leaving loaded weapons in caches they stake out, a potential danger to themselves? The statements then contain the usual emphasis that the soldiers thought their lives were in danger. Soldier 'A' was in the attic watching the stairs; the shooting was carried out by 'B' using his Sterling sub-machine-gun and 'C' using his Ingram sub-machine-gun. They were in the back bedroom. 'B' says he shouted, 'Don't move, Security Forces!'. 'B' continues – 'At the same time I came out of our room into the front room. I was aware of the silhouette of a person in the front room next to the wardrobe. The man appeared to push the door of the wardrobe closed. He spun round to face me bringing his right hand up. I thought he must have a gun in it and he was swinging it up to engage us. I believed my life was in danger. I fired at him with my SMG. My weapon was set on automatic as soon as I heard people coming because it seemed to me there was more than one'. He then hints that there was a back-up to the shot man. He looked out the window and saw two cars driving up the street and then coming back again; one stopped on the other side of the road but then the Quick Reaction Force came and this car drove off. Soldier 'C' gives the impression that he fired immediately after 'B'. He says, 'I heard Soldier 'B' shout 'Don't move, Security Forces' and there was a fractional pause. As I turned to face into the front room there were flashes and the noise of firing. I thought we were faced with armed men and I thought our lives were in danger. I fired into the front room. I only went a couple of steps into the front room. I did not touch the body. I think I fired 6 or 7 shots'.

The forensic report concludes from an examination of the spent bullets and cartridge cases that 2 weapons were discharged, the Sterling and the Ingram. All of the shots were discharged from the landing in front of the door leading into the bedroom. Some of the shots were directed towards the wardrobe and the remainder to the centre of the floor, passing through the corner of the bedroom door.

It will be remembered that the lady in the house next door calculated five minutes between the bursts of gunfire. An observer could conclude that Patrick Duffy was machine-gunned by the shots from the Sterling directed towards the wardrobe where he was standing. Five minutes later Soldier 'B' machine-gunned him as he lay on the floor. At the inquest on 10 April 1981 Mr Thomas V. Cahill, QC, representing the next of kin, pointed out that the wardrobe door had been locked and that the keys were lying on the ground; Mr Duffy who was unarmed was riddled with bullets.

The autopsy report shows that Patrick Duffy had 29 entrance and exit wounds in all on his body. Seven bullets struck the trunk; two had entered the left side of the the chest, four had entered the back and one had grazed the left side of the front of the lower abdomen. The combined effect of these injuries would have caused rapid death. Each forearm and the right thigh had also been traversed by a bullet whilst the left thigh had been struck by four bullets. He had been struck by at least 11 bullets and probably 14. They had come from the left, or from behind and to the left. The character of the two entrance wounds on the left side of the chest would suggest that these bullets were fired at close range.

One disturbing aspect affecting the grief of Mrs Moira Duffy and her children the night of the shooting was the attempt by the RUC and the Army to arrest Margarita at their home. One of the soldiers showed reluctance to carry out the distasteful operation. He protested at the searching of the Duffy house. The policeman in charge reprimanded him, 'You'll do your duty'. The Duffy family made phone calls and contacted a local priest. The raid was then called off. 'Thank God for that,' said the regular soldier. The police-woman present had been particularly officious towards Margarita – 'You can come now promptly or we will arrest you and hold you for three days'.

No prosecutions took place in the case of Patrick Duffy. The SAS did not appear at the inquest and there was no opportunity for cross-examination. Following Requiem Mass in St Columba's church, Long Tower, Patrick Duffy was buried with Provisional IRA honours. Four men in uniform fired two volleys of shots over the tricolour-draped coffin *en route* to the city cemetery. The graveside oration was given by Mr Seán Keenan of Derry.

PHASE V

Atkins' Secret Army

The SAS on the Antrim Road

In 1971 the British Government introduced torture in interrogation centres in Northern Ireland to force confessions and ensure that political opponents of the state were sent to prison for long terms. Cruel, inhuman and degrading treatment continued in the interrogation centres despite domestic and international reports. Fr Denis Faul and I exposed the brutality of the 1976-77 period in our book *The Castlereagh File*, published in 1978. Amnesty International followed and published a report in June 1978. A British domestic report known as the Bennett report was published in March 1979. Its findings of ill-treatment were backed up by police surgeons Dr Robert Irwin and Dr Denis Elliott and the Association of Police Surgeons. Just before the publication of the Bennett Report, Dr Irwin was interviewed on the *Weekend World* programme, London Weekend Television, 12 March 1979. He revealed that in the previous three years he had seen roughly between 150 and 160 prisoners with injuries which could not have been self-inflicted, ruptured ear drums, injuries to joints, bruising.

The programme had a powerful impact because of its timing and the status of the person interviewed. London Weekend Television and the Independent Broadcasting Authority came under enormous pressure from the British Government not to show it. This displeasure had a severe personal repercussion for Dr Irwin. The *Daily Telegraph* published a report on 16 March 1979 by Gerald Bartlett that a non-commissioned SAS officer raped Dr Irwin's wife at her home in Belfast in 1976. This information, leaked by the British secret service, was a propaganda operation to discredit Dr Irwin, implying that he was anti-RUC because they failed to catch his wife's rapist. Dr Irwin told Bartlett, 'Your information is correct. I am bitter against the Government officials who whisked the man responsible out of this province never to face inquiry or punishment. But the incident brought me even closer to the RUC for whom I have a great regard and admiration. It is nonsense to suggest that I am anti-RUC. They treated us with great kindness and were already there comforting my wife by the time I arrived home after the rape. There is absolutely no doubt in my mind that Government officials, worried by the finding of the Bennett Committee inquiry into RUC interrogation, are out to discredit me and cast doubts upon my motives for speaking out'.

Bartlett wrote that, 12 hours after Dr Irwin appeared on television, Whitehall officials sanctioned 'leakage' of the rape details. This alleged that hoodlum paramilitaries were responsible. Bartlett corrected the details; informed sources said that a non-commissioned SAS officer on undercover duties was responsible. On 17 March the *Daily Telegraph* published a report by Peter Fearon for the Press Association which supported Bartlett's story. Fearon added that Dr Irwin told him the RUC investigated the rape and traced a man to the Grand Central Hotel, the Army's Belfast HQ; he was a soldier on undercover duty; this soldier was removed to West Germany shortly after the offence. Bartlett gave the date of the rape as 27 November 1976, Fearon gave March 1976; further investigation of journalists established it as 26 March 1976.

Nine days after the rape of Mrs Irwin, in the early hours of 4 April 1976, Mrs Margaret Gamble was found dying, dressed in an evening dress and fur-trimmed coat, at the junction of Antrim Road and Glandore Gardens in North Belfast. She had been stabbed. She died an hour later in hospital. The RUC had said publicly that they had wanted to interview Mrs Gamble's sister, Mrs Róisín McLoughlin, in connection with the murder of three British soldiers in an Antrim Road flat on 23 March 1973. Suspicion falls on the SAS for accepting RUC accusations and carrying out a revenge murder. A third 'Antrim Road' murder carried out by SAS/loyalists has already been described, the shooting dead of Niall O'Neill at Thirlemere Gardens on 22 January 1976.

The British secret service 'plant' was counter-productive in two ways. A politicised public in Northern Ireland knew that it was propaganda and resented the 'dirty trick'. Support and sympathy for Dr Irwin soared. Also investigative journalists uncovered the SAS involvement and the SAS top brass were very hurt. A statement by the officer commanding the SAS, denying that any of his men were involved in Mrs Irwin's rape, appeared in the *Daily Telegraph*, 19 March 1979. *Mars & Minerva* also published it in Vol. 4, No. 1, June 1979, in the following editorial:-

> We have all, at one time or another, been incensed by the manner in which much of the news media has reported on the SAS. Our readers will, therefore, be more than pleased to read the following statement, issued to the Press Association on the evening of 18 March 1979, by our Colonel Commandant, Colonel B.M.F. Franks, DSSO, MC, TD:
>
> As Colonel Commandant of the SAS and therefore its titular head, I believe the time has come to rebut the ever-growing, ill-informed comment in the press and elsewhere about my Regiment.
>
> In particular, of course, I refer to the spurious reports suggesting an SAS Soldier was involved in the rape of MRS IRWIN in Belfast in 1976.
>
> At that time, no SAS Soldier is known to have been in Belfast. Evidence is quite conclusive on this point and the whereabouts of every

man in the Regiment serving in NI at that time has been checked and accounted for.

Some newspapers have suggested that the culprit was 'Spirited Out' of NI. So far as the SAS is concerned I am satisfied that there is no vestige of truth in this allegation.

I am disturbed at the increasing tendency to report on the SAS as if it were some secret undercover organisation. In fact, it is a Corps of the British Army subject to both military and civil law in exactly the same way as any other Corps listed in the Army List.

I have, in the past, refrained from comment in public on the wild stories published about this well-tried young Corps, believing that rebuttal of such false rumour is the responsibility of Ministers and the Ministry of Defence.

It seems to me that the time has now come when I cannot allow the Regiment to be pilloried any longer without comment from me.

'Our Secret Army'

'I want to re-emphasise the Government's total commitment of ensuring that those responsible for these (the double explosion at Warrenpoint in August which killed 18 soldiers) and for all other acts of terrorism are brought to justice. The police and army are putting their all into the struggle. And I am backing them to the hilt.' So spoke the Secretary of State, Mr Humphrey Atkins, at a meeting of Newry and Mourne District Council on 3 September 1979. He said the Government had been deploying the forces' specialist units such as the SAS 'who are here to use their very special skills in coping with the terrorist'. The SAS he said would be strengthened on the border.[99]

Mr Atkins returned to the theme on 30 October 1979 at the annual dinner of the Northern Ireland Chamber of Trade, Belfast. 'Much of the activity of the security forces now directed against terrorist operations is necessarily an undercover operation,' he said. 'Painstaking surveillance, the investments of considerable amounts of time and manpower in gathering information and turning it into evidence – these techniques pay dividends. But they would cease to do so if we advertised the techniques used, their successes and the means by which they succeed.'[100]

Undercover Soldiers Shot Dead

'I was on my way for bread when I heard these shots. I couldn't say how many but I turned round and saw this car skidding in the middle of the road. There were two men inside and I heard a scream. I ran for cover. I wasn't sure where the shots were coming from, whether it was a car or the men at the bottom of the Whiterock. There seemed to be so many people about. It all seemed so unreal.'

The plain clothes British soldier shot dead in this attack was named by the British Army as Private Paul Anthony Wright (21) from Leicester of the 3rd Royal Anglian Regiment at Palace Barracks, Holywood.[101] Another soldier was seriously wounded in the chest and shoulder. The Army said that they were engaged in routine courier work between the MacRory Park Army base and the Fort Monagh base in Turf Lodge, Belfast. The attack took place at 4 pm on 8 October 1979. It was well planned. Three men armed with handguns took over Murray's do-it-yourself shop at the junction of the Whiterock and Falls Road. When the unmarked Mini car drove down Whiterock they stood in the doorway and fired some ten shots causing it to swerve and crash into the railings. Two men followed it firing shots through the rear window. The Army denied the soldiers were engaged in under-cover work. They did not, however, belong to locally-based regiments and suspicion immediately fell on the SAS. This sounds very like the incident described in *Soldier, Soldier* (by Tony Parker, 1985):

> The incident occurred when we were on our way across the city in a car in plain clothes. My mate Eddie was driving and we gave two others a lift. We dropped them off where they wanted to be, then we started off for where we were heading. Eddie drove down the hill to a crossroads: there were traffic lights and they were against us. I remember it all quite clearly, it still runs through my mind like a film. There was a big red car in front of us. When the lights changed, we expected it to move but it didn't. From the pavement side nearest where I was two men with pistols stepped out of a shop doorway, then a man with an automatic weapon came round the other side and started to fire. The red car moved, Eddie slammed his foot on the accelerator and we shot across the road hitting some railings, so I knew then he'd been injured. The men with the pistols had run across the crossroads after us. I felt one bullet go in my hand, and I knew another had hit me but I didn't know where. I didn't know that altogether I had got five bullets in me. I jerked open the car door and rolled out, then got up and started to run up the street. There was a graveyard on the opposite side of the road, and I somehow remember thinking if I was going to die the thing to do would be to go in the graveyard and die there. I tried to make for it but I fell over between some traffic bollards in the middle of the road. Then I staggered back on to the pavement and there were some small houses with their front doors on the street. One of them opened, and a big woman grabbed hold of me. She said, 'Come on son, I won't let the fucking Brits get you'. I started to scream at her, I said, 'You fucking cow, take your fucking hands off me' and she slammed the door shut. I don't know where it'd come from but then an armoured carrier pulled

up next to me. A soldier stuck his head out and he said, 'What's wrong, is something the matter?' I said, 'What do you think, you stupid fucker'. My language was, it was dreadful. A lot of soldiers jumped out and dragged me into the vehicle and they got me to the hospital a few minutes away. I was finding it hard to breathe then, because I'd got four bullets in my chest. The nurses and doctors were trying to get my clothes cut off so they could give me an injection, and I was screaming and swearing at them and telling them to leave me alone. I heard one of the soldiers say my mate was dead, he'd been shot through the head. Then I was moved to a military hospital. I'd no idea who the men were who shot me, but I was moved because they might have come in to finish me off when they heard I was still alive, because for all they knew I might have recognised them. I was in hospital two-and-a-half months.

My fiancée was a local Irish girl I'd met. A Catholic. We're married now.   *(Ken D., corporal)*

The soldiers were shot on the day Sir Maurice Oldfield, new 'security co-ordinator' specially appointed by the Prime Minister, Mrs Margaret Thatcher, arrived in Northern Ireland. The incident pointed at some of the difficulties facing the British security forces. After a lull in 1977 the IRA had reorganised into a cell system. Gerry Adams was released in 1977 and his leadership of republicans was looked upon as a new danger. 'We want', said a Ministry of Defence man at this time, 'to watch someone like Adams 100 per cent of the time. Now we know where he is 70 per cent of the time, but there are gaps – and they're left because our resources are mixed all over the place.'

In two other separate incidents undercover soldiers were killed and wounded in 1979, the year of Oldfield's appointment. Less then a year after the shooting dead of SAS soldier Lance Corporal David Jones in south Derry, another shoot-out with IRA volunteers occurred in the same area.[102] There were casualties on both sides. The brief gun battle took place at a crossroads on the Crewe Road near Maghera on 24 January. Two undercover soldiers were wounded. The undercover men travelling in an unmarked van noticed a car with two occupants apparently on a bombing mission and went in pursuit of the vehicle. Then the shooting broke out; one soldier was hit in the back, the other in the arm. The IRA car sped away; at a safe distance it stopped and two men, one of them wounded, clambered out and made their getaway leaving a trail of blood in the snow. Four rifles, two of them Armalites, and a small parcel bomb were recovered from the abandoned car. Traces of blood were also found in it. In their statement on the incident the IRA said they believed the soldiers were SAS and claimed that the van was the same make, colour and had the same number plate as one owned by a Catholic farmer in Derry.

At 11.30 am, 6 May 1979, half-way through the 11 am Mass in Lisnaskea

Church, County Fermanagh, Sergeant Robert Maughan (parent regiment, 9th-12th Lancers) and Detective Constable Norman Prue pulled in at the church gates. Sergeant Maughan got out of the unmarked green Fiat car to buy a copy of *An Phoblacht* from a bystander. A gunman opened fire from behind a wall 20 yards away killing him instantly. Before Constable Prue could do anything, two other gunmen ran over to the vehicle and opened fire, also killing him instantly. Some miles outside the village, the escaping men crashed into a van; they then hijacked a passing Opel car and continued on. Canon Charles Lydon, who was assisting at the Mass being celebrated by Fr John McCabe, described the scene inside the church: 'The Offertory was about to begin when we heard the shots. At the time I did not realise they were shots. I thought something had fallen in the church. Some people in the 500-strong congregation tried to rush out as they thought they were being fired on from inside the gallery. I later discovered two bullet holes in the wall of the Baptistery and a bullet hole just above the front outside door. The people were alarmed. They were frightened out of their lives. They panicked; there was pandemonium; children and young girls fainted and old people were very distressed. Some tried to run out and some children ran home screaming. There was consternation. One of the men was lying across the front seat of the car and partly on the floor. His brain was shattered. The side-window was smashed as if he had been shot at close range. The other man was lying dead on the road and I saw that there was nothing I could do for him either'.

Sergeant Robert Maughan was 30 years of age. He was from Newcastle-on-Tyne. Constable Prue was 29 and lived at Sylvan Hill, Lisnaskea; he was the father of two children, a boy aged eight and a girl aged seven. Both were in plain clothes. The IRA maintained that Sergeant Maughan was an SAS man on a spying mission and that the two men had been under observation for some time. The Church of Ireland bishop of Clogher, Rt Rev. Robert Heavener, expressed revulsion at 'this barbarous sacrifice'.[103]

The UDR and the SAS

In July 1979 a training camp for the UDR was set up within Ballykinler Army base, County Down. UDR recruits received basic instruction there. The new camp specialised in counter-insurgency tactics. Some of the instructors came from the School of Infantry at Warminster, Wiltshire, the RUC, and veterans of the SAS training camp at Bradbury Lines, Hereford. 200 full-time and part-time UDR took part in the special training in search procedure, ambush tactics, and night patrolling in rural terrain.

In November 1979 a number of full-time UDR NCOs took part in a weekend scheme run by the SAS, an excerise in urban and rural ambush techniques carried out at Hanley, a prototype Belfast, Stoke-on-Trent, and on the Derbyshire dales near the village of Warslow. The course included undercover operations. This was to improve the UDR intelligence system (UDR Int). Each of its companies has three to four intelligence men. Its intelligence HQ is in 10 UDR battalion at Malone Road, Belfast.

Sir Maurice Oldfield

Sir Maurice Oldfield, former head of MI6, was brought out of retirement to head a new service in Stormont that would heal the MI5/MI6 rift or at least stabilise the dispute and give special priority to the RUC now more dominant since the ending of internment; the new method of 'putting people away', necessitating a success rate in the courts, was guaranteed by ill-treatment processes in the interrogation centres of Castlereagh, Belfast and Gough, Armagh. David McKittrick reported in *The Irish Times*, 6 October 1979, 'According to one version of events, Gen. Creasey became almost unmanageable after the killings of his men at Warrenpoint, and the purpose of Margaret Thatcher's hastily arranged trip to the North was at least partly to calm him down. "The man freaked out" said one source, not usually given to exaggeration'. General Creasey resented the RUC's growing role. He felt frustrated that there was not an all-out-war. He spoke his mind, after leaving Northern Ireland in January 1980, in a BBC programme *War School* – 'I believe that, given the national will and efficient use of all our resources – both military, police and civil – that are at the disposal of the modern state, terrorism can be defeated, and in fact that defeat is inevitable'. Sir Maurice Oldfield did try to make efficient use of all resources. He set up Joint Ops rooms at Castlereagh, Derry and Gough Barracks, Armagh. He set up a Joint Ops Planning Committee comprising the SPG (Special Patrol Group, RUC) Bronze section, HQ Company (14 Co), Special Branch, RUC, MI5 and MI6, SAS (including a Special Tasks' team in Belfast called 'Whiskey').

General Sir Timothy 'Bull' Creasey was critical of the much-vaunted 'Ulsterisation' policy in Northern Ireland. He thought the British Army could have a quick victory if given more of a free hand. His thoughts, however, were out of favour with Mrs Thatcher. When he left Northern Ireland he was sent to command the Sultan's forces in Oman, a country so close to Britain as almost to appear a protectorate. Later in Oman he was joined by Colonel Richard Lea, SAS, who had been appointed British Defence Military Attaché. Colonel Lea joined the SAS from the Queen's Regiment in 1967 as a squadron commander and had risen to command 21 SAS Regiment when he was transferred in 1979 to Northern Ireland as GSOI Intelligence/Security Group. The holder of this important post is responsible to the GOC for all British Army intelligence activities in Northern Ireland. Colonel Lea was honoured with an MBE and in 1980 was awarded

the Distingished Service Order. In Oman, Lea had the unenviable distinction of being the first senior SAS officer to face a court-martial. In June 1984
he was summoned home to face an inquiry. The news broke in the English
papers in March 1985 (*Sunday Express*, 17 March 1985; *Daily Mirror*, 18
March 1985). A Ministry of Defence spokesman told the *Sunday Express* –
'Colonel Lea has been suspended from duty since June last year to assist the
investigation into the discovery of some classified documents at his house
in Kent'. Apparently the papers of the inquiry, which went on for nine
months, were found by police investigating a reported burglary at Colonel
Lea's home in Tunbridge Wells. The classified documents were understood
to have listed details, including names and dates, of top secret operations
in Northern Ireland. A former SAS officer told the *Daily Mirror*, 'Richard is
very popular with the soldiers, and as far as I understand there is no
suggestion of him being a spy'. According to reports in *The Times* and the
Daily Telegraph, 30 April 1985, Colonel Lea was severely reprimanded at a
court martial at Chelsea Barracks, London, after he pleaded guilty to
keeping 153 secret documents in his possession between 30 May 1982 and
16 June 1984. He pleaded guilty to six charges under section 2 of the Official
Secrets Act. He admitted acquiring the documents by virtue of his military
position and retaining them 'when he had no right to do so'. He was
described as serving in the SAS directorate. Colonel Lea (51) was awarded
the Distinguished Service Order in 1980.

It has been estimated that there were more than 600 British Intelligence
operators working in Ireland in the Oldfield period. The six-month training
programme for agents in Ireland was called 'Operation Banner' and took
place in the school of Secret Intelligence in Kent. British Army intelligence
men received extra training at Overhill, near Shorncliffe. Phone tappers and
technical spies were given further training at Harrogate at the Royal Signal
Corps School and at an RAF station in Nottinghamshire.

Signals Intelligence arranged phone taps. Two of them were attached to
each SO2 office at each brigade HQ in Northern Ireland.

One covert Ammunition Technical Officer (ATO) worked with the SAS
and crossed the Border when necessary. His function was to assist the
recovery of weapon caches and EOD (Explosives Ordnance Device) if
located just south of the Border. If an EOD fails it can be used as a bait in a
trap laid by the SAS. The ATO would defuse a bomb during darkness and
withdraw leaving an operation partly to cover it. The chance is that the IRA
would return to find out why it had not fired or to recover materials.

The most secret part of the Intelligence Cell was the Research Office. It
dealt with informers or other sources. The operator who dealt with a source
was called a 'handler'. A slush fund was available. When a source was first
contacted he was given a code name like that of a racehorse – 'Red Cracker',
'Bread Crumb'. All information from a source was recorded.

Despite the presence of the SAS, the IRA were once again rampant in South Armagh. They had dealt a shattering blow to MI6 by killing the British Ambassador, Mr Christopher Ewart-Biggs, on 21 July 1976. MI6 officers operated under cover from the British Embassy in Dublin. On 13 October a heavily-armed unit of Provisional IRA in full combat uniform put on a show of strength in South Armagh and set up a checkpoint in full view of journalists from Britain and Germany. On the same day a young British solider was killed by a booby trap at Ford's Cross near Crossmaglen and in the same vicinity the IRA fired at a helicopter with an M60 machine-gun striking the fuselage. They followed this up with a second public check-point near the British Army/RUC barracks in Crossmaglen. They had the cheek to tell journalists that their checkpoints in the North were for the purpose of intercepting the SAS. The propaganda war was deliberately aimed at Mr Humphrey Atkins, Secretary of State, who, as already mentioned, on 3 September spoke to a meeting of Newry and Mourne District Council. In his speech to Belfast Chamber of Trade, 30 October 1979, he said the police and the Army were taking action but he could not talk about it. The two things he could reveal, he said, were the appointment of Sir Maurice Oldfield and the discussions with the Irish Government to see ways of improving border security.

1980 came in with little luck for the undercover operations in South Armagh. Two soldiers at Forkhill fell victims to the 'Shoot-to-Kill' policy and were shot accidentally by their own side. The official story of the incident on 1 January was that a patrol led by Lieutenant Simon Bates split in two. When it came to regroup, colleagues lying in wait fired on the second party killing Lieutenant Bates and Private Gerald Hardy. They were members of the 2nd Battalion Parachute Regiment. The story is more vividly described by a Sergeant, 2 Para, in Max Arthur's *Northern Ireland Soldiers Talking*:

> When you prepare an ambush you put the boys in, check all the business and you give 'Ambush Set'. That means nobody moves unless a war happens. In front, you've a killing area. There we were: cold, wet, lying in a ditch, when two blokes walked into the ambush. We positively identified weapons and we had to open fire.
>
> Unfortunately, it was our young lieutenant and his signaller. He'd walked down the road and come back up the wrong side. They were both killed.

Based on this account there was no warning, no prisoners taken. On 16 December 1979 another member of the Battlion, Steven Grundy, was killed at Forkhill. The IRA claimed he was caught in an explosion at a house which they mined; it had been occupied by Paras and SAS as a 'spy post'.

On 2 May 1980 one of the officially recognised SAS casualties in Northern

Ireland, Captain Herbert Richard Westmacott (28), was shot dead in Belfast. Eight members of the SAS were on patrol in unmarked cars on the Antrim Road. They wore anoraks and jeans. Each wore a florescent armband for identification purposes. Captain Westmacott, who was leading the group, received a call on his personal radio to go to Antrim Road where something suspicious was going on. The lead car went to the front of the house and the second car to the rear. As soon as the five SAS got out of the car at the front of the house they came under fire from another house. Captain Westmacott was killed instantly, hit in the head and shoulder by two bullets from an M60 machine-gun fired from an upstairs window. The SAS returned fire. They were armed with sub-machine-guns, Colt Commando automatic rifles and Browning pistols. After negotiations helped by the intervention of a priest, the IRA men surrendered. Four men, Angelo Fusco (24), Robert Joseph Campbell (27), Joseph Patrick Thomas Doherty (28) and Paul Patrick Magee (33) were later charged and sentenced for the murder of Captain Westmacott and possession of the M60 and other firearms. On 10 June 1981 the four men with four others shot their way out of Crumlin Road Jail, Belfast, and made good their escape. There was another, less spectacular, sequel to the Westmacott shooting. The SAS caused a security risk in London in September 1980 by holding a £75 plate dinner at a London club in aid of Captain Westmacott's dependants. The good intention of the ex-SAS officer who organised it was frowned on by the Ministry of Defence who thought it would be a risk if attended by many SAS men. Westmacott was posthumously awarded the Military Cross.

Sir Maurice Oldfield retired in June 1980 from his post as co-ordinator of security in Northern Ireland. His biographer, Richard Deacon, says that he had a staff of about forty. He brought the Army and RUC closer together, strengthened the link with Dublin and the Gardaí. His main contribution was the side-wooing of sections of the Catholic community and the cultivation of the 'deep cover' informer, a practice that was to continue to the present. Deacon says, 'Within eighteen months of Oldfield's coming to Ulster some thirty informers had given evidence which led to the arrest of more than three hundred suspected terrorists. IRA bombings were reduced in number and terrorist murders were halved in two years'.

Some of these informers were to become household names in protracted trials in the 1980s, Christopher Black, Raymond Gilmour, Harry Kirpatrick, Kevin McGrady, Robert Quigley, Clifford McKeown, Joseph Bennett. People were jailed on the suspicion of agents of dubious character, many of them guilty of crimes themselves, even murder. One such person, who may have been a police agent as early as 1969, was Anthony O'Doherty.[104] He had SAS connections. O'Doherty was arrested on 3 August 1980 and subsequently, 29 October 1981, pleaded guilty to forty-seven charges. These ranged from robbery and blackmail to three attempted murders of police-

Seamus Wright
(† 2-10-72)

Daniel Rooney
(† 26-9-72)

Paul Tinnelly
(† 2-6-74)

Colin Wallace, 1975
(Pacemaker)

Fred Holroyd

John Francis Green
(† 10-1-75)

Patrick Campbell
(† 24-10-73)

Capt. Robert Nairac
(† 15-5-77) *Pacemaker*

Seamus O'Brien
(† 17-1-76)

John Martin Reavey
(† 4-1-76)

Brian Reavey
(† 4-1-76)

Anthony Reavey
(† 30-1-76)

Thompson

Ligari

McClean

Lawson

Rees

Nicholson

Sketches of six of the SAS soldiers in court by artist Jim Palmer *(The Sunday World, 13-3-77)*

Seamus Harvey
(† 16-1-77)

Michael McHugh
(† 21-1-77)

Colm McNutt
(† 12-12-77)

Paul Duffy
(† 26-2-75)

Denis Heaney
(† 10-6-78)

William Hanna
(† 21-6-78) *Pacemaker*

Denis Brown
(† 21-6-78) *Pacemaker*

William Mailey
(† 21-6-78) *Pacemaker*

Jim Mulvenna
(† 21-6-78)

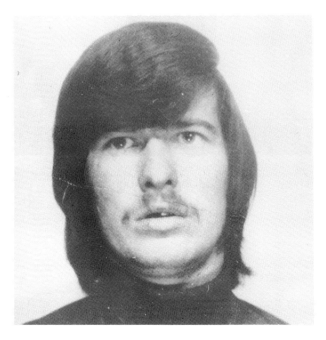

Peter Cleary
(† 15-4-76)

The walled garden where Peter Cleary was shot.

Funeral of James Taylor, 30-9-78 (Pacemaker)

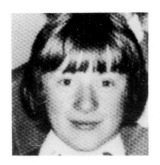

John Boyle
(† 11-7-78) *Pacemaker*

Patrick Duffy
(† 24-11-78)

John Turnly
(† 4-6-80)

Car of Frederick Jackson († 19-10-84) showing bullet hole *(Pacemaker)*

Funeral of John Turnly *(Pacemaker)*

Funeral of Miriam Daly († 26-6-80) *Pacemaker*

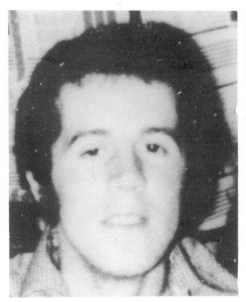 

George McBrearty
(✝ 28-5-81)

Charles Maguire
(✝ 28-5-81)

Funeral of George McBrearty and Charles Maguire *(Pacemaker)*

Sir Maurice Oldfield
Security Co-ordinator
N.I., 1979-80
(Pacemaker)

Ronald Bunting
(† 15-10-78)

Noel Lyttle
(† 15-10-80) *Pacemaker*

Neil McMonagle
(† 2-2-83)

Brian Campbell
(† 4-12-83)

Colm McGirr
(† 4-12-83)

Henry Hogan
(† 21-2-84)

Declan Martin
(† 21-2-84)

William Price
(† 13-7-84)

Funeral of William Price *(Pacemaker)*

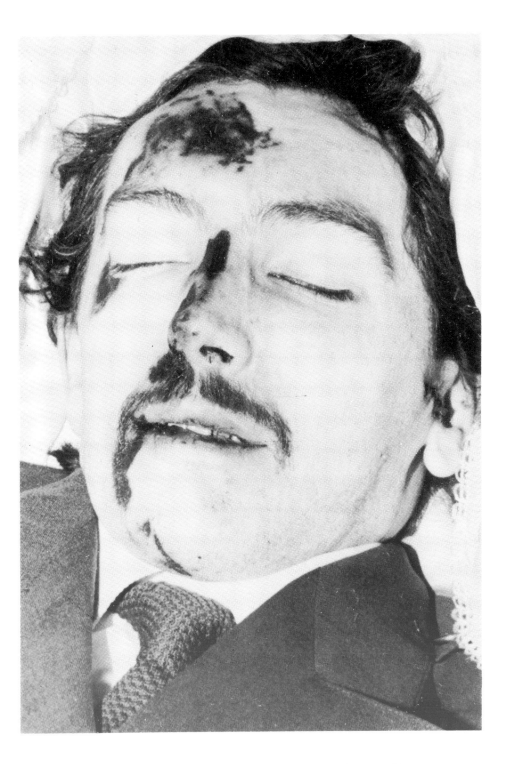

Signs of abuse on the face of Antoin Mac Giolla Bríde

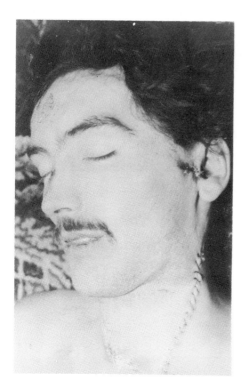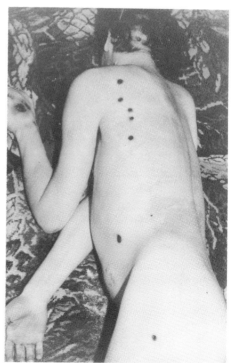

Wounds on the body of Antoin Mac Giolla Bríde

Entrance to Drumrush Lodge. Landmine was placed on near side of entrance.

Daniel Doherty
(† 6-12-84)

William Fleming
(† 6-12-84)

Charles Breslin
(† 23-2-85)

Michael Devine
(† 23-2-85)

David Devine
(† 23-2-85)

Francis Bradley
(† 18-2-86)

Seamus McElwain
(† 26-4-86)

Seán Lynch
(Wounded 26-4-86)

Anthony Hughes
(† 8-5-87)

**Volunteers
killed
at
Loughgall**

8 May 1987

Pádraig McKearney

Tony Gormley

Eugene Kelly

Patrick Kelly

Jim Lynagh

Seamus Donnelly

Declan Arthurs

Gerard O'Callaghan

Mairéad Farrell
(† 6-3-88)

Daniel McCann
(† 6-3-88) *Pacemaker*

Seán Savage
(† 6-3-88) *Pacemaker*

Martin Harte
(+30-8-88)

Gerard Harte
(† 30-8-88)

Brian Mullin
(† 30-8-88)

Ken Stronge
(† 1-7-88) Pacemaker

Funeral of Brian Mullin, St Mary's Church, Dunmoyle (The Independent)

men. At his trial O'Doherty revealed his work as a police agent; he was known as Agent 294. He also worked for the SAS and British intelligence. He underwent six months training with the SAS in their camp in County Tyrone. This included the skills of unarmed combat, surveillance and survival techniques. Before the IRA realised he was an informer, he had ingratiated himself to them by 'terrorist' attacks on security forces; one incident resulted in the wounding of two UDR men. At one time he possessed around a dozen weapons. The RUC provided him with a Sten captured from the IRA, a .303 rifle and a pistol. He had numerous short arms. O'Doherty carried out attacks and robberies outside his supervision. This led to his arrest. After three days interrogation he confessed to all the crimes laid against him except the murder of RUC Sergeant, Joseph P. Campbell, who had been shot dead outside Cushendall police station on 29 February 1977; he denied having guns on that day. He implicated his 'handler', Detective Sergeant Charles McCormick. McCormick was charged. He was found not guilty on all but three charges; these were the alleged hijacking of motor cars on 24 November 1974, the alleged possession of a rifle in suspicious circumstances on 25 November 1974 and an alleged armed robbery. McCormick was sentenced to twenty years. He was acquitted on appeal and all convictions against him quashed.

The controlling of paramilitary agents like O'Doherty and the use of informers brought short-term results in the conviction of people for political offences. However, it meant a long-term loss. The Diplock courts were suspect and the judges were thought to have failed in protecting the right of the citizen to life and liberty.

Sir Maurice Oldfield died 11 March 1981. In a parliamentary written answer on 23 April 1987 the Prime Minister, Mrs Margaret Thatcher, revealed in the House of Commons that he was a homosexual and 'a potential risk to security'. Allegations were made in a book by Chapman Pincher that he was a compulsive homosexual who lived a double life unknown to his colleagues.

Mrs Thatcher stressed that 'there was no evidence or reason whatsoever to suggest that security had ever been compromised; indeed he had contributed notably to a number of security and intelligence successes which would not have been achieved had there been a breach of security'. Mrs Thatcher said that reports were received which caused his positive vetting clearance to be reviewed. In March 1980 in the course of that review he made an admission that he had from time to time engaged in homosexual activities. His positive vetting clearance was withdrawn. According to Chapman Pincher his homosexual activities came to light when he was in Northern Ireland and subject to round-the-clock armed protection. Former MI6 men came to Oldfield's defence claiming that the accusations were part of an on-going campaign from the early and mid-70s against Oldfield from

MI5, the assertion being that MI5 resented interference from its rival agency. Mr George Young, a former deputy head of MI6, defended Oldfield. He said Oldfield had merely indulged in youthful peccadillos when he was at university; Oldfield's unsung achievements were drowned in smears. Anthony Cavendish, author of *Inside Intelligence*, former MI6 officer, also defended him. Colin Wallace who revealed the rivalry and hostility between MI5 and MI6 in Northern Ireland elicited motives for the smear: 'Oldfield had a Mr Clean approach in Northern Ireland, particularly against assassination plots and the dirty tricks war. There was a remarkable campaign of character assassination directed against Oldfield which could only have been co-ordinated by people who actually had very detailed inside information. Richard Deacon, in his biography of Oldfield, traces the source of the smears back to my old office in Army HQ Northern Ireland. He mentions an Ulster Defence Regiment source and he mentions HQ Northern Ireland. There was an attempt to smear Oldfield on two counts: first that he was a homosexual, which he wasn't, and secondly that he was a Russian agent... MI5 wanted him removed from Ulster because he would never have sanctioned the E4A-type activities. It was no secret to anyone who knew Maurice Oldfield that he was totally opposed to assassination. MI5 saw him as a threat to their activities in Northern Ireland'.[105]

The Secretary of State, Mr Humphrey Atkins, and Sir Maurice Oldfield were in agreement on military solutions and that covert action should play a vital role. Issue No. 33 (December 1979) of *The Leveller* magazine published a document, part of a Restricted Ministry of Defence guide to the administrative set-up of the SAS. The document, reproduced here, shows the administrative picture, the Regimental Headquarters at the top responsible through the Commanding Officer to the Director of SAS, then the Operations and Intelligence centre responsible for the squadrons and the Training Wing. In his book *The Soldiers* (1979) Henry Stanhope, analysing the organisation of 22 SAS, pointed out that the Training Wing had a special Northern Ireland cell. The commitment to Northern Ireland dictated a special cell in the Training Wing. The make-up of SAS squadrons is now fluid and some men are put back through training to become Northern Ireland 'specialists'.

The different agencies in the North, Army Intelligence, MI5, MI6 (in its lesser role) and Special Branch RUC were co-ordinated through a Joint Intelligence Operations Planning Committee. A special security directorate inherited from Oldfield, kept an eye on leaks from the different agencies; 14 Intelligence and Security Company acted as a 'Dirty Tricks' unit. The Northern Ireland co-ordinator, no doubt, reported to the security and intelligence co-ordinator in the Cabinet Office.

Operation 'RANC'

'Operation Ranc' was the name of a series of actions planned by British Intelligence against the INLA following their admitted assassination of Airey Neave, MP on 30 March 1979. Airey Neave played an important role in the British secret service during the Second World War and was OC, I.S. No. 9 TA and later the SAS TA, 1949-51. He was killed just before he was due to take charge of intelligence and security in Northern Ireland. 'Ranc's' 'chief' employed both official and unofficial personnel to execute operations. SAS personnel particularly from 'G' (Guards) 22 SAS were actively involved. 'Operation Ranc' is believed to have cost the lives of Ronnie Bunting, a very senior INLA officer and his non-INLA colleague Noel Lyttle, Miriam Daly (former IRSP), and John Turnly. It was terminated prematurely following strong but private protests from the Irish Government. The revolt of the political prisoners of the H-Blocks in Long Kesh (Maze) Prison was gaining momentum. Sympathy for their plight was widespread. Nationalists looked upon the special Diplock courts as a sham and resented the severe punishments imposed in Long Kesh (Maze) and Armagh prisons to break the prisoners' protest. One of the off-shoots of resentment was the growth of the INLA/IRSP movement. The small Irish Independence Party was also gaining ground. These parties combined with Sinn Féin to form a strong power of resistance. Working through the SAS and picking up their old allies, the UDA, once more, 'Ranc' engineered three assassination operations. Since it lacked hard evidence for the Airey Neave killing , soft targets were chosen.

The first victim was John Turnly, a highly-respected Protestant nationalist, former British Army officer from a unionist background.[106] John Turnly (44) was a founder member of the Irish Independence Party. He was a former Convention member and was a Larne councillor. On 4 June 1980 he was machine-gunned to death in front of his Japanese-born wife Miyoko and their sons at 8 pm on his way to a public meeting at Hamill's Hall in Carnlough. As he drew his car to a halt at the Bridge Tea Rooms, the gunmen's car pulled alongside and a door was opened with force hitting Turnly's vehicle. Two gunmen, one with a sub-machine-gun and the other with a pistol opened fire hitting him nine times on the body, leg and forearms. The murder was clinically planned and carried out with precision and ruthlessness.

Four UDA men were charged with the murder. Two brothers, Eric McConnell (21) of Garron Crescent, Larne and Robert McConnell (27) of Seacourt Road, Larne, and William McClelland (34) of Loran Avenue, were sentenced to life imprisonment on 10 March 1982. William McFettridge (34) of Gardenmore House, Riverdale, admitted manslaughter and was sentenced to 12 years. A fifth man, Edward Brownlee (23) from Ballygally, who hid the guns in question, was jailed for four years.

In a statement from the dock after their conviction Robert McConnell, also sentenced to life for the murder of Patrick Rodney McCormick, claimed he had been working for the SAS. He said he agreed to work for them two months before John Turnly's death. He said the SAS had given him weapons; these included two Army-issue Sterling sub-machine-guns, forty-eight magazines to fit them and around 3000 rounds of ammunition. He was given intelligence-gathering equipment, including a listening device which he once used to eavesdrop on Gerry Adams, Vice-President of Sinn Féin. He named the alleged two SAS soldiers he teamed with as Sergeant Tom Aiken, a Scot, and Corporal McGow. He said they discussed republican leaders, including Mr Turnly, Mrs Miriam Daly and Mrs Bernadette McAliskey. McConnell continued in court – 'They (SAS) said they had information that over a two-year period the republicans had a plan to escalate tension in the province by civil disorder, large-scale importation of arms and explosives, and by certain actions which would arouse the sympathy of republican people with the ultimate object of starting a civil war. We realise now that this involved the hunger-strikers'. McConnell added that he refused to accept money.

Two other features of the Turnly case aroused the suspicion of the public and the press. At the trial of the UDA men it was revealed that after the murder of John Turnly the McConnell brothers and McClelland were stopped at a UDR checkpoint. They were taken to Larne RUC Station where they allegedly told detectives they had been out drinking. They were released. Two months later, on 23 August, they murdered a Catholic, Patrick Rodney McCormick, recently released from Long Kesh (Maze) Prison. Two of the attackers held his wife Anne (Tilly) (21) down while a third pumped ten bullets into him.

During the Turnly trial RUC detectives admitted that notes from an interview with Robert McConnell's brother Eric had been destroyed on the order of a Chief Inspector because they contained 'sensitive information'.

At this time major changes had taken place in the UDA. The UDA was made up of a ruling eight-man inner council which included UDA brigadiers in charge of seven areas of Northern Ireland (the brigadiers came from north, south, east and west Belfast, south-east Antrim, Derry county and mid-Ulster).

A new committee, known as the 'Army Council' had been set up. This consisted of military commanders from each brigade area. John McMichael was appointed South Belfast commander in 1979. It was said that he had earned his pips on the ground by personally killing three Catholics. It is thought he played his part in forming a policy of attacking prominent republicans. The UDA, thanks to the help it always gave to the British in the war against republicans, has never been proscribed. The UDA, as the whole public of Northern Ireland knows, is a paramilitary organisation which has murdered hundreds of Catholics. The UFF (Ulster Freedom Fighters) does not exist. It is a flag of convenience for the UDA; still the Northern Ireland Office uses this as a way-out in not proscribing the UDA.

For example, Mr B. A. Blackwell, of the Law and Order Division, Northern Ireland Office, wrote to me on this point, 5 January 1987:-

> Turning to your remarks about the proscription of the Ulster Defence Association, the Government and the Security Forces keep under careful review the possibility of proscribing any organisation which is paramilitary in character or associated with acts of violence. While individual members of the UDA have been convicted of acts of terrorism, it is not itself a terrorist organisation. Sinn Féin is similarly not proscribed despite its close relationship with, and open support for, the Provisional IRA and the conviction of some of its members of terrorist crimes. The fact that membership of an organisation is not illegal does not, however, confer, any immunity from persecution on its members if they commit criminal acts.

Mr Blackwell's remarks contrast, for example, with those of Mr Justice Higgins who on 1 July 1988 launched a scathing attack on the UDA for involvement in murders and armed robberies when he sentenced a youth, Lee Francis Deery of Omagh, County Tyrone, to detention at the pleasure of the Secretary of State for involvement in the murder of a Catholic breadman, Dermott Hackett (37), shot at least 15 times at the wheel of his breadvan on 23 May 1987.

The real reason for the non-proscription of the UDA is its strong connection with British Intelligence. Since McMichael was never charged with murder but, on the contrary, was continually paraded on the British media, the logical conclusion is that he himself was a British agent brought up through the ranks and available to bring a lull or cull to the murder of Catholics as the general political situation so required. Such agents are always expendable.

The second victim in this precise targeting was Mrs Miriam Daly, lecturer in Queen's University, Belfast, an intelligent and respected republican. Although she had lately resigned from the IRSP, she remained an ardent advocate of civil rights and justice. Her murder followed close on that of John Turnly. Mrs Daly campaigned on behalf of the H-Block prisoners. Mrs Daly was seen at 2.30 pm on 26 June 1980 by different witnesses going into Brady's shop near her home. Her ten-year-old daughter coming into the house from school found her lying dead in the hall of the Andersonstown Road house. A neighbour said that Marie came into her home and told her that her mother was lying in the hallway. On entering, a neighbour found her face-downward in a pool of blood. Her legs were tied with string. A bloodstained pillow with bullet holes lay close by. It had been used to deaden the sound of shots. For half-an-hour before the shooting British soldiers and RUC patrolled the Andersonstown Road in large numbers. The killers came into the grounds from Dunmisk Park at the rear of the house and entered at the front door. The murder occurred between 2.30 pm and 3.30 pm. The 'professionals' cut the telephone wire in the hallway.

Nobody has been made amenable for the murder of Mrs Daly. The journalist Ed Moloney in the *Sunday Tribune*, 27 December 1987, quotes security sources as claiming that McMichael was directly involved in the planning of her death. The killing of Mrs Daly had an 'SAS' look. McMichael hankered after SAS tactics and even went so far as to give his 'soldiers' SAS-type training.

Another fixed target which bore the same 'SAS' hallmark and was carried out by the UDA was the murder of Ronnie Bunting, son of a former associate of Rev. Ian Paisley. He joined the People's Democracy when he was at Queen's University. Later he joined the Official IRA and took the INLA/IRSP side in the later split in the Officials. In 1980, like Mrs Daly, he was associated with the H-Block campaign. Like John Turnly, he and his wife Suzanne were republicans from a Protestant background. He and his friend, Noel Lyttle, IRSP member and H-Block campaigner, were shot dead in Bunting's home in the early hours of 15 October 1980. Suzanne was shot and seriously injured. The Buntings lived in a cul-de-sac in Downfine Gardens in Andersonstown. In an interview in the *Irish News,* 28 October 1980, Mrs Bunting said she told RUC detectives she believed the SAS were responsible for the murders. The detectives told her they were convinced a loyalist gang was responsible. Mrs Bunting said, 'They know, as I do, that the people who killed Ronnie and Noel knew where they could be found, in what rooms and how best to break the doors down. I told the police that I believe and know, with all my heart, that Ronnie and Noel were not killed by any republican group – it was the SAS. The attack was too well-planned, carried out by men who were cool and calm and knew what they were doing'. She said they were like animals without fear. They broke down the door of their home with sledges. Mrs Bunting also made a statement to her solicitor and made it available for the Association for Legal Justice. A friend, Noel Lyttle, was staying with them that night. He had come to their house at 10.30 pm. He had intended visiting Long Kesh Prison the next day. He wasn't sure if he was going to stay the night but came back later at 11.15 pm and said he would. She said her husband came to bed at about 1 am. They occupied the large front bedroom overlooking Downfine Gardens. Noel Lyttle was sleeping in the small front bedroom along with the baby. The other two children were in the back bedroom. The toilet light had been left on for the children. At about 3.15 am Suzanne and her husband heard banging downstairs. They both jumped out of bed and ran to bolt the bedroom door. Just as they reached the door two masked men reached it as well from the landing. They tried to push the door closed and the masked men tried to push it open. One of the gunmen fired at least one shot and Suzanne jumped away from the door on to the bed. The door opened and she saw the two men standing in the doorway. She heard more gunfire and when she looked up she saw one of the men continually shooting into Ronnie's body. She went berserk and ran over to the gunman who was still firing into Ronnie's body. She tried to pull him away shouting 'Leave him alone'. He fired at her and shot her through the shoulder and under the arm. She leaned against the landing wall above her husband's body. She saw the man who shot her walking backwards down the stairs towards his companion who was reaching the bottom of the stairs. The latter turned round and said , 'Come on Geordie'. He then raised his firearm and shot her in the mouth. She fell to the floor pumping blood. She knew Ronnie was dead; his eyes were wide open and staring. He had been hit with seven to nine bullets. Noel was shot but still alive; she could hear his strained breathing. The children appeared on the landing screaming. Her daughter Fiona ran on to the street for help.

There are a number of significant details about the killings. Three quarters of an hour before the shooting a neighbour saw a British Army checkpoint, a row of British Army vehicles, at the entrance of the street behind the cul-de-sac. That night the barrier across the Donegal Road had been open even though it had been closed for weeks previously. The killers' car was never found. There were seven doors in the landing in Buntings' home. The killers knew which bedroom door to head for. When the RUC came to the house they took away all photographic albums and bags of other personal effects. However, they did not bother, as in the case of Niall O'Neill, to pick up the spent cartridges. They left them lying on the floor. The gunmen were of medium build. Both wore khaki ski-masks, khaki corded jumpers with suede shoulder pads and khaki trousers tucked into army-type boots. In August 1980 Ronnie Bunting had been arrested under Emergency Laws and had been brought to Castlereagh Interrogation Centre. Afterwards in a statement he alleged that plain clothes interrogators made a number of death threats against him, 'You are a bad bastard and we'll get you'. He made a formal complaint to Queen Street RUC Station alleging ill-treatment. Ronnie Bunting took the threats and harassment seriously. He told a friend in September, 'Before Christmas I am going to be six feet under'.

The murder attempt on Bernadette McAliskey (34),[107] a leading H-Block campaigner in 1981, was planned in a room above a pub in Lisburn owned by John McMichael and, like the other UDA operations against Mrs Daly and Ronnie Bunting, bore McMichael's stamp. A UDA gang, Andrew Watson (25), Seymour Hill, Dunmurry, Belfast, Thomas Graham (38),

Carntogher Road, Lisburn and Raymond Smallwoods (31), Edenvale Gardens, Lisburn were sentenced for her attempted murder on 21 January 1982. Watson was jailed for life. Smallwoods was given 15 years and Graham 20 years. Present in court to hear the verdict was John McMichael. He declined to answer any allegations that the UDA could have been involved in the attempted killings. Bernadette McAliskey and her husband Michael (33) were shot and seriously wounded in front of their three young children at their isolated home in Derryloughan townland near Coalisland on 16 January 1981. The operation followed the pattern of the Bunting killing. Graham and Watson used a sledgehammer to smash in the front door at 8.15 am while Smallwoods remained outside. At the time Michael and Bernadette McAliskey were preparing breakfast for the children. Michael McAliskey tried to stop them coming in and was shot four times in the kitchen. Although conscious he pretended to be dead. Mrs McAliskey was shot eight times in the bedroom. Graham and Watson then ran out to their car which had been left with the engine running. Four paratroopers on undercover duty in a copse near the house captured them. Quick action by Lt Colonel Campbell Mac Farlane, a British Army surgeon, saved the lives of the McAliskeys. The gang were armed with a 9 mm Browning pistol and a .38 revolver. Watson was a former member of the UDR and son of a former H-Block prison officer. In his address at the end of the trial Mr Justice Mac Dermott said, 'You, Watson, were very much the leader of this team, whose purpose was murder and indeed you only stopped firing when the magazine of the Browning gun was exhausted'.

After the assassination attempt on her life, Mrs McAliskey spoke of many unanswered questions. Why were four paratroopers on hand almost as she hit the ground? Why paratroopers when the Argyll and Sutherland Highlanders were stationed locally? The four soldiers asked for a telephone but it had been cut by the assassins. The paratroopers claimed their radio was not working. They left without giving medical aid. For twenty minutes the wounded couple were without help while one of the soldiers set off to find a telephone. When the Argylls arrived they administered help at the bungalow and during the helicopter flight to the hospital. One Argyll saved Michael McAliskey's life by applying a tourniquet.

Another assassination bid on a prime target failed. Mr Gerry Adams, MP and three companions were shot and wounded in their car in Howard Street, Belfast, at 1.30 pm on 14 March 1984. It happened during a lunchtime adjournment of a case at Belfast Magistrates' Court in which Mr Adams was involved. Three UDA attackers were captured by an off-duty UDR man and by two members of the 'Royal Military Police' in plain clothes and in an unmarked car. This was of a pattern with the arrest of the UDA in the McAliskeys' murder attempt. The RUC denied British Intelligence or SAS involvement. Mr Adams said he believed the men who carried out the attack were 'set up' by British Intelligence. Mrs McAliskey said that, 'the members of the UDA, in whatever guise, had clearly been double-crossed by some of their leaders', and that a high-ranking British Army officer had been either 'party to or at least was fully aware of the plan to murder Gerry Adams'.

Three men were jailed for the shooting and wounding of Gerry Adams. Gerald Welsh (34), Monkscoole House, Rathcoole, and John Gregg (27) of Fernagh Drive, Newtownabbey, who between them fired 12 shots, were jailed for 18 years. Colin Gray (28) of Inniscarn Drive, Rathcoole, was jailed for 12 years. He was the driver of their Rover car.

The assassination attempt on Gerry Adams was planned by McMichael. UDA men were also involved in the killing of Mr Kevin McPolin in Lisburn on 8 November 1985. The murder came after the signing of the Anglo-Irish Agreement. In 1986 a wave of fire-bombing and the intimidation of hundreds of Catholics out of housing estates in Lisburn followed the loyalist March day of action against the Agreement. John McMichael organised the attacks. No protection was offered to the Catholics by the RUC or British Army. No action was taken against McMichael. In May 1986 the UDA shot and seriously wounded Mr Alex Maskey, a Sinn Féin councillor at his home in West Belfast. Another action against the Anglo-Irish Agreement planned by McMichael led to the imprisonment of three UDA members, one a former British soldier. Mr Justice McCollum described the fire-bomb plot against premises in Dublin on 7 February 1987 as, 'the type of crime intended to cause political instability, community strife and to invite retaliation'. He described the UDA as an organisation, 'which gives people power to engage in extortions, robberies and sectarian assassinations'. Jailed for 8 years were Francis Orr (31) of Mervue Street, Belfast, Roy Clements (48), formerly of the Engineers, British Army, and Raymond Verner (33) both of Sunningdale Gardens, Belfast.

John McMichael (39) was killed by an IRA booby-trap bomb under his car outside his home on 23 December 1987. Among those in the cortège at his funeral were Mr James Molyneaux, MP, leader of the Official Unionist Party and the Rev. Ian Paisley, MP, leader of the Democratic Unionist Party. Mr Harold McCusker, MP, Official Unionist, and Mr Peter Robinson, MP, DUP, helped to carry the coffin. Rev. Martin Smyth, MP, Official Unionist, was also present.

The Twinbrook Raid[108]

Four days after the killings of Bunting and Lyttle, the real SAS struck in West Belfast at IRSP/H-Block campaigners in an incredible exhibition of terrorism.

Dinner was just over in the Berkery home in Cherry Gardens, Twin-

brook, Belfast, Sunday, 19 October 1980. The family were having a late
dinner. Earlier they had taken part in a picket on the H-Block issue. They
handed out leaflets advertising an evening meeting. It was 6.30 pm. A
neighbour, Maura Campbell, came into the house with her baby. Mrs
Berkery and Maura sat down to chat in the dining-room. John Boyd was
washing the dishes. Two young men, Declan McDaid and Patrick Mc-
Caughey, were talking together in the living-room.

Suddenly a man was heard yelling and screaming at the front door. Milk
bottles were scattered. Mrs Berkery rushed to the door. A man was standing
there screaming and smashing through the glass door with a sledge
hammer. A second man was behind him with a long black gun. He was also
screaming. Mrs Berkery ran back into the dining-room. Maura Campbell
threw herself on the floor and pulled the baby under her for its protection.
Everybody thought loyalist assassins were invading the house. Mrs Berkery thought of her 15-year-old daughter Aisling upstairs and turned to
head up the stairs. It was too late. The room was already full of armed men.
They were dressed in anoraks and bomber jackets with orange florescent
armlets. One of them was gypsy-looking with long black greasy hair and a
dangling gold ear-ring. Another, blond, moustached, took up a position at
the door. Some ran upstairs. Mrs Berkery could hear them shouting at
Aisling. When she made to go up again, the blond man prevented her. He
ordered her to stand against the wall with her hands behind her back.
Another man ordered her to lie face down on the floor. As she turned he
pushed her down to the ground and taped her hands behind her back. One
who seemed to be in charge took her name, address and date of birth. She
could hear people screaming outside that shots had been fired and that a
young man was lying dead in the back garden.

When Declan McDaid and Patrick McCaughey heard the smash of glass,
McDaid ran to the door after Mrs Berkery. He saw the man with the long
black hair and the blond man with the gun. Instinctively he and Mc-
Caughey thought they were a loyalist gang and in panic both leapt through
the window of the living-room, breaking it as they went. McDaid went first,
cutting his hand badly and almost severing a finger. In the back garden they
were confronted by a man with long blond hair who shouted 'Stop you
bastards or I shoot'. He then fired shots. Both the lads ran round the garden
in semi-circles and then McDaid ran into the house again. He slammed the
inside door into the face of another SAS man heading into the room with a
sub-machine-gun. He tried to hold the door. At this stage he didn't even
notice his cut hand. The man was shouting, 'Open the door you bastard or
I'll shoot you through the door'. He kicked the door in. McDaid was
shouting, 'I'm not armed'. The SAS man pulled him down on the floor and
kicked him on the head dazing him. When he recovered consciousness he
was lying in a pool of blood and he saw that part of his hand was hanging

off. He shouted for a towel but the SAS man kicked him in the head again. Another SAS man bandaged his hand. Still the man guarding him kicked him, crying, 'Stop shouting you bastard, you bastard you'. Another SAS man gave an order, 'If you find the gear, we'll do them and get out quick'.

At the smashing of the front door John Boyd also looked into the front hall and saw the man with the long black hair carrying a gun. He too thought it was loyalists and that he was going to be shot. He ran into the living-room and saw another group coming down the garden path. Then McDaid dashed into the living-room again from the back covered in blood. Boyd tried to help him hold the door but seeing it was impossible he left him and jumped in behind the settee. The door burst open and McDaid fell to the ground screaming, 'Please don't shoot me. Don't shoot me. Have mercy on me. I haven't done nothing'. Boyd was frightened when they started kicking McDaid on the ground. The SAS did not realise he was behind the settee. Afraid that they might shoot him if they found out, he raised his head and called out that he was coming out from behind the settee. The SAS starting cursing and screaming. They threw him face down on the carpet. One put his foot on his back and pressed a gun into him. Another with a Belfast accent questioned him. He also heard a Scottish accent but the rest were English.

Outside, McCaughey in his frenzy had tried to get into the coal-bunker but it was locked. A man came running towards him with a small machine-gun. He was aged about 28, long blond hair, wearing a blue jacket and brown corduroy trousers, red-and-white-striped shirt. He had an English accent. He shouted, 'Don't move or you're dead'. McCaughey put his hands on the coal-bunker and took up the search position while he was being frisked. The soldier then forced him to lie spread-eagled, placing the barrel of his gun into his lower back and crouching down beside him. He told him to put his face on the ground and not move it or he would blow his head off.

Two women from the house next door came out and started shouting. One thought McCaughey was her son and that he was shot dead. McCaughey lifted his head and shouted, 'I'm not'. He was then searched and questioned. When asked what he was doing in the house, he said he was at a meeting. The SAS man said, 'You'll have no fucking meeting now'. Later the same man shouted, 'Have you found the stuff till we do him?'

Upstairs Aisling Berkery was standing on the landing doing some ironing when she heard the door being smashed in. She looked over the banister and saw two men in plain clothes wearing orange armbands and carrying guns. They ran up the stairs and pushed her into a bedroom. One of them shouted, 'Get in there, you bastard'. He had curly hair, a beard and wore an ear-ring. He told her to lie on the bed and then he tied her hands behind her back with white plastic tape. She heard a lot of shouting down the stairs and a shot fired. She was brought downstairs to the dining-room and made stand against the wall near where Maura Campbell was sitting facing the wall holding her baby. She counted ten men wearing orange armbands and carrying guns.

It would seem that five SAS men entered the house and were later joined by five more. There were others stationed outside. In all 18 SAS men took part in the raid. About 15 minutes after the raid had taken place, uniformed soldiers and uniformed and plain clothes RUC men arrived. The 'prisoners' listened to the SAS discussing the situation, where each person had been found and such detail. One SAS man was referred to as 'Joseph'.

About 15 minutes before the raid on the Berkery home, the house of Mrs Maureen Mooney of Cherry Park, some 150 yards away, was raided. She was standing in the dinette when she heard thuds and bangs. She saw a blond-haired man, aged about 30, average height, wearing a blue shirt and light-coloured bomber jacket. He entered the house and told her not to panic and to 'fucking sit down on the chair'. A black-haired man, 30-35, wearing jeans and a dark bomber jacket came into the dinette. He spoke with a Belfast accent. He asked her who else was in the house. 'There's only me wee baby,' she said. She saw men in balaclava helmets running up the stairs. They stayed about 15 minutes. Mrs Kathleen Robinson was alerted to Mrs Mooney's plight by her young daughter Lynda Mooney. She ran to Mooney's and saw four men coming from the house. Two wore balaclava helmets and orange armbands; they were armed. One said in a northern accent, 'If you want to see shooting, come round to Berkery's'. She ran behind them; they headed for Berkery's. She saw a transit van draw up with about 13 men in it. They went into Berkery's. All had guns and orange armbands.

From the testimony of other witnesses, a blue Volkswagen van, three cars and a white scooter were used in the SAS raid in Twinbrook. Doors of vehicles were left open and engines kept running. Neighbours collected and tried to enter the house. They continually shouted out and phoned the police. Then 8 to 10 RUC land-rovers arrived. When a major of the Royal Regiment of Fusiliers approached the back gate of Berkery's house, an SAS man pointed a gun at him and told him to 'fuck off'. Then an SAS officer shouted, 'Everybody out the back and in the van'. As they got into the van and cars, people noticed some wearing what looked like gas-masks hanging round their necks. A uniformed soldier went to the lead car and gave a clearway out of the estate. The detectives entered the house, searched it, confiscated H-Block leaflets and £37.20 collection money. Mrs Berkery, John Boyd, Patrick McCaughey and Declan McDaid were arrested and brought to Castlereagh Interrogation Centre. Mrs Berkery was interviewed about the hunger-strike and her son in Long Kesh (Maze) Prison. She was kept until 11 am on Tuesday. Boyd gave his opinion to the police that these same men murdered Ronnie Bunting and Noel Lyttle.

The injured McDaid was also taken to Castlereagh. His hand was bleeding heavily. The police said they would get a doctor. One came later and said McDaid would have to go to hospital. His hand was operated on. The next day three detectives took him from the hospital, still dressed in pyjamas, back to Castlereagh. There McDaid complained to a doctor and an inspector about ill-treatment. He was interviewed later that night. One of the detectives then said he was in no condition to be there and he would see an inspector. McDaid was released with McCaughey about 10.30 am on Tuesday morning. When they arrived home at Atlantic Avenue, an Army jeep was waiting for them. The soldiers laughed and jeered at them and followed them, taking photographs.

On Sunday night, 19 October, the RUC issued a statement defending the SAS raid. They said it was part of an operation to thwart an IRA attack on security forces. However, an outcry followed. Bishop William Philbin of Down and Connor visited the Berkery home and sympathised with them, 'My presence,' he said to reporters, 'is an indication of how I feel.' Belfast city councillor, Paddy Devlin, asked that the SAS guns be checked against those which murdered Miriam Daly, Ronnie Bunting and Noel Lyttle. Mr Gerry Fitt, MP raised the matter in the House of Commons. An SDLP delegation led by Dr Joe Hendron and councillor Billy McDonnell met the Deputy Chief Constable, Mr Harry Baillie. An *Irish News* editorial called it a 'nauseating example of gestapo tactics'. The *Irish Press* said it was 'licensed terror' and called on the Secretary of State, Mr Humphrey Atkins, to declare what the future role of the SAS in Northern Ireland would be since a top security source was quoted as saying, 'SAS men will be used more frequently. The flow of information is good and more emphasis will be put on covert work. We believe this is the most effective way of beating terrorism'.

On 14 November 1985 five of the Twinbrook people who suffered in the raid received £50,000 in an out-of-court settlement having sued the Chief Constable and the Minister of Defence.

John Boyd, Moyra Berkery (now Mrs Boyd), Aisling Berkery, Mrs Maureen Mooney and Maura Campbell received £12,000, £12,000, £10,000, £8,000 and £8,000 respectively. In a separate settlement Declan McDaid received £12,000. Shortly after the raid Patrick McCaughey entered a monastery and did not make a claim.

PHASE VI

Shoot-to-Kill

The IRA campaign in the North of Ireland is spasmodic. Operations are sometimes concentrated in one area, depending on the existence of a local unit or local intelligence officers. When the unit is broken up by casualties, capture, or forced flight, the campaign moves to another area which can provide personnel and resources. In the post-hunger-strike period of 1981-2 an IRA unit and an INLA unit operated in the vicinity of Armagh city. The motive was twofold, to take revenge for the hunger-strike deaths and deal a blow against the 'Ulsterisation' of military and police forces. The casualties around Armagh were numerous and savage. On 8 November 1981 Trevor Foster was killed by a booby trap bomb intended for another member of his family who was in the British security forces. On 10 November Charles Neville was shot dead. On 27 August 1982 Wilfred McIlveen, former member of the UDR, was killed in a booby trap explosion. On 7 October Private Frederick Williamson was shot at and died when his car crashed; in the same incident Elizabeth Chambers, prison officer, was killed when her car crashed. On 16 November two reserve constables, Samuel Snowden Corkey and Ronald Irwin, were shot dead in Markethill near Armagh. At Kinnego roundabout near Lurgan Sergeant Seán Quinn, RUC and Constables Alan McCloy and Paul Hamilton were killed by a land-mine explosion on 27 October.

In Armagh two youths were shot dead by the UDR in disputed circumstances, Tony Harker during a burglary on 24 January 1982 and Martin Malone on 30 July 1983. A UDR gang was convicted for shooting dead Adrian Carroll in Armagh on 8 November 1983.

The response from elements in the RUC and UDR to the murders of colleagues and friends in the Protestant community was to strike back, officially and unofficially, in and out of uniform. An out-of-uniform gang from the UDR attempted to kill Seamus Grew at his house in Armagh on 22 September 1982. An out-of-uniform UDR man and others murdered Peter Corrigan, an ex-internee, on 25 October 1982. Other attempted murders by the same gang resulted in woundings by gunfire.

Official attention came from the RUC. On 11 November 1982 the RUC shot dead three unarmed IRA men, Eugene Toman, Seán Burns and Gervaise McKerr near Lurgan. On 24 November they shot dead seventeen-year-old Michael Tighe and seriously wounded Martin McAuley in a hayshed near Lurgan. They shot dead two unarmed INLA members Seamus Grew and Roddy Carroll in Armagh on 12 December 1982. The RUC members who carried out these shootings were members of the Headquarters Mobile Support Unit (HQMSU), sometimes referred to as SSU (Special Tasks Unit), who came under E Department of the Special Branch RUC. Two of these units had been set up, each with 24 men trained at Hereford by the SAS. They were armed with rapid-firing automatic weapons. The units were controlled and directed by Special Branch officers.

In three articles on RUC undercover activities in South Armagh in *The Irish Times*, 21-23 January 1985, Ed Moloney argued that the military type activities of HQSMU had a forerunner in the Bessbrook Support Unit which was set up in 1979. This covert unit liaisoned with the SAS and Gardaí. It did not kill anybody but succeeded in curbing the IRA's free policing of South Armagh.

The Observer, 12 October 1986, gave a succinct account by David Leigh, Jonathan Foster and Paul Lashmar of the killings in 1982 by the RUC in County Armagh. It is to be borne in mind that it is one version of events; RUC men charged with murder in the cases were acquitted absolutely. After the policemen were killed at Kinnego, an informer, to be paid £20,000, gave three names, Toman, Burns and McAuley, which were passed on to secret southern region HQMSU command at Gough Barracks, Armagh. On the night of 11 November the Armagh command ordered one of its armour-plated Cortina squads to lie in wait at a road junction in Craigavon. This is an extract from *The Observer* account:

> An E4A surveillance man in an unmarked Japanese car had been following two of the suspects for three days. He had reported on his radio that Toman and Burns were on their way towards a republican housing estate. They would slow down to cross the Tullygally East Road. Two of the HQMSU team waited on foot in the darkness, guns in their hands. The other Cortina was around the corner, full of armed men, with its lights off and its engine running.
>
> As the Ford Escort containing Toman and Burns and driven by Gervaise McKerr approached, it appears to have spotted the ambush. As the men on foot opened fire it screeched to the right and away. The waiting Cortina roared in pursuit.
>
> As they closed from behind, the HQMSU man in front stretched out of the passenger window, pouring shots into the Escort from his machine-gun. His companion behind was simultaneously firing the Ruger out of the back window, and the driver himself, in a scene one policeman describes as 'like the Wild West', was holding the wheel with one hand and firing his pistol with the other.
>
> The chased car careered into a ditch, riddled with bullet-holes. No

fewer than 109 shots had been fired in a few minutes. Forensic evidence later proved that one of the men was shot through the heart, with his door open, presumably after the chase ended. Toman, McKerr and Burns were unarmed. All were dead.

The E4A eyewitness and his Japanese car disappeared. The death squad's cars, weapons and uniforms – the crucial forensic evidence – were transferred immediately to Armagh. Rapidly, an official RUC statement was put out. It said, untruthfully, that the men had been shot as they broke through a routine static police checkpoint...

It was 13 days later that an HQMSU team were ordered out again. This time it was to the area of the hayshed used as an IRA explosives' store. The pair of Cortinas were ordered by radio to patrol the area, and then to wait behind a high hedge which screened their view.

Martin McAuley was due to arrive on his motorbike. What seemed to have attracted him was the presence of three old rifles without ammunition lying on the hay-bales. The evidence points strongly to his having being lured there by the same informer who was to earn £20,000.

Quite unknown to the HQMSU team, their commanders at Armagh were listening intently through their head-phones. An MI5 bug in the hay-shed was ready to transmit sound of McAuley's arrival. The rustles and metallic noises were picked up inside a caravan parked a mile or two away in a secure police compound.

From there, a Special Branch constable and an Army intelligence officer with microphone and tape-recorder, radioed the news to Armagh. Armagh radioed the waiting Cortinas. The order was: 'In! Now!'

After the firing stopped, a seventeen-year-old boy, Michael Tighe, was found dead inside. He was innocent of republican connections, but had accompanied McAuley. On the evidence, no one at Armagh or in the Cortinas would necessarily have realised he was coming.

This time it was the surveillance caravan, the bug and the tape-recording that disappeared from the official version. An immediate cover story was issued, that armed men had been seen during a routine patrol to go into the shed, and that rifles had been pointed at the HQMSU squad.

A day or two later, an intelligence report was placed in the files at Armagh, purportedly from the same informant. It described Tighe as being on the fringes of the IRA. This was false. Internal evidence suggests it had been forged...

All the men, and more, thought to be behind the Kinnego bombing, were dead. But 18 days later the armour plated Cortinas rumbled into action again. This time the targets were suspected Irish National Liberation Army (INLA) men, and the informant may have belonged to the Army, who insisted on being involved.

On the night of 12 December a pair of cars were sent to mount a road-block in the town of Armagh, near the home of long-targeted INLA suspect Seamus Grew. An Army red Granada was to join them. Their orders were to expect... Dominic McGlinchey from across the border in the Republic.

Events were being controlled, as usual, from Armagh. This time things went badly awry, with the prospect of a diplomatic incident.

A plain Peugeot, without a giveaway radio, had been trailing the unarmed Seamus Grew and Roddy Carroll's yellow Allegro all day. The E4A inspector acting as 'shepherd' had followed them across the border as they took a relative home from a family funeral, and watched them pick up McGlinchey.

He then saw with disappointment that they dropped off McGlinchey inside the Republic. He dashed from his Peugeot to a phone, and managed to tell Armagh their main quarry had flown.

It seemed to make little difference to subsequent events. As the two cars, one behind at a distance, neared Grew's home, the road-block hurried to take up position on radio orders.

It went badly wrong. An Army private crashed his automatic car into an RUC Cortina, and broke a policeman's leg. As they milled about in the road, Grew drove by up the hill, past what seemed to be a mundane road accident.

Behind him, the E4A Peugeot screeched to a halt. The inspector excitedly told one of the squad they had allowed the quarry past. A constable leaped into the Peugeot with his machine-gun. They tore after the receding Allegro. As they slowed in front of it, the constable leapt out and pumped 15 shots in the direction of the passenger Roddy Carroll. He killed him. He moved round to the driver's side and killed Grew, who was found not in the car but lying in the road with a bullet in the back of his head.

The E4A inspector in the Peugeot ducked during the firing, then drove away hastily. Later his car was registered falsely as being on duty elsewhere.

The RUC man's broken leg was put to good effect; the cover story that emerged from Armagh was that the Allegro had crashed through a normal road-block, injuring an officer, and the squad had fired at the fleeing vehicle.

The Shoot-to-Kill policy has gravely affected the substantial nationalist population in the North of Ireland and caused misgivings among many people in the Republic of Ireland who think it is not possible to gain justice from the British Government. In *The Times* newspaper, 19 September 1988, the Chief Constable of the RUC Sir John Hermon in an interview denied a Shoot-to-Kill policy, calling it a misnomer; he did not regard the effects of the Armagh shootings as a lasting setback in the relations of the RUC with the Catholic community. In an article on the 'Abuse and Failure in Security Policies' in *Fortnight* magazine, September 1983, Kevin Boyle, Tom Hadden and Dermot Walsh wrote on disputed shootings. 'In almost every one there have been repeated demands for a public inquiry. But the response of the authorities has typically been to assert that the matter is being investigated by the police and that criminal proceedings will be considered in due course by the wholly independent Director of Public Prosecutions. In almost every case nothing more is heard until an inquest is held, usually more than a year later. These procedures are often referred to in official assertions that the security forces are subject to the rule of law in the same way as anyone else. The reality is rather different. In the first place members of the security forces are not subject to the same interrogation procedures as others and there is bound to be suspicion of a lack of impartiality and persistence in the investigation. In the second place the DPP is not independent, since he is formally subject to the Attorney-General and since it has been admitted that "difficult cases", like those involving the security forces, are regularly discussed with the Attorney-General. Since reasons for decisions by the DPP not to prosecute are never given, despite the recommendation to the Bennett Report in respect of interrogation cases, the possibility that political considerations prevail over purely legal ones cannot be dismissed.'

On 26 January 1988 the British-Attorney General, Sir Patrick Mayhew, announced that prosecutions would not be brought for reasons of public interest and national security against RUC officers in spite of evidence of attempting to pervert the course of justice in the cover-up following the shooting of the six unarmed civilians. Four RUC members were charged with murder in connection with the shootings and acquitted.

Following the debacle of the HQSMU's SAS-type killings of unarmed civilians in County Armagh, the units were stood down for ambush purposes and the SAS units set in action again.

IRA and SAS Casualties 1981-87

In the period 1981-87 the SAS shot dead as many as 26 people in Northern Ireland and one man drowned escaping from them. They were: two IRA volunteers, Charles Paul Maguire (20) and George Patrick McBrearty (24), Derry, 28 May 1981; Neil McMonagle (23), INLA, Derry, 2 February 1983; IRA volunteers Brian John Campbell (20) and Colm Anthony McGirr (24) Coalisland, 4 December 1983; IRA volunteers Henry John Hogan (20) and Declan Martin (18), Dunloy, County Antrim, 21 February 1984; IRA volunteer William Alfred Price (28), Mourne View, Carnan, Stewartstown, County Tyrone, 13 July 1984; Frederick George Jackson (43), Portadown, 19 October 1984; IRA volunteer Antoin Mac Giolla Bríde (27), Magherafelt and IRA volunteer Kieran Fleming (26), (drowned) 2 December 1984; IRA volunteers Daniel Doherty (23) and William Fleming (19), Derry, 6 December 1984; IRA volunteers Michael (22) and David Devine (16) and Charles Breslin (20), Strabane, 23 February 1985; Francis Bradley (20), Castledawson, County Derry, 18 February 1986; IRA volunteer Seamus Turlough McElwain (25), Scotstown, County Monaghan, 26 April 1986; nine were killed at Loughgall on 9 May 1987, a civilian, Anthony Hughes (36) of Caledon, County Tyrone, and eight IRA men, Declan John Arthurs (21), Galbally, County Tyrone, Seamus Donnelly (19), of Aughnaskea, County Tyrone, Michael Anthony Gormley (25), of Galbally, Eugene Kelly (25) Cappagh, County Tyrone, Patrick Kelly (30), Dungannon, Pádraig McKearney (32), Moy, James Lynagh, (32), Monaghan and Gerard O'Callaghan (29), Tullymore, Benburb.

In the same period four 'SAS' men were shot dead by the IRA. Sergeant Michael Burbridge (parent regiment, Royal Electrical and Mechanical Engineers) aged 31, from South Oxfordshire and 29-year-old Corporal Michael Ward (parent regiment, the Royal Corps of Signals), from southwest London were killed in a hail of bullets in an IRA ambush on 1 April 1982. They were dressed in plain clothes and were travelling from the Army/RUC post at Rosemount, Derry in a grey van, when the attack took place at 11.46 am at Creggan Street just outside St Eugene's Cathedral. Four IRA men took part in the attack. They occupied a second-floor flat at the junction of Creggan Road and Infirmary Road 15 hours before the shooting. As the van approached the junction, three of the IRA men, two of them armed with high velocity automatic rifles, and one with a handgun acting as back-up, stepped out in front of it and fired about 30 shots. The shooting was heard in the nearby parochial house. One of the priests gave the last rites. Priest and people lifted the men out of the van to the street. The Bishop of Derry, Dr Edward Daly, was also on the scene within minutes. He said, 'The men had been riddled. It was an awful sight. A lot of people were hysterical. It is another terrible deed which demeans us all'.[109]

Sergeant Paul Douglas Oram (26) of West Yorkshire was killed in a shoot-out with IRA volunteers.[110] He was a married man with a five-month old daughter Katie; his wife Julie never knew he was in the SAS. Army headquarters said he was a member of 9/12 Royal Lancers on attachment to 8th Infantry Brigade, Derry. He had been secretly awarded the Military Medal in 1983; there was no public citation. He had been mentioned in dispatches for his intelligence work in Northern Ireland. Victims who survived the shooting of Charles Maguire and George McBrearty (1981) and Neil McMonagle (1983), in Derry, thought he was involved in both incidents. When news of his death reached his home town, Leeds, West Yorkshire, relatives recalled that the last time they had seen him he told them, 'Don't worry. I'm just doing a job for Maggie'. He was described as being 6'2" tall and weighing 14 stone. His father, Douglas, said, 'The whole family is deeply upset by this tragedy'. His aunt, Mrs Joan Oram, said, 'He lived for the Army. He had served as a cadet since he was 17 and he never wanted to do any other job. His life was tragically short, but happy'. This was his second tour in Northern Ireland. He had been nearly a year on his second term. He also served in West Germany and Cyprus. The veil of secrecy on his Military Medal was lifted on 31 July 1984 when his 25-year-old widow received it publicly from Queen Elizabeth at Buckingham Palace.

In the gun-battle which followed the killing of IRA volunteer Antoin Mac Giolla Bríde by the SAS, 2 December 1984, the IRA shot dead Lance Corporal Alastair Slater (28) from Leicestershire. The Army officially stated that he belonged to the Parachute Regiment. It is clear, however, from the SAS magazine *Mars & Minerva* (issue Vol. 7, No. 2) that he was a member of the SAS. His obituary appears there. 'L/CPL. Alistair Ira Slater (1956-84), *Qui ante diem peruit sed miles sed pro patria*. Al was tragically killed in a contact with IRA gunmen in County Fermanagh, Northern Ireland, on 2nd December 1984. Despite being hit at point-blank range he managed to return fire. The operation was a success leaving two IRA gunmen dead, a further two captured, recovering 1000 lbs. of explosive, and saving countless RUC lives. The loss of Al however was a bitterly high price for us to pay. Al joined 22 SAS in November 1982. "Mr Angry" as he was known within 7 Troop (Free Fall) 'B' Squadron, was a man whose single-minded determination to soldier well rubbed off on all those around him and despite the short time that he served with the Regiment he was recognised as a man of great talent and considerable potential... He joined 1st Battalion, the Parachute Regiment and subsequently served in Berlin, Cyprus, Hong Kong and Northern Ireland. He started focusing on 22 SAS early in his career but took his time to ready himself. Meanwhile he rose to the rank of Sergeant in the Signals Platoon... In the months prior to his death he had shown himself to be a man of considerable cunning and courage during other operations. Having had to be encouraged to go on leave from Northern Ireland, he promptly proceeded to return early... He was posthumously awarded the Military Medal.' Slater's face was known to millions of TV viewers. He was the NCO training officer who appeared on a BBC series 'The Paras' shortly before his death.

In the period 1981-87 there were a number of incidents involving the SAS including the accidental death of Corporal Tommy Palmer.

On Friday, 19 October 1981 the IRA gunned down John Donaldson a young solicitor after he had visited Andersonstown Police Station on legal business. They mistook him for an undercover soldier. Following this there were a number of mysterious attacks on houses in Turf Lodge, Belfast. Windows were smashed in the homes of four republican sympathisers. At each house the young man seen carrying out the attacks left behind a neatly typed note accusing the occupants of being IRA sympathisers. The note read – '"On my knees I beg you, return to God" – Pope John Paul. You are an active supporter of the murderers. You are as responsible as the person who pulls the trigger or plants the bomb. If you are a Catholic you will heed Pope John Paul's words and help stop all forms of violence. An innocent young man was brutally murdered yesterday. Ask yourselves, what for? Of course the Provos apologised as they have done time and time before. 10 years of murder you bastard, are you not ashamed of yourself? What have you achieved? Fuck all and never will. I hope it's you next. Yours, Peace Person'. The attacks were carried out quickly by a man who raced around in a car. The car which had been stolen earlier that day in Lenadoon in West Belfast was found abandoned about two miles from Turf Lodge. An Army identity card was found in it.[111] Was there any connection?

SAS soldier Corporal Tommy Palmer (31) was killed in a car crash on the M1 motorway near Lurgan on 8 February 1983.[112] His unmarked car struck an embankment and overturned. His neck was broken. His companion was seriously injured. He joined his parent regiment, the Royal Engineers, in 1969 and served in the SAS behind the lines in the Falklands war. He was in 22 SAS for ten years. He was one of the SAS team who stormed the Iranian Embassy in London in 1980. He was one of a trio of SAS men who lost their lives in Northern Ireland and whose stories were written up by Andrew Parker and Paul Hooper in *The Sun*, 16 July 1985. The article said that he rang his wife Caroline from Ascension Island, 'I'm going in. Expect me home in a polythene bag...' That was his idea of a joke! Mrs Palmer said she recognised him on TV in the Iranian siege. 'After it was all over I saw Tommy come running out of the place with his shirt off.' When he first went into action his hood went on fire and his neck and shoulders were burned. He was one of five members of the Embassy squad decorated by the Queen for 'exceptional bravery'. He was survived by his wife Caroline and two daughters, Cara (7) and Shona (4). His wife tried to get him to quit the SAS. He was posted to a training squadron for a while but then returned to the action. 'He was SAS through and through,' said his wife, 'I knew he wouldn't be happy doing anything else.'

In April 1983 the Derry Brigade, IRA, claimed that they shot dead an SAS man in an attack on 11 April. The following is the text of their statement:- 'After an intensive surveillance operation carried out by an IRA Intelligence unit, the movements of SAS personnel in the centre of Derry were carefully noted and timed. On Monday morning at 8.30 a four-man ASU armed with semi-automatic rifles ambushed a green Sherpa van containing five SAS men at the junction of Strand Road and Governor Road. As the van approached the volunteers ran forward and sprayed it from point-blank range causing it to crash. Eyewitnesses at the scene have reported that one of the SAS men appeared lifeless while another lay seriously wounded'.

The IRA volunteers had taken over a house at Duncreggan Road at 8.30 on Sunday night, 10 April, holding the family captive all night. At 8.30 am they opened fire on the van with automatic rifles. Groups of schoolchildren ran screaming for cover into a nearby supermarket. The van crashed into a lamp post.

The RUC claimed that one soldier was slightly injured in the crash; none were shot dead. They claimed the soldiers were members of the Queen's Regiment being transferred from Ebrington Barracks to Fort George Army Camp about half-a-mile from the scene of the shooting. Local people, however, said that after the shooting two Army land-rovers with their sirens blaring, accompanied by an Army ambulance, sped away through the city centre. The IRA men drove off in the car belonging to the family they held captive. It was later found in the grounds of Carnhill High School. [113]

In its issue of 18 June 1985 the *Derry Journal* published what purported to be the first photographs of the SAS in action. The photographs were supplied to the paper by Sinn Féin. They appeared to show RUC officers talking to masked men beside a Ford Cortina car. The same newspaper on 30 April 1985 carried a story that on 26 April claims were made that a number of SAS men were involved in house raids in Derry following the release of a local bank manager who had been kidnapped from his home on 25 April; Mr Ronnie Brown was released at lunch-time on 26 April after a £15,000 ransom was paid by his bank. The day after the kidnapping, local people claimed that armed and masked men (presumed to be SAS) entered a house in Gartan Square and arrested four men who were subsequently released without charge. At the time of the Gartan Square operation the *Derry Journal* itself was refused permission to photograph the incident. Public representatives asked the RUC to clarify the matter. The RUC said that only RUC were involved in the operation.

Mars & Minerva, Vol. 7, No. 3, 1986, has a list of obituaries of SAS soldiers. They give insight into SAS background and culture. It is noteworthy that some of them, whether in SAS or parent regiment, served in Northern Ireland. The dates of service however are not given.

> S/Sgt James Drummond ('A' troop, 263 (SAS) Signal Squadron): It is with much sadness and deep regret that we report the death of Jim Drummond, tragically killed in a free-fall accident at Fox Covert DZ, Salisbury Plain, on 3rd June 1986. His many friends send their deepest sympathy to his widow, Maggie, and son James. Jim joined the Corps on 23rd March, 1970. His first posting after completing training as a Data Telegraphist was to 4 Armoured Division Headquarters and Signal Regiment. From December 1973 until January 1977 he served in 30 Signal Regiment and completed a roulement tour with UNFICYP. He was then posted to 22 Signal Regiment where he remained until

joining 264 (SAS) Signal Squadron in June 1980...

S/Sgt Kieran Joseph Farragher: Joe joined 'B' Squadron 22 SAS in 1972, coming to the Regiment from 29 Commando Light Regiment, Royal Artillery. Except for a tour away as an Instructor with 21 SAS (V) he served all his time with Mountain Troop. At the time of his tragic death on a climbing accident, he was the Troop-Staff Sergeant of his troop. During his SAS service he completed operational tours in the Oman and Northern Ireland, and served in the Falklands campaign. Joe was a quiet and thoughtful man – a true gentle giant...He was buried with Regimental honours at Hartley, in Kent, but a plaque stands to his memory in the Regimental Plot at St Martin's Church....

Sgt Stewart J. Windon: Stu Windon died on 26th June, 1986, as a result of a climbing accident on the Aiguille du Chardonnet in the French Alps. Stu joined the Parachute Regiment in 1972. During his career he saw service in Northern Ireland and in the Falklands Campaign. He was a keen sportsman and his interests included running , potholing and sailing. He excelled at cross-country running and competed at Army standard regularly...He was renowned for his enthusiastic approach, particularly with the Junior Para soldiers. This desire for excellence and a search for adventure led Stu to successfully complete selection in January 1986. He joined Mountain Troop 'D' Squadron...

Sgt Robert P. Arnott: Bob Arnott died on 26th June, 1986, as a result of a climbing accident on the Aiguille du Chardonnet in the French Alps. Throughout his career his professional approach and dedication to all aspects of his work won him many friends. He was a keen sportsman and his main interests were running and skiing. Bob saw service in Northern Ireland, but spent much of his service in BAOR...It was perhaps his desire for excellence and enjoyment of adventure that caused him to join 22 SAS. In January 1986 he completed selection. He then joined the Mountain Troop of 'D' Squadron...

The Shooting of Charles Maguire and George McBrearty[114]

Two IRA volunteers, George Patrick McBrearty (24) and Charles Paul ('Pop') Maguire (20) were shot dead and a third man seriously wounded, in an incident involving the SAS in Derry at 12.50 pm on 28 May 1981. There was a lot of tension in Derry at the time. Hunger-striker Patsy O'Hara of Derry had died on the night of 21 May and there was still a numbness with underlying bitterness after the funeral.

The IRA and the British Army issued conflicting statements on the shooting. The IRA statement, issued on the afternoon of the incident in the name of the Derry Brigade, said that one of their active service units had sighted a brown Opel car being driven by a known SAS undercover agent.

They pursued and opened fire on the car – 'Almost immediately two other cars, one a red Chrysler, the other a yellow Porsche with three SAS men, arrived at the scene and opened fire on the ASU. The two volunteers who had stepped from the vehicle were hit before the SAS sped off. Local people came to the assistance of the ASU and got them away'.

The British Army statement said that a soldier on duty in plain clothes was driving his car along Lone Moor Road when he was overtaken and stopped by another car containing four armed and hooded men. In the ensuing exchange of fire the soldier's car was hit and he shot and killed two gunmen and injured another before escaping. The soldier himself was not injured. The soldier used his own weapon, a 9 mm semi-automatic pistol. The British Army statement emphasised that he was all alone at the time.

The British Army vehicle in the shooting was put on display at RUC Headquarters at Strand Road, Derry. It was a brown (others report it as maroon) Opel Ascona. It had at least six bullet holes in it. Both windows on the driver's side were shattered and there were bullet holes in the bonnet and driver's door. There were also blood stains on the driver's door.

There were apparently no independent witnesses to the shooting although some youths informed journalists that a car turned and drove back to Creggan and cars drove from the scene along the Lone Moor Road towards the city centre.

The IRA account was expanded for the 6 June 1981 issue of *An Phoblacht/ Republican News*. It said that, in order to make certain that the driver of the brown Opel was a soldier, the IRA unit pursued the car into the Brandywell stopping it at the junction of Southway and Lone Moor Road. George McBrearty then approached the driver's window asking the occupant to identify himself. The soldier immediately opened fire hitting George in the heart, throat and hand. 'As he fell dying George managed to open fire into the car with his rifle. Almost simultaneously two other unmarked cars appeared on the scene. These riddled the volunteers' car with heavy automatic fire gunning down Pop Maguire who had opened the passenger-seat door of the brown Opel. The follow-up operation failed to uncover any of the volunteers' weapons.'

At the inquest on the two IRA men held in Derry on 9 March 1983 Mr Daniel Jude Moore said he was driving his company car along Iniscairn Road in Creggan at 11.30 am on the day of the shooting. A car containing three or four masked persons pulled up alongside him. The front seat passenger in the car got out holding a rifle and dressed in a combat jacket with a balaclava over his head. He told him he was going to take the car but that he would get the vehicle back in an hour. Two men accompanied him in the car instructing him to drive to Central Drive. Both men got out of the car at this spot and a man appeared out of an alley way and he was told to follow him. He was taken to a shed where he was locked up and released about an hour-and-a-half later. During this time he said he heard shooting. He said he was later told his car had been burned as two people had been shot.

It is apparent that the IRA unit had a particular target in mind. The target did not appear and the unit was anxious to return the car in case the man would be released and raise the alarm that his car was hijacked.

We turn now to the statement of the SAS soldier at the inquest, Witness 'A'. An article entitled 'The SAS Heroes who Dared and Died' by Andrew Parker and Paul Hooper in *The Sun*, 16 July 1985, indentifies him as Sergeant Oram. He was shot dead in an incident with IRA men in Dunloy on 21 February 1984. Soldier 'A' did not appear at the inquest. His statement to the police was read in his absence. He said he was serving with the 8th Brigade in Derry. On the day of the shooting he was on plain clothes duty driving an Opel Ascona in Creggan. At 12.50 pm he saw four masked men in a brown Ford Escort and transmitted what he believed to be their registration number to his base. He then continued along Circular Road towards Southway and as he approached the junction of Lone Moor Road and Coach Road the Ford Escort containing four masked men sounded its horn, overtook him and pulled in to his right hand side. Two masked men each armed with an Armalite rifle got out of the Escort. One of them took up a position to the right of his car with the Armalite at hit level pointing at him. The other was near the rear of the car also pointing the Armalite at him. Believing his life to be in danger he drew his 9 mm service pistol and fired at the man to his right. He then turned and fired through the rear off-side window at the other masked man. He fired two or three shots at the second gunman and realised that there were other shots being fired as well as his own. The gunman to his right had moved to the front of his car and was at the window. He fired through the window and as the gunman rolled along the side of his car and came in to an upright position he fired at him and believed he hit him in the back. He then pulled out of the area. He thought the other two men had remained in the other car and he did not know if they were armed. He drove off to RUC headquarters at Strand Road. He reported the incident and gave his pistol to a police sergeant. The magazine contained 20 rounds before the shooting and 9 were left. There were a number of bullet holes in his car and on the back seat was a .223 bullet case.

An RUC crimes officer told the inquest he went to the scene of the shooting at 2.30 pm and took two blood samples for examination by forensic scientists. At 3.45 pm he examined an Opel Ascona car. The rear passenger's window and the driver's window were smashed. There were perforations on the front of the car and blood on the outside of the driver's door. Cross-examined by Mr Brendan Kearney, solicitor for the family of the deceased, he said he forwarded 10 spent bullet cases to the forensic laboratory. He did not know where the .223 case came from nor had he any evidence that shots were fired at the soldier.

An RUC inspector investigating the shooting said that a third man received gunshot wounds in the incident and he later appeared in court when he was sentenced to five years imprisonment after he pleaded guilty to possessing two Armalite rifles with intent, two rifles under suspicious circumstances and attempting to hijack a car belonging to the Ministry of Defence.

The Northern Ireland Deputy State Pathologist, Dr John R. Press, in his written statement said that McBrearty died as a result of multiple injuries due to bullet wounds to the trunk. Six bullets entered the back and one entered the left side of the chest. He had been hit by at least seven and possibly nine bullets. Maguire sustained two gunshots wounds to his head. The injuries were caused by low velocity weapons.

Eamon McCourt was hit five times. This would mean that the three men were hit by at least 14 bullets. Soldier 'A' admitted to firing 11 bullets. Simple arithmetic indicates that the assertion of the IRA of the presence of more then one SAS man is correct. At the inquest Mr Brendan Kearney said there was no evidence to suggest that other shots fired had in fact been fired at the soldier in the car. He said that a spent round which had been found lying in the car was not consistent with the ammunition used by the plain clothes soldier and suggested that the soldier was not alone in the car. He also suggested that a number of bullet holes on the side of the vehicle came from shots which had been fired at the two men.

The IRA said that George McBrearty 'as he fell dying managed to fire into the car with his rifle'. It is difficult to accept either the SAS or the IRA official versions. The British Army statement had said only one soldier was involved. This soldier in his statement admits to shooting two IRA only. Yet three were manifestly hit.

Another reconstruction is as follows:

Sergeant Oram was on surveillance duty. The SAS were aware that a car had been hijacked. Oram was sent into Creggan to look for it. He spotted the car and the masked IRA men in it. Not to draw suspicion to himself, he waved at them as they passed him. But he had aroused their suspicion. They followed him and pulled up in front of him at the junction of Lone Moor Road and Coach Road. McCourt got out and walked round to the rear passenger window on the right hand side of the SAS man's car. The IRA did not know of course that he was SAS. The SAS man had already radioed that he had spotted the hijacked car and no doubt had pressed his 'contact' alarm when the IRA came after him. Maguire went to the driver's side and asked him to identify himself. The SAS man said – 'Can I get my licence?'

'Yes'. The SAS man reached up and got his licence above in the sun flap. As soon as Maguire took the licence he turned to McCourt and said, 'O.K.'. The IRA men lowered their guard. In a split second the SAS man drew his gun and shot Maguire through the side window. He turned quickly and fired through the rear window and hit McCourt in the chest. The force of the bullet spun him round on the road. The SAS man threw himself out of the car on to the road and kept firing at McCourt who was visible to him, hitting him again.

McBrearty had got out of his car and from the left fired through the front of the SAS car at the same time as the SAS man threw himself out. No doubt he thought in that instant that he had hit the SAS man. All this lasted seconds. The second SAS car, and perhaps a third, was on the scene with more SAS soldiers. They fired at McBrearty hitting him from behind and killing him. The shooting by the second SAS car and by McBrearty would account for bullet holes in the bonnet of 'A's' car. McBrearty's back wounds could not have been inflicted by 'A' lying on the road in front of him. After McBrearty was hit from behind 'A' got up off the ground and rolled over the bonnet of his car to McBrearty's side and fired a bullet into McBrearty.

When the shooting came from the second SAS car, the fourth IRA man, the driver, threw himself out of his car on the ground. When the second SAS car effected the rescue of 'A' they sped away. Andrew Pollak reported in *The Irish Times* from Derry, 29 May 1981, that there were no witnesses to the shooting other than local children playing in a garden nearby. One 10-year-old boy said he had seen two cars involved in the shooting. Pollak reports another youth saying there had been three cars coming down Southway from Creggan. After the shooting a Ford Escort (the IRA men) drove back towards Creggan and the other two cars (SAS) disappeared along the Lone Moor Road towards the city centre. Other locals agreed that there had been three cars and that the Ford Escort had more than one person in it. They also claimed that one of the people in the following car was hit in the exchange of shots.

Not only does the number of bullet wounds to the IRA men confirm more than one SAS man but in subsequent depositions for a court case there were six weapons returned for forensic, 3 Ruger revolvers, a sub-machine-gun, an M1 carbine and another weapon. There was no mention of these at the inquest nor at the subsequent trial since the charges were not contested.

The fourth IRA man put all his comrades into the car and drove to Creggan. Maguire and McBrearty were already dead. It was debated if McCourt should be taken across the border but it was clear he would not make it. They had come to the Creggan shops. McCourt was taken in a van to a person's house and an ambulance was called.

Rioting broke out in Creggan and the hijacked car was burned, not by the IRA but by youths. Despite the burning, bullet holes were still visible in it.

The SAS task was accomplished. They had come to 'A's' rescue and carried out that specific task. Two IRA men died as a result. It is highly unlikely that an SAS man would carry out city surveillance without a back-up and it seems the IRA members were caught in a pincer movement after inadvertently attempting to hijack an SAS car, as in the cases of Colm McNutt and Denis Heaney.

An Phoblacht/Republican News, 6 June 1981, described the two dead men as fearless Derry republicans. George McBrearty left behind a wife, Rosemary, and three young children, Orla, Kelly and Thomas. To his friends, the report said, he was good-humoured and good-natured; he joined Fianna Éireann in 1973 and was recruited into 2 Derry Brigade in which he was extremely active; he was interned in 1974 and released a year later; he became the first Derry man to be detained for seven days in Strand Road interrogation centre under the Prevention of Terrorism Act; Fr Denis Faul once described his home as the 'most raided house in the six counties'; in February 1978 he was arrested, charged and released on bail in the following October; since that time he was 'on the run'. Charles Maguire, said An Phoblacht, left behind a wife, Donna, and their baby girl, Clare; he was extremely kind and generous; a bricklayer by trade; he joined Fianna Éireann around 14 years of age; his sister Marie was imprisoned in Armagh Jail on two occasions and his sister Isobel in 1974; he was not 'on the run' as the RUC implied. Both men were buried with paramilitary honours.

About an hour after the shooting in which the two men died, there was a 10-minute gun battle in the same area. When the RUC arrived on the scene they came under fire. Local workmen who took refuge in a council workers' hut were searched and threatened. The gun battle and sporadic rioting later in Creggan and Bogside indicated resentment and anger in Derry at the shooting of the two men.

The Shooting of Neil McMonagle[115]

Neil McMonagle, or to give him his full name, Eugene Cornelius McMonagle, was 23 years of age when he was shot dead by an SAS man in Derry on 2 February 1983. He had five brothers and eight sisters. He was married and lived at Coshquin, a small housing estate at the Derry-Buncrana Road border checkpoint. At the time of the shooting he was 'on the run'; he was a member of the INLA and had served a term in prison. In 1981 he was charged with bombing the El Greco nightclub at Foyle Street, Derry, but the charges were withdrawn after he spent six months in custody. In 1977 he had been sentenced to four years imprisonment on charges of robbery, theft and possessing firearms. Two of his brothers, John and Jim, allege that the police threatened them that they would shoot Neil. This was when the two brothers were detained for interrogation, John in October 1982 and Jim a few weeks before Neil was shot. Neil had another brother, Martin, in Portlaoise Prison in the Republic and in fact intended visiting him on 4 February. On 5 February Martin got parole for Neil's funeral.

Neil McMonagle was in the company of Liam Duffy (then 19 years of age), a Derry man from Drumleck Gardens, the night of the incident. Neither knew that the man they accosted was a member of the SAS; they were 'checking him out' because he looked suspicious; the SAS man shot them, killing McMonagle and wounding Duffy.

The shooting took place at Leafair Park between 8.30 and 9 pm. Leafair Park is a complex of houses in the huge sprawling Shantallow estate in Derry. A great wide open green stretches away from the houses; in the distance one can see the lights of the inner city. The end of the complex where the shooting took place forms a block, the fronts of the houses facing in and a perimeter fence enclosing the back gardens on the outside. As one walks round the full block one enters into the inner street of front gardens and house fronts. An alleyway also cuts through to the inner street from the wide open space.

Liam Duffy gave me this account of the incident:

'Neil McMonagle was "on the run". He was back and forward to Derry and used to be in the Leafair area. I was involved with him only to a certain extent, hiding weapons for him. The night of the shooting he gave me a weapon and said "Could you hide that there?" It was a rifle sealed in a long plastic pipe. I went to a garden, dug a "hide" and when I had that done went back to a house in the estate to collect the weapon. This same house was later raided after the incident and other stuff was found there.

'I collected the weapon and walked back towards the "hide". I was on my own at this stage. I was just near it and was just coming to the alleyway when this man walked out from the alley at right angles to me. He was wearing a big duffle-coat. The minute he saw me he opened the bottom button of his duffle coat, put his hand inside his coat, which indicated that he knew who I was. I suspect now we were under surveillance. He was obviously watching me.

'At this stage he went on round the block and I walked the other side of the block and got rid of the weapon, threw it into a garden. Then we met head on again. I walked past him and he walked past me in front of the house where the other stuff was or the same row of houses; it was about 60 yards further down. We were now in the inner street. He walked across the street and I had come back and followed him about 30 yards behind. He cut into the alley again. I turned and walked back over the street, just saying to myself, "mustn't have been anybody". As I was walking back over the street I met Neil McMonagle coming out of another street. Neil says to me, "What's up?" I told him what had happened. He says "Where's the weapon now?" I walked to the end of the street and pointed to where I had thrown the weapon into the garden. So we were standing at the gable of a house looking over towards the weapon on the other side of the street. We were discussing what to do and as we were discussing this, the duffle-coat man came walking back over the street. He went round the block again and we

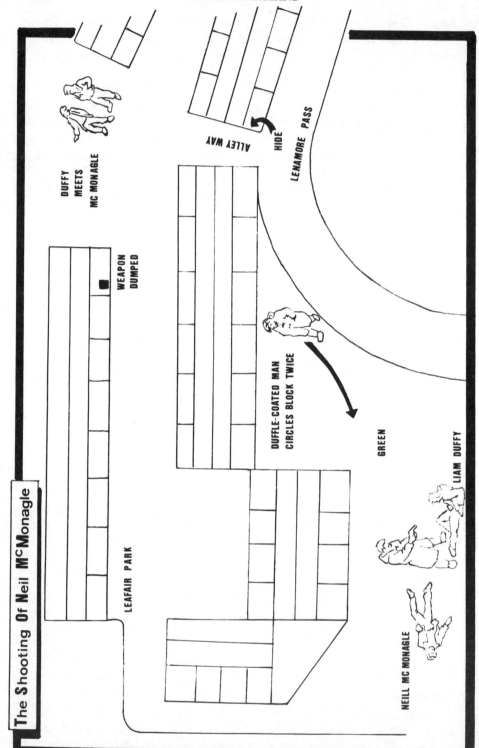

The Shooting Of Neil McMonagle

DUFFY MEETS McMONAGLE

WEAPON DUMPED

ALLEY WAY

HIDE

LENAMORE PASS

LEAFAIR PARK

DUFFLE-COATED MAN CIRCLES BLOCK TWICE

GREEN

LIAM DUFFY

NEILL McMONAGLE

went round the block in the other direction, round the back of the fences where the green is. We then met at the green at the back of the houses. As we met he started to cut across the green away from us. At this stage McMonagle called to him, "Hi there!" He stopped and looked round, showing the side of his face and Neil started walking towards him. I started following a short distance behind Neil. Your man turned again as if to walk away again, and Neil grabbed him by the corner of the coat. He turned around, knocked Neil with his arm and pulled a gun out of the band of his trousers. He fired two shots at me and then shot Neil. I was about 10 yards from him and Neil was right up beside him. After that I was lying on the ground and I looked up to see what was happening and he was standing "footering" with his gun. It seemed to have jammed on him. He saw me looking towards him and he came over and stood over me with feet apart and two hands on the gun and pointed it down at me. I said, "Please don't shoot me again". I started begging. He started asking details who we were and where we lived. I told him. Then he said, "Has that bastard got a gun?" I said, "I don't know. Search him". Then he said, "What did you want me for?" I didn't answer that. I just moaned as if I was in pain. He was radioing details. I asked him to call an ambulance. As he was standing over me, there were two women came out of a top corner flat; they were out at the doorway. I called for help, asked them to call an ambulance. He walked away. He took a glance at Neil as he went.

'I was hit by the first shot under the right armpit. A crowd started to gather and from then on I was too delirious. I had a severed artery. British medics were attending me at this stage but I don't remember them.

'The man had an English accent, dirty fair hair. I thought I recognised him as Sergeant Paul Oram when I saw the photograph later after he had been shot in Dunloy.'

Fr Joseph Carolan attended the two men at the scene soon after the shooting. When the ambulance arrived, he helped to place Duffy inside. When the driver moved off, soldiers who arrived on the scene blocked his path and refused to let the two men be brought to the hospital. A dispute took place between the priest and an Army officer. Fr Carolan contacted an RUC inspector and the ambulance was then allowed to proceed without delay.

The SAS man did not attend the inquest which was held on 16 April 1984. His statement was read out as in so many SAS cases. He said he was on duty alone in the Leafair Park area but in contact with his base at 8th Brigade, Ebrington, Derry. He was armed with a Browning 9 mm pistol with 20 rounds of ammunition. He had left his car at a supermarket car park nearby and was walking towards it when the men asked him to come over. He merely nodded, said, 'Right' and kept walking towards his car. He claimed:

'The same male who had spoken and was familiar to me, came towards me and, as I passed him, he came behind me and I could see him drawing what I could clearly see was a pistol from the waistband of his trousers with his right hand. This came from the front/right of his waistband and under his coat. At the same time he reached out with his left hand and caught me from behind on the left shoulder. I could feel he had put the pistol into the small of my back.'

He said the two men then made him walk towards a fence:

'It was about this time that I realised that as soon as I got to the fence I was a dead man. I knew they would have found my gun, personal radio and identification card easily and I would have been shot. The way the male was advancing towards me from my left front (*Duffy*) ... I was sure he was armed with a gun. I knew I had to act before I got to the fence so I drew my Browning pistol with my right hand from the front waistband of my trousers and immediately fired two rounds at the advancing male in front of me. This was a single-handed grip, because at the same time I immediately swivelled around and fired two rounds with my outstretched right hand into the gunman who was behind me. Both of the males fell to the ground.'

When Duffy gave McMonagle's name the SAS man said he then realised that McMonagle was on the run and a wanted member of the INLA. He said he carried out a quick search of the area but did not see any weapon so he went to his car and drove to the local police HQ. He said he only fired because he believed his life was in danger.

At the inquest an RUC inspector agreed that there was no evidence, save the SAS man's word, that McMonagle was armed. The state pathologist, Professor Thomas K. Marshall, in his *post-mortem* report said that McMonagle was killed by a bullet which entered his right side and traversed his chest; there was nothing to indicate the range. Duffy was later charged with possession of firearms in relation to the same day but not connected with the killing. No arms were found at the scene. It was recognised that the rifle in the plastic pipe was not used by McMonagle or Duffy, neither was there residue on their clothes.

At the funeral Mass Fr Seamus O'Connell criticised both the INLA and the SAS. It was a sad day for justice when questions had to be asked publicly about the apparent SAS Shoot-to-Kill policy which led to the man's death. It was a sad day for truth when the INLA first made him a hero on active service in their first statement but subsequently have made him a martyr. The mourners were headed by Neil's wife Patricia. The INLA provided a colour party and a guard of honour and shots were fired in a final salute.

There was some rioting in Derry in reaction to his death. It occurred at a time when there were protests in Armagh, Lurgan and Belfast against the Shoot-to-Kill policy also perpetrated by the RUC. Bishop Daly of Derry said that Neil McMonagle's killing bore similarities to other recent incidents in the North in which at least seven men had been shot dead and others seriously injured. The DPP ruled that there would be no prosecution in the case.

Sergeant Paul Douglas Oram of the SAS who shot Neil McMonagle was shot dead by the IRA in Dunloy on 21 February 1984. On 1 March 1989 in a ruling by Mr Justice Carswell Mrs Patricia McMongale, widow of Neil, lost her claim for compensation in the High Court.

The Shooting of Brian Campbell and Colm McGirr[116]

On the day he was shot dead by the SAS, Sunday 4 December 1983, Colm McGirr had dinner with his mother and sister Patricia at 2 pm. Then he left, heading for the Annual General Meeting of the local GAA club at their pavilion. He was immaculately dressed. His cousin Paul Hempsey was with him. Just as he was going through the gate into the pavilion ground, a car drove up with some friends in it. He turned to Paul, after speaking to them for a few minutes, 'I'll see you in half-an-hour,' he said. This was about 2.30 pm.

Colm was a bricklayer by trade. He was 23 years of age.

Brian Campbell, his friend, was 19 years of age. He lived with his parents. He was a mechanic, who learned the trade from his father, Brendan, a well-known garage man. Father and son were very close in affection. When Brian came from Mass that Sunday he had dinner with his father, sister Ursula and brother Donal. His mother had stayed on after Mass for the funeral of a parishioner, Paddy Kelly, as she wished to sympathise with the relatives. The last his mother saw of him alive was when she brought him up his shirt to dress for second Mass. After dinner his father asked him to wash the dishes. 'Da,' said he, 'I'll wash them when I get my tea,' meaning the evening meal. His father went to get chips for him for the evening tea. Brian went off; usually on a Sunday afternoon he went to the football field or like others played snooker; there is a tradition of snooker in the Coalisland district, home of world champion Denis Taylor. In the evening Brendan came home with the chips. There was no Brian.

On Thursday, 1 December, IRA members called off an operation. The weapons were dumped in a small field. One of them fired a shot from the shotgun to clear it before hiding it with the rest. Unknown to them at the time the shot was heard by a UDR patrol in the vicinity. The cache was discovered and reported to the RUC. The cache was then staked out by the SAS.

In the incident that day, when the SAS killed Colm McGirr and Brian Campbell, another man was wounded; he escaped in the car. He relates what happened:

'On the Sunday afternoon of 4 December 1983, while on my way to Annagher Petrol Filling Station, I met Brian Campbell who asked me for a lift to Annagher Club. On the road there we met Colm McGirr who was going through the Club gates. Colm got into the car and, after a few moments conversation between the two, they asked would I take them for a spin down the road as they wanted to check on something but they did not say what. They directed me to the Clough road and asked me to stop for a minute. At this point Brian got out of the front of the car and Colm out of the rear. They crossed the road and got under a wired fence and as they began to walk across the field there was the sound of heavy gunfire. The shooting began without any warning. As both men fell, I drove from the scene as fast as possible while shots were being fired in my direction, again without warning. When the two men were shot neither were armed nor were they at any time challenged to stop. As those who carried out these killings were on both sides of the road, they had every opportunity to stop and detain us all. This can be proven by the bullet holes in my car. But rather than stop any of us they chose to open fire without any warning.'

The SAS statements on the shooting were made available at the inquest on the two men. Soldier 'G', address given merely as Headquarters, Northern Ireland, makes it clear that the instigation for the mounting of the stake-out came from the RUC. He was briefed by Police Officer 'H'. The unit was asked to carry out a search on both sides of the Cloghog Road, and if weapons were found, to mount an observation on the hide with a view to apprehending any people who approached to take away the weapons.

The leader of the stake-out, Soldier 'A', stated that he went to the Cloghog Road in the townland of Maghermulkenny as a result of information received, to a small field overgrown with thistles and rushes. 'The field was surrounded by fairly thick hedges and there was a dyke from the centre almost all the way round. I also observed an old dwelling to the north-west of this field. The dwelling was overgrown with ivy and brambles. I entered the field. During the search I uncovered a weapons cache which appeared to have been pushed into a patch of brambles. I did not remove these weapons or disturb the hide, but I felt them and realised that one of these weapons was an Armalite with a magazine fitted, and the other was a shotgun. I could identify these weapons by experience and I did not need to remove them ... I observed another hole in bushes and I saw a bag which I removed. It was a clear plastic bag. I looked inside and I saw that there were two sets of trousers, which I think were black, two jackets, two hoods, black colour with eye and mouth holes cut out. Two sets of gloves ... I replaced this bag and the items...'

The SAS officer then related how he had set up an observation post to watch the cache and then went to Dungannon with others of the party for a briefing. They had arrived at the field at 11 pm on 1 December 1983 (Thursday) and the briefing took place in Dungannon in the early hours of the morning. For the operation the unit was divided into three groups with 'A' in overall command and 'E' second in command; group 1, 'A' and 'B', group 2, 'C' and 'D', group 3 was a cut-off group made up of 'E' and 'F'. The operation was carried out in military uniform and all members were in radio contact. They were back in the little field about 5.20 am. When the car arrived, it backed to the gap and Campbell and McGirr entered the field. He alleged that McGirr went to the bush where the cache was, pulled out the Armalite with magazine attached and handed it to Campbell; he then retrieved the shotgun. When Campbell turned as if returning to the car, 'A' said he shouted out 'Halt, security forces'. He continued, 'At this point the one in the tweed jacket (McGirr) who was holding the shotgun pivoted round, pointing the shotgun in my direction. I then thought that my life was in immediate danger, and fearing for my life and that of my comrades, I opened fire ... The one in the blue jacket (Campbell) who had the Armalite rifle, I noticed turned almost simultaneously with the man in the tweed jacket (McGirr). I fired another burst at him about 2 to 4 each time. I also heard other firing from other members of my group. Although the one in the blue jacket (Campbell) appeared to be hit, he went on a few more paces towards the gate. He still had the Armalite in his possession. I then saw him go down approx 5 metres from the gate. At that time I noticed that the car was moving off in an easterly direction, fairly fast. At that stage I shouted to the Group 3, soldiers 'E' and 'F', to stop the car. I also shouted to the Group 2 and my colleague in Group 1 to stop firing ... I then called for Soldier 'C' to move forward with me, while Soldiers 'B' and 'D' gave cover. As I moved towards the person in the tweed jacket (McGirr) at the same time, covering each other, I observed the person in the tweed jacket (McGirr) move as if to pick up the shotgun. I then fired again two short bursts at him to remove the threat. I missed with the first burst because I was running and fired a second burst. I also heard Soldier 'C' also fire...'

Soldiers 'B', 'C' and 'D' used similar language in their statements putting an emphasis, like 'A', on the threat to their lives. Soldier 'B':- 'Both men spun round very fast ... As the man in the blue jacket (Campbell) spun around he brought the muzzle of the rifle up and pointed it in my and Soldiers 'A's' direction. I realised we were being threatened ... I would like to stress that I only fired in what I believed to be in defence of my own life and those of my comrades'. Soldier 'C':- 'As the challenge was issued I saw the man in the blue jacket (Campbell) swivel round and point the Armalite in the direction of Soldier 'A'. At this point he was going to bring us under fire. I particularly noticed that when this man swung round he turned away from the gate and not as he would have done if he wished to run away. I fired four single aimed shots at this man ... As I moved out I got into a kneeling position in the field to cover Soldier 'A'. As I did so I noticed the man in the tweed jacket (McGirr) move his leg. I could see the shotgun and I thought he was about to open fire on us, so I fired 2 short bursts at him'. Soldier 'D':- 'A lot of things happened very quickly, the man in the tweed jacket (McGirr)

on whom I was concentrating looked up and pointed the shotgun in Soldier
'A's' direction. I was worried for the safety of Soldier 'A', so I immediately
fired one single aimed shot at this man. I heard other shots and saw him
drop back on his knees. Thinking he was about to fire from this position I
fired two further aimed shots. This sequence took 2 or 3 seconds. I saw him
pitch onto his face and did not fire at him again. I switched my attention to
the other bloke who was starting to run carrying the Armalite towards the
gate. I fired 2 shots in quick succession. They were aimed shots. I then fired
a further two similar shots. He staggered and dropped about 5 metres from
the gate'.

The same pattern of sentences emphasising 'threat to life' is present here
in the soldiers' statements as in the cases of the Ballysillan Four, John Boyle
and Patrick Duffy. One must again ask the question as in the cases of Boyle
and Duffy – why would élite professional soldiers leave an arms cache that
would pose a threat to themselves? Would it not be a simple thing to unload
them, confiscate ammunition and then take intruders captive? The weapons posed no danger to the soldiers; they were not booby-trapped; Soldier
'A' had already handled the packages.

Since the SAS were not obliged to attend the inquests that meant there
was little cross-questioning. As in most cases also, the DPP directed no
prosecution. The Army legal advisers were present for the statements of the
soldiers.

The third man escaped in the car. The cut-off group 'E' and 'F' failed to
stop the wounded man although they fired shots at the car. The car was later
found abandoned at Barrack Hill, Aghamullen.

The autopsy on Colm McGirr showed that he could have been hit by as
many as 13 bullets; the 4 in the trunk caused rapid death; he was also hit in
the face, right arm and right leg. Brian Campbell's autopsy showed he was
hit twice in the back; the more serious wound which caused his death
would not have been immediate.

On 14 March 1984 the inquest into the deaths of the two men was
adjourned when three of the soldiers involved in the shooting did not
appear at Dungannon. The coroner Mr J.P. Shearer was told that one of the
three soldiers had left the Army and was now out of the jursidication. Mr
Paddy Duffy, solicitor, described the inquest as a charade; it was incredible,
he said, that two men still bound by Army regulations failed to attend.

The families of the two men then released a statement. They said they
had intended to have it read in court and included in the record of the
inquest. The statement read:

> On Sunday, 4 December 1983, our two sons, Brian Campbell (19) and
> Colm McGirr (23) were murdered in a field in the vicinity of Coalisland
> and close to their homes by a number of men whose anonymity had

been protected by the British government and by the upholders of its law in Ireland.

Both of our sons had been threatened with assassination by the British Army and the RUC, Colm no later than the week before his death when he was held in Gough barracks on a Section 11 detention order for three days.

Both our sons were volunteers in the Irish Republican Army which, under British law, is a proscribed organisation and membership of which, upon conviction, could lead to a five year jail sentence.

Both of our sons were acknowledged as IRA volunteers and were on their way to inspect or collect a number of guns, illegal possession of which under British law is again an offence punishable with a heavy prison sentence. The law stops there, but the grim reality goes much further.

Brian and Colm had alighted from a car on Clough (=Cloghog) Road, crossed the road and got under a wire fence to begin crossing the field to where the arms were hidden.

Without being called upon to halt they were fired upon from both sides of the road and were killed ... by unknown gunmen who have since been blessed by the law as their actions have been defended by government representatives, and they have not been and will not be prosecuted.

We have absolutely no means of redress and have sought to have this statement read out at the inquest to at least put on official record the victims' side of the story.

Both our sons suffered horrific wounds and an act of savagery was carried out on the lifeless body of Colm McGirr.

It is quite clear that our sons could have been captured and taken alive ... Those undercover soldiers probably took the precaution of unloading and disarming the hidden guns so that they would be in no danger. Having been taken alive, full provision existed within the law to have Colm or Brian charged and imprisoned.

... Our sons were murdered as part of a Shoot-to-Kill policy operated officially by British forces but having absolutely no legality since parliament has not sanctioned summary executions as the penalty for intention to illegally possess firearms, the only possible charge that could have been laid against Colm and Brian.

That this Shoot-to-Kill policy is official can be seen from the consistent way it has been operated against nationalists in republican areas who have been cornered in compromising circumstances; for example, joy riding, or in the vicinity to a cache of weapons, or actually carrying weapons.

We accuse the British Government of murder and intimidation and

of having no right to be in Ireland except through the use of brute force
and illegalities.

Other bereaved families have experienced cover-up after cover-up,
and one inquest has been adjourned indefinitely and the coroner has
resigned over gross irregularities in RUC evidence.

We are protesting now at the official cover-up of the identities of our
sons' assassins and we accuse the British government of operating a
Shoot-to-Kill policy in the North of Ireland.

The inquest resumed in Dungannon Court House on Monday, 24 June
1985. It began at 10 am and ended at 6.30 pm. The men were shot at 3 pm
on 4 December 1983. It is clear from the inquest documents that the doctor
did not get to examine the bodies until 5.30 pm approximately and the priest
was not allowed to attend them until 6 pm. Two ambulance men arrived at
the scene at 3.45 pm but were held up and delayed in parking until 4.05 pm
when they were permitted to see the bodies. They were not permitted to
move them. One ambulance witness denied a suggestion from Mr Paddy
Duffy, solicitor, that he had told Jo Thomas of the *New York Times* (article,
'Shoot-to-Kill policy in Ulster?', 12 April 1985) that when he examined the
bodies one of the men seemed to be alive. Mr Duffy asked the RUC what
form the interviews of the soldiers took and the RUC agreed that the
soldiers met as a group with a legal adviser before making their statements.
Mr Duffy asked the RUC if any attempt had been made to immobilise the
cache of weapons; it would appear to have been a simple method to ensure
both men were taken alive. The RUC superintendent said that to do so
would have been dangerous and agreed to a suggestion from Mr Piers
Grant, counsel for the Ministry of Defence, that such arms caches were often
booby-trapped. (The fact that Soldier 'A' handled both packages was
ignored!) Mr Duffy said that allegations had been made that the soldiers
had shot the men as they went into the field and then laid the guns beside
them. The court also heard that the Armalite found in the cache had been
used in 4 murders and 18 attempted murders and the shotgun had been
taken from a house by masked men.

Mr Duffy commented that the only member of the unit who had
appeared at court, Soldier 'F', had been unable to see the shooting and they
were not going to hear from Soldiers 'A', 'B', 'C' and 'D' who did the
shooting.

Another soldier, 'G', who, at base, had received the radio report of the
confrontation and was flown to the scene by helicopter, was asked by Mr
Duffy if the men were dead when he arrived. He said they were and one had
been given first aid. Mr Duffy, 'Did your first report say if the men were
dead?' Soldier 'G', 'The radio report said two people had been killed'. Mr
Duffy, 'Have you brought the radio log with you?' Soldier 'G', 'No, it is a
classified report. I was not asked to bring it'. (In the Patrick Duffy case the

radio log details were brought to court.) Mr Duffy, 'Do you think it should have been brought as it is important?' Soldier 'G', 'No'. Mr Duffy, 'It is probably one of the most important documents at the inquest. It is certainly of vital importance'.

Both men received paramilitary funerals; volleys of shots were fired at both funerals. Brian Campbell was buried after 11 am Mass in St Patrick's Church, Clonoe, a short distance from the scene of the shooting. Fr Joseph Campbell, curate, said the Mass assisted by Fr John Mallon from Dungannon and Fr Peter Campbell, uncle of the deceased. In his homily Fr Joseph Campbell said, 'We call into question the circumstances of his death. We demand that the basic right to life be respected by all. It is only when this basic right to life is respected by all that there is a true foundation for justice and genuine peace'.

Colm McGirr's funeral took place at 12 noon on 6 December in the Church of the Holy Family, Coalisland. Fr Brian Mac Raois (brother of Réamonn Mac Raois who died on hunger-strike on 21 May 1981) spoke as follows:

> On behalf of our entire community, I offer to Colm McGirr's mother and father, brothers and sisters, his relatives and friends, his whole family circle and to those who knew him and mourn him, our deepest sympathy in their loss and their grief. We pray that God's Holy Spirit may support and strengthen them in this their time of trial, and that he may give them courage and comfort.
>
> Colm was a member of our parish. We bury him today as a fellow-parishioner, a fellow-Christian. We are united in offering up for him Christ's sacrifice of love in the funeral Mass. We pray for him, asking the Lord to forgive his sins and to take him to His own right hand in His kingdom.
>
> Death is always a tragedy but the death of a man at the hand of his fellow-man is something which must make us all grieve deeply. Since Cain killed his brother Abel, murder remains a terrible crime against the brotherhood of man, no matter what the circumstances are, no matter what the cause and what the motivation. Murder must always be something to make us all, members as we are of sinful humanity, hang our heads in contrite shame before God who is Father of us all, humbly calling upon Him for mercy and forgiveness.
>
> I would be failing in my duty to the truth if I did not on this occasion make some comment on the tragic circumstances in which Colm McGirr lived and died.
>
> Colm McGirr was an Irishman. He lived here in Coalisland, in Annagher. He died in the townland of Magheramulkenny in his native Tyrone, in the place where he and generation upon generation of his people before him were born and reared, and lived and struggled and

died, from time immemorial.

There is surely some law of nature which is offended and violated when Irishmen are struck down in the townlands where they belong, in their own ancestral fields, among their own kith and kin, and in the midst of the people who know them and recognise them as their neighbours' children.

There is surely some law of nature which is offended and violated when Irishmen are struck down in their native place by faceless, nameless strangers.

We are living in bad times, in times that are difficult. We need the Grace of Almighty God to help us as we make our pilgrim way through this valley of tears to our homeland which is in heaven.

We need to hear the words of Jesus as he hung upon the cross on Calvary: 'Father, forgive them for they know not what they do'.

We call upon the saints of Ireland, upon St Patrick, St Brigid, St Colmcille, St Columbanus, St Malachy, St Oliver Plunkett to guide and direct our generation of Irish people along the way that leads to life and salvation.

We call upon Christ our Saviour, who is seated at the right hand of the Father and who will come again in glory to judge the living and the dead, to protect us from all that is evil and harmful in ourselves and outside ourselves and to keep us and all his people in his loving care.

The shooting took place after the controversial killing by the RUC of Mary Foster (80) on 28 November 1983 during a post-office robbery in Pomeroy, County Tyrone, which again gave voice to the outcry of a Shoot-to-Kill policy.

Four Dungannon councillors said it was accepted locally that Brian Campbell and Colm McGirr were unarmed and could have been detained without loss of life. They expressed concern at the use of the SAS. They regarded it as an appeasement of the politicians demanding a Shoot-to-Kill policy, a criticism borne out by the comment of the DUP Press Officer who commended the SAS for their effective action. The shooting took place a few weeks after the Darkley Gospel Hall killings (20 November 1983) following which there were calls for greater SAS presence close to the border. The Secretary of State, Mr James Prior, speaking at Craigavon Hospital where he visited some of the injured survivors of the Darkley atrocity denied a Shoot-to-Kill policy or that the operation in Coalisland was to improve standing with a section of society. 'The SAS,' he said, 'have been here the whole time and it happens from time to time they have an opportunity of showing what they can do.'

Just more than a week later, Brigadier Michael Rose, who was in charge of 22 SAS in the Falklands, was appointed commander of the British Army's 39th Infantry Brigade which takes in Belfast and most of counties Down and

Antrim.

British Army HQ said it was 'purely coincidental' that his appointment followed an increase in SAS activity. Brigadier Rose (43) was a military assistant to the British Army GOC in the North, General Sir Timothy Creasey, between 1978 and 1979. General Creasey was a keen advocate of the SAS.

The Dunloy Killings[117]

On 21 February 1984 an engagement took place between an IRA unit and SAS soldiers which resulted in the death of Sergeant Paul Oram of the SAS and two IRA volunteers Henry John Hogan (20) who lived at Carness Drive, Dunloy, and his friend, Declan Dominic Peter Martin (18) of Bridge Road, Dunloy. Another SAS soldier was seriously wounded in the gun battle.

Henry Hogan was born at Moore Lake Cottage, Crediton, Devon, England. The family moved back to Ireland to Ballymena in 1973. They were intimidated there by loyalists and moved to Ballymoney. Again they were intimidated and moved to Dunloy only three weeks before the shooting. The family was republican in sympathy. A son, Michael, was serving a 12-year sentence in Portlaoise at the time of the shooting. The family thinks that the RUC alerted the British Army to their presence in Dunloy and this initiated an SAS observation post near their home at Carness Drive. Some weeks before the incident the UDR and British Army harassed local people. Hogan and Martin were also convinced that they were under surveillance. In a counter-surveillance test they drove to Maghera and Draperstown, halting at both places; a car following them also halted; they knew they were being followed. Carness Drive is a small housing estate off the Tullaghans Road. It is a bending cul-de-sac sweeping in to the left on entering, with an assortment of little bungalows for old people on the right and larger houses on the left. The Hogans had moved into one of the larger houses, a row that faced an open field; at that time work was not completed in the estate; not all the houses were occupied and the end of the cul-de-sac was in a rough state; there were three workmen's huts at the edge of the big open field behind the houses. Lighting had been installed in the Drive, the last lamppost being near a large telegraph pole which was situated behind a barbed wire fence close to the workmen's huts.

Declan Martin was going with Henry's sister, Margaret, and was therefore a constant visitor to the Hogan home. He worked as a plumber apprentice. When he came home from work on 21 February around 5.30 pm he brought his little brother Cathair, who was four years of age, out in the car for a spin. Cathair says he brought him to the bus station. It is thought that Declan picked up a member of the IRA at Ballymena railway station. He returned home with Cathair only and had a rushed meal. Mrs Martin

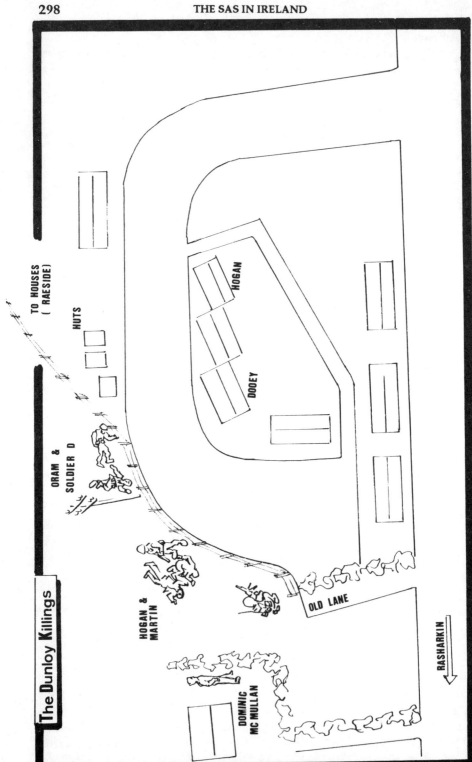

The Dunloy Killings

TO HOUSES
(RAESIDE)

HUTS

HOGAN

DOOEY

ORAM &
SOLDIER D

HOGAN &
MARTIN

OLD LANE

DOMINIC
MC MULLAN

RASHARKIN

remembers walking down to the 7.30 evening Mass; the snow had just gone; Declan was walking in front of her. The last she saw of him he was heading for the graveyard taking, as she surmised, a short cut to Hogans. She remembers that on that Tuesday Martin met Henry Hogan as he was coming from work and gave him a lift.

The IRA had caught on that the SAS were watching Hogan's house, probably on 21 February. Hogan and Martin realised that surveillance was coming to a point where they would be assassinated by the SAS. It was a matter of who moved first. An active service unit was formed to ambush them where they were hidden behind the storage huts. When Declan Martin entered Hogans' house that night he declared excitedly, 'They're there! They're there!' He had caught a glimpse of a torch or something shining. The IRA unit dressed in full combat uniform. They knew that there was a strong possibility that they might be killed. When Henry Hogan left the house shortly before 8 pm, he turned and looked at it almost with a sense of premonition, one long last backward look; then he saluted his home and went off. Three IRA men took part in the ambush, Hogan, Martin and a third unnamed person, probably the man Declan had picked up in Bally-mena. Hogan was armed with a Vigneron 9 mm sub-machine-gun, Martin with an Armalite and the third person with a shotgun. (The Armalite had been used in the murder of Constable John McFadden in Rasharkin on 5 November 1983). It is difficult to piece together the story but it would seem that the unit moved off from behind Hogan's house and succeeded in surprising the SAS soldiers where they lay in the field beside the telegraph pole, close to the workmen's huts, watching Hogan's house. The IRA in a statement said that they surprised three SAS men, opened fire, killing one, wounding another and the third escaped. It was stated at the inquest that Sergeant Oram sustained two bullet wounds in the neck, two in the trunk and two in the left leg; the neck wounds were probably caused from behind; the principal cause of death was injury to the heart. The IRA statement went on to say that, as the three IRA men withdrew, they were outnumbered by a back-up group of SAS who arrived in two cars; they got out of the cars and opened fire wounding Hogan and Martin; the third man got away. The statement continued: 'It was several minutes later as the situation cleared that Henry Hogan and Declan Martin, who were surrounded by the SAS, could be heard shouting. It was then that they were shot dead'.

From the evidence of witnesses it would seem that there were three bursts of gunfire and then single-type shots. There was a lull of three minutes between the first burst and the second burst; the second and third were almost in quick succession so that the second and third are classified by at least one witness as one burst. Mrs Bridie Dooey (23) said she heard one long burst of gunfire followed by two others. The front wall of her home, two doors from Hogans', was struck by a bullet. 'Suddenly two

Cortinas pulled up. Three men got out of one and another out of the second car. I could hear them shouting "Get the hell out of the way, get the hell out of the way". I couldn't make out for sure, but I think it was an English accent.'

Mrs Hogan thinks that the pattern of shots was as follows:

> 1. 8.12 pm. A long continuous burst of gunfire, perhaps 10 or 11 shots. Shouts and cries. A lull of 3 minutes. (I interpret this as Henry Hogan firing and killing Sergeant Oram and wounding SAS soldier 'D').
> 2. Another burst of gunfire. (To some two bursts of gunfire). (A third undesignated SAS soldier fires wounding Hogan and Martin as they dashed into the field). A lull. Two SAS cars arrive.
> 3. Gunfire in the field. (Soldier 'A' fires four shots into the wounded men lying on the ground. He sees that Oram is dead and immediately returns and fires two more shots into one of the men).

At the inquest Dominic McMullan who lived about 100 yards from the scene of the shooting at Tullaghans Road, on high ground overlooking Carness Drive, said that on the evening of 21 February he was working on a car at his house for about an hour. At about 8 pm he heard 7 or 8 shots which he took to be a car backfiring. A neighbour suggested to him that it sounded like gunfire. Some minutes later he heard more shots. He looked again in the direction of Carness Drive and saw two figures like black shadows running in the Drive and heading towards the barbed wire fence. They jumped over the fence into the big field. They ran about 10 or 15 yards. Then he saw sparks 'which appeared tight to the barbed wire fence but closer to our house than where the persons had crossed the fence'. He heard 8 or 9 or 10 shots. He saw the two figures fall. Then two cars drove into Carness Drive very fast. There were three persons in the first car and one in the second car. Two got out and jumped over the barbed wire fence. One of them pointed a gun down into the ground and fired 3 or 4 shots. He saw the sparks, as he thought, rising from the ground. He did not see the men on the ground move after they fell. One of the cars reversed up to the wire beside the telegraph pole. The boot was opened and the light in it came on. Something bulky was thrown into the boot.

It is difficult to assess the truth of the SAS soldiers' statements at the inquest. The line through them seems to be this. Soldier 'G' said that on 21 February a unit attached to HQ 8th Brigade at Ebrington Barracks had been deployed in North Antrim. Among them were soldiers 'A' and 'D' and Sergeant Oram. Each of them was armed with a 9 mm Browning pistol.

Soldier 'D' was the SAS man wounded in the gunbattle. He made a statement in the hospital on 6 March. He said that he had been on a uniformed foot patrol with Sergeant Oram at around 6.45 pm. At 7.15 pm they took up an observation position adjacent to the base of a telegraph pole near to the workmen's huts. The area was quite well illuminated from artificial lighting in Carness Park. Soldier 'D' said in his statement at the inquest, 'I was lying about a metre away from Sergeant Oram and to his right. Our position was in shadow caused by a mound of earth forming a small rise in front of us'. The two soldiers seem to have been distracted shortly after 8 pm by a blue Mini which pulled up; several people were seen around it. A man in dark clothing came from the rear of Hogans' to the front. (Was the car a decoy? Who was the dark figure?) Suddenly the two SAS soldiers heard loud voices from behind them. Soldier 'D' said he looked round and saw two masked men in combat dress pointing weapons at them. One of the masked men said, 'Are they armed?' They were ordered to stand up and put their hands on their heads. One of the men warned that if they moved they would get their heads blown off. They stood up. 'D', thinking that he was about to be shot, drew his pistol and fired at the man on the left; he saw Sergeant Oram firing at the same time. Henry Hogan also fired. 'D' was hit and fell; Sergeant Oram fell. Declan Martin's gun remained unfired throughout the whole incident. 'D' saw the IRA men on the ground moving away and still armed. 'D', though wounded, says he used the radio to call for assistance.

It is thought Hogan and Martin were not absolutely sure that the two men they saw in the hide were SAS men. They were afraid they might shoot two workmen or two other people. That is why they issued some challenge. The SAS then went for their weapons and Hogan shot them. Then there was the lull of some minutes as Mrs Hogan recounts. Hogan and Martin then ran down Carness Drive. There was a third SAS man in the unit who is not mentioned explicitly in the SAS statements. He was covering his two companions from a point along the barbed wire but could do nothing while the group was bunched together behind the huts. When Hogan and Martin broke cover he fired diagonally at them from his vantage point when they ran some ten yards into the field. That was the burst of gunfire that felled the two IRA men. Then almost immediately the SAS cars arrived at speed. This was the back-up SAS group described as being in plain clothes. Soldier 'A' was in one car and there were three SAS men in the other, 'E', 'B' and perhaps 'J'. They had received the 'Contact' alarm by radio and dashed to the scene from different points. Soldier 'A' arrived just before the second car. Later when the shooting was over a third SAS car, on patrol in the vicinity of Ballymoney, arrived with Soldiers 'F' and 'C'.

The rest of the shooting was done by Soldier 'A'. He was the soldier McMullan saw firing the weapon 'into the ground'. 'D' says when he saw 'A' approaching he shouted a warning to him – "A' turned round and engaged the terrorists'. Soldier 'A' did not appear at the inquest. His statement was read out. He said he was on patrol in an unmarked car when he received a report that two men had been wounded. He drove to the scene and arrived at the same time as 'E' and 'B' ('B' says 'A' was already there when he arrived). On entering the field he saw two wounded soldiers. Then he noticed a movement 5 or 6 metres in front of him in the field. He recognised two men with weapons in hand. Believing that they were about to fire at him, he engaged them with his Browning 9 mm pistol, firing 2 shots at each man.

Soldier 'B' (who must have followed close to 'A') – probably the two soldiers McMullan saw entering the field – called 'A' to return and check the other injured soldier (probably Oram); 'A' found no pulse. 'A' said that he then remembered that he did not remove the weapons from the IRA men and he went back. As he approached, he noticed one of them moving and 'pointing a weapon'; he engaged with 2 more shots and the man lay still.

Soldier 'B' said that prior to 8 pm he was stationed two kilometres north of Dunloy. He received the word 'Contact' by radio. He arrived at Dunloy at approximately 8 pm. He saw two soldiers in a firing position in the estate. One was Soldier 'A' but he does not identify the second soldier. If Soldier 'A' arrived alone in his car, which seems to be the evidence of local witnesses and he himself gives that impression, then who was the second soldier with him in a firing position? I think this points to the third SAS soldier who was on surveillance with Oram and 'D' in the vicinity of Hogans' house. He was responsible for felling Hogan and Martin as they fled from the scene. 'B' said that when he arrived Soldier 'A' went over to the fence; he heard 'D' shouting the message of warning to 'A' and saw two figures lying prone in the field. Both figures were moving their legs and arms. (Hogan and Martin lying wounded but alive). He saw 'A' go over to the two figures and heard him fire four shots. Soldier 'B' was giving first-aid to the wounded 'D'. 'A' at 'B's' bidding came over to assist Sergeant Oram who appeared to be dead. Then 'A' suddenly moved out into the field again ('A' said he went to retrieve the weapons) and 'B' heard 'A' fire another two shots.

'A' returned with the Armalite and sub-machine-gun and handed them over the fence to be put into the back of a car. Sergeant Oram's body was taken to the UDR centre at Ballymoney and thence by helicopter to hospital. Soldier 'D' was brought to Coleraine hospital.

The *post-mortem* carried out by Dr Derek Carson, Deputy State Pathologist for Northern Ireland, revealed that Henry Hogan was struck by 6 or 7 bullets, one in the left hand, 2 in the right arm, 2 in the upper abdomen, one in the right buttock and one in the left upper thigh. The trajectory of the latter 2 bullets suggested that he had been on his elbows and knees when they struck. The cause of death was laceration of the aorta which would have provoked massive internal bleeding. Declan Martin was struck by 6 bullets to the front of the chest, one in the back of the shoulder and another to the thigh. The cause of death was bleeding in the chest, due to massive injuries to the heart and lungs. The two bodies were not removed until 2.25 am.

The double barrelled sawn-off shotgun was found in a grassy unused lane off Tullaghans Road which was blocked by wire where it led to the big open field. It had been abandoned by the third IRA man. His role is not clear. He was not with Hogan and Martin when they engaged the SAS. One does not know the escape route planned by the IRA unit or what back-up they might have had. Something must have gone wrong with the operation for it is difficult to understand what prompted Hogan and Martin to run into the open field.

Browning pistols and spent bullets were retrieved by forensic experts. The bodies of Hogan and Martin were found face upwards. The brown masks had been removed, presumably by the SAS soldiers, and were lying beside the bodies. When the body of Declan Martin was lifted a scene-of-the-crime police officer found three depressions. A stone was placed over the depressions to preserve them. On a second search at daylight he found that where Declan Martin's body lay there were two holes and an indentation and on digging he found a 9 mm bullet. One gets the impression that Martin had been fired at from above as he lay prone and the bullets went through him into the ground. The bullets recovered from his body and clothing were from the pistols of Sergeant Oram and Soldier 'A'. Other bullets passed through his body and were not recovered. (From the gun of the third SAS man?) No bullets were recovered from the body of Henry Hogan.

The families were not represented at the inquest; not all the SAS soldiers attended; hence there was no cross-examination; there were no charges laid; a real investigation of exactly what happened was not carried out.

Fr Stephen McBrearty, one of the local curates who lived at Cloughmills at the other end of the parish, was driving on Tullaghans Road at 8.20 pm on Tuesday, 21 February. As he was about to turn into Carness Drive he saw a parked car across the Drive and an armed man in civilian dress crouched behind it. They exchanged words and Fr McBrearty was told to leave; he drove off but then turned back to ask what was happening and told the soldier he was a priest; he was told there was shooting going on and 'to get lost'. He dropped off a passenger in Hawthorne Crescent and was told that there had been shooting; he returned and on the way back heard two shots in quick succession. When he walked into Carness Drive he met a policeman who told him that several people were dead in a field. He left to fetch his oils and returned to administer the sacrament of anointing.

Local people can indicate the position of two of the back-up cars. One was parked near St Joseph's Parish Centre with a single bearded person in casual clothes in it (Soldier 'A'?). When the shooting broke out, a local who had just parked his car beside this man tapped the other's car window and said, 'There's shooting'. The stranger started up the car with a quick action and headed off at speed swerving badly as he went out the gate. By a strange coincidence Mrs Martin, mother of Declan, met the other back-up car. She left the 7.30 evening Mass before 8 pm and went with a friend on a Legion of Mary visit to 'McKillen's' to Dunloy Cross on the main Ballymena/Ballymoney Road, about a mile and a half from Dunloy. The SAS car was stationed in the lane she was about to enter; she had to reverse to let it out and it drove off at speed towards Dunloy (Soldier 'B's car).

The Rev. Ian Paisley, MP, in whose constituency the shooting took place, expressed his delight that 'the right men were brought under the fire of the British Army'. He praised the dead Sergeant Oram, a 'gallant sergeant of the British Army who died giving protection to the law-abiding citizens of that area'.

The RUC drafted 200 men into the village for the funerals. There were scuffles with the police as the body of Henry Hogan was removed from his home to be brought to St Joseph's Church. The tricolour was draped over his coffin. Mr Gerry Adams in his oration at the graveside described Henry Hogan and Declan Martin as freedom fighters and their killers as members of a 'British terror gang'. The funeral of Declan Martin took place a few hours later in St Joseph's Church. It was strictly private at the request of the family.

The Shooting of William Price[118]

Tyrone has lost a gallant soldier
A mother mourns a darling son
The little ones who call him brother
Their hearts are sad
Now Willie's gone

A carefree boy and gifted scholar
He loved the beauty of the land
And Ireland's glens and lofty splendour
Captured with an artist's hand.

It's well we know the price of freedom
Here in the land where Willie died
So Irishmen when you remember
All speak his name with pride

William Alfred Price (28) lived with his sister Mrs Eileen Maye, at Mourne View Cottages, Carnan, Stewartstown, County Tyrone. He came to live with her to keep her and her family company after her husband was killed in a car accident. His family and neighbours describe him as a second father to the children who returned his love. He was they say, 'quiet and modest and never bothered with anybody'. He was beloved by all creeds and even after his death when it was clear that he was an IRA volunteer, Protestant neighbours expressed their sympathy to the family. As a youngster in St Patrick's Boys Secondary School he came first in his class and excelled at drawing and painting and winning prizes in school competitions. It is not surprising that he chose painting as a trade. At the time of his death he was unemployed; many people, however, were in his debt for he was always willing to paint or decorate for charity. He enjoyed Gaelic football and played for the local Brockagh team. In fact he had done some football training the evening before he was shot dead by the SAS.

His family was aware that he was, as they said, 'an Irishman to the tip of his toes' but they did not know he was a member of the IRA. On the Friday of the weekend he was shot his sister went to Cookstown intending to stay for the weekend and took the youngest boy with her. Her two daughters were working in Portrush. Ronan (14) was at home with Willie. Ronan went to bed and took no notice that Willie had not come in. On Friday morning, 13 July 1984, his sister met a brother of a neighbour as she came out of a supermarket in Cookstown. He came over to talk to her assuming that she had heard the news. He had heard that a red-haired man from Carnan had been shot and presumed he was Willie. He accompanied her to a garage where he made a phone-call to confirm what had happened. He then accompanied Eileen to her mother's. She was in a state of shock. Her mother saw her through the window approaching the house crying. Her companion broke the news. No police ever officially informed them of Willie's death.

Martin Hurson from Galbally died on hunger-strike on 13 July 1981. His death greatly affected republicans in County Tyrone. To commemorate this event a co-ordinated series of incendiary attacks across Tyrone was planned by the IRA for 13 July 1984. Commerical premises in Cookstown and Coalisland were badly damaged by incendiaries. The burning of Forbes' Kitchens Factory at Ardboe was one of the IRA targets. At twenty minutes to twelve on the night of 12 July volunteers moved in to carry out the attack, timed to take place just after 12 midnight. The material found later at the scene gives an indication of the fire bombs prepared, four gallon cans of petrol with metal-cased explosive charges attached to each can by black tape; four timer power units in a white plastic bag were also found.

The republican version of what happened is as follows:

'The volunteers moved into position and headed towards the factory across the fields. On the way to the factory they heard a barley-banger which they had to pass to reach the factory. They knew that static electricity could set off the detonators and so they took time to guard against that by tying the ends of the detonator wires. While this was being done William

Price and another volunteer headed towards the factory to check it. They returned and by that time the wires had all been taped. The party then moved nearer to the factory to a spot about 200 yards from it, a vantage point to observe it. From this point they noticed an office light on but did not think it unusual and gave it no further thought. It was then decided that scouts would go forward and make an opening in the factory and then give the signal for the rest to follow.

'William Price and another volunteer headed towards the factory. Opposite the factory is a street light and at the bottom of that street light a cluster of bushes. They headed towards that cluster of bushes to keep in cover. They ran about three or four feet apart. When they got within 20 yards or so of the bushes three to four figures rose in front of them and suddenly the whole place lit up with gunfire. William Price fell moaning. The other volunteer crawled back through the long grass to the position he had left and made his escape.

'From the time William Price was shot and wounded to the time the other volunteer got out of the firing line the shooting never stopped. Some time after that shooting, the other volunteers heard the SAS whooping hysterically like Indians in an American wild-west film. A good three minutes after the firing there seemed to be one shot and then a burst of shots.

'Two volunteers headed towards the main road and towards Forbes' shop. Another group of SAS posted away from the factory fired at them. They kept running until they got into the light of Forbes' shop. The SAS followed them, running, and put them on the ground on the street. They would have been shot only Mrs Mary Forbes opened the window and shouted out at them thinking one of them was her son. The two men still think that is what saved them. Both these men, Raymond Francis O' Neill and Thomas McQuillan, were charged with having possession of two hand-guns, ammunition and incendiary equipment and were jailed for nine years. Another man, a fisherman, Francis Coleman, was arrested at the scene and held for a few days. He was an innocent passer-by and was released uncharged.'

Other details can be gleaned from the soldiers' statements and evidence at the inquest. Eight soldiers took part in the ambush. They are designated Soldiers 'A', 'B', 'C', 'D', 'E', 'F', 'G', 'H'. Soldier 'B' was in charge of the operation. Soldier 'A' says in his statement of 20 July 1984 – 'On Thursday, the 12th July 1984, I attended a briefing at my base given by Soldier 'B'. I was told a factory in the Ardboe area was a possible target for the P. IRA for a bomb-attack and we were to carry out an observation and arrest operation. The area was described by using an aerial photograph of the factory and the positions we were to take up were pointed out on a map'. Soldier 'E' in his statement of 7 August 1985 says, 'We were aware from our briefing that the factory was one of a number of potential targets for terrorists in the Tyrone

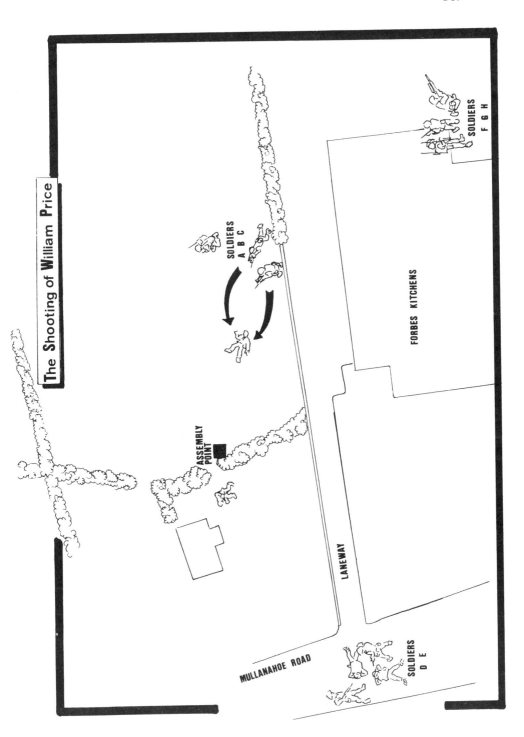

The Shooting of William Price

SOLDIERS
F G H

SOLDIERS
A B C

FORBES KITCHENS

ASSEMBLY
POINT

LANEWAY

MULLANAHOE ROAD

SOLDIERS
D E

area'. Soldier 'F' in his statement on 19 July 1984 said that at the briefing Soldier 'B' 'outlined this factory as a possible target for an incendiary bomb attack, that an ASU of the PIRA would carry out the attack which would include at least four men'.

Soldier 'B' (statement, 7 August 1985) outlines the setting up of the ambush. 'We had arrived in the area at approximately 23.10 hours and as soon as we arrived did a communication check. Having done this I divided the party into 3 groups, one 2 man group and two 3 man groups. I allocated one group of 3 men (Soldiers 'F', 'G', 'H') to the south-east corner of Forbes' Kitchens Factory. They were to keep an eye on the back of the building. Group 2, the one I was in, was positioned in the field in front of the factory (*Soldiers 'A', 'B', 'C'*). Group 1, the 2 man group (*Soldiers 'D' and 'E'*) was positioned beside the Mullanahoe Road; they were to observe the junction of the lane down to the factory. The 3 groups were in position to keep observation at approximately 23.18 hours. There was quite a bit of traffic moving from a club further on down the lane. There were people walking along as well'.

Since Soldier 'A' fired the fatal shot that killed William Price and like Soldier 'B' had a night sight on his rifle, we move to his statement to take up the SAS version. Statement, 13 July 1984:- 'I was dressed in Army camou- flage uniform and carried my issue AR15 rifle and three mags containing 90 rounds. We took up position at 11.30 pm on the 12th July 1984. I was in a field of long grass with Witness 'B' to my left and Witness 'C' to my right … I will refer to the field I was in as Field 1. The weather was dry and visibility was reasonably good. I was in a sitting position approximately 1m in front of a wooden fence and approximately 50m from the hedge to my west. There was a brick tower at this hedge. I could see through gaps in this hedge into Field 2…Witness 'B' was about 1m away from me and Witness 'C' about 10m behind me. There was a bird scarer in the area which gave off noise similar to gunfire approx. every 1½ to 2 minutes. At about 1.05 am I heard noises which came from the corner of the field (north-west). The noise was similar to that of a door knocker – metal. Three or four minutes later Witness 'C' crawled over to me and gave me a message. I then contacted Witness 'B' and told him that there were two armed men on the hedgerow to my left. I watched through the night sight of my rifle and saw two men at the brick tower. I believe that one had a hood on but because of the night sight I couldn't tell the colour. Approx. one minute later these men were joined by two others…I did not see any firearms being carried or any other articles. I spoke over to Witness 'B' and told him what I had seen. The four men were looking at the factory and at us as we were in a direct line with the factory. There was talking going on but I could not make out what was said or which one was doing the talking. About a minute later this group started to move towards us. They were crouched down and spread out in a line about 10m apart. I observed them through my night sight. I saw no weapons but had in my mind that they had spotted me when I had moved my position earlier. They still kept moving towards us in this crouching position. When the nearest one was about 30m away from me I called out a challenge, "Halt – hands up". This man raised his hands up very fast. I believed he was going to shoot at me so I fired one aimed shot at the centre of his body. I heard him scream. On firing my gun my vision was obstructed by the muzzle flash and when I regained vision he had disappeared. I fired a second aimed shot at the direction I had last seen him. I did not see a gun but he moved his hands into a position that suggested to me he was holding a gun. The other men had also disappeared from my view'.

Soldier 'B' says that when Soldier 'A' called out he heard a rustling in the long grass approximately north-west of him and then there was one shot fired by Soldier 'A'. He kept his head down and asked Soldier 'C' to radio a red alert report – 'Contact. Send QRF'. While this was going on he says there were approximately 3 more deliberate aimed shots fired by Soldier 'A'.

Soldier 'C' had also been viewing through his night sight. He said he saw 2 people moving from a gap in the hedgerow (probably William Price and another). They followed the line of the hedge to the tower. He could see them moving in soldier-like fashion. They kept about 10 metres apart. They stopped repeatedly and knelt down. He could see their heads moving from side to side as though they were very alert. They did not talk to each other but signalled to each other by using their hands. As they got nearer to the tower he was able to see more clearly through his night scope. As they got nearer to the tower they closed in together and he says, 'I was able to see that both persons were holding small dark objects in their hands which I had absolutely no doubt were handguns'. Both men returned to the gap in the hedge. He remarked to Soldier 'A' that there were armed men in the hedge. When he looked again he saw four men moving down the same hedgerow, the lead man just reaching the tower. He put his pocket scope away and was then only able to see blurred movement. He adopted a firing position. He heard Soldier 'A' shout 'Halt, Hands up', heard a number of shots being fired and simultaneously a scream. He says, 'I was convinced our group was being fired at from the enemy position. I therefore stood up and took a pace to my right and fired a short controlled burst of three rounds at the position where I had identified the enemy to be'. At 'B's command he radioed the 'Contact. Send QRF' alarm. Soldier 'B' then told him he was going to do a follow-up and Soldier 'A' and he were to remain as a cover group. He then sent a more detailed contact report – 'Four armed men at head of junction in front of factory. One scream. Three being chased'.

Soldier 'B' thought there was a possibility of other 'terrorists' in the vicinity of a derelict cottage north-west of the factory. He fired a burst of 5 rounds into the cottage. There was no reaction to this.

After he fired his two aimed shots at William Price, the man who had been hit and screamed, Soldier 'A' caught a glimpse of a person through a gap in the hedge in the next field, Field 2. He was running away up the hill towards the road. He says, 'I believed that this person was a threat so I fired one aimed shot at him. There was no reaction to the shot and he kept running up the hill out of sight. I then saw a second man going in the same direction so I fired another aimed shot at him. There was no reaction and he kept on running'.

Soldier 'B', after leaving 'A' and 'C' to cover him and firing into the cottage, linked up with Group 3, Soldiers 'F', 'G', 'H'. They worked in pairs and searched the area between the factory and the shop and filling station. Before they came to the shop he contacted a soldier in Group 1 (Soldiers 'D' and 'E') and joined them. He saw two persons lying on the ground at the junction of the factory laneway and the Mullanahoe Road. These were Raymond O'Neill and Thomas McQuillan. Soldiers 'D' and 'E' had been dropped off at 22.35 hours and had made their way to a point north of the junction of a lane leading to Forbes' factory and the Mullanahoe Road. Soldier 'D' says (statement, 7 August 1985) – 'Our job was to remain in position and if there was any trouble we were to move across to the top of the lane and set up caltrops on the lane. During this time there was a bird scarer operating nearby and there was a loud bang every couple of minutes. After about 2 hours there was a different sound of a shot which sounded like a rifle shot. I then believed the others had made some contact. We then moved immediately from our position to a point on the factory laneway near the junction and remained there. During this time Soldier 'E' tried to establish what had happened. Soldier 'E' appeared to have been alarmed by something on the road and then I heard footsteps coming along the road and 2 persons came into our view from the direction of approximately 100 yards north of our position. I saw one, the first one to appear, had a red pullover on and the other person who was about 5 metres behind was wearing a black jacket. I challenged them and said, "Stop or I'll fire". As soon as I shouted the fellow with the black jacket stopped immediately and put his hands in the air and stood there, the other fellow ran on quite fast. I pointed the rifle in his direction and called again for him to stop but he ran on and made a swing to his left towards some shrubs. I thought he was going to escape so I took 2 quick aimed shots and on the second shot he dropped to the ground. As soon as he did this I turned my attention to the first man and told Soldier 'E' to take care of the fellow whom I fired at. I then made the fellow in the black jacket to lie on the ground with his arms outstretched and I searched him for weapons but found none. Soldier 'E' then brought the other fellow up to where I was; he had searched him but found nothing. We then had both persons lying on the ground at the laneway junction. I heard Soldier 'E' ask them their names. They said they were O'Neill and McQuillan. Soldier 'E' asked them what they were doing. One of them said something about being with a girl and heard shots and ran. Just then 4 other members of the patrol (*Soldiers 'B', 'F', 'G' and 'H'*) came round the side of the buildings and joined us. About 2 or 3 minutes later QRF arrived and cordoned off the area and took charge of the two persons'.

We go back to Soldier 'A' to take up the SAS version of what happened after Soldier 'B' had left Soldier 'A' and 'C' to cover him when he moved off. Soldier 'A': 'I was told by Witness 'B' to give covering fire to the direction of the brick tower. Witness 'B' along with another patrol (*Soldiers 'F', 'G', 'H'*) moved off up the laneway towards the road, that is to my west. I then heard two shots from the direction Witness 'B' had gone but did not see anything. Witness 'B' returned a short while later and as a result of what he said I got through a hole in the wooden fence onto the laneway in front of the factory. Witness 'C'' joined me also. I told Witness 'B' that there might be a possible hit so he gave orders to check the area. We carried out a search of Field 1 (*where William Price was lying wounded*). I saw nothing, but Witness 'G' who was leading in the search pointed out petrol tins near the brick tower. I reported this to Witness 'B' and then I saw a path through the hedge between Field No. 1 and Field No. 2 ... There was a sleeve hanging on a branch; I think it was an orange colour. I went through into Field 2 beside the derelict house. Witness 'G' found a plastic bag. I didn't look in it but he told me what was inside. I assisted in carrying out a search of this field and was then told to return to Field 1 and search the NW corner. I found a track 2-3m from this hedge leading towards the corner – this led through a gap in the hedge into a cornfield (Field No. 3). There was a track through the cornfield which led to the north hedge. We followed it about halfway and then returned to Field No. 1.

'I then joined Witness 'B' at the brick tower and we walked in line towards my original position. Witness 'B' was on my right-hand side. About 25m from the brick tower I saw what appeared to be a body just showing through the grass. I saw the legs first. He was lying on his side with his head towards me. There was a sudden movement of his hands towards me and again I believed he was holding a handgun. I thought he was going to fire at me so I fired one round instinctively. I saw the injury to his head, so we closed in and on checking him found he was dead. I did a quick search of the body and immediate area. He had what I believed to be a box of matches in the inside pocket of his jacket and there was a pair of gloves beside the body. I found no firearms. We were then told to move to cover on the roadway where we were picked up and left the area. This was after the Police had arrived at the scene...'

Soldier 'B' says that they spent 20 minutes checking round the general area after leaving the 'two prisoners'. He says, 'At approximately 01.40 we decided to end the search and we were making our way across the field to my original position in front of the factory when Soldier 'A' fired one shot. I hadn't seen what he fired at just at the time but then I saw a body on the ground'.

It was this single shot from Soldier 'A' that killed William Price. Dr Derek Carson told the inquest that Price's death would have been instantaneous due to a high velocity gunshot wound to the top of the head. This was at 01.40 hrs as 'B' indicates. Price must have been wounded by the first two aimed shots by 'A' at approximately 01.10 hrs. That means he was lying wounded for 30 minutes. Price had three other wounds besides the shot to his head – to the left upper thigh, right leg and to the knuckle of one of his hands. One presumes that the first shot from 'A' hit Price in the upper left thigh. This was what made him scream and brought him down in the grass, 'disappearing' as 'A' put it. 'A' fired a second shot in the same direction. Soldier 'C' fired three rounds immediately after 'A'. Bullets from these last four shots could have caused the wounds to Price's right leg and knuckle of his hand. Replying to a question from Mr Martin Donaghy, solicitor for the next of kin, at the inquest in 1987, Dr Carson said the probability was that the deceased was standing up when shot in the legs. He could have been in a sitting position when struck later to the front of the head. The language 'A' uses in detailing his shooting of Price is common to all SAS statements, the 'sudden movements of his hands towards me'…'again I believed he was holding a gun – I thought he was going to fire at me so I fired one round instinctively'. 'A' says that Price was lying on his back on the ground, his head towards him when he shot him. How, unless he was an expert contortionist, could Price bring a gun round with movements of his hands to fire at a man behind him? Price was shot at close range in the top of the head; part of his head was blown off. His sister, who later identified the body, described the head as blown apart like the shell of an egg.

The Price family were not informed of the inquest into William's death held on 19 June 1986. Two RUC men came to his mother's house after the inquest. They told her that her son's inquest had been held that day. She asked what the verdict was. One of them said – 'You'll hear about it'. The RUC claimed that they could not earlier locate his mother's address. Obviously they knew where Price had lived and it would have been easy to find his mother's address from neighbours. Apparently a letter had been sent to Price's sister's address but she had moved. The family's lawyer applied for a second inquest and a judge heard the case in December 1986. Lord Justice Kelly ruled on 12 December 1986 that a new inquest should take place and that Price's mother should be notified in reasonable time of the date and place of the hearing. The judge said that she had suffered a disadvantage in not being able through her counsel to question witnesses called to that hearing. This however, he said, did not imply criticism of the coroner since there was no statutory obligation in Northern Ireland for the spouse or near relative of the deceased to be notified of an inquest.

The second inquest was held 17-18 June 1987. An RUC inspector's statement recorded that he had visited the scene on the morning of the shooting – 'On entering the field I was shown the body of a male person whom I know to be William Price, Mourne View, Carnan, Ardboe. I ascertained that he was dead and the body was still warm. He was lying face down and had received a head wound and further injury to the right thigh. I could not recognise him at this stage. On examining the area around the body I noted a .45 revolver lying partly under the deceased's feet which had socks placed over the shoes. A further .45 semi-automatic pistol was located some 5-6 feet from the body and a pair of wire cutters some 12 feet away in the same direction...' A member of the forensic science laboratory gave evidence of examining two weapons, a pair of yellow rubber gloves and a hood found at the scene. He said the rubber gloves were inside out. On examination of the revolver, a .455 Smith and Wesson, he found blood tissue. The revolver contained five rounds of ammunition. It showed no signs of recent discharge. It proved to be effective on tests. The semi-automatic pistol was a .45 and had two rounds. It showed no signs of recent discharge and on testing proved effective. It is noteworthy that the SAS found no weapons on the scene; one can only surmise that they made a cursory examination of the area only and left the scene in haste. If Price was accompanied by another volunteer in moving ahead to gain entrance to the factory, one guesses that the pistol belonged to his companion.

According to another forensic witness, examination of clothing of the deceased showed that fibres from Price's trousers were found in the front passenger seat of an abandoned Toyota car found nearby; he added, however, that the fibres could also have come from an identical pair of trousers. In his statement of 19 July 1984 Soldier 'F' admitted firing 2 aimed shots at the derelict cottage. On 12 July when he was interviewed by the RUC he said he did not fire his weapon.

The jury brought in a finding in accordance with the medical evidence that William Price died as a result of a high velocity gunshot wound to the head.

The funeral of William Price took place at St Brigid's Church, Brockagh, County Tyrone, on 15 July 1984. RUC officers baton-charged the mourners several times and injured dozens of people. No shots were fired during the interment and there was no colour party at the graveside. The aggressive batoning of mourners by the RUC was a policy adopted following the open display by the IRA at the funerals of Brian Campbell and Colm McGirr.

William Alfred Price belonged to a family of nine. He was the third generation of the Price family with the name 'William Alfred'. His uncle and grandfather were also so named. His father was an English soldier and there was a strong British Army tradition in the family. His father died three years before William. Since that the family have also been bereaved by the death of a sister. One of his brothers was taken off the plane on his way home for the funeral and held for 48 hours. He arrived home just when the funeral was over.

Some further details can be added to the story of William Price's death.

Although the SAS soldiers say they were dressed in camouflage military dress, local residents saw the soldiers who arrested O'Neill and McQuillan. All maintain that they were dressed in black clothes and that they bundled the prisoners into dark vans. Soldiers were also seen carrying what looked like pump-action shotguns.

It was several hours before a priest arrived on the scene to give William Price the last rites. The body was left lying in the field until midday 13 July.

After the 'Brighton Bombing'

In the early hours of Friday, 12 October 1984 a bomb placed by the IRA in room 629 of the Grand Hotel, Brighton, exploded. The blast ripped through the hotel bringing down a large part of it. The bomb was an attempt to kill the British Prime Minister Mrs Margaret Thatcher during the Conservative Party annual conference. She narrowly escaped. Four people died in the blast – Sir Anthony Berry (59), MP for Enfield and Southgate, Mrs Anna Roberta Wakeham (45), wife of Mr John Wakeham, the Government Chief Whip and MP for Colchester South and Malden, Essex, Mr Eric Taylor (54), chairman of North-West Area Conservatives, and Mrs Jean Shattock, wife of Gordon Shattock, chairman of Western Area Conservatives. Thirty others were injured including Mr Norman Tebbit, Secretary of State for Trade and Industry, and his wife Margaret. Mrs Muriel MacLean, who was badly injured in the blast, died in the Royal Sussex Hospital on 11 November 1984. She and her husband Donald were in room 629. A sixth victim, Mrs Gal Scanlon, a leading member of the Conservative Party, died at the age of 38 in July 1988; she was crippled a year after the blast by a back injury sustained in the bombing.

A period of ruthless killing by British forces followed the assassination attempt on the Prime Minister, not unlike the retribution that followed the killing of Mr Airey Neave, MP. Fred Jackson was killed during an SAS ambush of an IRA unit on 19 October. Two IRA volunteers, Antoin Mac Giolla Bríde and Kieran Fleming (drowned escaping) and an SAS soldier, Corporal Alastair Slater, died in an incident on 2 December. William Fleming and Daniel Doherty, IRA volunteers, were ambushed and shot dead by the SAS at Gransha hospital, Derry, on 6 December. A senior IRA bombing expert, Seán McIlvanna, was shot dead by the RUC at Blackwatertown, County Armagh, on 17 December. Three IRA volunteers, Charles

Breslin, Michael Devine and David Devine were shot down by the SAS at Strabane on 23 February 1985. The IRA responded in like manner to the intensification of the war. Nine RUC members were killed in a mortar attack on Newry RUC station on 28 February – Inspector Alex Donaldson, Sgt John T. Dowd, and Constables David Topping, Paul McFerran, Geoffrey Campbell, Rosemary McGookin, Ivy Kelly, Seán McHenry and Denis Price.

The Shooting of Frederick Jackson[119]

At 8.35am on the morning of 19 October 1984 Frederick Jackson (43), a businessman, was leaving Capper and Lamb haulage firm at Tamnamore, a district near Portadown, County Armagh, when he was fatally wounded by a low velocity bullet admittedly fired by an SAS soldier. The IRA had attempted a short time before to lay an ambush for an off-duty UDR major and in the subsequent action between the IRA and SAS soldiers Frederick Jackson was tragically shot dead. Frederick Jackson had just supervised a contract his firm was carrying out for Capper and Lamb. One bullet smashed through the windscreen of his bronze Ford Granada. The second pierced the driver's side door and struck him in the back. At the inquest into the circumstances of his death an employee at the yard said that he was driving a fork-lift truck when he heard gunfire. He stopped the machine and looking out saw Mr Jackson's car reversing and hitting a petrol pump. Jackson got out of his car and ran into the garage. He said he had been shot. Witness saw the blood on his hands. Jackson then fell to the ground.

At least eight soldiers in three cars, a silver Lancia, a maroon Renault, and a rust-coloured Saab were involved in a stake-out near the haulier's yard, acting, it was alleged, on a tip-off that a group of IRA men were coming to kill an off-duty major of the UDR who worked in Killyman milk factory. There were three soldiers in the Lancia, the commander of the SAS unit designated Soldier 'E' and Soldiers 'A' and 'B'. Two soldiers were positioned in bushes on the south side of the Tamnamore roundabout near the M1 motorway. One of these, Soldier 'K', in his statement at the inquest said he was dressed in Army jacket and trousers and was wearing a balaclava; he was armed with an Armalite rifle.

The Republican version of the incident is as follows:

On the night of 18 October masked men wearing green boiler suits took over the house of Daniel McIntyre of Washingbay Road, Coalisland. They remained the night there and next morning took a yellow Enterprise Ulster van from the household warning the residents not to report it until 10.30am.

It is confirmed that the operation was to shoot an off-duty major of the UDR on his way to work.

The operation began at Verner's Bridge near a petrol-filling station. The yellow van faced towards Tamnamore. The occupants saw the target's

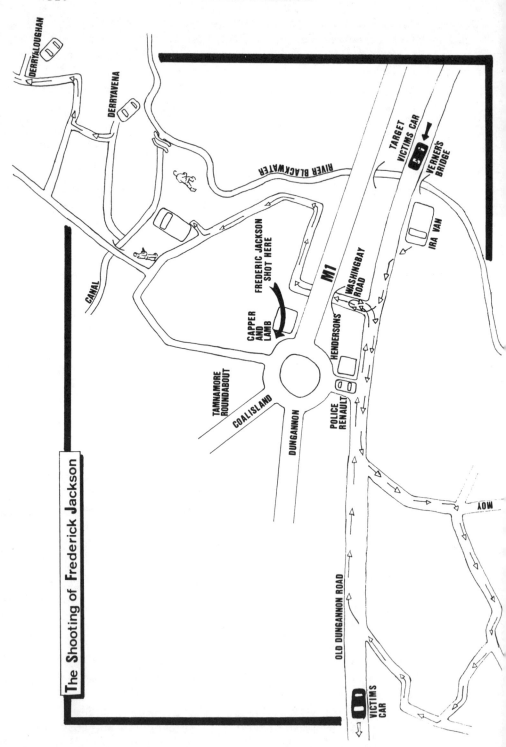

The Shooting of Frederick Jackson

vehicle approaching; they lowered the back windows of the van to prepare to shoot. The target either knew about the possible ambush or saw something suspicious from a distance. He slowed down and hesitated to come on. The van then moved off slowly but still the target did not move forward. The yellow van then turned right under a bridge that goes under the M1. The target then came forward and passed. The IRA driver turned, came out on to the Old Dungannon Road again and followed. He followed the target as far as Henderson's at the Tamnamore roundabout. At Henderson's the IRA noticed a maroon Renault 'police' car sitting in off the road. At the same time this car's occupants must have noticed the windows removed from the back of the van. It gave chase. The target then drove safely away towards Dungannon. The yellow van turned left down the Moy Road and second right down a narrow twisting road which wound back on to the Old Dungannon Road. The occupants (SAS) in the Renault fired across a field at an angle at the yellow van. Back on the old Dungannon Road the van with the IRA party headed back to the centre road that leads on to the Tamnamore roundabout. In front of them two cars were heading towards them blocking the road. One of the IRA men jumped into the front passenger seat of the van and opened fire on them. The two cars pulled to the one side as the van kept on coming towards them, the IRA man firing all the time. The yellow van swerved by the cars. The van then turned once again down the Washingbay Road near where the IRA had first hijacked it. A few miles down the road they turned right into a cul-de-sac and abandoned the car. They then took to the fields down towards the Blackwater river. As they ran a mysterious thing happened. They saw 'police' clearly on the road to the left who were staring down at them but remarkably the 'police' made no effort to come after them or fire at them. After resting they crossed the river by a footbridge. They hijacked a car at Derryavena. At the inquest on Frederick Jackson, Patrick Joseph Cullen of Derrytresk, Coalisland, said four men came into his yard dressed in army-style uniforms. One man put a rifle to the head of witness and told him not to say anything for five hours. They took the family car and asked for directions to the main road. About half-an-hour later police arrived at his home.

The IRA party then drove on to Derryloughan where they hijacked a second car and headed for Aughamullen and then escaped all cordons. At the inquest Mervyn McNulty of Derryloughan said that at 9 am there was a knock at the door of his home and two armed and masked men came into the kitchen. They asked for the keys of the wee van and warned witness not to say anything. Brian Robinson of Derryloughan was driving a lorry and described how he stopped his lorry at McNulty's yard where he was ordered into a van by a masked man. They drove off at high speed towards Washingbay. The men stopped at the Mountjoy road junction and told the witness to drive the van back to McNulty's yard.

The picture as it emerges from the SAS statements is as follows:

The commander of the SAS unit, Soldier 'E' in the Lancia, says he was suspicious of a yellow van when he saw it hanging round a junction for 5-10 seconds despite the way being clear. He then lost sight of it. Soldier 'K' at the roundabout received a radio message about the yellow van acting suspiciously. He then saw the SAS rust-coloured Saab passing his position followed by the SAS maroon Renault.

The yellow van turned and headed back towards where Soldier 'K' was posted at the roundabout and he saw the Lancia heading towards it. Soldier 'E' in the Lancia had been informed by radio that the yellow van was heading back. He ordered his driver to ram it. The IRA swerved round the Lancia firing at it and smashing the rear window. Soldier 'E' ordered 'A' and 'B' out of the Lancia and got out himself while still under fire from the van; he took up a kneeling position beside his car. Soldiers 'A' and 'B' fired their weapons, apparently a Heckler and Koch and a pistol, but 'E' did not fire. At this point the Renault returned to the scene at high speed and followed the yellow van, followed in turn by the Lancia with 'E', 'A' and 'B'. The van escaped. The Lancia unit returned to the haulage yard. A witness told the inquest that at one point there were six men in the yard with guns and that they had arrived in a 'silver' and 'brown' car.

An RUC statement said that the abandoned van contained a shotgun, a CB radio and 33 empty cartridge cases from an automatic weapon. The glass was missing from the doors.

At the inquest the Deputy State Pathologist, Dr John Press, was asked by counsel for the family of the deceased if immediate medical treatment would have saved Frederick Jackson's life. The pathologist said it was possible but that death would have been rapid and an operation difficult; the bullet had entered Jackson's body in the right side of his back, fracturing two ribs, lacerating a lung and an artery before lodging in his chest.

The jury at the inquest found that Jackson was a totally innocent victim and had been shot accidentally. None of the soldiers were ever prosecuted.

An IRA getaway car was parked at Annabeg and another one near the Tamnamore roundabout. The IRA intended switching to the cars from the yellow van but couldn't since they were being chased. The occupants of the Silver Lancia stopped with the car parked at Annabeg. The occupant Seán O'Neill was asked if he saw a yellow van. He said, 'No'. One of the Lancia men was bleeding from the face; obviously he had been hit in the exchange of fire. The Lancia then headed towards Tamnamore. O'Neill moved off towards Derryloughan. He was stopped by the UDR and taken for questioning. Later he was convicted of conspiracy to murder members of the security forces and was sentenced to seven years.

Republicans are adamant that they saw no men in 'soldier-type uniform' during the whole incident, only men in 'police-type' uniforms; in fact they thought they were dealing with police all the time. Were the SAS soldiers then disguised as policemen?

There were reports of a helicopter in the area before the shooting. When contact was made an RUC inspector directed units to the scene but subsequently redirected them away from the scene on the advice of the Special Branch, presumably on information coming to them that shooting had occurred. Later the District Mobile Support Unit of the RUC cordoned off the scene.

Before the inquest took place Ms Jo Thomas wrote an article in the *New York Times*, 17 March 1986, 'In Ulster, the "Shoot-to-Kill" rumours will not die'. She interviewed the Jackson family. She wrote that Alan Jackson, the victim's brother, and other members of the family said they thought the evidence they had uncovered showed that the undercover soldiers mistook Mr Jackson for an IRA man and shot him dead at close range. They said they had obtained evidence from reliable sources that he was shot only once, in the back with a handgun. 'The window on his side of the car had been smashed and his injuries suggest he was struck on the bridge of the nose with a blunt object. The family thinks Mr Jackson was shot because the Special Air Service mistook him for the IRA man who would normally have been waiting to pick up the gunmen. According to the family and people present that day, the workers in the trucking company who called for help as soon as they realised Mr Jackson had been shot were ordered by the soldiers to put their hands up. When an ambulance arrived, they say, the soldiers delayed it until the police could accompany Mr Jackson. He was dead on arrival at a local hospital and the family wants to know whether the delay cost him his life.'

It would take a thorough and vigorous investigation to answer these questions. Unfortunately the nature of inquests does not lend itself to answer them. There is no thorough investigation into 'Shoot-to-Kill' problems. That in itself is an indication that the policy is administrative.

Ms Jo Thomas also wrote an article 'Shoot-to-Kill Policy in Ulster? The Debate Rages' for the *New York Times*, 12 April 1985. In the May/June 1988 issue of the *Columbia Journalism Review* she reported how she left her job because of disfavour shown towards her coverage on Northern Ireland. She comments on the Stalker affair and then writes:

> What happened to me was quieter. A senior editor, who kept a home in London as well as New York and who had been enthusiastic about my initial dispatches from Belfast, began telling me to stay out of Northern Ireland. A high-ranking British official, who in the past has had close ties to the intelligence community in Northern Ireland, took me to lunch and suggested I drop my investigation in exchange for a lot of access to the secretary of state for Northern Ireland, the British

official who administers the place, as well as an exclusive first look at the Anglo-Irish pact then being negotiated between London and Dublin. I refused. Several American colleagues in London suggested I leave the difficult investigations to the local press: if there really were a story, British and Irish reporters would be on top of it. In fact, they were not – but some of them began treating me as if I were a member of the IRA. Then, too, the mail at my house in London started to arrive opened. In Northern Ireland, I was refused all official records, even transcripts on inquests and trials that had been open to the public...

Ms Thomas was abruptly ordered home in February 1986. She suspected that the cause was that she was paying too much attention to Northern Ireland. She has now left the *New York Times* to teach journalism and spend more time with her children.

Frederick Jackson was an innocent victim in a stake-out. How the RUC and SAS were aware of the intended IRA operation remains with them. It is hardly likely that it was routine guarding of a particular area. Perhaps the scouting of the scene by the IRA on a previous day was noticed and the stake-out followed. Mr Jackson was married with four children and lived in the Birches, County Armagh. At his death his brother Maurice said – 'The whole family circle misses him terribly especially his widow Sadie and his four children whom he adored. Freddie was a pillar of our business, and it will be very difficult to fill the vacuum left by his death'. His brother Alan said, 'He was highly respected, even loved, within his trade, and it was a great comfort to us all that people from all walks of life, and from all classes and creeds attended his funeral. It is incredible the number of messages of comfort and sympathy we received, some from as far away as the continent; and from his old school teacher Mr Brian Thomas, now living in Wales'.

The Shooting of Antoin Mac Giolla Bríde and the Death of Kieran Fleming[120]

Frank Mac Bride was not well in 1972. He was a contractor by trade and was anxious to return to work. He lived with his wife Nora and six children Antoin (Tony), Damian, Oistin, Lughaidh, Marie and Patricia on the Woodstock Road, Willowfield, in east Belfast. His health improved. The family was happy that their father was getting well again and would soon commence contract work. Then two men called at the house in May 1972. Mrs Mac Bride, with Patricia then a baby, went to the door and asked what they wanted. They told her through the closed door that they were looking for work. She opened the door. Her husband had walked up the narrow hallway behind her. As soon as he appeared in the hallway, they opened fire hitting him 7 times, in the shoulder making him lunge forward, in the hand, and in the thighs. Young Antoin had come out of a side room and got hit in the leg. The front door was raised some steps high from the footpath and the attackers were down on the footpath. This level difference saved the lives of the Mac Brides. The aim meant to hit them in the trunk of the body. The attack, however, did ultimately bring about the death of Frank Mac Bride, fourteen months later.

A series of attacks preceded the May 1972 shooting. Marie's bedroom was attacked with a petrol bomb. A bomb was found at the back door attached to a five-gallon can of petrol; luckily it did not go off. Then came the shooting attack. That was enough; the family fled for safety to Newtownards; it was the wrong place to go to; they were intimidated out of their home and moved to Magherafelt, County Derry.

Tony Mac Bride (Antoin Mac Giolla Bríde), the 14-year-old shot by loyalists in 1972, was arrested in possession of a rifle in 1979. He served 18 months of his 3-year prison sentence. He was in the Irish Army from February 1975 to June 1979; few people knew him in Magherafelt; local police brought a detective from Strabane to identify him on his arrest. On the last Tuesday in July 1984 he was arrested by plain clothes detectives at Queen's Avenue when he was walking into the centre of Magherafelt. He had been at home over the weekend, as was his custom; he was 'semi on the run'; although he was not wanted on specific charges, he studiously avoided all British forces; on this occasion the detectives were standing at a telephone box; he brazenly walked on ignoring them but they blocked his path. He was taken to Castlereagh Interrogation Centre and held until the following Friday. He was threatened; the interrogators said they would release him and say he gave information, in order to destroy his credibility with republicans, or alternatively they would 'put him in the way of the SAS'. He was severely abused; on the other hand he was very uncooperative; he did not eat or drink or speak during the three days detention. When his mother phoned Castlereagh and complained that a solicitor had not been allowed in, the policeman replied, 'How could he ask for a solicitor when he hasn't opened his mouth since he came in?'

There had been other arrests. He and his brother Damian were arrested and detained in Castlereagh in April 1981. In September 1981 Damian was arrested in possession of a rifle and pistol; he served 2 years of a 4-year sentence. When Damian was arrested the RUC came looking for Tony; for two or three weeks they called at the house as many as 15 times, sometimes twice a day; Tony just kept out of their way until he found out why they had arrested Damian. He was arrested in the Republic in 1982 and did a spell on Spike Island for desertion from the Irish Army. Until his arrest in July 1984 he prudently avoided police and Army. He came back home most weekends, however, and did his turn as drum-major in Kennaugh flute band. He lived in Bundoran. In November 1984, the month before he was shot, he went on a speaking tour in Norway at the invitation of the Irish Solidarity

Group, Trondheim. He had been in touch with this particular group for about four years.

He was home about three weeks before the fatal incident; he came back to Magherafelt a while and then went to Bundoran. On Wednesday 28 November 1984 Tony was at home. He and his mother were members of Cuairteoirí le Muire (CLM), a voluntary organisation which raised funds to bring handicapped children on pilgrimage to Lourdes. The annual meeting of the society was to be held at the weekend in Newbridge, County Kildare. On Sunday morning his mother arrived home in Magherafelt at ten minutes to nine. Tony had not turned up at the meeting in Newbridge. At the meeting she had chatted with Fr Leahy about Tony who had been in Lourdes the previous June. She was talking to Fr Leahy until about 1 am; coming home she was still thinking about Tony and got a presentiment that he was dead. At home she turned on the 9 am news. It carried a terse report that a soldier and a civilian had been shot in County Fermanagh; although no name was given she knew immediately that it was Tony.

There were two versions as to what happened in the incident that led to the shooting of Antoin Mac Giolla Bríde, IRA volunteer, Lance Corporal Alastair Slater, SAS soldier and the drowning of Kieran Fleming, IRA volunteer.

Republican Version
Five IRA men were involved in the laying of a landmine to catch British security forces on the night of 1-2 December 1984. A blue Toyota van was hijacked in Pettigo village, County Donegal at about 9.30 pm on Saturday night, 1 December. One man remained in the house until 12.30 am when the party returned and collected him. The family was warned not to raise the alarm for one-and-a-half hours. Four of the IRA men were dressed in combat uniforms. Mac Giolla Bríde wasn't; he was wearing two pairs of trousers, the outer ones green, a black hooded anorak and army-type boots. There was freezing fog and poor visibility. The landmine was planted near Drumrush Lodge Restaurant.

A call was put through to the RUC that firebombs were planted at the restaurant which was on the Kesh-Beleek Road. It was confirmed by an RUC constable at the inquest on Antoin Mac Giolla Bríde that at 00.25 am he received as duty officer in the RUC station at Kesh a telephone call with a Northern Ireland cultured accent, a female voice, which said, 'Listen carefully, this is the Fermanagh Brigade of the IRA; there is a number of blast incendaries in the Drumrush Lodge, Kesh. The reason for this is that they serve the bastard security forces'.

The shooting took place on a link road which joined the Kesh-Pettigo Road and the Kesh-Beleek road. The Toyota van was parked along the link road. Mac Giolla Bríde was the driver. It was by chance he had been called

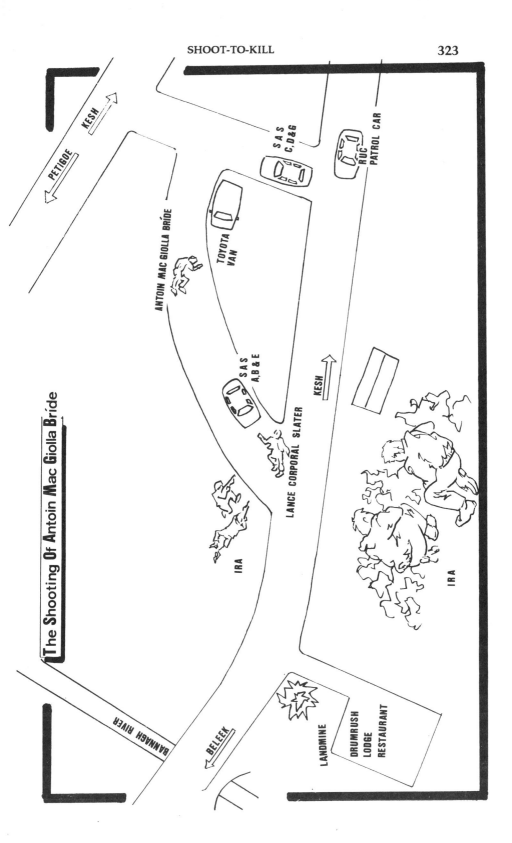

The Shooting Of Antoin Mac Giolla Bríde

in that night. The original driver backed out at the last minute; he had hurt his shoulder; none of the other IRA men could drive. This may account for Mac Giolla Bríde not being dressed in military uniform.

Two IRA men worked at the landmine. It consisted of kegs of explosives. It was placed in a culvert in the entrance to the driveway to the hotel. The command wire was run up a telegraph pole, then across the entrance to another telegraph pole, down the pole and then to a point some 300 yards up a hilly field. Two IRA on the Kesh side were positioned at this firing point. One of these was Kieran Fleming. Mac Giolla Bríde was at the van. He was equipped with a walkie-talkie. The van was parked on a piece of open ground at the side of the narrow road. There was no hedge and he had a view of the Kesh Road. He was not long there when an RUC patrol car came from the direction of Kesh. He signalled 'One' to the IRA men at the firing point. The RUC car passed the entrance to the hotel, made a U-turn further up the road, returned and drove into the hotel entrance. The IRA pressed the detonation but the bomb did not go off. Then the SAS in two cars came on the scene. One halted at the junction of the link road and the Kesh-Pettigo road. The other moved along the link road and spotted the van. Mac Giolla Bríde must have heard it coming and hid himself. According to the SAS statements they did not notice anybody in the van as they went by. The men at the mine heard the car coming and took cover in the nearby ditch. The SAS in the car sat for a while; the windows of their car were open. Then one of them got out and went round to the back of the car and radioed. Very shortly after that, the two IRA men in the ditch heard Tony coming walking up the road. They heard the SAS calling on him to halt. The SAS had sent a message by radio – 'We have located the van and have it under observation'. They called on Mac Giolla Bríde to stop and drop his gun. He is reputed to have replied, 'I'm not armed' and put his hands out. The SAS then approached him, one of them in front. They started questioning him. They asked, 'What are you doing? Who's "One"?' This latter question was interpreted as referring to Mac Giolla Bríde's radio message, an indication that they had monitored him. One then stepped forward and shot him in the left side. When he was shot he went down and then the two IRA volunteers opened up from the ditch. One was armed with a rifle and one with a shotgun. They were only about 10 feet from the nearest SAS men. They were so close they thought the SAS must have known they were there. This firing killed Lance Corporal Slater. The IRA men withdrew from the ditch. The SAS returned fire letting off guns in all directions. They sent up a flare; all of this happened instantaneously. The two IRA men kept moving until they got over the border.

The two IRA volunteers on the hill were within hearing distance but could not see on account of the fog. They heard Antoin being called on to halt. They could do nothing but wait. When the firing started and the flares went up they still waited. One of them attached the wires of the landmine and tried to detonate it but it didn't go off. One thought he heard Antoin shouting to blow the mine. They tried several times but failed. Kieran Fleming, it was said, was very cool and hard to ruffle. Finally they decided to move; just as they moved off they heard somebody screaming in pain. Then they heard another burst of gunfire about 15 minutes after the first shooting; this was one single burst of gunfire. There was no more shouting or crying out. They moved off and got as far as the Bannagh river. One of them entered the water to cross to the other side. When he got over he couldn't find Kieran Fleming. The river was only some 20 feet across but it was in flood and there were deep pools in it. Up or down from where they crossed, a mere 20 or 30 feet away, there was shallow water. Fleming was taken away in the flood.

SAS Version

The SAS version can be gleaned from their statements read out at the inquest of Antoin Mac Giolla Bríde.

Two SAS unmarked cars were patrolling the Kesh area of County Fermanagh at 23.30 hrs on the night of 1 December 1984. They were in plain clothes. Soldiers 'A', 'B' and 'E' were in one car and soldiers 'C', 'D', 'F' and 'G' were in the second. From information received they were on the look-out for a blue van of foreign make. At midnight 'A' says his car was instructed to drive past a suspect vehicle; the second car remained at the end of the link road. 'A' saw the parked van as they passed; as far as he could see there was nobody in it; it was stationary with no lights on and the driver's door was left slightly open. The driver turned at the end of the road and blocked it. He gave instructions to 'B' and 'E' (Slater) to get out of the car and take up positions by the side of the road. 'E' placed caltrops across the road to prevent vehicles driving past their position. After approximately 10 minutes 'B' heard someone walking down the road. 'A' switched off the radio and listened. They let the person walk to within 20 metres. 'B' shouted a warning and told the person to stand still and put up his hands; he said they were security forces. Mac Giolla Bríde said, 'It's O.K. It's only me'. 'A' got out of the vehicle and told him to stand still or he would fire. Mac Giolla Bríde then ran back up the road, jumped into a ditch and over a barbed wire fence. After 3 or 4 warnings 'A' fired a burst with his HK 53 rifle, firing to the right of the person running away. 'B' also fired. Mac Giolla Bríde then stopped but would not co-operate with instructions. 'B' then went forward to apprehend him. Mac Giolla Bríde came over the fence and was assisted on to the road. The SAS then placed him face down on the road. 'A' searched him while 'B' covered. He found no weapons or explosives. With the light of a flare he examined his clothing. He refused to answer any questions. 'B' and 'A' realised he was IRA. 'A' told him he was arresting him and he would be detained until the RUC came. He shouted at 'B' to bring forward the vehicle and the plasticuffs. 'B' did not answer and so he decided to bring him forward himself. When they arrived at the vehicle 'B' gave him ('A') his HK53 rifle and was looking for the plasticuffs. He noticed that 'E' (Lance Corporal Slater) was injured and lying on the road. He pointed this out to 'B'. At this stage Mac Giolla Bríde 'made a surge and attempted to try to get my rifle because I was holding both HK 53s. I dropped one on the road so that I could push him back. I fell to the ground, down the bank and the terrorist ran off and I thought he had picked up the spare rifle, as I could not see it. I told Soldier 'B' that the terrorist was armed and was escaping'. Both ran up the road in pursuit of him. 'Soldier 'B' fired several rounds and the terrorist fell to the ground. The terrorist then made a movement, tried to get up off the road and appeared as if he might be reaching for the weapon. At this I fired several shots at him as I feared he was going to open fire on me. When I fired these shots he slumped forward onto the road. I then went forward to check his condition. I lifted his shoulder, checked his pulse and looked into his eyes for any response. On examination I believed the terrorist was dead ... I could find no firearms on the body so I went back to the ditch where the struggle took place and I found the HK 53 there ...'

'B' adds little to 'A's' statement except to say that 'E' put up the flare when they wished to examine Mac Giolla Bríde's clothing. On the shooting of Mac Giolla Bríde when he was running away he says – 'He continued to run so I fired several shots at him with my 9 mm pistol. I was running as I did so. The terrorist appeared to stop and started to turn around. I believed he was going to open fire on me; I therefore fired several more rounds at him with my pistol. He then fell onto his face ...'

Soldier 'A's' account of Mac Giolla Bríde lunging forward to take his weapon bears a remarkable resemblance to the story of the SAS man who shot Peter Cleary in South Armagh. It is remarkable also that an unarmed man in the hands of the SAS should be able to escape twice! Is it possible that a highly-trained soldier would allow himself to cover a prisoner burdened with two weapons in his hands while 'B' went searching in a vehicle and 'E' lay injured? 'A' and 'B' include in their statements the familiar SAS sentences about their lives being in danger. The finishing-off of the victim as in other cases arises from a 'movement' of an injured man on the ground. It is also remarkable that neither 'A' nor 'B' heard the IRA shooting from the .303 rifle and the shotgun which killed 'E' (Slater). At least they do not mention it and they were quite close.

In a follow-up search of the area a small quantity of explosives was found in the blue Toyota van; nine beer kegs with approximately 900 lbs of explosives were found at the entrance to the road leading to Drumrush Lodge. A radio transistor and a pistol containing 6 rounds of ammunition were found at the wire fence where Mac Giolla Bríde had allegedly jumped into the field.

Fleming's companion finally made his way to safety over the border suffering severely from exposure. Kieran Fleming's body was found on Friday, 21 December 1984 in the Bannagh river.

Seamus Pius Clarke (28) of Old Town, Letterkenny, one of the Long Kesh (Maze) escapees of 1983, and Patrick Branley (34) were detained by Gardaí near Pettigo when they drove through a checkpoint a few hours after the shooting. The car had been hijacked earlier and the owner was still in the car. A Winchester rifle and 18 rounds of ammunition were found in it. Clarke was given an 18-months sentence and Branley a sentence of 3 years on the same charge.

There were vicious scuffles at the funeral of Antoin Mac Giolla Bríde, 4 December 1984, when the RUC, wielding batons, tried to remove a tricolour from the coffin on the outskirts of the little estate where the Mac Brides lived in Magherafelt. On Kieran Fleming, *An Phoblacht*, 3 January 1985, commented: 'Kieran Fleming (26), from Gobnascale in Derry's Waterside, died on active service on December 2nd 1984, just four days before his cousin William Fleming, also from Derry, was gunned down by SAS terrorists ... he was first arrested in August 1976 when he was 18 years old. He was sentenced in May 1977 to be imprisoned indefinitely under the 'Secretary of State's pleasure'. After six years in the H-Blocks, Kieran Fleming escaped with 37 of his comrades in September 1983. He returned to active service ...'

The autopsy on Antoin Mac Giolla Bríde showed that he had been hit by 9 and probably 10 bullets. One entrance hole was on the left flank 4 cm above the level of the umbilicus and 15 cm to the left of the midline in front. The interpretation of Antoin's family is that this was the first wounding of Antoin. The other 7 entrance wounds run in a line down the left side of his body from the back of his neck to his thigh, giving the impression of a directed burst of automatic fire on him as he lay on the ground. As his clothing was being removed in the mortuary, a copper-jacketed bullet with a flattened nose fell on to the mortuary floor. The family interpret that as a shot that went through his body while he lay on the ground and flattened against the hard road. The deceased had much bruising and laceration to the face including a gaping laceration measuring $3^1/2$ cm transversely by $1^1/2$ cm extending from the outer opening of the left ear. His family interpret these wounds as a sign of ill-treatment. He had also a gunshot wound to the hand.

About 30 people were injured during clashes between mourners and RUC at Kieran Fleming's funeral on 23 December 1984. Plastic bullets were fired by the RUC; BBC radio journalist Peter Somerville was struck in the face by one, sustaining a fractured jaw and facial and mouth injuries. It took almost three hours to complete the funeral from Fleming's home in the Waterside to the cemetery at Creggan. When the funeral turned into the

Bogside three IRA volunteers wearing uniforms and masks fired three volleys from handguns as British Army helicopters flew overhead.

Mystery remains as to why Antoin Mac Giolla Bríde walked up the road. Did he mistake the SAS car in the fog for the IRA scout car which was similar? Did he leave the pistol and radio behind deliberately and go up the road as an unarmed man to explore, placing confidence in himself to bluff his way? It will remain a mystery.

At the inquest, following representations by the family of the deceased, the coroner, Mr Rainey Hanna, agreed to list Antoin Mac Giolla Bríde's occupation as 'volunteer in the Irish Republican Army'.

The Shooting Of Daniel Doherty And William Fleming[121]

Daniel Doherty and William Fleming were committed IRA men. Both had joined Fianna Éireann when they were 14 years of age and later moved into the IRA. Doherty was only 18 months released from Portlaoise Prison, where he had served four years for IRA membership and possession of explosives, when he was shot dead. His sister Kay had served a term in Armagh Prison. She was visiting another brother, John, in Long Kesh on 6 December 1984 the day Danny and Willie Fleming were killed by the SAS. Doherty (23) was married; he and his wife Julie had an infant son Kevin-Barry; he was a joiner by trade and worked on the Derry docks. When he came out of Portlaoise, Doherty joined the IRA again; he believed in it; he thought that a new Ireland should be brought about quickly for a succeeding generation; his family were aware that this was his philosophy.

Willie Fleming (19) was also a keen IRA man; his brothers Gary and Paul were in prison. His cousin Kieran, an escapee from Long Kesh (Maze) in September 1983, had been missing (feared drowned) from the night of 1-2 December after fleeing from the SAS. Willie was unmarried and lived in Gobnascale in the Waterside, Derry. He worked for a while as a barman in the Rocking Chair Bar but had been out of work for a few months at the time of the shooting. From a young age he was continually harassed by the RUC and British Army; at Easter 1984 he spent a week in Hydebank Detention Centre, Belfast, for refusing to pay fines when found guilty of damaging a police car.

The two men were ambushed and shot dead by a party of five heavily-armed SAS men in plain clothes at 8 am on 6 December 1984 in the grounds of Gransha Psychiatric Hospital which also houses the administration headquarters of the Western Health and Social Services Board; the hospital is about four miles from the city centre. Shift changes took place in the hospital around 8 am and it may be that the two men, who were on active service for the IRA, had targeted an off-duty member of the UDR. There had been previous incidents in the vicinity. On 27 March 1984 a military policeman, Sergeant David Ross (31), was killed in a booby trap explosion near the hospital entrance and in 1980 a 49-year-old part-time UDR man was seriously injured after being shot when he arrived for work. On this occasion it would seem that the British Army had previous knowledge of the IRA mission. The major who briefed the SAS unit, 'F', said that they were on duty at the hospital two weeks before 6 December but that he had no specific information. The SAS team set up an ambush. Neither the RUC nor the hospital authorities were informed of their presence. The RUC did not arrive on the scene until after the shooting.

One is dependent on the SAS statements for a sequence of events but so unconvincing was their testimony at the inquest on 9 December 1986 that the jury took the unprecedented step of condemning them. Usually an inquest verdict is general and non-judgmental. In the case of the shooting dead of the two IRA men the jury said that they found, under the circumstances, that the five-man army unit should have tried to arrest them or at least have informed the RUC earlier and their lives might have been saved.

At the inquest Mr Brendan Kearney, solicitor, representing the families of the two men, said it was accepted that both were armed and were not in the hospital grounds for a lawful purpose, but the question remained whether it was necessary to kill them. In all 59 shots were fired by three SAS soldiers, 'A' 'B' and 'C'. None of these appeared at the inquest taking advantage of legalities to avoid cross-examination. Soldier 'F', a major, who was in charge of the operation, admitted that with hindsight two people might not have been dead if the RUC had been informed; however he said that was not a cause of worry to him; 'We trouble the police as necessary'.

An RUC detective, as has been the custom, read out the statements of the SAS who were absent. Soldier 'A' said he was on plain clothes duty alone in an unmarked car in the area of the Maydown roundabout. He received a radio message that there was a motor-cycle with a pillion passenger acting suspiciously in the area of Gransha hospital. Ten minutes later he overheard a second message to the effect that the motor-cycle had entered a road leading into the hospital. He drove to the main entrance of the hospital but knew that the motor-cycle had entered by another road. Daylight was breaking and he was driving with headlights; he saw the motor-cycle coming towards him not showing a front light; two people wearing crash helmets were on the motor cycle. He claims that the pillion rider had a handgun in his right hand. He stopped his car; his window was down; he shouted, 'Stop'; the motor-cycle accelerated and the pillion passenger 'raised the handgun and pointed it towards me...I believed at that time that he was going to fire at me through the windscreen. To save my life, I decided to ram the motor-cycle and I pulled my car across the roadway striking the motor-cycle'. He radioed contact; the motor-cycle had disappeared. 'I saw a man on the ground pointing a gun in my direction. I grabbed my gun, jumped out of the car and, thinking he was about to open fire at me, I fired 3 rounds at him...I glanced to my right and identified Soldier 'B'... I immediately noticed the gunman raising himself and pointing his gun towards me. I shouted to Soldier 'B', "Look out, he's still armed". At the same time I fired another 3 shots at the gunman. I realised that Soldier 'B' must have been firing at the same time because I could see strike marks in the area of the gunman...I saw the gunman slump to the ground... I removed the gun from the gunman's hand and placed it in a bag which was lying beside the gunman...'

Soldier 'B' says that he and Soldier 'C' were in plain clothes on foot patrol in the area of Gransha hospital at 7.45 am. He saw the motor-cycle acting suspiciously; he took his car from the grounds of the hospital and picked up 'C' at the main entrance; he then received a radio message that the motor-cycle was in the grounds en route to the main entrance; Soldier 'A' passed him in his car and he followed him; he saw 'A' colliding with the motor-cycle and saw the pillion passenger fall off; he received the 'contact radio-message from 'A' and knew that 'A's life was in danger' and 'A' was 'about to be involved in a gun battle'; he and 'C' got out of the car; he heard gunfire, 'The motor-cycle was coming towards me. I believed the motor-cyclist had been involved in a shooting with Soldier 'A'. I had already drawn my pistol and started to fire at the motor-cyclist as he came at me because I feared for my life. I fired several shots but the motor-cyclist continued towards me. I jumped clear...I could hear Soldier 'C' firing at the motor-cyclist and I then directed gunfire at a second man who I believed was engaging Soldier 'A' in a gun battle. I fired a total of 11 shots from my 9 mm Browning pistol at the motor-cyclist and the second gunman... knowing that I was running out of ammunition I grabbed my support weapon from the car and carried on engaging the second gunman...As I was moving forward towards Soldier 'A' I stopped firing and seconds later Soldier 'A' shouted to me that the gunman was still armed and warned me to watch out. I fired several more shots at the gunman until he stopped moving... the second weapon I used was a HK 53'.

Soldier 'C' gives a similar statement, using similar language, 'under attack', repetitive use of 'gunman', 'life in danger'. He said – 'I assumed that Soldier 'A' was under attack from the motor-cyclist and passenger... By this time the motor-cyclist was nearly upon us... Thinking that my own life and that of Soldier 'B' was in immediate danger, I opened fire at the motor-cycle. I was not sure at that time whether there was one or two persons on the motor-cycle. I was firing automatic with my MP 5K sub-machine-gun. I fired a burst. The motor-cycle kept on accelerating towards me and I was forced to jump to my left to avoid being run down. I kept on firing as the motor-cyclist was adjacent to me and just slightly past me. I couldn't be sure if I was striking him or not. Momentarily I lost my balance, stopped firing, spun round and continued firing again, running after the motor-cycle as I did so. I would probably have run a short distance before I started firing again. I continued to fire until the motor-cycle crashed near to a lamp post... When the rider came off... I dropped my MP 5K, drew my pistol and approached the now motionless body...from its rear, pulled the body which was lying on its left side back towards me and discovered that the person concerned appeared to be dead. I noticed a pistol in the area of his lap... During the engagement I fired a total of 30 rounds from my magazine...'

A Detective Chief Inspector stated at the inquest that he believed a total of 59 rounds was fired, 6 by Soldier 'A', 23 by Soldier 'B' and 30 by Soldier 'C'. A Senior Principal Scientific Officer at the Northern Ireland Forensic Science Laboratory said in his statement :-'From my observation of the scene, the motor-cycle and the car and, considering the injuries to the deceased, Paul [William] Fleming, I believe that the motor-cycle was being driven by Doherty, with Fleming on the pillion seat and that the cycle was travelling along Gransha Park in the direction of Clooney Road, when the right leg of the pillion passenger was struck by the Fiat car, causing the passenger to fall off. It is also clear that the cycle continued along the Gransha Park and that shots were directed towards it, at least two striking the cycle, and several others striking the rider. The cycle had then gone out of control and mounted the kerb, when the rider had come off...My examination indicates that Fleming was knocked off the cycle and was shot at and struck from two positions by two firearms. The cycle, ridden by Doherty, continued along the road and was probably fired at as it approached a second firing-position with a further two firearms and as it passed and drove away from this position. I believe the rider was struck by gunfire as he was driving away from this firing-position and that the cycle crashed. My examination also indicates that a further 6 shots were fired at Doherty whilst he was on the ground'.

The Police Surgeon reported, 'On arrival at 08.40 hours, I found the bodies of two adult males lying in the roadway; the first body was lying on the grass close to the carriageway leading to the Nurses' Home. He had injuries to the left upper arm and was bleeding from the area of the left ear...The second body was lying on the opposite side of the roadway, about 50 metres further into the hospital grounds. This man had wounds to the head and face and had a compound fracture of the left thigh bone'.

The autopsy on William Fleming showed that he had been struck by at least 4 bullets and numerous bullet fragments. One bullet had entered the left cheek and had passed up to lodge in the left temple. Three bullets and numerous fragments struck the trunk and lodged on the back causing internal lacerations, the combined effect of which would have caused rapid death. Besides the gunshot wound to the head, there were 56 gunshot wounds to the trunk and two gunshot wounds to his left upper limb.

Two bullets struck Daniel Doherty on the right side of the head, one lodging inside the skull and the other exiting on the left cheek. 12 bullets struck the back of the trunk causing rapid death. He had been struck by 19 bullets which had come from behind or to the right. Counting entrance and exit wounds, he had 3 gunshot wounds to the head, 21 to the trunk, 6 to the right upper limb and 6 to the left lower limb.

Although it was recognised that the two IRA men were probably on a mission to murder one of the armed forces, the Catholic public reacted strongly to the manner of the killing of William Fleming and Daniel Doherty. Their offence did not deserve 'capital punishment'. Nationalists are convinced that there is a Shoot-to-Kill policy backed and protected by the state. The enormity of the wounds inflicted on the men and the continous firing shocked them; such odds were stacked against the cyclists that it was incredible that they could not have been captured. Even after reading the accounts of the SAS, one wonders how they could not have captured them alive after Fleming was knocked off the cycle and it careered out of control. Had Fleming a gun in his hand? If he had did not Soldier 'A' break all the rules of a scene of a crime situation (and he was a member of security forces who should have known) by 'removing the gun from the gunman's hand and placing it in a bag'. This holdall contained a mask, a pair of gloves, five rounds of ammunition. Was it not more likely that the gun was also in the bag? Would Fleming, riding pillion, expose himself to detection by carrying his gun openly? Is it not more likely that he intended taking the gun out of the bag later when he had donned the mask and prepared for whatever action he was bound on?

Such questions were asked before the funerals. Bishop Edward Daly said, 'Do members of the Army here have the right to use more force than appears necessary when a crime is being committed or when it is suspected that a crime is about to be committed?' He protested against the glee with which the summary deaths had been received by some individuals, 'Every violent death, whoever the victim might be, lessens all of us and should bring sadness and sorrow rather than rejoicing'. Mr John Hume, MP called in the House of Commons for an emergency British Government statement but failed. He said the affair raised the fundamental question whether the authorities in Northern Ireland had abandoned the rule of law as the approach to the problem and whether there was a war situation. Derry City Council sent a telegram to the Republic's Minister for Foreign Affairs, Mr Peter Barry, asking him to take up the matter with the British Government. The *Irish Press* summed up the problem in its editorial, 'The security forces, having received information that a murder was planned, would naturally be expected to stop it. Had the circumstances arisen in Britain, the police would have lain in wait and attempted to make an arrest. But in Northern Ireland, under British rule, it was the Army who set the ambush – and it was an ambush, nothing else. No attempt at arrest was made. The men were shot dead without any chance of surrender'. Mr Neil Kinnock, leader of the British Labour Party, also called for an enquiry into the circumstances of the shooting at a press conference in Northern Ireland.

The IRA made their own protest. William Fleming's funeral from the Waterside joined up with that of Daniel Doherty's of Creggan. It was the largest funeral in Derry since that of hunger-striker Patsy O'Hara. The coffins were carried through the streets draped with tricolours. Four masked IRA men in full uniform fired volleys of shots over the coffins. More than three thousand people followed the cortège. In a graveside oration, Mr Martin McGuinness, Sinn Féin Derry Assemblyman, said that only the freedom fighters of the IRA could bring Britain to the negotiation table. At a Liam Mellows commemoration in Wexford the Sinn Féin president, Mr Gerry Adams, referring to the shooting said, 'These actions by the British have shown that they are not interested in their own discredited judicial system. They do not want to take prisoners; they only want dead bodies'. On 11 December 1984 the Secretary of State, Mr Douglas Hurd, was in Armagh to open an extension of a local college. The strong feelings of the nationalist people were put to him about the 'Shoot-to-Kill policy'. He merely stressed that security policy, along with the policy of the use of reasonable force and of law, remained unchanged.

Shoot-to-Kill in Strabane[122]

At 4.50 on the morning of 23 February 1985, three IRA men from Strabane, Charles Breslin (20) of Innisfree Gardens, and two brothers Michael Devine (22) and David Devine (16) of Coutrai Park, were shot dead when they walked into a trap set by the RUC and SAS. The stake-out was jointly planned by the two forces. The shooting was executed by the SAS. The men were shot in a high sloping field to the left of the Plumbridge Road as one leaves Strabane from Fountain Street in the Head-of-the-Town district of Strabane. A line of houses in the Springhill estate skirts the sloping edge of one side of the field. There are thick hawthorn bushes round the perimeter and the hedge forms the horizon of the top of the field. To the right of the Plumbridge Road is Innisfree Gardens. Strabane is usually named as the worst example of unemployment in western Europe. Unemployment is usually 40 per cent and half the men have no work. The one brightness was the self-help schemes of Fr Anthony Mulvey, who was also widely known for his criticism of the IRA.

For two weeks prior to 23 February, the RUC were aware of a possible IRA attack on a police land-rover. An RUC detective inspector at the inquest on the three men revealed that it was proposed to attack the land-rover with grenades fired from a launcher and then shoot any police survivors as they got out of the vehicle. Republican sources indicate that the target was a police car. On Monday, 7 October 1985 the IRA executed Damian McCrory, saying that he had confessed to working as an informer for 13 months and setting up the three murdered men. He was shot twice in the head. The murder brought condemnation from the local priests and there was a wave of sympathy for the 20-year-old youth who was known to be backward in intelligence. He was also known to hero-worship Charles Breslin. It would seem foolish that the IRA would allow the youth to be privy to the whereabouts of their arms cache. Republicans, on the other hand, felt that the RUC should not recruit vulnerable people like Damian McCrory. At the inquest on the three IRA men, Detective Sergeant Lawrence Cheshire said that he knew nothing of a tip-off which led to the British Army operation. He denied that he knew Damian McCrory. Under questioning at the inquest, Soldier 'E' said he had known the Breslin house for some months. He disclosed that there had been a photograph of Charles Breslin on a notice-board at Ebrington Barracks.

Mr William Devine, father of the Devine brothers, last saw Michael at the family home between 5 and 6 pm on 22 February; he saw David at tea-time. There were visitors in the Devine home; a daughter and her two children were staying and, as Michael had been sleeping on a camp-bed in the kitchen, not much notice was taken when he did not return. It was not unusual for him to stay with friends. David would often stay out late but he always phoned. That night he did not phone. Joseph Breslin, father of Charles, last saw his son alive at 10.10 pm on 22 February. The Breslins are staunch republicans although they were not aware that Charles was in the IRA. William Devine was opposed to the IRA. He was an ex-service man, having served in the British Navy.

There were five IRA men in the team which set out to ambush the RUC car. Besides Breslin and the Devines, there were Declan John Crossan (22) from Ballycolman estate, Strabane, and another. Crossan was later sentenced to 20 years imprisonment for conspiring to murder police at Fountain Street on the morning of 23 February. The attack was apparently scheduled for 4 am. IRA intelligence indicated that a police car had to come a certain way at a certain time. It did not come. The attack was called off. On looking back, one would imagine that the five should have been suspicious. They grouped together at the spot where Fountain Street runs into the Plumbridge Road. They split up, the Devines and Breslin moving into the field. They were carrying the weapons and had other material in a hold-all. They were heading for the arms dump situated about half-a-mile from Strabane beyond Springhill. Obviously the field provided some cover. They had only gone about twenty yards into the field when they were caught in heavy fire from a short distance of five or six yards. They were shot from behind and received multiple injuries. The two men on the road

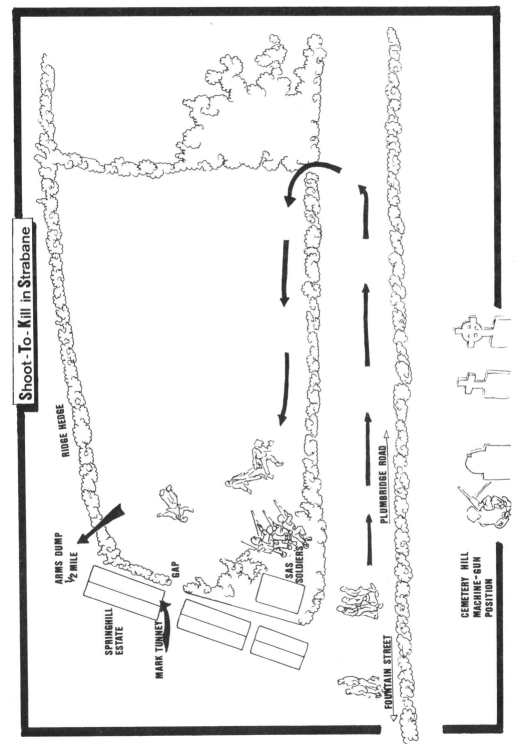

Shoot-To-Kill in Strabane

RIDGE HEDGE

ARMS DUMP
½ MILE

GAP

SPRINGHILL
ESTATE

MARK TUNNEY

SAS
SOLDIERS

PLUMBRIDGE ROAD

FOUNTAIN STREET

CEMETERY HILL
MACHINE-GUN
POSITION

had just turned off in the opposite direction. They were unarmed and made their escape.

There is a marked difference between the account of the shooting that can be gleaned from the evidence of local residents together with the arguments put forward by the solicitors of the deceased at the inquest and the official statements of the RUC and the soldiers of the British Army.

The 'local' account would seem to be as follows. Plumbridge Road lies in a narrow valley between the sloping field and another such field on the side where the men were shot and a hill opposite, some 150 yards distant, also sloping, on which is the cemetery. The cemetery hill commands a clear view of the road and the fields opposite. There are a few houses on the cemetery side of the Plumbridge Road but at some distance from the edge of the town and they do not block the view of the open field. Three SAS men, designated 'A', 'B' and 'C' at the inquest, were in hiding in the bushes in the Springhill-estate side of the open field. As they fired at the men from close range a general purpose machine-gun opened up a raking fire on the open field from the cemetery hill; flares went up; the tracer bullets from the machine-gun were distinguishable in sound and red flashes lit the sky. Soldiers were also stationed behind the 'horizon' hedge at the top of the field, a good number, perhaps as many as twenty. They, too, opened fire. The firing on the open field would obviously cut down anybody who made a run for it or would serve the purpose of driving anyone who entered the field into a corner. There is a theory that one of the IRA men had got some distance from the rest. He cried out for mercy but was shot down. All the witnesses describe two bursts of gunfire followed by single shots. The single shots were fired from short range. All the men were shot in the head. The IRA man who had made some distance was then dragged down the field and thrown alongside the other two at the bottom of the field. There was no warning or call to surrender. None of the IRA men returned fire.

Before 5 am Gerry Stevenson was wakened by his four-year-old son crying. His house is in Casement Place. He tended to the child and heard shooting. He looked out of his window facing the field and saw a soldier below on the street firing repeatedly with a rifle into the field. The area was lit up with red flashes. 'There were also tracer bullets coming from behind my house, which would have been from the direction of the cemetery, into the field. The soldier below emptied his magazine and reloaded. At one time he turned around and looking up at the houses shouted, "Get in or I'll fucking blow your head off". He was very agitated. When the shooting stopped, the SAS immediately took off and were replaced by others. From what I can work out, the volunteers would have been under observation all the time. I heard no warning or call to surrender. It would have been so easy to take them alive.'

Mark Tunney was in training for break dancing and had stayed up during the night practising. He looked out the window in Springhill Park. He saw soldiers taking up positions, running along the hedge and firing. He heard gunfire from both the top and the bottom of the field. It was clear to him that the open field was completely surrounded by soldiers. 'I could hear one of the lads shouting but with the gunfire I couldn't make out what they were saying. It sounded something like "Any chance, any chance".'

The shooting woke other people. Chris Brennan of Fountain Terrace says, 'First there was about five minutes of constant shooting, then pause, and I could hear cars reversing fast up the road. I heard somebody shouting, "Don't shoot", not loud, as if the person were wounded or already shot. Then there was a long burst of fire followed by three single shots'.

Elaine McNicholl from Springhill Park heard one of the soldiers between bursts of gunfire shouting, 'He's up here', and also one of the volunteers crying something like 'Don't shoot, don't shoot. I am wounded'. She saw a light in the graveyard and says she saw a red light high in the sky which she thinks was a helicopter. Her mother Margaret saw blue flares and heard somebody shouting about lights.

The Breslins in nearby Innisfree Gardens also heard the two bursts of gunfire and the three single shots.

From their statements and answers in cross examination at the inquest it is possible to cull details of the British Army/RUC version of the shooting. It is clear that information had been received regarding IRA activity in the Head-of-the-Town area two weeks before the planned IRA attack. SAS soldiers (though the fact that they were SAS is not officially admitted) carried out surveillance during that two weeks. A meeting took place in Ebrington Barracks before midnight on the night of 22 February when the SAS group was briefed for at least an hour by their major. It is not clear whether the major took part in the attack. The official version would seem to deny that he did. The major gave instructions that night on the Head-of-the-Town area. The patrol's task officially was to identify potential IRA men, abort any possible attack and apprehend if possible any suspects. The IRA retrospectively speak of a planned attack on an RUC land-rover. The group of six SAS soldiers left Ebrington between 10 and 11 pm. Soldiers 'A', 'B' and 'C' travelled to Strabane in unmarked cars and wore civilian clothes over their uniforms. They removed the clothing before they commenced their patrol. The major is identified as soldier 'G'. Soldiers 'D' and 'E' travelled in an unmarked car separately from the others. They both went to Strabane RUC Station where they were to liaise with the RUC district mobile support unit (DMSU) and act as a quick reaction force (QRF). They were in touch with 'A', 'B' and 'C' by radio and were to act immediately as a reinforcement on getting a 'Contact' signal. They were also dressed in civilian clothes but on arrival at Strabane RUC Station were provided with RUC waterproof jackets 'for ease of identification'. Soldier 'F' travelled alone in civilian clothes to Strabane and continued duty surveillance in an unmarked military vehicle at the 'Head-of-the-Town'. At the inquest he said he did not know why he was in civilian dress. When asked what roads he had patrolled, he said he could not recall the villages he had passed through.

Soldiers 'A', 'B' and 'C' were the soldiers who actually ambushed the IRA men from close quarters. They did not appear at the inquest. Their statements were read out by two detectives. In their statements they said they had been previously on patrol in the Head-of-the-Town for two weeks. They made a temporary stop in some bushes at the back of a house in the Plumbridge Road. 'A' said, 'We were about to move off from our position in the bushes when I saw three men with rifles walking in the field about 5 or 6 metres from our position. They were walking from my right in the direction of Springhill Park. On seeing the gunmen I immediately alerted my colleagues whom I refer to as Soldiers 'B' and 'C'. I think I said to my colleagues "Look out" or "Watch out". As I spoke to my colleagues, the gunmen obviously heard me as I saw two of the gunmen pull down previously positioned balaclavas which they were wearing. One of the three gunmen had the balaclava he was wearing pulled down over his face. All three gunmen swung their rifles towards us. I knew then we were in a contact situation and that the lives of myself and my colleagues were in immediate danger. I immediately engaged the gunmen with automatic fire and on doing so soldiers 'B' and 'C' also engaged the gunmen. I was firing with my HK53 rifle, serial number C111011. After my initial burst of 25 rounds, I fell back down the slope and into the back-garden of the house I have earlier described. When I opened fire, I was in the kneeling position at the edge of the bushes and exposed to the gunmen. Whilst in the back-garden of the house, I radioed my base and informed them that I had a contact situation. There was still firing as I was falling down the slope. After the radio transmission, I scrambled back up the slope with the assistance of soldier 'C'. All three of us were taking cover behind the bank out of view of the gunmen. The gunmen were shouting "Where are they?" or words to that effect. I fired a number of short bursts in the direction of the gunmen who were then lying on the ground. I think my colleagues were firing at the same time. After each burst, I took cover immediately behind the bank. The reason for taking cover after each burst I fired, was because I felt that my life and that of my colleagues were still in immediate danger. I then had a stoppage with my rifle. I just dropped my rifle and then drew my pistol, a 9 mm Browning, serial number BL79A24534. I fired a further seven rounds from my pistol in a similar manner towards the gunmen. I think that we all stopped shooting at the same time as we considered that the gunmen were no further threat to us. At this point in time, I was aware that QRF had arrived and were on the road immediately below our position. Shortly after the arrival of the QRF, I heard a number of shots coming from the direction of the roadway. I called for some assistance from the QRF and Soldier 'D' and a number of RUC officers came to our position. On their arrival I approached the three gunmen who were lying close together. I removed an SLR rifle which was lying close to one of the gunmen. He was the one lying closest to the hedge. I threw the rifle a short distance away from the body and to the right of the body. The gunman in the centre was lying face down. I turned him over. I went to the third gunman and turned him over as he was lying face downwards. All three gunmen appeared to be dead. I noticed a small hold-all which was zipped up. It was lying in the field to the left of the bodies. I opened it to reveal the contents and I saw a weapon magazine and two rocket-type projectiles. I handed the scene over to the RUC Officers present and then my colleagues and I left the area. The light was sufficient at the time of the contact for me to see clearly the gunmen and their weapons as I was only a short distance from them'.

'B' and 'C' gave similar statements, both emphasising that they thought their lives were in danger. 'B' said, 'All three gunmen brought their weapons to bear on us; I have no doubt by their actions that they were bringing their rifles up to shoot us'. 'C' said, 'All three looked in our direction...all three together brought rifles up into the aim at us'.

In Strabane Police Station 'D' and 'E' had settled into an empty room and listened in to the radio they had set up. Then came two quick messages of 'Contact'. They rushed down the stairs. Outside the station were two armoured RUC Cortina cars. They got into separate cars. There were three RUC men in each. 'D' gave instructions to go to the Head-of-the-Town. They arrived at the scene of the shooting within four minutes of the radio message that a contact had been made. 'D' heard shooting as he arrived. This indicates prolonged shooting for at least four minutes. He heard someone shout, 'Shoot out the street lights'. He fired two five-round bursts of tracer bullets from his HK rifle but missed the lights. The three-man patrol of 'A', 'B' and 'C' was located to the rear and above 36 Fountain Street. The policemen were ordered to hold fire. Then came the alleged incident with a civilian named Kelly from Strabane who accidentally drove into the scene in a red Fiesta car. Sergeant Stephen Pearson of the DMSU said that when he arrived he heard shooting coming from the field. He saw the red Ford Fiesta coming towards him and soldier 'E' shouted at him to stop it. He signalled the car to stop and the driver got out shouting 'Don't shoot, Don't shoot'. He searched the man as he lay on the ground and he said his name was Kelly from Plumbridge. He returned to his cover and gave instruction for the man to be released.

Soldier 'F' said that he heard the 'Contact' message from Soldier 'A' about 4.53 am. He drove immediately to the area and *en route* heard another 'Contact' from Soldier 'B'. He drove down Plumbridge Road towards

Strabane and parked his vehicle on the country side of the Community Centre. A short time later he heard soldier 'A' shout at him to bring his cutters to a gate. He brought bolt cutters to a gate and saw Soldier 'E' trying to gain entry into a house in Fountain Street. He assisted him with an axe. 'E' broke panes of glass to enter. The house belonged to two elderly brothers called Dunne. One of them, who had walked round the side of the house, was ordered to lie on the ground and the second, who was inside the house, was told to do likewise while the house was searched. No one was found. When 'A', 'B' and 'C' left the area immediately after the shooting, Soldier 'F' also went to Strabane RUC Station .

At the inquest into the deaths of the three men in Strabane on Tuesday 3 February 1987, Mr Frank Collins, solicitor, acted for the Devine family and Mr John Fahy, solicitor, acted for the Breslin family. The inquest attracted wide press coverage. The solicitors in persistent cross-questioning queried what they thought were restrictions on the procedures and rights of questioning, queried the thoroughness of the investigation into the deaths by the RUC, and emphasised the handicap of finding out the truth of the nature of the men's deaths since the principal witnesses , Soldiers 'A', 'B' and 'C', were not compelled to attend. There was tension when observers and relatives occasionally interrupted the proceedings and exception was taken to the conduct of the RUC towards relatives and solicitors. The solicitors withdrew from the inquest on the 15th day. One of the solicitors alleged that some of the jurors had left the courtroom during the proceedings without the coroner's permission. The solicitor withdrew because he disputed the decision of the coroner to further adjourn the proceedings until 22 April. He did not feel this adjournment was in the interest of justice. Many of the inquests involving killings by the SAS were summary affairs and, in fact, there were occasions when relatives were not even represented by solicitors. In this case the public felt that the efforts of the two solicitors were the only means of making some headway in finding out what really happened and seeking some redress by eliciting the truth.

At the inquest, the State Pathologist, Dr Thomas Marshall, revealed that Michael Devine had been hit at least 28 times, Charles Breslin had been hit by at least 13 bullets and David Devine was hit by 5 bullets. He described Michael Devine's wounds as a bizarre series of wounds which almost defeated interpretation; a lot of his wounds were sustained as he lay on the ground; death was due to bullet wounds in the head, trunk and limbs; one of the bullets went through the bridge of his nose. Charles Breslin's head-wound was caused by a bullet from a high velocity rifle which hit him as he turned away; his internal injuries were severe; death was due to bullet wounds to the head and trunk. David Devine's head-wound had been caused by a bullet from a high velocity rifle fired from above, as he lay on the ground or as he fell forward. The pathologist could not comment on the range but believed the bullets would not have been fired under two feet. In cross-examining the major, Mr Collins pointed out that David Devine had been shot in both the left and right arms while he had been standing up; he suggested that if someone was injured in such a manner he would not be capable of holding a weapon in his hand.

Soldiers 'A', 'B' and 'C', according to their statements fired a total of 117 rounds. Soldier 'A' fired a total of 53 rounds, 46 rounds of 5.56 from his HK 53 rifle and 7 rounds of 9mm from his Browning pistol. Soldier 'B' fired 45 rounds of 5.56 from his HK 53 rifle; he did not use his pistol. Soldier 'C' says he fired 19 rounds of 5.56 mm. Soldier 'D' said he fired two five-round bursts from his HK rifle in attempting to shoot out street lights. This would make a total of 127 rounds officially fired. 83 spent bullet cases were recovered from the scene. Constable Robert McCullagh from the RUC Mapping Section said that the three bodies were in close proximity to one another. Two of the men were virtually touching one another and the third body was less than two feet away. He outlined the position of the 83 bullet cases. 20 of them were 11 feet away from the nearest body and 9 were virtually touching one of the bodies and spread over a diameter of 5 feet 6 inches. 3 of the cases were also very close to one of the bodies and spread over an area of 3 feet 9 inches. 15 of the spent cases were some 4 feet from the nearest body and over a space of 12 feet by 8 feet. 8 were found on the road at Fountain Street. He said that spent cases were scattered over quite a large area, the furtherest being 30 feet from the nearest body and the nearest 5 feet 6 inches. Some were found in undergrowth behind a hedge. Mr Collins commented that the bullets were fired in very close proximity.

What happened the other cases of rounds admitted fired? A senior forensic scientist attached to the Northern Ireland Forensic Science Laboratory said that he did not realise that 42 spent cases had not been located. He had been satisfied with his initial search when 83 or 84 spent cases were found but when he read the soldiers' statements later it appeared more rounds had been fired. He realised that 42 spent cases had not been located. He said at the inquest that on 27 February, four days after the shooting, he rang asking for permission to return. The officer, who said he would ring him back the next day, refused the request. This was for 'operational reasons' and because locals had entered the scene after the RUC had pulled out. The scientist admitted he had not carried out an extensive search of the bank because it would have taken several days and extra manpower. He said he relied on the police to search the ground outside the area taped off by the police. From cases found in the area of the hedge and strike marks on the bank, it was apparent that shots could have come from the hedge. He said he had heard no mention of firing from the cemetery. The witness was able to match five bullets taken from Michael Devine's body to Soldier 'A's gun.

It emerged from the inquest that two of the IRA men were wearing jeans and Parka-type jackets. The third was wearing a boiler suit. All three were wearing gloves and had masks. Two more pairs of gloves were found in the hold-all beside the bodies and suggested that two more people were involved.

The three rifles found at the scene were a .223 FNC and a 7.6 FN, both Belgian-made, and a .223 Mini Ruger. In a statement the RUC said that ballistic tests proved that they were used in four separate attempted murders; the Ruger rifle was used, the statement said, in the murder of UDR man Robert Gregory Elliott at Castlederg on 2 January 1984. A forensic witness at the inquest said that the rifles all had bullets in their breeches; two had safety catches on. This implied that the men had not anticipated being fired on. The bodies lay between 15 and 20 feet from a wire fence. Two of the three bodies had been rolled over. The two grenade launchers found in the hold-all were hand-held and could be mounted on the shoulder; they had an armour-piercing capacity. There were also two grenade projectiles, two modified 12-bore Winchester cartridges, a loaded magazine probably for a rifle, rags, black tape, rubber gloves and a mask in the hold-all.

It was clear from the inquest that the IRA men had not fired their weapons. Speculation also remained that the limited search for spent bullet cases did not rule out firing from the cemetery or the top hedge of the field.

The solicitors for the families of the deceased put intense pressure on Soldiers 'D', 'E', 'F' and Major 'G', all of whom appeared at the inquest, to admit that they were covert SAS soldiers. They denied it. The solicitors argued their case from the fact that they wore civilian clothes, travelled in unmarked vehicles, used SAS-type weapons and had seen long service in the Army. Soldier 'E' was asked if he had been involved in the Gransha shootings, the killing of Daniel Doherty and William Fleming on 6 December 1984. He did not answer. Soldier 'E' said that 'A' had been the commander of the patrol; 'A' and 'B' had been of equal rank and 'C' had been junior; 'D' was under 'E's jurisdiction on the night of the shooting although they were both of equal rank; 'F' was junior again. Soldier 'E' was stationed in Northern Ireland for 21 months. Soldier 'F' admitted voluntarily that he was no longer a serving soldier and disclosed that he was a 'security consultant'; he was in Northern Ireland 21 months prior to the shooting. The Army major, Soldier 'G', said he had been in the Army 19 years and a major for 5 or 6 years. He said that Soldiers 'A', 'B' and 'C' were still serving soldiers but was not certain of their exact location. He said that to his knowledge they had not been notified of the hearing. In exchanges with the Coroner, Mr Collins claimed that the rules of the Coroner's Court had been breached if the soldiers had not been notified. The major disclosed that he himself had been 'on the ground a couple of times' in patrols at the Head-of-the-Town prior to the killings. He was present at the Strand Road but denied 'prompting' the soldiers before their statements; he said he was not the major present when they made their statements. Soldier 'E' said that he had returned to Ebrington Barracks on the night of the killings because he had not discharged his weapons; he made a statement a month later. He said however that the incident was discussed in great detail and that a debriefing session lasted some two hours. The statements of Soldiers 'A', 'B' and 'C' were taken at Strand Road RUC Station, Derry on 23 February 1985.

On 10 August 1987 Captain Simon Hayward, a Life Guards officer accused of smuggling 50.5 kilos of cannabis into Sweden, was sentenced to five years imprisonment. During his trial the story emerged in the media that he was an intelligence officer whose military training included a lengthy spell of dangerous work in Northern Ireland. The story was told in some detail by Neil Wallis in *The Sun* in 1987. Reporter Neil Wallis wrote:- 'Captain Simon Hayward, the young British officer facing drugs charges in Sweden, spent two years working as an undercover intelligence agent in Ulster. He laid his life on the line daily, master-minding a series of hush-hush hammer blows against the IRA. Among his many secret successes was the destruction of a notorious IRA death squad. Captain Hayward was in charge of a carefully planned ambush in which undercover soldiers shot dead three heavily-armed terrorists on their way to rocket attack a police station. Fears that his cover might have been blown – he is believed to be on the IRA death list – led to his transfer to a top secret senior post working for military intelligence in Whitehall. Captain Hayward was due to start this new job when he returned from the holiday which led to his arrest in Sweden...Some details of Captain Hayward's top-secret work in Ulster were hinted at after he was arrested on a charge of being a drugs courier in Uppsala, Sweden, in March...the young soldier forbade his lawyers to use his heroic undercover army activities in Northern Ireland in his defence. A senior Ulster Special Branch detective revealed last night: "Simon was a major lynch-pin in undercover operations against the IRA. He worked directly for the head of MI5 for Northern Ireland, co-ordinating, planning and seeing through sensitive hush-hush operations involving the SAS and undercover squads". Life Guards officer Captain Hayward was seconded to Ulster after his special talents were spotted. He served as a liaison officer between MI5, Army SAS units and the Royal Ulster Constabulary special branch undercover department E4. Hayward was based at the Army's Northern Ireland headquarters before being transferred to Gough Barracks, Armagh, as front-line communications and anti-terrorist liaison officer. The captain's patch included the notorious IRA killing ground along the County Fermanagh and South Tyrone border with the Republic'. Wallis maintained that Hayward master-minded the Strabane ambush and organised surveillance work to ensure the IRA men would be caught in the trap. The ambush he said had been set up following a tip-off from an IRA mole to the RUC who passed the information directly on to Hayward. Wallis wrote: 'We were told: "Typically Simon stayed on the scene long after he should have pulled out because he was determined to see the SAS guys got away safely."'

Commenting on the revelation in *The Sun* and other English newspapers Sinn Féin Councillor, Mr Ivan Barr, Strabane, said that, if it were true, then the scenario portrayed on behalf of the British Army and the RUC as to the circumstances surrounding the killings was nothing more than a contemptuous charade aimed at covering up the true facts about the events leading up to the slayings. In May 1989 it was announced that Hayward was to be released from the top security jail in Malmo, Sweden, after serving half of his five-year sentence for drug-smuggling. He was released on 12 September 1989.

However, in his book *Under Fire* (1989) Hayward says that he was posted to Northern Ireland twice, in 1982 when he was attached to the Coldstream Guards as Company Operations Officer during a four-month emergency tour to South Armagh, and in 1985 on a two-year posting to Headquarters Northern Ireland in Lisburn. He vigorously denies the claim in *Private Eye* magazine (July 1987) that he was a member of the SAS and played a leading role in the Strabane shooting. In fact Hayward says that he had only arrived in N. Ireland in June 1985, some months after the shooting.

At the inquest Mr Fahy cross-examined police witnesses regarding 'Kelly from Plumbridge' who it was said had driven into the scene of the shooting and had cried out 'Don't shoot! Don't shoot!' The man's identity had not been taken nor the registration number of his car. At the inquest a police sergeant said that further police investigations had failed to locate 'Kelly'. Mr Fahy put it to him that there had been a suggestion that the three men in the field were begging for mercy. Mr Fahy pointed out that the witness had twice mentioned in his deposition that 'Kelly' had shouted out. The witness said that he had done so. Mr Fahy asked whether he had mentioned it in his statement to counteract any suggestion that the shouting had come from the three men. The sergeant replied that he did not hear anything from the men in the field. He heard shouting from the man on the road.

On the morning of the shooting Mrs Devine brought her husband Billy a cup of tea to bed before going to work. She remarked that she heard on the news that three fellas had been shot in Strabane. She went to her work. Billy came downstairs. He never thought of his two sons being involved. He was clearing out the fireplace about 8.45 am when the RUC raided the house. They did not inform him that his two sons had been shot. One of the policemen, noticing all the trophies Michael had won at snooker, said, 'There must be a great snooker player in this house'. Fr Andrew McCloskey, one of the curates in the parish, then came and told him David had been shot. Billy then sent his son-in-law to look for Michael. While he was away Fr McCloskey came back again and asked, 'Has Michael blond streaks in his hair?' He said, 'Yes.' 'Well, I'm sorry to inform you,' Fr McCloskey said, 'Michael is dead too.'

At 7 am the RUC raided the Breslin home. They did not tell the family Charlie was dead, even though they knew.

Fr Oliver Crilly, the other curate, received a call from the RUC after the shooting. He was one of the first on the scene. He said, 'I found the bodies lying close together in the field. It was dark at that time and I was unable to identify any of them. I said the prayers for the dead'.

The bodies of the three men lay in the field for seven hours before they were released. A group of women marched to the field in protest. Some people who returned later to say the Rosary were prevented from going to the scene by the RUC.

The killings of the three men sparked off the Shoot-to-Kill controversy once again. Martin McGuinness of Sinn Féin said that the killings showed that the British forces were taking no prisoners. Paschal O'Hare, solicitor and Belfast City Councillor, called for an independent inquiry to investigate why the soldiers shot the men without challenging them. Mr Charles Haughey, TD, Fianna Fáil, leader of the opposition in the Dáil, speaking on Radio Éireann also called for an inquiry. He said, 'All constitutional nationalist politicians are deeply concerned about the level of alienation there is in the six counties area of a large number of people from the entire process of Government and the administration of justice. If there is to be an official policy of this kind by the security forces, then I can only see that as seriously exacerbating this already deep process of alienation. Western parliamentary democracies cannot in any way stand over a shoot-to-kill policy by its security forces. I think that is a basic principle'. Unionist politicians welcomed the killings. The Rev. Ian Paisley described them as 'judicial'. Mr Alan Kane, Mid-Ulster DUP Assemblyman, said, 'Such resolute action against the murderous enemies of our land is the only way back to peace and prosperity'. East Derry Unionist MP William Ross said, 'It is quite clear they were going out to murder another innocent victim. Thank God they didn't succeed'.

The parish priests of Strabane, Fr Anthony Mulvey and Fr John Farren, issued a joint statement: 'There is a great deal of uncertainty about the circumstances of this morning's events, and much scepticism and rumour. There are many questions to be answered and it is imperative that a full investigation take place, and the facts be made known as soon as possible. Those who are authorised to carry arms have the serious responsibility to exercise moral restraint at all times, and always to act with the moderation of blameless self-defence. For this reason, we must say that if no warning was given and no challenge offered, and no effort made to effect an arrest, then the shooting was murder. It is also true that whoever was responsible for putting these young men in such a position bears a heavy responsibility for their deaths'.

There were more condemnations of violence and killings following the murder on 24 February of Kevin Coyle (24), a married man with three children, by the IRA in the Bogside, Derry, on the allegation that he was an informer and the murder on the same day of an ex-UDR member, Douglas McElhinney (42) by the INLA in Rosemount, Derry. Following the five killings, Bishop Edward Daly of Derry said that he did not intend issuing future statements at the request of the media after such atrocities had taken place. He said vocabulary had been exhausted. The Church of Ireland bishop, Bishop James Mehaffey, said the violence had pushed the communities in the North further apart.

There were tense scenes at the funerals of the three men, more so at the funeral of Charles Breslin which was held up for more than an hour by the RUC. After Fr Oliver Crilly had negotiated with the RUC, the funeral cortège was allowed to move when a black beret and black gloves were removed from the coffin. The Devine funerals had no paramilitary trappings and were allowed to pass without interruption. Huge crowds attended the funerals. At the graveside of Charles Breslin, Gerry Adams, President of Sinn Féin said that the men had been shot by a 'British terrorist SAS gang' from concealed positions by volley after volley of firing and then after a lull one of the gang approached the bodies and fired one shot into the head of each. He described the Secretary of State, Douglas Hurd as 'the senior representative of the political wing of the British Army in Ireland' and added that he must bear responsibility for the killings.

At the Requiem Mass for the men, Fr McCloskey said, 'There are two reactions in particular on which we need to be questioned by the Gospel. Firstly, the reaction of those who abhor the attempt to solve political problems by violence and who may be tempted to think that the ruthless execution of these young men is acceptable and, because they were carrying arms, it is not open to moral question under any circumstances. This response can be so plausible at first that it needs to be questioned, and without attempting to exhaust the matter, I would like to suggest two factors that should be taken into account. Firstly, anyone who abhors violence and genuinely seeks a Christian response to our problems must with total integrity avoid any hint of rejoicing at the kind of violent end these three young men met on Saturday morning. Secondly, it is vital to realise that violence can only be overcome if the forces of law and order are seen to act with moral restraint and not to meet the problem of violence with ruthless and unrestrained violence. The second reaction on which we need to be questioned by the Gospel is the temptation to respond to the pain and anguish of the present situation by giving way to feelings of hatred or a resolve to seek or support the use of violence in pursuit of any political objective'.

Republican News/An Phoblacht in its edition of 28 February 1985 gave pen portraits of the dead volunteers. It said Michael Devine had joined the IRA early in 1984, was a fully-committed IRA volunteer for whom no task was too great or too small; he rapidly won the respect of his comrades as a careful planner who always did his utmost to ensure the safety of other volunteers. It said that David Devine joined Fianna Éireann at the age of fourteen and worked energetically with local IRA units who developed great trust in his scouting ability and in his intelligence gathering; he joined the IRA six months before his death. Charles Breslin it described as a highly politicised IRA volunteer who was active for two-and-a-half years before his death and took part in numerous attacks on crown forces; he was badly beaten while being interrogated in Castlereagh Interrogation Centre in 1984; 'His interrogators held a plastic bag over his head until he lost consciousness'.

On 25 February 1985 at 7.30 pm four masked IRA volunteers, two of them women, fired two volleys of shots over the coffin of Charles Breslin in the back-garden of his home. On 22 February 1987 a crowd of 1500 people attended a commemoration ceremony for the three men. Celtic crosses were unveiled at their graves.

On 22 April 1987 the inquest into the killings of the three IRA men ended. The jury of five women and six men unanimously found that the men had died as a result of gunshot wounds sustained in a field to the rear of 36 Fountain Street, Strabane. On Tuesday, 27 October 1987 a judicial review of the inquest was announced. This review was adjourned at the High Court in Belfast on 8 January 1988 after counsel for the dead men's families said they might want to cross-examine the coroner of the original inquest.

After the original inquest there was criticism of the inquest procedures regarding applications for car log-books, RUC officers' notebooks, and other items to be produced as evidence; regarding who was entitled to take notes; regarding the provision of crown witnesses' depositions; regarding the presence of witnesses in court before they gave evidence; regarding the exit of three jurors from the court; regarding the lengthy adjournments of the proceedings. The difficult task of the lawyers can be judged from the fact that the Crown witnesses answered 'I don't recall' to more than 300 questions.

In September 1988 the families of the three men failed to have the 1987 inquest quashed and reconvened. Mr Justice Carswell ruled: that the coroner had been in breach of the rules by not allowing the solicitors for the families access to plans and photographs relating to the killings; that the fact that the applicants' doctor had not been informed of the time and place of the *post-mortems* was irregular; that the soldiers' statements had been admitted under the wrong rule; that 'it did not appear that the proceedings were conducted at all times in as orderly or seemly an atmosphere as might be desired'. However, he said that these irregularities were not sufficient to invalidate the proceedings. His ruling was received with a great deal of criticism. Coroners' inquiries into deaths caused by the armed forces do not have a good image.

The Killing of Francis Bradley[123]

Francis Joseph Bradley was shot dead by the SAS at a farmhouse on the Hillhead to Toomebridge Road in the parish of Magherafelt, near Toomebridge, at 9.50 pm on Tuesday, 18 February 1986. The local curate, Fr James McNally, described him as 'as nice a youngster as you'd find anywhere, very good-mannered, very courteous; a man I would trust completely'.

Francis Bradley's funeral and burial took place on 21 February within days of his twenty-first birthday. The Requiem Mass was concelebrated by his uncle, V. Rev. John Bradley, PP and a cousin, V. Rev Francis Quigley, PP. The remains were received at St James' Church, Newbridge, by the parish priest, Canon Charles McKeone, who had administered the Last Rites to him. Fr McNally officiated at the graveside. At the end of the Mass Fr Bradley conveyed the thanks of the parents, brothers and sister of Francis to those who attended and said they were most grateful to all who had sympathised with them. There was no reference to the circumstances of the boy's death. His father, Mr Edward Bradley, was among those who carried his coffin the mile from his home at Derrygarve to the church.

There was a heavy RUC presence on the roads leading to the church, rows of land-rovers and many checkpoints. Their concentration was a reminder that his parents Edward and Rosemary Bradley dated the problems of the deceased with the police back to the funeral of Antoin MacGiolla Bríde on 4 December 1984. He was hit by the RUC with a baton on that day and required stitches in the hospital. Did this incident result in his being caught up in the dismal war between the IRA and the British forces and lead to his joining the IRA?

In May 1985 an RUC reservist, R.J. Evans, was shot and wounded at his house on the Aughrim Road. A young man in his company was also severely wounded. Bradley's parents say that two or three weeks after the shooting Francis was 'picked up by the police and questioned about that incident; he was kept for just about a day; we know that he was here at home with us that night when the shooting happened and he was not involved in this or anything else'.

Francis Bradley was arrested again at 5.30 am on Monday, 21 October 1985 under Section 11 of the Emergency Provisions Act and was taken to the Interrogation Centre at Gough Barracks, Armagh. After his release he made a statement to Fr Denis Faul, Dungannon, and a formal complaint was made at Castledawson RUC Barracks. He made allegations of undue pressure in a statement:

> I was taken into the Barracks. One said, 'Have fun for it will be a long time before we see you again'.
> *Monday:* Four interrogators ... normal.
> *Tuesday:* The line was, 'We're getting sick of you'...'We'll trail you through the muck'. They asked me about S. O'Connor, 'He'll not get his wedding at Easter'. In the evening they asked me to work for them. They gave me a number 32666. I was 'Dibble' and I was to ask for Top Cat (from TV). For two names for the shooting of Evans, they would give me the price of an Opel Manta, £8,000. They would turn a blind eye to motoring offences if I rung up and told them about the incidents.
> I jog. They said they would pull up and find out who debriefed me when I got out...
> *Wednesday:* My mother rang at 7 and was told I was safely in bed. In fact, I was awakened at 4.50 am and taken for interrogation. I got back to my cell about an hour before breakfast, which was at 8.30 am. I saw the interrogator's watch. One talked about Evans. He said he would arrest me for seven days and let me out and take me in the next day for another seven. He said I would be booked in on the 23rd December for Christmas; he wrote it down. Another said on Wednesday afternoon that they had an extension to keep me for four days. They said they would get a photo of S. O'Connor with another girl through his door. I feel I am under threat from the RUC. I know that an attempt has been made to blackmail me to work for them. I do not wish to work for them. My civil liberties have been interfered with and my health has been badly affected by my experiences in Gough Barracks. I feel I am already under threat from Protestants...

Mr Seamus O'Connor, whom Bradley referred to in his statement, was also arrested in June 1985 and taken to Castlereagh Interrogation Centre where he was held for three days during which time he was questioned about the shooting of Evans at Aughrim. Bradley and O'Connor were friends.

On Monday, 9 December 1985, 57 shots were fired at Castledawson Police Station. It was a cold frosty night with freezing fog and little or no visibility. O'Connor and Bradley were arrested again and brought to Gough Barracks. O'Connor in a statement to Fr James McNally, taken on 23 February 1986, made allegations of verbal abuse and threats:

> Monday 9th December 1985: There was a shooting at Castledawson Barracks. At 8.00 pm when I arrived home with my father two car-loads of police were searching at the house. Only my young sister, niece and

nephew were in the house when the police first arrived. The phone rang. One of the DMSU constables said to my sister, 'If you say we are here, I'll blow your fucking head off'. She replaced the receiver. During the search one constable said, 'Did you never see a fucking policeman before?' and told my nephew to get out of the way.

On my arrival I was arrested under section 12, and taken to Gough Barracks. It was a cold night but they drove with the windows down. On my way to Gough Barracks they asked me did I own a new house and did I intend to get married. I said I did own a new house and that I possibly would get married. A uniformed policeman…said, 'Boy, you're in for a shock, you'll never see Easter'. He talked to the driver and said, 'He'll be in a fucking coffin…' When I was taken to Gough Barracks, all my clothing was removed. I was given a boiler-suit and gutty slippers. My clothing was sent for forensic examination. On this occasion they only wanted to verify my movements. I was kept only one day…Francis Bradley and I travelled home in the same car…

Regarding the arrest of Francis Bradley on that occasion his parents stated (8 April 1986) that he was not involved; that he was in the house of his grandmother Mrs Mary Murray and the police checked this as being the truth. The statement continued, 'They arrested him a third time, and it was on the third occasion that they told him that he would be dead before his 21st birthday. When he got out he was badly shaken and very, very frightened. He did consider this particular threat to be a very real one. He was warned by a young Protestant man that a certain named person was out to get him with the help of a well-known policeman in Magherafelt. He was given a lot of trouble by the police who followed him about'.

Francis Bradley was of slight build, about 5 foot 7 inches tall. His family noticed that after this threat he failed a lot physically and became very thin. He was obviously suffering from nervous tension and mental suffering. Some RUC harassment of Francis is alleged by his girlfriend, Eilish Kennedy, and her sister Annette in a joint statement:

The Wednesday night after Francis got out of Gough Barracks after he was lifted for the shooting in Castledawson…Francis, Eilish and I came out of Taggarts' Hotel in Toomebridge. Francis went to the chip shop and I turned the car and parked it in the car-park. About five minutes later the police came down both sides of the street and pointed their guns into the car. Then a police car came and stopped beside us. A policeman got out and came over and asked Eilish questions about Francis: where he was, and how long she had been going with him.

Eilish and I went into the chip shop for Francis. As the three of us were walking back to the car, Francis turned to go back for minerals when a policeman caught him by the shoulder and said, 'Where do you think you're going?' Then he put him up against the wall and searched him. By this stage two of Francis's friends had come on the scene, and the police returned to their car. Francis and Eilish got into his friends' car and went over to Francis's house. The other friend and I got into Francis's car and, as soon as we started up the police car behind us also started up and, as soon as we were heading over the bridge, we were stopped by the sound of sirens and the flashing of lights. A policeman came over and he looked all surprised when he saw it wasn't Francis driving. He then asked where Bradley was. When we said he was away in the other car, he then asked the driver to show his insurance in the barracks within three days and not to be covering up for his friend anymore. He then let us go without any bother.

Saturday night: On the next Saturday night after Ballymaguigan Disco, we went into the Magherafelt Chinese restaurant. While we were sitting in the town, two police cars, one blue and one cream, kept driving up and looking into Francis's car. As I was driving out of the town I noticed the cream car following behind us. As I turned right to take the back road out of the town I noticed the blue car sitting at the exit of the road. Then the blue car also followed and passed us further up the road, the cream car still following. I turned down the Pound Road, and a short bit down that road they started to flash the lights; I pulled up and stopped. About five minutes later the police car bumped into us, and after about another five minutes they got out, came over and told us to get out. They then asked all our names, addresses, dates of birth. They searched the boot and the inside of the car. They even took out the cigarette lighter. Then they let us go.

In his statement Seamus O'Connor described further RUC surveillance of him and Francis Bradley:

Three weeks before Francis's death I had been coming from McLarnons' shop. I met Francis Bradley in McVeys' Cafe. When I was in the shop playing a poker machine, an individual was staring at us. He was 5'10" tall, well built, 30-35 years of age. When I went out and went towards my car, a blue Ford Sierra approached. There were four uniformed police in it – DMSU. On seeing us the Sierra pulled down the road a bit. Francis and I got into my car and drove off... there was another car, a silver Golf with a CB aerial. There were three men sitting in it. The Ford Sierra followed us to McLarnons' shop. There was a brown Colt sitting along the road when Francis and I returned to McVeys' shop for Francis's car. I followed Francis home for company. On my way back from Bradleys', the Silver Golf, the Colt and the Ford Sierra were at the Aughrim-Creagh Road junction.

I was afraid at that time that we were to be set up in the light of these movements.

On the night he was shot dead by the SAS at 9.50 pm, 18 February 1986, Francis Bradley arrived home from his work as a joiner at 5.40 pm. He had a meal and went shopping with his mother. They arrived back at 7.10 pm He had some business to do back at his work at Seán McElhone's factory. He was known to be in the company of an IRA man at 8.45 pm. The local unit of the IRA was badly organised, loose and confused. This man has been described as a rough illiterate person. Apparently this same man left some guns behind Walls' house on the main Toome road at 7.45 pm. They had been left there without the family's knowledge. They had been left just outside the back-yard on a rubbish dump beside a little house between the field and the back-yard. They were not hidden. One of the reasons advanced for leaving them there was that there was an RUC roadblock at Toome and it was necessary to move them. But why leave them lying in the open, behind a house on a main road? There is a maze of small roads off the main road leading to bogs and remote places where weapons could be well concealed. The night before he was shot, Bradley was told in the presence of others, 'Don't forget tomorrow night'. Bradley never left his work during the day, 18 February. It is evident that he never planted the guns there but was asked to collect them. He parted with the 'rough' IRA man shortly after 8.45 pm.

Francis Bradley called at two shops on the evening of 18 February before he got rubber gloves which suited his purpose. In the evening he called at McLarnons' house in Moyola View off the Black Park Road.

Bernard McLarnon, a middle-aged man recalls:- 'I helped my daughter to lock the shop (Newbridge Stores) at about 9.35 pm and drove her up home. We went straight into our house. I went into the bathroom and gave myself a quick wash. After about a quarter-of-an-hour, Francis Bradley came in. I spoke to him and I said I was going to see Kevin Walls to arrange a game of cards. Francis said, "I will go down with you". We went out and got into my car. I drove down to Walls's and parked my car at the gable. We got out of the car together and parted company. I turned my back and headed for Walls's front door. Before I got to the corner of the gable the shooting started. I hastened my step towards the front door, rapped it and said, "Colm, let me in"'.

Walls' house faces the main road and lies open at the front. As one looks at the house from the main road the garage is on the left, situated slightly back from the house, thus leaving an opening between the garage and corner of the gable, an entrance into the back-yard. The back-yard is boxed in with outhouses; a high wall connects the other gable with outhouses on that side. The house is two-storey. At the rear there are three upstairs windows, two downstairs windows and a back door. Immediately opposite this back door across the yard an open gateway leads out into a field. Just inside this field to the right is a small outhouse. An old round water tank and some timber and rubbish lies beside the little house. It is here the guns were lying, just at the corner of this little outhouse in the open. Forty yards across the rough field at this narrow part, for it opens out wide to the immediate left coming through the gateway from the yard, is an old railway cutting. A hedge and a deep drain form the fence between the field and the disused cutting. Here five SAS soldiers lay watching the house. They are designated 'A','B','C','D', and 'E'. 'B','A' and 'C', in that order, lay facing the farmyard. 'D' and 'E' were to their left at the junction of two hedges, the hedge running parallel to the railway cutting and the hedge which ran at right angles to it right up to the farmyard walls.

It is necessary now to turn to the statements of the SAS soldiers. Soldier 'A' was the commander in charge. Soldiers 'A' and 'C' were the only soldiers who fired shots. These did not appear at the inquest which was held in Magherafelt courthouse in March 1987. Their statements were read by a detective superintendent. Soldiers 'B','D' and 'E' did appear at the inquest.

Soldier 'A' in his statement said:

> I am a soldier attached to 8 Infantry Brigade at Londonderry. During the evening of 18th February 1986 I was operating a mobile patrol in a civilian car in the area of Toomebridge. I was accompanied by Soldiers 'B','C' and 'F', who was driving. I was wearing full military uniform which consisted of camouflage smock, trousers and boots. I was wearing no headgear. I was armed with an Armalite rifle serial No. 9604028 and one 30 round mag. which are my personal issue. Also attached to the rifle was a mini night-viewing aid.
>
> Prior to commencing our patrol we had been briefed that a general terrorist threat existed in the Castledawson, Toome, Magherafelt areas and we were operating as a double mobile patrol in the confines of that area. Our back-up vehicle, also a civilian vehicle, was manned by Soldiers 'D', 'E' and 'G'. At approximately 9.30 pm on the same date, as the result of information received, my driver, Soldier 'F', dropped Soldiers 'B' and 'C' and myself in the vicinity of a farmhouse...At this point Soldier 'F' withdrew from the immediate area and we were joined by Soldiers 'D' and 'E' who in turn had been dropped off by Soldier 'G'. We made our way to the rear of the farm referred to and took up positions to observe the rear of the farmhouse and outbuildings...I had a clear unrestricted view of the outbuildings. Visibility was good and it was a cold clear night with no cloud and a good moon. Furthermore light from a ground floor window illuminated the area. We had been told that there were gunmen in the vicinity of the farmhouse and we had been instructed to take up the most suitable positions to apprehend

them. As I was watching the rear of the farm, a vehicle drove into the driveway at the side of the dwelling-house. I only saw the headlights reflected off the buildings and after a few seconds they went out. I didn't hear the car doors open or close but after a short time I saw two men appear at a gap between the farm building referred to...I could see these men clearly in my night sights. One was quite young with reasonably short hair. He was wearing a bomber-type jacket, dark coloured, and dark trousers. The second person was elderly and slightly stooped. He was wearing a single-breasted type jacket and light-coloured trousers. This particular person stood at the corner of the building on the right-hand side of the gap when (*I was*) observing from my location. The younger walked through the gap and looked around in what seemed to be a visual check of the field and the rear of the outbuildings. The older man who had remained in the farmyard also seemed to be alert and looking round. The younger man returned to the older man and had a short conversation after which the younger man again returned through the gap. At the left-hand corner of the gap he bent down out of my view behind wood and rubbish. Seconds later he stood up and I saw that he was carrying a rifle in one hand, I'm not sure which. This person took a couple of strides towards the gap and I challenged him by shouting, 'Halt'. Before I could say anymore the gunman turned sharply as if to confront me and I saw that the rifle was now in both hands, traversing in an aggressive manner, in our direction. I believed that he intended to open fire on me and my colleagues and I fired one aimed shot. Almost instantaneously I heard a burst of shots fired from my right and I saw the gunman fall. Directly after this the other man ran off and I informed my base that we had contacted a gunman...

It was Soldier 'C' who fired at the same time as Soldier 'A'. According to the SAS statements, Soldiers 'A' and 'E' took off to the right and Soldiers 'B' and 'D' to the left in pursuit of the older man who had run away. 'A' and 'E' found the hedge too dense to cross. They returned to their original position by which time 'C' shouted he was moving forward. 'C' says, 'I quickly skirmished forward through the flat rough grass field and midway between my original location and the location of the gunman... I fired a further burst'. (This would mean, if what he says is accurate, that he was about 20 yards from Francis Bradley when he fired the second time). 'C' says of this second burst that it was impossible for him to use his night sights 'because of his actions' and as soon as he had detected movement in the shadows he instinctively fired – 'I did so fearing for my safety and (*it*) being completely open ground'. He then describes the circumstances of his firing a third time. He continues, 'Also as a result I darted to my right for (*the*)

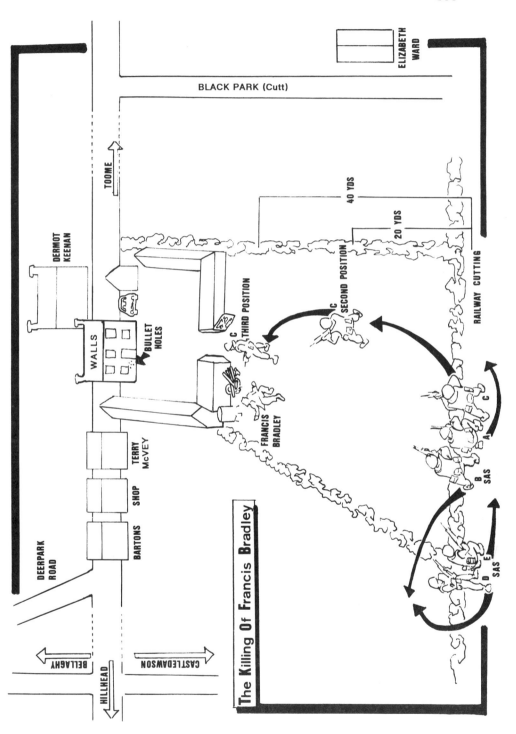

ELIZABETH WARD

BLACK PARK (Cutt)

TOOME

40 YDS

20 YDS

RAILWAY CUTTING

DERMOT KEENAN

THIRD POSITION

SECOND POSITION

C

C

C

A

B SAS

D E SAS

WALLS

BULLET HOLES

FRANCIS BRADLEY

TERRY McVEY

SHOP

BARTONS

DEERPARK ROAD

BELLAGHY

HILLHEAD

CASTLEDAWSON

The Killing Of Francis Bradley

cover of the outbuildings. At this time I knew the gunman was a bigger threat and possibly I had advanced too far forward. Having darted to my right at speed I had momentarily taken my eyes off the location of the gunman and, as I turned to relocate him, I was aware of a stream-light torch "attached to rifle" ('*E' had switched on the torch of his rifle*) sweeping the area. Instantaneously I again located the gunman and realised that he was moving into a position to engage me. I just opened fire instinctively and ran through the gap into the farmyard where I took cover by the farm buildings...'

The statements of the SAS soldiers contain the familiar phraseology of threats to their lives and movements. Bradley was shot many times and at close ranges, from 40 yards in the first two bursts from 'A' and 'C', at some 20 yards again by 'C' and then closer still. Was there a challenge at all? Were the IRA weapons loaded? Did Bradley actually take one in his hand? Did he raise it in a threatening manner? Did the SAS and the RUC receive definite information about the weapons? Could they have immobilised them? Francis Bradley was a nervous chap worn out by worry and harassment. He had probably been asked to move weapons to another location and so was wearing gloves. One surmises that he was on the fringe of IRA activity. The term 'gunman' seems loaded. Could he not have been taken prisoner after the gunfire bursts from 'A' and 'C' and even after the second burst from 'C'? It was the last burst from 'C' into the young man's stomach from close range that proved fatal.

A look at Dr J.L. Carson's deposition at the inquest indicates the gunshot wounds sustained by Bradley:

Trunk

1. An irregular area of abrasion, $1^1/2$ cm x 1 cm, on the front of the upper chest, through which could be seen part of the jacket of a bullet.

2. A group of three entrance wounds, all of similar size, shape and type, centred round the umbilicus.

Left Upper Limb

1. An elongated gaping but superficial wound, $7^1/2$ cm long and gaping by 3 cm, on the inner side of the upper arm, more or less horizontally directed and 13 cm below the apex of the armpit. It was not possible to say whether the bullet causing it had come from in front or behind.

2. A small circular wound, 3-4 mm diameter, on the radial border of the forearm...

3. A slightly oval and somewhat lacerated exit wound, 7 mm x 5 mm on the back of the forearm...

Right upper Limb

1. A small fragment wound, 5 mm x 3 mm, on the outer side of the shoulder...

2. A larger irregular circular gaping wound, 15 mm diameter, on the outer side of the upper arm...

Left Lower Limb

1. An elongated wound 5cm long and gaping by almost 2 cm on the outer side of the knee at a level 18½ inches above the sole... it was not possible to say which direction the bullet had been travelling when it caused this wound...

2. When the scrotum was elevated a further wound was revealed on the upper inner aspect of the left thigh... The lower part of the wound seemed to be the entrance wound... Some fragments of bullet were recovered.

Back

1. An oval somewhat lacerated exit wound, 11 mm x 9 mm, on the upper part of the right shoulder...

2. A neat circular entrance wound, 3-4 mm diameter, on the left buttock...

3. A lacerated exit wound, 7 mm by 3 mm, on the back of the right loin...

There were thus in all 8 gunshot wounds, 3 bullets entering the lower abdomen grouped round the umbilicus and passing upwards and backwards to emerge on the back of the right shoulder, on the outer side of the right shoulder upper arm, where a chip of bone had been dislodged from the posterior surface of the humerus causing the small wound above the larger one, and on the front centre of the upper chest. A fourth bullet had caused the lacerated track on the inner aspect of the left upper arm. A fifth had passed through the left forearm from front to back and upwards, whilst a sixth had lacerated the outer aspect of the left knee. A seventh bullet had passed through the right buttock behind, whilst the eighth had entered the left upper thigh, passing upwards and to the left, fracturing the pelvis and fragmenting before ending up below the skin...

Death was a result of gunshot wounds. In all he appeared to have been struck by eight bullets, but there was considerable variation in the position of the wounds and in the direction of the bullet tracks. Three wounds were apparently in one group, centred round the umbilicus. From here the bullets had passed sharply upwards through the abdomen and chest causing laceration of the intestines, stomach, liver, heart and right lung. The internal bleeding from these injuries would have caused rapid death. Two of these bullets had left the body, through the back of the right shoulder and upper arm whilst the third was found lodged and distorted in the breast bone. Considering the direction of these wounds, the deceased may have been lying on his back on the ground when the three shots were discharged.

Another bullet had ploughed a furrow across the inner side of the left upper arm and another had caused a similar injury on the outer side of the left knee. Because these bullets had not caused separate entrance and exit wounds it was not clear (in) which direction they had been travelling in relation to the deceased, but, with the body upright, their direction was more or less horizontal.

A sixth bullet had passed through the soft tissues of the left forearm, entering its radial border and passing upwards and backwards at about 45 degrees, and slightly to the left, before leaving the back of the forearm below the elbow.

A seventh bullet had entered the soft tissues near the inner aspect of the left upper buttock behind and it passed upwards to the right at 40 degrees to the horizontal plane, leaving through the back of the right loin. This wound was also peculiar in direction, suggesting that the deceased might have been on his knees at the time.

The eighth bullet had entered the inner part of the left upper thigh causing a rather irregular entrance wound. It had passed sharply upwards and to the left at 45 degrees to the horizontal plane, shattering the pelvis and fragmenting and causing considerable bleeding into the tissues around the groin. This wound track was also unusual in direction and could have been caused when the deceased was bending over or on his knees.

There were a number of linear abrasions on the right buttock and back of the left thigh, the cause of which was not clear. They were not caused by bullets.

The conclusion one could draw from the remarks of the pathologist is that Francis Bradley was hit twice in the left arm and once on the outside left leg in the initial burst of firing from Soldiers 'A' and 'C'. Soldier 'C' then ran forward and hit him twice in a burst of gunfire when Bradley was on his knees, his back to the firer and his body parallel to the ground. One bullet hit him on the top of the inner thigh and threw him forward with considerable force. The second bullet from 'C's burst hit him in the buttock and this spun him on his back. Then at a distance of 10 feet, with the aid of the light streaming from the torch attached to 'E's' rifle, 'C' fired the fatal wounds – three bullets into Bradley's stomach.

The following are the added remarks at the inquest on this matter from Dr Carson:

Discharge of a weapon from more than 2 or 3 feet away would be unlikely to result in powder burns on the body of the person fired at. The appearance of the wounds is consistent with the shots having been fired from a distance of 10 feet. If the deceased was on his back at the time, the angle of these three wounds (*the stomach wounds*) is consistent with the firer being a short distance away from the feet of the deceased in a standing or a crouched position.

The gaping wound on the inner aspect of the left upper arm could have been caused when the deceased was standing. That was not a fatal wound. The wound on the left forearm is more likely to have been caused when the deceased was standing. That was not a fatal wound.

The wound on the outside of the left leg was also more likely to have been caused when the deceased was standing. Again that was not a fatal wound.

Regarding the wound inside the top of the left thigh, it was untypical of entrance wounds in not being round and regular...This would indicate the bullet had been distorted – perhaps by heavy clothing or a zip or perhaps by a ricochet off the ground. The track was also most unusual. One possibility was that the deceased was bent over with his trunk more or less parallel to the ground and the firer was behind and to his right. The deceased would have had his back obliquely towards the firer. Prompt medical intervention might have saved his life as far as this wound is concerned.

Another alternative is that the deceased was lying on his back and this wound was caused by a bullet ricocheting off the ground. The wound is consistent with this but less likely.

Regarding the bullet wound to his buttock, the firer would have been behind him and to his left. This would not have proved fatal. The deceased was almost certainly kneeling when this was sustained.

If the deceased had been carrying a weapon in his right hand, the wounds to his left arm and leg would not necessarily have caused him to drop it but if he had been carrying it in his left hand I would expect him to have dropped it.

Regarding the three wounds in the stomach area I cannot pin down the range from which they would have been fired. The same comment is true of all his gunshot wounds.

The tendency is for wounds to one side of the body to turn the body away and that could bring the back or side of the person hit round towards the firer.

To clarify the position regarding the wound to the buttock, the deceased could have been kneeling or standing but the main point is that his trunk would have been more or less parallel to the ground and with his back towards the firer.

Regarding the wound to the top of deceased's left thigh, that wound could not have been sustained when the deceased was standing facing the firer.

If it was sustained in what I regard as being the more likely alternative, namely with the deceased bent over with his trunk parallel to the ground and the firer behind him and and obliquely to his right, I would expect the force of the bullet's impact to have thrown the deceased forward with considerable force.

After being struck thus, although the deceased would have been in considerable pain, I can see no reason why he could not have risen again as the wound did not involve the joint.

The wound to the buttock could have spun the deceased onto his back. Regarding the wounds to his stomach it seems more likely to me that the deceased was static when those were sustained and that they were also part of the same group of firing.

One could also say that since they were rapidly fatal it is unlikely that the deceased moved after they were sustained and hence they were almost certainly the last wounds sustained.

I would just like to add that the wound to the inside of deceased's left thigh is so untypical of an entrance wound that I would not like to draw any firm conclusion as to the position of the deceased when it was sustained. In particular, you could not draw as clear conclusions from its track as you could from the track of a bullet which had struck the deceased clearly.

Nevertheless the most likely conclusion is that the deceased had his back to the firer at the time.

The operation which ended in the death of Francis Bradley was quite an elaborate one, involving plain clothes soldiers, soldiers in uniform and uniformed RUC.

Terry McVey who lived beside the Walls family, proprietor of a café beside his house, says that a metallic blue Volvo 343 hatchback had been sitting in his yard at the café from approximately 6.30 pm until just shortly before the shooting. The occupants were a man and a woman. At approximately 8.00 pm he went to Cargin. On going through Toomebridge he passed through a checkpoint at which there was a blue Sierra. After he passed the checkpoint the Sierra apparently followed him to Cargin and was waiting in a laneway to follow him back home. He was sitting watching television at approximately 9.55pm when the shooting started. It seemed to him that there were four bursts of gunfire over a period of five minutes. He got the children down on the floor. Kevin Kelly, the cook, came running in from the café and he lay down on the floor also. When the shooting ended McVey went over to the door and unlocked it. When he opened the door he saw an armed man in civvies, with ginger hair, wearing white football boots and jeans. This man shouted, 'We want you', grabbed him by the hair, pulling out hair, and pulled him out of the house. He and another man pushed him to the ground. There was a helicopter on the scene within a minute. His 13-year-old son Stephen was spread-eagled against the wall while Terry was made lie on the ground. Stephen saw them throwing bread-baskets at his father where he lay. One of the men put a gun to Terry's head and said 'Make my day'. Another moved the bolt of his gun back and forward, thus springing live bullets on the back of his neck. Terry kept asking what was wrong but was persistently told to 'Fuck up'. He was made lie on the ground for two hours. After 15-20 minutes the RUC had arrived. He asked what he had done and was told by the RUC to 'Fuck up'. The RUC also clicked the triggers of their guns against his head. One SAS man stood on his wrists which were bruised against the gravel. Bags were put over his hands and he was handcuffed. When the CID arrived, he was allowed back into his house. The next day the CID took a statement but only up as far as the time he opened the door.

Colm Walls had not been well for a few days with 'flu. He got up from bed on the evening of 18 February at 6.30 pm. He was upstairs and did not hear the shooting probably because his mother had the television on. But he heard the knocking at the front door. He recognised Barney McLarnon through the glass door but could not let him in as it was locked and his brother Kevin had the key. Kevin had gone to bed that evening at 6.30 pm. He went round the back. As he passed through the kitchen his mother said that she had heard shooting. He told her it was probably the television and went out the back door. There was no sign of anyone or any activity in the yard. He saw absolutely nothing, but as he turned the corner another burst of shooting took place. He went on around to the front and when he reached the door there was another burst of shooting from the back. Then someone shouted a warning at him and Bernard McLarnon. Men came running over from McVeys'. They spread-eagled them against the wall, handcuffed them and put them down on the ground. They had very large paper bags put over their hands and, when they were face down on the ground, they were made lie in such a way that the bags blocked their vision. They were kept like that for two hours and then taken to Gough Interrogation Centre at Armagh. Both men were subsequently released.

Mrs Adeline McCann, who lives opposite Walls' and McVeys', heard a burst of gunfire as she sat in her living-room. This was at 9.55 pm. She looked out the window and saw a car drive up to McVeys' shop. It turned, facing the opposite side of the road. She saw no one and did not notice any one leave the car. She left the window when she heard two more bursts of gunfire. She immediately put out the lights and made a phone call. Mrs Mary Murray, Francis Bradley's grandmother, lived in a house in front of her to the left as she faced the road. There was a light in the window. She rang Mrs Rosemary Bradley, Francis' mother, and told her. She said her mother was not there. Obviously the raiding party were also in Mrs Murray's house because, when she returned, the curtain of the kitchen window had been caught in the window and part of it was hanging outside. In the meantime, as Mrs McCann observed the situation, two more cars parked facing across the road and a helicopter hovered over the area of Walls' and McVeys'. She watched through the windows and saw people running around McVeys' from the side of the house to the back. At Walls'

house there seemed to be a steady number of people running from the
house to McVeys'. More cars pulled up and parked along the main road. A
blue light flashed for a minute and eventually a light flashed around the
front of Walls's house and then she saw someone climb down off the wall
which adjoined the house; she could hear the raiders shouting at one
another.

John McCann noticed the build-up for the ambush. He lived also in
Aughrim Lane not far from Adeline McCann. Coming home on 18 February, as he was going up the lane towards his house at approximately 9.00
pm, he saw a man he did not recognise walk past the side of his house; he
did not pay much attention to him. This ties in with an intruder in Mrs
Murray's house. There was a helicopter overhead at the time. His sister-in
law Adeline rang him around 10.00 pm to tell him about the shooting. As
his brother Anthony was not at home he walked up to Adeline's, about
sixty yards. On his way he saw flares in the area of Colm Walls' house.
Laurence Walls arrived and he went with him to the main road. They
noticed a blue Sierra parked in the middle of the road opposite McVeys'.
They saw Colm and another man lying on the ground. The place was taped
off, a white tape running from the blue Sierra door-handle to the hedge.

Thomas Doherty, also of Aughrim Lane, and his family heard four bursts
of gunfire. He estimated from the moment of the first to the last gunfire two
minutes could have elapsed. Watching and listening from a window
upstairs he knew that someone must have been shot or injured; there was
a lot of running and shouting. Then the flares went up into the sky and in
about five minutes police cars started to arrive from all directions. Some
parked in the car-park and some along the road.

Richard Barton lived on the main road just beside McVeys'. He returned
from Belfast on 18 February at approximately 9.45 pm. A few minutes later
he went out to the shed to get a few sticks for the fire. He hear a short burst
of gunfire which seemed to come from the back of McVeys'. He returned to
the house and the rest of the family asked him if he heard the shooting. After
a few seconds there were up to three bursts of gunfire. The last seemed the
furthest away and was the longest of all. Almost simultaneously a helicopter could be heard overhead and flares were dropping which lit up the
whole area. The family did not go out for three to four minutes after the
shooting stopped. The first thing they saw outside was a police-car pulled
across the road with the emergency flashers on. There was only one policeman standing beside the car and he seemed very nervous. As they walked
towards the lane, two men in blue anoraks, wearing jeans and carrying
machine-guns, came out from the side of the shop and then disappeared.
There were then two police-cars parked at the front of the shop, one with
four doors and the boot open. Two soldiers in uniform and a few more
wearing blue anoraks and army trousers were walking around the front of

the shop. Some of these men were wearing arm-bands. Two or three wore balaclavas.

Richard Barton, Jr, says that when the shooting stopped he went out of the house and saw four men dressed in plain clothes at the front of the shop. They were wearing anoraks, jeans and had white arm-bands on their right arms. Three men were running about carrying machine-guns. Approximately five minutes after the shooting, men in plain clothes got into a Volvo 343, a new-type Audi 100 (maroon) and a light blue Cavalier. He thought there could have been up to eight men in this group including men in military gear who were wearing balaclavas; they headed towards Toomebridge.

Dermot Keenan lives on the main Hillhead road on the opposite side of the road to McVeys' and Walls'. He heard the shooting at approximately 9.50 pm and went outside to see what had happened. There was another burst of shooting as he came out of the house. He thought there were altogether four bursts of gunfire over a period of two or three minutes. As he went out the door, three separate flares were sent up. One arose from the Cutt road, just outside Wards' house. He found the flare casing on the road the following morning. Another went up on the old railway to the back and to the left of Colm Walls' house. The third was about one hundred yards further down the embankment to the right, somewhere to the back of McVeys' café. From the light of the flares he could make out several men all along the old railway line; some were police, some soldiers, and others were dressed in civilian-type clothes. All the action seemed to be at McVeys' café at that time. There was a lot of shouting and cursing; men were running to and from the café to Walls' house.

Miss Elizabeth Ward on the Black Park Road (the Cutt) also heard the shooting at about 9.55 pm. She went outside to see what had happened and a flare went up from the road just at her front door.

At the inquest into Francis Bradley's death in March 1987, Mr Liam McNally, who appeared for the next of kin, requested the names of Soldiers 'A' and 'C'. This was turned down by the coroner, Mr John Shearer. Mr McNally pressed hard on the question whether the soldiers were even summoned to attend the inquest. The coroner said he was exercising his right not to have the two soldiers summoned as it could have been taken as a form of intimidation of them to give evidence. Regarding the two rifles stated to have been found at the scene, an Armalite and an FNC, a detective-inspector said that both weapons had been used in an attack on Castledawson RUC Station on 9 December 1985 and, in addition, the Armalite which the RUC knew to belong to the Provisional IRA had been used in four murders and twenty other attempted murders of members of either the British Army, UDR or RUC. Mr McNally questioned the Forensic Science Laboratory witness, recalled regarding the weapons. He asked him why his evidence was being given at that stage. The witness said he had been asked by the detective-inspector to make tests and that had been done only that morning. Mr McNally then asked him, 'Are you telling me that the two guns found at the house have only been checked for the first time this morning to find out which other incidents these weapons have been involved in?' The witness said that was correct. The witness said that he had no evidence that the deceased had been involved in any of the incidents connected with the guns. Patrick J. Eastwood of the Belfast Weather Centre gave evidence of the weather conditions at Aldergrove and at Hillhead. In marked contrast to soldiers' statements, he said there was little or no moonlight on the night of 18 February. He said that the moon had not come over the horizon that night until 11.08 pm. Dermot Keenan and Miss Elizabeth Ward gave evidence of finding casings of the flares. Miss Ward gave one to Fr James McNally. It was presented to the forensic officer who examined it. Again this evidence contradicted SAS evidence. Mr Keenan pointed out that the police had never made any enquiries from him regarding the shooting, although he lived just opposite to where it had occurred.

Under questioning, Soldier 'B' said he was 16 years in the army and attached to the 8th Infantry Brigade. Mr McNally tried to find out what regiment he belonged to, suggesting the SAS, but this was objected to. 'B' however said that he had been involved in operations of the same nature prior to the Bradley shooting. He admitted all the soldiers had white arm-bands but denied any were wearing balaclavas or jeans. He said he did not see the deceased holding or carrying a gun. He saw deceased bend down out of sight and a few seconds later he heard the shout 'Halt' and the shot. Soldier 'E' said that some members of the patrol had flares with them but they were not used. He said he had been 10 years in the army and had been in similar operations for which he had received normal training.

Soldier 'B' revealed also that there was a set of car-keys beside the body. The observation could be made that if Bradley had car-keys in his hand and had also picked up one of the rifles he could hardly appear to have the weapon in an offensive way. After 'B's, examination Mr McNally said he had received a complaint from one of the dead man's family and others sitting in the public gallery, alleging that Soldier 'B' had put his hands behind his back as he passed and gave him the two-finger sign. The allegations were later denied by the lawyer appearing for the Ministry of Defence. The Coroner said that the people who made the allegation could be mistaken but if they persisted with it he would take evidence from both sides with a view to prosecution for contempt of court.

After the examination of Soldier 'E', Mr McNally asked that one of the weapons that killed Mr Bradley be produced in court. The coroner said that he did not see the relevance of the production of the rifle. Mr McNally said that it was simply to give the jury the full picture, especially the three shots which killed Mr Bradley.

Francis Bradley was a victim of a shoot-to-kill policy. His death looks like a set-up, whether the British forces acquired information regarding the two weapons from a renegade in the IRA or from some other source. It would seem that he had been asked to move the weapons. The SAS were in ambush positions a short time before he arrived. It is clear that these highly-skilled élite soldiers could have taken him prisoner. They proceeded to shoot him, wounding him and then murdered him from a short distance. The operation involved a huge back-up from other military and members of the DMSU, who had constantly harassed him in the weeks previous to his death. His death reveals the real face of the SAS, professional soldiers under orders from the British Government.

The Minister for Foreign Affairs, Mr Peter Barry, called for a report from the British authorities on the shooting. The Rev. William McCrea, the DUP MP for Mid-Ulster commented: 'The action of the Army in eliminating another gunman is commendable and heartening'. It was correct to follow a policy of 'taking no prisoners'. Fr Denis Faul condemned the killing of Francis Bradley as 'murder'. He said he had no doubt the undercover unit could have made arrests if it had so chosen. He said the British Army and the Provisional IRA leadership were both to blame for such killings.

The Killing of Seamus McElwain[124]

Just as dawn was breaking, on Saturday 26 April 1986, Seamus Turlough McElwain and Seán Lynch, two IRA volunteers, were ambushed by the SAS. Both were armed with rifles and one had a walkie-talkie radio. They were fired on. Both were wounded. Lynch escaped and lay hidden near the scene. McElwain was shot dead where he lay wounded.

The shooting happened at Mullaghglass, near Roslea, County Fermanagh, and only a few miles as the crow flies from McElwain's home at Knockacullion, near Scotstown in County Monaghan.

A culvert bomb of 357kg of home-made explosives packed in ten creamery cans had been placed at Mullaghglass by an IRA unit on 24 April to catch a passing patrol of British Army or RUC. Something had gone wrong with the detonation apparatus and Lynch and McElwain had been approached to take over the operation. The bomb apparently had been fixed up again and the IRA had watched it for a day. Then for some reason they could not stay and had to leave. Local residents were asked to watch out for British Army activity. To leave the bomb uncovered for a day was fatal. It was discovered. In the early hours of 25 April, four members of an SAS unit moved in and set up an ambush.

Both Lynch and McElwain took on the operation willingly but had doubts about it since others had initiated it. They talked about it as they set out. Something of that doubt can be read into a few lines of *An Phoblacht/ Republican News*, 1 May 1986. The paper commented on McElwain's own operations: 'Seamus had the good sense as O/C to seek the opinion of all volunteers on every aspect of an operation while steering the activity along the best lines possible. From an operational standpoint, he was absolutely meticulous, concerning himself with every detail in order to ensure the safety and security of his comrades'.

The commander of the SAS unit, Soldier 'A', said in a statement given on 8 August 1986: - 'On the evening of 24th April 1986 I was briefed that there was a possible culvert bomb west of Roslea, Co. Fermanagh. I was the Commander of a four-man patrol. In the early hours of 25th April 1986 we commenced our patrol. Our task was to locate any possible firing wire and trace it back to the firing-point. We were to observe the firing-point with the intention of arresting anyone who was seen acting suspiciously in that area. We located the wire and traced it back to a hedgerow which appeared to be the firing-point. The patrol then split into two two-man patrols, that is, Soldiers 'B' and 'C' took up positions in the firing-point, while myself and Soldier 'D' took up an observation position approximately one hundred metres east of the firing-point in a hedgerow. By the time we had located the firing-point it was first light. We stayed in those positions until nightfall. During the darkness hours we attempted to find better positions to observe the firing-point. There were no better positions, so myself and Soldier 'D' stayed in our original position. Soldiers 'B' and 'C' moved a very short distance into better cover which gave them a view of the firing-point. We remained in these positions for a number of hours until approximately 4.50 am on Saturday 26th April 1986 when I heard automatic gunfire from the area of the firing point'.

Seán Lynch, the IRA volunteer who survived, tells us his story of what happened:

'Around midnight Friday/Saturday, 25/26 April 1986, Seamus McElwain and myself moved out from a billet in County Monaghan. We were dressed in military combat dress. We were armed with rifles, a Ruger rifle and an FNC rifle, and four magazines. As we proceeded through the darkness everything seemed quite normal but as usual in such situations we approached our destination with extreme care, walking close to the hedge and covering each other at points of danger.

'At approximately 4.30 am we arrived at our destination. I knew where the point was, a mile outside Roslea on the Lisnaskea Road. It was dawning, the moon shining. So quiet. Feeling all was safe we broke cover and had a short discussion about the outline of the area. We decided to go down to the road to check it out. We were within 15 yards of the remaining ditch. I proceeded to cross first. There was a little wooden plank across the sheugh. I just had stepped on the plank about 15 feet in front of Seamus. Then I heard rapid machine-gun fire and saw flashes coming from a ditch or bushes approximately twenty feet away. Simultaneously I felt a burning sensation to the side of my body. The shots hit me in the stomach and right side, turning me round. I said to myself, "I mustn't go down". Immediately thoughts flashed through my mind that it was the SAS and to fall down would mean certain death. As I lifted my leg back across the ditch under continuous fire, I heard Seamus shout with pain and fall down. I think their objective was to shoot both of us in the lower body and legs to put us down so as to question us afterwards. They all fired at me at once. Then they switched their rifles on Seamus who was behind me but slightly to the right. It was in these few seconds I got a chance to escape. They could have shot us in the head. They were using night sights and were only 20 to 30 feet away. Running away from the scene up a field I felt weak and sickish. I was still in the line of fire and could hear the bullets whizzing by. About 50 yards up I was struck on the left leg by a bullet, almost bringing me to the ground. I managed to stay on my feet and stumbled on towards a gap, about 50 yards. I stumbled through the gap and turned left. I travelled up the back of a ditch which blocked the line of fire. Uppermost in my mind was to get away as far as possible and escape.

'The shooting stopped. Flares went up and brightened the sky as if it was day. Fearing being spotted I decided to roll into a ditch until the flares stopped. After several minutes they did. I was lying on my side. I tried to move knowing I was still within 100 yards from where the SAS were lying. I couldn't move. I felt paralysed from the stomach down. I thought I would be detected with little problem and killed. I tried my best to crawl but to no avail. A branch was hanging down over me. I lay on my stomach with my face downwards. I could see I had been shot in the finger.

'It was getting brighter. Approximately 15 minutes had passed in silence since the flares went up, when I heard branches being broken by people crossing hedges. I heard voices. The tone indicated they were questioning someone. There did not seem to be any response. Then there were three single shots from weapons similar to those used in the initial ambush. Around the same time a fancy jeep or truck came up the lane beside me. This lane led up from the main road. It stopped about 30 yards from where I was lying. Four or five people jumped out carrying rifles. They wore a mixture of military and civilian clothing, some with combat jacket and jeans, some with army trousers and ordinary civilian jacket. One of them stood guard at the vehicle. The other four walked by me and into the field where Seamus was lying. They did not see me. The uniform I was wearing blended into the ditch and foliage around me. I could hear the men talking. I could hear them searching on the other side saying I had been wounded and couldn't be far away.

'The next two hours passed with no sign of anybody but the one guarding the truck. All this time I kept total silence. Even breaking a twig would give away my life. I was getting weaker. I couldn't move. My body felt like a corpse it was so cold. I thought I was paralysed. I could see my watch. Then about ten of them came back through the gap and up by where I was. This was the first time I saw those who did the shooting. The ambush party was distinctive from the others. They were all in military fatigues and had large back-packs. One of them had a huge pack including a small shovel strapped to the back of it. They chatted and laughed for several minutes before a number got into the truck and drove off while the rest walked towards the road.

'This was the first time I thought I had a chance to live, knowing the SAS had left the area. My vision was beginning to fade. The farmhouse in the distance was blurred. Within minutes of the SAS withdrawing, two helicopters came soaring in a circle overhead, one of them flying very low, the other flying in a higher wider circle. Very few people would wish to be captured but I did, knowing as time passed I would die from injuries. Then I spotted several dozen soldiers and RUC closing in. A soldier with a dog followed the blood-stains from where the shooting took place. He pulled out a short-arm and pointed it, shouting to his mate that he had found a person... He said, "Have you been shot, mate?" I said, "I'm riddled". He put the gun away and put the leash on the dog. He said he would go down to the road and get medical help.

'After that two RUC men came up. They dragged me out. I felt a terrible pain in my spine like a sword going through me. They started asking questions – "What's your name? Who's with you? How many are with you? What were you going to do?" I answered only my name and gave my Fermanagh address. When I didn't co-operate they became agitated and started to kick me viciously. I squealed with pain. I still refused to answer and pretended I was on the brink of death. The pain was so bad I didn't care what happened. They debated whether to shoot me or let me die like a rat behind a ditch. One of the RUC men had his foot on my chest and a rifle pushed against my forehead. One of them said, "Don't shoot him. Just let him die". I said I was a soldier of war and shouldn't be treated with brutality.

'An Army doctor arrived with several soldiers. He told the RUC to stop mistreating me, that that was no way to treat a seriously-injured person. He ordered six of them to lift me carefully out of the ditch, very gently, two at each bending point and lay me down on the concrete lane running parallel. He put me on a drip and located each injury. He said there were serious abdominal injuries. He placed a large bandage right around the trunk. He said the leg was broken. He bandaged my knee and hand. While he was doing all this he told the RUC to watch carefully as it might come in useful some day if some of their colleagues were ever injured.

'An argument ensued between the RUC and the doctor as to how to remove me to hospital. The RUC said an ambulance would be best as I would be DOA (dead on arrival). He overruled them. He demanded on his radio one of the helicopters flying overhead. They said there were other 'suspected terrorists' in the area and they were needed. They finally agreed to send one from Omagh. I had to wait 15 minutes before it arrived. While we waited I listened to their comments, "How was it the first boys didn't find him? They must have been blind". It must have been the uniform saved me.

'When the helicopter arrived I was placed on the floor of it. The doctor ordered the pilot to fly to Enniskillen as there was too little time to fly to Belfast. In Enniskillen I went through a six-hour operation. I must have appeared as a British soldier to the nurses. I heard the medic explaining what he had done when I was brought in. After the operation I was flown to the intensive unit of the Royal Victoria Hospital, Belfast, that same evening. I was moved to the Musgrave Park hospital four days later and remained there two months'.

A priest was summoned at 8.30 am from Roslea. He walked to the place where Seamus McElwain was lying. The Army refused to let him turn the head for anointing as the dead man was lying face downwards. The priest, Fr McCabe, had known Seamus as a youth.

Seamus McElwain was the eldest of a family of eight. According to *An Phoblacht/Republican News* he joined Fianna Éireann at fourteen years of age and became OC of the IRA in County Fermanagh at the age of nineteen. He was captured from a house in 1981 in the same area where he was shot. He was sentenced to a recommended 30 years term for the murders of a UDR man and an RUC reservist. He was a candidate in the Republic's general election in February 1982 while on remand in Crumlin Road Prison, Belfast, and polled 4,000 first preference votes in the Cavan-Monaghan constituency. His father, Seamus McElwain senior, was a former member of Monaghan County Council, a builder and farmer. Seamus junior worked along with his father in the building trade.

The death of Seamus McElwain was welcomed by loyalist politicans. The Rev. Ian Foster of the DUP (Democratic Unionist Party) said, 'I welcome McElwain's removal. He had a lot of blood on his hands'. The SAS action was interpreted as building up the 'secret war' against the IRA. SAS operations had been ordered by the government in Westminster to sell the Anglo-Irish agreement to rebel unionists. The idea was to show that the agreement, which led to greater co-operation with the Gardaí, brought results.

Seamus McElwain's local popularity in County Monaghan, his highstanding among IRA men, his death at the hands of the SAS, the delight of loyalists, the blow to IRA prestige, ensured that he had a massive funeral.

Crowds turned out in Clones, Smithboro and Scotstown as his body was brought home. When the funeral arrived at his family home, three IRA men stepped forward from a guard of honour and fired what *Republican News* called 'defiant volleys of shots over the coffin of their comrade'. There was tension at his funeral on 28 April. Some 150 Gardaí in riot gear watched the cortège and some 3,000 mourners arrived at St Mary's church at Urblesh-anny. In a funeral oration Martin McGuinness of Sinn Féin said that after his escape from prison Seamus McElwain returned to active service when others would have thought of going to the United States to start a new life. He had been looked after during that time by the people of Fermanagh and Monaghan who had loved him and willingly gave up their time, their food and their homes to keep him safe. 'What happened,' he said, 'in the early hours of Saturday morning was that an Irish freedom fighter was murdered by British terrorists.'

On 29 April Seán Lynch was charged at a special court in Musgrave Park hospital, Belfast, on four counts relating to possession of weapons and explosives with intent to endanger life. At his trial he was sentenced to 25 years imprisonment. Lynch's phrase on his capture that he was a 'soldier of war' was brought up at his trial. Judge McDermott referred to it in his summing-up. He said he was no soldier but a criminal. This detail under-lines the British problem. If it is a war, then under the Geneva Convention captured IRA men would have to be treated as prisoners-of-war and criminal proceedings could not be taken against them. If it is not a war, then shooting to kill is not justified. If it is not a war, are not soldiers then bound by the civil law? If the SAS kill a wounded man, how then do they in practice face the law? The same answer emerges in McElwain's case as in so many others. Let us see how the SAS explain their action in their statements at Seán Lynch's trial. Italics are mine.

All four soldiers state that their intention was to *arrest* anyone seen acting suspiciously in the area.

Soldiers 'B' and 'C' were positioned at the bomb 'firing-point'. Soldier 'B' was armed with a Heckler and Koch self-loading rifle. Soldier 'C' was armed with a Colt M-16 rifle. 'A' and 'D' at an observation point 100 metres to the east were armed with Colt M-16 self-loading rifles.

'A' and 'D' heard a long burst of automatic gunfire at 4.40 am. This must have been Soldier 'B' firing his HK sub-machine-gun. *'B' and 'C' say 'B' challenged the men:* 'B' shouted 'Halt. Hands up. Army' before opening fire.

Next point. *Were the SAS men's lives in danger or did they think their lives were in danger?* Soldier 'B': 'One of the men stepped off the bank into the ditch which was the firing-point. I then challenged them by shouting "Halt. Hands up. Army". *As I was speaking I was aware that both men were taking up firing positions with their rifles. I believed that they were going to open fire on us.* So I fired a controlled burst firstly at the man in the ditch and then switched

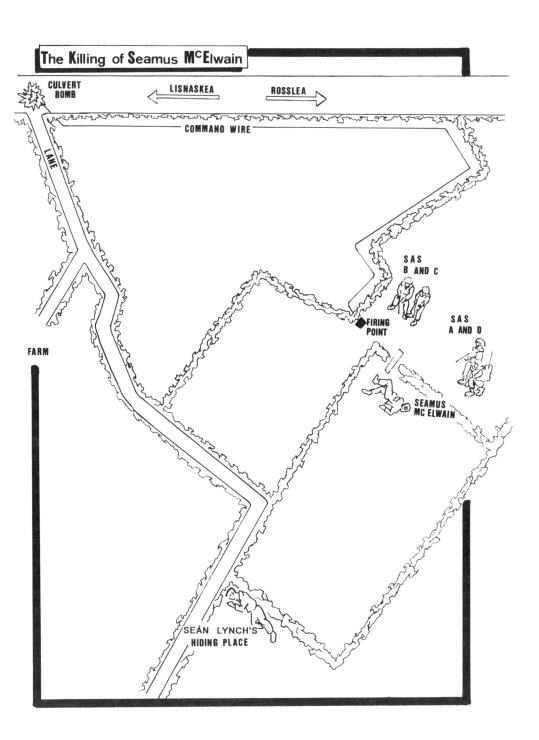

The Killing of Seamus McElwain

CULVERT BOMB

← LISNASKEA

ROSSLEA →

COMMAND WIRE

LANE

SAS B AND C

FIRING POINT

SAS A AND D

FARM

SEAMUS MCELWAIN

SEÁN LYNCH'S HIDING PLACE

my fire to the man on the bank. I was aware that Soldier 'C' had opened fire very shortly after me. At this time I heard screams but was unable to pinpoint where it had come from exactly. But I knew it was from the area where I had sighted the two armed men. I moved my position and I heard and saw further movement in the area of the firing-point and gunfire continued around me. I believed that I was under fire from the armed men. I continued to fire in the direction of the firing-point. During this I think I had two stoppages in my gun which I cleared. At this stage I advised Soldier 'A' and 'D' to approach our position.'

Soldier 'C' also at the firing-point says: 'There was a full moon with no cloud. At approximately 04.45 hours on 26 April 1986 I observed two armed men carrying rifles approach the firing-position from the south. One man was carrying a bag over his shoulder. He removed the bag from his shoulder and placed it on the ground behind him. I could see them clearly because the moon was behind them. They stood above the firing-point. One man pointed into the ditch and then down towards the road. He then climbed down into the ditch. At this point Soldier 'B' challenged them by saying something like "Halt. Hands up. Army". *The man in the ditch brought his rifle up as though he was going to open fire.* Soldier 'B' opened fire. I moved my position about two yards to the left of Soldier 'B' and opened fire at both gunmen. During the fire I heard both men scream. I covered the firing-point and put up a flare. Soldier 'A' and 'D' moved up behind me and then moved to my left.'

Forensic evidence at the trial of Seán Lynch showed that neither IRA man fired a weapon. The Ruger Mini-14 rifle which Lynch carried was found by the Senior Scientific Officer at the Northern Ireland Forensic Science Laboratory in the hedge. A few feet away in the field was McElwain's FNC rifle adjacent to his body. The FNC rifle had been hit by a bullet and the mechanism was jammed; there was a live round in the chamber. As recovered, the Ruger's safety-catch was still at 'safe' position. As in similar SAS killings, the SAS men thought they were being shot at! In fact it is their own gunfire they hear or unexplained phantom shots!

'B' says: '*Gunfire continued around me. I believed that I was under fire from the armed men...* I advised Soldier 'A' and 'D' to approach our position. As far as I was concerned I thought both armed men were still in the vicinity, one being in the ditch and one on top of the bank. I stayed in the hedge to give fire support if necessary while the other three moved forward to a hedge which ran beside the ditch I mentioned earlier. I saw Soldier 'A' cross into the next field and *I heard what I thought to be a low velocity shot being fired in our general direction.* I could not say for sure who it was aimed at. I also heard more shots from my colleagues. I then became aware that a body had been found nearby...'

Soldier 'B' also heard the 'phantom shot': 'Soldier 'A', 'D' and myself moved forward towards the hedge. We were covered by Soldier 'B'. When we reached the hedge Soldier 'A' was going through the gap in the hedge *when I heard what sounded like a shot.* At the same time *I saw a person on the ground who was crouching and facing Soldier 'A'. I thought that the shot had come from this armed man. I believed Soldier 'A's' life was in danger* so I fired one or two aimed shots at this man...'

This is the scenario for killing McElwain who had already been shot, who had screamed with pain. He is now a gunman facing 'A' whose life is in danger; indeed he is believed to have fired a shot. Much of the usual phraseology is in all the statements to ensure SAS immunity. It is a monotonous pattern.

Let us go back to 'C's statement: 'I believed Soldier 'A's' life was in danger so I fired either one or two aimed shots at this man. At the same time Soldier 'D' fired some shots. The man slumped to the ground after these shots were fired. We then checked the local area for the other man but I did not see him. During this time I saw two rifles. One was in the firing-point and the other was lying just behind and near to the body of the man...'

Soldier 'D' relates the shooting of McElwain in similar terms – 'Soldier 'A', 'D' and myself moved forward towards the hedge. I took cover at the hedge. Soldier 'A' fired what I believe to be two shots. *(In his statement Soldier 'A' says 'I want to say that what I fired at was a log in the hedgerow'.)* Soldier 'A' instructed me to cover him because he was moving down to the firing-position. I was lying covering him until he reached the firing-point. As he crossed the ditch I had to stand up to keep him within my view. As soon as I stood up *I heard what I thought was a shot* and at the same time I saw a man in a *crouching-cum-kneeling position.* I believed that this man was armed and he was facing Soldier 'A'. I fired two aimed shots at this person. At the same time Soldier 'C' fired shots. The man then slumped to the ground. Myself and Soldier 'C' moved forward to the firing-point. I covered the man lying on the ground...'

None of the IRA men fired their weapons. The *Sunday Telegraph,* 27 April 1986, referred to the 'early morning gun battle' and called the operation 'one of the most brilliant successes by the British Army in the "bad lands" of the border region... the stake-out bore all the hallmarks of a meticulously-planned SAS operation'. It said the IRA men were challenged by troops in camouflaged dress and that, according to Army HQ, shots were exchanged and McElwain died instantly. The role of the media and Army statements are important elements in the propaganda war. In this case they distorted the truth in saying that the men died in a fair fight.

Forensic evidence shows that no shots were exchanged. The IRA men did not fire. Both were seriously wounded in the initial burst of SAS firing. Lynch escaped. He says that he heard the SAS men interrogating McElwain where he lay wounded, 15 minutes after he had been first shot. Then he heard three single shots.

Seamus McElwain has now become a legend within republican circles as a soldier, somewhat like Francis Hughes. Seán Lynch wrote in *Borderline*, a Sinn Féin publication, August 1988: 'Operating with various active service units, Seamus soon became a fearless soldier. Faced with a problem others would fail to resolve, his famous words were "It can be done". This confidence and enthusiasm was an inspiration to his fellow-volunteers... Only those closest to Seamus knew his personal characteristics. He seldom talked of ordinary life and was quite shy though highly intelligent. He had little problem refraining from social activities, such as dances, though he did enjoy a few drinks and a good party. He looked forward to an occasional cigar and as much chocolate as you could carry to him...' In the same publication Bik McFarlane wrote of McElwain's part in the escape from H-Block, Long Kesh, in 1983:- 'Seamus played an important part in securing H-Block 7 on September 25th 1983, in terms of both the sound advice he had given in the weeks beforehand and in the active role he played on the day itself. But it was during the arduous and dangerous slog through the fields and rivers southwards that he displayed the qualities which distinguish the exceptional from the average. His wealth of experience from operating in country lanes and hedgerows was to prove vital for the survival of the small unit of eight volunteers who took to the fields with him that Sunday night. He was meticulous in studying our intended route, working with a small and none-too-detailed map, and displayed tremendous confidence as he led off at the head of our unit. During the following days he was a constant source of encouragement for men with weary limbs, urging them ever onwards. His rural knowledge at times seemed uncanny, but it is beyond question that it was his tact and experience which were major factors in ensuring that his comrades reached safety. For this he quite deservedly earned the respect and total admiration of each one of us...'

The Killing of Frank Hegarty

On 26 May 1986 the body of Frank Hegarty was found outside Castlederg, County Tyrone, some sixty yards from the Donegal border. His hands had been tied and he had been blindfolded, an obvious indication that he had been interrogated by his captors. The body was spotted by the Gardaí and they informed the RUC. In a statement the IRA said they had executed him because he had been working for British intelligence and had revealed the locations of major arms dumps. On 26 January 1986 the Gardaí had found 147 Russian-made rifles and a large quantity of ammunition in separate arms dumps at Carrowreagh, near Croghan, County Roscommon, at Mullaghroe, near the village of Gurteen, Sligo, and at Collera in the Strandhill area six miles from Sligo town. It was one of the biggest arms finds in the Republic. On that same day Frank Hegarty disappeared.

The IRA statement said:

'About seven years ago, while out walking greyhounds on the back road behind Glenowen in Derry city, Mr Hegarty was approached on several occasions by men with English accents. He was asked to work for British military intelligence and was persuaded to meet other Englishmen in a room at the White Horse Inn at Campsie. Although by this time a supporter of the republican movement, the men informed Mr Hegarty that that they knew that when he was a member of the Workers' Party, some years previously, he was responsible for planting a bomb in a car which exploded in Ebrington Barracks killing two civilians. After some questioning he admitted this and was assured that in return for becoming an agent he would be granted immunity from prosecution. He was given a payment of £400 and received weekly payments of £25 plus expenses incurred in meeting with his handlers in the Limavady or Waterside areas. On one occasion he was taken into Ebrington Barracks by one of five handlers to whom he reported or phoned over the years. During this period he was in no great position to pass on really valuable information and so, about two years ago, he was instructed to slowly ingratiate himself with the IRA and his offer of services was eventually accepted in the form of a "helper". Over a period of time he picked up pieces of information but in January of this year he became aware of a major movement of arms in the Free State. He contacted one of his handlers, "Brian", giving him the details and confirming the locations on an Ordnance Survey map. He was assured by "Brian" that, in order to protect him, the weapons would be monitored but would not be seized until they were broken down into smaller dumps and picked off at will. However, for the British and Irish governments the temptation of demonstrating to the loyalists the security value of the Hillsborough agreement was too great and so they decided to act on January 26. Within hours of the seizure, armed English agents, apparently without normal British Army or RUC cover, or without their knowledge, met Mr Hegarty as he came out of his home in Shantallow at 8.45 am. He took his car to the New Foyle Bridge where he transferred to an enclosed van. He was taken by private plane from Aldergrove to England... In this semi-detached house he was debriefed by his handlers. They also occupied the semi next door. He said that he was extremely angry that, contrary to assurances, his cover had been blown.'

The statement went on to say that Frank Hegarty maintained that he returned to Derry hoping that he could convince the IRA that he had not turned informer but that he had been kidnapped and compromised to look like the scapegoat for somebody else.

Mr Seamus Mallon, MP said that the killing of Frank Hegarty was part of a shoot-to-kill policy by the Provos against not only members of the nationalist community but against members of their own organisation.

At the Requiem Mass for Frank Hegarty in St Eugene's Cathedral, Derry, Fr Michael Canny said that the killing was a cruel, unjust and brutal act. He said that an excuse for the killing had been offered but that was no justification for what had taken place. His family believes him innocent. Others cynically asked – was he the only one in Derry at this time who gave information?

The Loughgall Massacre[125]

In 1921 twelve IRA volunteers were killed by the Black and Tans in Clonmult, County Cork, in the Irish War of Independence. On 8 May 1987 the IRA suffered its worst casualty in one incident since that engagement. Eight volunteers were shot dead in an SAS/RUC ambush in the village of Loughgall, County Armagh.

The IRA had renewed its activity from December 1986 following what seemed to be a winding down in its campaign. From the hunger-strike period 1980-81, the republican movement entered the political field in a more determined way. There followed then for some years a tactical balancing act between the 'ballot box and the Armalite'. On the whole, the political activity gained prominence over the military campaign. December 1986 saw a return to bombing and shooting in the south and south-west counties of the North. Up to the attack on Loughgall Barracks, there were 22 attacks on RUC stations. On 9 January 1987 RUC reservist, Ivan Crawford, was killed in a litter-bin explosion in Enniskillen. On 26 January Major George Shaw, UDR, was shot dead outside his home in Dungannon. Peter Nesbitt, an RUC reservist, was killed in an explosion in Ardoyne, Belfast, on 10 March. John Chambers, a Protestant man, was ambushed and shot in Rostrevor on 13 March. Leslie Jarvis, a prison officer, was shot dead in his car outside Magee College, Derry on 23 March. In the same incident Detective Inspector Austin Wilson and Detective Sergeant John Dennison were killed by a booby trap bomb that had been placed in Jarvis' car. On 30 March a soldier, Ian O'Connor of the Queen's Lancashire Regiment, was killed at the Divis Flats complex when two grenades blasted an armoured land-rover. Jim Oldman, UDR, was shot dead in his car as he entered the village of Ederney, County Fermanagh, at 8.45 am on 3 April. At 11.20 pm on the same day George Shaw, RUC reservist, was shot dead outside Ballinahinch RUC Barracks, County Down. Two RUC reservists, Robert J. McClean and Fred Armstrong, were shot down on the street in Portrush, County Antrim, on 11 April. Inspector David Ead, RUC, former British soldier, was shot dead in the street in Newcastle, County Down, on 20 April. On 23 April Sergeant Tom Cook, RUC, was shot dead in the car park outside the City of Derry Golf Club. On 28 April William Marchant, UVF leader, was shot dead on the Shankhill Road, Belfast.

In that period the IRA lost three men. Gerard Logue was accidentally shot at Gobnascale on 22 March. Finbarr McKenna died in a premature explosion on the Springfield Road, Belfast, on 2 May. Laurence Marley was shot dead by the UVF at his home on 2 April. The shooting of Marchant was a retaliation killing.

Sir Maurice Gibson (74), a Lord Chief Justice of Appeal (and the North's most senior judge after the Lord Chief Justice, Lord Lowry), and his wife Cecily (67) were killed in an explosion on Saturday 25 April at Killeen, County Armagh. A 500 lb bomb in a car parked on the hard shoulder of the Dublin-Belfast Road exploded at 8.35 am shortly after he crossed the border after leaving his Garda escort and before taking up with his RUC escort. The judge was a prime target for the IRA. Few members of the RUC and British Army and no members of the SAS have been convicted of murder. Lord Justice Gibson was for many years their ally. 'Shooting may be justified as a method of arrest,' he said in 1977, comparing security operations with a Wild West posse in pursuit. In 1984 he acquitted three RUC men of the murder of three IRA men. This was in the middle of a stormy Shoot-to-Kill controversy; the work of the SAS had been passed on to a section of the RUC. Acquitting the RUC members Sir Maurice Gibson commended them on their 'courage and determination in bringing the three deceased men to justice in this case, the final court of justice'. Another remark of Lord Justice Gibson was appreciated by the armed forces – 'When a policeman or soldier is ordered to arrest a dangerous criminal and in substance, as in this case, to bring him back dead or alive, how is he to consider his conduct now? May it not be that some may now ask: am I to risk my life carrying out this order, knowing that if I survive my reward will be the further risk of life imprisonment as a murderer?' In another case he acquitted a paratrooper of killing 12- year-old Majella O'Hare of Whitecross, County Armagh. He accepted the evidence of the soldier that he must have fired at a gunman as he claimed.

Following the publicity of the murder of Lord Justice Gibson and his wife, two notable interviews with IRA spokesmen appeared in the newspapers. Emily O'Reilly reported from Belfast in the *Sunday Tribune,* 3 May 1987, and Peter Murtagh for *The Guardian,* 5 May, talked to 'one of the men behind the campaign'.

One IRA spokesman admitted a major morale problem in Belfast due to 'lack of action' in the previous two years. Following the isolation of suspects, however, the killing of an alleged informer Charles McIlmurry, found shot dead at Killeen on 13 April 1987, and the release of IRA members who had been incarcerated under the discredited supergrass system, problems in Belfast, he maintained, had been overcome. This was further boosted by an IRA army convention under the guise of an Irish language seminar. The spokesman said, 'It was the first time that the leadership was democratically elected by the volunteers and it now directly mirrors the volunteers on the ground. A 12-person executive was elected first; they in turn elected a 7-person army council who then elected a chief of staff and then the GHQ'. The reporter commented that the real power of the movement lay with the GHQ and with the quarter-master general. Significantly the spokesman said that the current spate of IRA activity would shortly tail off; obviously the element of surprise had diminished and the British forces had become more alert. He added that nobody would be upset if there was a lull for two weeks, in the run-in to the British general election. The IRA spokesperson in *The Guardian* piece emphasised the 'reorganisation' nature of IRA activity, heralded the importance of operating again in Belfast, and admitted the difficulty of operating in South Armagh due to increased surveillance. He said, 'The IRA is fairly confident and stronger than at any time in the previous ten years. There are operations in the pipeline. Units are armed'.

Against all the cautionary philosophy put forward by IRA spokesmen in these interviews, a unit of the East Tyrone Brigade went ahead with a plan to bomb and attack by gunfire the RUC Barracks in the village of Loughgall. Loughgall has for two hundred years been the symbol of Protestant 'ascendancy', being the birth-place of sectarian disorder and the Orange Order. It was the centre of the 'Triangle of Death' murders of 30 Catholic civilians in the 1972-5 period. After the massacre of the IRA men, a spokesman of the East Tyrone Brigade explained, 'We attacked Dungannon courthouse a few days ago (Thursday 7 May) and the Loughgall attack was part of the IRA's plan to hit areas which had remained untouched. We want to show that there is no normalisation and the SAS action proves we are in a war situation. We have always maintained that; they have always practised it but never admitted it'.

Even before the murder of Lord Justice Gibson, British forces were inevitably on the alert. There had been a strong IRA campaign in the previous six months. Now the eyes of government looked to the military commanders to help hide their embarrassment and assuage unionist feeling. The Secretary of State, Mr Tom King, and the British Government were open to respond to demands for severe counter-measures. The British right-wing press was also in the mood for a backlash. The *Daily Mail* of 28 April 1987 carried the heading, 'Unleash SAS on the killer squads'. On the same day the *Daily Mirror* ran the banner headlines 'SAS set to Swoop' – 'Undercover army is briefed for battle'. Roy Mason, Labour MP and former Secretary of State, Northern Ireland, upholder of the SAS while in office, led demands for further security measures including the use of the SAS. Mr King said that the options recommended would be discussed with security chiefs. On 27 April he held a meeting with RUC Chief Constable, Sir John

Hermon, and the British Army Commander, Lt-General Sir Robert Pascoe at Stormont Castle. On 6 May Mr King presented his security package in the House of Commons. There would be an increase of RUC reservists and more UDR in a full-time role. On 7 May Sir John Hermon was more forthcoming on the role of the SAS. In a television interview he said it would be used when needed. He promised the security forces' 'approach would be tougher, different and sharper', and its capacity would be sharpened in 'an overt and covert way'. If he had already been briefed on a plan to attack Loughgall, would he have dropped a hint of SAS preparedness so publicly? Maybe so. Obviously Mr King's package would have included extra measures to improve intelligence-gathering by covert methods. There would have been a strengthening of the SAS at various isolated RUC stations like Loughgall; such a measure had been taken after a previous wave of IRA mortar attacks on police stations.

The British forces were in possession of precise information on the planned attack. An indiscreet phonecall made by an IRA man was overheard and relayed to the RUC.

The East Tyrone unit of the IRA was familiarly known as the 'A' team. They were a thorn in the side of the RUC and British Army. On 7 December 1985 they attacked Ballygawley RUC Barracks. The republician magazine *Iris* (No. 11, October 1987) described it thus: 'One volunteer took up a position close to the front gate. Two RUC men opened the gate and the volunteer calmly stepped forward, shooting them both dead at point blank range. Volunteers firing AK-47 and Armalite rifles moved into the barracks, raking it with gunfire. Having secured the building they planted a 100 lb bomb inside. The bomb exploded, totally destroying the building after the volunteers had withdrawn to safety.' In what was to be a carbon copy of the attack on Loughgall, the IRA bombed the RUC barracks at the Birches, County Tyrone, on 11 August 1986. A heavy mechanical digger was used as a tank to breach the security fence. *Iris* (No. 11) gives this account – 'The carefully co-ordinated attack involved a dozen volunteers using a comandeered low loader and a Volvo mechanical shovel. The IRA placed a 300 lb bomb on the shovel and rammed it against the wall, before detonating the bomb. The barracks was demolished and as the volunteers withdrew they raked the remains of the building with over 200 shots'.

After the massacre of the eight IRA men and also a civilian at Loughgall, the RUC alleged that the weapons had been used in seven murders. One of the weapons, a Ruger revolver, had been taken from one of the RUC reservists in the Ballygawley attack. The RUC reservists who died on that occasion were William J. Clements and George Gilliland. The seven murders mentioned were:- John Kyle a building materials supplier who was shot dead on 26 July 1986 in the Crossroads Bar, Greencastle, County Tyrone (the IRA tabbed him as a 'collaborator'); four UDR were killed –

Thomas Irwin shot at Mountfield, 26 March 1986, Martin Blaney shot on his farm at Eglish, County Tyrone on 6 October 1986, Major George Shaw shot outside his home in Dungannon on 26 January 1987, and William Graham shot on his farm at Pomeroy, 25 April 1987; two civilians killed by the guns worked for the same building firm – Ken Johnston shot dead at Magherafelt, 24 October 1986 and Harry Henry shot at his home in the Loup, County Derry, 21 April 1987.

The IRA men shot dead by the SAS in Loughgall on 8 May 1987 were Patrick Kelly (30), Mullaghmore Park, Dungannon, Pádraig McKearney (33), Moy, County Tyrone, James Lynagh (32), Monaghan, Declan John Arthurs (21), Roclain Road, Galbally, County Tyrone, Michael Anthony Gormley (24), Galbally, Seamus Donnelly (19), Cappagh Road, Aughnaskea, County Tyrone, Eugene Kelly (26), Lurgylea Road, Cappagh, County Tyrone, and Gerard O'Callaghan (29), Tullymore, near Armagh City. The civilian shot dead was Anthony Hughes (36) of Caledon, County Tyrone.

Declan Arthurs had been away from his home for some time and could be regarded as 'on the run'. Pádraig McKearney was a Long Kesh escapee. Jim Lynagh from Monaghan would have been regarded as a prime suspect if he had crossed into the North. Probably from Tuesday these men would have crossed into the North and billeted in Tyrone. Plans would have included the preparation and conveyance of the bomb and the procuring of a mechanical digger to use as a tank as in the Birches' attack. The OC, Patrick Kelly, would have had to have the attack passed from a higher command. In an article in *The Irish Times*, 5 June 1987, Jim Cusack reported that according to local sources up to 14 men would have been involved in the attack. If there were six others, that would have included those in the three scout cars and those involved in holding captive the owner of the mechanical digger and his family. Cusack mentions another strange detail – 'It is understood that the name of Pádraig McKearney was not on the list handed in, when representatives of the dead IRA men came to claim the bodies in the early hours of May 9th'. This list was published in the Saturday edition of the *Evening Herald* and may suggest changes in the team at a late hour. The driver of the van used in the attack was Eugene Kelly, who would have been intimate with the maze of small roads that make up east Tyrone and north Armagh. There is an indication of how aware the RUC was of what was going on. Fergal Keane in the *Sunday Tribune*, 10 May 1988, reported, 'Other locals said there is usually a high level of police and military activity in the area. This had intensified up until Wednesday of last week but from then no army or RUC landrovers had been seen in the village'. This is an indication that the SAS and RUC were in position from Wednesday, 6 May.

The mechanical digger was hijacked from Peter Mackle's farm at Lislassley Road on the Armagh side of Moy village, a small road running off the

Moy-Armagh Road, linking one might say two public-houses at each end, Trainors' and Chambers'. Mrs Mackle had just pulled into the farm with her sons and daughters when five IRA men arrived. They told her they wanted the mechanical digger and diesel oil. Two of them stayed behind and held the Mackle family captive to prevent them reporting the hijacking. Two left by car. Declan Arthurs drove the digger. His father had an agricultural contracting business and he had plenty of experience driving mechanical diggers. The three left Mackles' about 6.30 pm. By a direct line the distance from Mackles via Portadown Road, Collegeland, Hoggs' public house would be about four miles. Instead they went a circuitous route, Portadown direction, Ardress cross-roads and then right for Loughgall, a journey of about nine miles. Probably it was thought that a digger would not look out of place on a wider road; furthermore there was the matter of picking up the 200 lb bomb. The other seven men of the attacking unit travelled together in a van. The scout cars were presumably linked by radio to sound a warning in the event of a roadblock. The van, a blue Toyota Hiace, was hijacked from a business premises at Mountjoy Road in Dungannon by masked men at 2.30 pm on Friday, 8 May. It was obviously then hidden until evening. When the IRA attacked Ballygawley RUC Barracks in December 1985 and killed two RUC men at the front of the building, the other policemen escaped by running out of the back of the station. The larger unit of eight men to cover front and back of the barracks was to ensure that this would not happen. The JCB hijacked for Loughgall was not as heavy as the one used at the Birches; furthermore a low wall plus the security fence prevented full breach at Loughgall; a glance at photographs taken after the bombing shows the remains of the digger still on the road and the fence largely intact; the power of the bomb however was sufficient to destroy the barracks.

Loughgall is a sweet little village of some 350 inhabitants, all of whom are Protestant, an indication of its staunch loyalist history. In May-time the surrounding countryside is resplendent with apple blossoms, for this is orchard country. The police station is at the Armagh City end of the village. Normally it is manned by six officers including a sergeant and is opened on a part-time basis. 'Limited opening stations' was a measure introduced following IRA mortar-bomb attacks on country stations in recent years. Loughgall Station was opened for four hours daily, from 9 to 11 am and 5 to 7pm. On Fridays it closed 20 minutes earlier. Regular constables were withdrawn from Loughgall Station in preparation for the ambush and were replaced by the DMSU. The stake-out was composed of SAS men with blackened faces and RUC marksmen, all equipped with sniper scopes. It is most likely that the barracks was vacated.

At a point on the circuitous route to Loughgall, the bomb was placed in the bucket of the JCB; this did not take place at a derelict house as has been speculated. The digger approached Loughgall from the Portadown side. The van with its seven volunteers came from the Tyrone direction on to a road that merges into the Portadown side of Loughgall. It had been delayed and scout cars and digger waited for its arrival. Arthurs then drove the digger through the village on a scouting run; he passed the police station and observed the situation. He then turned and came back, passing the station once more. Meanwhile the van did the same thing. There must have been doubt whether to continue with the operation. One of the eight returned once again, this time in a scout car to observe the station and surrounding area. One can imagine a quiet village and the deathly stillness of the SAS and RUC waiting patiently to spring the ambush on the full team. The temptation would have been to open fire on the first passing of digger or van by the station. Patience prevailed; obviously the plan was to kill the attackers. They would be allowed to attack the station even to the point of destroying it and this to justify public opinion for the executions that would follow. It is easy to speculate from the events that followed that the IRA must have decided to 'half' abandon the attack. They would bomb the barracks and fire no shots, then make a quick getaway on a pre-planned route.

Residents say that at the time of the attack there was no sign of police or army. There was no helicopter. The village lay deadly still.

Declan Arthurs mounted the digger and set it in motion, the bucket raised on high, carrying the 200 lb bomb. It would have been a slow pace, the front wheels jolting under the weight. Gerard O'Callaghan, probably armed with a shotgun, and Tony Gormley armed with an automatic-rifle, mounted the digger to protect and encourage the driver. The van followed. No doubt the plan was to ram the protective fence as far as possible; then the driver would set alight the 40-second fuse; the three men would then run to the van which would have pulled in slightly in front of the digger, the back doors with the bolts cut free lying open; they would leap aboard and the party would speed away.

The digger reached the barracks at 7.20 pm. The driver crashed into the fence then set the fuse alight; then the three men ran for the van. Immediately shooting started. A withering fire was directed against the van. The three men would have turned and tried to run for it, perhaps firing a few shots. Then the bomb cracked in a great explosion blowing off the roof of the station and largely demolishing it. The withering fire continued for five minutes, an indication of the sustained nature of the firing. Some 1,200 rounds were fired. All the IRA men were killed within a small area. Four lay dead in the van which was riddled. Two men lay dead near the barracks about 20 or 30 yards apart. Another man lay dead about 60 or 70 yards from the barracks on the road on the village-centre side. These were the men who had ridden on the digger, Arthurs, Gormley and O'Callaghan. Only one man had made it out of the van, Seamus Donnelly. Seven of the IRA men were dressed in blue boiler suits and wore yellow gloves and balaclavas. Donnelly wore white trousers and this helped to identify him. He tried to escape into the football field opposite the barracks. The gate was locked and so he must have climbed it. SAS and police were stationed behind the hedgerow. They easily cut him down ten yards inside the field. Immediately the explosion was heard, a scout car picked up the volunteers guarding the Mackle family.

All the IRA men had multiple wounds and were shot in the head. Gerard O'Callaghan was shot front and back; he had a wound at the back of his ear. Declan Arthurs had, among other wounds, a bullet-entry straight down through the top of his head. Seamus Donnelly was literally riddled. Paddy Kelly's body was also riddled with wounds. There was one clear shot to his temple from a high velocity rifle which left a clear entry mark.

Anthony Hughes (36), an innocent motorist, was killed by gunfire 130 yards from the barracks on the Portadown side. His brother Oliver was severely wounded. On that splendid sunny day, they had gone to repair a lorry drive-shaft at John Guy's at Lissheffield. They finished the job on the lorry at his son Seán's yard. They went back to John Guy's house for their tea. John asked if they would leave his daughter Sheila up to a scallion field which he owned. They did this. They decided to drive home through Loughgall as it was a more direct road. Anthony drove the car. They were still wearing their blue overalls. They drove through Loughgall. Nothing appeared out of the ordinary. Just as they came over the hill at the church they heard a loud bang. Oliver says, 'I was aware that it was an explosion and saw smoke around the police barracks. Anthony stopped and was about to drive back when there was a heavy burst of gunfire from behind us. I heard the back window of the car smash and at the same time heard Anthony shout. At that same instant I felt a sharp pain in my back and a burning in my stomach. I lost consciousness'. Oliver, who miraculously survived the shooting, says there was no crossfire in their vicinity, contrary to the official RUC version. The gunfire that hit him and his brother came from behind. About 50 rounds hit the white Citroen (DIA 3428) from a garden ten yards to the rear. The IRA men were to the front a considerable distance away. The only window not shattered was the front windscreen which faced the IRA van and digger. The other windows were shattered and there were 17 bullet holes in the passenger side where Oliver was sitting. Obviously the brothers were mowed down by the SAS in ambush in mistake for IRA men. Coincidentally they also were wearing blue boiler suits. Oliver Hughes was hit twice on the right side of his back and in the left shoulder, his lungs collapsing under the impact; he was also hit in the left temple. There were no security checkpoints on the way to Loughgall. There was no one to warn motorists that they might be driving into an ambush. The stake-out forces did not want to give any alarm or alert that might spoil the surprise element. The risk led to Anthony Hughes's tragic death.

Just as the Hughes brothers drove towards the police station it was wrecked by an explosion. Anthony stopped the car. 'We can't drive past that,' he said. 'That looks like trouble.' Oliver suggested going back to the fork and making a detour. Then there was a roar of gunfire and both were hit. Throughout the whole of the next day, the RUC would not admit that the Hughes brothers were not members of the IRA team. 'They tried to blacken our names,' Oliver said. 'They tried to make out that we were IRA which was not right.' He called for a public enquiry. Mrs Brigid Hughes, wife of Anthony and mother of three small daughters, was bitter that the RUC did not clear her husband's name and did not offer sympathy, a point made by Fr Bernard Begley at Anthony Hughes's Requiem Mass. Fr Begley said that a *post-mortem* and inquest could reveal which guns fired at Hughes' car. He commented, 'The most tragic thing about it is that up to this moment no one on either side has said a word of apology or expressed sympathy to the widow and three children'.

The *Ulster Gazette* reported that the incident happened at 7.20 pm. 'One local man said he saw a white Citroen car with about five people on board at the station shortly beforehand.' Contrary to speculation this was not an IRA scout car. There was a surmise that since this was the same type and colour of car as the Hughes' car, the SAS made a ghastly mistake thinking it was an IRA scout car. Some twelve people were attending a parents' meeting of the Loughgall Girls' Friendly Society in St Luke's parish hall about 250 yards from the station. They were saved from injury from flying glass by the heavy curtains in the hall.

Just outside the hall, another motorist had a lucky escape. Mrs Beggs, a local woman, was driving into the village when the shooting started. Her red Mazda was hit three times from behind as she drove over the top of the hill. She escaped unhurt. Three members of the committee of Loughgall football club also had a miraculous escape. They were in the bar of the clubhouse, principally a wooden structure, preparing to open for the night, when they heard the shooting. They threw themselves on the ground and kept their heads down. Moments later the bomb went off. Pieces of glass and masonry rained down on them. Mr Victor Halligan said, 'The next thing we knew was that soldiers burst in and took us outside. At one stage I got the impression they thought we may have been involved as they had their guns trained on us. We were made to sit on the wall outside the club but were not allowed to look at what had gone on outside the station'. The three men were made to sit apart until a local RUC man identified them and they were allowed home at around 10 pm. 'As we walked home we saw two bodies, one lying against a wall and one lying beside a white car. However a policeman advised us to look the other way.'

Another motorist, a Catholic man in his forties from nearby Maghery, also drove into the scene. He was driving into Loughgall from the Armagh direction, the opposite direction to the attacking vehicles, on his way to a football match, when he heard the gunfire. He jumped from his car, 25 yards from the Toyota van. He took cover between the gable walls of two houses. He said, 'I lay there flat on the ground for what seemed like an eternity, praying to God for myself and my family'. When the shooting ended, he was arrested where he lay by soldiers with blackened faces and English accents. He was taken to Gough Interrogation Centre and interviewed by the police for five hours. His family only became aware of where he was when he phoned from Gough Barracks in the early hours of Saturday morning. Later he was treated by a doctor at home for severe nervous shock. An interview with him was published in the Tyrone paper *The Democrat*, 14 May 1987. He said, 'If I had driven another twenty yards, I'm sure I would be a dead man. I ran from the car when I heard the shooting; the explosion came later as I lay on the ground'.

Three young boys who came on the scene minutes after the shooting said in an interview with the *Sunday Tribune*, 10 May, that they were confronted by at least three men wearing military uniforms, speaking with English accents and wearing balaclavas. The youths said that they had been told by the Army that they had chased one IRA man up a road towards Portadown. They believed that this man was the one found furtherest from the RUC station. Soldiers were seen out on the Armagh side of the village firing continuously at the van. There were soldiers in the football field opposite the barracks who obviously shot Seamus Donnelly. There were soldiers in a garden on the village side who shot the Hughes brothers. It is clear that all exits were blocked and all parties of soldiers resisted firing until both digger and van had come into the net and had actually set about the attack on the barracks.

Only one empty magazine and one empty cartridge belonging to the IRA men were in the display of the IRA weapons set up by the RUC. If the IRA fired at all, probably only Gormley fired an automatic and O'Callaghan a shot from the shotgun. One of the strange remarks regarding the massacre was made by a senior officer in the RUC. He said that, after breaking through the wire with the JCB, the IRA opened fire on the station and were then 'engaged by the security forces' who returned fire before the bomb exploded. He then made the mysterious remark that at one stage police chased four men across nearby fields. If that is so, they were not IRA men. In the whole incident two policemen and one soldier were slightly injured by shrapnel.

Immediately after the shooting the RUC and British Army set up roadblocks at each end of the road leading to the barracks. Helicopters and

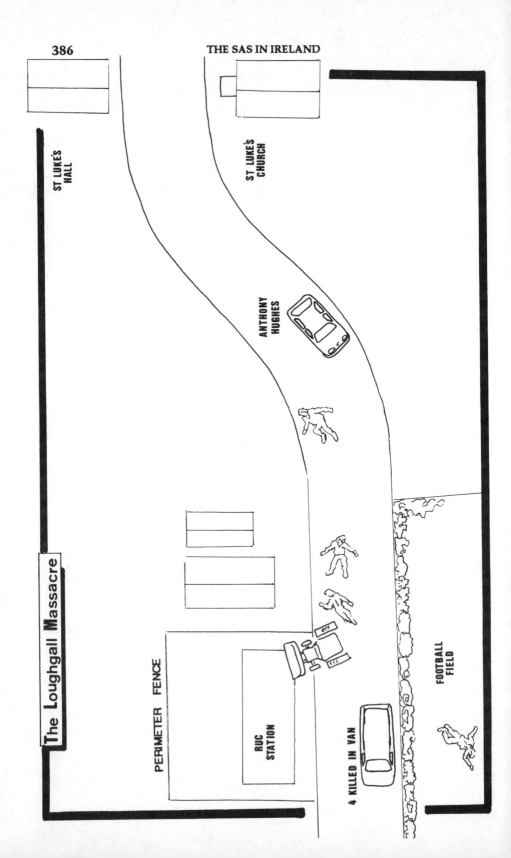

The Loughgall Massacre

ST LUKE'S HALL

ST LUKE'S CHURCH

ANTHONY HUGHES

PERIMETER FENCE

RUC STATION

4 KILLED IN VAN

FOOTBALL FIELD

personnel were coming and going for hours afterwards. However there was no searching helicopter. The cordon was confined to a small tight circle round Loughgall. There was no attempt to throw up a cordon in a wider circle to apprehend scout cars.The parish priest of Loughgall, Fr Charles Devlin, was washing his car outside his house in preparation for a wedding the next day when he heard the shooting. He went inside and some five minutes later heard the bang of the explosion. Different people from the area called with him, asking what happened. The telephone exchange beside the barracks had been damaged and so there was no possibility of making phone calls. The RUC sent a police car for him. He travelled to the village in the police car. The chief superintendent, however, was at the other roadblock on the Armagh side of the village. Another high-ranking policeman recognised Fr Devlin and let him through to adminster the last rites. Fr Devlin asked him if he knew any of the dead men. He said that he knew one of them, 'the man from Drumsallon' (O'Callaghan). Fr Devlin found the men in the positions I have already stated. He is adamant that there were four bodies in the van, not three as the RUC stated. His testimony that he attended Seamus Donnelly in the football field confirms the reports in the *Sunday Tribune*, 10 May, that locals claimed a body was lying in the football field. The same paper reported also that the RUC had discounted this. Fr Devlin noticed that all the men had been shot in the head, some in the face.

As is usual in Shoot-to-Kill cases, leaders of public opinion in the North divided on the issue. Nationalists pointed out that, if the RUC was privy to information, some or all of the attacking party could have been captured. They accused the Northern Ireland Office of sanctioning the setting-up of an ambush with the specific purpose of killing and taking no prisoners. The SDLP members were more hesitant than usual in their comments; they did not equate the Loughgall killings with the Shoot-to-Kill policy of 1983; they were saddened by the deaths and condemned the godfathers of the IRA for sending out young men to carry out dangerous attacks. Mr Austin Currie, SDLP called for an immediate inquiry into the killings. He repeated the question raised by his colleague Mr Seamus Mallon, MP as to why Mr Anthony Hughes and his brother Oliver were allowed to drive into an area allegedly staked out beforehand. He said, 'I understand many people's attitude has been tempered by the fact that there is a difference between someone who is completely innocent and someone involved in an attempted murder. I share those feelings myself but after all we live in a democracy. We live in a society where the attitude of my country, right or wrong, my army or police force, right or wrong, should not be allowed'. Fr Denis Faul, Dungannon, questioned the legal, moral and political aspects of the killings by British forces. He quoted the use of 'reasonable force' under Common Law and under section three of the Criminal Law Act. The Sinn Féin President Mr Gerry Adams, MP said, 'I am not making any accusations about "shoot-to kill". The double-speak and hypocrisy of those who condemn the IRA as terrorists and yet support the violence of the British forces is just contemptible'. The editorial in *An Phoblacht/Republican News*, 14 May 1987, commented, 'Republicans do not complain about the way in which the British forces carried out their operation. Centuries of British terror have taught us to expect it. The illegitimacy of the forces which carried out the Loughgall killings is not simply in their actions there but in their very presence in our country. It has always been and will always be illegitimate and unacceptable'.

Unionist leaders like Mr Ken Maginnis, MP rejected the need for a public enquiry. He sympathised with the Hughes family but said that all indications were that proper counter-measures had been taken. He said that he was encouraged by the actions in Loughgall, 'If it is necessary to kill these people then that is what must happen'. Sir Eldon Griffiths, Conservative MP and representative of the British police federations, said there should be no inquiry as this would undermine the effectiveness of the North's security forces in dealing with the IRA. He said it was a clear example of the security forces dealing with 'an attempt to carry out a murderous attack on a police station'. The Secretary of State, Mr Tom King, MP, commenting on Mr Gerry Adams' accusation of murder, said, 'I think that is the most total hypocrisy. I don't know who the godfathers were that planned that attack. The responsibility for that attack lies entirely with the people who decided to launch that attack and if people do launch terrorist attacks they must recognise that they have to face the consequences'.

The Tánaiste and Minister for Foreign Affairs in the Republic, Mr Brian Lenihan, TD, said that the Loughgall violence was initiated by the IRA and was met by a further violence from the British security forces. He did not publicly sympathise with the relatives of the deceased. The former Minister for Foreign Affairs, Mr Peter Barry, TD, said that it was important that the trust and confidence of the nationalist community built up through the structures of the Anglo-Irish Agreement should not be diluted as a result of Loughgall. In contrast with the attitude of the Irish government, which put the responsibility for the killings firmly on the IRA and failed to express concern about the way the IRA men had died, the Fine Gael leader, Mr Alan Dukes, TD, made a distinction. He deplored the loss of lives in Loughgall and the attack on the British security forces by the IRA group. That said, he pointed out that if the same security forces had acted before the ambush the loss of lives might have been averted.

In an editorial, 'Judge and Jury', 11 May 1987, *The Irish Times* commented – 'Whatever they (*the IRA men*) may have done or however suspect they may have been, the British Army were not entitled to act as judge, jury and executioner in their case. To do so would be to adopt the standards of the paramilitaries who brazenly complain when others employ their usual means of dealing with enemies, suspects and innocent bystanders'. On 14 May *The Irish Times* returned to the issue in an editorial – 'Those who composed the attacking party richly deserved to be taken out of circulation. But taking violent men out of circulation does not necessarily involve shooting them to death. There is a considerable body of opinion that the security forces might have succeeded in taking some or all of the attackers into custody. Their transportation was slow and cumbersome; there was no way off the roadway that leads past the barracks. If the security plan was other than to kill the attackers, the authorities have not attempted to demonstrate the fact. If there was an attempt to force a surrender, before or during the shooting , that has not been said. If there were circumstances in which the security forces believed they had no choice but to shoot and keep shooting until all the attackers were dead, they have not been set out. The Provisionals claim the North is at war. The lawful Governments of Dublin and London say otherwise; that it is a civil situation, with the Provisionals engaging in acts of criminal violence. In a civil situation, however dangerous and difficult, the forces of the State must act according to the civil law and not according to the rules of war. That means they must use reasonable force and seek to capture, where possible, for trial and imprisonment, those who commit crimes of violence. To do otherwise is to accede to the Provisionals' argument'.

Contrary to accusations that godfathers were responsible for the Loughgall attack, it is clear that the eight-man party was made up of seasoned volunteers. The OC of the party was Patrick Kelly. Jim Lynagh and Pádraig McKearney were also high-ranking officers over and above the unit. The quartermasters of the unit were also killed.

Patrick Kelly (30) was born in Carrickfergus, County Antrim. His parents, Vincent and Anne, moved to Dungannon when he was sixteen and he was brought up there. They were returning to their native locality. Patrick was a nephew of Liam Kelly who commanded Saor Uladh, a small republician military group active mainly in Tyrone and Fermanagh in the 1950s. Patrick's grandfather, Willie John Kelly, was a friend of the 1916 leader and Fenian Thomas Clarke, also a native of Dungannon. That simple example shows that anti-British resistance breaks out in every generation. Patrick Kelly was married; his wife was expecting their fourth child when he died. He lived near his parents. His father said, 'It was the RUC beatings which made Paddy a volunteer'. After his death he said, 'I am proud of him, that he went to do something about the plight of the nationalist people and died fighting for his country's freedom'. Patrick Kelly spent 22 months in prison on the word of informer Patrick McGurk, February 1982 to October 1983. When McGurk withdrew his evidence, Kelly was released and became commanding officer of the East Tyrone unit. At his funeral Fr Brian McNeice called for peace and justice in Ireland. He described Kelly as 'an upright man who loved his family, his Irish culture, his faith and his country'. He said that some leaders of society had been gloating over what had happened at Loughgall but no person or Government, only God, had the right to take life – 'There must be a rule of law impartially made and applied to every member of our land. The law of the jungle as we are now confronting it is not the solution to our needs'. Kelly, it was said, would never ask anybody to take a risk he would not take himself. He had a feeling for other volunteers and worried for their safety.

Jim Lynagh, the most senior IRA officer killed at Loughgall, was born on 13 April 1956. He was born and reared in Tully, near Monaghan town. He joined the IRA in his teens and operated with the East Tyrone Brigade. He was a close friend of Seamus McElwain who had been shot dead by the SAS. *An Phoblacht/Republican News*, 14 May 1987, said of him – 'So much was he feared by the crown forces that his name was repeatedly raised by RUC detectives interrogating people in Gough barracks. They offered massive bribes to set Jim Lynagh up and vowed that they would kill him before next Christmas'. His death was the second tragedy to strike the family; his younger brother Michael, politically uninvolved, died by his own hand in Mountjoy Prison on 10 September 1982; there were frequent official complaints made that he suffered from mental illness and had been harassed by the Garda Siochána. Another brother, Colm, is serving a sentence in Portlaoise Prison. His sister was married to Seamus Shannon in 1981; Shannon was one of the noted political prisoners extradited to the North from the Republic; the case against him in the North failed. Lynagh was arrested on 3 October 1973 when he was seriously injured by a bomb which exploded prematurely in a car in which he was travelling near Moy, County Tyrone. He served five years in Long Kesh for possession of explosives. He was elected as a Sinn Féin councillor to Monaghan Urban District Council in 1979. In April 1980 he was charged with membership of the IRA and was held for four months in Portlaoise Prison before being aquitted. In July 1980 he was the first person to be charged under the Criminal Law Jurisdiction Act; he was held again for four months before being acquitted for the murder of UDR member Harry Livingstone who was killed in Tynan on 6 March 1980. On 17 April 1982 he was arrested at Newbliss, County Monaghan, while carrying 12 rounds of ammunition. He was sentenced to three years. He was released from Portlaoise prison in April 1986. Lynagh combined a reputation as a fearless IRA man with a charming personality and was very popular in Monaghan district. *An Phoblacht/Republician News*, 14 May, said, 'His ready smile, love of the crack, his talent as a story-teller and his ready wit, made him immensely popular, a far cry from the image of a dour fanatic painted by sections of the media'.

Pádraig McKearney was also a high-ranking IRA member. He was one of the escapers from Long Kesh (Maze) prison in 1983. He was first arrested in 1972 and spent six weeks in Crumlin Road Jail before the charge was dropped. He was arrested again in December 1973 and sentenced to seven years for possession of weapons. He spent some of his term in Magilligan Prison in the company of Jim Lynagh. They were close friends and were later to join together in IRA operations. McKearney was released in August 1977. He was arrested again in August 1980 and received a 14-year sentence for possession of a loaded Sten gun. On 13 May 1974 his brother Seán and Eugene Martin, both from Moy, were killed by the bomb they were planting at a filling-station outside Dungannon. His brother Tommy, the eldest in the family of six, in prison in the North since 19 October 1977, went on the first hunger-strike, 27 October 1980, for the renewal of political status. His sister Margaret suffered trial by media in the British press following statements that she was wanted by the British police. *An Phoblacht/Republican News*, 14 May, said of Pádraig – 'He was a key figure in some of the most daring and innovative missions in the last few years in the East Tyrone Brigade's operational area'.

Gerard O'Callaghan (29) was a native of the Tullysaran district of Armagh parish, the youngest of eleven children. *An Phoblacht/Republican News*, 14 May, said of him, 'He was a carefree youth, had an outgoing personality, and had a special place in the hearts of all who knew him. Unknown to his family, Gerard joined the IRA when he was seventeen. In 1980 he and volunteer Pádraig McKearney were captured on active service when they were stopped at a crown forces' roadblock. They were held on remand in C Wing, Crumlin Road Jail, during which time they both went on the 'no wash' protest. He was sentenced to six years for possession of weapons and IRA membership and spent some months in Magilligan Prison before his release in 1983. Gerard O'Callaghan immediately reported back to the IRA on his release and resumed active service along the border, being involved in planning and carrying out some of the most daring attacks on barracks and commercial targets. He was not one for expressing his opinions. He was quiet and, in his own way, a bit of a loner. On active service, however, he was sharp and utterly reliable, qualities which impressed his comrades who trusted him completely'. O'Callaghan was probably the most serious loss in military terms to the IRA. He was a crack shot, ruthless in battle and had nerves of steel. His grumpy temperament did not antagonise his friends but rather amused them. He loved a 'game of cards and, being a single man, was fully devoted to the republican cause. His friends say he "lived for it"'.

The four other IRA volunteers came from the same district around the village of Galbally, County Tyrone. They were companions and had been deeply affected by the death in 1981 of the hunger-striker Martin Hurson, their friend.

Declan Arthurs (21) was the third eldest of the family of Patrick and

Amelia Arthurs. He had a sister Mary and four brothers, Paul, Brian, Patrick and Dominic. *An Phoblacht/Republican News*, 14 May, said that he was fifteen years old when he resolved to join the IRA and waited impatiently until he could do so the following year – 'He soon revealed astounding leadership qualities despite his youth and inexperience and gave his total attention and commitment in every operation he was involved in. "Dec", as he was known to his friends, was very security-conscious, particularly about the safety of other volunteers. He made certain, to the best of his ability, that arrangements for operations were checked and rechecked, that there were no loose ends which could endanger or jeopardise the lives of his comrades. Because of this he was held in the highest regard by the volunteers of the East Tyrone Brigade who knew he was absolutely reliable and capable of making on-the-spot decisions regardless of the pressures. Last Christmas he was held in Gough Barracks for seven days, released on a Saturday, then rearrested on Monday and interrogated for seven days. The RUC beat him up and told him they were going to shoot him. During the month of January Declan had one week of freedom, being held on a succession of seven-day detention orders for the rest of the month. His family's home was constantly raided and on one occasion the floors were dug up'. It was after one of these raids that he decided to leave home. The reference to his 'security-conscious' nature may be an indication as to why he drove by the barracks in Loughgall to inspect the scene. In the months before Loughgall, Arthurs and Donnelly had 'proved' themselves in major operations and both moved up through the IRA ranks very quickly.

Seamus Donnelly (19) was the youngest member of the volunteers killed. He was very fond of traditional Irish music and was a musician and singer. He was the fourth child in Patrick and Lette Donnelly's family. As a youth of fifteen he was frequently beaten by British security forces. His mother said that he had been picked on and harassed from an early age by the RUC. 'There was one policeman in particular who used to kick him. That was part of it. He wanted to get his own back on them for what they had done to him.' *An Phoblacht/Republican News*, 14 May, relates that he and Declan Arthurs were stopped by the UDR at Kilnaslieve when coming from a dance. On that occasion in February 1987 a gun was put to his head. The report continues, 'The following month, during a seven-day detention in Gough Barracks, the RUC threatened that they would shoot him. They showed him detailed plans of his own room and indicated they knew where he slept. In the three years he spent as an active volunteer Seamus Donnelly was regularly involved in IRA operations'.

Tony Gormley (24) was the second eldest of a family of three boys and three girls and lived with his parents Anthony and Annie Gormley. *An Phoblacht/Republican News*, 14 May, says that he joined the IRA at eighteen years –'He rarely raised an opinion on politics or the struggle. He had a happy-go-lucky nature generally but he would think before he attempted to say anything or take any action'; he also had been arrested and interrogated many times in Gough Barracks; Gormley could have been a prosperous, rich man; at one time he had twelve men working under him as a subcontractor for Powerscreen Factory; he sacrificed all this 'for the cause'. He is described in the article as a big, tall, strong, fighting man with big hands and a flair for practical jokes; he combined physical strength with a ready wit and a strong will.

Eugene Kelly (25) was the second eldest in a family of three boys and four girls. Like his father Michael, he was a building contractor. He was a member of the IRA for five years. *An Phoblacht/Republican News*, 14 May, said he was involved in numerous operations in the Cappagh area and, like other young nationalists, was frequently harassed by the RUC and British Army. He also was frequently interrogated on seven-day detention orders in Gough Barracks. Willy Clingan reported in *The Irish Times*, 11 May 1987, from Galbally – 'On Saturday afternoon his brown Nissan Bluebird car was still sitting on the side of the road where he had parked it on Friday evening. "He came home for his dinner," his mother said. "Then he went out and I never saw him again. I didn't think anything of him going out – it was a Friday night and maybe he was going to the pub or something." Word of her son's death came about two o'clock in the morning when neighbours called at the house with the news. More and more people came throughout the night to sympathise. "The house was full all night," she said. The stream of callers continued on Saturday as the house settled into a routine of handshakes, quiet words and cups of tea. "Everybody in the area is stunned," she said, "people are going from house to house, round the four houses. It's not the easiest thing to do."'.

The Loughhall massacre sparked off disturbances in nationalist areas throughout the North, in Lurgan, Portadown, Downpatrick, Coalisland, Strabane and Newry. There were public demonstrations in Derry and West Belfast. As news of the deaths spread, the worst rioting for years in West Belfast broke out and lasted from 11.00 pm to 5.00 am. Hundreds of youths threw petrol bombs. The RUC fired plastic bullets. A bomb was thrown from a passing car at the home of Judge John Curran in the Old Cave Hill area of north Belfast. The commemorative hunger-strike march on Sunday 10 May in West Belfast was the largest for many years. Soldiers and RUC lined the route. A journalist heard an RUC man call out laughing, 'Galbally, we must have wiped out half the population'. Clare County Council, 11 May 1987, voted sympathy to the relatives of the eight men 'executed by British forces in Loughgall, occupied Ireland'. Leitrim County Council and Tralee Urban District Council passed similar votes of sympathy. Castleblayney, County Monaghan, Urban District Council adjourned its monthly meeting as a mark of respect for the eight IRA men and civilian killed.

On Saturday, 9 May the RUC Chief Constable Sir John Hermon visited the scene of the massacre and talked to local RUC men. At the week-end he issued an extraordinary statement suggesting that there could be liaison between families, clergy and police with the aim of avoiding police involvement at a time of private grief and avoiding paramilitary displays. The families of the deceased immediately rejected the idea of discussions with the RUC. Catholic priests were also astounded by the statement, having on occasions received the promise from RUC inspectors of low-key police intervention only to be presented on the day of the funeral with a massive display of RUC force, scores of land-rovers and police entering the cemeteries with plastic-bullet guns.

As it turned out, there were paramilitary demonstrations at some stage of the funerals of Jim Lynagh, Pádraig McKearney, Gerard O'Callaghan, Tony Gormley, Patrick Kelly, Seamus Donnelly and Declan Arthurs. There was scuffling between mourners and Gardaí at the funeral of Lynagh and a Garda pressed by the crowd fired shots in the air. Mr Gerry Adams, MP said at his funeral, 'On Friday night the forces of British oppression lowered their sights. After ten minutes of sustained firing, nine corpses lay in the area around Loughgall barracks. Jim Lynagh was one of those corpses. He wouldn't complain about the enemy action. He probably would have thought that they did not have to shoot some of the younger volunteers, but he wouldn't have complained. He knew the risks. He didn't have to go into the Six Counties. No one intimidated him into taking up arms'. These words showed the dichotomy between regarding the massacre at Loughgall as a series of executions breaking the civil code on reasonable force and a military attitude that the IRA and the British forces are at war and war is a bloody affair. Five thousand people attended the funerals of Donnelly and Arthurs. RUC men stationed at the side of the Cappagh Road jeered at mourners as they walked to the Donnelly home. On different occasions shots were fired by firing parties and prominent members of Sinn Féin spoke at the funerals. The funeral of Eugene Kelly was free from paramilitary signs at the request of his family. In his oration at the funeral of Gerard O'Callaghan Mr Danny Morrison of Sinn Féin said that the RUC was quick to point out that people had been killed by the weapons recovered at Loughgall but one did not hear of the forensic tests on the SAS weapons responsible for a very long list of deaths.

In the course of his homily at the Requiem Mass for Gerard O'Callaghan Fr Patrick Campbell said:

A Phobal Dé, yesterday in this church we celebrated the funeral Mass of John McKeever, a man of nearly eighty years of age, who died a natural death. Today's funeral is very different. The remains of Gerard O'Callaghan of Tullymore, still in his twenties, lie before the altar, his body riddled with bullets, one of nine Irishmen shot dead in Loughgall last Friday evening by British armed forces in the conflict that continues to engulf this part of our island.

All violence is frightening and terrible. Every war is ugly and obscene and brings with it mountains of human pain, anguish and suffering and the irreplaceable loss of human life. All human tears are much the same – Catholic or Protestant, British or Argentinian, Russian or American. Most of us manage to keep out of the arena of war. Others are not so fortunate.

It is a fact, however regrettable, that as long as injustice exists in any of the areas that touch upon the dignity of the human person there will be violent reaction. If politicians do not decide and act for just change then the field is open to violence. 'Violence thrives best when there is political vacuum and a refusal of political movement' (Pope John Paul II, Drogheda 1979). We Catholic nationalists of the North have been the victims of gross injustice since the partition of this island. That oppression, which has continued now for nearly seventy years, is no more legitimate, no less immoral now than then. This is what we know. This we must not be afraid to say, welcome or unwelcome, because it is the truth. Everybody on this island must hear us, and in Britain and in the world. Our political situation is intolerable and there is little sign of redress.

I say these words because it is out of this situation that many deaths have come – Gerard O'Callaghan is one of thousands. How many more will there be before we can hope to live out our lives in some kind of political normality? Is there to be any end to the pain and suffering and loss of life?

In a letter, dated 7 November 1988, to Mr Kevin McNamara, MP, spokesman on Northern Ireland for the British Labour Party, Mr Tom King, Secretary of State for Northern Ireland, said that the Northern Ireland Director of Public Prosecutions had decided that there would be no prosecution of any of those involved in the killings of the nine people at Loughgall. Friends of the Hughes family said it was a disgrace that the security forces would not be prosecuted for the murder of an innocent man.

On 20 March 1989 the IRA in South Armagh ambushed and shot dead two senior RUC officers, Chief Superintendent Harry Breen, the divisional commander of 'H' division which includes Newry, South Armagh and Armagh City, and Superintendent Bob Buchanan, who had special responsibility for RUC liaison with the Gardaí on border operations against the IRA. They were shot near Jonesborough as they returned from a meeting with senior Garda officers in Dundalk. The IRA regarded Supertintendent Breen as a prime target since he was in charge of the Armagh area at the time of the Loughgall shootings; he had been pictured in the press beside the display of IRA weapons captured at Loughgall. *Irish News*' reporters, 19

June 1989, have speculated that information gleaned from the RUC men's documents had led the IRA to identify a County Tyrone woman as the informer who supplied information on the plan to attack Loughgall. In an interview to *Sunday Life* (3 December 1989) this woman said that on 21 May 1989 she was visited at her home by three men who said they wanted to ask her some questions; she left with them in a car which shortly afterwards was stopped at an RUC checkpoint. Three men were later charged with kid-napping and the woman was taken into protective custody at Thiepval Barracks, Lisburn and later transferred to Nottingham. She alleged in the interview that she returned home and after entering into a pact with the IRA withdrew her evidence against the accused. She said that the phone call giving the go-ahead for the Loughgall attack was made from her home, though not by a member of her family. She said she was in the bathroom and overheard the call but at that time did not realise what it meant.

It was more than two years later before the IRA committed a large number of men to one operation. On 13 December 1989 a unit of 12 volunteers launched a carefully-planned attack against a permanent check-point at Derryard in County Tyrone killing two soldiers of the 1st Battalion, The King's Own Scottish Borderers, Lance Corporal Michael John Patterson (21) and Private James Houston (22), and severely wound-ing a third.

Death in the Afternoon: Gibraltar[126]

It had always been expected after the Loughgall killings that the IRA would take revenge and in particular against regular British forces rather than the RUC or UDR, a more difficult task since the local forces were in the front line. Targets could still be pin-pointed in the North but British forces' casualties in Britain or on the continent would obviously bring massive publicity. Just before one considers the shooting of three IRA volunteers in Gibraltar by the SAS on 6 March 1988 it is useful to look at the background of events in the new year 1988. Anglo-Irish relations were at a low ebb. It seemed that Britain was the stronger partner. In the matter of security *vis-á-vis* justice the British were winning every time. The failure to obtain justice from an uncomprising Prime Minister, Mrs Thatcher, was frustrating the nationalist community in Northern Ireland.

January 26: The British Government announced that it would not prose-cute RUC officers who allegedly covered up the facts regarding the shoot-ing dead of six unarmed civilians by the RUC in County Armagh in 1982. The British Attorney General said that they would not be prosecuted in the interest of 'national security'.

January 28: The British Court of appeal upheld the convictions of the six men sentenced for the Birmingham pub bombings of 1974. There is widespread belief at home and abroad that they are innocent.

February 16: The British Government announced that the Prevention of Terrorism Act, until then renewable annually, would be made permanent. The Act had since 1975 discriminated against Irish people and was considered in legal circles a violation of human rights.

February 21: Aidan McAnespie (24), as he walked from a border checkpoint to a Gaelic football match on the northern side of the Tyrone/Monaghan border, was shot dead by a British soldier from a look-out post. The British Army described it as an accident.

February 23: Private Ian Thain, the only British soldier to be sentenced to life imprisonment for killing a Catholic civilian in Northern Ireland, was released after serving only over two years of his sentence. It was revealed that his services had been retained by the British army during his imprisonment. On release he returned to his regiment, the First Battalion, The Light Infantry.

Those who died in the 'troubles' in the North from January 1988 were:

15 January: Billy Kane, a Catholic shot dead in his home in the New Lodge Road, Belfast, by the UVF.

16 January: Captain Timothy Armstrong, UDR, shot dead by the UDA on the Ormeau Road, Belfast, in mistake for a Catholic.

16 January: John Stewart, UDR, ambushed in his car by the IRA at Coalisland.

19 January: Anthony McKiernan, a Catholic, was found shot dead, killed by the IRA.

25 January: Jack Kielty, a Catholic businessman, was shot dead in his office in Dundrum, County Down, by the UDA.

25 January: Colin Gilmore, RUC, was killed in an IRA ambush on the Falls Road, Belfast.

15 February: Cpl Alan Johnston, UDR, was shot dead at his work in Kilkeel, County Down, by the IRA.

24 February: James Cummings and Fred Starrett of the UDR were killed in an IRA explosion at Royal Avenue, Belfast.

29 February: Two leading IRA bomb-experts in South Armagh, Brendan Burns and Brendan Moley, were killed accidentally in an explosion at Cregganduff near Crossmaglen. An iron bar which had been left aside after being used to break the lock of a garage, in which an IRA team was about to shelter since British soldiers were thought to be in the area, slipped and hit the timer of the bomb sending it speeding through its circuit and causing the explosion. Brendan Burns was a close friend of Mairéad Farrell. She broke down and wept when she heard of his death. She probably worked in close co-operation with him. Her entry into the Gibraltar team was a late one, maybe even as late as 29 February.

On 6 March three unarmed Irish citizens were shot dead at close range in the head and back by the SAS in Gibraltar as they walked along the public street on a sunny afternoon. The three were from West Belfast and were IRA volunteers. Mairéad Farrell (31), an intelligent good-looking woman passionately concerned about the oppressed, was from Andersonstown. She was a popular figure in her local community and always greatly loved by those with whom she closely associated, fellow-prisoners and students. She was convicted in 1976 of planting a bomb at the Conway Hotel, Belfast, and served 10 years of a 14 year sentence. She was the first woman to be sentenced after the ending of special category ('political') status in 1976 and so lost remission for her prison protest; in prison she joined the first hunger-strike, 1 December–19 December 1980. The incident for which she was convicted was particularly tragic; one companion on that occasion, Seán McDermot, was shot dead by an RUC man, while another, Kieran Doherty, died on hunger-strike in prison in 1981. In Armagh prison she acted as leader and steered the women through a difficult time of hostility and oppression from the authorities. She was released in September 1986. She took up politics and economics again as a student in Queen's University, subjects she had begun in an open university course in Armagh prison. *An Phoblacht/Republican News*, 10 March 1988, says, 'She reported back to the IRA. Her ten-and-a-half years in prison had, as she said herself, strengthened her resolve'. She was the only girl in her family.

Daniel McCann (30) from Clonard, Lower Falls, Belfast, came from a popular respected family in the Falls Road. He was a life-long republican. In 1973 he was sentenced to six months for 'riotous behaviour'. In the same year he joined the IRA and gave up his job in the Royal Victoria Hospital to work full-time in the republican movement. In January 1979 he was sentenced to two years imprisonment for possession of a detonator. He joined the 'no-wash no work' protest in the H-Blocks and spent two years 'on the blanket'. He was released in January 1981 but from May 1981 spent four months on remand for alleged possession of a gun. He was arrested in November 1981 and released again in April 1982; the charge was dropped. He was arrested in July 1982 on the word of a 'supergrass'. When this man retracted, McCann was released. While he was in prison, on remand, he married Margaret Doherty. They had two children at the time of his death, Daniel and Maeve. He was badly beaten by the British Army in October 1982 and was continually harassed by them and the RUC. He featured in the Amnesty International Report of June 1978 as one who had been ill-treated in Castlereagh Interrogation Centre. *An Phoblacht/Republican News*, 10 March 1988, said of him, 'He was a life-long activist. He knew no compromise and was to die as he had lived in implacable opposition to Britain's criminal presence in our land'.

Seán Savage (23) was a young man of many talents. His activity in the

IRA was unknown. He, like Daniel McCann, had been arrested in July 1982 on the word of a 'supergrass'; he was released after a month. He was an Irish language enthusiast, rambler, cyclist, Gaelic footballer, cook. He was single, did not smoke or drink, rarely expressed political views; he was never seen at republican functions. His great love for Ireland prompted him to travel the country on bicycle and learn his native language. Both Daniel McCann and Seán Savage were expert IRA engineers.

On 7 March the IRA admitted that the three people shot dead by the SAS were IRA volunteers on active service, that they were unarmed at the time of the shooting and that they had 140 lbs of Semtex explosives under their control. On 8 March Spanish police found 141 lbs of Semtex explosives in a hired white Ford Fiesta car in an underground car park in Marbella, Spain. Alan Feraday, a British military scientist at the Royal Armaments Research establishment at Kent, described the cache in the subsequent inquest as containing 141 lbs of Semtex in 25 blocks of 2.55 kilos each, four instantaneous electric Canadian detonators, two 991 'Ever Ready' batteries and two timing-devices. The two timing-units, he said, were set for 10 hours 45 minutes and 11 hours 15 minutes which meant that, when either one completed its run, it would detonate the bomb. The box of the timing-devices was inscribed 'test this unit, 11 Hr 15 Min'. A bomb was obviously being prepared to explode at the time of the changing-of-the-guard and band parade ceremony of the 1st Battalion The Royal Anglian Regiment which was to take place at Ince's Hall in Main Street, Gibraltar, on Tuesday, 8 March. There has been no indication from the IRA as to what the intended target was or whether there was to be one bomb or many bombs but it is clear that the soldiers were the target when they completed the ceremony and dispersed in the cul-de-sac at the back entrance. It is thought the IRA would have wanted to avoid civilian casualties as happened in the Enniskillen atrocity on 8 November 1987 when eleven people died in the Remembrance Day explosion.

In the context of the Gibraltar affair one remembers that the French customs seized tons of explosives, ammunition and weapons destined for the IRA on board the ship MV *Eksund* off the French coast on 30 October 1987. Other shiploads of weapons and explosives, however, reached their destinations and the IRA continued to build up a continental offensive against the British. This meant, of course, taking on continental and international intelligence networks and walking the security tightrope at a time of a developing intelligence co-operation.

The central theme of the British version of what happened in Gibraltar on 6 March, put forward in the House of Commons by Sir Geoffrey Howe, the Secretary of State for Foreign Affairs and at the inquest into the deaths of Seán Savage, Daniel McCann and Mairéad Farrell is as follows: Seán Savage drove a white Renault 5 car across the border into Gibraltar and parked it at 12.50 pm in the second bay of the car park in the square opposite Ince's Hall just off Main Street. At 2.30 pm Mairéad Farrell and Daniel McCann crossed the border on foot. They had left the red Ford Fiesta in the car park at La Linea. When it was later found it was said to contain electrical tape, wire, an alarm clock and false passports. They met up with Savage about 2.50 pm in the Gibraltar car park and it is said they looked at his car. The three walked south towards Almeda Gardens about 200 metres away. At 3.25 pm they returned to Referendum gates and reportedly 'stared' at Savage's car. Their presence and actions aroused suspicion that the car contained a bomb which could be triggered off by remote control. They then moved north towards the border. They were challenged by the security forces. Sir Geoffrey Howe stated on 7 March 1988 in the House of Commons, 'When challenged, they made movements which led the military personnel operating in support of the Gibraltar police to conclude that their own lives and the lives of others were under threat. In the light of this response, they were shot. Those killed were subsequently found not to have been carrying arms'. The military personnel were soldiers of the SAS. This version has since been contradicted in vital aspects by Spanish police sources.

On 6 March the IRA team entered Gibraltar on a reconnaissance mission unarmed and without a bomb. In fact no firearm relating to their activity was ever found. Information on an intended IRA attack in Gibraltar had been in the hands of British Intelligence for over four months. It would appear it was a matter of waiting to catch the team in a trap and then shoot them dead. Gibraltar like the Falklands is symbolic of the last vestiges of British imperialism and 'greatness'. In that sense, as with the *Belgrano* in the Falklands war with Argentina, the IRA were to be taught a bloody lesson. The circumstances of the shootings would be irrelevant to the central policy of the inner committee of the British cabinet. None of the team was to escape from Gibraltar, no prisoners, only corpses.

The Thames television programme, 'Death on the Rock', 28 April 1988, and various articles by investigative journalists in the *Observer*, *Sunday Telegraph*, *Times*, *Guardian*, *Independent* and *Sunday Tribune* have to an extent traced the movements of the IRA in planning their operation. SAS, RUC, E4A, MI5, MI6, Scotland Yard Special Branch and Anti-terrorists Squad were all involved in the gathering of information to make up a final report for the Prime Minister towards the end of February 1988. SIE, the Spanish counter-terrorist unit, played the major role in the surveillance operation in Spain, backed up to a lesser degree by the Spanish special branch. *The Independent*, 23 May 1989, reports, 'Spanish Government sources say the British Embassy in Madrid acted as liaison between the British intelligence agencies and the Spanish Interior Ministry. A counter-terrorist expert from Belfast, code-named F-5, arrived in Madrid to oversee the setting of the trap...nor were the British prepared to rely exclusively on Spanish police surveillance. *The Independent* has learnt that at least one British police officer and another intelligence expert surfaced in Marbella the day before the Gibraltar shootings'.

The Spanish police were first alerted by the British to the possible presence of an IRA unit in southern Spain in September 1987. It is alleged that Daniel McCann arrived at Malaga airport on 5 November 1987 using a false passport under the name of Reilly. The British already had wind of a Gibraltar operation at this time and had supplied the Spanish authorities with names, descriptions and possible aliases. Spanish police noted McCann's entry, having been directed by the Ministry of Defence in Madrid to co-operate with the British in carrying out surveillance on suspects. McCann was followed to Torremolinos. By mid-November three IRA suspects had been pin-pointed, McCann, Savage and a woman who travelled under the name of Mary Parkin (a passport belonging to Mary Parkin, wife of a Press Association journalist, had been stolen). It is alleged that eaves-dropping Spanish police heard them discussing a bomb-attack but the police were not clear about the details of the target. On 15 November Daniel McCann and Seán Savage flew from Malaga to Madrid and then back to Dublin. McCann travelled as R.W. Reilly and Savage as Cohen. On consultation with the British no arrests were made.

In February 1988 the IRA resumed their operation. British Intelligence alerted Spanish police in Valencia that at least two IRA suspects, a man and a woman, had flown in to Valencia. They were kept under surveillance but gave the Spanish police the slip in their hired car. By design or by accident the area of the Gibraltar changing-of-the-guard was closed so that the guardhouse could be painted. On 10 February the Spanish police were requested by the British to keep 'Mary Parkin', described as having long hair, under surveillance. She had checked into the Hotel Buena Vista in Estepona, a town on the Costa del Sol situated between Gibraltar and Marbella. On 23 February British soldiers paraded again. 'Mary Parkin' was noticed studying the changing of the guard ceremony. The following Tuesday, 1 March, she was seen there again. On Thursday, 3 March (it was her birthday) Mairéad Farrell left her home at 2.15 p.m. and got a lift to Dublin. She flew to Brussels from Dublin on that day and then to Madrid and Malaga on Friday, 4 March. She travelled under the names of Mary Johnston and Katherine Alison Smith née Harper. Actually she was in a hurry on her journey from Belfast to Dublin and nearly missed her flight. Her driver was stopped by the Gardaí for speeding. Daniel McCann and Séan Savage flew to Paris from Dublin on 3 March and on to Malaga on 4 March arriving at 20.50 on flight IB-657. Séan Savage left Belfast after 3 pm on 3 March. He had waited until his mother had come home from work. He told her he intended staying the weekend in a caravan in the Galway Gaeleacht. As in the previous November McCann travelled under the same passport in the name of Robert Wilfred Reilly. This would have been enough to alert the authorities. The two men were noted by the police and followed. Contrary to British claims and what purported to be a sworn affidavit by the number two special branch officer in Malaga, Chief Inspector Tomás Rayo Valenzuela, they were never 'lost'. (This affidavit said that on their arrival McCann and Savage went to the Banco Exterior at the airport where they met Mairéad Farrell. The police lost both men when they took a taxi and lost sight of Mairéad Farrell in the airport building. The taxi-driver was traced and he said he had taken both men to the Hotel Florida in Fuengirola. On inquiry it was found out that the men were not guests at that hotel. There followed a fruitless search by Spanish police along the Costa del Sol. Their hotel, Hotel Escandinavia, was only traced in the early hours of Monday, 7 March when police found an hotel key in the trio's car at La Linea.) At home in Ireland McCann's driver was stopped at the border on the way back to Belfast.

The Independent, 23 May 1989, says that 'MI5 had already passed on the trio's ID photographs to a police command hastily set up in the Marbella' two days before they arrived. The same newspaper report says, 'Spanish police have described to *The Independent* how, at a Marbella command centre, they collected all the intelligence relating to the movement of the IRA team, such as their false identities, their cars and hotel hide-aways. This data, they say, was always passed swiftly to British intelligence'.

In a series of articles in *The Irish Times*, 25-26 April, 10 May, 1989, Andy Pollak and Geraldine Mitchell reviewed the extent of Spanish surveillance and the co-operation of the Spanish police with the British. Their startling revelations that probably six members comprised the IRA team was backed up by *The Independent*'s report by Tim McGirk and Heather Mills on 23 May 1989. Three members of the IRA team were already in the Costa del Sol before the arrival of McCann, Savage and Mairéad Farrell. The whole team used the same aliases indiscriminately in order to confuse police who might ask for descriptions.

Seán Savage and Daniel McCann booked in to Hotel Escandinavia at Avenida de Palma de Mallorca 49 in Torremolinos on Friday night, Savage under the name Brendan Coyne and McCann under Edward McArdle. Mairéad Farrell also stayed in the same room; there were three beds in it and some female items of clothing were later found in it.

At midday on Saturday, 5 March a man using the name John Oakes (not Savage nor McCann) hired a red Ford Fiesta in Torremolinos from Autoluis, a car-hire firm. This man had booked in to the Al-Andalus hotel at Torremolinos on 3 March for two nights, paying cash in advance. He drove off in the car with a woman. This car was not followed by the Spanish police. The car registered 1594 kilometers from the time 'Oakes' hired it until it was found at La Linea near Gibraltar on 6 March. This car picked up the explosives in Valencia on Saturday.

On Saturday night a woman using the name Katherine Smith, described as slightly built with short curly hair (probably Mairéad Farrell) hired a white Ford Fiesta at a car hire firm called Rent-a-Car Marbesol at Avenida de Ricardo Soriano. (The affidavit purporting to be from Chief Inspector Tomás Rayo Valenzuela, says this car was hired at 10.00 hours on Sunday, 6 March and that an employee recognised Mairéad Farrell 'without a shadow of doubt' as the woman who used the name Katherine Smith.) On Saturday night this car, immediately after it was hired, was driven to the Sun car park at Edificio Marbeland in Marbella and parked in the basement area. In the early hours of Sunday morning, unknown to the Spanish police, the red Ford Fiesta returned from Valencia with explosives and unknown members of the IRA team transferred them to the white Ford Fiesta in the underground car park. This car and explosives remained undetected until found by Spanish inspector Feliz Sanchez at 5.30 pm on 8 March.

The third car, a white Renault 5, was hired at 1 pm on Saturday, 5 March from the Avis firm in Torremolinos. In their article on 10 May 1989 Andy Pollak and Geraldine Mitchell say that the car was not hired by Savage nor McCann. According to the employee the customer had two fingers missing from his right hand. *The Independent,* 23 May 1989, alleges that this car was driven on Saturday, 5 March to Gibraltar and was used as the blocking car to reserve a place for the white Ford Fiesta bomb car (all the British evidence says that the car was parked at 12.50 pm in Gibraltar by Seán Savage on Sunday, 6 March) – 'a senior Spanish police officer involved in the operation told *The Independent:* 'the white Renault (the suspect bomb car) was driven in to Gibraltar a day before the shooting. We told the British we were 90 per cent certain that the car contained no bomb'.

On the afternoon of Sunday, 6 March Daniel McCann, Seán Savage and Mairéad Farrell drove to Gibraltar in the red Ford Fiesta followed the whole way by plain clothes members of the Spanish anti-terrorist élite squad.

On 25 September 1988 The Observer published an article 'Challenge to SAS line at IRA inquest', by Ian Jack and Simon de Bruxelles. Harry Debelius, a senior American correspondent in Madrid who covered Spain for British newspapers for twenty years, sent a statement to Felix Pizzarello, the Coroner at the inquest on the three, giving an account of the briefing he received from Agustin Valladolid, then chief spokesman for Spanish state security. He went to see him as chief consultant for the TV programme 'Death on the Rock'. His meeting lasted an hour and twenty minutes. Valladolid outlined the method of surveillance of Savage's car. *The Observer* says: '1. Four or five police cars "leap-frogged" each other on the road while trailing the terrorists to avoid arousing suspicion. 2. A helicopter spotted the car during part of the route. 3. Police agents were in constant contact with their headquarters by radio. 4. Agents were placed at fixed observation points along the road.' Valladolid said that the British in Gibraltar received 'minute by minute details' of the car's movements directly from the Spanish police. The British were aware of the arrival of Savage at the border. Debelius said he had a further conversation with Valladolid by telephone a few days later. 'Either during this conversation or a later conversation Valladolid informed me that during the Spanish surveillance operation two members of the British security service had worked with the police in Malaga.' On 24 September Valladolid, then chief spokesman for the Interior Ministry, told *The Observer*, 'I did indeed have an interview with these people in the same way that I had interviews with others on the subject at about that time. In this interview, the co-operation between the British and Spanish police forces was emphasised. Out of respect for the legal proceedings in Gibraltar it is not possible to make any further comment'.

The article 'The SAS and the Spanish connection' by Rory Godson and Ed Moloney in the *Sunday Tribune*, 25 September 1988, said: 'Before the inquest started there was ample evidence that there had been a considerable Spanish input. Spanish interior official, Luis Aranz, confirmed to Thames TV "Death on the Rock" that there had been complete co-operation...Three days after the shooting members of Spain's Terrorismo Internacional police squad confirmed the extent of their operation to the Madrid weekly magazine *Interviú*. 'They told me up to ten officers were tailing each of the IRA members, a total of maybe 25 men". *Interviú* reporter Enrique Yeves told the *Sunday Tribune*, "They had their own interests in the IRA. They wanted to know if there were any links with ETA and whether the IRA had bases in Spain". He added that he was "dumbfounded" by British claims to the contrary.' At the inquest Detective Constable Charles Huart admitted that he was allowed to sit inside the frontier post on the Spanish side of the border to monitor the IRA's arrival. His superior, Detective Chief Inspector Joe Ullger, head of the Gibraltar Special Branch, said at the inquest: 'The only way for the operation to succeed was to allow the terrorists to come in.'

The Independent, 29 September 1988, quoted Valladolid as saying, 'When the terrorists entered Gibraltar, the British authorities knew they were coming in. It's logical that they only would have known this if there had been surveillance on the Spanish side'. There was speculation in September 1988 when Mrs Thatcher was on an official visit to Spain that she discussed the future of Gibraltar and European defence co-operation with the Spanish Prime Minister, Mr Felipe Gonzales, and diplomatic moves were made to persuade the Spanish government not to allow a Spanish police officer attend the inquest and relate the full story of the Spanish part in surveillance. In any case there was no question of the Spanish government doing anything that might show recognition of Britain's possession of Gibraltar. After the shootings Mrs Thatcher and British Intelligence sent messages of congratulations to the Spanish Prime Minister and the Spanish police force for their part in the operation. The Chief Minister of Gibraltar, Mr Adolpho Canepa, described the Spanish police as brilliant. After the Thames Television programme 'Death on the Rock' in April 1988, with its analysis of the shooting and outline of Spanish surveillance, the British Government, realising the serious implications for British Intelligence and the SAS, changed its attitude and began to minimise the Spanish dimension. It was hard for Spanish officialdom to deny completely the part of the Spanish police. In a modest manner it has counteracted the British cover-up. When the Spanish Interior Minister, Mr José Luis Cocuera, met the Home Secretary in London in January 1989, he told Spanish journalists that when the Spanish police followed the IRA trio they were 'completely under our control, we did not lose them'. He would say nothing about what happened in Gibraltar. At the same briefing Spain's director of state security at the time of the shootings, Mr Rafail Vera, was asked why Spanish officials did not challenge the British assertion that the Spanish surveillance operation was botched. He said, 'Not always by keeping quiet does one agree with what is being said'.

The Independent, 23 May, elaborated on the Spanish surveillance – 'One officer described how those tailing the cars would change at distances of between 16 and 32 kilometres. Although it was felt unlikely that all three would risk a journey with the explosives, it was possible that the red Fiesta had picked up the bomb. However, it was left on the Spanish side of the border, the three crossing on foot'. Surveillance details were passed on to the British.

Two miles from the Spanish border the car entered a car park at La Linea. It is possible that Seán Savage crossed the border first on foot and was not detected. The transcripts of the inquest reveal that no one saw Savage actually cross the border on Sunday in a white Renault (this fits in to The Independent's allegation that it was driven in on Saturday.) Little is revealed of his movements in the next hour and a half. At 2.30 pm Mairéad Farrell and Daniel McCann crossed the border on foot. They were noted and allowed to pass through.

If The Independent allegation that the white Renault was in position in the car park in Gibraltar from Saturday is true, then the British authorities had plenty of time to check whether it contained a bomb, evacuate the area, and if it did contain a bomb, render it safe. On 7 March 1988 Sir Geoffrey Howe said in the House of Commons, 'The suspect white Renault car was parked in the area in which the band of soldiers would have formed for the Tuesday parade. A school and an old people's home were both close by. Had a bomb exploded in the area, not only the 50 soldiers involved in the parade, but a large number of civilians might well have been killed or injured. It is estimated that casualties could well have run into three figures'. Did Sir Geoffrey Howe and other ministers know the truth or were they deceived? Were they subsequently caught in a cover-up for an execution? Even without the knowledge that the white Renault was parked on Saturday, it would have been obvious to bomb experts that it did not contain a large bomb. The car was high on its springs. Even the *Sunday Times*, so prejudiced in favour of the British official version in its early reporting, showed a turning away in its Insight article of 2 April 1989; it alleged that Soldier 'G', who gave evidence at the inquest that he thought the car contained a bomb, being suspicious of its aerial, was opposed in his view by two other experienced officers who were adamant that there was no bomb; their view was not revealed at the inquest and 'G's' suspicion was transferred into a definite message of a car bomb.

Following the collation of surveillance details from the Spanish police on Friday and the parking of the white Renault on Saturday, the Gibraltar Commissioner of Police, Joseph Canepa, held a midnight briefing for intelligence personnel, police and SAS soldiers. The trap was set.

Four SAS soldiers designated 'A', 'B', 'C' and 'D' were assigned to do the killing. Their tactical commander 'E' was in a secret Joint Operations Room with Soldier 'F' the SAS commanding officer and senior military advisor to the police, Soldier 'G' a bomb disposal advisor, MI5 surveillance officers, other SAS soldiers and other surveillance people and experts of different kinds. The Gibraltar police present played a subsidiary role. The SAS soldiers consisted of two units each with four men; some had served in Northern Ireland. They were seasoned members. Soldier 'A', from north London had served 12 years, Soldier 'B' 6 years, Soldier 'C' 11 years and Soldier 'D' 2 years. The plot to attack the IRA team was named 'Operation Flavius'. One MI5 officer who briefed all the military and police personnel on the operation, known as Mr 'O', gave evidence at the inquest; he was the first MI5 officer known to give evidence in court. His role was that of supplying information. He said that he had spent 7 years in the service and had knowledge of counter-terrorism and the activity of the IRA.

There were two teams of armed plain clothes Gibraltar police, three in each team. Each team supported a plain clothes SAS team. 'A' and 'B' formed one SAS team. Each carried a radio, 'A' being in contact with the military network and 'B' in contact with the surveillance network. They were armed with Browning 9 mm pistols. 'A' had four magazines, each containing twelve rounds, one of which was on his pistol. Soldier 'B' had two magazines. In the second team 'C' was linked with the military network and 'D' with surveillance. 'C' carried his Browning 9 mm in the back waistband of his trousers. He had two magazines with twelve rounds in each, one attached to his gun. 'D' also had a Browning 9 mm pistol and three magazines of twelve rounds each. David Leigh and Paul Lashmar revealed in an article 'Inquest doubts on Gibraltar' in *The Observer*, 20 November 1988, that the officer designated to take charge of Firearms Team 1 was Inspector Luis Revagliatte. The three armed policemen in the police team gave evidence at the inquest as 'P', 'Q' and 'R'. Mr Dick Spring, leader of the Labour Party in the Irish Republic, told the Dáil in Dublin on 16 November 1988 that he had documents which threw light on the Gibraltar affair on three vital parts, one of them being an operation order signed by the Gibraltar Commissioner of Police naming Inspector Luis Revagliatte as the officer in charge of two armed firearms teams. This may refer to the operation planned for 8 March. Revagliatte's Christian name is variously given in newspaper reports as 'Luis' and 'Joseph'.

Duncan Campbell in his article 'Panic in the street', *New Statesman & Society*, 17 June 1988, asserts that the original intention was to shoot the three IRA members in the middle of the airstrip across which runs the road from Gibraltar to Spain. This would ensure against independent witnesses. In his opinion they moved to kill the three when British and Spanish intelligence officials lost track of the fourth member of the team, 'Mary Parkin'. They could no longer be sure of the timing of a bomb with one of the band on the loose and so they decided to move lest they too should escape. Campbell says, 'An "over-exuberant" reaction by the Gibraltar police provoked panic in the street and the three killings by the SAS soldiers'.

The three had walked about a mile when they were attacked. They passed through the bridge linking Line Wall Road to Smith Dorrien Avenue. They reached the junction of Winston Churchhill and Smith Dorrien Avenue. Seán Savage split from the other two and began walking back towards the landport tunnel, the pedestrian route leading into the town centre. Daniel McCann and Mairéad Farrell continued walking towards the Shell garage on the right hand side of Winston Churchhill Avenue. The garage was closed on Sunday. *The Observer*, 20 November, points to some coincidences: 'Inspector Joseph Revagliatte arrives at the scene with three colleagues in a police car, close behind the men previously designated as his police firearms teams, although he is on unconnected "general patrol".' (*he maintained this at the inquest*); 'Inspector Revagliatte decides to set off his siren at the precise moment the SAS and his firearms team are closing in on the suspects, thus making them look round. All three suspects individually made sudden, unexplained jerky movements.'

To go back to Campbell. The security chiefs panicked when 'Mary Parkin' skipped surveillance and disappeared: 'Orders were radioed to the Gibraltar police and to the SAS soldiers tracking the bombers to move in without waiting for them to approach the Spanish border. Hence the Gibraltar police car with its blaring siren. Hence the very public killings.' It is hardly likely that the alarm at 'Mary Parkin's' disappearance meant that she was being tracked in Gibraltar. By Sunday, 6 March 'Mary Parkin' was probably back in Ireland.

When Mairéad Farrell and Daniel McCann turned startled at the sound of the siren, 'A' and 'B' shot them dead. Almost immediately 'C' and 'D' gunned down Seán Savage a hundred yards away. After the shooting the SAS soldiers donned black berets. 'A' and 'B' were driven towards the airport and then back to the Operations Room and reported to 'E'. 'C' and 'D' also put on black berets and went on foot to the Operations Room to report. At 5.20 pm the four soldiers were brought to the office of Detective Constable Mario Busto at the Central Police Station. They handed in weapons and ammunition but did not give their names. A fifth man said he was an Army legal adviser. After he received a report at 3.47 pm of the 'apprehension' of the trio, Soldier 'E' left the Operations Room and went to the scene of the shootings. He saw Soldiers 'A', 'B', 'C' and 'D' later in the Operations Room. All the SAS soldiers left Gibraltar about 11 pm on Sunday night and returned to Britain.

The IRA trio would have been surveillance-conscious. That fact was explained by police and Army witnesses at the inquest, who noted them looking around, looking in car mirrors, Savage walking behind the others. Why did the three head back towards the border? It can only be a matter of speculation. Maybe as follows: the trio already had 'Mary Parkin's' report and probably details from other unknown members of their team but wanted to see the ground for themselves, smell the atmosphere, look to details, gauge the power, the size and the effect of the bomb (with a view to avoiding civilian casualties). Their reconnaissance mission accomplished, they walked back to the border, Savage walking behind as a counter-surveillance measure. When he saw them to within half-a-mile of the border, he probably intended returning to the centre, hoping to follow after a reasonable time on foot and meet up with them in the car park at La Linea. The other possibility is that they decided for some reason to abandon the mission. Going on that theory, Savage turned back to the centre to pick up the white Renault to show to possible watchers that it certainly did not contain a bomb; to abandon it would leave them open to identification and a red alert. Savage's parting from the two combined with Revagliatte's siren (whether accidental or intentional) would have been enough to signal a strike. Winston Churchhill Avenue was not the best place to shoot them even on a Sunday when many people were in Spain for the day and business places were closed. There was the problem of witnesses in the flats over-looking the area and passers-by. Anyhow the air strip would not have been entirely free of witnesses either. The siren blared. The SAS went into action.

The shooting of the trio meant the escape of 'John Oakes' and probably other back-up members of the team. Andy Pollak and Geraldine Mitchell wrote in *The Irish Times*, 10 May 1989, 'Spanish sources also suggested to *The*

Irish Times that one of the other two men in the six-member IRA unit may have been in Gibraltar's Ince Square, the scene of the targeted military ceremony, hours before Savage, McCann and Farrell were shot dead on Sunday March 6th. This would appear to be borne out by the record of last September's Gibraltar inquest. Detective Constable Albert Viagas of the Gibraltar police told that inquest on September 20th that while he was on surveillance duty in the Hambros Bank offices adjoining the square shortly after 12.30 pm, he had heard a member of the security forces commenting that the driver of the white Renault car that had just been parked in the square "had taken time and fiddled with something between the seats". British press reports at the time, quoting security forces, claimed that he was making last-minute adjustments to the car bomb. However, neither Constable Viagas nor the other two men on surveillance duty with him, could identify the man as Savage at that time, even though they had photos of Savage in front of them, according to the policeman's testimony. A more senior 'field officer', whom they contacted for an identification, was also unable to recognise him. "He was not the person we were supposed to be keeping surveillance on", said Constable Viagas'. However, if another male member of the team was present in Gibraltar on 6 March, how did he escape?

The Spanish police were shocked by the killings. They thought the IRA trio would have been arrested. Since they were dead, how were they expected to trace the bomb? On 8 March 1988 Spanish 'Terrorismo Internacional' inspectors, Juan Carlos X and Ferando Y told three Spanish journalists Enrique Yeves, José Maria Alegre and Tomás Casquero they had been in the cars following the trio to the frontier and that police were shocked when told of the killings. One said, 'The brutes (*bestias*). What have they done?' In subsequent months the pride of the Spanish police was hurt by British slighting of their surveillance and especially when the SAS and British Intelligence testified to their incompetence at the inquest. In a move to placate them, 22 Spanish police officers, including the head of SIE, Manuel Reverte, two superintendents, six chief inspectors and inspectors, were awarded what the Interior Ministry described as special commendations for 'meritorious service in the field of intelligence'. They came from Madrid, Malaga, Cadiz, Valencia and La Linea. Such awards would enhance their future promotions. The commendations were not given in public. They were then leaked, probably by Spanish police, to *El Pais* in mid-March 1989. At that time Mr Miguel Martin Pedraz, president of the Spanish Professional Policemen's Union (SPP) emphasised the thouroughness of the Spanish surveillance and was quoted as saying, 'It's too risky for me to say whether or not I think that the SAS expected the IRA or not but there is no doubt that the Spanish police would have liked to end it differently. A good terrorist isn't a dead one, it's one that is behind bars'.

Besides the commendations, the police authorities took the unusual step of paying cash bonuses to the police who took part in the surveillance.

The evidence suggests the intention was always to shoot the members of the IRA team when caught in a compromising situation. Let us turn now and look at the background of the intelligence people, the Prime Minister and members of the cabinet. Much is revealed in the article by Simon O'Dwyer-Russell and Donald Macintyre and Walter Ellis, 'A Job for the SAS', *Sunday Telegraph*, 13 March 1988: '...the critical decision to entrust the SAS with the task of foiling probably the biggest ever terrorist operation planned against a British target was taken at Downing Street in late February. Only three members of the Cabinet would have been involved at that stage. The Foreign Secretary, Sir Geoffrey Howe, the Defence Secretary, George Younger and, most crucially, the Prime Minister herself were given the top secret report of a four-month surveillance operation ... Mrs Thatcher approved rules of engagement which provided for the arrest of the terrorists if possible. But if SAS soldiers carrying out the operation believed arrests were impossible without endangering either their own or civilian lives, then they were empowered to shoot. Military sources confirmed that instructions were unequivocal: once the IRA unit was in Gibraltar it was not to be allowed to re-enter Spanish territory. "Our orders were clear," said one officer, "they were to be arrested or, if necessary, shot".'

The Observer, 13 March 1988, made similar remarks (article, Mary Holland, Simon de Bruxelles and Ian Mather): 'So who did sign the "death warrant"? The decision to send in the SAS was taken with the approval of Mrs Thatcher, acting on information channelled through the Cabinet's Joint Intelligence Committee. A large number of government agencies were involved. They included the Foreign Office, Ministry of Defence and Northern Ireland Office. MI5 and MI6, who operate in Northern Ireland, liaised with the Spanish authorities through the British Embassy in Madrid.'

Months later, 5 September 1988, *The Guardian* underlined where responsibility lay in an article 'Power behind the scene':

'The surveillance of the IRA team during the months and weeks before its planned attack in Gibraltar was co-ordinated in London by MI5, backed up by the Joint Intelligence Organisation, and in particular, its relatively new Current Intelligence Group responsible for Irish terrorism. Current Intelligence Groups (CIGs) are made up of officials from MI5 and MI6 and GCHQ with support from the Special Branch. They send regular reports to the Joint Intelligence Committee which, in turn, sends weekly assessments to the Prime Minister who decides which other members of the Cabinet need sight of them.

'The CIG on terrorism is helped by the EEC's so-called Trevi Group of interior and justice ministers, and in Britain's case, the Home Secretary... Co-operation by the Spanish security authorities was essential in keeping

MI5 in close touch with the movements of the IRA team. London and Madrid communicated via coded faxes, now installed by security services throughout western Europe... While British embassy officials in Madrid were lubricating the machinery there, at the London end MI5 built up a file on the movements of Farrell, Savage and McCann, assessing their aims and their likely target.

'MI5 officers visited Gibraltar and briefed the military authorities, including the Governor-General. A handful of Gibraltar police officers, including Joe Canepa, the police commissioner, who is appointed by the Governor and responsible to him, were also briefed. The key decision was then taken to draw up a contingency plan to bring in the SAS. The SAS Counter Revolutionary Warfare (CRW) team and its commanders, chosen to keep on standby for a possible operation, was detached from the rest of the SAS – which is technically under the command of the conventional Ministry of Defence military structure. From then on the SAS team in effect became an instrument of the Security Service. MI5 officers were directly involved in the operation and it is understood drove the Gibraltar police cars which took the SAS to the scene of the shooting on March 6. For political reasons, Mrs Thatcher and Sir Geoffrey Howe, the Foreign Secretary, were told at a relatively early stage about the proposal to bring in the SAS. The SAS was anxious to get political sanction for the plan as soon as possible. The final decision to commit the SAS was taken by the Prime Minister...It is now firmly established as a convention that the Prime Minister has to agree to military action overseas, and security and anti-terrorist measures abroad involving military personnel.'

Colin Brown in his article on the Gibraltar killings in *The Independent*, 5 September 1988, states also that the Prime Minister agreed to the operation in principle at a highly secret meeting in Downing Street which included Geoffrey Howe and George Younger. The preferred option was to allow the IRA team into Gibraltar under surveillance rather than have them arrested in Spain where charges would be difficult to prove – 'The briefing was organised by the Ministry of Defence and given by a senior member of the security services. MI5 was also present. But as the operation would be taking place abroad, the Foreign Secretary was the lead minister...The crucial question which is never likely to be answered by the Cabinet papers is whether the Prime Minister and her colleagues sanctioned the actual killings. Those close to the Cabinet ministers involved insist this was covered in the rules of engagement. The balance of probability is strongly against the SAS team being told to kill the IRA team. However, there is little doubt among ministers that the rules of engagement left it open to the SAS to kill if their own lives or the lives of others were at risk...Security sources say the SAS would have sent back a situation report on the day of the operation which would have been relayed to Downing Street. It could be argued, at this stage, the SAS could have asked for permission to kill the terrorists. But the security sources insist that this would not have been necessary. A pre-arranged code word was all that was required to tell the SAS to go ahead. One former member of the security forces who had served in Northern Ireland said that, as a result of the eyewitness reports, he believed the SAS team had gone in to kill the IRA team. The killings took place close to the airport, where the SAS had a transport aircraft waiting to fly them out. The operation was upset when a siren was used by a Gibraltar police car, shadowing the IRA team. This forced the SAS to go into action, killing all three members of the IRA in the street, before they reached the airfield'.

The theory of a conspiracy to kill, of a power behind the SAS killers themselves, motivated the questioning and summing up of Mr P.J. McGrory who was the legal representative of the families of the victims at the inquest. Before the inquest he said, 'Those who killed publicly enough in the sunlight should not be allowed now to seek the shadows'. In his summing-up Mr McGrory drew an image from the *corrida* in Ernest Hemingway's book *Death in the Afternoon*. He said that many English people disliked the bullfight, 'because it interferes with and offends against their sense of fair play because they think the victim is condemned to die once it enters the arena. There is no chance of living against the superior skills of the matador. It was a little like that, was it not, in Gibraltar on 6 March? There were differences. There was no music, no grace of movement, no remarkable exhibition of courage, no colour save for the blood that eventually stained the pavements of Gibraltar but it wasn't fair. If it was not fair it was not reasonable and if it was not reasonable it was not lawful and that is an image of legal principle with which we are all in fact dealing. It may be that the three who died may have said *c'est la guerre* because they regard themselves as Irish soldiers but we are lawyers and we must keep foremost in our minds that we are not interested in rules of engagement but in the rule of law and I hope it is foremost in the minds of the jury...The SAS were chosen and the evidence, the little that there was of it, shows that they were not chosen in Gibraltar, for what was conceived to be, as presented, an arrest operation which is essentially a police matter. What I am submitting to you is that it was wholly unreasonable and led to a lot of what happened afterwards as a whole chain of unreasonableness which in the end led to three killings which I would submit were illegal criminal killings. Indeed I would submit that they were contemplated at the inception when the SAS were chosen'.

The coroner Mr Felix Pizzarello asked: 'In other words conspiracy to murder?'

'Precisely,' said Mr McGrory, 'and there were counsellors and procurers. One of the features of the inquest that struck me has been the vigorous efforts of how the soldiers of the SAS tried to portray their regiment and themselves as ordinary soldiers with no special status. It seems to be a matter of contemporary history that it is no such thing. It is a highly-trained and motivated attack force which is wholly unsuited to arrest procedures. It is particularly trained for special tasks such as hostage-taking and hijacking. It is my submission that the choice of this force is highly significant and the jury must decide if the real object was merely to arrest or were the events of 6th March intended and shown to be intended by the choice of this force. If the killing of the active service unit was in fact contemplated by the people who choose the SAS as a counter-terror or vengeance that is stepping outside the rule of law and is murder and is a proper matter for the jury. Alternatively if the choice of instrument for the arrest operation was wholly unreasonable with their training in speed, firepower and aggression, those who chose the instrument must be taken to have intended the consequences of that choice'.

The fact that the choice of the SAS sealed the fate of the trio was in the mind of the writer of the editorial in *The Independent*, 10 September 1988:

> The British Army manuals define the successful ambush as one in which all enemy soldiers are killed. The SAS are among the toughest and best-trained fighters in the world and the prime task of such men is to kill other soldiers in war, giving them as little choice as possible to defend themselves. Maximum violence, instantly... The concept of shooting to wound is not one which comes easily to soldiers and it certainly does not loom large in the training and experience of members of the SAS... Politicians who authorise the use of the SAS do so in the knowledge that they are employing a deadly weapon which lacks an adequate safety-catch.

Having shot the three IRA members dead in the head and back from a close range in cold blood, the British prepared their defence. First by misinforming the media, tabloid and quality alike. Secondly by delaying the inquest to September on a flimsy excuse, to cool the atmosphere, to give more time for more disinformation, to nobble and intimidate key witnesses. One of the most significant pieces of disinformation was paradoxically to hide behind the 'humiliation' of making three mistakes. These were an invention and were given by the MI5 agent Mr 'O' at the inquest. These errors (so-called), he said, were conveyed to the SAS hours before they killed. The SAS were allegedly told that the trio were almost certainly armed, that the car contained a bomb which would cause great carnage and devastation and that it would be detonated by remote control.

This last is a classic *post-hoc* invention. If the SAS were so worried about a 'button job' as they called it, why did they risk setting it off by continually firing into the bodies or risk the bodies falling? They made no attempt to look for a device on the bodies after the shootings. If their intelligence believed there was a bomb why did they risk an atrocity by not clearing the area for two-and-a-half hours, a half-an-hour after the three were dead? (If the white Renault was installed from Saturday, then the British have no case.) It was after 7 pm before controlled explosions had been completed on the parked white Renault and the area declared safe. Dr Michael Scott, a lecturer at the National Institute for Higher Education in Dublin, an electronics authority, called at the inquest by Mr McGrory, said that a radio signal sent from where the three had been killed would not have detonated a bomb in the Renault which was a mile and a half away. He said that the Crown witness, Mr Alan Feraday, 'had' given some misleading information on radio wave propagation 'and had introduced evidence that was quite unnecessary and irrelevant'. A year later, October 1989, Michael Scott in a technical article in *Fortnight* magazine again rebutted the Crown case.The SAS statements have an uncanny consistency and pattern. The SAS members were well rehearsed and gave out the statements pat, sometimes staccato fashion, at the inquest; they exuded a tremendous confidence. Readers of this book are familiar with the phraseology of SAS statements which ensure that they come within the wide parameters of the special rules of engagement. The rules in Gibraltar included – to open fire if they had reasonable grounds for believing that an action was about to be committed which was likely to endanger life and if there was no other way to prevent that; a warning was to be given which was to be as clear as possible and include a direction to surrender and a clear indication that fire would be opened if the directive were not obeyed; they could fire without warning if the giving of such a warning was 'clearly impracticable' or 'likely to cause a delay in firing which might lead to death or injury'. With such a safety-valve it was easy to find excuses of 'danger to life'. There was also the added benefit of sucking people into sidetracks on details of the shootings, even when from the start there was every intention of shooting to kill.

Let us look at some of the phraseology of the SAS soldiers in Gibraltar:

The commanding officer Soldier 'F' said they were mindful of the priorities to arrest the offenders, disarm them and to defuse the bomb.

Soldier 'E' said Savage was killed because he swung around in a crouching stance and put one hand to his hips when challenged. He was 'dangerous and lethally aggressive': 'By his movements, however they were motivated, the soldiers had reasonable grounds for believing he was a lethal threat. It's as simple as that.' Soldiers 'C' and 'D' shouted the first part of an agreed warning before opening fire. The second part of the warning was obliterated because they opened fire when Savage swung round.

'E' said soldiers were standing behind Farrell and McCann. When a warning was shouted Farrell brought her hands up to the middle of her body and clutched at her handbag; what precipitated the action was McCann turning to look over his shoulder while he was having a conversation with Farrell and staring 'fully in the eye of Soldier 'A''. The stare, 'E' said, indicated that McCann knew or recognised Soldier 'A'.

Soldier 'A' in his testimony repeated this eye-to-eye contact – 'The look was alertness and very aware. At that stage, I was just about to shout a warning to stop and at the same time was drawing my pistol. I went to shout "stop" and I actually don't know if it came out. The look on McCann's face, the alertness, then all of a sudden the right elbow moving what I would call aggressively across the front of his body. I thought McCann was definitely going to go for a button. To me the whole worry was the bomb in the debussing area...I was drawing my weapon and fired at McCann one round into his back. I was about three metres away. We'd come up at a relatively brisk pace...Then I caught out of the corner of my eye a movement of Farrell who had a handbag under her left armpit, and grabbed at her bag. I thought she was going for the button and I shot Farrell in the back. I then engaged McCann with a further three rounds, one in the body and two in the head. He was falling all the time. His hands were away from his body...'

Soldier 'B' includes the danger to 'A'; at the sound of gunfire he didn't know if 'A' had been shot. He said he heard a shout from 'A' which he presumed was the start of an arrest process. At the same time almost instantaneously there was firing on his right. At the same moment he saw Farrell, whom he had been watching, draw her shoulder bag across her body and with all the information he had been given it was in his mind that she was trying to detonate a bomb. He thought of the public of Gibraltar and he did not know if Soldier 'A' had been shot, 'So I opened fire. I drew my weapon as the shouting started and firing began. It was all in a split second. She made a movement to the right and I decided they were movements to detonate the device. I opened fire on Farrell and then I switched firing to McCann. I did not know if Soldier 'A' had been shot. I believed McCann to be an equal threat to myself, to the public and to my comrades'.

Regarding the shooting of Seán Savage, Soldier 'C' said he was moving forward to effect an arrest when he heard shots behind him:- 'Savage spun round very fast. I shouted "stop". At the same time as I shouted, he went down to the right area of his jacket. At this stage, I had my weapon out to effect an arrest and I fired. I was about five to six feet away. I carried on firing until I was sure he'd gone down and was no longer a threat to initiate that device...I fired to the mass, to the body. He was full frontal because he had spun round. I could not take any more chances of effecting a physical arrest. I fired six rounds. Four went into the chest area, two went into the head. Savage spiralled down and then fell backwards'. He denied firing at Savage on the ground, 'All my shots I finished firing as he was falling down like a corkscrew. He got one in the neck and one in the head'.

Soldier 'D' also said that Savage spun round after the sound of shots and 'C's cry of 'stop'. He also feared detonation of the bomb and when shots were fired he didn't know if 'A' and 'B' had been shot. He said Savage did not stop and 'his arm went to the hip area on the right or to his jacket pocket'. He denied a suggestion from Mr McGrory that he had stood on Seán Savage's chest as he lay on the ground and fired into his head.

After considering these statements laced with threats, movements suggesting going for weapons or detonating a catastrophic bomb, shots fired by companions thought to be shots from the enemy that may have killed some companions, one can turn to assess them against the medical evidence and some of the statements of independent witnesses.

One of the witnesses of the Gibraltar shootings was Mr Stephen Bullock, a practising barrister. He gave evidence at the inquest. He had gone out for a walk with his wife Lucinda, then nine months pregnant, and with his young daughter who was in a pushchair. He told the inquest they were walking south down Smith Dorrien Avenue past a children's playground. He noticed a police car over at a zebra crossing with four uniformed officers inside and a radio blaring out messages. 'A man pushed past us very roughly but he did actually say "Excuse me". I noticed that he had the butt of a very large pistol sticking out of the waistband of his jeans. At this point I was fairly worried because he didn't look like a policeman. When I have seen people carrying weapons they are generally in holsters and not in the back of their trousers. I must say this man seemed to be looking over his shoulder towards the police car. I thought maybe he was running away from the police. At the bottom of the avenue he met up with another person. They both peered in the direction of the landport tunnel through some bushes (*They were Soldiers 'C' and 'D'*). As the second person turned I could see that he also had a butt of a pistol in the back waistband. At this stage I started to slow down, thinking something very strange was going on. The police car we had passed earlier pulled out of the line of traffic and as it got almost level with us it turned its siren on and almost simultaneously there was a sudden burst of shots from the direction of the petrol station, which is I suppose, about 50 yards from where we were standing. Given the fact that it was much closer to us – and so the sound would have travelled faster from the car than from outside the garage – I would say that as far as I was concerned the siren came first but within almost a split second there was a burst of shots. When I heard the bangs I looked in the direction they were coming from and outside the petrol station I saw a man standing in the road (*Soldier 'B'*), almost I suppose against the edge of the pavement, with another man who was maybe four feet away from him, facing on to him at this stage, (*Daniel McCann*). The man on the pavement was reeling backwards and the man standing on the road was firing very rapidly.' Mr Bullock demonstrated how McCann was reeling backwards with his hands thrown back. 'He hit the ground and his legs came right off the ground. I could vaguely see something lying on the ground. I can't be certain what; it could have been an article of clothing. As the shooting stopped I looked back to the two men at the corner (*Soldiers 'C' and 'D'*). They were watching very intently what was going on there. As the shooting stopped they both suddenly turned and ran around the corner in the direction of the landport tunnel. Out of my sight and within a matter of seconds there was another very, very long burst of shooting. At which point I dived down behind the wall. I dragged my wife and pulled the pushchair down behind the wall in order to get some sort of cover.'

Mrs Josie Celecia spoke on the TV programme, 'Death on the Rock', and at the inquest. She said she was standing at the bedroom window overlooking the petrol station where Mairéad Farrell and Daniel McCann were shot dead. She said she saw them walking along the pavement: 'Well, I saw two couples, and I was standing at the mantlepiece. He had spikey blond short hair, you know. Then all of a sudden I took my sight off him and looked to the adventure playground. Suddenly I heard two shots – there were about two shots. So I was just looking from where that came from. And all of a sudden I saw the woman, you know, the couple on the floor.' At the inquest she said she heard further shots when the couple were on the ground; she saw a man standing over the bodies with his hands outstretched and pointing downwards at the same time as she heard a second burst of shots; she didn't see any pistols but heard the bangs coming from that direction.

On 'Death on the Rock' Mrs Carmen Proetta (44), a translator for two Spanish lawyers, said:- 'I looked out of the window, and all of a sudden I saw a car – police car. It stopped all of a sudden and the doors were open, all of them the four of them, and three men came out dressed in jeans and jackets, jumped over the intersection barrier in the road, guns in hand...They didn't do anything, they just jumped with their guns in their hands and they just went and shot these people. That's all. They didn't say anything, they didn't scream, they didn't shout, they didn't do anything. These people were turning their heads back to see what was happening, and when they saw these men had the guns in their hands they just put their hands up. It looked like the man was protecting the girl, because he stood in front of her, but there was no chance. I mean they went to the floor immediately, they dropped'. She saw a gunman fire at the two people who were lying on the ground, 'Yes, he bent down and with the two hands he got his gun like that and went on shooting at them'. At the inquest she stuck to her story that she saw the couple put up their hands 'in surrender or shock' just before they were shot (her husband Maxie thought they put their hands up more in shock than surrender). She told *Independent* reporter Heather Mills (14 May

1988) she could see the blood spurt out when the gunman fired on the pair on the ground, 'It is something I will never forget. It was horrible, it made me feel bad. I keep thinking I will wake up and this will be a dream'.

Mrs Proetta was subjected to the most terrible vilification in the British tabloid press. She was called 'The Tart of Gib', by *The Sun* newspaper. Its front page paraded a gruesome picture of her and an ugly story, 'The Sun discovers shock truth about IRA deaths witness Carmen... she's an ex-prostitute, runs an escort agency, and is married to a sleazy drug peddler'. The *Sunday Times*, like *The Sun* owned by Rupert Murdoch, published stories designed to discredit her as a witness, quoting other witnesses as describing her version of events as untrue (these witnesses later denied they said any such thing). John Waters for *Magill* (June 1988), and Thames Television found no shred of evidence to substantiate *The Sun*'s serious allegations (*The Sun*, 30 April, 2 May 1988). In the first of five libel actions against British newspapers, Mrs Carmen Proetta on 16 December 1988 received substantial damages (believed to be over £50,000) and legal costs after *The Sun*'s editor Kelvin Mackenzie and journalists Michael Fielder and Martin Smith accepted that the allegations were untrue and should never have been published. *The Sun*'s solicitor expressed sincere regret and apologised for the distress and embarrassment caused. On 15 June 1989 Mrs Proetta won 'substantial' undisclosed libel damages from Mirror Group Newspapers over articles in the *Daily Mirror* in April and September 1988. Allegations were withdrawn and apologies were made.

The crown pathologist at the inquest, Professor Alan Watson of Glasgow University, examined the three bodies at the Royal Naval Hospital, Gibraltar, 24 hours after they had been shot. He found the equipment in the *post-mortem* room poor; there was no X-ray machine available in the room. Two local doctors attended and watched but did not offer any help. Two members of the Royal Navy assisted as morticians but neither had assisted at a *post-mortem* before. Professor Watson had to prepare his report in an unprofessional way. He did not see the ballistic reports, the forensic science report or the results of the blood and urine tests he had handed over. The absence of details of strike marks and the distribution of spent cartridges hindered him in his post-mortem. Furthermore the Coroner's Officer revealed at the inquest that the bodies had been stripped before the *post-mortem* to enable photographs to be taken to highlight the wounds. The pathologist should have had the opportunity to examine the bodies before they were undressed. He said that Daniel McCann had 2 wounds in his back and on the front of his body and 3 wounds to the head. It was likely that a wound on top of his head was an entry which came out on the left side of the neck. Two bullets which entered his back passed between his ribs and came out at the front of his body. He died from 2 gunshot wounds to the back and 2 to the head. The wound to the left of the jaw raised the suspicion that he must have been facing the person shooting when he received it but because of extreme damage he could not be absolutely sure. The first shot to the head was probably to the face and the second shot to the top of the head while McCann was lying down, but the chest wounds would have come before either of these. McCann could have been shot while falling down or even lying down.

Mairéad Farrell, Professor Watson said, died from internal haemorrhage when 3 bullets entered her back, passed through her chest and exited in the front. There were 5 wounds to her face, head, and neck which had been produced by 2 bullets but which did not do any more than superficial damage. Her heart was shot to pieces. Shots to her body went in her back and out the front. He suggested that she was shot in the face first and that she had her body, or at least the upper part towards the person shooting. He thought it was reasonable to conclude that she fell away and she was shot in the back, killed by 3 shots to the back from a distance of between 2 and 6 feet. He agreed with Mr McGrory that Mairéad Farrell could have been lying down when some of the shots were fired. Someone shot, even superficially, in the face would be stunned, shocked and in pain and would immediately turn away and begin falling. Mr McGrory said that the angle of the bullets entering her back was upwards and for someone like her who was only 5 feet 1 inch in height, the gunman would have needed to have been bending down or she, the victim, would have to have been lying on the ground on her face. Professor Watson agreed. Professor Derek Pounder, professor of medical science at Dundee University, a second pathologist, was called at the inquest by Mr McGrory. He had the benefit of seeing the ballistic report and examining pictures of the scene. He agreed that she had been shot 3 times in the back from about 3 feet. The wounds in her face and back could have been caused when she was on the ground. 'She could not have been conscious for more than 10 to 15 seconds. She would probably have been stunned and bewildered.'

Michael O'Higgins and John Waters have written in detail on the evidence given at the inquest on the three victims in *Magill*, October 1988. In his summing-up the coroner said that if the jury found that any of the three had been shot on the ground after being effectively put out of his action 'that would be murder if you come to the conclusion that the soldiers continued to shoot to finish him off'. The authors say, 'On the basis of this, together with the evidence of Soldiers 'A' and 'B' themselves, the conclusion that this precise act of murder was carried out in the case of Mairéad Farrell seems inescapable'.

This is their analysis:

'The precise sequence of events leading up to this is disputed, but there are, nevertheless, a number of eyewitness accounts which suggest that a more likely scenario was as follows. Farrell and McCann, walking past the

Shell station, are approached from behind by Soldiers 'A' and 'B'. Soldier 'A' is directly behind, on the footpath, and Soldier 'B' is standing out on the road. (Officer M/Officer I/Stephen Bullock/Carmen and Maxie Proetta/ PC James Parody); Soldier 'A' or 'B' shouts a warning; Soldier 'B' opens fire from the road (Proettas/PC Parody); he fires first at Farrell's face (Proettas/ Professor Watson, the pathologist/various witnesses who say that Farrell was first to fall); Farrell raises hands to her face (Proettas), having been only superficially wounded (Professor Watson) and is hit again in the face, falling to the ground face-down (various); McCann having moved to protect Farrell, is himself hit once or twice in the head (Professor Watson), and falls also; Soldier 'B' stops shooting, having fired 7 rounds, 2 hitting each Farrell and McCann, the others ricocheting off petrol pumps four and five which are directly behind; Soldier 'A' moves in and fires 5 shots from close range; 3 into the back of Farrell and 2 into the back of McCann as they lie on the ground (Officer I/Proettas/Josie Celecia).'

In the case of Seán Savage the soldiers say they fired only 15 shots. After the shooting they did not hand in all their magazines. Fifteen bullet cases were found in the vicinity of his body. However, another one was found in his left-hand trouser pocket. Also Professor Derek Pounder, who had access to the forensic report and examined the clothing of the deceased, established that the wound on Savage's left shoulder was an exit wound; Professor Watson had been in doubt about this since he had not the clothes nor the forensic report at his disposal for his report. This made 17 shots. The area where Savage's body lay was outlined with chalk; within that area were four strike marks delineating his head. The soldiers admitted shooting him in the head as he corkscrewed to the ground. The *Magill* authors point out, 'Both Professor Watson and Professor Pounder said that in their opinion some at least of the shots to the head had been fired while Savage was lying on his back on the ground. Professor Pounder advanced the view that the shots were fired from the direction of the feet. One of the two groups of spent shells mentioned by Sergeant Acris as being in the vicinity of Savage's body were found about 4 feet to the right of the head. The inquest also heard evidence that the Browning pistols used by the SAS soldiers eject cartridges to the right usually to a distance of about 4 feet...'

Professor Watson said that Seán Savage was killed by 16 to 18 bullets. It took him more than fifteen minutes to read the chilling list of his wounds. Entry wounds included 5 to the head, 5 in the back, 5 in the front and one to the hand. There were 27 wounds. Cause of death was gunshot wounds to the head, resulting in extensive brain damage. There were gunshot wounds to the left leg, and right and left arms. Professor Watson said that there were two surprisingly 'symmetrical' wounds to the top of both shoulders. There were multiple fractures of the skull. An arm and a leg had been broken. In cross-examination Mr McGrory asked Professor Watson if, in fact, Savage had been riddled with bullets. He said, 'Yes, I can concur. I do not like to use unscientific terms but it was like a frenzied attack I would say'.

Diane Treacy, a bank clerk, was the first independent witness to see a soldier firing at Savage. She said she was walking north when she passed a group of men at Landport Bridge on their way towards town, in the opposite direction. Behind them she saw Savage running towards her. He passed by her. Then she saw a second man coming. He was running awkwardly because he had a gun in his left hand. He was four or five feet away from her and in front when she saw him open fire. She heard no shout. She said, 'When I heard the first shot I looked back and I saw the first man falling back as he was being shot. I got so frightened I ran away'. Savage, she said, had been shot through the back and he fell on his back. After the first shot she saw him with his back arched backwards: he was 'bouncing on the floor' and then she heard more shots. The inescapable conclusion is that Savage was shot while he lay on the ground.

Mr Robyn Mordue, a British holidaymaker in Gibraltar in March, told the coroner's court that he was walking to the beach on 6 March when a man carrying newspapers (Seán Savage) passed him by. A man (not identified) leapt out from the left and pushed a woman on a bicycle (not called as a witness) into him. He heard bangs and somebody shouted, 'Stop. Get down'. As he moved to get up there were more shots. He said, 'I think, I can't quite remember, but I think I did say to this girl: "He is a madman and is going to kill us all"'. In cross-examination he said he did not see the shooting, although he was aware of Savage being on the ground. He saw a man bleeding and lying at the foot of a tree. Then there was the sound of more shots. He hid behind some cars and was sick. When he was asked specifically about the man he saw standing over Savage's body and pointing his gun at it, he said the man had stopped firing at that stage. Mr Mordue received threats before he gave evidence. Men with English accents telephoned his ex-directory number, called him a 'bastard' and told him 'You've got to stay away!'

One of the witnesses who aroused consternation and frustration at the inquest was the bank clerk Kenneth Asquez (20). He had said in the Thames programme 'Death on the Rock' that he had seen the shooting of Savage from a car: 'The man on the ground was lying on his back, the man standing over this man had his foot on the man's chest. I could see that he also had a gun in his hand. I then saw the gunman point his gun deliberately at the man that was lying on the floor and fire 2 or 3 times into him at point-blank range. I was horrified by what I saw.' *The Observer*, 20 November 1988, points out that he gave this same description three times: to Major Bob Randall, who was doing research for the TV programme, the day after the shooting at the bank where he worked; in a handwritten statement to

Randall and to Christopher Finch, a Gibraltar lawyer whose confidence he sought because he was frightened to go in to court because 'of the people involved'. He retracted the damaging part of his statement. One part of his statement had never been revealed until the inquest. He had said in his original statement that the soldier who shot Savage had shown an identity card. This was corroborated by a statement of PC Douglas Colombo who was on duty near the shooting. The coroner said at the inquest: 'The trouble is…that this question of…the ID card…has only come out for the first time in this court.' Asquez just said he was confused and his thoughts were vague. Lawyers for the families did not have the original police statements and were not able to cross-examine Asquez on this point. *The Observer* says that Asquez's lawyer then said that Randall did not offer him money but only 'mentioned money'. Randall, of course, would totally deny this and he has challenged Asquez to repeat outside the court his allegations of harassment. Asquez has refused to do this. Another person who was in the car with Asquez gave a statement that he had seen nothing. *The Observer* reported that he was the son of a Gibraltar police officer. The driver of the car in which Asquez was a passenger and two women passengers were not called to give evidence at the inquest. This would have been helpful in assessing the evidence of Asquez. Evidence was not heard either from the man to whom Asquez made his original handwritten statement.

Since the inquest controversy has surrounded the affidavit tendered in the name of Chief Inspector Tomás Rayo Valenzuela to the Gibraltar inquest. He was number two in the Provincial Special Branch in Malaga which played a lesser role than the Spanish élite anti-terrorist squad, 'Terrorismo Internacional'. It supported the British version that the IRA trio had been 'lost' by Spanish police and took the British by surprise when they arrived in Gibraltar. An unsigned English 'translation' of this affidavit was not admitted at the inquest but was leaked to the British press. British authorities have said a number of times that a Spanish version sworn before a Spanish judge in Malaga on 9 August 1988 was lost. Finally in June 1989 the British Foreign Office produced what it said was the original. It had never got past the British Embassy in Madrid and had not been sent to the Gibraltar coroner's office. The Chief Inspector has contradicted this affidavit several times to journalists. Two Spanish journalists have claimed that it is a forgery.

Misinformation

David Miller and Dave Maguire of the Department of Sociology, University of Glasgow, wrote a study, 'Truth on the Rocks: The Media and the Gibraltar Shootings' in 1988 analysing the media stories of the 'Bomb Gang', 'Shoot-Out', 'Fourth Members', the 'Death on the Rock' programme, the 'Insight' articles in the *Sunday Times*. David Miller and the Glasgow University Media Group presented an expansion of this paper to the British Sociological Association Annual Conference in Plymouth on 21 March 1989.A few quotations from their study will show how false statements prepared the minds of the public to accept that the three who were shot dead deserved to die. This misinformation was allowed to continue for more than a day.

Here are some examples:

> 'They were challenged by, it appears, plain clothed policemen... Then the shoot out happened' (BBC1, 21.00, 6.3.88)
>
> 'A fierce gun battle broke out' (ITN, 21.15, 6.3.88)
>
> 'A 500lb car bomb close to the governor's residence' (ITN, 12.30, 7.3.88)
>
> 'Army explosives' experts used a robot to defuse the bomb'(ITN, 12.30, 7.3.88)
>
> 'A 500lb bomb was later defused' (*The Guardian*, 7.3.88)
>
> 'One of them was a woman and they were both armed' (*Today*, 7.3.88)
>
> 'They were armed' (*The Sun*, 7.3.88)

Sir Geoffrey Howe, Secretary of State for Foreign and Commonwealth Affairs, made a statement on the shooting in the House of Commons, 3.30 pm, 7 March. He admitted the three Irish people were unarmed and that there was no bomb. He defended the killings in words familiar from other cases of disputed shootings: the three were challenged, 'They made movements which led the military personnel operating in support of the Gibraltar police to conclude that their own lives and the lives of others were under threat. In the light of this response they were shot dead. Those killed were subsequently found not to have been carrying arms'.There was no bomb but it must appear that the three were evil people about to commit a terrible crime and therefore they deserved to die. He said: 'The suspect white Renault was parked in the area on which the band of soldiers would have formed for the Tuesday parade. A school and old people's home were both close by. Had a bomb exploded in the area, not only the 50 soldiers involved in the parade, but a large number of civilians might well have been killed or injured. It is estimated that casualties could well have run into three figures.' This statement from a senior minister pre-empted any inquest, judicial inquiry or prosecution. The government which had sanctioned the use of the SAS had a vested interest in protecting itself. At the inquest three Public Interest Immunity certificates, from the British Home Secretary, the Secretary of State for Defence and the Deputy Governor of Gibraltar enabled the Crown to claim immunity from answering questions that would reveal classified intelligence information or endanger national security. The truth revealed at the inquest was limited. One could not learn of the surveillance operation in Spain. The official line was that there was none

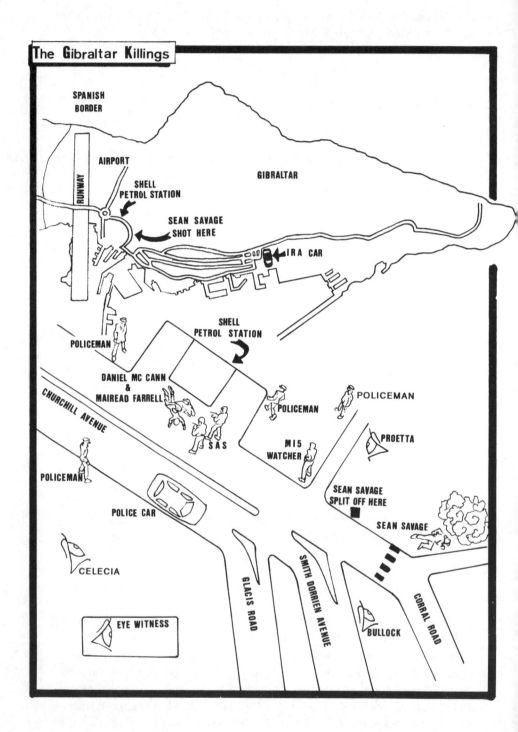

The Gibraltar Killings

SPANISH BORDER

AIRPORT

RUNWAY

SHELL PETROL STATION

GIBRALTAR

SEAN SAVAGE SHOT HERE

IRA CAR

POLICEMAN

SHELL PETROL STATION

DANIEL MC CANN & MAIREAD FARRELL

POLICEMAN

POLICEMAN

CHURCHILL AVENUE

SAS

MI5 WATCHER

PROETTA

POLICEMAN

SEAN SAVAGE SPLIT OFF HERE

SEAN SAVAGE

POLICE CAR

CELECIA

GLACIS ROAD

SMITH DORRIEN AVENUE

BULLOCK

CORRAL ROAD

EYE WITNESS

before 6 March.

The use of the media to get across the first story is 'time-honoured'. The first story runs ahead and it is very difficult to catch up. Colin Wallace who has featured in an earlier part of this book and who worked in 'Psychological Operations' in the North in the 1970s described the potential of misinformation in influencing public opinion a few days after the shootings:

> The important thing is to get saturation coverage for your story as soon after the controversial event as possible. Once the papers have printed it the damage is done. Even when the facts come out the original image is the one that sticks. (Quoted in *What the papers say*, Channel Four, 11.3.88).

Mr George Robertson, Labour's foreign affairs spokesman, supported Sir Geoffrey Howe's statement. The one dissenting voice was Mr Eric Heffer, MP (Lab. Liverpool Walton). He asked if Sir Geoffrey could explain why three people although on active service had been killed 'when they didn't have guns and didn't plant a bomb? How will this help the fight against terrorism? Won't this help terrorism?' Later he was to assert that he received dozens of letters from ex-SAS men, ex-colonels, and Tories, also expressing great disquiet. On 10 March he tabled a motion signed by 60 Labour MPs describing the Gibraltar shootings as an 'act of terrorism and as tantamount to capital punishment without trial'. The dissent began to mount. Mr David Owen, MP asked the Prime Minister to hold an enquiry, 'People can't be given a license to kill'. Mr Kevin McNamara also called for an inquiry. On 8 March the Taoiseach Mr Charles Haughey told the Dáil that he was gravely perturbed over the shooting dead of three unarmed Irish people in Gibraltar when it appeared they could have been arrested, 'I have already said that the shooting of unarmed civilians is unacceptable to this Government and I think it should be unacceptable to democratic governments everywhere'. He said that the Gardaí were not involved in surveillance of the IRA unit. Mr Haughey was bitterly attacked by Mr Norman Tebbit, MP in an article in the *Sunday Express*, 13 March, where he defended the action of the SAS: 'Personally I have had more than a bellyful of Mr Haughey, the Prime Minister of Southern Ireland. What's wrong with the man?'

The quality press also began to ask questions in editorials and articles by correspondents disturbed by the action. *The Guardian* editorial of 9 March 1988 was headed 'An open but not a shut case'. *The Independent* spoke of 'unacceptable secrecy'. On 8 March the editorial in the *Daily Telegraph* criticised the government: 'The government must tell why it gave a succession of contradictory accounts to the world about Sunday's events. Unless it wishes Britain's enemies to enjoy a propaganda bonanza, it should explain why it was necessary to shoot dead all three terrorists on the street, rather than apprehend them with the considerable force of police and SAS which appeared to have been deployed in the locality.' Robert Kilroy-Silk contributed an article 'Licensed to Kill?' to the 11 March edition of *The Times*: 'We are in danger, not only of being perceived to have double standards, but also of having a flexible attitude to the rule of law. This is the quickest way to authoritarianism.' Mr Bill Speirs, chairman of the Labour Party in Scotland, while condemning the IRA at the Perth conference on 11 March said that the 'Stalker affair led directly to what happened on the streets of Gibraltar'. He said that the IRA's monstrous campaign did not provide a license for agents of the British state to engage in summary executions of unarmed people. Labour MP Mr Tony Benn also described the killings as 'summary executions' at a meeting of Hammersmith Trades' Council. A number of students' unions regretted that Queen's University where Mairéad Farrell was an arts student did not publicly recognise her death. The author Mr Auberon Waugh wrote in the *Sunday Telegraph*, 13 March: 'What surprised me was the number of Saloon Bar Britons who reckoned it was all right to gun down suspected terrorists, even if they were not engaged in terrorist activities at the time. If the majority of Britons feel like this – and my own soundings suggest they do – what is to stop Mrs Thatcher setting up murder squads in the South American model?' On 14 March the Labour MEP for Luton Central Mr Stan Newbus called for a resolution in the European Parliament on a public inquiry into the Gibraltar killings. He claimed support from his own party and from Greek, Dutch and German MEPs as well. He said, 'One cannot claim a moral mandate against terrorism if one goes beyond the rule of law. Even the Geneva Convention which applies to war time does not allow the execution of unarmed personnel'. Richard Ingrams has continued to ask questions on the Gibraltar incident in *The Observer*.

Spanish papers also criticised British forces. Following the killings *El Pais* said they had 'gravely violated every moral code of a civilised society by undermining fundamentally the laws it is supposed to uphold. It said that if the Spanish authorities had acted in the same way against Basque terrorists there would have been a 'scandal of immense proportions'. *Diario 16* said they operated on a principle of 'Kill first, ask questions later'.

At the end of March, Amnesty International called for a public explanation of the killings and announced that it would also investigate them. This aroused the fury of Mrs Thatcher and other Conservative members of Parliament but Amnesty was defended by Mr David Steele, MP. Then followed the two television programmes, ITN's Thames Television programme, *This Week*, 'Death on the Rock' on 28 April 1988 and BBC's *Spotlight* programme on 5 May 1988. Sir Geoffrey Howe tried to have the Thames programme postponed until after the inquest by appealing to Lord Thomson of Monifieth, chairman of the Independent Broadcasting Authority (IBA), but failed. Likewise Mrs Thatcher reiterated her Government's opposition to the BBC programme on the day of the programme but to no avail. The programmes created further unease of conscience regarding the policies of 'Shoot-to-Kill' and 'the end justifying the means'.

On 5 October 1988 Thames Television invited Lord Windlesham to conduct an independent inquiry into its programme 'Death on the Rock'. Lord Windlesham asked Mr Richard Rampton, QC to assist him. After an investigation which took three and a half months to complete, the report of 145 pages was published on 26 January 1989. The report, contrary to the opinion of the Prime Minister, Mrs Margaret Thatcher, and the Foreign Secretary, Sir Geoffrey Howe, found that the TV programme was not 'trial by television' and had not prejudiced the inquest. It cleared the programme of a long list of more than twenty criticisms and found fault in only two areas. The British Government immediately denigrated the report. The report not only vindicated Thames' *This Week* team in making the programme but also concluded that Thames Television and the Independent Broadcasting Authority were correct not to bow to Government pressure to ban 'Death on the Rock'. The report was a slap in the face to the *Sunday Times* which had constantly abused the programme. Jolyon Jenkins in 'Truth on the rocks' (*New Statesman & Society,* 27 January 1989), pointed out the shameful record of Fleet Street itself, especially the *Sunday Times,* in spreading misinformation on what had happened in Gibraltar.

The Funerals

There was much apprehension in Ireland while awaiting the return of the bodies of the three IRA volunteers. The parents of Mairéad Farrell and the families of the two men issued a statement on 12 March: 'We appeal to the British forces to permit us dignity to bury our loved ones in peace.' The bodies were brought back by a specially chartered aircraft and arrived in Dublin airport at 4.40 pm on 14 March. Large crowds, reminiscent of the funerals of the hunger-strikers of 1981, lined the villages *en route* to the border, massive crowds turning out at Drogheda and Dundalk. At the bridge into Dundalk, Gardaí saluted as the tricolour-draped coffins passed, symbolic of the sense of feeling throughout Ireland at the outrage. Security was low-key and there was no demonstrative paramilitary display. A firing party of the IRA had already paid tribute to them with three volleys of shots over a memorial consisting of flowers and photographs of the three in Rodney Drive, West Belfast. It was a different matter when the cortège crossed the border. Mourners were harassed by the RUC the whole way to Belfast and only arrived safely home in West Belfast at 3 am having been diverted and delayed many times by the police. While the bodies were *en route,* Kevin McCracken (30), an IRA volunteer, was shot dead by British soldiers at 7.45 pm in an alleyway in Turf Lodge, Belfast. A rifle was found near him.

I celebrated the funeral Mass of Mairéad Farrell in St Oliver Plunkett's Church, Lenadoon, Belfast on Tuesday evening, 15 March. I had been chaplain of Armagh Prison and knew her well. In my homily I said:

'Just beyond her family and close friends there is another little family over which she acted as a kind of mother and sister combined: myself and the little band of girls who shared life together for ten years. Shared joys and sorrows, ups and downs, hardships and friendships for ten years in Armagh Jail. Mairéad was a great and loyal friend. She was a generous companion to all the girls. They suffered a lot. Mairéad herself served three extra years of punishment. It is impossible for me to prise open that world. The depth of solidarity of people who suffer together is too great to explain. Therefore her companions and I have a grief of our own. Our faith however prompts us ever to remember the sunny days. I will always remember Mairéad's searching intelligent eyes, twinkling between seriousness and humour, and her ready smile. The banter, joviality, the good-humoured slagging matches, the fair debates and arguments, the laughter will break always through the walls and bars of prison and memories.

Mairéad – cailín, gáiriúil, díograiseach, cróga
        cliste, croíúil, aigeantach, beoga.

'Mairéad's death was sad and tragic. Done to death, barbarously assassinated by a gunman as she was walking in public on a sunny Sunday afternoon. There was no respect for law and morality. In the words of the leading Spanish paper El Pais – "The British forces have gravely violated every moral code of a civilised society by undermining fundamentally the laws it is supposed to uphold".

'During Lent we are meditating on the passion and death of Jesus. His mysterious failure shows that love is stronger than death. From his poisonous wounds comes healing. From his death comes life. His open arms on the cross are an open embrace to gather all pain and suffering and tragedy to himself. A victim of violence himself he gathers all victims, young and old into the bosom of God.'[127]

At the Mass for Seán Savage and Daniel McCann in St Agnes' Church on the morning of 16 March Fr Tom Toner spoke of the lies that had been told about the killings, about 'people in high places gloating over these murders'.

At the Mass for Kevin McCracken, Fr Aidan Denny told the packed congregation in Holy Trinity Church that Kevin McCracken and Seán Savage, natives of the parish, grew up knowing only the 'Troubles': 'It is a world without hope for the young. They are constantly being abused, harassed, and humiliated by the forces of law and order. They see the institutions of the State perpetrating and turning a blind eye to great injustices. They have friends in prison for years, yet discovered recently a soldier released from prison after two years for murdering another parishioner 'Kidso' Reilly. Is it any wonder some of them vent their anger and desperation and frustration in throwing stones or petrol bombs, hijacking and burning vehicles or even joining the IRA?'

Regarding the SAS killing of three people in Gibraltar he said: 'Everybody here was shocked by the death of three unarmed Irish people in Gibraltar. The fact that they were shot dead rather than maimed or arrested makes us call it murder. The Christian cannot condone murder, no matter by whom it was done. But it has an even more sinister dimension when done by the State security forces or is approved of by the State. We are shocked by the obvious injustice and self-righteousness of people in power over the past few weeks. Is their sin not a greater wrong than the sin committed by people without power? If we say that it is wrong for them to practise violence, must we not also say that the people of West Belfast are more sinned against than sinning? The people of West Belfast want peace as much as people anywhere in the North of Ireland. Yet so long as they feel they are being unjustly treated they will feel aggrieved.'

The British press, including the Catholic periodical *The Tablet*, did not like the home truths contained in the priests' homilies. They misquoted them. On the morning of 16 March the three funerals converged outside St Agnes' Church. There had been constant negotiation between clergy and RUC for a low profile of Army and RUC at the funerals. The three hearses moved off followed by gigantic crowds. For those in the procession there was a sense of foreboding as well as heavy sorrow. One had been prepared for a watch from a discreet distance by British forces. But not a single policeman or soldier was in sight!

At the funeral, just as Mairéad Farrell's body had been lowered into the grave, at 1.20 pm, a UDA man armed with a Ruger revolver, Browning pistol and grenades launched an attack. He was accompanied by a second man who made off when the crowd panicked and some young men surged forward to apprehend them. Three men were killed by the principal attacker, later identified as Michael Stone (33) of Ravenswood Park in the Braniel Estate in East Belfast. Those killed by him were Kevin Brady (30), John Murray (26), Thomas McErlean (20). Some seventy people were injured.

When the attack happened heavily-armed RUC men in a white Transit van parked on the MI motorway moved off. As Stone was captured by some of his pursuers and bundled into a car, land-rovers of RUC arrived on the scene and took charge of him. The presence of the white van, the complete visible absence of military and RUC, led to accusations of collusion of the RUC and British soldiers with the killer. Just before the attack I myself passed a plain clothes man at some few hundred yards distant from the main crowd. He was crouched down behind a tombstone and was relaying a commentary by radio on the proceedings in the cemetery. He had an English accent. I took him to be an undercover British intelligence officer.

On 2 November 1988 the *Irish News* reported that, besides the three murders in Milltown cemetery, Stone was also charged with the murders of Patrick Brady (36), a milk rounds man, Boucher Road, Belfast, on 16 November 1984, Kevin McPolin (27), a joiner, at Lisburn (territory of UDA leader John McMichael) on 8 November 1985 and Dermot Hackett, a bread server, at Drumquin, County Tyrone on 23 May 1987. Four charges of attempted murder were also put to him: Robert McAllister, a taxi-driver in Belfast whose car was booby-trapped; John James Bloomfield, another taxi-driver from Ballynahinch, whose car was raked by gunfire; John Joseph Davey of Gulladuff, Magherafelt (shot dead by loyalists on 14 February 1989) and John Augustine O'Kane of Kilrea, County Antrim on whose farm a booby trap was planted. He was accused of plotting to kill Sinn Féin leaders Martin McGuinness and Owen Carron and ex-prisoner Peter John Bateson of Toomebridge. He intended killing Gerry Adams at St Agnes' Church on the day of the funeral but decided against it since he had no chance of escape. The grenades, Browning automatic pistol and Ruger revolver he used in the cemetery attack were from a consignment of loyalist guns imported through contacts with South African agents seeking secrets of the Star Streak missiles at Shorts' aircraft factory in Belfast. On 3 March 1989 Michael 'Flint' Stone was jailed for 30 years for the funeral murders and concurrent sentences totalling 648 years for other crimes including three other murders. At his trial for the murder of Dermot Hackett, of which he was found guilty, Stone said, 'I read his file. He was a legitimate target'.

Another horrible atrocity followed the Milltown cemetery massacre. Just as thousands lined up behind the coffin of Kevin Brady, the IRA man killed by Stone, two undercover British soldiers who drove into the cortège were beaten by a mob, stripped and then shot by the IRA. The horror and terror of their deaths was clear from TV film and the pictures of their dead bodies. The victims were Corporal Robert Howes (23) and Corporal Derek Wood (24) of the Royal Corps of Signals, a regiment which works closely with the SAS and military intelligence. British military spokesmen said they had driven into the funeral by mistake. The soldiers drove their car at speed with its headlights on along the pavement of the Andersonstown Road after passing front-line stewards of the funeral and a number of black taxis. Instead of turning right, up Slemish Way, beside the hearse, they reversed back in front of the hearse where they were blocked by black taxis. The action sparked off panic. People thought it was another loyalist attack. Others thought they were SAS (some Sunday newspapers reported them as such on 20 March). The British Army gave no adequate explanation why the undercover soldiers were there. Corporal Howes was only a week in the

North. Corporal Wood was ending a four-year term; his experience dispelled the theory that they were 'lost'. In an article 'The questions our muzzled press should be asking on Gibraltar', Mr Enoch Powell wrote on the possibility that the Gibraltar shootings could be deliberate, cold-blooded premeditated murder. He upbraided a supine press who did not make it their business to hunt for truth and justice. He said: 'Staying for a moment with terrorism there was the event of the corporals murdered in Andersonstown and the two questions that have gone unurged since then. The happening, however horrifically terminated, was a military catastrophe, the result of military default, by incompetence or worse. Whose and what that default was ought to be determined, so that responsibility may be duly assigned. The other question is: who took the underlying decision on policing policy, and at whose instigation was it taken? If it was the Secretary of States, he ought to be made resign: men of honour have resigned before for less.'

On 19 March another atrocity occurred. Gillian Johnston (21), a young Protestant, was shot dead in her car and her boyfriend Stanley Ligget (25) seriously injured at Belleek, County Fermanagh, in an attack by the IRA. She was mistaken for her brother. Her brother was mistakenly thought to have been a member of the UDR. The killings continued. Clive Graham, RUC, was shot dead in Creggan estate, Derry on 21 March.

In the aftermath of Gibraltar the IRA continued its campaign on the continent and in Britain. On Sunday, 1 May 1988 three RAF servicemen were killed in Holland. In the first incident at Roermond gunmen opened fire on three men in a car killing Senior Aircraftman Ian Skinner (20) and seriously injuring two others. In the second attack a short time later two men were killed and a third injured when a bomb exploded under their car at Nieuw-Bergen. The men killed were Senior Aircraftmen John Baxter (21) and John Miller Reid (22). On 3 May a bomb found under a captain's car (with forces' plates) outside the officers' mess at Rippon Barracks, Bielefeld, Germany, was defused. On 12 August Regimental Sergeant Major Richard Heakin of the Royal Regiment of Wales was shot dead in Ostend in Belgium. In West Germany on 5 August an explosion at Roy Barracks, Ratingen near Düsseldorf, the base of the 14th Topographical Squad of the Royal Engineers, injured three soldiers and a civilian. On 13 July nine soldiers had been injured when a bomb exploded inside the perimeter fence of the RAF barracks at Duisburg.

On 31 August two men were arrested by a West German customs official near the Dutch-German border. On 19 June 1989 an IRA team planted five Semtex bombs, each containing 66 lbs, at the Quebec barracks at the Osnabrück base in West Germany. A civilian worker disturbed them before all the bombs where primed. The unit escaped. One bomb went off wrecking part of a building. On 2 July Corporal Steve Smith (31), Ist Royal

Tank Regiment, was killed, his wife Tina and three children injured, when a Semtex bomb, attached magnetically to the underneath of his car, exploded in the Hindenberg suburb of Hanover. A second bomb was found nearby attached to a car belonging to a soldier. On 12 July a man and a woman were arrested at Rosslare as they disembarked from the Cherbourg ferry. On 14 July two men and a woman were arrested in France not far from the German border. On 28 August a British soldier discovered a 3 lbs Semtex bomb under his car in the Bothfeld district of Hanover. The device was defused. On 1 September two British soldiers were shot and seriously wounded by two gunmen using a revolver and an AK47 Kalashnikov rifle. The shooting took place near Münster barracks. On 7 September Mrs Heidi Hazell (26), wife of a British Army Staff Sergeant, was shot dead in her car in the Unna-Messen suburb of Dortmund by a gunman using an AK47 rifle. On 9 September two shots were fired at the British Army base at Minden. Corporal Maheshkumar Islania (34) and his baby daughter Nivruti Mahesh were shot dead by the IRA on 26 October at a filling station near Widenrath, the site of an RAF base close to the Rhine Army headquarters at Mönchengladbach.

One of the results of the co-ordination of intelligence in Northern Ireland by Sir Maurice Oldfield, and following the IRA bombing of eight British Army barracks in West Germany in 1978, was the recruitment of informers within the Irish community in 1979 by the Intelligence and Security Group (G), an Army Intelligence Corps based at Rheindalen. Two newspapers, the *Sunday Tribune* (8 October 1989) and *An Phoblacht* (12 October 1989) revealed details of two operations against the IRA, one code-named Ward in 1981, involving MI5 and MI6, and a second code-named Scream, also a joint MI5/MI6 plan – drawn up without the knowledge of British military intelligence – designed this time to place agents from Britain and Ireland among the Irish community in Germany. The unit of Ministry of Defence civilian intelligence at Rheindalen is called the British Services Security Organisation or BSSO and links with the British Joint Intelligence Committee in Bonn and the German Bundesamt für Verfassungsschutz. The renewal of the IRA campaign against British forces in Germany is an indication of the failure of both operations.

On 1 August 1988, in Britain, Lance Corporal Michael Robbins (23) of the Third Training Regiment of the Royal Engineers was killed in an explosion at Mill Hill barracks near London. Nine soldiers were injured. On Wednesday, 21 December police found weapons and more than 100 lbs of Semtex explosives in a flat in Northcote Road, Battersea, London, following a shooting incident in a car outside the flat. Two men escaped from the flat. Fifty paratroopers narrowly escaped death after an alert at Tern Hill Barracks, Shropshire, on 22 February 1989. Large sections of the barracks were destroyed by Semtex bombs placed inside. Four packets of Semtex explosives were found at Stoke Newington, north London on 27 February and 25 lbs of the same explosive were found on 7 March near Scarborough in North Yorkshire where Mrs Thatcher was due to attend a Conservative Party national council conference on 18-19 March. Following the Scarborough find the British Home Secretary said of the IRA on 9 March, 'They are professional killers. That is their occupation and they will go on doing it. No political solution will cope with that. They just have to be extirpated'. On 22 September 1989 ten members of the Royal Marines School of Music were killed when an IRA bomb exploded at 8 .20 am at Walmer Barracks, Deal, Kent. Sixty others were injured. The bomb was planted the night before. The Marines killed were Robert Simmonds (34), 'Taff' Jones (27), Richard George Fice (22), Mark Timothy Petch (26), Timothy John Reeves (24), Trevor Davis (39), Dave McMillan (26), Dean Pavey (32), Andrew Clitheroe (25) and Michael Ball (24). Another Marine, Christopher Nolan (21), died from injuries on 18 October. On 10 October a cache of some 50 lbs of Semtex explosives , detonators and timers were found accidentally in two holdalls at Hamstead Heath, London. On the night of 13 November a large Semtex bomb was found under a car in Kelso Close, Kensington, London. It was defused. The target was Lt General Sir David Ramsbotham, one of the most senior members of the British Army. He had served as commander of the 39th Infantry Brigade, covering Belfast, in 1979 and in 1989 was appointed UK Field Army and inspector-general of the Territorial Army. As commander of the Field Army he is administratively responsible for the SAS base at Hereford. On 18 November Staff Sergeant Andrew Mudd lost both his legs and his wife Margaret was injured when his car was blown up by a bomb near Army married quarters at Goojerat Barracks, Colchester. Sergeant Mudd had been mentioned in dispatches when, as a Military Police corporal, he helped to capture three loyalist gunmen who tried to shoot Gerry Adams. On 3 November police acting on a tip-off found a large amount of Semtex explosives, detonators, automatic rifles and handguns near the village of Newgate, Pembrokeshire, west Wales. Police watched the scene and detained two men on 21 December. The two men, named as Mr 'A' and Mr 'B', appeared at Bow Street Magistrates Court, London, 24 December, accused of conspiring to cause an explosion likely to endanger life or cause serious injury to property, and further charged with having a single-barrelled pump action shotgun with cartridges intending to resist arrest.

Attacks in Northern Ireland were also concentrated against regular British forces. Six soldiers died when their van, left unattended, was booby-trapped in a car park in Lisburn on 15 June 1988. They were: Sgt Michael Winkler (31), Royal Corps of Signals; Signalman Mark Clavey (24), Royal Corps of Signals; L/Cpl Derek Green (20), Royal Army Ordnance Corps; Cpl Ian Metcalfe Ist Battalion, the Green Howards; L/Cpl Graham Patrick

Lambie (22), Royal Corps of Signals; Cpl William John Paterson (22), Royal Corps of Signals.

On 20 August eight members of the 1st Battalion Light Infantry were killed and many injured in an attack on their service bus on the Bally-gawley-Omagh Road, County Tyrone. Those killed were Private Jayson Burfitt (19), Private Richard Greener (21), Private Mark Norsworthy (18), Private Stephen Wilkinson (18), Private Jason Winter (19), Private Blair Bishop (19), Private Alexander Lewis (18) and Private Peter Bullock (21). On 22 August a Royal Navy recruiting officer, Lieutenant Alan Shields (45), was killed in Belfast by a bomb attached to his car.

The Inquest Verdict

The inquest on the three shot dead by the SAS in Gibraltar on 6 March 1988 opened on 6 September 1988 and the inquest jury gave its verdict on 30 September by a majority of nine to two that the trio were lawfully killed. Afterwards Mr McGrory said, 'The full facts have not been presented at this inquest. But the truth has a way of getting out in the end'. Mr Niall Farrell, brother of Mairéad, said the families of the deceased would be asking the Irish Government to refer the case to the European Commission for Human Rights at Strasbourg.

An inquest is not a public inquiry. It is not a full inquiry into the many implications of a death. The Prime Minister Mrs Thatcher ruled out a public inquiry. A public inquiry can examine in detail issues surrounding the immediate cause of death. An inquest is limited in its reference, limited to 'how, where and when' a particular death or deaths occurred. At the end lawyers can not sum up the facts but can only give a summary of points of law. This casts a burden on the coroner. Mr Pizzarello went out of his way to be fair and had an excellent grasp of the minutiæ of the case. However, one of the disappointments of Mr Pizzarello's summing-up, for example, was his failure to emphasise the evidence of the pathologist Professor Watson.

One can point to serious inadequacies in the police investigation and the working of the inquest itself.

1. The bodies of the three were removed in haste before scene-of-the-crime police officers and forensic experts arrived. Bullet cases and other items were collected without marking or mapping their positions. This would have been important in determining the positions of the soldiers when they fired and the sequence of shots. The outlines of the bodies of Mairéad Farrell and Daniel McCann were not marked. An outline, how-ever, was made of the body of Seán Savage and it showed that a number of strike marks lay within the outline of his head.

2. Photographs were not taken of the bodies before they were moved, nor were photographs taken of the areas of ground where bullet cases had

fallen. There was no video evidence at the inquest. It is inconceivable that such a major security operation would have neglected to set up cameras in advance of the IRA operation, at least in the changing-of-the-guard area.

3. There was no urgency to take statements from independent witnesses; there was a preponderance of witnesses from the Crown side who confused the issue or had seen little, some of them off-duty policemen. On the other hand, TV investigative journalists found it easy to get witnesses. Some witnesses were intimidated by the police and smeared by the press. In contrast the SAS were not formally interviewed and their statements were taken not in Gibraltar but weeks after the event in Britain. The impression the SAS gave in their evidence was of 'extremely careful schooling. All four of the shootists used the same expressions again and again'. (Mr McGrory on the ITV current affairs programme *The question is,* 23.10.88). In reports (1989) on the inquest into the deaths in Gibraltar the National Council for Civil Liberties and Amnesty International strongly crticised the police's failure to gather eye-witness evidence. There was no incident centre. Amnesty remarked, 'Although a police witness testified that they had twice gone from door to door looking for witnesses, the witnesses found by journalists claimed the police had not visited them'. The NCCL report commented, 'It was clear from the evidence that there were witnesses to the shootings who had not come forward, or who might have been traced after a thorough investigation. A woman cyclist, and passers-by and bystanders, who on the evidence were witnesses to the shooting of Seán Savage, were not available. No information was given to what efforts, if any, had been made to trace those individuals. It was probable that many people had seen the separate shootings of McCann and Farrell. It is clear that members of the public were unwilling to come forward, but the evidence that was given by inquiries that were made by the police did not reassure that this problem had been properly addressed'.

4. As Mr McGrory, unlike the coroner and the lawyers for the Crown and the SAS, did not have beforehand the order of witnesses, he therefore did not have the overall picture of the opposing lawyers and coroner and could not foresee the relation of evidence which would help him in cross-questioning.

5. When the jury was divided, the coroner exerted inexplicable pressure on them to return a verdict. His action can only be described as 'unholy haste' or as one commentator called it 'a stop-watch verdict'.

6. The families of the deceased in an inquest do not receive legal aid. Mr McGrory did not take a penny but, one must contrast his situation with the Crown, who had vanloads of advisers, unlimited finance, copies of the transcripts daily. The court transcript increased from 10p a sheet to £5 a sheet just before the inquest; it would have cost the families £300 a day to acquire these. Their lawyer's junior counsel had to resort to taking notes.

Mr Jack O'Sullivan, from whose article in *Fortnight* magazine, October 1988, I have drawn some of the above points, has a second article in the same magazine, November 1988, in which he comments on the final verdict:

> For a few hours it appeared possible that the jury might be unable to return a verdict, so making another inquest necessary. As it turned out – despite the lateness of the decision – the government escaped the ignominy of morning newspaper headlines reading, 'Jury deadlock over killings'. The popular perception engendered was that the SAS had been vindicated and all was right with the world.
>
> In fact, behind closed doors for at least six hours that Friday afternoon, three of the jurors had argued that the trio – Daniel McCann, Mairéad Farrell and Seán Savage – had been unlawfully killed. A fourth backed an unlawful killing just for Savage.
>
> The jury was deadlocked, 7-4. Two hours later after the coroner, Felix Pizzarello, warned them that they had taken enough time, the jurors finally returned a minimum majority verdict of 9-2 in favour of lawful killing in all three cases. The dissenter on Savage and one of those who thought all three had been murdered swung over to the majority.
>
> This verdict, and the subsequent political reaction, has tended to overshadow two important elements of the case; the final legal submission to the coroner and Mr Pizzarello's summing-up. Study of these reveals what amounts to an ... unsuccessful attempt by the government counsel, John Laws, to 'stitch up' the soldiers in the unlikely event of an unlawful killing verdict.
>
> Mr Laws urged the coroner to direct the jury that, on the evidence, it was entitled to return an unlawful killing verdict aimed only at the SAS soldiers. In other words, the possibility of high-level conspiracy or of responsibility of senior authorities was not even to be entertained...
>
> In the event, the coroner ignored this final attempt to get the government off the hook. In his summing-up he inserted this professional suicide note concerning alleged conspiracy to murder: 'If I thought that in law there was no evidence at all to support that proposition I would withdraw it from your consideration but in my view, little as it is, there is, and you must consider it'.

Inquest, the annual report of the United Campaign for Justice, who had observers at the inquest, commented on the coroner's urging of the jury to avoid an open verdict: 'Where the coroner's direction was fundamentally flawed was in his legal analysis of the verdicts available. The law, in our submission, is quite clear and logical. Unlawful killing requires proof beyond a reasonable doubt. Lawful killing requires proof on the balance of probabilities. If the jury decides that the killings were unlawful on the balance of probabilities, but not beyond reasonable doubt, then neither standard is reached and the proper verdict is an open one. Unfortunately the coroner mistakenly directed the jury that, if they were not satisfied beyond reasonable doubt that the killings were unlawful, they should bring in a verdict of lawful killing because "in the nature of the circumstances of this incident this is what you will have resolved". In our view this direction must be incorrect because it totally ignores the logical "gap" between the two verdicts. Although the coroner did say that an open verdict would be the only alternative if the situation could not be resolved either way, he did not explain how this proposition fitted in with his earlier direction, which it appears to contradict.

'On the subject of an open verdict, two successive English Lords Chief Justice, Widgery and Lane, have stressed that such a verdict does not suggest that the jury is not performing its proper function, and that there are "many, many cases where there is real doubt as to the cause of death and where an open verdict is right, and where anything else is unjust to the family of the deceased". Despite this clear guidance, Mr Pizzarello told the jury: "I must urge you, in the exercise of your duty, to avoid this ... verdict".'

And *Inquest* sums up:

'What, then, do the verdicts establish? The most that can be said is that a majority of the jury was not satisfied, on the evidence before them, and in the time available, that any of the killings was unlawful beyond a reasonable doubt. Whether the authorities have proved that they were lawful, even on a balance of probabilities, is a more difficult question. Whatever the outcome of any legal challenge to the verdicts, the fact remains that this inquest could not, by its nature, answer questions of fundamental importance. Only a public inquiry with wide terms of reference could begin to address them. To maintain that the issues raised by the killings have been settled and the government totally vindicated would be at the very least misleading.'

The Shooting of Ken Stronge: A Mistake[128]

On 1 July 1988 the SAS shot and fatally wounded a taxi-man, Mr Ken Stronge (46) from Olympia Drive, Belfast. On that night, just after midnight, Thursday/Friday, 30 June/1 July, Mr Stronge, a Protestant, was taking bar staff from a nearby public house home. He had just dropped off one woman passenger and was approaching the North Queen Street RUC Barracks when the IRA launched an attack on the heavily fortified station. Three IRA men in a Volvo car had come from the opposite direction. The car drew to a halt not far from Stronge's taxi. An IRA man emerged from the car's sun-roof and fired an RPG-7 Rocket. A second man raked the station with Armalite gunfire. The attack was expected. Six SAS soldiers and two RUC men were in a Sanger at the base when the rocket was fired. Four of the soldiers fired more than 80 high velocity bullets at the attackers. The IRA drove on a short distance, and then abandoned the car and fled. Ken Stronge was hit three times in the neck and arm. He shouted to his passenger, Angela Coyle, to get down as bullets hit the windscreen of his Sierra. He then said he had been hit. Although critically wounded he still managed to radio for help. At the inquest on 25 October 1989 forensic scientist Leo Rossi said that because of fragmentation it was impossible to say which of the soldiers' guns the fatal bullet had been fired from. A bullet from one of the SAS soldiers had passed through the Volvo car and then through the windscreen of the taxi. One of the soldiers in his statement to the inquest said that when he got to the Volvo he saw a rocket on the back seat and a taxi approaching slowly; he called on the taxi to halt and then saw the driver slumped over the seat. The RUC gave first aid and the wounded man was then taken by ambulance to the Mater Hospital. Later Army bomb-disposal men carried out a controlled explosion on the Volvo car. A second rocket was found in the car and in a further search the RUC found a rocket-launcher, a mask and a blood-stained jacket. The Volvo car had been taken from a house in the New Lodge Road where a family had been held prisoner by men claiming to be from the IRA. Over the week-end Mr Stronge seemed to make a good recovery in hospital but died on Monday night, 4 July from a heart attack.

None of the soldiers appeared at the inquest. The coroner, James Elliott, said, 'All the soldiers are overseas at present'. Their statements were read by an RUC man. In their statements the four soldiers who opened fire said they discharged 'aimed shots' because they felt their 'lives were in danger'.

David Hearst commented on the shooting in *The Guardian*, 14 August 1989: 'Not all SAS operations are clinical, and when blunders are made tensions between the RUC and the British Army can surface. The RUC got word that North Queen Street police station would be the target of a gun and rocket attack.

The SAS was given the task. The commanding officer of the team insisted on having full operational command of the station and turfed out the police reservist who operated the gold coloured levers which activated the steel doors. The plan was to leave the doors slightly ajar, so that when the unit struck, the SAS would rush out and engage the car in rapid fire. When the attack came, the SAS pulled the wrong lever, closing the door instead of opening it. By the time they got out, it was too late. An innocent taxi-driver was killed in the crossfire.'

Mr Stronge was the fourth Protestant to be killed by SAS 'mistakes'. The others were: William James Hanna, 20 June 1978, James Taylor, 30 September 1978, and Frederick Jackson, 19 October 1984. On 2 September 1989 British undercover soldiers shot dead a UVF gunman, Brian Robinson (27), after he and another gunman on a motorbike had gunned down a Catholic,

Patrick McKenna (40), at Ardoyne, Belfast. The two undercover Army cars were noticed on surveillance for quite a while before the shooting. Could they not have prevented the shooting of Patrick McKenna? The soldiers crashed a car into the motorbike and then shot Robinson dead. Could he not have been taken prisoner? There is speculation that British intelligence risked the action to win some public favour after the UDA had disclosed their collusion with the British forces following the murder of Loughlin Maginn, a Catholic, at his home in Rathfriland on 25 August 1989. It is not the policy of British forces to shoot loyalist paramilitaries. In fact it is extremely rare. On 16 March 1983 the RUC shot dead William Millar of the UVF in a car on University Road, Belfast, and the UDA blamed the 'dirty tricks' department of the security forces for the blowing up of Michael Wright on 15 April 1980 while handling explosives in a community centre on the Highfield estate, Belfast.

Because of the milieu in which they live, families of Protestant victims shot by the British Army and RUC in unjustified circumstances are reluctant to protest publicly.

Ambush at Drumnakilly[129]

On Tuesday, 30 August 1988 three IRA men, Gerard and Martin Harte, brothers from Loughmacrory, County Tyrone, and Brian Mullin from Foremass, Sixmilecross, County Tyrone were shot dead in an SAS ambush in revenge for the IRA bomb attack on a British Army coach on 20 August 1988 when eight soldiers of the Light Infantry were killed and twenty-seven injured. The British media interpreted it as such. The first headline in the article of John Burns and Peter Hooley in the *Daily Express* read, 'Armed terrorists shot in gun battle as bus-bomb avengers swoop from dugout'. Paul Vallely wrote in *The Times*, 'Yesterday's Army action comes in the wake of calls for tougher action to curb an IRA offensive that began at the beginning of this month and has claimed a succession of servicemen's lives in Ulster, Britain and the Continent'. 'IRA men shot dead by Army avengers', wrote Ian Hepburn and Trevor Hanna in *The Sun*. A huge heading, 'SAS rub out IRA rats', dwarfed the story of Robert Brady and Peter Welbourn in *The Star*. The headline for writers Joe Gorrod and John Hicks in the *Daily Mirror* easily competed with *The Star*: 'Revenge! SAS kill three bus bombers'. *Today* also identified the three men as the bombers of the coach: 'Revenge of the SAS. IRA bombers of 8 boy soldiers shot in cottage ambush.' Jim McDowell reporting from Belfast expanded on this, 'The SAS would not comment on the operation last night but one insider said: "The boys look after their own. If they have avenged the deaths of those young soldiers killed on the coach they'll be happy". *Today* also quoted comment from the parents of one soldier killed in the coach bomb that, if the men ambushed by the SAS had anything to do with it, then justice would have been done. Newspapers referred to the IRA men as suspects for the coach bombing; one mentioning Gerard Harte as having being detained for questioning after it, another mentioning Brian Mullin. All the papers regarded the shooting as a carefully-planned ambush, the first sign of a tougher policy to deal with the upsurge in the IRA campaign. The *Evening Standard* leader writer set the tone of satisfaction: 'The first reaction of most people to the shooting dead of three IRA terrorists will have nothing to do with politics or the law. It will be a simple satisfaction that the IRA have had to pay.' The Prime Minister Mrs Margaret Thatcher gave an interview to the *Daily Express*, 1 September 1988: 'When you are faced with terrorism you obviously do not let the terrorists know precisely what steps you are taking to counter their terrorism. Nor shall we. But my message to them is this: *Do not doubt our resolve to defeat terrorism.*' Not one of the papers quoted advanced a single piece of evidence that the three men killed had a part in the Ballygawley coach bombing.

On 4 September the Northern Ireland Secretary of State, Mr Tom King, speaking on BBC Radio 4's *The World This Weekend* promised a full investigation into the killing but restated the Army's case that the IRA had fired first. 'There is no question of any change in the rules. This was a particularly nasty murder gang. They were out to kill and it was a courageous act on behalf of the security forces to prevent more killing.' On the same day Labour MP Mr Tam Dalyell wrote to Mr King asking whether the security forces were now acting as *agents provocateurs* in Northern Ireland. He was referring to a report in the *Sunday Telegraph* suggesting that the lorry to be attacked by the IRA was parked as a decoy. He asked, 'If it is true that *agents provocateurs* are being used by the state does this not raise serious issues? Does such a policy, if it exists, have the *imprimatur* of the Cabinet?'

The SAS action was an ambush. The lorry was a decoy. The operation against the Tyrone IRA was planned *before* the Ballygawley coach bombing. That atrocity hastened the massacre at Cloughfin, Drumnakilly. There is no evidence that any of the men killed had anything to do with the coach bombing.

The large white covered lorry, with its distinctive blue streak painted along the side, belonged to the British Army. It was demonstrably driven around Tyrone by a UDR man. It was seen calling at coal depots and bringing cargo to Carrickmore joint Army/RUC Barracks and the UDR Barracks in Omagh. The IRA marked it as a target. Having shown the bait, the British Army then set the trap to beat the IRA at their own game as they would see it.

The lorry was seen as early as 10 am on the morning of Tuesday, 30 August. It was parked on the Omagh-Carrickmore Road (called Drumnakilly Road in the misleading new road designations) in the townland of

Cloughfin. It was parked on the left-hand side of the road facing Carrickmore beside a deserted and boarded-up two storey house, known as 'Sarah's shop', once owned by Sarah Kerr. It was well out on the narrow road causing traffic to slow down to pass it. A man in civilian clothes, really an SAS man and described by a passer-by as 'Army-looking', ostentatiously walked round the lorry, worked with a spare wheel (which was noticed to be inflated) on the road and waved on anybody who stopped to help. On the ditch side of the lorry were two entrances, an open entrance into the street of the house and its long separate row of joined-up out-offices whose low gable faced the road, and another open entrance on the other side of the out-offices' gable which led into a small field. Here the SAS were in ambush. One soldier manned a machine-gun placed in a pillar-box aperture which had been simply made by pushing out a few rows of bricks and raising the edge of the corrugated roof of the shed. Part of the lorry blocked the view of the field entrance but the SAS soldier had a clear vision to shoot in a narrow vision-alley at a vehicle or person who might approach from either direction. Impressions in the grass showed, even weeks after the event, that at least three other soldiers lay in the shallow ditch where openings had been made in the hedge to give vision to the road. There are no indications that soldiers were on the other side of the road; perhaps this was to avoid crossfire. Weeks after the shooting, bags and cardboard cartons of the soldiers' snacks still lay beside the grass impressions. The soldier in the shed conveniently stood on an old car wheel to help fix his position. Another soldier had pulled an old iron bedstead into the drain at the hedge to avoid wetting his feet. There the SAS waited patiently to draw the IRA into a snap-operation. The decoy worked. The lorry and its customary UDR driver were known to IRA intelligence. The man prowling about the lorry was obviously not the 'known' target but the IRA probably assumed he was Army personnel, perhaps an 'intelligence' man. In what looks like a quickly planned operation, the local IRA decided to act. This was rash since the obvious policy of the IRA in Tyrone would have been to lie low after the coach bombing and the subsequent high-level of surveillance.

At 2 pm three IRA men were let off at the house of Justin McBride about half-a-mile from the lorry. They were dressed in blue boiler suits and wore black masks. They were armed with two AK47 Kalashnikov rifles and a Webley .38 revolver. The McBride family was ushered into a back room and told to keep quiet. The curtains were then pulled. One man smashed the phone with his rifle. The IRA then left in McBrides' red Fiat car. It was only some 200 yards from there to the main Omagh-Carrickmore Road. They turned left towards Omagh and almost immediately turned into the yard of McAleers' house, known as the Brick House. The procedure was the same as in McBrides'. Two masked men ran into the kitchen from the backyard and ordered the elderly lady of the house into the sitting-room.

They gathered all in the house into this room and ordered them to pull down the blinds and relax. It was 2.05 pm. They ran upstairs and checked out all the rooms. They pulled out the phone in the sitting-room and entrance hall. Two doors led into the sitting-room from the hall. They kept these pulled tight. From time to time one would peep in to check. One man kept guard in the yard. The intention was obviously to ambush the lorry from the hall of the house. Inevitably, the men thought, the lorry facing in the Carrickmore direction would be repaired and pass by. They would then attack it with automatic rifle fire. At 2.30 pm the milkman drove his milk-bulk tanker into the yard. He was apprehended and taken into the sitting-room. Just before 3 pm Thaddeus McAleer drove into the yard on a digger. He was likewise conducted into the sitting-room. All these people thought at first the men were UDA or UVF and were terribly frightened. The masked men repeatedly told them to relax. At 3.10 pm Eamon McCullough, a salesman, came to see about McAleers' microwave oven. He drove into the yard and was also taken prisoner and like the rest was told not to move or speak. His two children were with him and they were also put into the room. At 3.35 pm the IRA returned the red Fiat to McBrides. The McBrides had stayed in the back room of their house, afraid to move and under the impression that there was a guard in the garage or at the back. One of the IRA men came into the room, threw the keys on the floor and said, 'Your car's OK – its a bit dirty. Sorry for putting you to inconvenience. You can go out in five minutes'. At 3.40 pm one of the IRA men rushed into McAleers' sitting-room and announced, 'We're leaving. Don't report anything to anybody. Stay here about twenty minutes. Sorry for annoying you'. Five minutes later one of them rushed in again and said 'Pull your blinds over again. There is a change of plan'. Those in the room heard the smashing of glass. The conclusion is that the IRA men pushed out the back window of the salesman's white Sierra. The owner recognised its sound starting up. Some of those in the room peeped out and saw the car pass the house in the direction of the lorry and Omagh. One man was driving and two were in the back seat. These two probably intended to fire out the back window. As time dragged on, the IRA men obviously had grown impatient and decided to abandon the idea of an ambush from the house. But did they just in these last five minutes at the house suddenly decide to take the more suitable white car and drive down to the lorry to investigate or possibly launch an attack?

We are dependent on a local farmer for much of the rest of the story. He was in a field about 300 yards from the scene of the shooting. The field was opposite to 'Sarah's shop'. He had been working on his mother's farm. He knew every inch of the ground. He often went out from Omagh to help at home. He and his brother saw the lorry there at 11 am. He passed no remarks; he thought it belonged to a neighbour. He saw no police or army activity. He went to his own home in Omagh for lunch, 1 to 2 pm, and arrived back around 2 pm. He was working on his own at this stage. Then he heard the shots. His description is detailed.

1st Burst. A long burst like a panic burst. Rapid firing. Shooting unusual. Seemed to be a vibration or echo coming off the gun and that seemed to make it louder. Like a diesel tractor inside a tin shed. Puzzled me. In a place with tin. Very strange. Loud burst. I thought, 'Is that not going to stop?'
2nd Burst. More controlled. Not as fast. Then a single shot – pop, like a squib going off.
3rd Burst. Controlled. Think you could count the shots. Then pop.
4th controlled burst. This was the last burst – slower rapid fire. Again think you could count the shots.
Silence.
Then final single shot, same pop sound. The delay meant that it sounded out of place – it could have been ten to twenty seconds after the last burst.

The witness continues:
'I was stunned and shocked. I headed towards the shooting as I knew about First Aid. I thought, "There is somebody lying there. Maybe I could do something". I got 100 yards across the field. Then I heard a helicopter. There had been a brightness before the shooting. Now a good heavy shower was coming on. The helicopter dipped off a bit from view due to the bank in the bog nearby. The helicopter was about 200 yards from me. It was flying very low, about 40 yards in the air. It seemed to swerve round. Then it popped down, touched lightly on the ground. I could see the rotators. This was in the boggy field on the Omagh side of the white car on the road. It only touched down for seconds. I got the impression it may have left people off but I did not see anybody from where I was. There was time, one could say, to let somebody off but not to pick anybody up. Then it was off within seconds heading towards Omagh.

'The first helicopter was no sooner gone than I saw another one heading up, same type, same procedure. It came down the same way, then off again but came round once more and landed again. At this stage I was about 100 yards from the helicopter. When it came down the second time it stayed down and stayed open. I saw a machine-gunner sitting in the helicopter. I had the feeling he was watching me but now on hindsight I think he mustn't have seen me. The machine-gun was pointing at me. I didn't move. I was on my hunkers. Then down the road came a group of men from the front of the lorry. I thought they had taken prisoners the way they were crouched as they came from the gate but it must have been because of running low to go under the rotators. I thought three of them were police; they had black uniforms and police hats. Others, maybe four, were in jeans and boiler-suits-type clothes, blue-coloured clothes. They came through the gate, an open gap, and boarded the helicopter from the other side from where the machine-gun was pointing at me. As they ran the helicopter was revving up. When the helicopter took off I expected it would do a U-turn and come across over the top of me but it did not come back in the Omagh direction. Maybe it went the Carrickmore direction but I was hiding at this stage and the bank hid my view in that direction.

'I came out of hiding into the open, taking my time. I was startled by two young lads who came up behind me from another farm-house. For a split second I thought they were soldiers. They were young Protestant lads about fifteen-years-old wearing white shirts. I was wearing a long purplish pullover and probably it was difficult to see me in the heather. Two groups of police were running towards us. The two lads took off and ran a few yards, then stopped. I ran on. One group of police, the one furtherest away, stopped. I was running towards the second group which was still coming on but I was heading at an angle and had the cover of the bog bank for 100 yards. I knew that as they got to one bank I would be at the second bank and then I would only be some yards from my mother's house. I didn't stop at the house. I jumped into the car and went to the scene of the shooting by road. I wanted to find out who was shot, to see what had happened. When I arrived at the checkpoint with the man whose car had been taken, whom I had lifted on the way, the uniformed police there took his name and address but they never asked who I was. I asked, "What's going on here?". A policeman said, "Don't you worry. They are dead anyway". I drove home to Omagh and phoned the parish priest Fr Murray and told him three men were dead. Then I phoned the media.'

First media reports said that a lorry driven by a UDR man had broken down on the road and had been ambushed. The news items then departed from this story and ceased to mention the UDR man. The witness had also phoned Fr Denis Faul and he also had contacted the media. Next day the newspapers printed a short statement issued by the RUC the previous day, 'Shortly before 4 pm a shooting occurred on the Omagh to Carrickmore Road. Three people died. There are no security force casualties'. When a Catholic is shot dead, whether an IRA or civilian victim of sectarian killers, the death is invariably announced by the RUC in indirect fashion: 'The victim had no connection with the security forces.'

Fr John Cargan and another priest went to the scene to administer the last rites. Fr Cargan was visibly shocked when he spoke briefly on television. He said there were two weapons to be seen, one on the road and one in the ditch on the other side of the road, 'but I couldn't say who was carrying these arms'. 'It is quite horrific. It is just a tragic situation in which people seem to die in this part of the world. Irrespective of who they are, it is not a way that people should die.' He was asked whether the men could be identified; he said two could but the third man was fairly badly dismembered. He had limited access to the bodies.

Two bodies were seen by witnesses in the back seat of the car, one partly out of the opened back door. Six feet from the car-front two pools of chalk marks were visible, made by security investigators in recording the position of spent bullet cases. These would indicate that the SAS came from behind the ditch after the machine-gun had brought the car to a halt with probable casualties. These SAS soldiers then pumped more bullets into an already riddled car. No doubt the short-range firing accounts for the horrific mutilation of Gerard Harte, the driver of the vehicle.

Mr Tom King, Secretary of State, prejudged the issue by saying that the IRA fired first. The RUC in a subtle, reserved statement released 25 hours after the shooting gave the impression that the IRA had fired. It said, 'A number of spent rounds at the scene appear to be consistent with the recovered terrorist weapons. Tests are being carried out'.

Fr Denis Faul took Mr King to task on the statement he made, a statement based on the RUC allegations that the IRA had opened fire and spent cartridges found were from one of the Kalashnikov rifles. Fr Faul doubted this. All the evidence so far available, he said, indicated that the intention of the government forces was to carry out an assassination ambush and a revenge killing.

The description of the independent witness to the shooting makes it clear that the SAS machine-gun was the first weapon fired. It was a prolonged burst from short range. The IRA men could not have fired after that. No description of the sound of firing indicates that they fired.

The *Sunday Times* 'Insight' report gave a version of the shooting 'from sources in the security forces'. Considering the *Sunday Times* right-wing stance, its pro-Government prejudice in recent years in reporting the Northern Ireland conflict and its source, the report must be treated with great caution. The theme is that the IRA fired first: the man in the boiler suit working at the spare wheel was not warned about the white Ford Sierra; he jumped from the spare wheel when he saw the car coming and ran for the gates of the house, bullets spraying around him from the IRA in the car; the car drove past the lorry and was then raked by gunfire from the SAS lying in wait on both sides of the road.

The two Harte brothers were married with one child each. They were natives of Loughmacrory, County Tyrone. Gerard Harte (29) was survived by his wife Róisín and his infant son Colm. He was not, as alleged by the RUC, IRA OC in Mid-Tyrone. Martin Harte (21) was married to Briege, a sister of Brian Mullin, who also died in the shooting. Martin also had an infant son Declan. Brian Mullin (26) came from Foremass, Sixmilecross, County Tyrone, sixth youngest in a family of seven brothers and three sisters. His eldest brother Pat is serving a life sentence in Long Kesh (Maze) Prison. He was granted parole for his brother's funeral. The IRA in Mid-Ulster issued a short statement on the deaths: 'Brian Mullin, Gerard Harte and Martin Harte were Volunteers of the Irish Republican Army. They were killed on active service. We salute their courage and extend deepest condolences to their families.'

The Harte brothers were buried after Requiem Mass in Loughmacrory Church on 2 September. The previous evening the IRA fired a salute. The RUC with plastic-bullet guns lined the lanes and road. Mourners complained that they and British Army personnel damaged scores of cars with their weapons. At the Mass Fr Peter Taggart said, 'One of the prime teachings of the Catholic Church is that human life is sacred from conception until the moment of death. This principle is binding on everyone, not just on ordinary citizens, but also on the Government and those charged with the administration of the law... There are many young people here. Let us pray that they may love life and respect life and that they do not listen to the voices which speak of hatred, revenge and retaliation...Since disturbing questions have been raised about the circumstances in which these young men died, it's necessary to point out that the law of the land must obey the moral law'. In the funeral oration at the graveside Sinn Féin president Gerry Adams spoke of the 'criminal conspiracy which passes for British Law in Ireland. Thatcher and King claim that these young men were killed within the law. What law? No one in Ireland has given them the right to enact legislation or to pass repressive laws aimed at subverting the national rights of the people of this island'.

Brian Mullin was buried on Saturday, 3 September after Requiem Mass celebrated by Fr Anthony Lambe in Dunmoyle church, Altamuskin. Fr Lambe said that his life had been tragically cut short in his prime. An RUC officer video-taped the mourners from the top of a land-rover beside the church wall. Phil Reeves of *The Independent* graphically described the disgraceful conduct of the RUC at Brian Mullin's funeral. His article was headed in deep black letters, 'Police laugh and joke as IRA man is buried'. He wrote: 'As the funeral Mass was performed for the IRA terrorist Brian Mullin, two policemen stood among mourners outside the tiny country church whistling and humming. Raucous laughter intermittently arose from behind a clump of bushes six yards away, where members of the Royal Ulster Constabulary were sitting on the grass having lunch. The smell of chicken curry was detectable. Dozens of police officers, wearing visored helmets and carrying shields and batons, sat along one wall of the churchyard dangling their legs inside as they watched mourners. When Mullin's coffin emerged and the service moved to the graveside, a piper played a final lament. "Still taking lessons", one RUC man commented loudly. Several officers tapped the churchyard wall with their truncheons. Plastic-

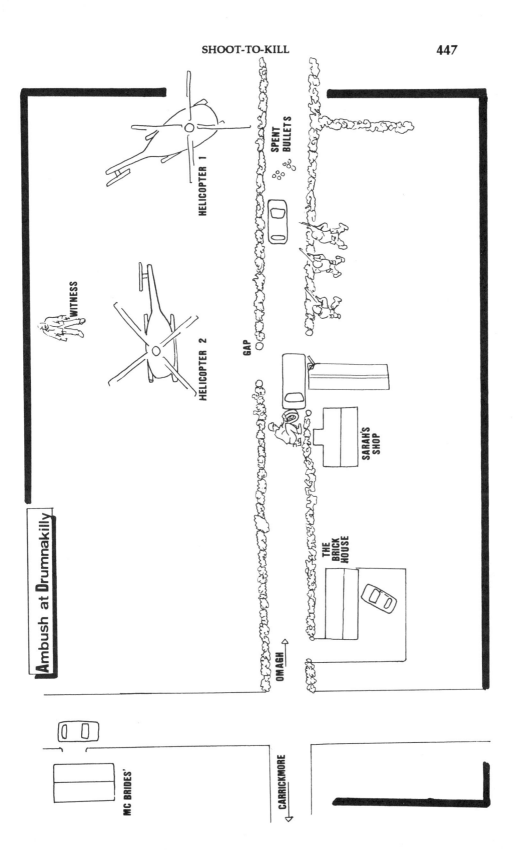

Ambush at Drumnakilly

bullet guns were ready to fire if necessary. A message from the IRA was read out at the graveside: "The Mullins' door was always open, the house always known for its hospitality, each of the children growing up with a sense of justice and each has suffered dearly as a result in terms of raids, arrests and harassment...This has to be the last war of Irish independence. We have suffered enormous tragedies and it is our task to drive Britain to the brink of despair".'

The Government in the Republic of Ireland called for an urgent and full report on all circumstances surrounding the shooting. The request was made through the Anglo-Irish Secretariat in Belfast. Mr Ken Maginnis, Unionist MP who had once described the shooting by the SAS of Tyrone IRA members Brian Campbell and Colm McGirr in the words 'two swallows do not make a summer', said of the killings of the three men: 'One would be foolish to gloat on this particularly successful operation because, in the very nature of things, there are many more godfathers and leaders within the IRA organisation. Nonetheless, one is grateful to the security forces for pre-emptive action which has obviously saved the lives of innocent people.'

The *Daily Express,* 1 September, in a profile on Mr Maginnis said: 'In the wake of the Ballygawley coach carnage, where eight soldiers were slaughtered, he told Mrs Thatcher the IRA's top assassins must be caged. And he named names.' Later on radio Mr Maginnis said that one of the names was that of one of the men shot by the SAS.

In a propaganda statement to emphasise that the men deserved to die the RUC issued new profiles of the three men describing them as ruthless dedicated terrorists. This was a variant on issuing a statement on the criminal history of weapons found.

The shooting of the three IRA men was followed in subsequent months by intense harassment of the Catholic people in Tyrone. Numerous complaints followed of assaults, harassment and house-wrecking by the RUC, British Army and UDR.

Surveillance and Collusion

In the 1980s the British Army and RUC designated four military zones in the North – West Belfast, Derry City west of the Foyle, East Tyrone and South Armagh. A low profile is kept by the Army and RUC outside these areas and people there, since they enjoy a welcome normality, are inclined to ignore the severe problems of victims of harassment and house searching in the military zones. In the zones there is a demonstrative British Army and RUC presence on the streets; republican families are continually harassed. In South Armagh permanent checkpoints and look-out posts have been erected on the summits of hills and mountains. Special plain clothes surveillance units are deployed by the Army and RUC. The RUC uses the Special Branch E4A unit and draws also on the three HMSU (Headquarters Mobile Support Unit) groups based in Belfast, Derry and Armagh. The HMSU is trained by the SAS. The RUC also relies on units of MI5 and MI6 for special assistance. The 12th Intelligence Company provides the Army with information. Separate from the SAS, the Army has 300 men in a special unit under the covert name 14th Intelligence Company. Together with the SAS they form the Intelligence and Security Group or 'Int and Sy Group'. 14th Intelligence Company was formed in the 1970s and is trained in a philosophy of speed and aggression by the SAS at Hereford.

Within the military zones, senior members of the IRA are sometimes directly assassinated by security forces or killed through collusion with loyalist paramilitaries; some are arrested and have forensic evidence placed on them. A number of murders in 1989 have aroused the public's suspicion of British intelligence complicity. At midnight 3-4 April two men dressed in black balaclavas and plain green army-type jackets burst into the home of Gerard Casey (29), an IRA leader, and shot him at point-blank range with a shotgun and pistol where he lay beside his wife in bed. Gerard Casey had been arrested and brought to Castlereagh Interrogation Centre in October 1988. At the time of his arrest his legally-held shotgun was removed and a sketch map of the interior of his house was drawn by the RUC. This parallels the case of Loughlin Maginn (28) shot dead on 26 August 1989. While accepting that there was no official collusion behind the killing, his solicitor said he had completed a dossier of harasssment suffered by his client. Detailed in the dossier was the regular photographing of his house by the RUC and a plan of the house drawn by RUC men on the morning he was arrested and taken to Gough Interrogation Centre in October 1988. Following his death, two full-time private soldiers in the UDR (one of them formerly a regular soldier from Scotland) and another man have been charged with Maginn's murder. One of the soldiers was also accused of the murder of Liam McKee in Lisburn on 24 June; the attack followed a familiar pattern – his front door was smashed down and he was shot dead in his bedroom; the murder was claimed by the UFF. Following the disappearance of security files on the IRA and the disclosure that the UDA had used such files to target Loughlin Maginn, Cambridge deputy Chief Constable John Stevens was requested by the RUC Chief Constable Hugh Annesley to conduct an inquiry into collusion of the security forces with loyalist paramilitaries. On the night of 29 November, two Catholics, Liam Ryan (39), a republican, and Michael Devlin (33), were shot dead at Ryan's public house on the shores of Lough Neagh at Ardboe, County Tyrone. Local people allege that the area was scouted by two UDR men for two days before the murder; a decoy getaway car was seen and heard departing before the murders; the suspicion is that the murderers came in and departed by boat;

local people point out that the British Army has three patrol boats on the lough and that these may have been used by the killers. Francis McNally, a Sinn Féin councillor, whose brother Phelim had been shot dead on 24 November 1988 at his house at Coagh, alleged after the murders that the RUC had informed Ryan that his name appeared on two missing security files and had told him that he would be shot dead by Christmas. A Detective Inspector revealed at the inquest on Phelim McNally, 19 April 1990, that the rifle and revolver used to shoot McNally were also used in the murders of Ryan and Devlin. Pat Finucane, solicitor, Belfast, was shot dead on 12 February 1989. He had been prominent in the legal battle to compel the three RUC officers who shot dead three unarmed men in Co. Armagh in 1982 to give evidence at their inquest.

As a result of John Stevens' inquiry a number of UDR and UDA men have been arrested and some have been charged with possession of sensitive intelligence documents and illegal possession of arms. Some UDR members have been charged with murder. Collusion of security forces with loyalist paramilitaries in the late1980s reflects the picture of similar collusion in the early 1970s.

The Shooting of Desmond Grew (37) and Martin McCaughey (23) at Lislasley, on 9 October 1990

Desmond Grew, Charlemont, Co. Armagh, and Martin McCaughey from Galbally, Co. Tyrone, both members of the IRA, were shot dead by undercover British soldiers, presumed to be the SAS, on 9 October 1990, at Lislasley, about two miles from Loughgall and about seven miles from Armagh City. Their families claim that up to 200 rounds were fired as they were unarmed near a disused mushroom shed. Autopsy reports revealed at least 48 gunshot wounds on Desmond Grew and at least 12 gunshot wounds on Martin McCaughey. The soldiers claimed that both men were shot as they emerged with rifles from the shed. Relatives claimed that soldiers planted the rifles beside the bodies after they had shot them.

At a quarter to three in the morning, three hours after the shooting, I received a telephone call while on pastoral duty in my parish of Armagh informing me that there had been a shooting and a priest was needed. The policeman who phoned gave me directions to the scene. I published an account in my book *State Violence: Northern Ireland 1969–1997* and I include an extract here:

> I followed the directions. I met no car or person. Then as I turned right at the school, a red car halted at the junction coming from the other direction. A man in civilian clothes, but obviously a policeman, called out to me that I was on the right road. The white house soon showed up in the dark and then the waving blood-red light. I was directed by gestures to park my car. A group of uniformed

police stood in the shadows. Nobody spoke. There was white tape, familiar sign of an incident, across a lane leading down by another house. A policeman came forward from the other side of the tape and introduced himself to me as an inspector. He was polite and friendly, so different from the sullen phalanx of uniforms I had just passed through. He guided me to the scene, past a farmhouse to an open yard. He told me that two men were dead and that one of them was Desmond Grew. There was an open empty mushroom shed, of the old arc-shaped type. It had no frontage. A light was shining inside and there was a white car in it. In front of the shed was an apron yard of concrete. In the half-light, I looked down on the black forms of two bodies lying within a few yards of one another, sprawled out. Beyond their heads, lying on the ground, were two Kalashnikov rifles. I said the Act of Contrition, gave them conditional absolution and anointed them. I recognised Dessie Grew. He was very badly shot in the head. The blood from the heads of the two men was thick and clotted and the dark intestinal-looking brain matter shone slightly red in the poor light. They were dressed in casual denim-like clothes, unmasked. The butt of a pistol protruded from a trouser pocket of Martin McCaughey. All was silence. I prayed at length. The bodies looked so small and thin and even vulnerable in death. We seemed to stand towering over them like giants. Such an impression I have experienced before at scenes of fatal accidents. Perhaps it is psychological, the power of life lording it over death.

I never asked any questions while I was there. I was on a spiritual mission. Anyhow, I knew I would not get answers. I learned, however, that they had been shot at midnight. What happened? From my experience of writing a book on the SAS, I would ask: Were the weapons discovered and were they staked out? Did the two men come to move the weapons only or to pick them up for an IRA action? Could they have been taken prisoner, considering the soldiers were in a strong superior position? Were they shot in cold blood and were the guns then planted beside them? To date, 1997, there has been no inquest and no explanation given. Only the police and soldiers who were present at the shooting know the full truth. Will they tell it?

At the High Court in Belfast on 19 December 2003 the fathers of the two men successfully judicially reviewed the chief constable for failure to provide the coroner conducting the inquest with a copy of the RUC investigating officer's report and unredacted intelligence reports in connection with the shooting.

No inquest has as yet been held into the deaths of Desmond Grew and Martin McCaughey. Papers were forwarded by the police to the office of the DPP and in April 1993 the DPP directed that no soldier should face criminal charges as a result of their actions. Despite retaining papers since October 1994, the coroner has yet to hold the inquest into the two men's deaths.

A lawyer representing the families of both deceased had argued that the chief constable was under a duty to provide the coroner with the investigating officer's report to the DPP. Séamus Treacy QC argued that the chief constable was obliged by domestic, European and common law, and Justice Weatherup rejected arguments on behalf of the chief constable that the reports were confidential, irrelevant, and likely to influence the candour with which police officers might conduct their investigations. He also rejected suggestions that to disclose the investigating officer's report would create a 'chilling effect' on the public co-operating with police inquiries.

Justice Weatherup also ordered that the chief constable provide the coroner with unredacted intelligence reports leading to the shooting of both men. It would then be for the coroner to decide on their relevance and whether they should then be provided to the lawyers for the next of kin.

Fearghál Shiels of Madden & Finucane Solicitors, who represent both the Grew and McCaughey families, said at court: 'There is no evidence that the RUC/PSNI at any stage took the initiative in progressing the inquest, a process in which they are intimately involved, given their statutory obligation to provide documentation relating to their investigations to the coroner. We welcome the decision of the High Court and this will have profound implications for the way in which this and other inquests involving lethal force by the State will proceed in future, and with regard to how inquests have been conducted in the past'. This inquest and others related to SAS and RUC killings are still held up because of the failure of the state to provide proper disclosures. Coroners are not satisfied with the material supplied so far, large parts of which have to date been blocked out. Procedures to obtain full disclosure are still going through the courts.

Desmond Grew was a brother of Séamus Grew who with Roddy Carroll was shot dead by the RUC, 12 December 1986, in one of the Co. Armagh shoot-to-kill incidents. Martin McCaughey had already been shot and wounded by undercover soldiers in Cappagh, Co. Tyrone, on 24 March 1990, after which he went 'on the run'.

The Shooting of Tony Doris (21), Lawrence McNally (38), and Pete Ryan (35) at Coagh, Co. Tyrone, 3 June 1991

Tony Doris left his home in Meenagh Park, Coalisland, Co. Tyrone about 3 pm on Sunday 2 June 1991. He was allegedly called in at a late stage to take part in an IRA operation which, it appears, was to be the shooting of a UDR member in Coagh whose movements had been observed there over a few weeks. This man in documents is variously described as a 'member' and an 'ex-member'. The assigned driver apparently did not know the roads and pulled out and, it is claimed, Doris being the OC (officer in command) stepped in. Having left home he went to Moortown, Ardboe. That night accompanied by three other men he allegedly went to the Loop, Moneymore, to take a car, gaining entry to the home at ten minutes to midnight with the excuse of looking for a can of petrol. Three of the men went into the house. One other left. They were masked in black balaclavas and wore blue boiler suits. Two of them were described as having 'long guns'. Next morning, 3 June, just before 7.30 am the three, Tony Doris, Lawrence McNally and Pete Ryan, the claimed IRA men involved, took the family car, a red Vauxhall Cavalier, from the house they had taken over and headed for Coagh. Before they left they disconnected the phone and took it with them. They told the family not to report their car missing until 8.30 am. Tony Doris, it was said, was driving. Lawrence Mc-Nally, native of Ballinderry, Co. Derry, and Pete Ryan from Ardboe, Co. Tyrone, were 'on the run' and were living in Monaghan. It is believed they had crossed the 'border' on the previous Thursday 30 May and had billeted in the Ardboe area.

The SAS were waiting for them. Information of the IRA operation apparently had reached the RUC on 30 May 1991, as recorded in their reports: 'East Tyrone PIRA in the Ardboe area intend to carry out an attack against an ex-member of the UDR in the Coagh area during the weekend 31.5.91 to 3.6.91'. A further report on Sunday 2 June read, ' … the attack on the ex-member of the UDR planned for the weekend by East Tyrone PIRA will take place on Monday, 3.6.91, in Coagh village'. The intended 'target' apparently was in the habit of waiting for a lift at a particular place, perhaps joining up with some one else. Information as far back as 15.5.91 had read, 'Source states that Pete Ryan OTR (on the run) from Ardboe still has an active interest in PIRA activities in East Tyrone'. Tony Doris' home had also been under observation and the family and neighbours had more than once seen black-clothed figures hiding near the house. A well-known feature of Coagh is the Hanover House Restaurant. Shortly after 7 am the SAS had parked a red flat-backed Bedford lorry beside the restaurant. They had so arranged the body of the lorry that they could lie concealed, observe and mount an ambush. The lorry faced the bridge. Four SAS soldiers designated 'A', 'B', 'C' and 'D' were concealed in the lorry. According to one of these, Soldier 'A', a gold coloured Maestro car arrived in the car park on the opposite side of the street, reversed into a parking spot near the public toilets and the driver got out and began to read the newspaper beside the car. This man apparently was 'the target'. The SAS were now using him as a decoy, probably unknown to him. Although soldier 'H' would not state where he was positioned, it appears he was in the vicinity of the car park. Six other SAS men were positioned towards the rear of the restaurant. The IRA car came over Coagh Bridge at the entrance to the village at 7.35 am and approached the lorry to its right. Soldier 'A' said in a statement that when the red Cavalier appeared he received the 'Standby. Standby' radio signal and then almost immediately the 'Go. Go. Go' transmission. Soldiers 'B' and 'D' dropped the sides of the lorry. When the IRA car appeared 'A' says he saw one man in the back right passenger seat holding an AK assault rifle. 'He was holding the rifle in the alert position and it was pointing towards the car park. I knew there was a man in the car park who I believed whose life was in immediate danger. I started firing at the person in the back seat who was holding the rifle. At this stage I was aware that other shots were being fired'. There was sustained firing. A witness who lived nearby said that it sounded like at least one machine-gun was being used. It was soldier 'H' who radioed the 'Standby. Standby' and the 'Go. Go. Go' alert that initiated all the firing. He did not fire any shots. In his statement he said that the IRA car had at first attempted to turn immediately left into the car park but then swung right and halted. 'The left door swung open, a man started to get out of the vehicle and he was armed with a rifle. The butt was in his shoulder and the weapon was pointed in the direction he was looking which was [at] the man reading the newspaper. I then gave the "Go. Go" on the radio. The Cavalier started to accelerate and the man fell back into the car and at the same time I heard shots'. By this time the six soldiers, 'E' (patrol commander), 'F', 'G', 'I', 'J', 'K' positioned behind the restaurant ran to the street and engaged also in the firing. The car burst into flames having been hit by many shots, travelled 20 to 30 metres out of control and crashed a short distance away into a stationary car and a garden wall on the right of Hanover Square. Tony Doris, the driver, was burned in the car. According to the SAS the doors of the crashed car were open and two bodies lay burning beside the burning car. The two rifles beside them were burning. Bodies and rifles were badly burnt when the RUC later examined the scene.

The autopsy reports carried out in Craigavon hospital describe the bullet wounds and burns. Tony Doris' body was received inside several body bags. His body was grossly charred, only the lower part of the facial skeleton of his head and part of the base of the skull remaining. He was identified by dental examinations and comparisons carried out by an expert. 'When the charred debris was brushed and washed from the back there were two wounds which were possibly gunshot wounds. One was an elongated, lacerated wound, 4cm x 1cm, over the right side of the lower chest, its long axis vertical and centred 5.5 cm to the right of the spine. The other was a roughly circular wound, 7 mm diameter, on the lower part of the right loin, centred 2 cm to the right of the spine and 8 cm above the upper limit of the natal cleft. A little blood was seen at its margins ... Spine: Intact above the sacrum, where there was a ragged hole, 3.5 cm x 2 cm, where a bullet had come through from behind. There was also a ragged hole through the right pubic ramus near the symphysis, measuring approximately 2 cm diameter ... There could have been bullet wounds in other situations, the evidence now lost through the destruction caused by burning. For example the head could have been so damaged although it was now impossible to say. No other bullet tracks could be located within the trunk, but the limbs could also have been involved for all one could say'.

Lawrence McNally's body was also badly burned and he was identified again by dental work. There was evidence that he had been struck by at least several high velocity bullets. 'There was a small circular hole, consistent with the entry wound of a bullet, on the back of the head ... Another ragged hole, probably made by a bullet, was noted on the inner end of the left eyebrow. Thus it seemed probably that at least two high velocity bullets had struck the head. The tissues of the trunk were also quite badly burned but one hole could be identified in the vicinity of the left loin and internal examination revealed several ragged holes in the rib cage ... There were also lacerations of the right half of the diaphragm, the heart, lungs, stomach, liver and right kidney indicating damage due to several high velocity bullets ...'

Pete Ryan's death was due to a bullet wound of the chest ... 'A bullet or bullet fragment had also lacerated the liver whilst a bullet had also struck the right thigh. The body was severely burnt and as a result it was impossible to say whether or not he had been struck by any other bullets or bullet fragments. The bullet which had struck the chest had come from in front and slightly to the left but the direction of the others was uncertain'. Pete Ryan's baptismal name was 'Michael' but his father had given him the pet name 'Pete' when he was a child and it was by this name that he was familiarly known.

In a RUC report it was recorded that 2 AKM rifles and 4 magazines were found outside the IRA car, with spent cases. Some questions: why could arrests not have been made? Did not an ambush endanger the life of the targeted man? Why wasn't he simply warned of an intended attempt on his life? Why is there not a statement from the intended victim who obviously witnessed the scene? Perhaps the mystery is deeper – did soldier 'H' act as a decoy himself and take the place of the intended target and so was in a position to alert the rest of the patrol to shoot immediately without warning? If so it would explain why he did not fire any shots and, standing outside the car shielded with a newspaper, he could easily use his radio to sound the alert.

On-going research and inquiry is still going on in the case of these three men. On Tuesday 20 May 2003 at a preliminary hearing at Dungannon court to determine the relevance of material being requested by legal representatives of those killed at Coagh a PSNI spokesman told the coroner that the handwritten interview notes of questions and answers sessions with soldiers involved in the Coagh killings could not be found and might have been destroyed. Coroner Roger McLernon told the court that the documents were 'central to the court' and that this was clearly unsatisfactory. The PSNI spokesman said the evidence might have been destroyed in 1996 while in Gough barracks. It was claimed that the documents had been stored in an area that had been contaminated by asbestos dust and therefore in the interest of health and safety had to be destroyed. Following a High Court ruling East Tyrone coroner Roger McLernon on 7 January 2004 told a preliminary inquest into 10 killings (which included the killings by the SAS in Coagh and Clonoe, and the killings by loyalists of pensioner Roseanne Mallon at her sister-in-law's home in Dungannon and of Jack and Kevin McKearney at their family shop in Moy) that the British Ministry of Defence had agreed to hand over documents and video footage to him. The coroner said he would decide what material was relevant to the cases and should be made public to the families and their legal representatives. However he added that any decision he made could be open to challenge by the PSNI or the Ministry of Defence 'if they decide that security grounds override public interest issues'.

The full inquest is still pending.

The Shooting of Kevin Barry O'Donnell (21), Seán O'Farrell (23), Peter Clancy (19) and Daniel Patrick Vincent (20) at Clonoe, Co. Tyrone, 16 February 1992

At 7.30 pm on Sunday, 16 February 1992, twelve members of the SAS took up observation positions at the rear of a low-lying hedge on the southern edge of the car park of St Patrick's church, Clonoe, Co. Tyrone. The church is near a busy staggered crossroads, with lines to Coalisland, Stewartstown, Ardboe, and the M1 motorway. With the church, a garage, a few shops and a sprinkling of houses it is a centre point of a heavily populated rural parish. Soldier 'A' the leader of the patrol had already been briefed by Captain 'A' at British Army Headquarters, Lisburn. Information had been received that the IRA were to carry out an attack on Coalisland RUC station and they would form up at Clonoe church car park prior to the attack. It had been further learned that they would use a heavy machine-gun, possibly a 12.7 MM and Russian assault rifles. It is an indication that remote preparations were being made at Coalisland and Clonoe as in a statement made on 16 June 1992 a British Army sergeant who was to deploy troops on a regular patrol in the Washingbay and south Coalisland area received a radio message at 1600 hrs detailing it as an 'out of bounds area' for them on that day. The SAS claimed they were dressed in full British Army uniform and armed with Heckler and Koch G 3 rifles and 9mm pistols but the pistols were not used.

Shortly after they had concealed themselves a dark blue Cavalier car entered the car park, made a sweep of the grounds and departed. It was followed a short time later by a red Cavalier which repeated the performance. These scout cars came back and forward regularly to check that the car park was clear, and were later joined by a third car, a dark blue Vauxhall Astra. Sometimes the occupants engaged in snatches of conversation with one another. The SAS were content to watch their movements and wait for the attackers.

About 8.30 pm four masked men called at a house near Coalisland and demanded the owner's 'pick-up' vehicle. When they found out that it was not there they took his lorry and three of them left shortly after 9 pm. They gave a warning not to report it missing for two hours. One remained until 9.45pm and then left. This Ford Cargo Tipper lorry was used by the IRA to mount the attack on Coalisland police station. The machine gun they erected on the lorry was referred to subsequently by the RUC as a 12.7 MM Dagtyarev heavy machine-gun.

At 10.45–10.50 pm the attack took place, a few bursts of machine-gun fire and some automatic rifle fire. Different witnesses saw the tracer bullets lighting up the sky. There was no return fire. The police station was empty since the attack was expected. The assault was brief. People heard the men cheering and saw them waving their rifles as they sped off.

The SAS heard the shooting and saw the red tracer in the sky. The Astra car hurriedly left the car park. Very shortly a car was seen approaching at speed from Coalisland and was followed almost immediately by the lorry with a great roar as if it was being driven in a lower gear. The car turned into the car park. At this stage there were three cars nose to tail in the car park facing the rear exit. The SAS watched the lorry enter the car park, one man holding on to the handles of the machine-gun mounted on the tailgate, some others bearing rifles. It was a clear moonlit night and there was some light in the car park thrown in from the street lighting on the main road and the house and garage at the crossroads. Some of the SAS reported seeing three or four in the lorry, some thought there were five or six. No warning was given by the SAS and there was no attempt to arrest those now trapped within the car park. The SAS statements contain the usual phraseology of fearing for their lives and seeing and hearing 'movement'. Detailed examples are given here from Soldiers 'A', 'B', 'D' and 'F' and they are illustrative of all the SAS statements.

Soldier 'A': 'I then stood up and started to move through the gap in the hedge towards the car park. I was satisfied that the gunmen in the back of the lorry presented a very serious threat to my life and that of the rest of my patrol. Bearing in mind the weapon I saw and the lack of any hard cover and hearing gunfire I engaged the man on the back of the lorry who was holding the machine-gun. The lorry continued to move from left to right along the back of the church and the gunman at the machine-gun went out of view. I then engaged the other gunman on the back of the lorry. Whilst engaging this gunman I saw movement from the red Cavalier and I believed that the occupant of the red Cavalier was a threat as I considered that he and the occupants of these vehicles were part of this group of gunmen. I believed that the occupant of the red Cavalier was about to exit the car and I engaged the occupant of the car with short bursts. At this stage the blue Cavalier, the first one in the line, began to move off towards the rear exit. I believed the occupants of this car to be armed and to have just come from the attack from Coalisland. I opened fire on the driver. The blue car exited the car park and headed towards Stewartstown. The red Cavalier then started to move forwards towards the exit. I fired a number of shots at this vehicle but the vehicle exited the car park and went off in the direction of Stewartstown. I fired at both vehicles on the Cloghog Road whilst they escaped from the car park as I was still satisfied that these persons were armed terrorists. During the time that I engaged the blue Cavalier and the red Cavalier I was aware of movement of the occupant of the dark blue Cavalier and of the fact that he could still kill me. I saw this person get out of the car and taking up a position behind the front of the vehicle which to me looked to be a firing position and that he was about to fire at me. I then fired at him and he disappeared from my view behind the car. My attention was then drawn to two persons running down the left side of the church towards the road. It appeared to me that they had come from behind the dark blue Cavalier. As they ran into the light I could see that both were wearing dark tops and what appeared to be balaclavas. I believed that they were part of this group of terrorists and that they had come off the back of the truck. I fired at them until they went out of my view. I then moved forwards towards the dark blue Cavalier and became aware of other soldiers to my left and to my right. As we were advancing towards the dark blue Cavalier I heard shouting from behind the Cavalier, "Don't shoot! Don't shoot!" We then moved around to the driver's side of this car where I saw a man lying on the ground. I told him to stand up and put his hands in the air. He was lying in the prone position and I couldn't see his hands. He refused to get up and I warned him if he didn't stand up I would shoot him as he was part of this armed terrorist gang and could shoot. He again shouted "Don't shoot! Don't shoot!" and he got up and put his hands into the air. I then searched him for weapons. He was unarmed. I saw that he was wounded and told him to lie down. I then checked the inside and rear of the car and found nothing. I then saw that the church roof was on fire. The shooting had stopped and my patrol regrouped in the car park near the exit and arranged for the ambulance to deal with the injured man and a member of my patrol who had been shot. I left the scene a short time later and afterwards handed my gun to a scenes of crime officer at Gough barracks (Armagh)'. On being questioned during his police interview 'A' admitted that shots fired before he fired himself came from his patrol and could not say that the IRA fired shots. He was between the hedge and the fence of the car park when he fired his shots.

Soldier 'B': I stood up and saw the lorry slow down. The car that was fronting the lorry turned in my direction and I was illuminated in its headlights. The men in the back of the lorry brought their weapons from being raised and I believed I had been seen. I engaged the terrorists on the back of the lorry along with the other members of the patrol as I had seen flashes from the lorry and I believed the armed terrorists were firing at us from the lorry. I fired short bursts of automatic fire at the lorry until my magazine was empty. I then done a magazine change down on one knee and moved through the gap in the hedge. I climbed over a fence and moved into the car park. I then had a clear view of the front of the lorry. There were soldiers to my right and left and I then dropped down on one knee and fired 3 to 4 single shots at a terrorist in the driver's side of the cab of the lorry. I then moved forward towards the lorry and was still observing the cab of the lorry. I was aware that soldiers on my left had gone to the rear of the truck. I could hear gunfire from the other side of the lorry and I knew that two soldiers at the rear of the lorry had not gone around to the other side of the lorry. I shouted at the soldiers to my right to stop. I then fired a short burst through the gap between the cab and the back of the lorry because I believed that the armed terrorists who had been in the back of the lorry had got out and were firing at the other soldiers. I could still hear someone moving about in the cab of the lorry. I was concentrating on the cab of the lorry and as I hadn't seen anyone leave it I still believed there were armed terrorists in the cab. I then fired a short burst into the cab through the door of the driver's side. I didn't hear any more movement. I then went around the front of the lorry with Soldier 'F' to my left. As I came through the headlights I saw two terrorists on the ground. The one furtherest away from me was sitting up. The top half of his body was up and alert. There was still firing going on and believing him to be a threat both to me and Soldier 'F' I fired a short burst at him. I then moved towards the main road with Soldier 'F' to my left. On reaching the main road I assisted other soldiers in carrying out a search of the fields off the main road opposite the church. When I was scanning the field with my nite sight I heard shots to my left. I looked to my left and saw other soldiers in that area. Along with Soldier 'E' I diverted cars away from the scene until the arrival of the RUC. I then went back to my original position in the hedgerow and collected a number of magazines. On my way back to collect the magazines I saw a dark coloured Cavalier in the car park. Later I handed my rifle and magazines to a police officer at Gough barracks, Armagh'.

Soldier 'D': 'As I approached the rear of the lorry I saw a terrorist dressed in dark coloured clothing on the ground and I was satisfied that he was one of the occupants of the lorry. I saw him lurch forward and I believed that he was armed and taking into consideration what had happened and what was still happening I believed that my life or the life of other members of the patrol were in danger and I fired one round at him'.

Soldier 'H': 'At this point I could clearly see two terrorists on the ground. I believed the weapons were within reach of them and felt unable to try and remove the weapons without adding further risk to myself and my colleagues. I fired 5 or 6 single shots at them. Soldier "F" then moved back along the lorry towards the area of the cab and I followed. I was also aware of soldiers to my extreme right. Soldier "F" then fired into the cab. He then moved around the front of the cab and I followed him. Soldier "F" was to my right and I was aware of colleagues behind me. Soldier "F" then moved out to the right past the cab and fired again. I moved towards him and immediately saw a terrorist on the ground who was moving towards his weapon. I immediately felt there was a threat to my life and I fired at this terrorist. Both Soldier 'F' and I then went past both terrorists on the ground and as I was approaching the second terrorist he made a move towards his weapon. I fired 1 or 2 single shots at the terrorist. I then followed "F" to the eastern side of the church and we made our way onto the road at the front of the church. Soldier "F" told me there was a possible terrorist lying on the verge some 30–40 metres from our position. I then also saw this possible terrorist and both Soldier "F" and myself skirmished towards him. As we came closer I could see his paramilitary dress and as I ran towards him I could see him immediately go for a metal object which was very close to his right arm. I felt he was going for a weapon. I fired at him 3 to 4 automatic shots'.

Following a phone call *c.* 10.30 pm informing him of a lot of shooting around Clonoe church and the fire at the church, Fr Kieran McKeone, parish priest of Clonoe, went to the scene. A policeman brought him to the bodies. He administered the last rites to the four dead men and also spoke to the injured man. Patrick Vincent who had been the driver of the lorry was shot five times in the cab. Peter Clancy and Kevin Barry O'Donnell had managed to get out of the lorry. They lay beside the lorry. Peter Clancy had been shot

ten times, Kevin Barry O'Donnell twice. O'Donnell had been about to dismantle the machine-gun on the lorry. The screwdriver lay beside him on the
ground. Fr McKeone says he drove straight to the church where he saw those
whom he thought were SAS. He relates, 'I met a white car blocking the
Mountjoy Road at Dernagh Crossroads. I had come along the Moor Road
and I can't remember whether I met any vehicles or people. My first recol-
lection is the white car ... I could see a soldier dressed in full army uniform.
That soldier was standing beside or near the white car. I could see maybe half
a dozen men come towards the car from the direction of the chapel and go
away again several times. These men were wearing small peaked caps with
"Army" written across the front of the caps. These may not have been caps.
They may have been bands around the foreheads. I could see these men were
wearing camouflage trousers and anoraks or jerseys. I can't be sure. I took
these men to be SAS'. Fr McKeone also describes attending Seán O'Farrell
who had tried to make his escape, and as we have seen from the statements
of the soldiers themselves, though wounded, appears to have been shot
down in cold blood, 'At that stage a policeman who I think was with me all
the time, told me there was another body on the Mountjoy Road across the
road from the chapel. That policeman brought me down to a body. There was
light where that body was lying. The body was on the grass verge. His feet
were on the roadway and he was face up lying on his back. He was on the
right of the road, a few yards from McGraths' shed, between the shed and
the bottom gates giving access to the front of the chapel. I could see that man
had blood about his face. I gave him the last rites'. Two IRA men who were
injured escaped. Two others who had been in the cars and who were also injured were later charged with attempted murder of RUC officers at Coalisland RUC station and with possession of firearms with intent. They received suspended sentences.

In April 2003 the families of the four men shot dead at Clonoe made the
following points in an outline statement for Relatives for Justice's preparation of reports and information to the United Nations Special Rapporteur on
Summary or Arbitrary Executions:

1. According to the soldiers' statements they were all in place between
   19.00 and 20.00.
2. There was no warning of any kind. The soldiers shot and killed these
   men without any attempt to arrest them.
3. A total of 514 spent cartridges were recovered and allocated to the soldiers' rifles.
4. Contrary to reports of a gun battle, nothing was found to indicate that
   any of the firearms from the lorry had been discharged in the car park
   at Clonoe Chapel.
5. When Coalisland barracks was attacked there was no return fire or no
   pursuit; in fact solders patrolling the area in cars were warned to stay
   away.

6. At 20.14 a soldier identified Kevin Barry O'Donnell driving into Clonoe car park. Why was he not arrested?

7. Car teams (a–h) were in position by 20.00 and were told by C/S40 to hold off until PIRA team had reached Clonoe Chapel car park, then to move along designated routes towards target location as soon as the contact was initiated by the ground team. This proves that the British Army intended to kill these men.

8. It is obvious from documents dated 15/2/92 that the Army knew exactly what the plan was that night including the guns to be used and where they came from. Why was the attack not prevented?

9. The RUC knew that the IRA would move to Clonoe to dismantle the machine-gun and leave the area. If the British Army wanted to arrest these men they could have waited, but it is obvious that there was a shoot-to-kill policy in Clonoe that night.

10. Seán O'Farrell had fled 100 yards before he was shot. He was running for his life but apparently had time to lift and run with a magazine as one was found under his body!

11. The RUC carried out an investigation into these killings and a decision was made on 15 October 1992 that there would be no prosecutions even though some soldiers involved that night did not make statements until December 1992.

Envoi 1990

Four years after the Anglo-Irish Agreement, despite periods of great tension but with a noticeable defusion in 1989, the political strategists on both sides seem to have adopted a policy of treading water, though the Secretary of State for Northern Ireland recently was trying to promote once again the notion of devolution, awaiting, perhaps, the potential spin-off from European developments anticipated within the next few years. One is constantly amazed at the changes of mood manifested in the relationship between the two sovereign powers, modulating in response to specific events and making it difficult to assess accurately what is the real political intention of those who wield political power.

In the unionist camp the old artificially bolstered sense of security, power and superiority continues to diminish. The old guard hanker after the good old days of Stormont. The younger ones don't remember it and, since the violence broke out many more Protestants are emigrating to Britain as their fellow Catholics have always done. Unionists generally feel a lessening British interest in them as a people and more of a British determination to remain in Northern Ireland for logistical and defensive motives. To withdraw under seeming pressure from the IRA would be unthinkable for the British but, nonetheless, the unionist crisis of identity intensifies.

Nationalists are divided: some republicans believe in the moral legitimacy and tactical value of the use of armed force; others abhor the use of force and think that it prolongs the political impasse. Despite strikes on the continent and in England, the 'physical force' movement has lost some of its impetus, influenced by such factors as civilian casualties, war weariness, confusion on the political/military alliance, media censorship and the improvement of prison conditions in both Portlaoise and Long Kesh. Despite improving conditions for Catholics, the old discrimination dies hard as, for example, the recent Fair Employment Agency's damning indictment of employment practices at The Queen's University, Belfast, proves beyond all possibility of lofty demur. The reality of discrimination was always known. Statistics now can prove it.

Antipathy to IRA violence and the reality of British governmental power and control combine to force some Catholics to acquiesce uneasily in the run-of-the-mill violations of human rights which are perpetrated by a state that is held together by its armed forces. The SAS in its operations typifies most acutely the worst features of state-sponsored crime and, of course, against its excesses every Irish Catholic strongly protests. When, after long years campaigning, corruption and gross injustice are incontrovertibly exposed, as in the cases of the Guildford Four and the Birmingham Six, practically everybody climbs on the bandwagon, most typically elements of the media in the Irish Republic.

The incidents recorded in this book form only the tangible face of a vast undercover operation of intelligence-gathering, surveillance, harassment and bloody action. The British Prime Minister, Mrs Margaret Thatcher, sometimes speaks of the 'more than 2,000 people murdered by the IRA since 1969'. IRA violence is the only violence she chooses to mention. Her statement is inaccurate. While it is true that republican groups have been responsible for the majority of deaths in the Northern Ireland conflict, it is also a fact that, of the 2,775 deaths, 1969 to 31 December 1989, 127 uninvolved civilians have been killed by British Army / UDR / RUC; these security forces have killed 119 republicans and 15 loyalists; 613 civilians have been assassinated by loyalist paramilitary groups and loyalists have also killed 14 members of the security forces; 111 civilians have been killed in loyalist explosions; 13 civilians have died in loyalist cross-fire and 'accidents' and 27 loyalists have died by their own action; 46 people have died in riot situations and 51 deaths are unclassified; 450 civilians have been assassinated by republicans; 167 civilians have been killed in republican explosions and 61 civilians have died in cross-fire and 'accidents' due to republican action; republicans have killed 843 members of the security forces and 118 republicans have died by their own activity. Most of the deaths in 1989 were caused by the IRA. The SAS are estimated to have been involved in 45 shootings in the Northern Ireland conflict, 1969–89. Some SAS soldiers also played their part indirectly in some of the murders committed by loyalist paramilitaries. SAS violence is a British reaction to IRA violence. IRA violence was a reaction to the partition of Ireland and to the resulting injustice and violence of the state.

Young people, Catholic and Protestant, have been manipulated by British Intelligence personnel and have spent long years in prison as a result. On the other hand, the state allows its covert army to operate with immunity. If their operations are probed, it is prepared to go to incredible lengths to defend them even in the face of overwhelming criticism from the more independent and self-respecting journalists.

I hope that the cumulative effect of reading the various accounts of SAS / Undercover activity in Ireland during the past twenty years will be to convince the reader of the ruthless and unprincipled British military action that has been and is being conducted – from the case of Peter Cleary in 1976, 'Shot while trying to escape', to the Gibraltar killings of 1988 when no prisoners were taken. (Most recently, 13 January 1990, plain clothes soldiers, reportedly members of the 14th Intelligence Company, shot dead three men, Edward Hale (25), John McNeill (42) and Peter Thompson (21) while they were robbing a bookmakers on the Falls Road, Belfast. An eyewitness said that one of the soldiers fired pistol shots into the bodies of the wounded men where they lay on the ground. Bishop Cahal Daly's call for an independent inquiry into the shootings was refused by Peter Brooke, Secretary of State. Bishop Daly in a lengthy statement said, 'The incident has aroused grave and widespread concern, and not just within the Catholic community. Among those who have expressed the greatest concern are people who have spoken the most consistently and worked the hardest against republican or loyalist paramilitary violence, but who now, with dismay, see their efforts sabotaged by this operation'.) Richard Ingrams wrote in *The Observer*, 17 December 1989, that it was the SAS killings in Gibraltar and the subsequent lying statements put out by various government spokesmen that had a critical effect in altering Margaret Thatcher's public image for the worse. He continues – 'Taken with the Stalker affair, it confirmed the extent to which our politics and our legal system had been corrupted by Mrs Thatcher's obstinate determination to defend the indefensible division of Ireland'.

The cycle has moved from the intelligence-gathering of 1969 to the destabilising of the Catholic community, through the pseudo-gang alliance with the loyalist paramilitaries, the surveillance with the odd kill, to an active 'terrorist' role blossoming in a shoot-to-kill policy, actively promoted at cabinet and prime-ministerial level and equally actively covered up by the most flagrant techniques and the co-operation of compliant elements in the media. The effects of this policy in nationalist, economically deprived areas are an alienation from the institutions of state and a resulting anarchy that is fatalistically endured by the people.

The British seek a policy of containment in Northern Ireland. In a depoliticised atmosphere there is greater emphasis on winning a 'war'. The influence of the British Army and the RUC is greater than any of the political parties in the north and Margaret Thatcher has given a very special role to the SAS in her military strategy. In her 'move to beat the terrorists' she is prepared to sacrifice liberties like the right to silence, the enforcing of a non-violence oath for elections, the reduction of remission on sentences from the Diplock courts, the ending of interviews with Sinn Féin and paramilitaries on radio and television.

After the SAS storming of the Iranian embassy in London on 30 April 1980, Mrs Thatcher pronounced the SAS operation absolutely wonderful and said it made her proud to be British. In her speech on the final day of the Conservative party annual conference at Brighton on 14 October 1988 she praised the SAS who, she said, had demonstrated conclusively that they had at all times acted within the law to save lives. She proclaimed a military goal, 'We will never give up the search for more effective means of defeating the IRA. If the IRA think they can weary or frighten us, they have made a terrible miscalculation. People sometimes say that it is wrong to use the word "never" in politics. I disagree. Some things are of such fundamental importance that no other word is appropriate. So I say once again today that this government will never surrender to the IRA. Never'. In an interview with *The Times* on 26 October 1988 regarding the ban on radio and television interviews, she characterised the conflict in Northern Ireland as a 'War'; 'In order to beat off your enemy in war, you have to suspend some civil liberties for a time'.

If war were declared, the way would be open for an open conflict. Since, however, no war has been declared, are the SAS justified in killing IRA members in planned ambushes? The answer must be no. Consequently the SAS are forced by the logic of government policy to retrospectively justify 'a risk of death' situation. In their evidence they will lace the circumstances of a killing with exempting phrases: they intended to arrest; there was a threat to life and limb; the other party 'fired first'. It is their word against the word of a paramilitary witness, or a civilian witness or a witness or witnesses who have been intimidated. Sometimes, even when there is no independent witness, the medical and other forensic evidence challenges the version of events presented by the SAS and RUC.

The SAS rarely attend inquests. Faced only with statements not open to cross-examination, what is a coroner to do? Who is there to enunciate and apply international human rights law in the case of SAS unjust killings and murders? Who is there to enunciate and apply the moral law?

As there was no domestic remedy for the problem of torture used by the agents of the state in Northern Ireland in the 1970s until the European Commission for Human Rights and the European Court of Human Rights ruled on the issue, there may be no halt to the policy of setting the SAS on a war footing in the north of Ireland with a licence to shoot-to-kill until Europe probes for the truth and makes a ruling once again.

It may be recalled that the SAS star was somewhat in decline after the Second World War but that there came a revival in the 1950s when it was invested with a markedly secret mystique. With the siege of the Iranian embassy and the Falklands War, however, a new Thatcher-inspired glorification of the SAS was promoted. Glorification and immunity went hand in hand. How could such an élite, such highly-principled and crack paragons possibly do anything wrong? Perish the thought!

It would be consoling to think that we had entered another waning period in the history of the SAS because the political judgement had been made that overall its activities in Ireland had proven counter-productive but, despite Gibraltar and other bloody actions, the glorification policy appears to survive. Proof of this seems to emerge from the New Year Honours' List for 1990 published in *The Independent*, 30 December 1989:

> Less predictable than the peerage for the retired Admiral of the Fleet Sir John Fieldhouse of Falklands fame, is the knighthood for Colonel David Stirling, founder of the SAS. The award comes not in the military division of the honours list, where colonels become Commanders of the British Empire and where knighthoods are reserved to lieutenant-generals and above, but in the Prime Minister's list.

Less predictable? I shouldn't have thought so.

Epilogue

Since *The SAS in Ireland* was first published in 1990 there have been positive steps towards social and political advancement in Northern Ireland. Reforms to bring about equality for all in society, really the early root of the conflict, have been almost completed and are bearing fruit. Human rights organisations such as the Committee on the Administration of Justice, the British Irish Rights Watch, the Pat Finucane Centre and Relatives for Justice are still monitoring the actions of the government and its institutions in relation to human rights and are committed to a Bill of Rights, an all-island Charter of Rights, the dismantling of emergency legislation and criminal justice reform. Only the last pieces of the visionary Patten Report on the reform of the police remain to be put in place, especially the abolition of the life-threatening plastic bullets and total disbandment of the Special Branch which had been a 'force within a force' and lacked accountability. One hopes for final demilitarisation by the government and decommissioning of arms by paramilitaries. Town and mountain military posts in South Armagh still scar the region and appear provocative. The decommissioning process between the IRA and General John de Chastelain is incomplete and has been arduous and torturous. The loyalist paramilitaries have made no serious effort to disarm and have carried out numerous sectarian murders. The Good Friday Agreement signed in 1998, following the IRA ceasefires in 1994 and 1997, provided an assembly with a balanced executive formed from the largest parties. The new ministers proved themselves capable and naturally understood local problems. Although the assembly has had a chequered career since 1998 and is at present, 2004, again awaiting re-establishment, perhaps, following the assembly election on 26 November 2003, the classical colonial deal between the two polarised parties, the Democratic Unionist Party and Sinn Féin will mark the climax of the political peace process. It remains to be seen whether all the substantial political parties can again come to an agreement. There is, paradoxically, more and more co-operation among parties at local government level. North-South co-operation in economics, cultural exchange and education is growing apace with the world's globalisation trend. The authorities of all the main Church denominations are making greater efforts than ever before to advance good relations and promote reconciliation and there are admirable examples of clergy and community workers combining to promote peace and culture sharing at local level. It is a major task. Once the conflict formally ended sectarianism burst to the surface, leading to a six year July conflict between members of the Orange Order and police and military at Drumcree in Portadown, random sectarian murders by the UDA, LVF and UVF, clashes at the interfaces of nationalist and loyalist areas in North and East Belfast where complex issues resulted in the innocent suffering, notably the targeting of Catholic schoolchildren at Ardoyne. The UDA has carried out a sustained pipe bombing campaign against Catholics where they live as a minority, especially in areas in Belfast, Larne, Ballymena, Ballymoney and Coleraine. It has once again, February 2004, renewed its ceasefire. On 15 August 1998 republican dissidents, the 'Real' IRA, were responsible for one of the major massacres of the conflict, a bomb in Omagh that killed 29 people and injured many others. This atrocity has become the catastasis of the pain and pathos of the northern tragedy. Although the IRA since its ceasefires has not committed any sectarian murders or carried out attacks against police and military in the north, they have murdered some drug dealers, and murdered Charles Bennett on 29 July 1999 and Joseph O'Connor on 13 October 2000. Like other paramilitaries they have engaged in punishment beatings. Their response to the repatriation of the 'disappeared', those murdered by them in the past and buried secretly, has been less than thorough or gracious. Ferocious murderous feuds have erupted among loyalist paramilitaries as rival bands strive to control territory or battle over the spoils of racketeering. Having practically dispensed with their political wings they have become isolated, and sadly the ghettoes in which they live are now lost wastelands abandoned by government and politicians. Release of prisoners and associations to explore the needs of prisoners have created some controversy but have obviously been necessary components of peace and those working for the welfare of ex-prisoners have proved themselves compassionate and politically far-seeing. Wider dimensions have been catered for in north-south institutions in Ireland and links between Britain and Ireland, and of course the external influence of the European Union steadily and inexorably brings about economic and social change.

The wounds of the injured and bereaved may never be healed. Victims' associations offer counselling and support, but how to pursue and find truth and justice in the many unsolved murders is still a dilemma. The decision to retain in the British Army the two released British soldiers, Scots Guards Ian Wright and Mark Fisher who were convicted of the 1992 murder of Peter McBride in Belfast, seems to add insult to injury. It has often been asked why there were so few prosecutions for the sectarian murders of Catholics in mid-Ulster. In what might be taken as a symbolic example of police neglect, Ms Nuala O'Loan, the Northern Ireland Police Ombudsman, in her report, 19 January 2004, on the murder on 12 May 1997 of Seán Brown, a prominent GAA figure in Bellaghy, Co. Derry, found 'significant failings' in the investigation mounted by the then RUC, and said that the investigation was 'incomplete and inadequate'. One calls to mind that MI5 officers destroyed a secret tape containing potentially vital evidence regarding the shooting dead by the RUC of 17 year old Michael Tighe, a lad with no IRA connections, in a hayshed a few miles from Lurgan, Co. Armagh, on 24 November 1982.

Neither the state, nor loyalists, nor republicans are anxious to reveal the truth of what happened in the political murders and killings of thirty years. All find common cause in hiding the truth. The British government would like to see an 'amnesty' all round and is anxious to bring a 'closure' to the past and leave the Saville Inquiry into the killings by British Army paratroopers of 13 civilians on 'Bloody Sunday' in Derry as the sole absolution of the bad conscience of state violence. The British government's strategy, in responding to the campaigns for truth and justice, symbolically highlighted so often in the campaigns demanding public inquiries into the deaths of the leading human rights lawyers Pat Finucane and Rosemary Nelson, is to deny access to sources on a plea of protecting national security. Even the inquests have been so curtailed as to shut out the deceit on the part of the security forces. Delay and playing for time is also a constant tactic. The British government wishes to escape a responsibility for murder, unjust killing and 'collusion' with loyalists. Responsibility obviously went higher than military and police protagonists and authorities and approached institutional conspiracy. The Stalker/Sampson Report and the various Stevens Reports have essentially been ignored or thwarted. The Stalker Report did result in the British government returning the main responsibility for covert operations to the British Army. Stevens One, set up when Sir John Stevens was assistant commissioner with the Cambridgeshire police, reported in the early 1990s concerning security force/paramilitary collusion. A campaign of obstruction against the inquiry itself included leaking of information and an arson attack on the offices of Sir John Stevens and his team. Stevens Two was an elaboration of One. The Stevens Interim Report of April 2003 (Stevens Three), which took four years to complete, made it clear that the British Army colluded in dozens of murders and that the system of recruiting and handling 'agents' was 'out of control'. Sir John Stevens defined collusion as 'the failure to keep records, the absence of accountability, withholding of intelligence and evidence and the involvement of intelligence agents in murder'. His 3,000 page full report contains names, accusations and recommendations. However only a very short summary has been published. Like Stalker/Sampson it remains a secret and has so far been suppressed by the British government. The Stevens team claimed to have interviewed 15,000 people, catalogued 4,000 exhibits, taken 5,640 statements and seized 6,000 documents. None of this is available for public scrutiny. In an interview given to Jackie Ashley in *The Guardian*, 20 January 2003, Sir John Stevens referred to his inquiry then, after 13 years, as 'the longest and most complex criminal investigation that has ever been undertaken in this country'. He said that he and his officers had discovered 'a massive amount of documentation I had never seen before'. On the Finucane case he said that investigation had taken so long because of the 'secrecy and the fact that we are investigating not just the army, and what was the RUC, but MI5 activity as well. It goes to the very heart of what takes place in terms of intelligence gathering in this country'. He made it clear that he would not flinch from investigating even those at the very top – 'We will go where the evidence takes us'. One awaits the prosecutions! In advance of the delivery of the Stevens Report, Michael Finucane, son of Patrick Finucane and a practising solicitor, said on behalf of the Finucane family:

This report is widely believed to be some sort of 'systems analysis', an examination of what went wrong in Northern Ireland and how that can be prevented in the future. On this level also, Stevens' work is flawed. Nothing went wrong. The 'system' worked exactly as intended and, in the British government's eyes, it worked perfectly. The policy in Northern Ireland was – and may yet be – to harness the killing potential of loyalist paramilitaries, to increase that potential through additional resources in the shape of weapons and information and to direct those resources against selected targets so that the government could be rid of its enemies. Simple policy. Simple operation. Simply chilling. We are convinced beyond any doubt that Britain's policy included amongst its victims one lawyer the rule of law could not stop. I refer, of course, to my late father, Patrick Finucane. His murder is just one example of what the British government was prepared to do to further its own ends, but he is not the only casualty. My family and I call upon the British government once again to establish a full independent judicial public inquiry into the murder of Patrick Finucane and the policy of collusion with loyalist paramilitaries.

The Guardian on 28 April 2001 carried an article with headline 'Sinister role of secret army unit: Police investigate claims of collusion with paramilitaries'. It described the organisations involved in covert operations in Northern Ireland including the British Army's Force Research Unit (FRU) – 'The FRU was one of three army-sponsored undercover intelligence squads in Northern Ireland. The others were 22 Squadron SAS and 14 Company. The FRU, which was set up in Northern Ireland in 1980, dealt with recruiting and handling agents in paramilitary organisations'. 14 Company specialised in surveillance while 22 SAS undertook 'executive actions'. 'That means they killed people', said an army source. It is significant that there is little evidence of the SAS being used to combat loyalist paramilitaries. By the end of the 1980s British Military Intelligence and Special Branch RUC were practically in charge of the UDA in North and West Belfast. This is evident from the information squeezed from the leakages of the Stevens' Reports, from police, soldiers and the courts. The FRU's headquarters is based at Repton Manor, within Templar barracks, Ashford, Kent, which is the headquarters of the British Army's Intelligence Corps. Its trainees operating in Northern Ireland controlled *agents provocateurs*, some of them ex-British soldiers, within the IRA and the loyalist paramilitaries. Special Branch RUC also controlled informers within these organisations. IRA men, Catholic citizens and a few loyalist paramilitaries were singled out to be killed. In the 'dirty war' other Catholics and even some members of the security forces were not given protection in the interest of shrouded secrecy and so lost their lives. Who were the British officers and who were the British politicians who sanctioned this strategy and these operations? The British government is still trying to avoid the answers to these vital questions.

The FRU used Brian Nelson (died 11 April 2003), a former British soldier of the Black Watch regiment, to infiltrate the Ulster Defence Association. He was responsible for at least 30 murders, among them Patrick Finucane and many other victims not involved in violence. The Force Research Unit reported directly to the senior British commander in Northern Ireland. The *Sunday Herald*, which for more than two years investigated the role of Brigadier Gordon Kerr, former commanding officer of FRU, in the 'dirty war' in Northern Ireland, reported on 23 February 2003 that he had been sent to the Gulf to head up British spying activities in the Middle East as part of preparations for action in Iraq. The move followed a decision on 13 February 2003 by Sir John Stevens to forward papers on Kerr and some 20 members of the security forces who served in Northern Ireland to the DPP. A senior military source told the *Sunday Herald*, 'This posting makes Kerr untouchable. He is not going to be dragged away from essential war work in an operational theatre to talk to police or prosecutors. Kerr has landed on his feet with this posting'. The newspaper commented, 'It shows that the whole Stevens inquiry is nothing but a whitewash. He is never going to end up in a court of law. The posting keeps him safe and protects those in the army above him – and those politicians who were in power when the FRU was carrying on these activities in Ulster – from ever having to answer nasty questions that might arise through him being arrested or charged'.

The activity of the British Army's double agent in the IRA, code-named 'Stakeknife', is still under investigation. The stories of undercover agents 'Stakeknife' and Brian Nelson are already the subject of a book, *Stakeknife: Britain's secret agents in Ireland* (2004), by Martin Ingram, former British intelligence officer and FRU handler, and journalist Greg Harkin.

Following the Weston Park talks in July 2001, a dialogue to restore confidence after David Trimble resigned as First Minister of the Assembly on the decommissioning issue but also due to the pressure on him of the right wing of unionism which cannot bear to share an equal relationship with nationalists, Judge Peter Cory, a former Canadian Court justice, was, as part of a balanced deal, appointed by the British and Irish governments to inquire into six alleged cases of collusion north and south. London and Dublin governments pledged to carry out a public inquiry into any of the murders if that was what was recommended.

On 7 October 2003 Judge Cory handed over his reports to the British and Irish governments. The two cases in the south were the murders of Judge Gibson and his wife and two senior RUC officers Bob Buchanan and Harry Breen. The judge, because of insufficient evidence, did not recommend a public inquiry into the Gibson case but he did in the killing of the two police officers. On 18 December 2003 the Irish government published Judge Cory's Reports in these cases and said it would hold an inquiry. In the Breen/Buchanan Report Judge Cory outlined his principle in assessing collusion and this was also his principle in the northern investigation:

> Because of the necessity for public confidence in the police, the definition of collusion must be reasonably broad when it is applied to their actions. This is to say that police forces must not act collusively by ignoring or turning a blind eye to the wrongful acts of their servants or agents or by supplying information to assist

others in committing their wrongful acts. Any lesser definition would have the effect of condoning, or even encouraging, state involvement in crimes, thereby shattering all public confidence in these important agencies.

This broad definition of collusion, which can be either active or passive, is not dissimilar to that of Sir John Stevens. Among the criteria necessary for a public inquiry Judge Cory included full powers to subpoena witnesses and documents together with all the powers usually exercised by a commissioner in a public inquiry.

The northern cases were: Patrick Finucane shot dead by the UDA before his family at Sunday dinner in his own home, 12 February 1989; Robert Hamill, a Catholic, attacked by a loyalist group near an armoured RUC vehicle in Portadown on 27 April1997, died in hospital without regaining consciousness on 8 May 1997; Billy Wright, leader of the Loyalist Volunteer Force, shot dead by the INLA in the Maze prison on 27 December 1997; Rosemary Nelson killed near her home by a loyalist booby-trap bomb in her car on 15 March 1999.

On 12 January 2004 Judge Cory contacted the families of Patrick Finucane, Robert Hamill, Billy Wright and Rosemary Nelson to inform them that he had recommended public inquiries into each of their cases to the British government.

On 31 March 2004, after a delay of three months and an initiative by the Finucane family to seek a High Court decision to force the British government to set up a public inquiry into the Patrick Finucane case, the families received copies of the individual reports under pledge not to divulge their contents, and on 1 April 2004, the British government published Judge Cory's Report. Some parts of the report were withheld in publication, presumably for 'legal' and 'security' reasons. Despite the fact that Taoiseach Bertie Ahern was an equal partner in commissioning the Cory Report, he was also given the censored version. Although his findings were provisional, Judge Cory, who had access to 'sensitive' RUC and British Army records, pointed strongly to a mass of evidence in the collusion with loyalist paramilitaries of sections of the British Army and RUC, and members of the RUC, the Special Branch, MI5, the Prison Service and the Northern Ireland Office. His reports portray sections of the British security forces as regarding themselves above the law and conducting a one-sided 'dirty' war. They depict agents allowed to set up murders and loyalists given British Army intelligence that may have been used to kill nationalists.

It is noteworthy that at this time, on 31 March 2004, the Oireachtas Joint Commission on Justice in Dublin, which had examined the Barron Report on the Dublin and Monaghan bombings of 1974, concluded that the probability of British security force collusion in the attacks was 'exceptionally high' and recommended the holding of a series of inquiries including a public one in Britain or Northern Ireland.

Here are some extracts from Judge Cory's Reports:

[Patrick Finucane] They (FRU) were aware that (Brian) Nelson was a central play-er within the UDA, and that he had considerable influence in directing targeting operations. They were also aware that Nelson often played a direct and active role in reconnaissance missions. The provision of information to Nelson in these circumstances may be seen as evidence of collusive behaviour that had the po-tential to facilitate the deadly operations planned by the UDA.

The documents I have examined disclose that Army handlers and their su-periors turned a blind eye to the criminal acts of (Brian) Nelson. In doing this they established a pattern of behaviour that could be characterised as collusive.

Similarly, they indicate that Special Branch rarely took any steps to docu-ment threats or prevent threats by the UDA, whereas pro-active steps were taken in connection with PIRA and other Republican threats. The failure to issue warn-ings to persons targeted by the UDA often led to tragic consequences. This is in-dicative of attitudes with RUC Special Branch.

If criminal prosecutors are to proceed the practical effect might be to delay the public inquiry for at least two years. The Finucane family will be devastated. A large part of the Northern Ireland community will be frustrated. Myths and misconceptions will proliferate and hopes of peace and understanding will be eroded. This may be one of the rare situations where a public inquiry will be of greater benefit to a community than prosecutions.

[Robert Hamill] Police officers must not act collusively by ignoring or turn-ing a blind eye to the wrongful acts of their officers or of their servants or agents. Nor can the police act collusively by supplying information to assist those com-mitting wrongful acts or by encouraging them to commit wrongful acts.

First and foremost the actions of Reserve Constable 'B', if established, are capable of being found to constitute the most flagrant type of collusion. His actions did not constitute the simple turning of a blind eye. Rather they could be found to be carefully planned and premeditated actions taken to frustrate a murder in-vestigation and to protect or to exonerate an individual who might have been guilty of murder.

Steps should have been taken to obtain the clothing of Robert Hamill and those identified at the scene as taking part in the assault ... the failure to take steps may indicate a bias in the police force that could amount to institutional collusion.

[Rosemary Nelson] I am satisfied that there is evidence of collusion by gov-ernmental agencies in the murder of Rosemary Nelson that warrants holding a public inquiry.

RUC officers are alleged to have made highly demeaning and threatening re-marks about Rosemary Nelson while questioning her clients. Among other things, they are said to have questioned her morality, made insulting sexual innuendos, described her facial scarring in cruel and debasing terms, belittled her ability as a lawyer and, perhaps most disturbingly, to have threatened her life. It is for a public inquiry to determine whether or not these remarks were made. If it is found that they were, this could constitute strong evidence of collusion.

The NIO's (Northern Ireland Office's) mishandling of documents that were directly pertinent and vitally important to the safety of Rosemary Nelson may also indicate a level of neglect or disregard that could be found to be collusive.

[The NIO's] failure to take any action to protect Rosemary Nelson could be found to be troubling when it is considered against the background of the earl-ier murder of Patrick Finucane. By disregarding a significant body of evidence of

threats against Rosemary Nelson, it could be found that the NIO engaged in conduct that was collusive in nature.

[*Billy Wright*] This case will turn primarily on the response to these questions. First, and most importantly, did the Northern Ireland Prison Service turn a blind eye to the very dangerous situation they knew or ought to have known would arise from billeting the INLA and LVF (Loyalist Volunteer Force) prisoners in the same H bock in the Maze? Similarly, did another governmental agency fail to advise or supply to the Prison Service information they had received and considered reasonably reliable which indicated that a dangerous situation had arisen or was arising in the prison?

One or two of the incidents that occurred on the day of the murder may, in themselves, have little significance. On the other hand when they are all considered together, the resulting effect may be sufficient to take them out of the realm of coincidence and make them components of a plan to murder Billy Wright that was collusive in nature.

There is, in my view, sufficient evidence of acts or omissions that could, after hearing the testimony of witnesses, coupled with a review of the relevant documents result in a finding that there had been acts of collusion by Prison Services, their directors, officers or employees.

In a statement in the British House of Commons, I April 2004, the Secretary of State for Northern Ireland, Paul Murphy, announced immediate public inquiries into the murders of Rosemary Nelson, Robert Hamill and Billy Wright under the Northern Ireland's Police Act of 1978. The Cory Reports would form the basis of the investigations and the edited sections would be made available to the inquiries. The inquiries would be given powers to summon witnesses and compel the production of official documents. The families welcomed the announcement. It seemed to them and their supporters that their long campaign for truth and justice had borne fruit at last. Hope was expressed that the mode of the inquiries would be to the satisfaction of the families.

The British government did not commit itself to an inquiry into the Patrick Finucane case on the excuse that it was committed firstly to current and possible future prosecutions arising from the on-going Stevens inquiry into his murder. Geraldine Finucane, widow of Patrick Finucane, responding for the family said:

This is a very disappointing but expected statement. The British government continue to cover up the truth about the death of my husband with their delaying tactics. We did not ask for the Stevens investigation. We did not ask for Justice Cory to prepare a report and we certainly have never asked for prosecutions. We have always said that these were delaying tactics and the delay continues. But the campaign for a public inquiry will also continue. Paul Murphy quoted Justice Cory as saying '... Society must be assured that those who commit a crime will be prosecuted and if found guilty punished'. However he did not refer to the fact that Justice Cory also said in his report that 'this may be one of the rare situations where a public inquiry will be of greater benefit to a community than prosecutions'. Justice Cory confirms that there was a State policy of targeting and assassination. The public should read the details of his report. It is unbelievable but the official documents that he examined show that it is all true.

A criminal prosecution is pending in connection with the murder of Robert Hamill and in spite of that an inquiry was sanctioned. It is to be remembered also that the Prime Minister, Tony Blair, gave an undertaking at the Weston Park talks to establish public inquiries on the recommendation of Judge Cory's Reports. Michael Finucane, a son of Patrick Finucane, said on 2 April 2004, that the decision to reject Judge Cory's recommendation to immediately establish a judicial inquiry appeared to have been made at the highest level of the British government. A spokesperson for Amnesty International said, 'In failing to establish an immediate public inquiry into the killing of Patrick Finucane, the UK government is making a mockery of its commitment to ascertaining the truth and to the rule of law'. Both Taoiseach Bertie Ahern and Foreign Minister, Brian Cowen, in the Irish government expressed disappointment on 1 April 2004 at the British government's decision to delay action in setting up a public inquiry in the case of Patrick Finucane. Likewise Judge Cory himself, in interviews on RTÉ and BBC on 5 April 2004, said he was disappointed that the Patrick Finucane case was being deferred. He said that a public inquiry would not necessarily affect a prosecution and that it was more important to hold the public inquiry than the trial and prosecution, 'not just for the Finucane family but for the community as a whole ... I would have thought,' he said, 'that in the light of the manner in which terrorist trials are held, that is to say in front of a judge alone, that they could proceed at the same time'. The public inquiry had been promised at the Weston Park talks and the Finucane family had already been waiting 15 years. Key witnesses could die; the criminal case could take an interminable time, with the possibility of appeals and of others being charged. The Committee on the Administration of Justice noted in its press release that the stance of Judge Cory, and the frequently stated desire of the family to hold a public inquiry, led one to the unavoidable conclusion that it was fear of revealing the depth and breadth of collusion that appeared to be the motivation for the government's continuing prevarication on the Finucane case. Param Cumaraswamy, a former senior UN representative, also criticised the failure to hold an immediate public inquiry.

Judge Cory's Report is of supreme importance since it is the first official report ordered by the British and Irish governments that details the British security and intelligence establishments' efforts to withhold the truth about the scale of collusion over thirty years. Coming from a respected outsider it has an international dimension to it.

On 18 February 2004 Professor Desmond Rea, chairman of the north's Policing Board, and his deputy Denis Bradley, suggested a truth commission and an amnesty for those involved in the thirty years of violence. This in effect is in line with the thinking of the chief constable of the PSNI (Police Service of Northern Ireland), Hugh Orde, who pleads lack of resources, money and personnel, to investigate the some 1,800 unsolved deaths by violence during the conflict. Prior to Paul Murphy's statement on Judge Cory's Report in the House of Commons on 1 April 2004 the Prime Minister, Tony Blair, at his monthly press conference expressed the British government's desire to draw a line through history and move on. He said he had asked Mr Murphy to begin consultations about finding 'some way of trying both to allow people to express their grief, their pain and their anger in respect of what has happened in Northern Ireland without the past continually dominating the present and the future'. This nervous reaction to Judge Cory's Report is obviously an intention to create an escape route for the government from an avalanche of requests from families and human rights' organisations for disclosure of documents on state killings, murder and collusion in the government's possession. However, any idea of closure is not acceptable to the victims' families. Collusion is part of the context of state killings of which those murders and unjust killings by the police and army, including the SAS, are part. In his Report Judge Cory criticised the RUC Special Branch for paying little attention to loyalist paramilitaries. He said, 'The documents indicate that in some instances Special Branch failed to take any steps to prevent actual or planned attacks on persons targeted by Loyalist terrorist groups'.

The allegations over years of British state terrorism including actions of the SAS were well founded and those who made allegations of collusion are vindicated by the Stevens and Cory Reports. British governments and security chiefs must be made judicially responsible for extra-judicial killings if it is found in public inquiries that they were complicit in such crimes. Human rights standards were needed most at a time of conflict and that is where successive British governments failed. It is important now to promote public confidence in security services. This will only happen when the British state opens up the sources it has kept locked up over the years of a long-running conflict. The revelation of the truth would in fact hasten the pace of healing and reconciliation and brighten the vision of peace in a new Ireland. Justice must be seen to be done for the sake of law, morality and democracy.

Appendix I

Rulings of the European Court of Human Rights

Completely inadequate investigations into state crime in Northern Ireland remains a deep grievance, and this was highlighted in four cases brought to Strasbourg in April 2000 and also in a decision by the European Court of Human Rights on 7 January 2003 in the case of Patrick Finucane.

In May 2001 the European Court of Human Rights ruled that human rights were violated in the cases of eleven people killed by the security forces in Northern Ireland. These were Gervaise McKerr and Pearse Jordan who were unarmed when shot dead by the police, and eight IRA members and one civilian, Anthony Hughes, killed by the SAS in Loughgall in 1987. At the inquest in June 1995 into the Loughgall deaths the SAS admitted not giving any warning before opening fire. The court gave the same ruling in respect to Patrick Shanaghan (31) who was killed by loyalist paramilitaries on 12 August 1991. Pearse Jordan (23), unarmed, was shot in the back three times by the RUC when he tried to run away after his car was rammed by the police in West Belfast on 25 November 1992. To mark the gravity of its decisions the court for the first time ordered the British government to pay £10,000 compensation to the relatives of each of the victims. The seven judges did not rule on whether the men had been unlawfully killed leaving that to domestic law but they did rule that the authorities had failed to conduct the proper investigation into the deaths, thus violating Article 2 of the European Convention on Human Rights. They said:

> If the aims of fact-finding, criminal investigation and prosecution were carried out or shared between several authorities, as in Northern Ireland, the court considered that the requirements of Article 2 might nonetheless be satisfied if, while seeking to take into account other legitimate interests such as national security or the protection of material relevant to other investigations, they provided for the necessary safeguards in an accessible and effective manner. However, in all four cases the available procedure had not struck the right balance.

The judges condemned the lack of independence of the investigating police officers from the security forces implicated in the incidents and recommended the creation of a fully independent agency to investigate complaints against the police. There was a lack of public security and victims' families were not given enough information. In the case of the Loughgall killings the court was severely critical of the fact that the SAS who fired the shots could not be required to attend the inquest as witnesses. The inquest procedure did not allow for any verdict or findings which could play an effective role in securing a prosecution in respect of any criminal offence which might have been disclosed. The court upheld the complaint of relatives of Patrick Shanaghan who was murdered by loyalist paramilitaries in 1991, that the inquest excluded an investigation into alleged collusion between the security forces and loyalist paramilitaries:

> In all four cases the court observed that the shortcomings in transparency and effectiveness identified ran counter to the purpose identified by the domestic courts of allaying suspicions and rumours. Proper procedures for insuring the accountability of agents of the state were indispensable in maintaining public confidence and meeting the legitimate concerns that might arise from the use of lethal force. Lack of such procedures would only add fuel to fears of sinister motivations, as was illustrated among other things by the submissions made concerning the alleged shoot-to-kill policy.

In the case of Gervaise McKerr, one of three unarmed IRA men shot dead near Lurgan on 11 November 1982 by the RUC, the court complained that the inquest did not allow for any verdict that might secure a prosecution for a criminal offence. The police officers, who had fired 109 rounds into the car, could not be required to testify at the inquest.

The criticisms of the court included: lack of independence of the investigation carried out by the RUC; lack of public scrutiny and information to the victim's family concerning the independent (Stalker/Sampson) investigation, including lack of reasons for the failure to prosecute any police officer for perverting or attempting to pervert the course of justice; the inquest procedure did not allow verdicts or findings which might play an effective role in securing prosecutions in respect of any criminal which might be disclosed; no advance disclosure of witness statements at the inquest; the Public Interest Immunity Certificate had the effect of preventing the inquest examining matters relevant to outstanding issues; the police officers who shot Gervaise McKerr could not be compelled to attend the inquest as witnesses; the inquest proceedings did not start promptly, and neither they nor the Stalker/Sampson investigation proceeded with reasonable expedition. The domestic courts commented that the inquest was not the proper forum for dealing with the wider issues in the case. No other public-accessible procedure, however, was forthcoming to remedy the shortcomings.

Jonathan Kerr, who was eight years old when his father was shot, said, 'We always knew our loved ones were victims of a shoot-to-kill policy which the British government, adding insult to injury, has been denying existed up to this day. We are pleased that the European Court, unlike any other, has not let us down and we would encourage the families of other victims of the security forces to take their cases as far as they can'.

The British government did not appeal the European Court's decision. Paul Mageean of the Committee for the Administration of Justice said he believed the court's ruling would prepare the way for a revision of the inquest system in Northern Ireland, including the compulsion of witnesses who pulled the trigger to attend and the jury's ability to deliver verdicts. To date the deeply flawed inquests, many delayed for many years, have been obstructed by the non-disclosure of facts and reports.

Despite the ruling of the Human Rights Court in Strasbourg the British government confirmed that they did not propose to carry out further investigation into the circumstances of the McKerr case. The McKerr family have been forced to take further proceedings, first in the High Court and then in the Court of Appeal in Belfast to force the British government and the Secretary of State to live up to their international obligations and their obligations under the Human Rights Act. The British government continued to defend their position and appealed to the House of Lords, arguing that they should not be obliged to investigate murders, committed by their own security forces, which occurred prior to October 2000, the date the Human Rights Act (enacted 1998) came into effect. On 11 March 2004 the House of Lords decided in favour of the government. The main issue remains – apart from the Saville inquiry there has been no proper public hearing into deaths involving the security forces. The Stalker/Sampson Report itself has not been made public.

On 7 January 2003 the family of Patrick Finucane welcomed the judgement of the European Court of Human Rights in Strasbourg, the first judicial determination on the murder of Patrick Finucane. The court had the benefit of all relevant material on the case since it was submitted in 1995, including the recent report by Sir John Stevens, Commissioner of the London Metropolitan Police. The claims by the family and many others worldwide that the RUC and British Army colluded in his murder have now been judged so serious that the court ruled that the United Kingdom government violated Article 2 of the Convention, the right to life, in not responding to them adequately or at all. The European Court was persuaded that the actions of the British State 'failed to provide a prompt and effective investigation into the allegations of collusion by security personnel'.

Amnesty International, British Irish Rights Watch and the Committee on the Administration of Justice welcomed the ruling. The court found that Patrick Finucane's right to life, which is protected under Article 2 of the European Convention on Human Rights, had been violated in a number of ways:

The RUC, who were suspected of issuing threats against Patrick Finucane, were not sufficiently independent to conduct an effective investigation into the murder. The court concluded that there were 'serious doubts as to the thoroughness or effectiveness with which the possibility of collusion was pursued'. The court observed that, 'as later events were to show, however, there were indications that informers working for Special Branch or the security forces knew about, or assisted in, the attack on Patrick Finucane'.

The inquest, which had refused to accept evidence of threats made against Mr Finucane, 'failed to address serious and legitimate concerns of the family and the public and cannot be regarded as providing an effective investigation into the incident or a means of identifying or leading to the prosecution of those responsible'.

The court criticised the DPP for failing to give reasons for the many decisions taken in relation to cases touching on the murder. The court noted that where the police investigation is itself open to doubts about its independence, 'it is of increased importance that the officer who decides whether or not to prosecute also gives an appearance of independence in his decision-making'. They found, 'Notwithstanding the suspicions of collusion however, no reasons were forthcoming at the time for the various decisions not to prosecute and no information was made available either to the applicant or the public which might provide re-assurance that the rule of law had been respected. This cannot be regarded as compatible with the requirements of Article 2 ...'

While the first and second Stevens Reports apparently did not focus on the Finucane case, in any event the reports were never made public and the Finucane family were never informed of their findings, 'the necessary elements of public scrutiny and accessibility of the family are therefore missing'. The Stevens 3 investigation, coming some ten years after the murder, 'cannot comply with the requirement that effective investigations be commenced promptly and conducted with due expedition; it is also not apparent to what extent, if any, the final report will be made public, though a summary overview has recently been published'. The European Court of Human Rights concluded, 'The court finds that the proceedings for investigating the death of Patrick Finucane failed to provide a prompt and effective investigation into the allegations of collusion by security personnel. There has constantly been a failure to comply with procedural obligation imposed by Article 2 of the Convention and there has been, in this respect, a violation of that provision'.

The human rights groups, Amnesty International, British Irish Rights Watch and the Committee for the Administration of Justice, called on the British government to take immediate action to give effect to the judgement of the court. They called on the government: to publish the reports of Stevens 1, 2 and 3; to ensure that the DPP gives full reasons for the many controversial decisions that have been made in relation to the Finucane case, and, most important of all, to immediately establish an independent, international public inquiry with full judicial powers of discovery and subpoena. As the European Court itself notes, international standards suggest that 'in cases where government involvement is suspected, an objective and impartial investigation may not be possible unless a special commission of inquiry is established'.

Speaking on behalf of the family, following the ruling, Michael Finucane, eldest son of Patrick Finucane, Dublin, said, 'My family have never been afraid to put our case forward to be tested. Now, we have a judgement from the highest court in Europe that his right to life was violated. The UK have been found wanting because they did not properly protect his life nor investigate his death. It is easy to see why they didn't want to investigate this murder: they were the instigators and facilitators of it'. He called for a full independent judicial public inquiry.

Appendix II

Interim Report on the Report of the Independent Commission of Inquiry into the Dublin and Monaghan Bombings

Extra and corrective material on the Dublin and Monaghan bombings and the shooting of John Francis Green is to be found in the *Interim Report on the Report of the Independent Commission of Inquiry into the Dublin and Monaghan Bombings.*

On 19 December 1999, the Taoiseach Bertie Ahern, TD, announced the appointment of Mr Justice Liam Hamilton to head the inquiry. Justice Henry Barron succeeded him. The terms of reference were:

> To undertake a thorough examination, involving fact finding and assessment, of all aspects of the Dublin/Monaghan bombings and their sequel, including
> – the facts, circumstances, causes and perpetrators of the bombings;
> – the nature, adequacy and extent of the garda investigation, including the co-operation with and from the relevant authorities in Northern Ireland and the handling of evidence, including the scientific analyses of forensic evidence;
> – the reasons why no prosecution took place, including whether and if so, by whom and to what extent the investigations were impeded; and
> – the issues raised by the *Hidden Hand* TV documentary broadcast in 1993.

The inquiry had largely come about through the persistent campaign of Justice for the Forgotten and their legal team. It was a thorough investigation considering the limitations it had to work under. Justice for the Forgotten will be able to further build up their campaign for truth and justice and will pursue its call for a full public independent inquiry. Due to a parsimonious attitude and the inadequacy of material supplied from the British authorities the Inquiry had to thoroughly inquire into the background of former members of the British security forces and analyse and assess their allegations. Two of these are already featured in *The SAS in Ireland,* namely former British Army Senior Information Officer Colin Wallace and former British Army Captain Fred Holroyd. Since the book was published in 1990 another informant has come to the fore, John Weir a former RUC Sergeant. Weir had been imprisoned for his part in the murder of William Strathearn on 19 April 1977. The report states:

> He claims to have been part of a group of policemen, UDR officers and loyalist extremists who carried out a series of attacks in the mid-1970s. He says many of their operations were planned and prepared at a farm owned by RUC reserve officer James Mitchell at Glenanne, Co. Armagh. He claims that both Mitchell and UVF member Stewart Young confessed their own involvement in the Dublin and Monaghan bombings to him, and gave him the names of a number of others who they said were also involved.

Weir's information fills in part of a wide background of sectarian murder and collusion in the mid-1970s and much of it refers to contexts and killings already mentioned in *The SAS in Ireland*. Weir was born and educated in Co. Monaghan. He joined the RUC in March 1970 and on 1 August 1973 was transferred to a Special Patrol Group (SPG) for an area roughly covered by Co. Armagh. Here are some of his allegations as stated in the report:

> Most of Weir's allegations stem from his involvement with the group of RUC Special Patrol Group officers who he says were collaborating with well-known loyalist paramilitaries from the Portadown area in acts of sectarian violence.
>
> Sometime between January 1975 and September 1976, while he was stationed in Castlereagh, Weir was visited by two of his former colleagues in the Armagh SPG – Gary Armstrong and Ian Mitchell. They said that a group of policemen had decided that the time had come to take direct action against not merely known republicans or IRA activists but against the Catholic population in general; that the only way to stop the IRA murder campaign was to attack the Catholic community itself so that it would put pressure on the IRA to call off its campaign. Weir agreed to join the group in its activities aimed at the Catholic community. Although senior members of the RUC were not involved, and did not sanction their activities, Weir says they were aware of what this group was doing, but took no steps to stop or discourage their actions. This acquiescence, it is said, amounted to approval and unofficial sanctioning of their activities.
>
> A few days later, there was a meeting of SPG officers in Armstrong's house. Armstrong and another officer named Laurence McClure explained that the group had connections with UVF members through a farm at Glenanne, near Markethill. Together they had already carried out a number of sectarian attacks on both sides of the border. The Glenanne farm was the place where most of these attacks were planned, and where explosives, weapons and ammunition were stored and prepared. The farm owner, James Mitchell (who was a member of the RUC Reserve) was fully involved in this.
>
> Weir said he was given details of these activities by a few of the RUC officers, 'so that I would have a proper understanding of the character of the organisation I was joining'. Some of these stories were later confirmed by UVF members of the group and by the farm owner. The Dublin and Monaghan bombings were among the atrocities for which they claimed to have been responsible. Weir claims that members of the gang (often but not always including RUC officers) were involved in the following sectarian attacks:
>
> 1. The Dublin and Monaghan bombings, 17 May 1974.
> 2. A gun and bomb attack on two pubs in Crossmaglen on November 1974.
> 3. The murder of a well-known PIRA member John Francis Green near Castleblayney on 10 January 1975.
> 4. The murder of John Farmer and Colm McCartney, at Tullyvallen, 24 August 1975.
> 5. A gun and bomb attack on Donnelly's Bar, Silverbridge, 19 December 1975.
> 6. A car bomb at Kay's Tavern, Dundalk on the same date.
> 7. The murder of three members of the Reavey family at Whitecross, 4 January 1976.
> 8. The shooting of three members of the O'Dowd family at Ballyduggan on the same night.

9. A car bomb at Castleblayney in March 1976.

10. A bomb attack on Tully's Bar, Beleek, Co. Armagh in May 1976.

11. A bomb and gun attack on the Rock Bar, near Keady, 5 June 1976.

12. The planning of a bomb attack on a pub in Clontibret, Co. Monaghan, 15 August 1976.

13. A bomb attack at the Step Inn, Keady, 16 August 1976.

14. The murder of RUC Sergeant Joseph Campbell at Cushendall, 25 February 1977.

15. The murder of William Strathearn, 18 (r.19) April 1977.

For each of these attacks, he named the persons whom he believed to have carried them out. Weir claims his only involvement was in the planning of the Beleek and Clontibret attacks, and in the murder of William Strathearn.

He says that these attacks were not sanctioned or claimed by the UVF or UDA. Instead, the Glenanne group used cover names such as the Protestant Action Force, the Red Hand Commandos or the Red Hand Brigade.

Weir stated that whenever bombs were used by the group, the explosives for them were supplied by a named UDR officer. Weir claims to have seen him bringing explosives to the Glenanne farm on a number of occasions. He told journalist Liam Clarke: '[He] would have brought the explosives. Where did [he] get them from? Nobody asked that. Nobody wanted to know where he was getting such large amounts of explosives … He had gelignite, fertiliser, detonators, the whole lot. Fertiliser-based explosive with a gelignite detonator'.

Weir also claimed to have seen James Mitchell mixing homemade ANFO (Ammonium Nitrate and Fuel Oil) explosive in the farmyard on one occasion.

On Colin Wallace's evidence the report says:

Based on his knowledge and experience, Wallace claims that the security forces in Northern Ireland knew the names of those most likely responsible for the bombings within days of the attacks taking place. He believed then and now that some of those involved had links with either the RUC Special Branch, military intelligence or MI5. Finally, he believes there are reasons for suggesting that elements of the security forces acted to discourage a proper investigation into the bombings, in order to protect certain loyalist extremists.

Fred Holroyd:

He has claimed to have received reliable information during his period in Northern Ireland concerning the perpetrators of the Dublin and Monaghan bombings. He has also made other allegations that are important to the Inquiry because they have been frequently used to support the theory that the bombings were part of a pattern of collusion between elements of the security forces in Northern Ireland and loyalist paramilitaries … A number of Holroyd's allegations are not completely true, but they relate to events that did happen. Insofar as they raise serious questions concerning the behaviour of the security forces, North and South during the 1970s, they are of relevance to the work of the Inquiry, and have contributed to the Inquiry's view on the possibility of collusion between elements of the security forces and loyalist paramilitaries.

Among the conclusions of the inquiry it states:

The Dublin and Monaghan bombings were carried out by two groups of loyalist paramilitaries, one based in Belfast and the other in the area around Portadown/Lurgan. Most, though not all of those involved were members of the UVF. It is likely that the bombings were conceived and planned in Belfast, with the mid-Ulster element providing operational assistance.

The bombings were primarily a reaction to the Sunningdale Agreement – in particular to the prospect of a greater role of the Irish government in the administration of Northern Ireland …

The loyalist groups who carried out the bombings in Dublin were capable of doing so without help from any section of the security forces in Northern Ireland, though this does not rule out the involvement of individual RUC, UDR or British Army members. The Monaghan bombing in particular bears all the hallmarks of a standard loyalist operation and required no assistance.

It is likely that the farm of James Mitchell at Glenanne played a significant part in the preparation for the attacks. It is also likely that members of the UDR and RUC either participated in, or were aware of, those preparations …

A number of those suspected for the bombings were reliably said to have had relationships with British Intelligence and/or RUC Special Branch officers. It is reasonable to assume that exchange of information took place. It is therefore possible that the assistance provided to the Garda investigation team by the security forces in Northern Ireland was affected by a reluctance to compromise those relationships, in the interest of securing further information in the future. But any such conclusion would require very cogent evidence. No such evidence is in the possession of the Inquiry. There remains a deep suspicion that the investigation into the bombings was hampered by such factors, but it cannot be put further than that.

The Garda investigation failed to make full use of the information it obtained. Certain lines of inquiry that could have been made [and] pursued further in the jurisdiction were not pursued. There were other matters, including the questioning of suspects, in which the assistance of the RUC should have been requested, but was not.

The State was not equipped to conduct an adequate forensic analysis of the explosions. This was because the importance of preservation, prompt collection and analysis was not appreciated. The effect of this was that potentially vital clues were lost.

There is plain disappointment in the report with the response of the Northern Ireland Office to its request for information. Reading behind the courteous civil service language it is obvious that there was a cover-up:

Correspondence with the Northern Ireland Office undoubtedly produced some useful information but its value was reduced by the reluctance to make original documents available and the refusal to supply other information on security grounds. While the inquiry fully understands the position taken by the British government on these matters, it must be said that the scope of this report is limited as a result.

The information came in the form of a ten-page letter from the Secretary of State Dr John Reid dated 26 February 2002 and a further six pages append-

ed to the letter giving details regarding the structure and control of intelligence gathering in Northern Ireland during the relevant period. No copies of
any original documents were forthcoming!

Disappointment is obvious too concerning missing files in the Republic:

> Firstly, some relevant security files that should have been retained at Garda
> Headquarters were missing. The Inquiry was furnished with the Monaghan se-
> curity file, but not with that for Dublin. In relation to loyalist paramilitary organ-
> isations, the general file started in 1966 contains no information prior to the early
> 1980s. While there are annual files relating to the UVF/UDA, none are available
> for the years 1974 and 1975. The Special Detective Unit kept files on these bod-
> ies, and those have been made available to the Inquiry. But the files kept by
> Security and Intelligence (C3) at Garda Headquarters would have included more
> than just the files kept by the Security and Intelligence (C3) division, of which
> SDU was merely a part. These have not been seen by the Inquiry. Secondly, annu-
> al files relating to payments were not available. Of particular interest to the In-
> quiry were payments made to confidential sources, but full information on this
> matter no longer exists.

Regarding information from the Irish government it states:

> Government departments have provided all the relevant files in their possession
> and have answered all requests for follow-up information, with one exception:
> the Department of Justice, Equality and Law reform has found that files are miss-
> ing from its archives. A copy of the investigation report into the Monaghan
> bombing is the only contemporary document relating to the Dublin and Monag-
> han bombings of 17 May 1974. It is not only the Dublin investigation report that
> is missing, but also what must have been a considerable amount of security in-
> formation. Extensive files have been provided relating to matters arising after the
> 'Hidden Hand' programme in 1993. This emphasises the extent of the documen-
> tation which is no longer available.

Amongst the information supplied by the PSNI to the inquiry were the files
on the two guns used in the murder of John Francis Green on 10 January
1975. The Inquiry gives a lengthy report on the murder of Green.

The Shooting of John Francis Green

The inquiry analyses the evidence regarding the claim by Captain Holroyd
that Captain Robert Nairac had killed Green:

> In his statement to the Essex police dated 21 July 1982, Holroyd set out the his-
> tory of his attempts to have his removal from Northern Ireland reviewed. He
> then set out his allegations, and concluded by saying: 'There are also more sen-
> sitive allegations I would be prepared to make in the event of no action being
> taken in this case'.
>
> Speaking to the RUC in September 1982, he said that these allegations con-

cerned an illegal SAS operation in the Republic, and finally admitted that they referred to the killing of Green.

The picture derived from this is of a man increasingly frustrated with the failure of the British Authorities to take his claims seriously; who saw the threat to reveal a cross-border SAS assassination as perhaps his only remaining weapon in the fight to secure a proper review of his own case. His allegation regarding Nairac must be read with that in mind.

The evidence before the Inquiry that the polaroid photograph taken by the killers after the murder was actually taken by a Garda officer on the following morning seriously undermines the evidence that Nairac himself had been involved in the shooting. However, it is still possible that, having obtained the photograph from the RUC, Nairac used it to persuade Holroyd that he had killed Green. This, if true, raises the question as to why a British Army officer would attempt to claim responsibility for an illegal, cross-border assassination. If one assumes he was not in fact involved, the only answer that presents itself is that he must have considered it desirable to have it thought by other members of the security forces that he was involved. This could only be the case if such illegal acts were already being tolerated or encouraged by an element within the security forces.

According to RUC officers with whom the Inquiry has spoken, the general view amongst the security forces in Northern Ireland within weeks of the shooting was that members of the UVF were responsible for it.

Former RUC Sergeant John Weir is also of the view that members of the UVF killed Green. However, he told journalist Liam Clarke of information received from a named UVF source which said that Nairac had been with the killers on the operation:

'The men who did that shooting were Robert McConnell, Robin Jackson and I would be almost certain, Harris Boyle who was killed in the Miami attack. What I am absolutely certain of is that Robert McConnell, Robert McConnell knew that area really, really well. Robin Jackson was with him. I was later told that Nairac was with them. I was told by … a UVF man, he was very close to Jackson and operated with him. Jackson told [him] that Nairac was with them'.

Even if this information was not true, there remains the possibility that Nairac's unit might have assisted Green's killers with surveillance, but there is no evidence for this other than Holroyd's assertion that Four Field Survey Troop had Green under surveillance from the time he first gave Nairac a photograph of him. The presence of a British Army vehicle in the area on a number of days before and after the shooting could be significant in this regard; but Garda inquiries have failed to link that vehicle directly with either the Green murder or with Nairac's unit, Four Field Survey Troop.

The inquiry gives details of the forensic analysis of the two guns used in the murder of Green. It emphasises the involvement of members of the UDR with the UVF:

The two firearms used in the Green murder were subsequently found. On 18 May 1978, police searched the home of Edward Sinclair, a suspected UVF member from Dungannon. They uncovered a Luger pistol, serial number 4, and also a second pistol along with other illegal material including explosive substances.

The Luger, with four rounds of ammunition and silencer, was found in the milking parlour. On 3 August 1979 a number of firearms were found at Portadown which included a Star pistol, serial number 344164. The owner of the farm upon which the weapons were found was a part-time UDR member. He received a seven year sentence for possession of the weapons and was also given a concurrent four year sentence for membership of the UVF.

The finding of the two guns enabled a fuller ballistic investigation to take place. Reports were furnished by Victor Leslie Beavis, a Forensic Scientist employed at the Northern Ireland Forensic Science Laboratory, and from D/Garda Niland, now a Detective Sergeant.

From the report of Victor Beavis it appears that both guns were test fired and that spent bullets and cartridge cases were retained in the possession of the Northern Ireland Forensic [Science] Laboratory. The firearms themselves were returned to the RUC for ultimate disposal.

On 15 September 1983, Beavis received the Star pistol from the RUC for re-examination. Again, there were test firings and the spent cartridge cases and bullets together with the test five cases and bullets collected in 1979, were compared microscopically with the material recovered from the incidents listed in his report. He was satisfied that the cartridge cases in the following incidents were discharged from the Star pistol. The incidents were:

1. the attempted murder of J. Turley near Lurgan on 10 March 1973;
2. a shooting incident at Loughgall, near Portadown on 24 March 1973;
3. the murder of John Francis Green on 10 January 1975; and
4. the murder of Mrs D. Trainor and attempted murder of Mr M. Trainor in Portadown on 1 April 1975.

He was also satisfied that the bullets recovered from the following incidents were fired from the Star pistol:

1. the murder of Green and
2. the murder of Mrs D. Trainor and attempted murder of Mr M. Trainor.

The markings on other bullets – those relating to the attempted murder of J. Turley and the Loughgall incident – indicated that although they were all fired from a single firearm, they had not been fired from the same barrel as the bullets in the other two incidents. He concluded that since the cartridge cases from all four incidents indicated a single firearm and that the bullets from the 1973 incidents are different from later incidents, this would indicate that the barrel had been altered or replaced.

He then examined a number of 9 mm Parabellum cartridge cases taken from the Green murder and the Miami Showband attack of 31 July 1975. He said the markings on them were 'indistinct', but continued: 'Nevertheless, there are sufficient details to enable me to say that they were discharged in the Luger pistol Serial No. 4'.

However, he refrained from making a 'definite conclusion' owing to the availability of only one test bullet from the Luger pistol. The pistol had been destroyed by the RUC on 28 August 1978.

As part of the Garda investigations into former British Army Captain Fred Holroyd's allegations in 1983/84, D/Sgt Niland prepared a further report. It includes a more detailed history of the weapons and the relevant incidents than was given in Beavis' Report. He noted that the Star pistol was licensed to a member of the UDR stationed at Portadown. It had been reported stolen from him on 2nd March 1973 at 11 o'clock in the evening while walking at Loughgall Road,

Portadown. The Luger pistol was not recorded as having been licensed in Northern Ireland.

D/Sgt Niland's report directly linked the Luger pistol, not only to the murder of John Francis Green but also to the Miami Showband killings. He referred to the recovery of bullets and cartridge cases from the respective crime scenes and stated: 'Subsequent ballistic comparison showed that they were discharged from and fired in the Luger pistol No.4'.

As we have seen, Mr Beavis was more cautious in his conclusions owing to the fact that only one test fired bullet from the Luger was available to him. While he was prepared to say that cartridges found at both the Miami and Green incidents were discharged from the Luger, he felt unable to make a definite conclusion concerning the bullets. He noted a similarity of rifling characteristics on the bullets recovered at the Green murder, but made no comment as to those found at the scene of the Miami Showband attack.

These two ballistics reports were sent by C/Supt Daniel Murphy to the Assistant Commissioner, C Branch, by letter dated 24th February, 1984. In the above letter, C/Supt Murphy commented: 'The position regarding this investigation is unsatisfactory and the destruction of such a very important exhibit as the Luger pistol is difficult to comprehend'.

In the same letter he also indicated that he had received information in November 1983 from RUC Inspector Mack that the owner of the Star pistol had been interviewed with no positive result. Inspector Mack also told him that he had further enquiries to make and hoped to have a complete investigation file ready at Christmas when he would send a copy to Garda Headquarters. The file, in so far as it related to the murder of John Francis Green, was sent to the Garda Síochána on 18 May 1984.

Note: One of the 'prime suspects' in the Dublin–Monaghan bombings, David Alexander Mulholland, formerly of Portadown and a senior member of the UVF, died in England on 10 December 2003 just hours after the publication of the Barron Report.

On 9 March 2004 Greg O'Neill, solicitor for the Justice for the Forgotten Group representing the relatives of those killed in the 1974 Dublin and Monaghan bombings, told a sub-committee of the Joint Oireachtas Committee on Justice set up subsequent to the Barron Report, that he would not rule out prosecutions for the atrocities. He said, 'There is still a moral and criminal complicity in this crime. I predict that because of garda action or rather, inaction, and mismanagement we can make the assumption that it is unlikely, but I will not rule it out'. He said that the garda investigation at the time had been a 'shambles' and issues of British MI5 and MI6 collusion could not be used as a charter for the garda and the state to allow those involved to escape punishment. Counsel for Justice for the Forgotten, Mr Cormac Ó Dúlacháin, said the families were seeking, and the atrocity warranted, a full public tribunal of inquiry.

The Joint Oireachtas Committee on Justice concluded that there was a high probability of collusion by British security forces with the UVF bombers and recommended that the Irish government should therefore insist on a public inquiry in Britain or Northern Ireland. It said that the government should consider instituting proceedings in the European Court of Human Rights in Strasbourg if the British government failed to carry out an appropriate investigation. It concluded that private investigation by a judge should precede such an inquiry; commissions should be set up to examine why the garda investigation into the attacks was wound down in 1974 and to examine the loss of a Garda security file on the bombings. The committee also wanted its findings to be endorsed by the Dáil and the British parliament.

The Dublin and Monaghan bombings inquest is to open on 27 April 2004. The victims and victims' relatives of the bombings are set to press for a full public inquiry into the atrocities.

Desmond Grew
† 9-10-90

Martin McCaughey
† 9-10-90

Tony Doris
† 3-6-91

Lawrence McNally
† 3-6-91

Pete Ryan
† 3-6-91

Barry O'Donnell
† 16-2-92

Peter Clancy
† 16-2-92

Seán O'Farrell
† 16-2-92

Patrick Vincent
† 16-2-92

Chronology

1941

July SAS founded by Captain David Stirling

1945

October SAS regiments disbanded

1947

Formation of 21 SAS (Artists), a territorial unit

1950

Malayan Scouts formed; from these emerged 22 SAS, a regular regiment

1959

23 SAS, a territorial unit, formed

1969

SAS sent to Northern Ireland

1970

3–5 July Falls Road Curfew

SAS soldiers attached to 39th Brigade at Lisburn formed the core of intelligence officers and helped to organise and operate the Military Reconnaissance Force (MRF) (sometimes called the Military Reaction Force)

1971

MI6 in Northern Ireland

9 August Internment

1971–72

Torture and ill-treatment of detainees in the Palace barracks, Holywood, Girdwood Park barracks, Belfast and Ballykelly barracks

1972

6 February David Seaman found shot dead in South Armagh

March Amnesty International Report into Interrogation Methods in Northern Ireland

15 April Conway brothers, Belfast, shot and wounded by plain clothes soldiers

12 May Patrick McVeigh, Belfast, shot dead by plain clothes soldiers

29 May Official IRA ceasefire

14 June Punishment shooting of two SAS soldiers by Official and Provisional IRA in Belfast

22 June Four men shot and wounded by MRF at Glen Road bus terminal, Belfast; Captain James Alistair McGregor and Sergeant Clive Graham charged and acquitted

29 August British Army undercover soldiers involved in incident in Bawnmore estate, Belfast

26 September Daniel Rooney, Belfast, shot dead by plain clothes soldiers

2 October Four Square Laundry van ambushed by IRA

19 October Kenneth Littlejohn arrested in London

1973

Late April Trooper Louis Hammond shot and wounded in Belfast

14 September UDA leader Tommy Herron assassinated by pseudo-gang

15 October Albert Walker Baker, UDA, sentenced to life imprisonment

1974

18 March Robert Fisk, in *The Times*, reported the presence of SAS in Northern Ireland

20 March Plain clothes soldiers Corporal Michael Francis Herbert and Corporal Michael John Cotton shot dead by RUC at Mowhan, Co. Armagh

1 April Jim Hanna, UVF and SAS collaborator, shot dead in Belfast

17 April Undercover soldier Captain Anthony Stephen Pollen shot dead by Provisional IRA in Derry

14 May Ulster Workers' Council strike

17 May UDA bomb attacks killed 28 people and injured 100 in Dublin, and killed 5 people in Monaghan

2 June Paul Tinnelly shot dead in Rostrevor by Official IRA

20 July Ex-British soldier Brian Shaw shot dead by Provisional IRA in Belfast

5 October Eugene McQuaid killed by doctored bombs at Killeen, near Newry

23 December Provisional IRA ceasefire

1975

10 January IRA commander John Francis Green assassinated at Mullyash, near Castleblayney, Co. Monaghan

4 April British Army intelligence officer killed in car accident near Trillick, Co. Tyrone

18 April Plain clothes soldier shot and wounded by IRA in Belfast

8 July Undercover soldier in incident on Falls Road, Belfast

31 July Three members of the Miami Showband were shot dead by the UVF after two UVF men Harris Boyle and Wesley Somerville were blown up by their own bomb while placing it in the band's van

14 August Norman 'Mooch' Kerr, friend of Harris Boyle, shot dead by IRA in Armagh

1976

4 January In loyalist attacks two men of the Reavey family (a third died later), Whitecross, South Armagh, and three members of the O'Dowd family, Gilford, Co. Down, were shot dead

5 January Ten Protestant workers were shot dead and one seriously injured by armed men at Kingsmills, Co. Armagh

7 January Prime Minister Harold Wilson publicly announced the sending of the SAS to South Armagh

17 January Seamus O'Brien shot dead by IRA in Belfast

22 January Niall O'Neill shot dead in Belfast

12 March Seán McKenna, IRA, kidnapped by SAS in Irish Republic and brought across the border into Northern Ireland

19 March Undercover soldiers Sergeant M.G. Peacock and Corporal Douglas Whitfield killed in a car crash near Newry

4 April Mrs Margaret Gamble stabbed to death in Belfast

15 April IRA captain, Peter Cleary, taken prisoner and shot dead by SAS near Forkhill, South Armagh

1 May Séamus Ludlow shot dead near Dundalk, Co. Louth

5 May Eight SAS soldiers arrested by garda in the Irish Republic

6 July Vincent Hetherington shot dead by IRA

12 July Kevin Byrne and Patrick Mooney abducted from the Irish Republic to Northern Ireland by the SAS

21 July Christopher Ewart-Biggs, the British ambassador to Ireland, killed by

IRA explosion

2 December Prime Minister James Callaghan extended SAS patrols throughout Northern Ireland

1977

16 January IRA volunteer Seamus Harvey shot dead by SAS near Crossmaglen

21 January Michael McHugh shot dead near Castlederg, Co. Tyrone, by UDA gang with British Army link

March Certification that a full squadron of SAS was engaged in Northern Ireland

9 April Myles McGrogan shot dead by IRA

15 May Captain Robert Nairac shot dead by IRA

November Major-General Timothy Creasey appointed commanding officer in Northern Ireland

25 November Sergeant Hubert Shingleston, undercover soldier, accidentally shot dead near Lurgan

12 December Colm McNutt, INLA, shot dead by undercover soldier in Derry

14 December Undercover soldier Lance Corporal Paul Harman shot dead by IRA in Belfast

1978

17 February Former SAS soldier Lt Col Iain Gordon-Lloyd killed when his helicopter was shot down by the IRA in South Armagh

26 February IRA volunteer Paul Duffy shot dead by SAS near Ardboe, Co. Tyrone

16 March Desmond Mackin and Robert Gamble shot and wounded by SAS soldiers in Belfast

Engagement between SAS and IRA near Maghera, Co. Derry, in which SAS soldier Corporal David Jones was killed and Lance Corporal Kevin Smyth and IRA volunteer Francis Hughes were wounded

7 June Staff Sergeant D. J. Naden SAS killed in road accident at Shanalongford Bridge, Co. Derry

10 June IRA volunteer Denis Heaney shot dead by SAS in Derry

20 June IRA volunteers, Jim Mulvenna, Denis Brown, William Mailey and passer-by William James Hanna ambushed and shot dead by SAS and RUC

11 July John Boyle shot dead by SAS soldiers in Dunloy, Co. Antrim

11 August Undercover soldier Lance Corporal Alan David Swift shot dead by IRA in Derry

31 August Undercover soldiers Sergeant John Roeser and Corporal Michael Bloor killed in car accident near Nutt's Corner, Co. Antrim

28 September Two youths, Anthony Fisher and Samuel McHugh killed, and Peter Lavery injured, by hit and run undercover soldier in Belfast

30 September James Taylor shot dead by SAS near Coagh, Co. Tyrone

5 October Undercover soldier shot and wounded by IRA in Dungannon

24 October William Smyth shot dead in mysterious circumstances in Belfast

24 November Patrick Duffy, IRA Auxiliary, shot dead by SAS in Derry

1979

24 January Brief gun battle between IRA and SAS near Maghera

12 March Police Surgeon Dr Robert Irwin interviewed on *Weekend World*, London Weekend television on ill-treatment of detainees at Castlereagh Interrogation Centre

30 March Airey Neave, MP assassinated by INLA

6 May Undercover soldier Sergeant Robert Maughan and Detective Constable Norman Prue RUC shot dead by IRA at Lisnaskea

September Humphrey Atkins, MP, Secretary of State, emphasised the deployment of SAS-type specialist forces

October Sir Maurice Oldfield appointed co-ordinator of security and intelligence in Northern Ireland

'Operation Ranc' to avenge the death of Airey Neave, MP, former Conservative opposition speaker on Northern Ireland who had been assassinated by INLA

8 October Undercover soldier Private Paul Anthony Wright shot dead by IRA in Belfast

1980

2 May Captain Herbert Richard Westmacott, SAS, shot dead by IRA in Belfast

4 June John Turnly, Irish Independence Party member, shot dead by UDA in Carnlough, Co. Antrim – 'Operation Ranc'

Robert McConnell, convicted for the murder, named two SAS soldiers he teamed with

26 June Mrs Miriam Daly, lecturer in Queen's University, Belfast, shot dead by UDA – 'Operation Ranc'

15 October Ronnie Bunting, INLA and Noel Lyttle, IRSP, shot dead by UDA – 'Operation Ranc'

19 October SAS terror raid on Twinbrook estate, Belfast

1981

16 January Attempted assassination of Bernadette McAliskey and her husband Michael near Coalisland by the UDA – 'Operation Ranc'

28 May IRA volunteers Charles Maguire and George McBrearty shot dead by SAS

1982

1 April Undercover soldiers Sergeant Michael Burbridge and Corporal Michael Ward shot dead by IRA in Derry

11 November IRA volunteers Eugene Toman, Seán Burns and Gervaise McKerr shot dead by SAS trained HQSMU, RUC, in Craigavon

24 November Michael Tighe shot dead and Martin McAuley wounded by HQSMU near Lurgan

12 December Séamus Grew and Roddy Carroll, INLA, shot dead by HQSMU in Armagh

1983

2 February Neil McMonagle, INLA, shot dead by SAS in Derry

8 February Corporal Tommy Palmer, SAS, killed in car crash near Lurgan

10 April Undercover soldier shot and wounded by IRA in Derry

4 December IRA volunteers Brian Campbell and Colm McGirr shot dead by SAS near Coalisland

1984

21 February Sergeant Paul Oram, SAS, shot dead by IRA and IRA volunteers Henry Hogan and Declan Martin shot dead by SAS in Dunloy.

13 July IRA volunteer William Price shot dead by SAS near Ardboe

12 October Four people killed and many injured in IRA explosion at Grand Hotel, Brighton during Conservative party annual conference

19 October Frederick Jackson shot dead by SAS near Portadown

2 December IRA volunteer Antoin Mac Giolla Bríde shot dead by SAS and Lance Corporal Alastair Slater shot dead by IRA in incident in Co. Fermanagh

IRA volunteer Kieran Fleming drowned

6 December IRA volunteers Daniel Doherty and William Fleming shot dead by SAS in Derry

1985

23 February IRA volunteers Michael and David Devine and Charles Breslin shot dead by SAS in Strabane

1986

18 February Francis Bradley shot dead by SAS near Toomebridge

26 April IRA volunteers Seamus McElwain shot dead and volunteer Seán Lynch wounded by SAS near Roslea, Co. Fermanagh

1987

25 April Lord Chief Justice Sir Maurice Gibson and his wife Cecily killed by IRA bomb at Killeen near Newry

8 May Anthony Hughes, a passer-by, and 8 IRA volunteers – Patrick Kelly, James Lynagh, Declan Arthurs, Seamus Donnelly, Anthony Gormley, Eugene Kelly, Pádraig McKearney and Gerard O'Callaghan – shot dead by SAS at Loughgall, Co. Armagh

1988

6 March IRA volunteers Mairéad Farrell, Daniel McCann and Seán Savage shot dead by SAS in Gibraltar

16 March Kevin Brady, John Murray and Thomas McErlean shot dead by UDA in Milltown cemetery, Belfast

19 March Corporal Robert Howes and Corporal Derek Wood shot dead by republicans in Belfast.

15 June Six British soldiers killed in IRA booby trap in Lisburn

1 July Ken Stronge shot dead by SAS in Belfast

20 August Eight British soldiers killed on Ballygawley–Omagh Road, Co. Tyrone, in IRA bomb attack

30 August IRA volunteers Gerard and Martin Harte and Brian Mullin shot dead by SAS at Drumnakilly, near Omagh, Co. Tyrone

1989

12 February Pat Finucane, solicitor, shot dead in Belfast

14 February John Joe Davey, Sinn Féin councillor, shot dead at Gulladuff, Co. Derry

4 April Gerard Casey, IRA, shot dead at Rasharkin, Co. Antrim

25 August Loughlin Maginn shot dead at Rathfriland, Co. Down.

2 September Brian Robinson, UVF, shot dead by British undercover soldiers in Belfast

22 September Ten Royal Marines killed by IRA bomb, Deal, Kent

29 November Liam Ryan and Michael Devlin shot dead at Ardboe, Co. Tyrone

13 December Two British soldiers killed at Derryard, Co. Tyrone

1990

13 January Peter John Thompson, Edward Paul Hale, John Joseph McNeill shot dead by soldiers from 14th Intelligence Company in Belfast

20 January Brian Nelson, army undercover agent, arrested at request of Stevens inquiry

17 May Summary of Stevens Report said there had been collusion between security forces and loyalist paramilitaries

18 September Air Chief Marshal Sir Peter Terry shot and wounded in an IRA attack. As Governor of Gibraltar he had authorised the use of the SAS that led to the shooting dead of three IRA volunteers in 1988

9 October IRA volunteers Desmond Grew and Martin McCaughey shot dead by SAS at Lislasley, near Loughgall, Co. Armagh

9 November Secretary of State Peter Brooke's declaration that Britain has no 'strategic or economic interest' in Northern Ireland and would accept the unification of Ireland on consent

1991

14 March 'Birmingham Six' freed

3 June IRA volunteers Tony Doris, Lawrence McNally and Pete Ryan shot dead by SAS at Coagh, Co. Tyrone

26 June The Maguire Seven cleared by Court of Appeal in London

1992

22 January Army agent Brian Nelson sentenced to ten years' imprisonment

16 February IRA volunteers Kevin Barry O'Donnell, Seán O'Farrell, Peter Clancy and Patrick Vincent shot dead by SAS at Clonoe, Co. Tyrone

5 May Reopening of inquest into the deaths of Seán Burns, Gervaise McKerr and Eugene Toman

4 June Conviction of Judith Ward quashed

1 July Amalgamation of Ulster Defence Regiment and Royal Irish Rangers into Royal Irish Regiment

10 August After a long history of committing hundreds of sectarian murders UDA officially declared illegal from midnight

1993

15 July UVF admitted carrying out the Dublin and Monaghan bombings of May 1974

15 December The Downing Street Declaration

1994

8 May Roseanne Mallon, 76 years of age, shot dead by UVF. Surveillance cameras discovered near the house on 27 July

2 June Twenty-five senior security personnel in Northern Ireland killed in Mull of Kintyre helicopter crash

31 August IRA announced ceasefire as of midnight

13 October Combined Loyalist Military Command announced ceasefire as of midnight

28 October Opening of Forum for Peace and Reconciliation in Dublin

10 November Frank Kerr shot dead by IRA. The IRA later said it 'was not sanctioned by IRA leadership'

1995

22 February Documents *Frameworks for the Future* published

27 September The European Court of Human Rights in Strasbourg ruled that the shooting of three unarmed IRA volunteers in Gibraltar in March 1988 breached the Human Rights Convention. The British government was ordered to pay the legal costs of the case, but no damages were awarded. On 24 December the British government paid £38,700 to cover the legal costs of the families of the three IRA volunteers

30 November Visit of Bill Clinton, President of the United States of America, to Northern Ireland

1996

9 February IRA ended its ceasefire. Explosion at Canary Wharf Tower, London

7 June Detective Garda Jerry McCabe shot dead by IRA

23 September IRA volunteer Diarmuid O'Neill shot dead by police in controversial circumstances in London

1997

12 February Stephen Restorick, the last British soldier to be killed by the IRA before its second ceasefire

8 May Death of Robert Hamill from injuries received on 27 April from a loyalist mob in Portadown. Family has accused RUC of failing to intervene to stop the attack

19 July IRA announced renewal of its ceasefire from midday on 20 July

9 September Sinn Féin signed the Mitchell Principles and joined all-party talks

24 September Launch of the International Commission on Decommissioning headed by John de Chastelain

7 December Launch of 32-County Sovereignty Committee, republicans opposed to the 'peace process'

27 December Billy Wright shot dead by INLA in the Maze Prison

1998

11 April Good Friday Agreement

22 May Referendum on the Good Friday Agreement

25 June Elections to the Assembly

19 July Andrew Kearney, Belfast, died after being beaten and shot by IRA

15 August Twenty-eight people killed and many injured by Real IRA bomb in Omagh; another died from injuries on 5 September

2 September Scots Guards Ian Wright and Mark Fisher, convicted for the murder of Peter McBride, released from prison

8 September Real IRA announced ceasefire

16 October John Hume and David Trimble awarded the Nobel Peace Prize

4 November Scots Guards Ian Wright and Mark Fisher permitted to remain in British Army

1999

25 January Relatives of IRA volunteers killed at Loughgall met Security Minister Adam Ingram

11 February On the tenth anniversary of the murder of solicitor Patrick Finucane a petition signed by more than a thousand legal figures and supported by Amnesty International called for an independent inquiry into his death

15 March Human rights solicitor Rosemary Nelson killed by bomb

18 March John Stevens, Deputy Commissioner of the Metropolitan Police, asked to investigate new collusion claims in the murder of Patrick Finucane

24 March Revealed that Independent Commission on Police Complaints had listed concerns regarding the RUC's investigation of alleged threats against Rosemary Nelson by the RUC

12 April Param Cumaraswamy, special rapporteur of the United Nations, called for an independent inquiry into the murder of Patrick Finucane

17 April Chief Constable Ronnie Flanagan announced a fresh inquiry by John Stevens into the murder of Patrick Finucane

29 July Charles Bennett, Belfast, shot dead by IRA

5 August Victims Commission, Dublin, recommended private inquiry into the Dublin & Monaghan bombings of 1974 and the 1976 murder of Séamus Ludlow in Co. Louth

8 August Declaration by INLA –'War is over'

9 September Release of Patten Report on Policing in Northern Ireland

30 September DPP decided no charge against policemen in case of killing of Robert Hamill

11 October Peter Mandelson replaced Dr Mo Mowlam as Secretary of State, Northern Ireland. Ms Nuala O'Loan appointed Police Ombudsman

1 December Hugh Orde of London Metropolitan Police new head of Stevens investigation into the murder of Patrick Finucane

2 December British-Irish Agreement signed into effect and new Articles 2 & 3 of Irish Constitution ratified

9 December Six human rights organisations called for independent inquiry into murder of Rosemary Nelson

13 December Inaugural meeting of North-South Ministerial Council in Armagh City

2000

1 February Inquest into the 1996 fatal shooting of IRA Volunteer Diarmuid O'Neill in London

11 February Suspension of institutions of Good Friday Agreement

18 February Inquiry into death of Diarmuid O'Neill ruled that he had been 'lawfully killed'

5 March Chief Constable Colin Port reaffirmed his commitment to arrest the murderers of Rosemary Nelson

10 March Article in *The Guardian* regarding role of Major General Robert Forde in 'Bloody Sunday'

15 March Petition signed by 100,000 calling for an independent inquiry into the murder of Rosemary Nelson given to British prime minister

20 March Peace Centre in memory of children Tim Parry & Jonathan Ball, died in IRA explosion in 1993, opened in Warrington, Cheshire

2 April Report in *Sunday Times* of effort of British government to suppress book by 'Martin Ingram' former FRU member

3 April European Court of Human Rights hears four cases alleging British government's failure to uphold the right to life of its citizens

3 May William Stobie, facing charges of involvement in Patrick Finucane's murder, also charged with the 1987 murder of Adam Lambert

4 May Death of Kieran Nugent, first 'on the blanket' prison protester in 1976

30 May After Hillsborough accord, devolved powers restored to Northern Ireland Assembly & Executive

3 June Param Cumaraswamy, UN Special Rapporteur on the Independence and Impartiality of Lawyers and Judges, called for an independent inquiry into the deaths of lawyers Patrick Finucane and Rosemary Nelson

7 June Belfast coroner John Leckey cancelled inquest into death of Robert Hamill because of threats to witnesses' lives. Taoiseach Bertie Ahern called for an independent judicial inquiry into the killing

8 June Visit of President McAleese to Greysteel where seven people were shot dead by UDA on 30 October 1993; an eighth person died later

26 June IRA announced it had opened its arms dumps to inspection. Confirmed by international inspectors

4 September Meeting of Finucane family with Prime Minister Tony Blair

6 September Opening of inquest into Omagh bombing

8 September International Relations Committee US Congress called for full implementation of Patten Report on policing

14 September Irish government raised issue of policing in Northern Ireland in

United Nations

30 September Maze [Long Kesh] prison closed

2 October Human Rights Act 1998 enacted

13 October Joe O'Connor, Belfast, shot dead by IRA

21 November The Police (Northern Ireland) Bill Act cleared in House of Commons. Law at end of month

2001

18 January Meeting of family of Robert Hamill with Prime Minister Tony Blair

24 January Dr John Reid succeeded Peter Mandelson as Secretary of State

5 April UN Rapporteur Param Cumaraswamy submitted reports on police investigations into Patrick Finucane and Rosemary Nelson to UN in Geneva

4 May European Court of Human Rights ruled that human rights were violated in the cases of eleven people killed by the security forces in Northern Ireland – Gervaise McKerr and Pearse Jordan shot dead by RUC, eight IRA volunteers and one civilians shot by the SAS in Loughgall. Inquest opened on death of Charles Bennett

28 May New York Times called for independent inquiries into deaths of Patrick Finucane and Rosemary Nelson

30 May Devolution restored

9 July Weston Park talks

23 July Meeting of Relatives for Justice with Dr John Reid and retinue of civil servants on plastic bullets, state killings and RUC investigations

7 August Northern Ireland Bar Association to accept International Rule of Law award on behalf of Rosemary Nelson from American Bar Association

9 August IRA announced it had agreed to decommissioning scheme

10 August Power-sharing executive suspended. 3 IRA 'suspects' arrested in Colombia

14 August IRA withdrew its plan for decommissioning

20 September SDLP, UUP and DUP signed up to new Northern Ireland Policing Board

21 September Northern Ireland Assembly again suspended

28 September Journalist Martin O'Hagan shot dead in Lurgan by LVF

4 October Police Ombudsman released contents of Drury Report 1971 to family of Samuel Devenny, died 16 July 1969, 3 months after an RUC attack on him in his house

13 October After series of UDA/LVF murders, Dr John Reid announced end of their ceasefire

23 October International Commission witnessed an IRA decommissioning

3/4 November Midnight PSNI replaced RUC

26 November William Stobie ex-quarter master of UDA and RUC Special Branch informer cleared of murders of Patrick Finucane and Adam Lambert. DPP decided not to call witness Neil Mulholland

3 December Part of Brian Nelson's journal in Crumlin Road Prison, Belfast, revealed in *Irish News*

12 December Ombudsman's critical report on Omagh bombing investigation William Stobie shot dead by UDA/LVF

2002

17 January Dr John Reid, Secretary of State, agreed to co-operate with inquiry into Dublin and Monaghan bombings

29 January Crown solicitors informed the High Court that the law would 'soon'

be changed compelling soldiers and police to give evidence to inquests – case taken by family of Pearse Jordan shot dead by RUC in 1992

5 February Death of Sister Sarah Clarke who campaigned for rights of Irish prisoners in Britain

13 February USA Lawyers Committee for Human Rights published a report on the killing of Patrick Finucane and called for an inquiry

17 February Three Irishmen formally charged with training FARC guerrillas in Colombia

19 February Chief Constable Ronnie Flanagan, RUC, to become Inspector of Constabulary on retirement at end of February

17 March Break-in at headquarters of RUC Special Branch, Castlereagh

23 April Judge Peter Cory, retired judge, Canada, asked by British & Irish governments to inquire into deaths of Patrick Finucane, Rosemary Nelson, Robert Hamill, Billy Wright & RUC officers Harry Breen and Bob Buchanan

17 July IRA apologised for killing 'non-combatants' on 'Bloody Friday', Belfast, 21 July 1972

3 September Sir Hugh Orde appointed Chief Constable of PSNI (Police Service of Northern Ireland)

4 October PSNI raided Sinn Féin Office at Stormont in sight of the cameras of alerted media

14 October Northern Ireland Assembly suspended

24 October Paul Murphy succeeded John Reid as Secretary of State

2003

13 February Papers forwarded by Sir John Stevens to DPP on members of security forces

29 March Chief Constable Hugh Orde promised new PSNI team to investigate unsolved murders

11 April Death of FRU agent Brian Nelson

17 April Third Stevens Report revealed collusion between British Army, RUC and loyalist paramilitaries. Sir John Stevens said, 'from Day One, my inquiry team was obstructed in its work ... it should not have taken 14 years to get to where we've gotten now'

May A month dominated in media by question of identity of 'Stakeknife', the highly placed British agent in IRA since 1978

7 October Judge Cory handed his Reports to British and Irish governments

26 November Northern Ireland Assembly Election

18 December Irish government published Cory Reports on cases in Irish Republic and said it would hold a public inquiry

2004

12 January Judge Cory told families of northern cases that he had recommended a public inquiry into all cases

19 January Report of Ombudsman, Nuala O'Loan, on 'significant failings' of RUC investigation into murder of Seán Brown in 1997

1 April British government published Cory Reports on cases in Northern Ireland and announced public inquiries into murders of Rosemary Nelson, Robert Hamill and Billy Wright but did not commit itself to public inquiry into case of Patrick Finucane

26 April Three Irish republicans acquitted of training FARC guerrillas in Colombia.

References and Notes

The Untellable Story
1.   *Siege!*, p. 126–7. cf. Mary Holland, 'Super power and super people', *Hibernia*, 15 May 1980; Michael Maguire, *The Sunday Tribune*, 15 February 1981; Stephen Webbe, 'Is Britain's SAS too quick to pull the trigger?', *The Christian Science Monitor*, 3 October 1988.
2.   Andrew Parker and Paul Hooper, 'The SAS heroes who dared and died', *The Sun*, 16 July 1985; *The Irish News*, 12 February 1983. An SAS man who took part in the siege and who was killed in an accident was Sgt Leslie Barker (34) of Wheatley Hill, Co. Durham. He was killed during a training exercise in Oman on 21 November 1981 when his parachute failed to open. His funeral took place in St Martin's Church, Hereford on 27 November. Six colleagues bore his coffin to his grave which was surrounded by 150 wreaths, including a centrepiece in red, white and blue flowers of the winged dagger emblem of the SAS. The Rev. John Boulch, rural dean of Hereford and chaplain to the SAS told the congregation, 'He was a good man and a brave man, and I thank God for him'. cf. *The Daily Telegraph*, 24, 25 November 1981; *News Letter*, 28 November 1981.
3.   Michael Maguire, 'The many-headed British intelligence operation in Ireland', *Camerawork*, No. 23, December 1981, p. 14.
4.   *The Daily Telegraph*, 24 May 1982; Martin Middlebrook, *Task Force: The Falklands War* (1982), Appendix 1, p. 408.
5.   cf. Account of the farewell regimental party for Major C. L. D. Newell, OBE, regimental adjutant SAS Group, *Mars & Minerva*, Vol. 6, No. 4.

Unravelling the SAS
6.   Tony Geraghty, *This is the SAS*, p. 8.
7.   Virginia Cowles, *The Phantom Major*, dust-jacket quotation.
8.   'The Golden Road to Samarkand', *CPAR* 6, Summer 1982, p. 2.
9.   *Mars & Minerva*, Vol. 7, No. 2, p. 51.
10.   cf. B.A. Young, *The Artists and the SAS*.
11.   Tony Bunyan, *The Political Police in Britain*, pp. 293–6; Tony Bunyan, 'Policing British politics', *Time Out*, No. 318, 16–22 April 1976.
12.   cf. Wilfred Burchett and Derek Roebuck, *The Whores of War*; Jonathan Bloch and Patrick Fitzgerald, *British Intelligence and Covert Action*, pp. 43–52; 'The Golden Road to Samarkand'; 'Soldiers for Smith', *The Leveller*, No. 2, December 1976 – 'the men now serving in the Rhodesian Light Infantry from the Royal Marines, Paratroop Regiment and the Royal Green Jackets – all of whom are closely connected with the Special Air Service. The Greenjackets was the SAS sponsor regiment and provides many of its recruits; the Paratroops provide the highest proportion of SAS recruits of any regiment'. Bob Taylor and Denis Cassidy, 'Who's behind the secret soldiers?', *The People*, 6 August 1967; Tony Geraghty and David May, 'British firm sells know-how on silent killing', *The Sunday Times*, 10 July 1977; Nigel Nelson and John Dale, 'The ransom commando', *Daily Mail*, 17 September 1977 – 'British experience in North Ireland has bred some of the world's top experts in counter-terrorism'; Nick Davies '"Angola soldier" with Rhodesian forces', *The Guardian*, 3 August 1979; Duncan Campbell, 'The pedigree dogs of war', *Time Out*, No. 43, 21–27 July 1978; 'Covert Operations in British Politics 1974–78', *Lobster*, No. 11; Nick Davies, 'SAS network offered chance for action', *The Guardian*, 3 August 1979; David Clark, Andy Weir & Jonathan Bloch,

'Zimbabwe and Britain', *The Leveller*, No. 32, November 1979; David Graves, 'Ex-SAS men hired as mercenaries', *The Daily Telegraph*, 27 June 1980; 'Finally chained … a dog of war', *The Sunday Tribune*, 1980; 'Ex-SAS charged with coup attempt', *The Irish Times*, 10 February 1981; 'North points to British specialist', *The Guardian*, 14 July 1987; 'Irangate figure "is out of the country"', *The Guardian*, 15 July 1987; 'Briton set off Beirut car bomb', *The Observer*, 27 September 1987.
13. Patrick Marrinan, *Colonel Paddy*, Introduction.

Six Phases of the SAS in Northern Ireland
14. Gery Lawless, '1970: Mission Ireland', *Sunday World*, 23 May 1976.

Phase I: Intelligence Gathering and Torture
15. Denis Faul, Raymond Murray, *The Hooded Men*, pp. 36–42.
16. Denis Faul, Raymond Murray, *British Army and Special Branch RUC Brutalities*, pp. 27–8.

Phase II: The Sectarian Murders
17. Based on 'Report on shooting of John Conway and Gerard Conway, Ballymurphy Road, Belfast on Saturday 15 April 1972,' Association for Legal Justice (ALJ) document, 9 May 1972. cf. Robert Fisk, 'Plain clothes Army patrols "have killed unarmed men"', *The Times*, 3 March 1973.
18. Based on 'Report on the shooting incident at Glen Road Bus Terminal at noon on Thursday 22 June 1972', documents of ALJ. cf. 'Story of MRF man accused of three attempted murders', *The Irish News*, 28 June 1973.
19. Statement by Mrs Kathleen Wright to Rev. Brian J. Brady, 13 May 1973, ALJ; Chapman Pincher, 'Army "spy" vanishes', *Daily Express*, 11 October 1972. cf. 'Military petticoat brigade spy on Catholics', *The Irish News*, 10 November 1973. Robert Lennon, 'SAS girls on trail of Provos', 4 May 1978.
20. Based on 'Report on the shooting dead of Daniel Rooney (18), Rodney Parade, Belfast on Tuesday 26 September 1972 by a surveillance patrol of British soldiers in plain clothes', ALJ, 3 October 1972; Inquest report, *The Irish News*, 7 December 1973.
21. Frank Doherty, 'The S.A.S. in N. Ireland', *Hibernia*, 30 March 1973.
22. *Idem.*
23. cf. Kennedy Lindsay, *Ambush at Tully-West* (1979); Vincent Browne, 'Why did agents try to murder this man?', *Sunday Independent*, 24 February 1974; David Blundy, 'Why did the Army shoot this man?', *The Sunday Times*, 24 February 1974; Colin Wallace, Appendix 4, *Lobster*, No. 11; 'Paisley seeks probe into Army shooting', *The Irish News*, 31 January 1974; 'Paisley claims Army shot ex-UDR man', *The Irish News*, 1 February 1974; 'Military tried to kill ex-UDR man? – Lindsay', *The Irish News*, 5 February 1974; David Pallister, 'How a UDR man became SAS target', *The Guardian*, 2 February 1990.
24. Frank Doherty, *op. cit.*; Dossier of Bawnmore & District Tenants' Association; 'Is S.A.S. in North – NICRA', *The Irish News*, 31 August 1972.
25. Frank Doherty, *op. cit.*; local interviews.
26. Frank Doherty, *op. cit.*
27. cf. Niall Kiely, 'War which Britain cannot win', *The Irish Times*, 11 August 1979; Tony Geraghty, *Who Dares Wins*, pp. 170–3.
28. 'Where's my son, plea by mother,' *Sunday News*, 20 May 1973; Desmond Hamill, *Pig in the Middle*, p. 136.
29. cf. 'M15 and M16' below.
30. *Derry Journal*, 16 April 1974; *The Irish News*, 15 April 1974.
31. *Northern Ireland 1968–74. A Chronology of Events*, Vol. 3, 1974, p. 121a.
32. John Deering, 'Soldier's death raises Fermanagh suspicions', *The Irish Times*, 7 April 1975.

33. 'Dangerous secret that made soldier run away', *Irish Independent*, 22 August 1975; 'Ulster death-list soldier dismissed', *The Guardian*, 22 August 1975.

34. Christopher Walker, 'IRA says it shot "spy" soldier', *The Times*, 23 April 1975; Christopher Walker, '"Seized tape" played by Provisionals', *The Times*, 24 April 1975.

35. '"Spy car" set alight by crowd on Falls', *The Irish News*, 9 July 1975; 'Soldier in attacked car no spy – Army', *Belfast Telegraph*, 9 July 1975; 'Army rejects a "ludicrous" story', *Belfast Telegraph*, 15 July 1975; Christopher Walker, 'SAS controversy reopened by pistol discovery in Ulster', *The Times*, 16 July 1975.

36. cf. Jonathan Bloch and Patrick Fitzgerald, *British Intelligence and Covert Action*, pp. 217–25; Roger Faligot, *The Kitson Experiment*, pp. 102–108; *Spies in Ireland* (Clann na hÉireann). There was extensive coverage of the Littlejohns' Affair in newspapers and journals. Attention is drawn to a select number here:– Bryan Trench, 'Bank robbers or British agents', *Hibernia*, 3 August 1973; *The Irish News*, 4–11 August 1973; 'Brothers claiming "secret agents" role get 35 years', *The Guardian*, 4 August 1973; Denis Taylor, 'Two brothers jailed...', *The Times*, 4 August 1973; Peter Gladstone Smith, 'British agents in Eire recalled', *The Sunday Telegraph*, 5 August 1973; 'Spy sensation wife talks', *News of the World*, 5 August 1973; 'Yes, my husband is a spy, says robber's wife', *Sunday People*, 5 August 1973; 'IRA bid to kill Keith Littlejohn', *The Sunday Press*, 5 August 1973; Dick Walsh, '20-year jail sentence, but who was in the dock?', *The Irish Times*, 6 August 1973; 'Banished servants of the Crown?', *The Guardian*, 6 August 1973; 'Spy brothers and IRA: the facts', *Evening News*, 6 August 1973; Martin Woolacott and Derek Brown, 'IRA threat to brothers', *The Guardian*, 6 August 1973; 'Britain silent on Littlejohn case', *The Irish Times*, 6 August 1973; 'Whitehall admits link', *The Irish Press*, 7 August 1973; 'Defence ministry admits Littlejohn meeting', *The Times*, 7 August 1973; 'Littlejohn spy deal admitted by Whitehall', *The Guardian*, 7 August 1973; 'Carrington backs talks with "spies"', *Evening Standard*, 7 August 1973; 'Why Britain must use men like these', Chapman Pincher, *Daily Express*, 8 August 1973; James McManus & Jackie Leishman, 'Four new facts back demands for spy inquiry', *The Guardian*, 8 August 1973; 'I did my duty – Carrington', *The Daily Telegraph*, 8 August 1973; 'I'll walk free', *Daily Express*, 8 August 1973; 'Littlejohn row grows', *The Irish Press*, 8 August 1973; Robert McGowan, John Pender & Joe Hall, 'Carrington "made mistake" over spy', *Evening Standard*, 8 August 1973; 'Spy taken off wanted list', *Irish Independent*, 8 August 1973; 'The Littlejohn Affair', *The Times*' editorial, 8 August 1973; Jim Nicoll, 'Governments "to keep lid on"', *Irish Independent*, 8 August 1973; Robert Fisk, '"Walter Mitty" life of Littlejohn brothers', *The Times*, 9 August 1973; Angus Macpherson, 'Why Carrington went into this hare-brained escapade', *Daily Mail*, 9 August 1973; Gordon Greig & Brian Park, 'Speak up or get out Wigg tells Carrington', *Daily Mail*, 9 August 1973; Norman Luck, 'How I spied for Britain', *Daily Express*, 9 August 1973 (Littlejohn's gun described as a .22 Beretta, with high velocity ammunition); 'The Littlejohn affair', *Time Out*, No. 181, 10–16 August 1973; 'Did Littlejohns help in Woolsey killing?', *Irish People*, 10 August 1973; 'Spies shock for Donegan', *The Sunday Press*, 12 August 1973; Frances O'Rourke, 'Questions to be answered', *The Sunday Press*, 12 August 1973; 'Now Lynch admits he knew', *The Irish News*, 14 August 1973; Conor McAnally, 'Revealed: the spy mission that passed almost unnoticed', *Irish Independent*, 17 August 1973 (story of an agent provocateur in Belfast in 1969); 'Littlejohn affair tip of the iceberg – claim', *The Irish Times*, 22 September 1973; Renagh Holohan, 'Littlejohn affair raised in Commons', *The Irish Times*, 17 October 1973; '*Habeas corpus* move in Littlejohn case', *The Irish Press*, 20 October 1973; 'Littlejohn appeals adjourned', *The Irish Times*, 20 October 1973; ; 'Littlejohns: were they let out?', *Hibernia*, 29 March 1974; 'Littlejohns' escape probe to be secret', *The Irish News*, 22 March 1974; 'No Littlejohn probe – Wilson', *The Irish News*, 2 April 1974; 'Littlejohns' brother-in-law gets 10 years', *The Irish News*, 21 March 1974; 'Littlejohn remanded in custody', *The Irish Press*, 14 December 1974; 'The spy marked

down for death', *Sunday People,* 29 September 1974; David Pallister, 'Irish release the Littlejohn brothers', *The Guardian,* 19 September 1981; 'Three IRA men guilty of attack on Littlejohn', *The Guardian,* 20 June 1984; interview with members of Tinnelly family; BBC *Spotlight* programme.

37. *The Irish Press,* 6 October 1973; *Evening Press,* 6 October 1973; *The Sunday Times,* 7 October 1973; *The Guardian,* 8 October 1973.
38. Faligot, *op. cit.,* p. 105.
39. Faligot, *op. cit.,* pp. 104–5.
40. *The Sunday Press,* 12 August 1973.
41. Faligot, *op. cit.,* pp. 107–8.
42. *The Irish News,* 22 December 1972, 14 February 1973, *The Irish Times,* 21–23 December 1972; 14, 27, 28 February 1973.
43. Faligot, *op. cit.,* p. 102; *Spies in Ireland* (pub. Clann na hÉireann) p. 11; 'Diplomat accused by IRA is recalled', *News Letter,* 13 September 1973.
44. cf. Christopher Walker, 'More army dossiers on IRA suspects "missing"', *The Times,* 13 June 1975.
45. 'Prisoner was offered a deal – Paisley', *Belfast Telegraph,* 29 August 1973; Frank Doherty, 'The Baker file … I made deal says killer … Dublin probe uncovers car bombers', *Sunday World,* 4 January 1976; Frank Doherty, 'MP will visit killer', *Sunday World,* 18 January 1976; Tom Wilson, 'Mass killer "silenced" with drugs', *Sunday News,* 25 November 1984; 'The Complete Story of the RUC's First Super-Grass – Guinea Pig', Albert Walker Baker, Memorandum, (1986); letter of Albert Walker Baker to Fr Denis Faul, November 1985. Paul Connolly in the *Sunday News,* 22 January 1989, reported an interview with Ken Livingstone, MP who visited Albert Baker recently in prison; Mr Livingstone said, 'I have not the slightest doubt that he killed people after he was fed information by RUC and Army intelligence'.
46. *Belfast Telegraph,* 30 August 1973.
47. *Belfast Telegraph,* 15–17 October 1973.
48. *Belfast Telegraph,* 16–17 October 1973.
49. Sandra Chapman, 'The case of the missing 70 minutes', *Belfast Telegraph,* 17 October 1973.
50. 'Shankill guns turn on Paras', *The Irish News,* 12 June 1972; 'Devlin letter to Wilson on Army policy', *The Irish News,* 16 October 1972; 'Horse-trading end to UDA "war"' on Army – Devlin', *The Irish News,* 19 October 1972; 'Lay off, UDA tell Military', *The Irish News,* 25 October 1973; 'Army-UDA versions of East End shootings', *The Irish News,* 18 February 1974.
51. 'The Tommy Herron shooting', *Hibernia,* 21 September 1973; 'Brown link in Herron murder says UFF', *Sunday News,* 16 May 1976; Alan Murray, 'UFF killed Brown over Herron plot', *The Irish Press,* 17 May 1976; David McKittrick, 'East Belfast killing linked with Herron case', *The Irish Times,* 15 May 1976.
52. *The Irish News,* 12–15 February 1974; *The Irish Press,* 13–15 February 1974.
53. cf. Articles by David McKittrick, *The Irish Times,* 22–24 April 1980.
54. *The Portadown News,* 22 March 1974.
55. *Northern Ireland 1968–74. A Chronology of Events,* Vol. 3, 1974, p. 59a.
56. cf. Brian J. Brady, Denis Faul, Raymond Murray, *Corruption of Law,* Memorandum to the Gardiner Committee on the working of emergency legislation in Northern Ireland, September 1974.
57. cf. various newspaper reports – David McKittrick, 'Former British Army PRO jailed, *The Irish Times,* 21 March 1981; Duncan Campbell, 'British Army's secret war across the Border', *The Sunday Tribune,* 6 May 1984; David McKittrick, 'Nairac "boasted of killing IRA man in Republic"', *The Irish Times,* 21 May 1984; 'Dirty tricks at top claim', *News Letter,* 10 December 1986; Brendan O'Brien, 'M15 in Ireland', *Irish Independent,* 20 January 1987; Barrie Penrose, 'MP go-between in M15 pay-off', *The Sunday Times,*

22 February 1987; Martin Cowley, 'Ex-British intelligence man says he used Garda, *The Irish Times*, 28 February 1987; Brendan O'Brien, 'Dukes' denial as M16 "smear" is raised again', *Irish Independent*, 6 March 1987; 'My years as a secret soldier', *Sunday News*, 8 March 1987; David Pallister, 'Paisley was "M15 target"', *The Guardian*, 28 April 1987; Liam Clarke, 'Garda "spy" now a hero', *Sunday World*, 3 May 1987; Liam Clarke, 'The M15 plot to smear Paisley', *Sunday World*, 17 May 1987; Seán Flynn, 'New inquiry on Holroyd claims', *The Irish Times*, 18 May 1987; 'Airey Neave in "M15 plot"', *The Irish Press*, 14 July 1987; John Ware, 'Parachutist who was all waffle and no action', *The Independent*, 2 September 1987; David McKittrick, 'Unravelling the truth in Ulster's dirty war', *The Independent*, 2 September 1987; Liam Clarke, 'Putting Wallace to the truth test', *The Irish News*, 21 September 1987; 'Former agent calls for RUC men's extradition', *Sunday World*, 6 December 1987; reports on interviews with Colin Wallace and Fred Holroyd on Barry Cowan's *Talkback* programme BBC, Martin Cowley, *The Irish Times*, Alan Murray, *The Irish Press*, 28 February 1988. Important TV programmes included Channel 4, *Diverse Reports*, 2 May 1984 researched and reported by Christopher Hird and Duncan Campbell, and *Today Tonight*, RTE, 18 March 1987. Important also are the speech by Ken Livingstone, MP in the House of Commons, 7 July 1987 and questions tabled by him in parliament, March 1988 and 24 April 1988.

58. Professor Kennedy Lindsay editor of *Ulsterman*, a monthly paper, alleged this, and also accused the SAS of sending letterbombs to a number of Catholic homes in West Belfast – reported in *Andersonstown News*, 13 December 1975, where a republican opinion is also given that the SAS planted three 'radio' booby trap bombs, one of which killed a man in a book-shop off Castle Street, Belfast.

59. cf. Fred Holroyd, 'The trial of Colin Wallace', *Lobster*, No. 11; Frank Doherty, 'Black propaganda and black murder', *Magill*, December 1986; James Campbell, 'The case of Colin Wallace', *Gate Fever* (1986).

60. cf. Duncan Campbell, 'Booby traps and bank raids', *New Statesman*, 11 May 1984.

61. cf. an assessment in Robin Ramsay & Stephen Dorril, '*The Independent*'s vilification of Colin Wallace – a refutation', 1988.

62. cf. *Craigavon Times (Portadown Times)*, 6 August 1975.

63. *Portadown Times*, 21 February 1973.

64. *Dungannon Observer*, 9 March 1974; *The Irish News*, 16, 21 March 1974.

65. *The Irish News*, 12 January 1976.

66. *Craigavon Times (Portadown Times)*, 6 August 1975

67. *Portadown News*, 22 August 1975.

68. Inquest report, *Belfast Telegraph*, 24 July 1976.

69. *The Catholic Standard*, 12 September 1975.

70. *The Irish News*, 24, 25, 27 July 1974; 6 August 1974.

71. Account of Captain Robert Nairac based on – interviews; book of evidence for the trial of Liam Townson; reports of trial and appeal of Liam Townson in *The Irish Times*, 1977–8; *The Times*, 17, 18 May 1977; David Blundy, 'Death of a secret soldier', *The Sunday Times*, 3 November 1977; Irish newspapers 27 May, 30 May, 3 June 1977, 7–11 November 1978; *The Daily Telegraph*, 16 December 1978; Duncan Campbell, 'Victims of the dirty war', *New Statesman*, 4, 11, 18 May 1984.

Phase III: The SAS in South Armagh

72. Account based on interview with Reavey family.

73. cf. Denis Faul, Raymond Murray, *SAS Terrorism – the Assassin's Glove*; *The Irish News*, 29 April, 14 May 1977; *Belfast Telegraph*, 30 April 1977.

74. Inquest documents on the death of Peter Cleary; Denis Faul, Raymond Murray, op. cit. Brigadier Peter Morton commanded 3 Para in South Armagh, 15 April–17 August 1976. In his book *Emergency Tour* he refers to the death of the Peter Cleary. He says that,

supported by the Chief Superintendent RUC, he delayed releasing the news of his death, or the body to Daisyhill Hospital, Newry, for a few hours, so that the story would be late for the newspapers and the Army account would be the first received by the media. His book also deals with the Paras' shooting of Liam Prince and Majella O'Hare, their placing of a hoax bomb on the main Dublin–Belfast railroad, and the Army's keeping secret the death of Private William Snowdon killed in an IRA landmine explosion.

75. Pathologist's report, inquest documents; Denis Faul, Raymond Murray, *op. cit.*

76. Denis Faul, Raymond Murray, *op. cit.;* Irish and British newspapers, 7–17 May 1976, 5–9 March 1977.

77. *Birmingham Evening Mail,* 16 January 1986.

78. *The Irish Times,* 14 July 1976; *The Irish Press,* 15 July 1976.

79. cf. Irish national newspapers, 17, 18 January 1977.

Phase IV: SAS Terrorism 1977–78

80. *The Irish Times,* 22 January 1977; *The Irish News,* 22 January 1977; *The Irish People,* 29 January 1977; interview with family; *The Irish Times,* 21 November 1987; *The Irish News,* 21 November 1987.

81. cf. *Belfast Telegraph,* 5 May 1978.

82. *The Irish Times,* 31 October–1 November 1977, 2 November 1977; *Hibernia,* 27 September 1979.

83. *The Lurgan Mail* (1977).

84. *The Irish News,* 15 December 1977; *The Irish Times,* 15 December 1977.

85. *Belfast Telegraph,* 17 March 1978.

86. *The Irish News,* 12 August 1978; *Hibernia,* 17 August 1978.

87. *Belfast Telegraph,* 1 September 1978.

88. *Irish Independent,* 7 October 1978.

89. cf. *Irish Independent,* 30 October 1978; *The Irish Press,* 11 December 1979; *The Irish News,* 11 December 1979.

90. Trial papers of Patrick Heslin Phelan; interview with family; Irish newspapers 13–15 December 1977; *The Irish News,* 17 April 1980.

91. Interview with family and solicitor; inquest papers; Paul Duffy *v.* Chief Constable and another, 1978; Peter Taylor, *Beating the Terrorist?* (Penguin special, 1980), pp. 115–120; *The Irish Times,* 27, 28 February 1978; *The Irish News,* 27, 28 February 1978; *The Irish Times,* 1 March 1978; *Tyrone Courier,* 1 March 1978; *The Democrat,* 24 August 1978; *An Phoblacht/Republican News,* 14 July 1979; *The Democrat,* 2 August 1979.

92. Trial papers, 'Regina *v.* Robert Joseph Gamble'; 'Memorandum of law in support of motion to dismiss request for extradition', United States District Court, Southern District of New York; interview; Dossier on shooting by ALJ; Irish newspapers 17–28 March 1978; *Belfast Telegraph,* 6 October 1979; *The Irish News,* 29 February 1980; *The Irish Press,* 6 October 1980; *The Irish Times,* 24 December 1981; *The Irish News,* 30 December 1981; *The Irish Press,* 31 December 1981; *The Irish Press,* 1–2 January 1982.

93. Denis Faul, Raymond Murray, *The British Dimension;* interviews with family; Eamon McCann, *War and an Irish Town,* pp. 161–4; documents, Elizabeth Heaney and the Ministry of Defence, High Court; statements taken by local human rights' groups; *Republican News,* 24 June 1978; *The Derry Journal,* 30 November 1979; inquest papers.

94. Inquest documents; Irish and British newspapers, 22, 23, June 1978; *Republican News,* 24 June 1978; *The Irish News,* 13 September 1980.

95. The John Boyle case was heavily reported in Irish newspapers. cf. Tony Geraghty, *Who Dares Wins,* pp. 154–60; Liz Curtis, *Ireland: The Propaganda War,* pp. 76–7.

96. Irish and British newspapers, 2–4 October 1978, 19–20 April 1979, 6–7 September 1979.

97. *The Irish News,* 26 October 1978; *Republican News,* 4 November 1978; ALJ, 'Report on the killing of William Smyth', November 1978.

98. Inquest papers; interviews with family; *Belfast Telegraph*, 25 November 1978; *The Irish News*, 28 November 1978; *The Irish Times*, 28 November 1978; accounts in *The Derry Journal*; *Republican News*, 2 December 1978.

Phase V: Atkins' Secret Army
99. *The Irish News*, 4 September 1979.
100. *The Irish News*, 31 October 1979; *Daily Mail*, 31 October 1979.
101. *The Irish News*, 9–10 October 1979.
102. *Belfast Telegraph*, 25 January 1979; *The Irish News*, 25–26 January 1979.
103. *Irish Independent*, 7 May 1979; *The Irish Times*, 7 May 1979.
104. cf. Andrew Boyd, *The Informers*, pp. 34–40.
105. *The Guardian*, 18, 20, 24 April 1987; *The Observer*, 26 April 1987; *The Guardian*, 4 January 1988; *The Sunday Times*, 17 January 1988. There have been other notable names linked with British intelligence in Northern Ireland. The M15 'spy' Michael Bettaney (alias 'John Edmonds'), jailed for 23 years in April 1984 for passing secret information to Russia, worked in Northern Ireland for two years, 1976–78, in counter-IRA activities. *The Guardian* (17 April 1984) claimed, 'The experience set off an intellectual and emotional earthquake in him and he began to have serious doubts about the British role in Northern Ireland. However, he seems to have believed that M15's role in gathering intelligence on terrorists was not in itself objectionable'. Sir Philip Woodfield (64), former head of the Northern Ireland Office and former Home Office deputy secretary, well-versed in the operations of M15, was appointed on 2 November 1987 'staff counsellor' to the security and intelligence services. The new internal and secret complaints procedure was opened to the c. 2,000 officials in M15, the c.3,000 in M16 and the c. 7,000 civilians working in GCHQ, the electronic intelligence-gathering centre based in Cheltenham. In 1988 Patrick Walker, who rose to prominence in the intelligence world in Northern Ireland, became the first Catholic to head M15.
106. Denis Faul, Raymond Murray, *The British Dimension*, p. 69; Irish newspapers, 1–3 October 1980; *News Letter*, 5, 17 February 1982; *The Guardian*, 11 March 1982; *The Daily Telegraph*, 11 March 1982.
107. *Belfast Telegraph*, 16 January 1981; *The Times*, 10 March 1981; *Belfast Telegraph*, 20, 22 January 1983; *The Guardian*, 22 January 1982.
108. Dossier compiled by ALJ, 22 October 1980; Irish newspapers, 20–23 October 1980.

Phase VI: Shoot-to-Kill
109. *Belfast Telegraph*, 1 April 1982; *Irish Independent*, 2 April 1982; *An Phoblacht/Republican News*, 8 April 1982.
110. *News Letter*, 23 February 1984; *Daily Mail*, 1 March 1984.
111. *Hibernia*, 1 November 1981.
112. *The Irish News*, 12 February 1983; *The Irish Times*, 12 February 1983.
113. *The Irish News*, 12 April 1983; *The Irish Press*, 12 April 1983.
114. Interviews; Irish newspapers, 29 May 1981; *Daily Mail*, 29 May 1981; *The Derry Journal*, 29 May 1981; *An Phoblacht/Republican News*, 6 June 1981; *The Irish News*, 10 March 1983; *The Derry Journal*, 11 March 1983.
115. Interview with family and Liam Duffy; *Belfast Telegraph*, 3 February 1983; Irish newspapers, 4, 5, 7 February 1983; *The Irish News*, 27 April 1984, 2 March 1989; *The Irish Times*, 27 April 1984.
116. Interviews with families; inquest papers; Irish newspapers 5–9 December 1983; *Dungannon Observer*, 15 March 1985; *Tyrone Courier*, 20 March 1985; *The Democrat*, 21 March 1985; *The New York Times*, 12, 19 April 1985; *The Irish News*, 25 June 1985; *Tyrone Courier*, 26 June 1985; *The Democrat*, 27 June 1985; *An Phoblacht/Republican News*, 27 June 1985; *Dungannon Observer*, 28 June 1985.
117. Interview with families; Irish newspapers, 23–25 February 1984; *Daily Mail*, 23 Feb-

ruary 1984; *Belfast Telegraph,* 29 February 1984; *The Irish News,* 29 February 1984; *Irish Independent,* 29 February 1984; *An Phoblacht/Republican News,* 23 February, 1 March 1984; *Ballymena Guardian,* 22 May 1986.

118. Interview with family; inquest papers; *Belfast Telegraph,* 13 February 1984; Irish newspapers 14–16 February 1984; *An Phoblacht/Republican News,* 18 December 1986; *The Irish News,* 19 June 1987; *Dungannon Observer,* 19 June 1987; Irish Information Partnership Agenda.

119. Interviews; *Portadown Times,* 26 October 1984; *Armagh Observer,* 15 May 1986; *Craigavon Times (Portadown Times),* 23 May 1986.

120. Interviews with families; inquest papers; Irish newspapers 3–5 December 1984, 17, 18, 22, 24 December 1984; *The Irish News,* 20 March 1986; *An Phoblacht/Republican News,* 6 December 1985, 3 January 1986, 27 March 1986.

121. Interviews with families; inquest papers; Irish newspapers 7–10 December 1984; *The Guardian,* 10 December 1984; *The Irish News,* 12 December 1984; *The Irish Times,* 10 December 1986; *The Irish News,* 10 December 1986.

122. Interviews with families; inquest papers; Irish newspapers 23–27 February 1985; *The Guardian,* 25 February 1985; *An Phoblacht/Republican* News, 28 February 1985; *The Strabane Chronicle,* 2 March 1985; *The Irish Press,* 12 December 1986; *The Strabane Chronicle,* 14, 21, 28 February, 7, 14 March, 11 April 1987; *Workers Press,* 21 November 1987; Irish newspapers, February, March 1987; Captain Simon Hayward – *Sunday Mirror,* 19 July 1987; *The Strabane Chronicle,* 25 July 1987; *The Sun,* 5 August 1987; *Daily Mirror,* 11 August 1987; *The Guardian,* 11 August 1987; *Fortnight,* October 1988.

123. Interview with family and other witnesses; dossiers of Fr James McNally – 'Television reports', 'Statements concerning the Death of Francis Bradley, 18 February 1986'; 'Report of a public inquiry by The Community of Justice'; Irish newspapers, 20 February 1986; *The Guardian,* 20 February 1986; *Ballymena Guardian,* 27 February 1986; Irish newspapers, 26–28 February 1987; *The Mid-Ulster Mail,* 5 March 1987; *Northern Constitution,* 7 March 1987.

124. Interviews with family and Seán Lynch; trial papers of Seán Lynch; *The Observer,* 27 April 1987; The Sunday Press, 27 April 1987; *The Irish Times,* 28–29 April 1987; *An Phoblacht/Republican News,* 1 May 1987. cf. Colm Tóibín, *Walking Along the Border,* Derek Dunne, *Out of the Maze.*

125. Interviews; *Evening Herald,* 9 May 1987; *The Sunday Press,* 10 May 1987; *The Sunday Times,* 10 May 1987; *The Observer,* 10 May 1987; *The Sunday Tribune,* 10 May 1987; Irish and British newspapers, 11–14 May 1987; *The Ulster Gazette,* 14 May 1987; *The Democrat,* 14 May 1987; *Craigavon Times (Portadown Times),* 15 May 1987; *An Phoblacht/ Republican News,* 14 May 1987; *The Irish Times,* 9 September 1987; *Iris,* October 1987; *The Irish Times,* 10 November 1988; statement of Oliver Hughes, 12 August 1987.

126. cf. special 'Gibraltar' section in bibliography.

127. This theological thought on the universal and infinite love and mercy of Christ was distorted by Independent Radio News, London, and became a headline 'IRA bomb girl "died like Jesus"' in John Passmore's front-page story in the *Evening Standard,* 16 March 1989. It was then picked up by TV AM, Michael Mates, MP, Ken Magennis, MP, Sir John Biggs-Davison, MP, John Junor (*The Sunday Express,* 20 March 1988), *The Daily Telegraph,* 21 March 1988; Lord Fitt wrote in *The Daily Express*: 'One priest, Father Raymond Murray, said that one of the Gibraltar terrorists died in violence, "just like Jesus". I am a Catholic and preparing for Easter. Let me tell you this: We will not be celebrating the fact that Jesus died because he was planning to bomb Bethlehem.' The distortion was carried on by Ian Jack in his article 'Gibraltar' in *Granta* 25, Autumn, 1988.

128. *The Independent,* 6 July 1988; *The Irish Press,* 7 July 1988; *The Irish News,* 8 July 1988; *News Letter,* 26 October 1989; *The Guardian,* 14 August 1989.

129. Interview; Irish and British newspapers, 31 August 1988, 1–5 September 1988; *An*

Phoblacht/Republican News, 1 September 1988; *The Sunday Times,* 4 September 1988; *Fortnight,* October 1988.

Bibliography

Ackroyd, Carol, Margolis, Karen, Rosenhead, Jonathan, Shallice, Tim, *The Technology of Political Control*, Pelican, Penguin Books, 1977.

Adams, James, *Secret Armies. The full story of S.A.S., Delta Force & Spetsnaz*. Hutchinson, London, 1988. Revised edition 1989.

Adams, James, Morgan, Robin & Bambridge, Anthony, Ambush. *The war between the SAS and the IRA*, Pan Books, 1988.

Agenda: Information Service on Northern Ireland and Anglo-Irish Relations. Irish Information Partnership, 5th edition, Volume One, Volume Two, (1987).

Amnesty International, United Kingdom, *Northern Ireland: Killings by Security Forces and 'Supergrass' Trials*, June, 1988.

Amnesty International, United Kingdom, *Killings by Security Forces in Northern Ireland*. Update., April, 1990.

Arthur, Max, *Northern Ireland Soldiers Talking. 1969 to today*, Sidgwick & Jackson, London, 1987.

Barzilay, D., *The British Army in Ulster*, Vol. 3, Century Services, Belfast, 1978.

Beresford, David, *Ten Men Dead. The story of the 1981 Irish Hunger Strike*, Grafton Books (A division of Collins Publishing Group). 1987.

Bew, Paul, Gillespie, Gordon, *Northern Ireland: A Chronology of the Troubles 1968–1999*, Gill & Macmillan, 2nd edition, 1999

Bloch, Jonathan & Fitzgerald, Patrick, *British Intelligence and Covert Action*, Bradshaw, Ireland; Junction, London, 1983.

Boyd, Andrew, *The Informers, A chilling account of the supergrasses in Northern Ireland*, Mercier Press, Cork & Dublin, 1984.

Bradford, Roy & Dillon, Martin, *Rogue Warrior of the SAS. Lt-Col 'Paddy' Blair Mayne*, John Murray, 1987.

Bunyan, Tony, The *History and Practice of Political Police in Britain*, Quarter Books, London, 1977.

Burchett, Wilfred & Roebuck, Derek, *The Whores of War*, Penguin Special, 1977.

Campbell, James, Gate Fever, *Voices from a prison*, Sphere Books Limited, London, 1986.

Clark, A. F. N., *Contact*, Secker & Warburg, London, 1983.

Cowles, Virginia, *The Phantom Major, The story of David Stirling and the S.A.S. Regiment*, Collins, London, 1958.

Cramer, Chris & Harris, Sim, *Hostage*, John Clare Books, London, 1982.

Curtis, Liz, *Ireland: The Propaganda War, The British media and the 'battle for hearts and minds'*, Pluto Press, London & Sydney, 1984.

Deacon, Richard, *A History of British Secret Service*, Granada, 1980.

Deacon, Richard, *'C', A Biography of Sir Maurice Oldfield. Head of M16*, Futura, London, 1985.

Dillon, Martin & Lehane, Denis, *Political Murder in Northern Ireland*, Penguin, London, 1973.

Doherty, Frank, *The Stalker Affair*, Mercier Press, Cork & Dublin, 1986.

Dunne, Derek,*Out of the Maze, The true story of the biggest jail escape since the war*, Gill & Macmillan, Dublin, 1988.

Faligot, Roger, *British Military Strategy in Ireland, The Kitson Experiment*, Zed Press, United Kingdom; Brandon, Ireland, 1983.

Farran, Roy, *Winged Dagger*, Collins, London, 1948.

Faul, Denis & Murray, Raymond, *British Army & Special Branch RUC Brutalities*, 1972.

Faul, Denis & Murray, Raymond, *The Hooded Men*, 1974.

Faul, Denis & Murray, Raymond, *The Triangle of Death*, Third edition, 1975.

Faul, Denis & Murray, Raymond, *The Castlereagh File*, 1975.

Faul, Denis & Murray, Raymond, *H Blocks*, 1979.

Faul, Denis & Murray, Raymond, *Hunger Strike*, 1980.

Faul, Denis & Murray, Raymond, *The British Dimension*, 1980.

Faul, Denis & Murray, Raymond, *SAS Terrorism – the Assassin's Glove*, 1976.

Fegan, Artúr, Murray, Raymond, *Collusion 1990–1994, Loyalist Paramilitary Murders in Northern Ireland*, Relatives for Justice, 1995

Fisk, Robert, *The Point of No Return. The strike which broke the British in Ulster*, Times Books, André Deutsch, London, 1975.

Foot, Paul, *Who Framed Colin Wallace?* Macmillan, London, 1989.

Geraghty, Tony, *Who Dares Wins, The story of the Special Air Service 1950–1980*, Arms and Armour Press, London-Melbourne, 1980.

Geraghty, Tony, *This is the SAS. A pictorial history of the Special Air Service Regiment*, Fontana, Collins, 1982.

Hamill, Desmond, *Pig in the Middle, The Army in Northern Ireland 1969–1985*, Methuen Paperback, London, 1986.

Hayward, Simon, *Under Fire. My Own Story*, W. H. Allen, London, 1989.

Holland, Jack, and Phoenix, Susan, *Phoenix: Policing the Shadows*, Coronet Books, Hodder and Stoughton, 1996.

Holroyd, Fred (with Nick Burbridge), *War without Honour, Medium*, Hull, 1989.

Hunter, Robin, *True Stories of the SAS*, Weidenfeld & Nicholson, London, 1985

Ingram, Martin and Harkin, Greg, *Stakeknife: Britain's Secret Agents in Ireland*, O'Brien Press, Dublin, 2004

Jeapes, Colonel Tony, *SAS: Operation Oman*, William Kimber, London, 1980.

Jeffrey, Keith (ed.), *The Divided Province. The troubles in Northern Ireland 1969–1985*, Orbis Publishing, London, 1985.

Kitson, Frank, *Gangs and Counter-gangs*, Barrie & Rockliff, London, 1960.

Kitson, Frank, *Low Intensity Operations. Subversion, insurgency, peace-keeping*, Faber & Faber, London, 1971.

Ladd, James D., *SAS Operations*. Robert Hale, London, 1986.

Lewis, David, Sexpionage, *The exploitation of sex by Soviet Intelligence*, Harcourt Bruce Jovanovich, New York, 1976 & Heinrich Hanau Publications, London, 1976.

Lindsay, Kennedy, *Ambush at Tully-West. The British Intelligence Services in action*, Dundrod, Dundalk, 1979.

Livingstone, Ken, *Livingstone's Labour*, Unwin Hyman, London, 1989.

McArdle, Patsy, *The Secret War*, Mercier Press, Cork & Dublin, 1984.

McCann, Eamonn, *War and an Irish Town*, Pluto Press, London, 1980.

McKeown, Michael, *De Mortuis*, Irish Information Partnership, London, 1985.

McKittrick, David, Kelters, Seamus, Feeney, Brian, Thornton, Chris, *Lost Lives: The stories of the men, women and children who died as a result of the Northern Ireland troubles*, Mainstream Publishing Company (Edinburgh) Ltd, 1999

Marrinan, Patrick, *Colonel Paddy*, The Ulster Press, Belfast, 1986.

Middlebrook, Martin, *Task Force: The Falklands War*, 1982, Penguin edition, 1987.

Moloney, Ed, *A Secret History of the IRA*, Allen Lane, The Penguin Press, 2002

Morton, Brigadier Peter, *Emergency Tour. 3 Para in South Armagh*, William Kimber, 1989.

Mullan, Don, *The Dublin & Monaghan Bombings*, Wolfhound Press, Dublin, 2000

Murray, Raymond, *State Killings in Northern Ireland*, Relatives for Justice, 1991

Murray, Raymond, *Hard Time: Armagh Gaol 1971–1986*, Mercier Press, 1998

Murray, Raymond, *State Violence: Northern Ireland, 1969–1997*, Mercier Press, 1998

Ó Cuinneagáin, Mícheál, *The Nairac Affair*, Published privately, 1981.

Parker, Tony, *Soldier, Soldier*, Coronet Books, Hodder & Stoughton, 1985.

Pincher, Chapman, *Too Secret Too Long*, Sidgwick & Jackson, London, Edition 1987.

Rees, Merlyn, *Northern Ireland: A Personal Perspective*, Methuen, London, 1985.

Report of an International Delegation of Lawyers, *Legal Defence in Northern Ireland*. Following the murder of Patrick Finucane on 12 February 1989.

S.A.S. Elite Forces, Series Editor: Ashley Brown, Consultant Editors: Brigadier-General James L. Collins Jr (Retd), Dr John Pimlott, Brigadier-General Edwin H. Simmons USMC (Retd), Orbis publishing, London, 1986.

Segaller, Stephen, *Invisible Armies. Terrorism into the 1990s*, Michael Joseph, London, 1986.

Shoot to Kill? International Lawyers' Inquiry into the lethal use of firearms by the Security Forces in Northern Ireland, Chairman: Kadar Asmal, Mercier Press, Cork & Dublin, 1984.

Siege. Sunday Times Insight on the great embassy rescue, Hamlyn paperbacks, London, 1986.

Spies in Ireland. Printed and published by Clann na hÉireann, London.

Stanhope, Henry, *The Soldiers. An anatomy of the British Army*, Hamish Hamilton, London, 1979.

Strawson, John, *A History of the S.A.S. Regiment*, Secker & Warburg, London, 1984.

Taylor, Peter, *Families at War*, BBC Books, 1989.

Tóibín, Colm, *Walking Along the Border*, Queen Anne Press, 1987.

Warner, Philip, *The Special Air Service*, William Kimber, London, 1971. New edition, 1982.

Wilkinson, Paul & Stewart, A. M., ed., *Contemporary Research on Terrorism*, Aberdeen University Press, edition 1989.

Young, B. A., *The Artists and the SAS*, Published by 1st Special Air Regiment (Artists), T. A., London, 1960.

Selected Articles

Blundy, David, 'Why did the Army shoot this man'?, *The Sunday Times*, 24 February 1974.

Blundy, David, 'The Army's secret war in Northern Ireland', *The Sunday Times*, 13 March 1977.

Blundy, David, 'Death of a secret soldier', *The Sunday Times*, 3 November 1977.

Boyle, Kevin, Hadden Tom, Walsh, Dermot, 'Abuse and failure in security policies', *Fortnight*, September 1983.

Brown, Vincent, 'Why did agents try to murder this man?', *Sunday Independent*, 8 October 1972.

Brock, George, Chesshyre, Robert, 'Battle over new Ulster policy starting', *The Observer*, 7 October 1979.

Bunyan, Tony, Hosenball, Mark, 'Policing British politics', *Time Out*, No. 318, 16–22 April 1976.

Campbell, Duncan, Page, Bruce, Anning, Nick, 'Destabilizing the "decent" people', *New Statesman*, 15 February 1980.

Campbell, Duncan, 'Victims of the dirty war', *New Statesman*, 4, 11, 18 May 1984.

Campbell, Duncan, 'British Army's secret war', *The Sunday Tribune*, 6 May 1984.

Campbell, Duncan, 'M15 subverts "dirty tricks" investigation', *New Statesman*, 14 December 1984.

Campbell, Duncan, 'Dirty Tricks: rubbishing the rogues', *New Statesman*, 25 September 1987.

Charters, David A., 'Intelligence and psychological warfare operations in Ireland', *Journal of the Royal United Services Institute for Defence Studies*, September 1977.

Clark, David, Weir, Andy, Bloch, Jonathan, 'Zimbabwe and Britain: sticky fingers in the white honeypot', *The Leveller*, No. 32, November 1979.

CPAR, 'The Golden Road to Samarkand', No. 6, Summer 1982.

Cockerell, Michael, 'General Kitson's College', *The Listener*, Vol. 103, No. 2644, 10 January 1980.

Cockburn, Alexander, 'US press goes easy on "death squads" in Northern Ireland', *The Wall Street Journal*, 26 May 1988. Connolly, Frank, 'The UDR – a litany of crimes', *Magill*, October 1989.

Cusack, Jim, 'IRA men may have been lured into ambush', *The Irish Times*, 5 September

1988.

Daily Mail, 'Inside the SAS', 19, 20, 21 May 1980.

Doherty, Frank, 'The S.A.S. in N. Ireland', *Hibernia*, 30 March 1973 (reprinted in *Andersons-town News*, 25 April 1973).

Doherty, Frank, 'Belfast's dept. of "dirty tricks"', *Hibernia*, 16 November 1973.

Doherty, Frank, 'Edgar Graham – was he set up?', *Sunday News*, 18 December 1983.

Doherty, Frank, 'Black propaganda and bloody murder', *Magill*, December 1986.

Dorril, Stephen, 'A Who's Who of the British Secret State', *Lobster*, special edition, May 1989.

Downey, James, 'The meaning of the Flagstaff', *The Irish Times*, 11 May 1976.

Ford, Richard, 'Intelligence accused of link in Dublin bombing', *The Times*, 2 March 1987.

Geraghty, Tony, 'How to train a hit team', *The Sunday Times*, 11 May 1980.

Hadden, Tom, 'Drumnakilly: the issues raised', *Fortnight*, October 1988.

Hearst, David, 'Inner city doubling as war zone', *The Guardian*, 14 August 1989.

Hibernia, 'Behind the loyalist bombs', 16 November 1973.

Hibernia, 'UDR: too many bad apples', 3 December 1976.

Hoggart, Simon, 'The army PR men of Northern Ireland', *New Society*, 11 October 1973.

Holland, Jack, 'Strasbourg: the men behind the torture', *Hibernia*, 8 October 1976.

Holland, Mary, 'Super power and super people', *Hibernia*, 15 May 1980.

Hudson, Christopher, 'SAS: heroes or villains?', *Daily Star*, 3 October 1988.

Hunter, John, 'Assassinations were revenge for Neave?', *Sunday World*, 26 October 1980.

Lawless, Gery, 'SAS: mission Ireland', 23 May; 'We protect your workers', 30 May; 'Operation Kerrygold', 6 June; 'The Great Train Robbery', 13 June; *Sunday World*, 1988.

The Leveller, 'Northern Ireland torture bosses named', No. 2, December 1976.

The Leveller, 'The deal behind the Dublin SAS trial', No. 5, April/May 1977.

The Leveller, 'How the British Army trained me in torture techniques', No. 6, June 1977.

The Leveller, 'SAS – restricted document details regimental structure', No. 33, December 1979.

Lewis, David, 'On her majesty's sexual service', *Penthouse*, Vol. 10, No. 12, 1976.

Lindsay, Kenneth, Extracts from Ambush at Tully-West: the British Intelligence Services in Action, in *The Irish Times*, 5, 6, 7 November 1979.

Lobster, 'Kitson, Kincora and counter-insurgency in Northern Ireland', No. 10, 1986.

Lobster, 'Wilson, M15 and the rise of Thatcher; covert operations in British politics 1974–78', No. 11, 1986.

Magill, 'The day of the bagman: the British Secret service in Ireland', June 1979.

Maguire, Michael, 'The SAS: new glamour but old style', *The Sunday Tribune*, 15 February 1981.

Maguire, Michael, 'The many-headed British intelligence operation in Ireland', *Camerawork*, No. 23, December 1981.

McKay, Ron, 'What makes the Special Air Service special', *Time Out*, No. 451, 8–14 December 1978.

McKay, Ron, Peak, Steve, Margolis, Karen, 'Terminal surveillance', *Time Out*, No. 469, 13–19 April 1979.

McKittrick, David, 'East Belfast killing linked with Herron case', *The Irish Times*, 15 May 1976.

McKittrick, David, 'Oldfield's job sets the tongues wagging', *The Irish Times*, 6 October 1979.

McKittrick, David, 'British spies in Ireland', 22 April, 'Information for sale', 23 April, 'Setting spy against spy', 24 April, *The Irish Times*, 1980.

McKittrick, David, 'Unravelling the truth in Ulster's dirty war', *The Independent*, 2 September 1987.

Moloney, Ed, 'The SAS in Northern Ireland', *Magill*, September 1978.

Moloney, Ed, 'The victims of Mason's secret war', *Hibernia*, 8 February 1979.

Moloney, Ed, 'The hidden force', *The Irish Times*, 21, 22, 23 January 1985.

Moloney, Ed, 'How the UDA's John McMichael earned his pips', *The Sunday Tribune*, 27 December 1987.

Moriarty, Gerry, 'Shoot-to-Kill in Strabane?', *The Irish Press*, 12 December 1986.

Murray, Alan, 'The 'crack' regiment that made bungle after bungle', *The Irish Press*, 5 July 1979.

Murray, Raymond, 'The SAS in Northern Ireland', *The Irish News*, 1 September 1980.

Murtagh, Peter, 'Trail that led from sunny Ibiza to Swedish solitary,' *The Guardian*, 11 August 1987.

Myers, Kevin, 'British intelligence: the loyalist links,' *Hibernia*, 13 June 1975.

New Hibernia, 'Undercover murder', December 1985.

Norton-Taylor, Richard, 'Picking the lock of Britain's security', *The Guardian*, 6 April 1988.

Ó Gadhra, Nollaig, 'Seóiníní in Éirinn': na Littlejohns agus spiairí eile', *Inniu*, 9 October–11 December 1981.

The Phoenix, 'SAS dirty tricks', 9 December 1983.

The Phoenix, 'SAS man to tell all', 2 March 1984.

Platow, Alexander, 'The SAS, their early days in Ireland and the Wilson plot', *Lobster*, 18 October 1989.

Ramsay, Robin, 'Loyalty is what they stab you in the back with', *Tribune*, 23 January 1987.

Ramsay, Robin, 'Smearing Wallace and Holroyd', *Lobster*, No. 15.

Ramsay, Robin, Dorril, Stephen, '*The Independent*'s vilification of Colin Wallace', privately circulated, 1987.

Republican News, 'SAS', 7 July 1973.

Republican News, 'The SAS', 19, 26 November, 3, 12 December 1977.

Riley, Morris, 'Smiley's people – the SAS men return', *Anarchy*, No. 37, Winter, 1983–4.

Ryder, Chris, 'Bond has nothing on the IRA spy catchers', *Sunday Independent*, 8 October 1972.

Scott, Stephen, 'The secret war in Ireland', *New Statesman*, 13 July 1979. (reprinted in *Hibernia*, 19 July 1979).

Shatter, 'Spyfile'.

Sunday World, 'The SAS men they wouldn't let you see', 13 March 1977.

Thomas, Jo, '"Shoot-to-Kill" policy in Ulster?', *The New York Times*, 12 April 1985.

Thomas, Jo, 'In Ulster the "Shoot-to-Kill" rumours will not die', *The New York Times*, 17 March 1986.

Thomas, Jo, 'Bloody Ireland: a reporter chronicles her attempt to investigate in Northern Ireland – and describes the forces that conceal the secrets of a dirty war', *Columbia Journalism Review*, May/June 1988.

Time Out, 'A good week for the KGB?', No. 181, 10–16 August 1973.

Time Out, 'The pedigree dogs of war', No. 433, 21–27 July 1978.

Tóibín, Colm, 'Ghosts of the killing fields', *M, the Observer* magazine, 22 November 1987.

Troops Out, 'Army. Get out!', 29 July 1978.

Urban, Mark, 'Fighting terrorism: the making of an SAS man', *The Independent*, 6 September 1988.

Wallace, J. C., Letter to *The Listener*, 27 August 1987.

Ware, John, Letter to *The Listener*, 27 August 1987.

Webbe, Stephen. 'Is Britain's SAS too quick to pull the trigger'? *The Christian Science Monitor*, 3 October 1988.

Winchester, Simon, 'How the SAS moved in on the terrorists', *The Guardian*, 11 December 1976.

Workers' Research Unit, 'Repression', Bulletin No. 2, Winter 1977.

Gibraltar Killings

Amnesty International, United Kingdom. *Investigating Lethal Shootings: The Gibraltar Inquest*, April 1989.

Ascherson, Neal, 'No morals, please, we're English', *The Observer*, 10 April 1988.

Bolton, Roger, *Death on the Rock and Other Stories*, W. H. Allen/Optomer, 1990.

Brooks, Richard, Harris, Robert, 'Television on trial', *The Observer*, 1 May 1988.

Campbell, Duncan, 'Whose finger on the trigger?', *The Sunday Tribune*, 1 May 1988; 'Panic in the street', *New Statesman & Society*, 17 June 1988.

Cockerell, Michael, 'Between a rock and a hard place', *The Sunday Times*, 29 January 1989.

Connolly, Frank, 'Death without end', *Magill*, April 1988.

Court Report: The Gibraltar Inquest. Channel Four Television. Post production script, October 1988.

'Death on the Rock', *This Week:* Thames Television, 28 April 1988, reporter Julian Manyon; producer, Chris Oxley; researchers, Eamon Hardy, Alison Cahn; editor, Roger Bolton.

Donlon, Lorna, Godson, Rory, Trench, Brian, 'Gunned down in Gibraltar', *The Sunday Tribune*, 13 March 1988.

Dunne, Derek, 'Breaking the silence', interview with Gerry Adams, *In Dublin*, 28 April 1988.

Editorial: 'Gibraltar – rock of press freedom?', *The Sunday Tribune*, 29 January 1989.

Editorial: 'The horror and the pity', letter, *The Tablet*, 20 March 1988.

Editorial comment: 'The Ides of March', *The Month*, May 1988.

Faul, Denis, 'The horror and the pity', Letter, *The Tablet*, 16 April 1988,

Godson, Rory & Moloney, Ed, 'The SAS and the Spanish connection', *The Sunday Tribune*, 25 September 1988; 'The Gibraltar verdict: it was a close run thing', *idem*, 2 October 1988.

Hebert, Hugh, 'Don't knock the Rock', *The Guardian*, 9 September 1988.

Hislop, Ian, 'Questioning the Gibraltar killings', *Marie Claire*, May 1989.

Hogg, Andrew, 'Whitewash or vindication?', *The Sunday Times*, 29 January 1989.

Hopper, John, Murtagh, Peter, 'Anti-terror officers win awards', *The Guardian*, 14 March 1989; 'Police awards played down', *idem*, 15 March 1989; 'Spain rejects Gibraltar evidence', *idem*, 16 March 1989; 'Questions linger over Rock shooting', *idem*, 25 March 1989.

Inquest, Annual report 1987–8. Special report on Gibraltar inquest.

Insight, 'Ambush on the Rock', *The Sunday Times*, 13 March 1988; '60 seconds that put the SAS in the dock', *idem*, 8 May 1988; 'TV Lie, part 1, 2,', *idem*, 8 May 1988; 'Doubts emerge over key Gibraltar evidence', *idem*, 2 April 1989 .

Jack, Ian, 'Gibraltar', *Granta* 25, Autumn 1988; 'Deaths that cannot be buried away', *The Observer*, 28 May 1989.

Jenkins, Jolyon, 'Truth on the rocks', *New Statesman/New Society*, 27 January 1989

Jenkins, Peter, 'The press must not back the covert state', *The Independent*, 4 May 1988.

Kee, Robert, 'Foundering on the Rock', *The Observer*, 29 January 1989.

Kellner, Peter, 'Power wields bigger guns than truth', *The Independent*, 30 January 1989.

Kennedy, William V., 'The truth about war', *The Christian Science Monitor*, 28 April 1989.

Kilroy-Silk, Robert, 'Licensed to kill'?, *The Times*, 11 March 1988.

Lashmar, Paul, Hopper, John, 'FO has "lost" key Rock document', *The Observer*, 28 May 1989; ('FO reveals Gib document', *idem*, 4 June 1989).

Leigh, David, 'TV reporter "mislaid" by Defence Ministries', *The Observer*, 18 December 1988.

Leigh, David, Lashmar, Paul, 'Inquest doubts on Gibraltar', *The Observer*, 20 November 1988; 'Insight into a distortion', *idem*, 15 January 1989.

Leigh, David, Lashmar, Paul, Hopper, John, 'Spanish explode M15 "Rock" story', *The Observer*, 19 February 1989: 'Madrid angry at UK "lies" on IRA deaths', *idem*, 21 May 1989.

McGeever, Jenny, 'The story of Mairéad Farrell', *Magill*, October 1986.

McGirk, Tim, Mills, Heather, 'Spain honours police in IRA surveillance', *The Independent*, 14 March 1989; 'Spanish police contradict British line on IRA deaths', 'SAS shootings allowed others to escape', *idem*, 23 May 1989.

McGirk, Tim, Mills, Heather, McKittrick, David, 'Spanish challenge on Gibraltar shootings,' *The Independent*, 16 March 1989.

McKittrick, David, 'The last hurrah for Paddy McGrory', *The Independent*, 7 September 1988.

Miller, David, 'Whose truth? The media and the Gibraltar killings', (Glasgow University Media Group), 21 March 1989; 'The damage was done', *Magill*, April 1989.

Miller, David, Maguire, Dave, 'Truth on the rocks', *Magill*, February 1989.

Mills, Heather, 'Witness defies "smear" campaign', *The Independent*, 14 May 1988.

Mills, Heather, Urban, Mark, 'Many secrets stay hidden on the Rock' and other reports, *The Independent*, 1 October 1988.

Mitchell, Geraldine, 'Britain denies Spanish claims on IRA trio', *The Irish Times*, 16 March 1989.

Mitchell, Geraldine, Pollak, Andy, 'The Spanish policeman rejects British version of IRA killings', *The Irish Times*, 24 April 1989; 'Spanish unease over IRA surveillance claim', *idem*, 25 April; 'Gibraltar report withdrawn but not denied', *idem*, 26 April; 'Six took part in IRA's Gibraltar operation', *idem*, 10 May.

Moloney, Ed, 'Gibraltar witnesses attack "Sunday Times' distortions"', *The Sunday Tribune*, 15 May 1988; 'Profile: Paddy McGrory', *idem*, 10 July 1988; 'Spain undermines British version of Gibraltar killings', *idem*, 19 March 1989; 'Spanish police leaks undermine British version of Gibraltar killings', *idem*, 28 May 1989.

Morgan, Robin, Letters, *The Guardian*, 4, 10 January 1989.

National Council for Civil Liberties. Kitchen, Hilary, *The Gibraltar Report*, London, 1989.

Norton-Taylor, Richard, 'Truth founders on the Rock', *The Guardian*, 5 December 1988.

O'Dwyer-Russell, Simon, Macintyre, Donald, Ellis, Walter, 'A job for the SAS', *The Sunday Telegraph*, 13 March 1988.

O'Higgins, Michael, Waters, John, 'The anatomy of an afternoon', *Magill*, October 1988.

O'Sullivan, Jack, 'The Rock keeps its secrets', *Fortnight*, October 1988.

O'Sullivan, Jack, 'Death at a glance', *Fortnight*, November 1988.

Oxley, Chris, Letter, *The Guardian*, 6, 13 January 1989.

Oxley, Chris, 'A broadcaster in the dock', *The Guardian*, 2 February 1989.

Pallister, David, Norton-Taylor, Richard, 'Knocking on the door of the secret world', *The Guardian*, 5 September 1988.

Pallister, David, Norton-Taylor, Richard, 'Inquest leaves trail of open questions', *The Guardian*, 1 October 1988.

Parliamentary debates (Hansard), 'Gibraltar shootings', Monday, 7 March 1988.

Powell, Enoch, 'The questions our muddled press should be asking on Gibraltar', *The Independent*, 1 April 1988.

Profile. Lord Windlesham. *The Sunday Telegraph*, 29 January 1989.

Report. *The Windlesham/Rampton Report on Death on the Rock*, Faber and Faber, 1989.

'Rock Bottom', *Private Eye*, February 1989.

Rusbridger, Alan, 'Pulpits of faith and fury', *The Guardian*, 26 March 1988.

Scott, Michael, 'The "button" comes unstuck', *Fortnight*, October 1989.

Spotlight: BBC TV, programme on the Gibraltar killings, 5 May 1988.

Sunday Times, 'Scoops, revelations – and some errors', 29 January 1989.

Tiernan, Joe, *The Dublin and Monaghan Bombings, and the Murder Triangle*, 2002.

Valenzuela, Chief Inspector Tomás Rayo, English and Spanish version of his statement placed in House of Commons Library following parliamentary question by Andrew F. Bennet, MP.

Waterhouse, Rosie, Letter, *UK Press Gazette*, 2 January 1989.

Waters, John, 'The vilification of Carmen Proetta', *Magill*, June 1988.

Webbe, Stephen, 'Is Britain's SAS too quick to pull the trigger?', *The Christian Science Monitor*, 3–9 October 1988.

Worsthorne, Peregrine, 'Why shield the SAS?', *The Sunday Telegraph*, 29 January 1989.

Yeves, Enrique, Alegre, José, M., 'La policia Espanola informo que los terroristos del IRA iban desarmados', *Interviú*, April 1989; Townson, Nigel, 'Deceit on the Rock' (translated and adapted from *Interviú*), *New Statesman & Society*, 21 April 1989.

Index

Abbots, Ray, 198.
Acris, Sgt, 420.
Adams, Gerry, 195, 251, 260, 264–265, 304, 333, 346, 387, 388, 394, 430, 433, 446.
Adams, James, 12.
Aden, 11, 34, 37, 232.
Adriatic, 21.
Africa, East, 87.
Africa, North, 13.
Africa, South, 20, 430.
Ahoghill, 133, 235.
Aghyaran, 186.
Agnew, Kevin, 80, 188.
Ahern, Bertie, 471, 474, 480, 498.
Aiguille du Chardonnet, 279
Albania, 21.
Albany Prison, 93.
Aldershot, 78, 82.
Alegre, José. Maria, 409.
Ali, 9.
Alison, Michael, 235.
Alps, French, 279.
Altamuskin, 446.
Amateur Photographer, 196.
Ambush, 12.
Ambush at Tully-West, 67, 502.
Amery, Julian, 19.
Anarchy Magazine, 19.
Andersonstown News, 125, 505, 513.
Andrews, Alex, 62.
Angola, 20.
Ankara, 195.
Annabeg, 318.
Annagher, 289, 296.
Annaghmore, 146, 147.
Antrim, 99, 108, 110, 225, 231, 232, 233, 235, 260, 300, 376, 389, 430,493, 494, 459.
Arabia, South, 11, 19.
Arabian Gulf, 31.
Arabistan, 9.
Arabs, 9.
Aranz, Luis, 404.
Archer, Geoffrey, 87.

Ardboe, 194, 201, 202, 207, 305, 306, 313, 449, 450, 452-453, 456, 493-495.
Ardoyne, 467.
Ardress, 381.
Ardstraw, 53.
Argentina, 9, 10.
Armagh, 29, 31, 41, 64, 72, 78, 82, 99, 106, 110, 116, 118, 121, 122, 126, 127, 130, 133, 140, 141, 142, 146, 159, 163, 198, 253, 270, 271, 272, 273, 274, 288, 315, 320, 333, 344, 349, 361, 376, 377, 380, 385, 387, 391, 395, 396, 449, 450, 458, 459.
Armagh Observer, 508
Armagh Prison, 35, 37, 39, 78, 80, 259, 284, 328, 398, 428.
Armagh, South, 29, 30, 63, 71, 75, 81, 82, 89, 90, 103, 119, 122, 136–143, 149, 150, 153, 163–184, 185, 188, 189, 196, 222, 231, 255, 271, 326, 344, 378, 395, 448, 449.
Armaghbreague, 128.
Armoy, 235.
Armstrong, Fred, 376.
Armstrong, Gary, 481.
Armstrong, Raymond, 10.
Armstrong, Timothy, 397.
Arnott, Robert P., 279.
Arthur, Max, 255.
Arthurs, Amelia, 392.
Arthurs, Brian, 392.
Arthurs, Declan John, 275, 376–396, 495.
Arthurs, Dominic, 392.
Arthurs, Mary, 392.
Arthurs, Patrick, 391.
Arthurs, Patrick (Jr), 392.
Arthurs, Paul, 392.
Arthy, John, 10, 11.
Ashford, 30, 115, 149, 469.
Asquez, Kenneth, 421–422.
Athens, 13.
Atkins, Humphrey, 31, 247, 249, 255, 258, 269, 494.
Atkinson, Malcolm, 10, 11.
Aughamullan, 124.

Augher, 144.
Aughnacloy, 123, 137.
Aughnaskea, 275, 380.
Augustine, St, 27.
'Austen, Kenneth', 77, 81, 83, cf.
    Littlejohn, Kenneth, 77, 81, 83.
'Austen, Keith', 83, cf. Littlejohn, Keith.
Australia, 18, 38, 111.

Babbington, Judge, 93, 169.
Bad Kohlgrub, 34.
'Badger, The', 119, 124.
Bahrain, 198.
Baillie, Harry, 269.
Baird, Ernest, 185.
Baker, Albert Walker, 88, 91–102, 188,
    491, 504.
Baldonnel, 178.
Ball, Jonathan, 498.
Ball, Julian A., 116, 117, 118, 119.
Ball, Michael, 433.
Ballinahinch, 376, 430.
Ballinderry, 236.
Ballinderry Bridge, 143.
Ballydougan, 165.
Ballyduggan, 481.
Ballygally, 259.
Ballygawley, 143, 379, 381, 440, 448.
Ballyhalbert, 94.
Ballykelly, 30, 33, 40, 72, 80, 110, 178,
    227, 491.
Ballykinler, 33, 252.
Ballymaguigan, 351.
Ballymena, 91, 99, 233, 297, 299, 467.
Ballymena Guardian, 508.
Ballymoney, 226–227, 230, 297, 467.
Ballymoyer, 141.
Ballysillan, 221–225, 292.
Balniel, Lord, 37.
Bambridge, Anthony, 12.
Banbridge, 132, 137, 140.
Bangor, 51, 55, 155, 156.
Banks, John, 20.
Bann, 123.
Bannagh, 327.
Bannon, Roderick, 170.
Barber, Alice, 62.
Barber, John, 62.
Bari, 21.
Barker, Leslie, 501.

Barr, Ivan, 344.
Barrett, Robert, 216.
Barron Report, 471, 480–488.
Barry, Peter, 332, 365, 388.
Bartlett, Gerald, 247–248.
Barton, Richard, 362.
Barton, Richard (Jr), 363.
Barzilay, David, 21.
Bates, Ernest, 62.
Bates, Simon, 255.
Bateson, Peter John, 430.
Baty, Brian, 179–180.
Bavaria, 11, 34.
Baxter, John, 431.
Beating the Terrorist? 506
Beattie, Paul, 139.
Beavis, Victor Leslie, 486-487.
Beggs, Mrs, 384.
Begley, Bernard, 384.
Begley, William, 10.
Beirut, 464.
Beleek, 482.
Belfast, 10, 22, 29, 30, 31, 33, 34, 35, 39,
    41, 43, 48, 50, 51, 54, 55, 56, 60, 61, 62,
    64, 65, 66, 68, 70, 73, 74, 80, 81, 82, 83,
    84, 88, 92, 93 95, 96, 97, 98, 99, 100,
    103, 105, 106, 109, 110, 112, 118, 119,
    125, 138, 144, 148, 149, 150, 151, 155,
    156, 157, 158, 159, 161, 182, 185, 186,
    194, 195, 196, 197, 199, 207, 208, 214,
    221, 231, 247, 248, 249, 252, 253, 255,
    256,260, 261, 263, 265, 266, 276, 277,
    288, 320, 328, 345, 347, 369, 370, 376,
    377, 378, 393, 397, 398, 400, 401, 402,
    427–428, 429, 430, 433, 434, 437, 439,
    440, 448, 449, 450-451, 466-467, 469,
    476, 478, 483, 491-495, 497-500, 503,
    504, 505.
Belfast Telegraph, 48, 62, 94, 100, 146, 147,
    221, 232, 503, 504, 505, 506, 507, 508.
Belgium, 13, 431.
Belgrano, 10, 400.
Belize, 18.
Bell, Brian Edward, 98.
Bell, James, 227.
Bell, John, 141.
Belleek, 431.
Belleeks, 169, 170.
Bellaghy, 467.
Benburb, 275.

Benn, Tony, 426.

Benner, Robert Malcolm, 63, 64.

Bennett, Charles, 467, 497, 499.

Bennett, Marie, 158.

Bennett Report, 247, 274.

Beragh, 145.

Beresford, David, 196.

Berkery, Aisling, 265–269.

Berkery, Moyra, 265–269.

Berlin, 111, 276.

Berry, Anthony, 314.

Bessbrook, 89, 139, 149, 151, 152, 165, 167, 169, 170, 174, 175, 176, 177, 179, 182.

Bethlehem, 508

Bettaney, Michael, alias 'John Edmonds' 507.

Bielefeld, 431.

Biggs-Davison, John, 163, 508.

Birches, 320, 381.

Birmingham, 17, 50, 76, 89, 179, 462.

Birmingham Evening Post, 506

Birmingham Six, 462, 496.

Bishop, Blair, 434.

Black, Alan, 167.

Black, Christopher, 256, 377.

Black, Mrs, 66.

Black, Tom, 67.

Black, William, 65–68, 106, 112, 193.

Blacktown, 144.

Blackwater, 317.

Blackwatertown, 315.

Blackwell, B.A., 261.

Blair, Tony, 474-475, 498-499.

Blaney, Martin, 380.

Bleakley, Rosemary, 161.

Bleary, 137.

Bloch, Jonathan, 501, 503.

Bloomfield, John James, 430.

Bloomhill, 144.

Bloor, Michael, 197, 493.

Blundy, David, 193, 505.

Boal, Desmond, 212.

Boer, 17.

Bohan, Alan Michael, 225–235.

Bonn, 432.

Bonnett, Alan, 197.

Borderline, 374.

Borneo, 11, 37.

Boulch, John, 501.

Bowen, Marion, 137.

Boyd, Andrew 507.

Boyd, John, 265–269.

Boyle, Cornelius, 226–227, 231.

Boyle, Evelyn, 141.

Boyle, Harris, 124, 137, 138, 140, 141 143, 485, 492.

Boyle, Hugh, 226–227, 231.

Boyle, John, 194, 225–235, 236, 292, 493, 506.

Boyle, Kevin, 274.

Boyle, Mrs, 227.

Boyle, Owen, 137.

Brace, Trevor, 188.

Bracknell, Trevor, 142, 165.

Bradford, Roy, 12.

Bradley, Denis, 474.

Bradley, Edward, 348.

Bradley, Francis Joseph, 275, 348–365, 495, 508.

Bradley, John, 348.

Bradley, Rosemary, 348, 361.

Brady, Brian J., 33, 52, 99, 502, 504.

Brady, Kevin, 429, 430, 495.

Brady, Patrick, 430.

Brady, Robert, 439.

Branley, Patrick, 327.

Brazil, Patrick, 179.

Bredin, William, 188.

Breen, Harry, 395, 470, 500.

Breen, James, 136.

Brennan, Brendan, 57, 58, 59.

Brennan, Chris, 337.

Breslin, Charles, 275, 315, 333–348, 495.

Breslin, Joseph, 334.

Brighton, 31, 314, 464, 494.

Brigid, St, 296.

Britain's Military Strategy in Ireland: The Kitson Experiment, 154, 503, 504.

British Army and Special Branch RUC Brutalities, 78, 502.

British Army in Ulster, The, 21.

British Dimension, The, 506, 507.

British Intelligence and Covert AAction, 503

Brockagh, 305, 313.

Brooke, Peter, 463, 496.

Brown, Bob, 180.

Brown, Colin, 411.

Brown, Denis Emmanuel, 194, 221–225, 493.

Brown, Derek, 180, 503.
Brown, Gregory, 97, 98, 99, 504.
Brown, James, 140.
Brown, Robert C., 114, 185.
Brown, Ronnie, 278.
Brown, Seán, 467, 500.
Brown Vincent 502.
Brownlee, Edward, 259.
Bryson, James, 46, 61.
Buchanan, Bob, 395, 470, 500.
Buchanan, Raymond, 140.
Buchanan, Winston, 146.
Buchwald, Namoi, 214.
Bullock, Lucinda, 416.
Bullock, Peter, 434.
Bullock, Stephen, 416, 417, 418.
Bunch of Five, 41.
Bundoran, 72, 322.
Bunker, Paul, 10, 11.
Bunting, Fiona, 263.
Bunting, Ronnie, 259, 262–263, 265, 268, 269, 494.
Bunting, Suzanne, 262–263.
Burbridge, Michael, 275, 494.
Burchell, Nigel Anthony, 177.
Burchett, Wilfred 501
Burfitt, Jayson, 434.
Burns, Brendan, 397.
Burns, John, 62, 439.
Burns, Robert, 10.
Burns, Seán, 270, 271–272, 494. 496.
Burntollet, 29.
Burt, Tom, 22.
Buskhill, 137.
Busto, Mario, 408.
Byrne, Kevin, 30, 181–182, 492.
Byron, 13.

Cadiz, 409.
Cahill, Joe, 63.
Cahill, Thomas V., 80, 205, 206, 246.
Caledon, 275, 380.
Callaghan, James, 31, 37, 185, 231, 493.
Callan, Mary, 172.
Calvert, J.M., 14.
Cambodia, 19.
Cambridge, 449.
Camerawork 501
Cameron, Ian, 102, 121.
Campbell, Brendan, 289.

Campbell, Brian John, 274, 289–297, 448, 494.
Campbell, Donal, 289.
Campbell, Duncan, 19, 116, 130–133, 135, 407, 501, 504, 505.
Campbell, Geoffrey, 315.
Campbell, James, 505.
Campbell, Joseph, 295.
Campbell, Joseph P., 257.
Campbell, Maura, 265–269.
Campbell, Patrick, 132.
Campbell, Patrick, 394.
Campbell, Peter, 295.
Campbell, R. B., 218.
Campbell, Robert Joseph, 256.
Campbell, Seán, 119, 150.
Campbell, Ursula, 289.
Canada, 94, 150, 399, 470, 500.
Canepa, Adolpho, 405.
Canepa, Joseph, 406, 411.
Canning, Mrs, 57.
Canny, Michael, 376.
Cappagh, 122, 145, 275, 380, 393, 452.
Cardiff, 37.
Cargan, John, 445.
Cargin, 360.
Carlisle, Norman, 140.
Carman, 201, 274, 305, 313.
Carnlough, 259, 494.
Carolan, Joseph, 287.
Carr, Robert, 77.
Carrickfergus, 50, 143, 156, 160, 389.
Carrickmore, 144, 145, 207, 440, 442.
Carrington, Lord, 76, 77, 81, 86, 87, 503.
Carroll, Adrian, 270.
Carroll, Roddy, 127, 133, 271, 273, 452, 494.
Carron, Owen, 430.
Carrowreagh, 375.
Carson, Derek, 302, 312.
Carson, Elizabeth, 158.
Carson, J. L., 356, 358.
Carswell, Justice, 348.
Carver, Lord, 20.
Carville, Gerry, 128, 129, 130, 131, 142.
Carville, Jerry, 129.
Cary, 17.
Casey, Gerard, 449, 495.
Casquero, Tomás, 409.
Cassidy, Denis, 501.

Castlebellingham, 84.

Castleblayney, 62, 72, 126, 127, 128, 131, 133, 135, 141, 393, 482, 492.

Castledawson, 142, 235, 275, 349, 350, 353, 363.

Castlederg, 186–187, 188, 342, 374, 493.

Castledillon, 116, 117, 124, 137, 148.

Castlereagh, 99, 133, 153, 253, 263, 268, 269, 321, 347, 349, 398, 449, 481, 493, 500.

Castlereagh File, The, 247.

Catherwood, Gordon, 100.

Catholic Standard, The 505.

Cavan, 369.

Cavendish, Anthony, 258.

Celecia, Josie, 417, 420.

Chalfont, Lord, 165.

Chamber, Richard, 147.

Chambers, Elizabeth, 270.

Chambers, John, 376.

Chambers, Robert, 167.

Chapelizod, 86.

Chapman, Reggie, 167.

Chapman, Sandra 504

Chapman, Walter, 167.

Charlemont, 450.

Charles, David A., 189.

Chastelain, John de, 466, 497.

Chelsea, 77, 87.

Cheltenham, 507.

Cherbourg, 432.

Cheshire, Lawrence, 334.

Chinese, 14.

Christian Science Monitor, The, 501.

Churchill, Winston, 13.

Clancy, Peter, 456, 459, 496.

Clare, 126, 393.

Clark, David, 501.

Clarke, A. F. N., 148, 149, 182.

Clarke, Hugh William, 129–130, 142.

Clarke, Liam, 482, 485, 505.

Clarke, Sr Sarah, 500.

Clarke, Seamus Pius, 327.

Clarke, Thomas, 109, 124.

Clarke, Thomas, 389

Clavey, Mark, 433.

Cleary, Peter, 23, 30, 150, 168–175, 180, 185, 326, 492, 505.

Clements, Roy, 265.

Clements, William J, 379.

Clingan, Willy, 393.

Clinton, Bill, 496.

Clitheroe, Andrew, 433.

Clogher, 144.

Clogherhead, 83, 84.

Clones, 72, 118, 370.

Clonmult, 376.

Clonoe, 455-456, 459-461, 496.

Clontibret, 482.

Clontygora, 127.

Cloughfin, 440, 441.

Coagh, 194, 236, 238, 450, 452-453, 455, 493, 496.

Coalisland, 29, 122, 124, 139, 144, 145, 264, 274, 289, 296, 305, 315, 317, 393, 397, 456, 460, 494.

Cockburn, Claud, 164, 222.

Cocuera, José Luis, 405.

Colchester, 197, 314, 433.

Coleman, Francis, 306.

Coleraine, 54, 112, 467.

Collegeland, 381.

Collera, 375.

Collett, David Allan, 149, 150, 152.

Collins, Alexander, 188.

Collins, Frank, 340, 341, 343.

Collins, Gerry, 102.

Collins, Seán, 78, 80.

Colmcille, St, 296.

Colombo, Douglas, 422.

Colonel Paddy, 12, 502.

Colombia, 499, 500.

Columbanus, St, 296.

Columbia Journalism Review, 319.

Combat, 143.

Compton, 36, 37.

Conaghan, Rory, 125, 138.

Condon, Colm, 85.

Congo, 122, 144.

Connolly, Patrick, 123.

Connolly, Paul, 504.

Contact, 148, 182.

Convery, Michael, 161.

Conway, Gerard, 45–48, 456, 491, 502.

Conway, John, 45–48, 456, 491, 502.

Conway, William, 35, 38, 39, 141.

Cook, Tom, 377.

Cookstown, 144, 145, 202, 205, 305.

Cooldery, 184.

Cooper, Edward, 88.

Cooper, Ivan, 60.
Corgary, 186.
Cork, 376.
Cork Examiner, 175.
Corkey, Samuel Snowden, 270.
Cornascriebe, 147.
Corrigan, Leslie, 147.
Corrigan, Peter, 270.
Corrigan, William, 146.
Corruption of Law, 504.
Cory, Judge Peter, 470-471, 473-475, 500.
Cosham, 17.
Coshquin, 284.
Costello, Maolíosa, 201.
Costello, Seamus, 81, 82, 201.
Cotton, Michael John, 71, 104, 492.
Counter Revolutionary Operations, 23.
Cowen, Barry, 507.
Cowen, Brian, 474.
Cowles, Virginia, 11, 501.
Cowley, Martin, 505.
Coyle, Angela, 438.
Coyle, Kevin, 346.
Coyle, Marion, 187.
Coyle, Michael, 161.
'Coyne, Brendan', 402.
CPAR, 463.
Craig, William, 107, 108, 185.
Craigavon, 99, 124, 155, 195, 271, 296,
    454, 494.
Craigavon Times, 139, 505, 508.
Cramer, Chris, 9.
Crawford, Ivan, 376.
Creasey, Timothy, 194, 235, 253, 297, 493.
Crediton, 297.
Cregagh, 99.
Cregganduff, 397.
Cres, 22.
Crilly, Oliver, 345, 346.
Crinnion, Patrick, 86, 87.
Croghan, 375.
Crossan, Declan John, 334.
Crossmaglen, 30, 84, 141, 148, 149, 156,
    170, 174, 182–183, 184, 196, 255, 397,
    493.
Crozier, Thomas Raymond, 124, 138.
Crumlin Road Prison, 168, 369, 391.
'Cuhen', 401.
Culfore, 175.
Cullen, Patrick Joseph, 317.

Culloville, 62, 63.
Cumaraswamy, Param, 474, 497-499.
Cummings, James, 397.
Cummings, Wilfred, 124.
Curran, Judge John, 393.
Curran, Noel, 85.
Currass, Philip, 10.
Currie, Austin, 387.
Curtis, Liz, 107, 506.
Cusack, Jim, 380.
Cushendall, 257, 482.
Cutting, Stephen, 70.
Cyprus, 18, 34, 41, 195, 276.

Daily Express, 52, 86, 163, 178, 439, 440,
    448, 502, 508.
Daily Mail, 178, 378, 501, 503, 507.
Daily Mirror, 197, 222, 254, 378, 418, 508.
Daily Telegraph, 22, 24, 247–248, 254, 425,
    501, 502, 503, 505, 507, 508.
Dale, Eric, 127.
Dale, John, 501.
Dalmatian, 21.
Daly, Cahal, 463.
Daly, Edward, 231, 241, 275, 288,
    332–346.
Daly, Marie, 261.
Daly, Miriam, 259, 260, 261–262, 494.
Daly, Tom, 72.
Dalyell, Tam, MP, 9, 440.
Damocles, 16.
Darkley, 128, 142, 296.
Davey, John Joseph, 430, 495.
Davidson, Sarah, 104.
Davidson, Sid, 10, 11.
Davidson, William, 104.
Davies, Nick, 501.
Davies, Rhys, 179.
Davis, Trevor, 433.
Deacon, Richard, 256, 258.
Deal, 433, 495.
Dearsley, Bernard ('Bunny'), 120.
Death in the Afternoon, 412.
Debelius, Harry, 403, 404.
de Bruxelles, Simon, 403, 410.
Deering, John, 502.
Deery, Lee Francis, 261.
Democrat, The, 385, 506, 507.
Dennison, John, 376.
Denny, Aidan, 428.

Derby, 88.

Derbyshire, 252.

Derry, 29, 41, 43, 60, 68, 71, 75, 78, 80, 88, 99, 105, 142, 143, 144, 185, 188, 194, 196, 197, 199, 205, 214, 216, 220, 221, 231, 241, 251, 253, 260, 274, 275, 277, 279, 280, 281, 284, 285, 315, 321, 327, 328, 332, 333, 345–346, 353, 375, 376, 377, 380, 393, 431, 448, 449, 453, 467, 468, 492, 493, 494, 495.

Derry Journal, 278, 502, 506, 507.

Derryard, 396, 495.

Derryavena, 317.

Derrygarve, 348.

Derryloughan, 264, 317.

Derrytresk, 317.

de Valera, Eamon, 21.

Devenney, Samuel, 41, 499.

Devenney, William Robert, 236–239.

Deverna, 166.

Devine, David, 275, 315, 333–348, 495.

Devine, Michael, 275, 315, 333–348, 495.

Devine, Mrs, 344.

Devine, William, 334, 344, 345.

Devlin, Charles, 387.

Devlin, Daniel, 221, 222.

Devlin, Gertrude, 122, 123, 144.

Devlin, James, 122, 123, 144.

Devlin, John, 50.

Devlin, Michael, 449, 450, 495.

Devlin, Paddy, 95, 164, 185, 269, 504.

Devlin, Patricia, 122, 123, 144.

Devon, 297.

Dhofar, 11, 198.

Diario 16, 426.

Dillon, Martin, 12.

Dillon, Viscount, 76.

Diverse Reports, 116, 121, 467.

Doherty, Daniel, 275, 315, 328–333, 342, 495.

Doherty, 'Dutch', 79.

Doherty, Frank, 47, 61, 88, 96, 502, 504, 505.

Doherty, John, 328.

Doherty, Joseph, 256.

Doherty, Julie, 328.

Doherty, Kay, 328.

Doherty, Kevin-Barry, 328.

Doherty, Kieran, 398.

Doherty, Margaret, 398.

Doherty, Ronnie, 340.

Doherty, Thomas, 362.

Donabate, 120.

Donaghmore, 144.

Donaghy, Martin, 312.

Donaldson, Alex, 315.

Donaldson, John, 276.

Doncaster, 17.

Donegal, 88, 96, 187–188, 322, 374.

Donegan, Mr, 175, 176.

Donegan, Mrs, 175, 176.

Donegan, Patrick, 503.

Don Juan, 13.

Donnelly, Lette, 392.

Donnelly, Michael, 142–165.

Donnelly, Patrick, 392.

Donnelly, Patsy, 142, 165.

Donnelly, Seamus, 275, 376–396, 495.

Dornan, Mary Ellen, 161.

Dorril, Stephen, 134, 505.

Doris, Tony, 452-454, 496.

Dortmund, 432.

Douglas-Home, Alec, 19.

Dowd, John T., 315.

Dowling, Mr, 180.

Down, 65, 75, 80, 81, 82, 88, 89, 90, 104, 156, 165, 196, 252, 376, 397, 492, 495.

Down & Connor, 269.

Downpatrick, 393.

Doyle, Eugene, 136.

Doyle, Sammy, 97.

Draperstown, 235, 297.

Drimnagh, 64.

Drogheda, 395, 427.

Dromad, 181.

Dromintee, 149, 151, 152, 175.

Dromore (Down), 196.

Dromore (Tyrone), 145.

Drumcree, 466.

Drummond, Deane, 18.

Drummond, James, 278.

Drummuckavall, 183.

Drumnakilly, 439–448, 495.

Drumnasoo, 146.

Drumquin, 430.

Drumsallon, 387.

Drury Report, 499.

Dublin, 21, 30, 62, 63, 64, 74, 76, 77, 80, 83, 84, 85, 86, 87, 88, 96, 98, 107, 109, 110, 113, 120, 142, 169, 174, 178,

179–180, 193, 202, 255, 256, 265, 320, 389, 401, 427, 470, 471, 479, 480-484, 487-488, 492, 496, 497, 499.
Duddy, Gerald, 47.
Duffy, Anthony, 109, 124.
Duffy, Liam, 284–292, 507.
Duffy, Magarita, 241, 246.
Duffy, Moira, 246.
Duffy, P. A., 203–207, 292, 294, 295.
Duffy, Patrick, 75, 194, 241–246, 292, 493.
Duffy, Paul, 194, 201–207, 493, 506.
Duisburg, 431.
Dukes, Alan, 388, 505.
Duncan, James, 183.
Dundalk, 62, 72, 78, 80, 84, 85, 150, 151, 153, 156, 168, 169, 175, 177, 182, 395, 427, 481, 492.
Dundee, 419.
Dundrum, 397.
Dungannon, 29, 61, 122, 123, 124, 125, 137, 138, 139, 143, 144, 145, 146, 197, 202, 206, 290, 292, 294, 296, 317, 349, 376, 378, 380, 381, 387, 389, 391, 455, 485, 493.
Dungannon Observer, 146, 505, 507.
Dunleer, 83.
Dunloy, 194, 225, 226, 230, 231, 274, 281, 289, 297–304,493, 494.
Dunmoyle, 446.
Dunne, 340.
Dunne, Derek, 508.
Durham, 101, 501.
'Durverne, Charles', 77, cf. Littlejohn, Kenneth.
Düsseldorf, 431.

Ead, David, 376.
Eastaugh, John, 10.
Ebrington, 99, 196, 226, 244, 278, 287, 300, 343, 375.
Economist, The, 107.
Edendork, 144.
Edentubber, 168.
Ederney, 376.
Edinburgh, Duke of, 25.
'Edmonds, John' 507, cf. Bettany, Michael.
Eglinton, 188.
Eglish, 380.
Egypt, 13.

Eksund, 399.
ELAS, 13.
Elisworth-Jones, William, 180.
Elite Forces, The SAS, 12.
Elizabeth II, Queen, 25, 276, 277.
Elliot, Ernie 'Duke', 95.
Elliott, Denis, 247.
Elliott, James, 438.
Elliott, Robert Gregory, 342.
Ellis, Walter, 410.
El Pais, 409, 426, 428.
Emergency Tour, 505.
Encyclopaedia Britannica, 155.
Enfield, 314.
Enniskillen, 163, 369, 376, 399.
Errington, 72.
Erwin, Laurence, 141.
Eskaraghlough, 144.
Evans, Clifford, 234.
Evans, E. W., 25.
Evans, R. J., 348, 349.
Evelegh, Robin, 56–59.
Evening Herald, 87, 380, 508
Evening News, 503.
Evening Press, 504.
Evening Standard, 440, 503.
Ewart-Biggs, Christopher, 30, 86, 175, 255, 492.
Ezzatti, Dr, 9.

Fagan, Lorraine, 172.
Fagan, Mark, 172.
Fagan, Rachel, 172.
Fagan, Raymond, 170, 173.
Fahy, John, 340.
Faligot, Roger, 154, 155, 503, 504.
Falklands, 9, 10, 11, 25, 277, 279, 400, 465, 501.
Fallahi, Abbas, 9.
Falls, Patrick Aidan, 124, 125, 145.
Faloon, Mervyn Joseph, 147.
Farmer, John, 481.
Farmer, Seán, 141, 142, 143.
Farnborough, 198.
Farnes, Keith, 121.
Farragher, Kieran Joseph, 278.
Farran, Roy, 12.
Farrell, Laurence, 178.
Farrell, Mairéad, 396–437, 495.
Farrell, Niall, 434.

Farren, John, 345.

Faul, Denis, 33, 37, 38, 39, 93, 122, 143, 183, 186, 188, 213, 231, 247, 284, 349, 365, 387, 444, 445, 502, 504, 506, 507.

Faye, Philip Anthony, 92, 93.

Feakle, 126.

Fearon, Patrick, 153.

Fearon, Peter, 248.

Feeney, Michael John, 137.

Fennalog, 141.

Feraday, Alan, 399, 414.

Ferguson, David, 170.

Fermanagh, 144, 251, 276, 322, 325, 344, 365–366, 368, 369, 370, 376, 389, 431, 494, 495, 502.

Fice, Richard George, 433.

Fielder, Michael, 418.

Fieldhouse, John, 465.

Finch, Christopher, 422.

Fintona, 145.

Finucane, Geraldine, 473.

Finucane, Michael, 468, 474, 479.

Finucane, Pat, 450, 466, 468-469, 471-474, 476, 478-479, 495, 497, 498, 499, 500.

Fisher, Anthony, 197, 493.

Fisher, Mark, 467, 497.

Fisk, Robert, 68, 103, 105, 106, 108, 164, 193, 492, 502.

Fitt, Gerry, 104, 164, 233, 235, 269, 508.

Fitzgerald, Garret, 180.

Fitzgerald, Patrick, 501, 503.

Flanagan, Ronnie, 497, 500.

Flecker, James Elroy, 53.

Fleming, Gary, 328.

Fleming, Kieran, 274, 314, 320–328, 495.

Fleming, Joseph, 88.

Fleming, Paul, 328.

Fleming, William James Paul, 275, 314–315, 327, 328–333, 342, 495.

Florida, 11.

Flurry, 151, 152, 168, 181.

Flynn, John, 119.

Flynn, Séan, 505.

Foley, J. P., 23.

Foot, Paul, 102, 109.

Forbes, Anne, 202, 207.

Forbes, Gerry, 202, 203, 207.

Forbes, Mary, 306.

Forde, Major General Robert, 498.

Foremass, 439, 446.

Forkhill, 150, 152, 170, 176, 255, 492.

Formby, 197.

Fortnight, 43, 274, 414, 436, 508, 509.

Fort Bragg, 34.

Foster, Ian, 369.

Foster, Jonathan, 271.

Foster, Mary, 296.

Fox, Billy, 118.

Frameworks for the Future, 496.

France, 13, 21, 432.

Franks, B. M. F., 248.

Fraser, Hugh, 148.

Frazer, Robert, 141.

Freeburn, Robert, 167.

Freeland, Ian, 29.

Freeman, Mr, 114, 115, 116.

Fuengirola, 402,

Fusco, Angelo, 256.

Galbally, 275, 305, 380, 391, 393,

Gallagher, Eddie, 187.

Gallagher, Ian, 161.

Gallagher, John, 29, 41.

Gallagher, Lawrence, 10.

Gallagher, William, 216.

Galway, 76.

Gamble, Margaret, 161, 248, 492.

Gamble, Robert, 208–214, 493, 506.

Gangs and Counter-gangs, 41, 42.

Garvagh, 196.

Garvey, Edmund, 120.

Gate Fever, 505.

Geneva, 370, 426.

Geraghty, Tony, 12, 19, 163, 165, 196, 230, 501, 502, 506.

Geraghty, Tony, 137.

Germany, 21, 45, 53, 92, 105, 111, 248, 255, 276, 431, 432.

Ghadaffi, Col, 19.

Gibraltar, 11, 23, 31, 396–437, 463, 464, 465, 495, 496.

Gibson, Cecily, 377, 470, 495.

Gibson, Maurice, 153, 214, 377–378, 470, 495.

Gilford, 165, 492.

Gilliland, George, 379.

Gilmore, Colin, 397.

Gilmour, Raymond, 201, 256.

Gilvarry, Maurice, 221.

Girdwood, 30, 33, 35, 38, 40, 178, 491.

Glasgow, 422–423.
Glassdrummond, 84.
Glenanne, 103, 167, 480-483.
Glencull, 137.
Glengormley, 97.
Gloucestershire, 148.
Godson, Rory, 404.
Golan, 145.
Gonzales, Felipe, 404.
Goose Green, 9.
Gordon-Lloyd, Iain, 196, 493.
Gorman, Denis, 123.
Gormley, Annie, 392.
Gormley, Anthony, 392.
Gormley, Michael Anthony, 275, 376–96, 495.
Gorrod, Joe, 439.
Gortavale, 136.
Gortnaglush, 139.
Gough, 153, 253, 271, 344, 349, 350, 361, 385, 390, 392, 393, 455, 458, 459.
Graham, Clive, 431, 491.
Graham, David Alexander, 224, 225.
Graham, Thomas, 263, 264.
Graham, William, 380.
Grant, Francis, 46.
Grant, Piers, 294.
Granta, 25, 508.
Graves, David, 502.
Gray, Colin, 265.
Greece, 13, 21.
Greek Islands, 13.
Green, Ann, 126.
Green, Derek, 433.
Green, Francis, 126.
Green, Gerard, 126.
Green, Gerry, 126.
Green, John Francis, 68, 110, 116, 122, 125–136, 137, 138, 141, 142, 143, 480-481, 484-487, 492.
Green, Ursula, 126.
Greencastle, 379.
Greener, Richard, 434.
Greer, Jack, 161, 162.
Gregg, John, 265.
Greig, Gordon, 503.
Grew, Desmond, 450-452, 494, 496.
Grew, Seamus, 118, 119, 120, 127, 133, 270, 271, 273, 452, 494.
Grey, Lord, 52.

Greysteel, 498.
Griffin, James, 142.
Griffiths, Sir Eldon, 388.
Grimes, William, 179.
Grundy, Steven, 255.
Guardian, The, 167, 178, 180, 185, 377, 378, 400, 410, 423, 425, 438, 468, 469, 498, 501, 502, 503, 504, 508.
Guernsey, 19.
Guildford, 125, 462.
Guinea Pigs, The, 33.
Gulladuff, 80, 430, 495.
Gullan, Hector, 22.
Gurteen, 375.
Guy, John, 383.
Guy, Seán, 383.

Hackett, Dermot, 261, 430.
Hadden, Tom, 274.
Haldane, Lord, 17.
Hale, Edward, 463, 495.
Hale, Margaret, 142.
Hall, Joe, 503.
Halligan, Victor, 384.
Hamill, Desmond, 502.
Hamill, Robert, 471-474, 497, 500.
Hamilton, Archie, 68, 134.
Hamilton, David, 188.
Hamilton, Joe, 129, 130, 142.
Hamilton, Justice Liam, 480.
Hamilton, Paul, 270.
Hammersmith, 426.
Hammond, Louis, 491.
'Hamnan, Paul Edward', cf. Harman, Paul, 195.
Hanley, 252.
Hanna, Jim, 74, 492.
Hanna, Rainey, 328.
Hanna, Trevor, 439.
Hanna, William, 146.
Hanna, William James, 194, 221–225, 439, 493.
Hannastown, 98.
Hannaway, Kevin, 32.
Hanover, 432.
Hardy, Gerald, 255.
Harker, Tony, 270.
Harman, Paul, 195, 493.
'Harper', 401.
Harris, Sim, 9.

Harkin, Greg, 470.
Harrogate, 254.
Harte, Briege, 446.
Harte, Colm, 446.
Harte, Declan, 446.
Harte, Gerard, 439–448, 495.
Harte, Martin, 439–448, 495.
Harte, Róisín, 446.
Hartley, 279.
Harvey, Patrick, 183.
Harvey, Seamus, 30, 183–184, 185, 493.
Hassan, 53.
Hassett, Mrs, 49.
Hastings, Stephen, 163.
Hattersley, Roy, 37.
Hatton, William, 10.
Haughey, Charles, 345, 425.
Hawkins, Garth, 10.
Hayden, Robert, 179.
Hayes, Daniel, 47.
Hayward, Simon, 343, 344, 508.
Hazell, Heidi, 432.
Heakin, Richard, 431.
Heaney, Bernard, 215.
Heaney, Denis, 68, 194, 214–220, 284, 493.
Heaney, Denis, (Sr), 219.
Heaney, Elizabeth, 215, 217, 219, 506.
Heaney, Gabrielle, 215, 217.
Heaney, Paula, 217.
Heaney, Seamus, 215, 217.
Heany, Sheila, 83.
Hearst, David, 438.
Heath, Edward, 52, 102.
Heavener, Robert, 252.
Heenan, Patrick Eugene, 93.
Heffer, Eric, 425.
Hegarty, Frank, 374–376.
Hemingway, Ernest, 412.
Hempsey, Paul, 289.
Henderson, Betty, 217.
Hendron, Joe, 269.
Hennigan, Aidan, 143.
Henry, Harry, 380.
Hepburn, Ian, 439.
Herbert, Michael Francis, 71, 104, 492.
Hereford, 10, 15, 16, 18, 24, 25, 53, 67, 105, 196, 252, 501.
Herefordshire, 10.
Hermon, John, 273, 379, 394.

Heron, William, 141.
Herrema, Tiede, 187.
Herron, Tommy, 95, 96, 97, 99, 457, 491, 504.
Hertfordshire, 197.
Hetherington, Vincent Patrick, 98, 100, 492.
Hibernia, 34, 47, 61, 74, 113, 197, 501, 502, 503, 504, 506, 507.
Hicks, John, 439.
Higgins, John, 20.
Higgins, Justice, 261.
Higgins, William, 108.
Hill, Charles, 48.
Hillsborough, 375, 498.
'Hilton Operation', 19.
Hippo, 27.
Hird, Christopher, 116, 505.
History of the S.A.S. Regiment, A, 12.
Hitchin, 17.
Hitler, 21.
Hogan, Henry John, 274, 297–304, 494.
Hogan, Margaret, 297.
Hogan, Michael, 297.
Hogan, Mrs, 300.
Holland, 112, 431.
Holland, Jack, 34.
Holland, Mary, 47, 410, 463, 501.
Holloway, 85.
Holohan, Renagh, 503.
Holroyd, Fred, 102, 103, 109, 110–121, 124, 130, 131, 133, 134, 135, 136, 137, 141, 149, 480, 482, 484-86, 505.
Holywood, 30, 33, 35, 38, 40, 42, 43, 51, 52, 59, 64, 79, 178, 196, 250, 491.
Hong Kong, 111, 276.
Honiton, 29.
Hooded Men, The, 33, 502.
Hooley, Peter, 439.
Hooper, Paul, 277, 281, 501.
Houston, James, 396.
Howe, Geoffrey, 400, 405, 406, 410, 411, 423, 425, 426, 427.
Howes, Robert, 430, 495.
Huart, Charles, 404.
Hucker, Michael, 436.
Hughes, Anthony, 275, 376–396, 476, 495.
Hughes, Barbara, 76.
Hughes, Brendan, 69, 70, 98.

Hughes, Brigid, 384.
Hughes, Daniel, 122.
Hughes, Felix John, 123.
Hughes, Francis, 196, 374, 493.
Hughes, Michael Philip, 174.
Hughes, Oliver, 376–396, 508.
Hughes, Patrick, 142.
Hughes, William, 10, 11.
Hulme, Damian, 172, 173.
Hulme, Patricia, 172.
Hulme, Shirley, 172.
Hume, Basil, 148, 154.
Hume, John, 61, 332, 497.
Hunter, Robin, 12.
Hunter, William, 178.
Hurd, Douglas, 333, 346.
Hurson, Martin, 305, 391.
Huston, 9.
Hutchinson, Jackie, 193.
Hutchinson, James Henry, 146.

Independent, The, 133, 134, 135, 136, 400,
    402, 403, 404, 405, 411, 413, 417, 425,
    446, 465, 505, 508.
Informers, The, 507.
Ingram, Adam, 497.
Ingram, Martin, 470, 498.
Ingrams, Richard, 426, 464.
Inquest, 436, 437.
Inside Intelligence, 258.
Interviú, 404.
Iran, 9, London embassy, 9, 11, 277, 464, 465
Iraq, 470
Ireland: The Propaganda War, 107, 506.
Iris, 379, 508.
Irish Independent, The, 89, 119,503, 504,
    505, 506, 507, 508.
Irish News, The, 55, 100, 146, 147, 197,
    262, 269, 395, 430, 501, 502, 503, 504,
    505, 506, 507, 508.
Irish People, 503, 506.
Irish Press, The, 103, 143, 156, 157, 232,
    269, 332, 503, 505, 506, 507, 508.
Irish Times, The, 34, 39, 99, 108, 133, 135,
    164, 174, 194, 222, 233, 253, 271, 283,
    380, 388, 389, 402, 408, 409, 502, 503,
    504, 505, 506, 507, 508.
Irwin, Evan Alexander, 146.
Irwin, Mrs, 161, 247–248.
Irwin, Robert, 161, 247–248, 493.

Irwin, Thomas, 380.
Islania, Maheshkumar, 432.
Islania, Nivruti Mahesh, 432.
Italy, 13, 21.

Jack, Arthur, 233.
Jack, Ian, 403, 508.
'Jackal, The', 132, 133.
Jackson, Alan, 319, 320.
Jackson, Frederick George, 274, 314,
    315–320, 439, 494.
Jackson, Maurice, 320.
Jackson, Robin John, 140, 485.
Jackson, Sadie, 320.
Jameson, Robert, 144.
Jarvis, Leslie, 376.
Jeapes, Tony, 12.
Jebel, Akhdar, 14, 198.
Jenkins, Jolyon, 427.
John Paul II, Pope, 277, 395.
Johnson-Smith, Geoffrey, 57, 76, 77, 78,
    82, 85.
Johnston, Alan, 397.
Johnston, Gillian, 431.
Johnston, John, 141.
Johnston, Ken, 380.
Johnston, Peter Gerald, 162.
Jones, David, 196, 251, 493.
Jones, Philip, 10.
Jones, 'Taff', 433.
Jonesborough, 150, 181.
Jordan, Pearse, 476, 499, 500.
Jordan, Peter, 179.
*Journal of the Royal United Services
    Institute for Defence Studies,* 189.
Junor, John, 508.

Kane, Alan, 345.
Kane, Billy, 397.
Kane, Kevin, 161.
Keady, 126, 128, 141, 142, 482.
Kealy, Amy, 198.
Kealy, Maggi, 198.
Kealy, Mike (John Anthony), 197, 198.
Kealy, Mrs, 198.
Kealy, William, 198.
Keane, Fergal, 380.
Keane, John, 175.
Kearney, Andrew, 497.
Kearney, Brendan, 281, 282, 329.

Keeley, William James, 147.
Keenan, Dermot, 363.
Keenan, Seán, 246.
Kelly, 339, 340, 344.
Kelly, Anne, 389.
Kelly, Bernard, 60.
Kelly, Eugene, 275, 376–396, 495.
Kelly, Ivy, 315.
Kelly, James Joseph, 97.
Kelly, Judge, 219.
Kelly, Kevin, 360, 361.
Kelly, Liam, 389.
Kelly, Michael, 393.
Kelly, Paddy, 289.
Kelly, Patrick, 143, 145.
Kelly, Patrick, 275, 376–396, 495.
Kelly, Vincent, 389.
Kelly, Willie John, 389.
Kennaugh, 322.
Kennedy, Annette, 350.
Kennedy, Derek, 188.
Kennedy, Eilish, 350, 351.
Kennedy, Mary, 196.
Kenny, Hugh, 48.
Kent, 30, 115, 149, 195, 254, 279, 399, 433, 495.
Kenya, 18, 41, 42.
Kerr, Frank, 496.
Kerr, Gordon, 470.
Kerr, Norman 'Mooch', 140, 492.
Kerr, Robert John, 138.
Kerr, Sarah, 441.
Kesh, 322, 324, 325.
Kettering, 77.
Khuzestan, 9.
Kielty, Jack, 397.
Kiely, Niall, 174, 502.
Kildare, 322.
Kildress, 60.
Kilkeel, 397.
Killeen, 119, 127, 150, 169, 193, 377, 492, 495.
Killeter, 187.
Killygonland, 202.
Killylis, 137.
Killyman, 315.
Kilnasagart, 119.
Kilnaslieve, 392.
Kilrea, 430.
Kilroy-Silk, Robert, 426.

Kilskeery, 72.
Kinawley, 144.
King, Frank, 129.
King, Gerry, 193.
King, Tom, 115, 378, 379, 388, 395, 440, 445, 446.
Kingsmills, 167, 170, 492.
Kinnegar, 49.
Kinnego, 270, 271, 272.
Kinnock, Neil, 333.
Kirpatrick, Harry, 256.
Kitchen Hill, 195.
Kitson, Frank, 41, 42, 61, 102, 106, 194.
Knockacullion, 365.
Kurds, 34.
Kyle, John, 379.

Ladd, James, D., 12.
La Linea, 400, 403, 405, 408, 409.
Lambe, Anthony, 446.
Lambert, Adam, 498, 499.
Lambie, Graham Patrick, 434.
Lancaster, 106.
Lands Operation Manual, 23.
Lane, Chief Justice, 438.
Langley, James, 17.
Larne, 97, 154, 259, 260, 467.
Lashmar, Paul, 271, 406.
Lassen, Andy, 21.
Latimer, 115.
Laverty, Tommy, 129.
Lavery, Michael, 228.
Lavery, Peter, 197, 493.
Lawless, Gery, 502.
Laws, John, 436.
Lawson, John Michael, 176.
Lea, Richard, 253, 254.
Leahy, Fr, 322.
Leckey, John, 498.
Leeds, 17.
Leicester, 250.
Leicestershire, 276.
Leigh, David, 271, 406.
Leishman, Jackie, 503.
Leitrim, 393.
Lenihan, Brian, 388.
Lennon, James, 167.
Lennon, Kenneth, 105.
Lennon, Robert, 464.
Leonard, William Thomas, 122, 123, 144.

Letterkenny, 123, 327.
Leveller, The, 20, 33, 34, 258, 501, 502.
Le Williams, Alan, 185.
Lewis, Alexander, 434.
Lewis, David, 54.
Ley, John, 178.
Libya, 13, 19.
Ligari, Illisoni Vanioni, 176, 177.
Ligget, Stanley, 431.
Lightfoot, Paul, 10, 11.
Limavady, 375.
Limerick, 187.
Lindsay, Kennedy, 67, 68, 502, 505.
Lislasley, 450, 496.
Lisburn, 42, 44, 51, 61, 68, 72, 73, 74, 96, 98, 102, 109, 110, 116, 127, 144, 196, 263, 264, 265, 344, 396, 430, 433, 456, 491, 495.
Lisnaskea, 251, 252, 494.
Lissheffield, 383.
Litterick, Mr, 114.
Littlejohn, Christine, 75, 78, 83, 85.
Littlejohn, Keith, 75–91, 503, 504.
Littlejohn, Kenneth, 75–91, 102, 105, 112, 159, 491, 503, 505.
Liverpool, 197, 425.
Livingstone, Harry, 390.
Livingstone, Ken, 101, 114, 115, 116, 117, 504, 505.
Livingstone's Labour, 102.
Lloyd, Selwyn, 14.
Lloyd-Owen, David, 13.
Lobster, 110, 111, 113, 134, 501, 502, 505.
Lockhart, Roger, 146.
Logue, Gerard, 377.
London, 9, 15, 17, 18, 31, 41, 76, 77, 81, 85, 86, 87, 102, 178, 189, 247, 254, 256, 277, 320, 389, 406, 411, 432, 433, 464, 470, 478, 491, 493, 496, 498.
Long Kesh [Maze] Prison, 80, 126, 130, 169, 176, 188, 196, 259, 260, 262, 268, 327, 328, 374, 380, 390, 446, 471, 473, 497, 499.
Loop, 452.
Losinj, 22.
Lough Neagh, 449.
Loughgall, 23, 142, 275, 376–396, 450, 476, 486, 495, 497, 499.
Loughmacrory, 439, 446.
Loughran, Seamus, 73.

Loughrey, James, 119, 150.
Loughrey, James, 188.
Loughlin, Patrick, 118.
Loup, 380.
Lourdes, 322.
Louth, 75, 84, 175, 176, 184, 458.
Lovat, Lord, 148.
Love, Michael, 10.
Low Intensity Operation, 41, 61, 106.
Lowry, Robert, 91, 101, 229, 230, 377.
Luck, Norman, 503.
Ludlow, Seamus, 30, 175–176, 492, 497.
Lurgan, 10, 110, 119, 123, 124, 126, 127, 128, 131, 132, 133, 136, 138, 139, 142, 143, 144, 146, 195, 270, 271, 277, 288, 393, 467, 477, 483, 486, 493, 494, 499.
Lurgan Mail, 146, 506.
Luton, 105, 426.
Lydon, Charles, 252.
Lynagh, Colm, 390.
Lynagh, James, 275, 376–396, 495.
Lynagh, Michael, 390.
Lynch, Jack, 52, 84, 86, 87, 503.
Lynch, Seán, 365–376, 461, 495, 508.
Lyttle, Noel, 259, 262–263, 265, 268, 269, 494.

Mackensie, Kelvin, 418.
Macintyre, Donald, 410.
Mack, Desmond, 493.
Mack, Insp., 487.
Mackin, Desmond, 208–214, 493.
Mackin, Mrs, 213.
Mackle, Mrs, 381.
Mackle, Peter, 380.
Macmillan, Harold, 14, 19.
Macpherson, Angus, 503.
Madden, 129, 141.
Madden & Finucane, solicitors, 452.
Madrid, 400, 401, 403, 409, 410, 411.
Magee, Paul Patrick, 256.
Mageean, Paul, 477.
Maghera, 188, 196, 251, 297, 493.
Magherafelt, 79, 80, 274, 321, 322, 327, 348, 353, 380, 430.
Maghermulkenny, 290, 296.
Maghery, 385.
Magill, 48, 86, 418, 419, 420, 505.
Magill, Michael, 80.
Magilligan, 146, 391.

Maginn, Loughlin, 439, 449, 495.
Maginnis, Ken, 388, 448, 508.
Maguire, Charles Paul, 274, 275, 279–284, 494.
Maguire, Clare, 284.
Maguire, Dave, 422.
Maguire, Donna, 284.
Maguire, Francis, 35, 36.
Maguire, Isobel, 284.
Maguire, Marie, 284.
Maguire, Michael, 501.
Maguire Seven, 496.
Maidstone, 45.
Mailey, William John, 194, 221–225, 493.
Main, Christopher, 119.
Malaga, 401, 402, 404, 409, 422.
Malaya, 11, 14, 15, 18, 491.
Malaysia, 37, 111.
Malden, 314.
Mallon, Dominic, 38.
Mallon, John, 295.
Mallon, Roseanne, 455, 496.
Mallon, Seamus, 142.
Mallon, Seamus, MP, 185, 376, 387.
Malmo, 344.
Malone, Martin, 270.
Malvern, 15.
Manchester, 18, 51, 62, 63, 179.
Mandelson, Peter, 498, 499.
Mao Tse-Tung, 23.
Marbella, 399, 401, 402, 403.
Marchant, William, 377.
Mark, Robert, 18.
Markethill, 103, 270, 481.
Marks, Howard, 112.
Marley, Laurence, 377.
Marrinan, Patrick, 12, 502.
Mars & Minerva, 10, 14, 20, 21, 22, 23, 28, 117, 198, 248, 276, 278, 501.
Marshall, Thomas K., 218, 238, 288, 340.
Martin, Cathair, 299.
Martin, Declan Dominic Peter, 274, 297–304, 494.
Martin, Eugene, 391.
Martin, Eva, 144.
Martin, Seán, 391.
Martin, Mrs, 299, 304.
Maskey, Alex, 265.
Mason, Roy, 31, 163, 184, 185, 193, 198, 222, 231, 232, 233, 378.

Masterson, Elsie, 162.
Masterson, Gerard, 162.
Mates, Michael, 508.
Mather, Ian, 410.
Mathers, Brian, 85.
Mathers, Kay, 89.
Mau Mau, 42.
Maughan, Robert, 251, 252, 494.
Maye, Eileen, 305.
Maye, Ronan, 305.
Mayhew, Patrick, 274.
Mawhinney, Brian, 114.
May, David, 463.
Mayne, 'Paddy' Blair, 12, 22, 23, 29.
Maze [Long Kesh]Prison, 124, 188, 196, 259, 260, 268, 327, 328, 390, 446, 471, 473, 497, 499.
Meaklin, William, 141.
Meehan, Martin, 79.
Mehaffey, James, 346.
Mellows, Liam, 333.
Mercer, W. J. Crossley, 236, 239.
Metcalfe, Ian, 433.
Middle East, 21, 178, 470.
Mitchell, Ian, 481.
Mitchell, James, 480-483.
Middlesex, 17.
Middletown, 72, 120.
Mid-Ulster Mail, The, 508.
Millar, Robert George, 226, 227, 228.
Millar, William, 439.
Miller, David, 422, 423.
Mills, Aubrey, 188.
Mills, Heather, 402, 417.
Minden, 432.
Min Yuen, 14.
Mitchell, Geraldine, 402, 403, 408.
Moffett, Robert, 144.
Moley, Brendan, 397.
Molloy, Patrick, 122.
Moloney, Ed, 48, 262.
Molyneaux, James, 265.
Molyneux, 116.
Monaghan, 72, 88, 96, 107, 109, 110, 118, 120, 126, 130, 143, 275, 365, 366, 369, 370, 380, 390, 393, 397, 471, 480-484, 487-488, 492, 496-497, 499.
Monasterevin, 187.
Mönchengladbach, 432.
Moneyglass, 235.

Moneymore, 236, 452.
Monica, St, 27.
Mooney, Lynda, 268.
Mooney, Maureen, 268, 269.
Mooney, Patrick, 30, 181, 492.
Moore, Charles, 60.
Moore, Daniel Jude, 280.
Moortown, 452.
Mordue, Robyn, 421.
Morgan, Robin, 12.
Morgan, Thomas P. J., 153.
Morris, Thomas, 142.
Morrison, Danny, 394.
Morton, Peter, 174, 505.
Moscow, 22.
Moss, Robert, 107.
Mountbatten, Earl, 30.
Mount Everest, 25.
Mountfield, 380.
Mount Pleasant, 175.
Mountjoy, 318.
Mountjoy Prison, 89, 90.
Mourne, 31, 249, 255.
Moville, 188,
Mowhan, 71, 104, 492.
Mowlam, Mo, 498.
Moy, 122, 139, 140, 141, 142, 275, 380,
    390, 391, 455.
Mudd, Andrew, 433.
Mudd, Margaret, 433.
Mulgrew, Colm, 162.
Mulhern, Kevin, 188.
Mulholland, Arthur, 136.
Mulholland, David Alexander, 487.
Mulholland, Neil, 499.
Mulkearns, Paul, 172.
Mullaghbawn, 142.
Mullaghglass, 365.
Mullalish, 146.
Mullan, Bernadette, 122.
Mullan, Denis, 142.
Mullan, Francis, 122.
Mullen, Arthur, 181.
Mulley, Fred, 194, 233.
Mulligan, Michael, 158.
Mullin, Brian, 439–448, 495.
Mullin, Pat, 446.
Mullinahoe, 207.
Mullyash, 126, 128, 143, 492.
Mull of Kintyre, 496.

Mulvenna, James Gerard, 194, 221–225,
    493.
Mulvenna, Patrick, 61.
Mulvey, Anthony, 333, 345.
Münster, 432.
Murdoch, Rupert, 418.
Murphy, Daniel, 487.
Murphy, Inspector, 205, 206, 207.
Murphy, James, 144.
Murphy, James, 174, 176.
Murphy, Paul, 473, 475, 500.
Murphy, Thomas, 161.
Murray, Alan, 156, 157, 504, 505.
Murray, Fr, 444.
Murray, Garda, 176, 177.
Murray, Jim, 48, 49.
Murray, John, 429, 495.
Murray, Mary, 350, 361, 362.
Murray, Raymond, 502, 504, 505, 507,
    508.
Murtagh, Peter, 377.
Muscat, 15, 41.
Myers, Kevin, 74.

McAlea, Des, 137.
McAleavey, Mary, 158.
McAleer, Thaddeus, 442.
McAleese, David, 60.
McAleese, President Mary, 498.
McAlinden, Joseph, 161, 162.
McAliskey, Bernadette, 260, 263–264,
    265, 494.
McAliskey, Michael, 264, 494.
McAllister, Robert, 430.
McAnally, Conor, 503.
McAnespie, Aidan, 397.
McAnoy, Agnes, 158.
'McArdle, Edward', 402.
McAree, Sheila, 49.
McAuley, Martin, 270, 271–272, 503.
McBirney, Martin, 125.
McBrearty, George Patrick, 274, 275,
    279–284, 494.
McBrearty, Kelly, 284.
McBrearty, Orla, 284.
McBrearty, Rosemary, 284.
McBrearty, Stephen, 303.
Mac Bride, Damian, 320, 321.
Mac Bride, Frank, 320, 321.
McBride, Justin, 441.

Mac Bride, Lughaidh, 320.
Mac Bride, Marie, 320, 321.
Mac Bride, Nora, 320.
Mac Bride, Oistin, 320.
Mac Bride, Patricia, 320.
McBride, Peter, 467, 497.
McCabe, Anthony, 154.
McCabe, Fr, 369.
McCabe, Jack, 123.
McCabe, Jerry, 496.
McCabe, John, 252.
McCafferty, Charles, 60.
McCaffrey, Eddie, 38.
McCall, George, 140.
McCall, Sandra, 140.
McCann, Adeline, 361, 362.
McCann, Daniel, 396–437, 495.
McCann, Daniel, (Jr), 398.
McCann, Eamon, 506.
McCann, Joe, 82.
McCann, John, 362.
McCann, Maeve, 398.
McCann, Thomas, 64.
McCarron, Francis, 60.
McCarron, Richard, 216, 217, 219, 220.
McCartan, James Patrick, 92, 93, 101.
McCartan, Paul, 92, 93.
McCartney, Colm, 141, 142, 143, 481.
McCaughey, Martin, 450-452, 496.
McCaughey, Patrick, 265–269.
McClay, Peter, 188.
McClean, Neill Garvock, 177.
McClean, Paddy Joe, 40.
McClean, Robert J., 376.
McClelland, William, 259, 260.
McCloskey, Andrew, 345, 346.
McCloskey, B. W., 218.
McCloy, Alan, 270.
McClure, Laurence, 481.
McCollum, Justice, 265.
McCollum, William George Hamilton, 236–239.
McConnell, Eric, 259, 260.
McConnell, Nevin, 141.
McConnell, Robert, 259, 260, 485, 494.
McConnell, Robert, 142.
McConville, John, 167.
McConville, Joseph Denis, 146.
Mac Cormack, Douglas, 10.
McCormick, Anne, 260.

McCormick, Charles, 257.
McCormick, Patrick Rodney, 260.
McCorry, Kevin, 60.
McCourt, Eamon, 282, 283.
McCourt, Michael, 123.
McCourt, Michael, 145.
McCoy, Brian, 137.
McCoy, Michael Joseph, 153.
McCracken, Kevin, 427.
McCrea, William, 365.
McCreery, Edward, 94.
McCrory, Damian, 334.
McCullagh, Robert, 341.
McCullough, Eamon, 442.
McCullough, William, 119.
McCusker, Harold, 197, 235, 265.
McCutcheon, William, 234.
McDaid, Declan, 265–269.
McDermot, Seán, 398.
McDermott, Justice, 264, 370.
McDonagh, Martin, 161.
McDonagh, Mrs, 161.
McDonald, Peter, 183.
McDonnell, Alastair, 231.
McDonnell, Billy, 269.
McDowell, James Roderick, 124, 138.
McDowell, Jim, 440.
McElhinney, Douglas, 346.
McElhone, Patrick, 203.
McElhone, Seán, 352.
McElwain, Seamus, 369, 495.
McElwain, Seamus Turlough, 275, 365–376, 390, 461.
McErlean, Daniel, 60.
McErlean, Thomas, 429, 495.
McFadden, John, 299.
McFarlane, 'Bik', 374.
Mac Farlane, Campbell, 264.
McFerran, Paul, 315.
McFettridge, William, 259.
McGarry, Fr, 160.
McGeown, Alphonsus, 61, 122.
McGinley, Michael, 60.
Mac Giolla Bríde, Antoin, 274, 276, 314, 320–328, 348, 494.
McGirk, Tim, 402.
McGirr, Colm Anthony, 274, 289–297, 448, 494.
McGirr, Patricia, 289.
McGleenan, John, 142.

McGlinchey, Dominic, 133, 273.
McGonigal, Ambrose (Lord Justice), 21, 147.
McGonigal, Ian, 21.
McGookin, Bill, 136.
McGookin, Rosemary, 315.
McGowran, Robert, 503.
McGrady, Kevin, 256.
McGrath, Thomas, 147.
McGregor, James Alistair, 49, 491.
McGrogan, Myles Vincent, 98, 100, 493.
McGrory, P. J., 412, 414, 416, 419, 420, 434, 435.
McGuckin, Martin, 202, 203, 207.
McGuffin, John, 33.
McGuigan, Francis, 33.
McGuinness, Martin, 333, 345, 370, 430.
McGuinness, Mrs, 49.
McGurgan, Eamon, 118, 127, 128.
McGurgan, Kathleen, 127, 128.
McGurk, Patrick, 389.
McHenry, Seán, 315.
McHugh, Mary, 187.
McHugh, Michael, 10, 11.
McHugh, Michael, 185–188, 493.
McHugh, Samuel, 197, 493.
McIlmurry, Charles, 377.
McIlvanna, Seán, 315.
McIlveen, Wilfred, 270.
McIntyre, Daniel, 315.
McKay, Howard, Henry, 123.
McKearney, Jack and Kevin, 455.
McKearney, Jennie, 142.
McKearney, Margaret, 391.
McKearney, Pádraig, 275, 376–396, 495.
McKearney, Peter, 142.
McKearney, Tommy, 391.
McKee, Billy, 195.
McKee, James, 141.
McKee, Liam, 449.
McKee, Ronald, 141.
McKeever, John, 394.
McKenna, Finbarr, 377.
McKenna, Michael, 137.
McKenna, Patrick, 439.
McKenna, Seamus, 137.
McKenna, Seán, (Jr), 30, 168–169. 492.
McKenna, Seán, 33, 168.
McKeone, Charles, 348.
McKeone, Fr Kieran, 459-460.

McKeown, Clifford, 256.
McKerr, Gervaise, 270, 271–272, 476-478, 494, 496, 499.
McKiernan, Anthony, 397.
McKittrick, David, 99, 108, 133, 134, 135, 136, 233, 504
McLarnon, Bernard, 352, 361.
MacLean, Donald, 314.
MacLean, Muriel, 314.
McLernon, Roger, 455.
McLoughlin, Patrick, 176.
McLoughlin, Róisín, 248.
McMahon, Eamonn, 123.
McManus, James, 503.
McMichael, John, 260, 261, 262, 263, 265, 430.
McMillan, A. H., 174.
McMillan, Dave, 433.
McMonagle, Jim, 284.
McMonagle, John, 284.
McMonagle, Martin, 284.
McMonagle, Neill, 274, 275, 284–292, 494.
McMonagle, Patricia, 288, 289.
McMullan, Dominic, 300, 301, 302.
McMullen, Frank, 179.
McNabb, Sheila, 218, 220.
McNally, Lawrence, 452-454, 496.
McNally, Francis, 450.
McNally, James, 348, 350, 508.
McNally, Liam, 363, 364, 365.
McNally, Phelim, 450.
McNamara, Kevin, 395, 425.
McNeice, Brian, 389.
McNeill, John, 463, 495.
McNicholl, Elaine, 337.
McNicholl, Margaret, 337.
McNulty, Mervyn, 317, 318.
McNutt, Colm, 194, 199–201, 283, 284, 493.
McNutt, Mrs, 199.
McNutt, Una, 199.
McParland, Fr, 207.
McPolin, Kevin, 430.
McQuaid, Eugene, 119, 492.
McQueen, David, 94.
McQuillan, Thomas, 306, 310, 311, 314.
Mac Raois, Brian, 295.
Mac Stiofáin, Seán, 82.
McVeigh, Martin, 137.

McVeigh, Patrick, 45, 47–48, 491.
McVerry, Michael, 126.
McVey, Stephen, 360.
McVey, Terry, 360, 361.

Naden, D. J., 196, 493.
Nairac, Barbara, 148.
Nairac, Maurice, 148.
Nairac, Robert, 15, 68, 110, 116, 119, 121,
    127, 130, 131, 133, 134, 135, 136, 138,
    140, 147–154, 169, 182, 195, 484-485,
    493.
Nairac, Rosamund, 154.
Nation, The, 125.
Neave, Airey, 17, 31, 164, 184, 233, 259,
    314, 493, 494, 505.
Neeson, Cornelius, 162.
Nelson, Brian, 469-470, 472, 495, 496,
    499, 500.
Nelson, Nigel, 501.
Nelson, Rosemary, 468, 471-473, 497,
    500.
Nesbitt, Joseph, 142.
Nesbitt, Peter, 376.
Neville, Charles, 270.
Newbliss, 390.
Newbridge (Derry), 348.
Newbridge (Kildare), 322.
Newbus, Stan, 426.
Newcastle, (Down), 104, 376..
Newcastle-on-Tyne, 252.
Newell, C. L. D, 23, 501.
Newgate, 433.
New Hibernia, 131, 132, 133.
Newmills, 144
Newry, 31, 78, 79, 119, 139, 140, 166, 167,
    168, 169, 249, 315, 393, 395, 492, 495,
    506.
News at Ten, 165.
News Letter, 100, 501, 504, 507, 508.
News of the World, 83, 503.
New Statesman, 20, 116, 121, 130, 135,
    136, 505.
New Statesman & Society, 407, 427.
Newton, John, 10.
Newtownabbey, 265.
Newtownhamilton, 128, 141, 142.
New York, 214.
New York Times, 294, 319, 320, 499.
New Zealand, 18, 111.

Nicholson, Michael, 218, 226, 228, 230.
Nicoll, Jim, 503.
Nieuw-Bergen, 431.
Nightingale, Andrew, 20.
Niland, D/garda, 486-487.
Nimmons, John, 123.
Nolan, Christopher, 433.
Nolan, Frank, 162.
Norsworthy, Mark, 434.
North Devon, 29.
Northern Constituition, 196, 508.
*Northern Ireland 1968–74. A Chronology of
    Events,* Vol. 3, 1974, 502, 504.
Northern Ireland Soldiers Talking, 255.
Northolt, 101.
Northamptonshire, 77.
Norway, 11, 322.
Nottingham, 105, 396.
Nottinghamshire, 254.
Nugent, Kevin, 128.
Nugent, Kieran, 498.

'Oakes, John', 402, 408.
Ó Brádaigh, Ruairí, 126, 127.
O'Brien, Brendan, 119, 504.
O'Brien, Seamus, 98, 154–158, 159, 161,
    492.
O'Brien, Sheila, 154.
Observer, The, 47, 76, 271, 400, 403, 404,
    407, 410, 421, 422, 426,464, 502, 507,
    508.
O'Callaghan, Gerard, 275, 376–396, 495.
O'Clery, Conor, 34, 189.
O'Connell, Seamus, 288.
O'Connor, Catherine, 162.
O'Connor, Ian, 376.
O'Connor, Joe, 467, 499.
O'Connor, Patrick, 10, 11.
O'Connor, Seamus, 349, 350, 351.
O'Doherty, Anthony, 256, 257.
O'Donnell, Kevin Barry, 456, 459-461,
    496.
O'Donnell, Turlough, 188.
O'Dowd, Barry, 165, 166, 492.
O'Dowd, Declan, 165, 166, 492.
O'Dowd family, 481, 492.
O'Dowd, Joseph, 165, 166, 492.
Ó Dúlacháin, Cormac, 487.
O'Dwyer-Russell, Simon, 410.
O'Farrell, Seán, 456, 460-461, 496.

O'Hagan, Bernadette, 119.
O'Hagan, Feilim, 127, 128.
O'Hagan, Kevin, 119.
O'Hara, Brendan, 137.
O'Hara, James, 119.
O'Hagan, Martin, 499.
O'Hara, Patsy, 279, 333.
O'Hare, Gerry, 48.
O'Hare, Majella, 377, 506.
O'Hare, Paschal, 78, 80, 239, 345.
O'Higgins, Michael, 419.
O'Kane, John Augustine, 430.
Oldfield, Maurice, 31, 189, 251, 253–259,
    432, 494.
Oldman, Jim, 376.
Old Sarum, 115.
O'Loan, Nuala, 467, 498, 500.
Omagh, 72, 186, 261, 369, 441, 442, 443,
    444, 492.
O'Malley, Desmond, 85.
Oman, 11, 15, 18, 31, 34, 41, 118, 198,
    253, 279, 501.
Omeath, 81, 176–177, 180.
O'Neill, Diarmuid, 497, 498.
O'Neill, Greg, 487.
O'Neill, Niall, 158–162, 248, 263, 492.
O'Neill, Paddy, 160.
O'Neill, Raymond Francis, 306, 310, 311,
    314.
O'Neill, Róisín, 160.
O'Neill, Seán, 318.
Onslow, Earl of, 76.
Onslow, Lady Pamela, 76, 82, 85.
Operation 'Banner' 254.
Operation 'Corporate', 10.
Operation 'Motorman', 82.
Operation 'Ranc', 31, 259–265, 494.
Oram, Douglas, 275.
Oram, Joan, 275.
Oram, Julie, 275.
Oram, Katie, 275.
Oram, Paul Douglas, 275, 279–284,
    284–292, 297–304, 494.
Orde, Hugh, 474, 498, 500.
O'Reilly, Emily, 377.
O'Reilly, Noel, 45.
O'Rourke, Daniel, 153.
O'Rourke, Frances, 503.
Orpington, 195.
Orr, Francis, 265.

Osanbrück, 431.
O'Shea, Cathal, 72.
O'Shea, Máire, 179.
O'Sullivan, Jack, 436.
O'Toole, Fran, 137.
Out of the Maze, 508.
Overhill, 254.
Owen, David, 425.
Oxford, 41, 148.
Oxfordshire, 275.

Paisley, Ian, 97, 232, 233, 235, 262, 265,
    304, 345, 502, 504, 505.
Palley, Claire, 39.
Pallister, David, 502, 504, 505.
Palmer, Cara, 277.
Palmer, Caroline, 277.
Palmer, Shona, 277.
Palmer, Tommy, 10, 276, 277, 494.
Parade, 154.
Park, Brian, 503.
Parker, Andrew, 277, 281, 501.
Parker, Tony, 250.
Parkhurst Prison, 101.
'Parkin Mary', 401, 407, 408.
Parody, James, 420.
Parry, Tim, 498.
Pascoe, Robert, 379.
Passmore, John, 508.
Patrick, St, 296.
Patterson, Michael John, 396.
Patten Report, 466, 497, 498.
Pavey, Dean, 433.
Payne, Denis, 102.
Peace Keeping in a Democratic Society, 56.
Peacock, M. G., 492.
Pearson, John, 170.
Pearson, Stephen, 339.
Pedraz, Miguel Martin, 409.
Pembrokeshire, 62, 433.
Pender, John, 503.
Penn, Arthur, 158.
Penrose, Barrie, 108, 124, 504.
Penthouse, 54.
People, The, 501.
Perks, Brian, 77.
Persian, Gulf, 91, 92.
Perth, 426.
Petch, Mark Anthony, 433.
Pettigo, 322, 327.

Phantom Major, The, 11, 501.
Phelan, Patrick Heslin, 199–201, 506.
Philbin, William, 269.
Phoblacht, An, 73, 157, 252.
Pig in the Middle, 502.
Pincher, Chapman, 52, 86, 163, 257, 502, 503.
Pizzarello, Felix, 403, 412, 434, 436, 437.
Plough, The, 82.
Plumbridge, 344.
Plunkett, St Oliver, 296.
Plymouth, 423.
Point of No Return, The, 108.
Police Gazette, 77.
Political Police in Britain, The, 501.
Pollak, Andrew, 283, 402, 403, 408.
Pollen, Anthony Stephen Hungerford,
    15, 71, 492.
Polson, Charles, 422.
Polson, Terence, 422.
Pomeroy, 123, 296, 380.
Port, Colin, 498.
Portadown, 106, 107, 109, 110, 116, 118,
    119, 121, 122, 123, 124, 126, 127, 130,
    133, 136, 137, 139, 140, 143, 144, 146,
    147, 196, 274, 315, 382, 393, 466, 471,
    481, 483, 486-487, 494, 497.
Portadown News, The, 146, 504, 505.
Portadown Times, The, 139, 505, 508.
Portavogie, 94.
Portglenone, 235.
Portlaoise, 284, 297, 328, 390.
Portrush, 305.
Portsmouth, 17.
Pounder, Derek, 419, 420.
Powell, Enoch, 113, 431.
Press, John, 228–229, 233, 282, 318.
Price, Denis, 315.
Price, Mrs, 305, 312, 313.
Price, William Alfred, 23, 274, 304–314,
    494.
Prince, Liam, 506.
Princes Gate, London, 9.
Pringle, Justice, 178.
Prior, James, 296.
Private Eye, 344.
Proetta, Carmen, 417, 418, 420.
Proetta, Maxie, 417, 420.
Prue, Norman, 252, 494.

Quaile, Patrick J., 161.

Quigley, Francis, 348.
Quigley, Robert, 256.
Quinn, Seán, 270.

Rafferty, Joseph, 35, 37, 39.
Rampton, Richard, 427.
Ramsay, Robin, 121, 134, 505.
Ramsbotham, David, 433.
Randall, Bob, 421, 422.
Rasharkin, 299, 495.
Rathfriland, 439, 495.
Ratingen, 431.
Ravensdale, 168, 175.
Rea, Desmond, 474.
Reavey, Anthony, 165–167, 458, 492, 505.
Reavey, Brian, 165–167, 458, 492, 505.
Reavey family, 481, 492.
Reavey, John Martin, 165–167, 458, 492,
    505.
Reavey, Oliver, 167.
Redmond, James, 106.
Rees, Malcolm, 177.
Rees, Merlyn, 104, 108, 121, 136, 193.
Reeves, Phil, 446.
Reeves, Timothy John, 433.
Reid, John, 483, 499, 500.
Reid, John Miller, 431.
Reid, Joseph, 141.
Reilly, 'Kidso' 429.
'Reilly, Robert Wilfred', 401, 402.
Reluctant Judas, 81.
Republican News, 75, 99, 100, 157, 158,
    195, 221, 506.
Republican News: An Phoblacht, 280, 284,
    327, 347, 366, 369, 388, 390, 391, 392,
    393, 398, 432, 506, 507, 508, 509.
Restorick, Stephen, 497.
Revagliatte, Luis, (Joseph), 407, 408.
Reverte, Manuel, 409.
Rheindalen, 432.
Rhine, 117.
Rhodes, Carsten, 177.
Rhodesia, 20, 463, 501.
Rice, Bernard, 47.
Richhill, 146, 231.
Riley, Morris, 19.
Ritchie, David, 146.
Robbins, Michael, 432.
Robertson, Geoff, 81.
Robertson, George, 425.

Robinson, Brian, 317.
Robinson, Brian, 439, 495.
Robinson, Constable, 133.
Robinson, Kathleen, 268.
Robinson, Peter, 97, 265.
Rock, 136.
Rocks, Owen Francis, 153.
Roebuck, Derek, 501.
Roermond, 431.
Roeser, John, 197, 493.
Rogue Warrior of the SAS, 12.
Rooney, Daniel, 56–60,491, 502.
Rooney, John, 57.
Rooney, Mary, 57.
Rooney, Mary, 58.
Rooney, Patrick, 29.
Roosevelt, 13.
Roscommon, 375.
Rose, Michael, 297.
Roslea, 365, 366, 369, 495.
Ross, David, 329.
Ross, John Malcom, 98.
Ross, William, 345.
Rossi, Leo, 438.
Rosslare, 432.
Rostrevor, 80, 81, 82, 83, 88, 376, 492.
Rouse, David, 97.
Russia, 469.
Rutherford, Robert, 188.
Ryan, Liam, 449, 450, 495.
Ryan, Pete, 452-453, 455, 496.
Ryder, Chris, 54, 55, 165.

Saintfield, 65, 67.
Salisbury, 115, 278.
Samarkand, 53, 501.
Samson, Michael, 183.
Sampson Report, 468, 477, 478.
Sanchez, Feliz, 403.
Sandhurst, 77, 198.
SAS in Ireland, 466, 480, 481.
SAS Operations, 12.
SAS: Operation Oman, 12.
SAS Terrorism – The Assassin's Glove, 505.
Saudi Arabia, 188.
Savage, Seán, 396–437, 495.
Saville Inquiry, 468, 478.
Scanlon, Gal, 314.
Scarborough, 433.
Scene Around Six, 107.

Scotland, 16, 17, 426.
Scotstown, 275, 365, 370.
Scott, Michael, 414.
Scott, Stephen, 113.
Seaman, David, 62–64, 159, 491. (alias 'Hans Kruger', alias 'Barry Barber')
Secret Armies, 12.
Sexspionage: The Exploitation of Sex by Soviet Intelligence, 54.
Shanaghan, Patrick, 476-477.
Shannon, Seamus, 390.
Shannon, Thomas, 65.
Shatter, 158.
Shattock, Gordon, 314.
Shattock, Jean, 314.
Shaw, Brian, 49.
Shaw, Brian, 71, 492,
Shaw, Eileen, 48.
Shaw, George, 380.
Shaw, George, 376.
Shaw, Thomas, 48.
Shearer, J. P., 292, 363.
Shields, Alan, 434.
Shiels, Fearghál, 452.
Shingleston, Hubert, 195, 493.
Shivers, Patrick, 33.
Shorncliffe, 198, 254.
Shropshire, 432.
Shuter, Given, 236, 237, 239.
Siege, 9, 501.
Silkin, Sam, 233.
Silverbridge, 142, 165, 481.
Simmonds, Robert, 433.
Simpson, David, 188.
Sinclair, Cameron, 77.
Sinclair, Edward, 485.
Sinnamond, David, 144.
Sixmilecross, 439, 446.
Skinner, Ian, 431.
Slater, Allastair Ira, 276, 314, 320–328, 494.
Sligo, 375.
Smallwoods, Raymond, 264.
Smellie, Craig, 102, 116, 120, 121.
Smethwick, 76, 77.
Smith, Ian, 501.
Smith, Joseph, 48, 49.
Smith, 'Katherine Alison', 401, 403.
Smith, Martin, 418.
Smith, Peter Gladstone, 88, 503.

Smith, Steve, 431.
Smith, Tina, 432.
Smith, Willie, 129.
Smithboro, 370.
Smyth, Kevin, 196, 493.
Smyth, Martin, 265.
Smyth, William, 194, 493, 506.
'Smythe, Douglas', 77, 78, 82, 86. (alias 'Michael Teviott', 'John Wyman').
Snowdon, William, 506.
Soldier, 149.
Soldier, Soldier, 250.
Soldiers, The, 258.
Somerville, James Joseph, 124, 125, 138, 139, 145.
Somerville, Peter, 327.
Somerville, Wesley, 124, 137, 138, 139, 143, 492.
Southgate, 314.
Spain, 399, 404, 407, 408.
Sparbrook, 37.
Sparkhill, 179.
Special Air Service, The, 12.
Speirs, Bill, 426.
Spies in Ireland, 503.
Spike Island, 321.
Spring, Dick, 407.
Spycatcher, 113.
'Stakeknife', 470, 500.
Stakeknife: Britain's secret agents in Ireland, 470.
Stalin, 13.
Stalker, John, 319, 426.
Stalker Report, 464, 468, 477, 478.
Stanhope, Henry, 258.
Star, The, 439.
Starrett, Fred, 397.
State Violence in Northern Ireland, 1969–1997, 450.
Steele, David, 426.
Sterling, Edward, 17.
Stevenge, 197.
Stevens, John, 449, 450, 468-471, 473, 475, 478-479, 495, 497-498, 500.
Stevenson, Gerry, 336.
Stewart, John, 397.
Stewartstown, 144, 201, 274, 305, 457.
Stirling, David, 11, 13, 19, 21, 148, 465, 491.
Stirling, William, 13.

Stobie, Willaim, 498, 499.
Stockman, Robert, 85.
Stoke-on-Trent, 252.
Stone, Michael, 429, 430.
Stonehouse, 148, 154.
Stormont, 61, 82, 102, 193, 253, 379, 462, 500.
Strabane, 315, 321, 333–348, 393, 495.
Strabane Chronicle, The, 508.
Strandhill, 375.
Strasbourg, 30, 33, 34, 40, 178, 434, 476, 478, 488, 496.
Strathearn, William, 133, 480, 482.
Strawson, John, 12.
Stronge, Ken, 437–439, 495.
Stuart, Ted, 53, 55.
Sun, The, 174, 277, 281, 343, 344, 418, 423, 439, 501, 508.
Sunday Express, 254, 425, 508.
Sunday Free Press, 154.
Sunday, Herald, 470.
Sunday Independent, 43, 54, 85, 165, 502.
Sunday Life, 396.
Sunday Mail, 54.
Sunday Mirror, 508.
Sunday News, 65, 99, 109, 143,502, 504, 505.
Sunday People, 504.
Sunday Press, 43, 63, 64, 504, 508.
Sunday Telegraph, 88, 373, 400, 410, 426, 440, 503.
Sunday Times, 9, 73, 74, 89, 108, 124, 136, 165, 178, 180, 193, 194, 406, 418, 423, 427, 445, 501, 502, 504, 507, 508, 509.
Sunday Tribune, 262, 377, 380, 385, 387, 400, 404, 432, 502, 504, 508.
Sunday World, 72, 88, 96, 110, 133, 145, 175, 502, 504, 505.
Sunningdale, 107.
Sussex, 314.
Sutherland, Peter, 178.
Sweden, 343, 344.
Swift, Alan David, 197, 493.
Sykes, Stephen, 10.

Tablet, The, 429.
Taggart, Peter, 446.
Talkback, 505.
Tamnamore, 315, 317, 318.
Tandragee, 147.

Task Force: The Falklands War, 501.

Tate, Laurence, 123.

Taylor, Bob, 501.

Taylor, Denis, 289.

Taylor, Denis, 503.

Taylor, Eric, 314.

Taylor, James, 194, 236–239, 439, 493.

Taylor, John, 82, 83.

Taylor, Peter, 506.

Taylor, Richard, 34.

Tebbit, Margaret, 314.

Tebbit, Norman, 314, 425.

Technology of Political Control, The, 106.

Temperley, Joseph, 225–235.

Templer, Gerald, 14, 20.

Ten Men Dead, 196.

Terry, Sir Peter, 495.

'Teviott, Michael', 77, cf. 'Smythe, Douglas'.

Texas, 91.

Thain, Ian, 397.

Thatcher, Margaret, 31, 114, 122, 251, 253, 257, 275, 314, 396, 404, 405, 410, 411, 426, 427, 433, 434, 440, 446, 448, 463, 464.

The Question is, 435.

These Men are Dangerous, 12.

This is the SAS, 12, 501.

This Week, 426.

Thistle Cross, 153.

Thistlewood, 175.

Thomas, Brian, 320.

Thomas, Jo, 294, 319–320.

Thompson, 88.

Thompson, Lord, 426.

Thompson, Peter, 463, 495.

Thompson, Vincent, 177.

Tievecrum, 170.

Tighe, Michael, 270, 271–272, 467, 494.

Time Out, 19, 81, 82, 501.

Times, The, 68, 103, 104, 105, 106, 109, 163, 164, 165, 170, 178, 186, 189, 254, 273, 400, 426, 439, 464, 492, 502, 503, 505.

Tinnelly, Jack, 89.

Tinnelly, Kathleen, 89.

Tinnelly, Paul, 81, 82, 88, 89, 90, 492

Tinnelly, Seán, 90.

Today, 423, 439, 440.

Today Tonight, 138, 505.

Todd, John, T., 95.

Toland, John, 188.

Toland, Thomas, 46.

Toman, Eugene, 270, 271–272, 494, 496.

Toman, Joseph, 137.

Toner, Tom, 428.

Toomebridge, 234, 348, 350, 353, 360, 430, 495.

Topping, David, 315.

Torremolinos, 402, 403.

Townson, Liam, 152–154, 505.

Trainor, Dorothy, 136, 137, 486.

Trainor, Malachy, 137, 486.

Tralee, 393.

Travers, Stephen, 137.

Treacy, Diane, 421.

Treacy, Séamus, 451.

Trench, Bryan, 503.

Trent, Richard Brooking, 233.

Triangle of Death, The, 122.

Tribune, The, 121.

Trillick, 72, 143, 144, 145, 492.

Trimble, David, 470, 497.

Trondheim, 322.

Troops Out, 44.

True Stories of the SAS, 12.

Tucker, Ray, 20.

Tully, 390.

Tullymore, 275, 380, 394.

Tullyroan, 122, 140.

Tullysaran, 391.

Tullyvallen, 128, 141, 143.

Tullyvalley, 481.

Tully-West, 65.

Tunbridge Wells, 254.

Tunney, Gilbert, 145.

Tunney, Mark, 337.

Turbitt, William, 231.

Turkey, 195.

Turley, J, 486.

Turley, Patrick James, 124.

Turnly, John, 233, 259–261, 494.

Turnly, Miyoko, 259.

Tuzo, General, 35, 52.

Tynan, 120.

Tyneside, 17.

Tyrie, Andy, 97.

Tyrone, 53, 60, 72, 123, 142, 143, 144, 145, 185, 186, 187, 194, 201, 202, 206, 207, 236, 257, 261, 274, 275, 296, 304, 305,

308, 313, 344, 374, 378, 379, 380, 382, 385, 389, 390, 391, 392, 396, 397, 430, 434, 439, 446, 448, 450, 452-453, 455, 456, 492, 493, 495, 496.
Tyrone Courier, 506, 507.

Ullger, Joe, 404.
Ulster Gazette, 384.
Ulsterman, 505.
Under Fire, 344.
USA, 11, 115, 154, 214, 370.
Uppsala, 343.
Urbleshanny, 370.
Ustashi, 21.

Valencia, 403, 409.
Valenzuela, Tomás Rayo, 402, 403, 422.
Valladolid, Augustin, 403, 404.
Vallely, Paul, 439.
Vanishing Derry, 215.
Vera, Rafail, 405.
Viagas, Albert, 409.
Verner, Raymond, 265.
Verner's Bridge, 317.
Vietnam, 18.
Vincent, Daniel Patrick, 456, 459, 496.
Vindicator, The, 125.
Virginia, 34.
Visor, 100.

Wade, Margaret Isobel, 242.
Wakeham, Anna Roberta, 314.
Wakeham, John, 314.
Wakerley, J. C., 164.
Wales, 320.
Walker, Christopher, 163, 170, 186, 504.
Walker, Patrick, 507.
Walker, Robert, 167.
Walker, Walter, 19.
Walking along the Border, 508.
Wallace, Colin, 20, 102, 103, 109, 110–115, 121, 122, 133, 134, 135, 258, 425, 480, 482.
Wallis, Neil, 343.
Wallis-King, Brigadier, 116.
Walls, Colm, 351, 352, 361, 362, 363.
Walls, Kevin, 352, 361.
Walls, Laurence, 362.
Walpole, Edward, 10.
Walsh, Dermot, 274.

Walsh, Martin, 169.
Walton, 425.
War on the Mind, 16.
Ward, Elizabeth, 363.
Ward, Judith, 496.
Ward, Michael, 275, 494.
Ware, John, 134, 174, 505.
Warminster, 91, 252.
Warner, Philip, 12.
Warrenpoint, 30, 80, 81, 84, 253.
Warrington, 498.
Warslow, 252.
Washingbay, 318, 456.
Washington DC, 60.
Waterfoot, 78.
Waters, John, 418, 419.
Waterside, 144.
Watson, Alan, 418, 419, 420, 434.
Watson, Andrew, 263, 264.
Watson, Peter, 16.
Watters, Kirk, 95.
Waugh, Auberon, 426.
Weatherup, Justice, 451-452.
Webbe, Stephen, 501.
Weekend World, 247, 493.
Weir, Andy, 464.
Weir, John, 480-482, 485.
Weir, Joseph, 123.
Welbourn, Peter, 439.
Welsh, Gerald, 265.
West Virginia, 11.
Western Desert, 13, 21.
Westmacott, H. R., 10, 196, 255, 256, 494.
Westminster, 369.
Wexford, 333.
Wharton, Kenneth, 167.
What the papers say, 425.
Wheatley Hill, 463.
Whitecross, 141, 165, 377, 481, 492.
Whitehall, 343, 465.
Whitelaw, William, 52, 60, 68, 93, 100.
Whitfield, Douglas, 492.
Who Dares Wins, 12, 196, 502, 506.
Who Framed Colin Wallace?, 102, 109, 113.
Whores of War, The, 501.
Who's Who, 106.
Widenrath, 432.
Widgery, Lord, 85, 437.
Wigg, Lord, 77, 503.
Wiley, Jack, 122.

Wilkinson, Stephen, 434.
Williams, Clive Graham, 49.
Williamson, Frederick, 270.
Wilson, Austin, 376.
Wilson, Bill, 136.
Wilson, Harold, 30, 52, 98, 108, 109, 165, 492, 503.
Wilson, Michael, 97.
Wiltshire, 17, 252.
Winchester, Simon, 167, 185.
Windlesham, Lord, 427.
Windon, Stewart J, 279.
Winged Dagger, 11.
Winkler, Michael, 433.
Winter, Jason, 434.
Wood, Derek, 430, 431, 495.
Woodfield, Philip, 507.
Woodford, David W., 152.
Woolacott, Martin, 503.
Wooley, Nicholas, 56.
Woolsey, Edmund, 81, 84, 503.
Woolsey, Peter, 147.
Worcestershire, 15, 196.
Workers Press, 508.
Workers Research Unit, 43.
World in Action, 40.
World this Weekend, The, 440.

Wright, Billy, 471, 473, 497, 500.
Wright, Ian, 467, 497.
Wright, John, 139.
Wright, Kathleen, 50, 51, 502.
Wright, Michael, 439.
Wright, Paul Anthony, 250, 494.
Wright, Peter, 113.
Wright, Seamus, 50–52.
Wright, T. B., 227.
Wright, William, 50, 51.
Wright, William Ashton, 138.
'Wyman, John', 77, 82, 86, 87, cf. 'Smythe, Douglas'.

Yemen, North, 19.
Yeves, Enrique, 404, 409.
York, 27.
Yorkshire, 27, 115, 148, 433.
Young, B. A., 463.
Young, George, 258.
Young, Kenneth, 147.
Young, Stewart, 480.
Younger, George, 410, 411.
Yugoslavia, 21.

Zadar, 21.
Zimbabwe, 502.